Praise f
Four Battleg

"[Paul] Scharre is a thoughtful, knowledgeable, and capable guide. He explains why AI matters and charts the areas that will determine which country gets the most out of its investments."

—Lawrence Freedman, *Foreign Affairs*

"Scharre covers the exciting advances of the last 5 years in an accessible style. . . . [A] well-balanced and detailed assessment of the state of the art and a useful critique of just how fast and far the Pentagon is moving."

—Frank G. Hoffman, *Joint Force Quarterly*

"Excellent. . . . Scharre applies his unique personal combat perspective as a former U.S. Army Ranger, combining it with research visits to key artificial intelligence conferences, labs and development programs around the world, as he leads readers along the cutting edge of militarizing AI."

—Scott Gourley, *Army* magazine

"How will AI change the balance of power between authoritarian states and democracies? . . . [A] farsighted and comprehensive survey of the issues involved and the paths forward."

—Pedro Domingos, author of *The Master Algorithm*

"In this riveting book on AI and power by one of the leading strategists of our time, Paul Scharre highlights an existential challenge: as Americans and Chinese militarize ever more powerful AI to avoid ceding control to each other, they risk ceding too much power to machines."

—Professor Max Tegmark, MIT AI researcher and author of *Life 3.0*

FOUR
BATTLEGROUNDS

ALSO BY PAUL SCHARRE

Army of None

FOUR BATTLEGROUNDS

POWER
IN THE AGE OF
ARTIFICIAL
INTELLIGENCE

PAUL SCHARRE

W. W. NORTON & COMPANY
Independent Publishers Since 1923

For information about permission to reproduce selections from this book, write to Permissions,
W. W. Norton & Company, Inc., 500 Fifth Avenue, New York, NY 10110

For information about special discounts for bulk purchases, please contact
W. W. Norton Special Sales at specialsales@wwnorton.com or 800-233-4830

Manufacturing by Lakeside Book Company
Book design by Chris Welch
Production manager: Anna Oler

ISBN 978-1-324-07477-9 pbk.

W. W. Norton & Company, Inc., 500 Fifth Avenue, New York, N.Y. 10110
www.wwnorton.com

W. W. Norton & Company Ltd., 15 Carlisle Street, London W1D 3BS

1 2 3 4 5 6 7 8 9 0

In memory of Jim Hornfischer

Author, agent, mentor, and friend

Artificial intelligence is the future, not only for Russia, but for all humankind. It comes with colossal opportunities, but also threats that are difficult to predict. Whoever becomes the leader in this sphere will become the ruler of the world.

—RUSSIAN PRESIDENT VLADIMIR PUTIN

Science and technology has become the main battleground of global power rivalry.

—CHINESE GENERAL SECRETARY XI JINPING

CONTENTS

LIST OF ILLUSTRATIONS

PREFACE

There was a singular moment when I realized robots would transform warfare. It was the spring of 2007 and I had just begun a one-year tour in Iraq during the height of the U.S. troop surge. Iraq was a chaotic, violent place. The country was ripping itself apart in civil war. I'd been on three prior deployments to Afghanistan and my unit had taken casualties every time—I'd been an Army Ranger and we didn't shy away from combat—but I had never seen violence like this. For my Iraq tour I was part of a civil affairs team deployed to Forward Operating Base Warhorse in Diyala province. Diyala's population was split among Sunnis, Shias, and Kurds, like a microcosm of Iraq. The groups warred with each other and with U.S. troops for the future of the country. Improvised explosive devices (IEDs), or roadside bombs, had taken a heavy toll on U.S. troops in the area. The base had a makeshift monument erected by the 1st Cavalry Division unit operating out of Warhorse with the names of soldiers killed during their tour, and when I arrived in country I was taken aback by the long roster of names stenciled on the concrete barriers. It was a difficult time.

One day on patrol we came across a roadside bomb (as one did at the time). We saw it first, which is the preferred way of discovering one rather than running into it, and we pulled the Stryker armored vehicle over to wait for the bomb disposal techs to arrive. I had occasionally seen U.S. troops handle roadside bombs by simply shooting at them to detonate the bomb while leaning out the side of the Humvee, but waiting for the bomb disposal professionals certainly seemed like the more prudent course of action to me.

It took a while for the explosive ordnance disposal (EOD) team, as they were formally known, to arrive as they were in high demand at the time, but eventually they rolled up in their large Buffalo mine-resistant ambush protected (MRAP) armored vehicle. I had only been in theater maybe a month or so and had yet to see an EOD team in action, so I popped my head out of the Stryker hatch to watch with interest. I expected to see the bomb tech emerge from the MRAP armored vehicle in a giant protective suit. Instead, out came a little robot. And the light bulb went off in my head: *Send the robot to defuse the bomb!*

It seemed obvious, afterwards, to use a robot for such a hazardous mission. Why put a human at risk if you didn't need to? My mind went to all of the missions in war that might someday be done by robots, sparing the need to put soldiers in harm's way.

After I left Iraq, I worked at the Pentagon on emerging technologies and helped push for U.S. investments in military robots. I believed then, and still do, that these machines would help save American lives and defend the nation. The military's plans for increasingly advanced robots led inevitably to questions about the scope of autonomy in future systems, a thorny issue with important legal, ethical, and strategic dimensions. I was involved in drafting the official Defense Department policy on autonomy in weapons, which gave guidance to weapons developers. In the years following, I had the opportunity to participate in multiple rounds of diplomatic discussions at the United Nations on autonomous weapons, which was the topic of my first book, *Army of None*. But even as nations debated the role of autonomy in weapons, the ground was shifting beneath our feet.

The robotics revolution that unfolded in the early 2000s, enabling Roombas and military robots, has given way to something far deeper and more profound: a revolution in artificial intelligence (AI). The combination of exponential growth in data and computer processing power (compute) has fueled a renaissance in machine learning, an AI technique in which machines learn from data, rather than follow an explicit set of preprogrammed rules of behavior. Machine learning is now being applied to medicine, finance, transportation, and other industries. Many have argued that AI could be the next industrial revolution. Given the enormous geopolitical disruptions caused by prior industrial revolutions, it makes sense that AI is also a fast-growing arena of competition between nations who are vying for dominance. AI is changing global security and power dynamics. The consequences of this competition may not be as immediate as that of the roadside bomb back in Iraq, but the stakes are just as high. AI is likely to have profound effects on human freedom and global security. Whoever leads in AI will have a tremendous advantage in shaping the future, if the technology can be controlled at all. AI will bring about a new digital order, and this book is the story of those fighting for control over that future.

FOUR
BATTLEGROUNDS

INTRODUCTION

"Fight's on, fight's on!" The two aircraft twisted in the blue, each furiously maneuvering to gain advantage. In one simulated cockpit, a human pilot. In the other, an AI agent.

Less than thirty seconds into the fight, the AI had scored the first kill. The human pilot's simulator flashed red as the AI's guns hit their mark. Both aircraft dove furiously, but mere seconds later, the AI scored another hit. Then another. And another.

In under ninety seconds, it was over. The AI had racked up four kills and the human none.

The fight was the culmination of DARPA's AlphaDogfight Trials, which pitted an AI agent against a flesh-and-blood highly experienced F-16 pilot who goes by the call sign "Banger." Eight AI teams competed in a tournament against one another, with the thirty-person Heron Systems beating out defense giant Lockheed Martin in the finals. Victory over the other AI agents earned Heron Systems' algorithm, call sign "Falco," the opportunity to compete 1v1 against a human pilot. It performed flawlessly. In five total rounds, the AI racked up fifteen gunshot kills against Banger. Banger couldn't get a single shot on the AI.

Dogfighting, or air combat maneuvering, is one of the most challenging skills for human fighter pilots. Even while air combat has evolved to increasingly rely on air-to-air missiles shot beyond visual range, close-in dogfighting remains a key crucible in which to test AI performance in aerial combat. DARPA, the Defense Advanced Research Projects Agency, is the U.S. military's "department of mad scientists" that develops technology breakthroughs, and DARPA's Air Combat Evolution (ACE) program is taking air combat to the next level.

Launched in 2019, the ACE program capitalizes on the explosion in AI under way since 2012 as part of the deep learning revolution. Improvements in data, computing hardware, and algorithms have enabled rapid improvements in machine learning, a method for creating intelligent machines by training algorithms on data. Deep learning, a machine learning technique that uses deep neural networks, has yielded tremendous successes, including superhuman performance in games such as the Chinese strategy game *go* and complex computer games such as *StarCraft II* and *Dota 2*. With the ACE program, the U.S. military aims to use machine learning to build more effective AI assistants for human pilots. Not only did AlphaDogfight achieve superhuman performance in a simulated environment, it demonstrated some of the superior strengths of AI systems in combat.

Heron Systems' algorithm, Falco, displayed superhuman precision in its flying and fighting, giving it an unbeatable edge over its human opponent. In an aerial dogfight, planes circle one another in tight spirals seeking to gain a positional advantage over their opponent so they can maneuver into a kill shot with short-range missiles or guns. Carefully managing the aircraft's energy so they can turn tighter and faster than the enemy is a critical skill in dogfighting. Pilots must fly the aircraft at the peak of its performance. This can be challenging for humans, who must not only pay attention to the velocity and position of their aircraft but also keep track of the enemy fighter and anticipate next moves. The AI agent flew with superhuman precision, keeping the aircraft at the peak of its performance and never wasting energy in suboptimal maneuvers.

The AI agent also demonstrated superhuman precision in employing its weapons. The AI agent showed a strong favor for what pilots call forward-quarter gunshots, when the two aircraft are racing toward each other head-to-head. Human pilots tend to be bad at forward-quarter shots because they rarely practice them. In training, forward-quarter gunshots are banned because of the danger of flying directly at another airplane at several hundred miles per hour. (In combat, there are no rules.) Even with training, forward-quarter shots would be incredibly difficult. They offer only a split-second window of opportunity to hit the target, which usually arrives at the moment when pilots most need to be thinking about avoiding a mid-air collision. For this reason, human pilots tend to favor rear-quarter shots, where a fighter pulls in behind another plane at the six o'clock position. The AI agent had none of these disadvantages. It quickly and precisely executed forward-quarter shots, all while deftly maneuvering to avoid a collision. Lieutenant Colonel Justin "Glock" Mock described the AI agent as executing "a gunshot that is almost impossible," demonstrating "superhuman capability . . . to aim that accurately and to be able to do it in such a dynamic situation." The AI's use of a tactic banned in training for humans might seem unfair, but war isn't fair. One of the best advantages of AI systems isn't just their ability to fight better than humans but to fight differently.

Lastly, the AI agent could pull maneuvers that a human pilot simply could not physically withstand, sustaining g-forces that would cause a human to black out. In their last engagement, the two simulated aircraft circled each other for nearly two minutes at roughly 9 Gs (nine times the force of Earth's gravity), a level of g-forces that even trained fighter pilots can only withstand for a few seconds. Not only could AI systems exploit the lack of human physical limitations for superior tactics, future robotic combat aircraft could be designed to handle far more aggressive maneuvers. In analyzing AlphaDogfight, Navy fighter pilot Commander Colin "Farva" Price noted, "The human will always be the limiting factor in the performance of an aircraft." By handing over some tasks to AI, militaries can build more effective combat systems with superhuman performance.

AI systems have seen impressive gains in recent years but still have many limitations. In the AlphaDogfight Trials, the AI agent was given perfect situational awareness of the simulated environment, including the location of the opposing fighter. In the real world, an AI system would need to rely on sensors and data processing algorithms to find enemy aircraft, identify them, and correctly distinguish them from friendly or civilian aircraft. But classification algorithms that can identify objects are improving as well. DARPA is continuing to mature more capable AI-enabled autonomy, with the goal of evolving to a live flight demonstration on a trainer jet. DARPA's goal isn't to build a completely autonomous combat airplane, however. The ACE program manager, Lieutenant Colonel Dan "Animal" Javorsek, explained that the goal was to build more effective AI systems that could be used by human pilots. "We envision a future in which AI handles the split-second maneuvering during within-visual-range dogfights," Javorsek said, "keeping pilots safer and more effective as they orchestrate large numbers of unmanned systems."

AI is changing war, and it is also changing surveillance, disinformation, and other aspects of global peace and security. Nations around the globe are racing to capitalize on AI technology to gain an advantage over others. The world is just beginning to grapple with the implications of a technology that could herald another industrial revolution.

AI is not a discrete technology, like railroads or airplanes. It is a general-purpose enabling technology, like electricity, computers, or the internal combustion engine, with many applications. Those earlier general-purpose technologies brought sweeping economic, social, and political changes. Likewise, the scale of potential change from artificial intelligence is staggering. By one estimate, nearly half of all tasks currently being done in the U.S. economy could be outsourced to automation using existing technology. *Wired* magazine cofounder Kevin Kelly has argued that "[AI] will enliven inert objects, much as electricity did more than a century ago. Everything that we formerly electrified we will now cognitize." AI has applications in cybersecurity, surveillance, defense, border security, disinformation, and economic warfare, yielding major geopolitical advantages to whoever best harnesses these tools.

The first and second industrial revolutions brought about a societal process of mechanization that saw the creation of machines that were stronger than humans for specific tasks. While today's AI systems are a far cry from the C-3POs and Terminators of science fiction, AI technology is real today and a powerful tool. Today's "narrow," or task-specific, AI allows the creation of machines that are smarter than humans for specific cognitive tasks and will spark a broad process of cognitization across society. While the process of industrialization transformed society with physical machines, cognitization will transform society with intelligent machines. AI has many constructive applications. AI will save lives and increase efficiency and productivity. It is also being used as a weapon of repression and to gain military advantage.

This book is about the darker side of AI.

The dangers from AI aren't the dangers science fiction warned us about. We needn't fear robots rising up to throw off their human overlords, or at least not anytime soon. The dangers from AI today come from people using the technology maliciously or carelessly, causing harm to others. Militaries around the globe are investing in AI technology, and authoritarian regimes are using it to tighten their grip for internal repression. The Pentagon is applying the same AI techniques used to achieve superhuman intelligence in poker to much higher-stakes strategic game theory, such as analyzing what weapons to invest in to deter nuclear war. China is building a techno-dystopian surveillance state to monitor and repress its citizens through facial recognition and an Orwellian "social credit" system. Deepfake video and audio continue to improve, and long-term trends are likely to lead to fakes that are indistinguishable from reality, undermining truth. And AI technology could radically alter the nature of war, ushering in a battlefield "singularity" in which war moves too fast for human control.

Like prior industrial revolutions, the cognitive revolution will reshape geopolitics in the twenty-first century. AI is likely to lead to shifts in power on the global stage, empowering some actors and even changing the key metrics of power. During the industrial revolution, coal- and steel-producing nations became more powerful and oil became a global strategic resource. Today, computing hardware, data, and AI talent make up the key resources in the global struggle for AI dominance.

More than fifty countries have signaled their intent to capitalize on AI for national advantage, but nowhere is the competition fiercer than in the accelerating rivalry between the United States and China. China has launched a national-level AI development plan with the intent to be the global leader in AI by 2030. China is spending billions on research, training more AI scientists, and aggressively courting top experts from Silicon Valley. The White House and Pentagon are undertaking their own initiatives, reaching out to tech firms and launching billion-dollar cloud computing projects to build out AI infrastructure.

The U.S.-China AI competition is complicated by the fact that their AI ecosystems are deeply intertwined. U.S. military leaders have raised alarm at China's model of "military-civil fusion" and the fear that U.S. firms working in China could, even indirectly, benefit the Chinese military. Some U.S. tech firms have undoubtedly contributed to the growth of the AI ecosystem in China including, in at least a few instances, working with researchers from Chinese military institutions. Partnerships between the Chinese military and U.S. academia are equally problematic. Since 2007, an estimated 500 Chinese military scientists have studied in the United States. From 2006 to 2017, Chinese military scientists coauthored over 1,100 research papers with U.S. scientists. Major U.S. universities including MIT and Princeton have worked with Chinese companies that have later been sanctioned for human rights abuses. These ties have led U.S. policymakers to increasingly push to "decouple" the United States from China to stem the tide of intellectual capital flowing from U.S. businesses and academia into the arms of a strategic competitor.

But Chinese tech firms like Baidu, Alibaba, and Tencent are global leaders in AI in their own right, and China has a vibrant AI start-up ecosystem. China boasts some of the most highly valued AI start-ups in the world, including SenseTime at over $16 billion and ByteDance at $350 billion. In some areas, such as facial recognition, Chinese companies such as SenseTime and Megvii are global leaders and have a major leg up on U.S. companies such as Amazon, IBM, and Microsoft, which face a much stricter regulatory environment. Chinese AI firms, meanwhile, benefit from the Chinese Communist Party's aggressive domestic surveillance. The Chinese government is building a burgeoning panopticon with over 500 million cameras deployed nationwide by

2021, more than half of the world's surveillance cameras. Even more significant than government cash buoying China's AI industry is the data collected, which AI companies can use to further train and refine their algorithms. With facial recognition deployment stalled in the United States, Chinese firms are poised to dominate the global facial recognition industry.

China today is not the China of twenty years ago. While China's AI ecosystem has benefited enormously from deep ties to the United States, both from legitimate research collaboration and intellectual property theft, China today doesn't need to steal U.S. research to be a global technology leader. China already publishes more AI papers than the United States and is on track to surpass the United States in the top 1 percent most-cited papers by 2025. More broadly, given current trends China will overtake the United States in total national research and development (R&D) spending (across all fields, not just AI) in the next decade.

The tsunami of change that AI is bringing is crashing into the deepening U.S.-China rivalry, making AI a focus of geopolitical competition. U.S. policymakers are taking steps to sever what they see as problematic connections between the two nations, such as banning students from Chinese universities with military ties, at the same time as making renewed investments in American competitiveness. In 2022, a bipartisan cadre of lawmakers passed a massive investment of over $50 billion in the U.S. semiconductor industry, a foundational hardware underpinning AI and other digital technologies.

Even as the United States and China race to stay ahead in AI research, successfully implementing AI for national defense, intelligence, surveillance, or information operations will require more than basic research. Governments looking to apply AI for national power will need to rapidly spin-in and adopt a technology that has largely been invented in the commercial sector. This book will pull back the curtain on the U.S. military's efforts to harness AI and will dive deep into new organizations, such as the Defense Department's Joint AI Center and the Pentagon's Silicon Valley outpost, Defense Innovation Unit. But despite their best efforts, these new organizations may not be enough. If the United States moves too slowly, it could cede military dominance in a critical new technology to a rising and revisionist China.

Whichever nation leads in AI will have tremendous advantages in setting the terms of the geopolitical order for the twenty-first century. The United States and China are vying for military dominance in the Asia-Pacific region, and AI could help tip the scales to either side. U.S. and Chinese tech firms are competing for social app dominance, a high-stakes contest to control the information seen by billions of people. And China is pioneering a new model of AI-enabled surveillance and repression that is increasingly being adopted around the world, threatening global freedoms. On the eve of Russia's 2022 invasion of Ukraine, Russia and China announced a "no limits" partnership that encompassed, among other issues, artificial intelligence. If the United States and other democracies do not work together to lead in AI and shape the rules for how it is used, they risk a creeping tide of techno-authoritarianism that undermines democracy and freedom around the globe.

If China achieves its goal of becoming the world's AI leader by 2030, it would empower a regime guilty of gross human rights abuses, threatening its neighbors, and bullying countries around the world. As China's power rises, other nations may seek to adopt its authoritarian tendencies, eroding global freedoms.

Democracies must work together to lead in AI and present an effective model for AI governance. Democratic nations have many advantages over authoritarian regimes in a long-term contest to shape how AI is used. Collectively, democratic nations have greater talent, military power, and control over critical technologies. Yet this power is fragmented among different countries and actors, including governments, corporations, academics, and tech workers.

Democratic societies will need to manage their internal divisions to harness their strength. Democratic governments will need to work with tech firms to govern surveillance technology to ensure that authoritarian regimes *or* corporations don't undermine individual liberties. National security experts who want to stem the flow of AI technology to competitor nations will need to work with academics who favor openness. And militaries in democratic societies will need to demonstrate they will use AI responsibly to win over skeptical scientists concerned about what their own government may do with AI.

Caution is warranted, because even as nations race to leverage AI technology for national advantage, there are risks. AI technology is powerful but has many vulnerabilities. Machine learning systems can learn the wrong thing if the data they are trained on is biased or has been poisoned by an adversary. AI systems can be manipulated by exploiting vulnerabilities in how the system "thinks," cognitive hacks that are analogous to cyberattacks on computer software. These features make AI technology simultaneously transformative and brittle. Systems may work brilliantly in one setting, then fail dramatically if the environment slightly changes. The "black box" nature of many AI methods means that it may be difficult to accurately predict when they will fail or even understand why they failed in retrospect. Potentially even more dangerous, the global competition in AI risks a "race to the bottom" on safety. In a desire to beat others to the punch, countries may cut corners to deploy AI systems before they have been fully tested. We are careening toward a world of AI systems that are powerful but insecure, unreliable, and dangerous.

But technology is not destiny, and there are people around the world working to ensure that technological progress arcs toward a brighter future. The contest for who controls AI is global, with many radically divergent visions for the future. European nations are leaning into regulating AI, aiming for a "race to the top" on regulatory standards. Grassroots movements against facial recognition have sprung up across the United States. Conscientious-objector tech employees have said "no" to militarizing AI, while defense experts are pushing the military to use AI responsibly. The fight to control AI includes powerful megacorporations that control the content for billions of people, human rights activists who've uncovered abuses using AI technology, researchers who are working to build deepfake detectors, and scientists who are trying to build the next generation of safer, more robust AI systems. The diversity of voices in democratic societies debating the future of AI is a strength that can lead to social benefit in the long run, but only if they build a responsible tech ecosystem together. Democratic societies need to establish a positive model of AI governance, or risk a future dominated by authoritarian uses of AI that undermine truth and personal freedoms.

The future of humanity will be determined in large part by the shape of AI technology as it unfolds in the world and who determines its destiny. AI can be used to strengthen democratic societies or authoritarian ones, to bolster individual freedom or crush it. Russian president Vladimir Putin has said, "Whoever becomes the leader in [artificial intelligence] will become the ruler of the world." The race is under way to lead in AI and write the rules of the next century to control the future of global power and security.

PART I
POWER

1

THE NEW OIL

P̲ower is the currency of international relations. It is the difference between weak states and strong ones, between those who set the terms of the geopolitical order and those who must accommodate the will of others. Stronger states don't always prevail in international disputes, just like my children don't always listen to me, despite my power over their screen time. Strategy, alliances, a willingness to absorb costs, and sheer force of will also matter in settling disputes, among people and states alike. But being the bigger dog has its advantages. Germany is a more powerful state than Luxembourg, for example, giving it more sway over the direction of European—and global—economics and politics.

Technology is an enabler of both hard (economic and military) and soft (culture and values) power. Technology can be used to build weapons to coerce or defend, material goods to trade, bribe, or bolster other states, and media platforms to spread messages around the world. Technological revolutions have, in the past, not only transformed the global balance of power but even the key metrics of power. AI promises to do the same.

One of the starkest illustrations of a technology's transformative effect on global power is nuclear technology, whose advent in the mid-twentieth century quickly divided the world into nuclear haves and have-nots. Nuclear weapons have awesome destructive power, but translating that power into political outcomes is hardly straightforward. Threats to use nuclear weapons are rarely seen as credible except in the most extreme cases. AI is in many ways the opposite of nuclear technology. AI technology is widely available, proliferates rapidly, and has a multitude of uses.

Many experts have suggested that AI, like earlier general-purpose technologies, could cause changes on the scale of another industrial revolution. The first and second industrial revolutions saw nations rise and fall on the world stage based on how rapidly and effectively they adopted industrial technology. By the time the second industrial revolution ended in the early twentieth century, the world order and even the key building blocks of national power had been transformed.

The industrial revolution occurred in two waves: the first industrial revolution from around 1760 to 1830 and the second industrial revolution from around 1870 to 1914. Each revolution encompassed a set of mutually reinforcing technologies. In the first industrial revolution, steam engines, improvements in iron production, machine tools, and interchangeable parts, among other inventions, helped to fuel an explosion in economic productivity, leading to a wave of factory-building and urbanization. The second industrial revolution was enabled by the internal combustion engine, electrification, steel, and oil, and led to the construction of railways, telegraphs, automobiles, and more efficient factory production. These technological revolutions had an immense effect on global power. As Paul Kennedy observed in his landmark work, *The Rise and Fall of the Great Powers*, "Dramatic changes occurred in the power balances, both inside Europe and without. Old empires collapsed, and new ones arose."

The industrial revolution began in Britain and then spread across continental Europe and beyond, leading to major shifts in the balance of power. Russia lagged the other European powers in industrialization, with the result that by 1830 it had a per capita gross national product (GNP) (a measure of national income-per-person) that was 70 percent that of Germany and half that of Britain. Yet, for a time, Russia's superior population made up for its economic backwardness. Russia was not just the largest European power by population, it was far and away the largest European power by GNP, with nearly 30 percent more economic output than Britain and 45 percent more than Germany. Yet Russia's size could only help for so long as other nations surged in industrial productivity. From 1830 to 1890, Britain and Germany both more than doubled their per capita GNP while Russia stagnated, increasing by a mere 7 percent total over a sixty-year period. The result was that while Russia was the largest European economic power (measured in GNP) in 1830, by 1890 Russia had been eclipsed by Britain and Germany.

Similar shifts happened worldwide with even more profound consequences for global power dynamics. In 1790, Europe (collectively), China, and India (including what is now Pakistan) held roughly the same shares of global manufacturing output. They all had approximately equivalent levels of per capita industrialization. But the industrial revolution skyrocketed European economic productivity and, by extension, military power. By 1900, Europe collectively controlled 62 percent of global manufacturing output, while China accounted for 6 percent and India less than 2 percent.

The resulting European military dominance fueled a wave of colonial expansion. The effect of technological dominance on military power was put on stark display in the Battle of Omdurman in 1898. British, Egyptian, and Sudanese troops were outnumbered two to one by Sudanese Dervishes yet won the battle by a lopsided sixty-to-one casualty ratio due to superior firepower. The British troops had better training, but even more significant was their possession of forty-four Maxim guns, the first machine gun, which, by virtue of industrial technology, could fire 500 rounds per minute. By 1914, Europeans had translated their economic and military might into occupying or controlling over 80 percent of the world's land surface.

The industrial revolution not only grew some nations' economic and military power while leaving others behind; it also changed the key metrics of power. In a preindustrial era, military power was measured chiefly in men under arms. As a consequence, national power—and *potential* military power—was measured by population. Larger nations could, all things being equal, field larger armies. And larger armies were more powerful. There were, of course, many other secondary factors affecting military power, including geography, alliances, economic and financial power, technological development, and military organization and training, but population was a reasonable first-order proxy for potential military power. The industrial revolution shifted the main metric of military power from numbers of men under arms to numbers of war machines, such as tanks and airplanes. Industrialization eclipsed population as the major factor in potential military power.

By World War II, a nation's coal and steel production counted far more toward potential military power than their national population alone. Scholars of industrial-age national power measure not just national population and GNP, but also iron/steel production, energy consumption, manufacturing output, and industrial potential. While economic productivity does not directly translate to military power, it is a good approximation of potential military power for industrialized nations. Factories can be—and were—repurposed for building tanks and airplanes as nations mobilized for war. In World War II, the Allied powers had three times the industrial "war potential" of the Axis powers. Once mobilized, Paul Kennedy explained, "these figures of *potential* power were being exchanged into the hard currency of aircraft, guns, tanks, and ships." At the height of the war, Allied factories were producing over 3.5

times as many aircraft and tanks as the Axis powers, burying them beneath an onslaught of iron.

The information revolution, which began in the 1960s with the introduction of integrated circuits, or computer chips, brought another shift in economic and military power. The United States benefited by being a first mover in the information revolution, which translated into advantages in both hard power, such as military dominance, and soft power, such as setting the initial terms of the internet. The military advantages of digitally enabled systems such as smart bombs, stealth aircraft, GPS satellites, and computer networks were on full display in the 1991 Gulf War, when the U.S. military dismantled Saddam Hussein's Soviet-equipped army with a thirty-to-one casualty ratio. Iraqi forces were so helpless against American airpower that the White House eventually ended the war earlier than planned because media images of the so-called "highway of death" made American forces seem as if they were "cruelly and unusually punishing our already whipped foes," in the words of Gulf War air commander General Chuck Horner. Yet as information technology proliferated, it leveled the playing field among nations, allowing other countries to procure their own precision-guided weapons and build their own balkanized, censored portions of the internet.

Even as information technology diffuses around the globe, the information revolution continues to mature. Big data, Internet of Things (IoT) devices, high-speed wireless networking, autonomous systems, and machine learning are just some of the digital systems transforming industries and society today. The current wave of digital innovation is highly globalized, with centers of gravity in the United States, China, and Europe. Each power center is vying to realize their own vision for how digital technologies should be used in society. This struggle for geotechnical dominance points to the importance of assessing national *digital* power. As the AI revolution unfolds, which countries will benefit the most, and what digital elements will become key determinants of national power, like coal, steel, and oil did during the industrial revolution?

Machine learning systems depend on a few key inputs: data, computing hardware (compute), algorithms, and human capital. Machine learning is often data- and compute-intensive, using large amounts of computing power to train an algorithm on enormous datasets. The process isn't magic, and it can often be difficult work to get machine learning systems to function properly, so having talented AI scientists and engineers is crucial to building effective machine learning systems. When considering AI power, some of these inputs matter more than others. It's hard to limit the spread of algorithms, so the relative availability or scarcity of data, talent, and compute are major factors (although not the only ones) that affect national AI capacity. Additionally, social institutions, from the availability of funding for AI start-ups to public perceptions of AI technologies, also influence AI adoption. Nations that lead in these four battlegrounds—data, compute, talent, and institutions—will have a major advantage in AI power.

A number of independent analysts have built global AI indices in an attempt to comprehensively measure countries' national AI power. While the specific metrics vary, many researchers have come to similar conclusions, which one group summarized as: "the United States currently leads in AI, with China rapidly catching up, and the European Union behind both." These indices consider national AI capabilities across a number of areas, including funding, data, hardware, research, development, talent, and adoption. Some indices also include infrastructure, the operating environment, and government strategy. Two efforts in particular stand out as noteworthy for their analytic rigor.

Researchers at the Center for Data Innovation evaluated China, the United States, and the European Union across thirty quantitative metrics in 2019 and again in 2021. These included the number of top AI researchers, field-weighted research citations, highly cited patents, R&D spending, AI start-ups, venture capital and private equity funding, and semiconductor firms. Their conclusion was that the United States led overall and in the subcategories of talent, research, development, and hardware, but that China led in data and adoption.

Researchers at Tortoise released a "Global AI Index" in 2019 and 2021, assessing sixty-two countries across 143 metrics. They similarly concluded that the United States led the world overall in AI and in the subcategories of talent, research, development, and commercial activity, but that China was the number two country overall and in research, development, and commercial activity. Additionally, Tortoise researchers ranked China far ahead of the United States in government strategy and an operating environment conducive to AI, which includes regulation and public opinion.

Some caution is warranted in interpreting these results. First, there are important asymmetries between the American, European, and Chinese AI ecosystems that can skew results. The biggest among these is size. Like Russia in the nineteenth century, China has a much larger population, so metrics that look at raw size, such as internet users, will heavily benefit China, even if raw size may not be the most relevant indicator in all cases. Conversely, metrics that are size-adjusted, such as per capita or per worker, tend to benefit the United States and Europe, which have smaller populations, even if in other cases sheer size may matter more. Most importantly, size-adjusted indices discount China's *potential* power, which is enormous if it continues to modernize and harness the potential of its 1.4 billion people.

Another important difference is that, across many metrics, the Chinese AI ecosystem tends to emphasize quantity over quality compared to the United States and Europe. For example, the United States has a modest (1.5×) advantage over China in terms of the overall number of AI researchers, but it has an overwhelming (5×) advantage when it comes to top AI researchers. A similar asymmetry exists in publications. Chinese researchers publish nearly 1.5 times as many papers as U.S. researchers, but U.S. papers were cited roughly 70 percent more on average, an indication of their higher average quality. The U.S.-China balance in research and talent can look very different depending on whether one is looking at quality or quantity, and both matter in different ways.

There are other ways in which these indices are valuable, but imperfect, yardsticks for measuring national AI power. While most of the metrics are quantitative, there is some subjectivity in deciding what to count and, in particular, how to weight or combine various indices. The indices are also only a snapshot in time. They capture metrics based on data available when they were produced, which often is 2017–2020 data, but sometimes are cumulative metrics dating back several decades. The choices of what to measure are based on an understanding of AI technology at the time. As AI technology continues to evolve, its future evolution may change the relative value of some metrics. For example, the increased use of synthetic data may diminish the value of real-world data as an input to AI power and increase the value of computing power, which both analyzes and creates synthetic data.

The indices generally don't capture trends, although in some cases trends can be seen by looking at the underlying data sources. Even if China is behind in many areas as of 2017 to 2020, the trends heavily favor China. The Chinese economy has been on a rocket-like trajectory for the last several decades and has rapidly emerged as a global powerhouse in AI. Just because China is number two today doesn't mean that they are destined to stay there. China's goal to be the global AI leader by 2030 looks very achievable based on current trends, absent a course correction by the United States.

Finally, these indices don't capture the agency that individuals and organizations have to chart their future. Governments, corporations, universities, and civil society groups all have choices about how they respond to AI technology. These choices can accelerate, shape, or stall AI adoption. AI indices capture a moment in time; they are not a prediction of the future.

To better understand which countries have an advantage in military, economic, and political power in the age of AI, we'll need to dive deeper into four key areas: data, compute, talent, and institutions.

2

DATA

Of all the inputs to machine learning, data has perhaps received the most attention as an element of national power. In 2017, *The Economist* proclaimed, "The world's most valuable resource is no longer oil, but data."

The digital revolution has created a globe-spanning network of digital devices, which in turn are creating unprecedented amounts of data. There are an estimated 24 billion connected devices in use in 2021, growing 10 percent annually to an estimated nearly 30 billion devices by 2023. As the internet expands, it is bringing both more people and devices online. By 2023, there will be an estimated 5.3 billion internet users, or two-thirds of the world's population. IoT devices, which include smart meters, medical devices, home appliances, and industrial applications, are growing even faster than users and by 2023 are expected to account for over half of all connected devices. These devices create data and share it across a global network that trafficked an estimated over 250 exabytes of data per month in 2020. Global internet protocol (IP) traffic is growing even faster than connectivity, at a rate of 26 percent annually, and was projected to increase to nearly 400 exabytes per month in 2022. Network speeds are increasing to accommodate this data. Broadband speeds are expected to more than double and wireless speeds more than triple between 2018 and 2023.

It can be hard to wrap one's mind around the scale of data that is created and transmitted over the internet. An exabyte is 10^{18}, or a million trillion (1,000,000,000,000,000,000), bytes. To give a sense of scale, if the amount of data transmitted through global networks every day in 2020 were represented on paper, it would be a stack of paper that would stretch from the earth to the sun and back. Every day. By 2022, that stack of paper would have grown roughly 50 percent taller, doing one and a half round trips from the earth to the sun every day.

This explosion of data creates enormous opportunities for companies and governments that can harness it. Data has value both directly as a resource to be mined and analyzed for information but also for training machine learning systems. Many of the recent advances in AI are due to machine learning, an AI method in which algorithms are trained on data. This method contrasts with rule-based AI systems that follow a set of hand-crafted rules to govern their behavior, sometimes called "good old-fashioned AI" (GOFAI).

A subfield of machine learning behind much of the recent AI progress is deep learning, which uses deep neural networks. Neural networks are loosely inspired by mammalian brains, in which artificial "neurons" pass signals to one another through a network. The neural network "learns" by adjusting the strength of the connection between neurons in the network. "Deep" neural networks are those with many intermediate layers between an input layer and an output layer.

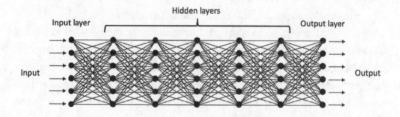

Deep Neural Network. *Deep learning is a subfield of machine learning in which deep neural networks are trained on data. Loosely inspired by mammalian brains, neural networks "learn" by adjusting the weights of connections in the network. Some of the largest neural networks have billions of connections.*

Many of the datasets used to train deep neural networks are massive. ImageNet, the image database that kicked off the deep learning revolution in 2012, includes 14 million images. In order for a neural network to learn what an object looks like, such as a "cat," "car," or "chair," it needs many examples to develop an internal representation of that object. For any given object, ImageNet contains roughly 500 to 1,000 images of that object to allow for a rich set of examples. Deep learning is a more data-intensive process than writing a set of rules for behavior, but deep learning can also be vastly more effective at building intelligent systems for some tasks.

Imagine trying to create an AI system to tell the difference between a picture of an apple and a picture of a tomato. It would be difficult to write a set of rules to determine the difference. Both are round, shiny, and red (but some-times green). Both sometimes have a green stem on top. Yet a child can tell the difference between them and so can deep neural networks if they are trained on sufficient numbers of labeled images of apples and tomatoes. Deep learning image classifiers surpassed human performance on benchmark tests of image identification back in 2015.

As deep learning has continued to evolve, AI researchers have turned to ever-larger datasets to train more advanced AI systems. In 2019, OpenAI announced a language model called GPT-2 trained on 40 gigabytes (GB) of text. At the time, it was the largest language model that had been trained, with 1.5 billion parameters. Two and a half years later, Microsoft and NVIDIA announced Megatron-Turing NLG, a 530 billion parameter language model that drew its training data from an 825 GB text database. AI researchers con-tinue to see performance gains from ever-larger models and datasets, demon-strating the value of large datasets.

The search for historical analogies to understand the geostrategic signifi-cance of digital power, such as data, is understandable, even if such analogies are bound to be imperfect. "Data is the new oil" became a common refrain for a brief period, spawning articles and op-eds in outlets such as *Wired, Forbes,* and the *New York Times.* (Not long after came a counter-wave of data-is-*not*-the-new-oil articles, including in many of the same outlets.) Data, of course, is not oil. But it can be a useful metaphor in certain ways. Not only are data and oil both valuable, they are both critical inputs into the technological revolutions of their age. Oil is used to fuel engines that can be used for mechanical work. Data is used to train machine learning algorithms that can perform cognitive labor. Both data and oil are resources that can be extracted, pooled, and traded. Both need to be refined to be used. Amassing data, like oil, confers advantages to those who can find ways to use it.

Yet there are important ways in which the comparison breaks down. Oil is consumed when used, while data is not. Data can be freely shared and cop-ied, while oil is a scarce resource. But the most consequential difference—and where claims that China is "the Saudi Arabia of data" fall apart—is that data is not a fungible resource. Whereas oil can be refined into different fuels that can be used to power cars, semitrailers, cargo ships, commercial airliners, tanks, fighter jets, warships, and power plants, data's uses are very specific to the type of data that is collected. Data on faces can be used to train facial recognition systems but won't be of much use for training AI-enabled fighter jets in air combat. Imagine, if instead of refining crude oil into gasoline, propane, and

other products, companies had to drill for the oil to make gasoline, diesel, propane, and jet fuel in different places. Furthermore, imagine if each make and
model of car required its own type of gasoline. Oil would be less valuable than
it is now. ("Data is the new natural gas" might better draw attention to some
of the limitations of data but is not nearly as catchy a phrase.) Oil remains the
new oil.

In fact, machine learning systems are often so narrowly constrained by the
datasets on which they've been trained that their performance can often drop
if they are used for tasks that are not well-represented in the training data. For
example, a facial recognition system may perform poorly on people of races or
ethnicities that are not adequately represented in its training data. A machine
learning algorithm used for predictive maintenance on one aircraft won't work
on another aircraft—it would need to be retrained on data for the new aircraft. It may not even be effective at predicting maintenance needs on the same
aircraft in a new environment, since maintenance needs may differ based on
environmental conditions, such as in a desert where sand can clog parts or in a
maritime environment where there is saltwater corrosion.

Nevertheless, data, like oil, has enormous geopolitical significance. Do
some nations have a national advantage over others in how they use data? The
United States, China, and Europe operate under vastly different regulatory
regimes when it comes to personal data. Europe has leaned the most into regulating data collection, with its General Data Protection Regulation (GDPR).
The U.S. government, by contrast, has taken a more laissez-faire approach to
regulating technology, allowing the growth of "surveillance capitalism" in
which big tech companies collect and store massive amounts of personal data.
(Although political winds in Washington are starting to shift with a growing
"techlash" against big tech firms.) China represents the starkest difference, with
the Chinese Communist Party building an intrusive and expansive techno-
authoritarian surveillance apparatus, which is imperfect and fragmented for
now but will become increasingly capable over time. Yet China's data advantage, which has been espoused both by proponents of China's AI development
and those who fear it, is overstated. There are some ways in which Chinese
companies and the Chinese government will have access to more data than
their American or European counterparts, but this does not necessarily translate to a major national advantage, and it certainly doesn't directly translate to
a military advantage.

In theory, the argument for China's data advantage stems from the combination of China's large population and lax data privacy regulations. The truth,

as always, is more complicated. China has the largest number of internet users in the world, with an estimated 900 million internet users as of 2020. India comes in second, with roughly 750 million internet users in 2020, the European Union (collectively) in third with around 400 million users, and the United States a distant fourth with roughly 290 million internet users. China and India have an even higher internet user potential than Europe and the United States simply by virtue of their larger populations: roughly 1.4 billion for China and India each compared to just under 450 million in the European Union and 330 million in the United States. More people means more data, but far more relevant than national internet user metrics is the size and diversity of the datasets available to tech companies. Major U.S. tech firms like Meta (formerly Facebook) and Google have global reach and are hardly constrained by the size of the U.S. population. Facebook has 2.7 billion users and YouTube over 2 billion, compared to WeChat's 1.2 billion. The diversity of data also matters a great deal for training robust machine learning systems, and, with the exception of ByteDance's TikTok, Chinese apps have struggled to gain a foothold outside of China. Tencent, which owns WeChat and other Chinese social media apps, will be in an overwhelmingly dominant position to leverage its user data to train algorithms to predict the behavior of Chinese social media users, but those predictions may not hold for markets outside China.

Additionally, Chinese citizens' alleged "cultural nonchalance about data privacy," in the words of Chinese AI pioneer Kai-Fu Lee, is also overstated. For one, American citizens have acquiesced without much pushback to U.S. tech companies hoovering up their personal data. Data privacy issues in China are also more complex than they might first appear. While the Chinese government exercises enormous surveillance powers over its citizens, many police databases are decentralized and localized. The Chinese government has also taken steps to increase privacy protections from corporate (although not government) surveillance, and the government may see advantages in reining in the independent power of tech companies. The Chinese Communist Party has begun cracking down on the power of Chinese big tech firms, reeling in once-powerful moguls like Alibaba cofounder Jack Ma.

There are some areas in which Chinese firms will have major data advantages over U.S. companies, which are likely to translate into technical advantages in some AI applications. The most notable among these is facial recognition, which is being widely deployed in China while a grassroots backlash in the United States has slowed deployment. Several cities and states across America have banned facial recognition for law enforcement. In 2020, Amazon and

Microsoft placed a moratorium on selling facial recognition to law enforcement and IBM cancelled its work on facial recognition. These national differences are likely to give Chinese firms a major edge in future facial recognition development. This edge in facial recognition may also help to lift China's AI ecosystem somewhat overall, although it isn't clear how much these advantages will carry over into other AI applications.

Data is vital to AI, but its advantage is likely to be constrained to narrow applications. When comparing countries, tech companies' dominance of global markets is far more important than national population.

Finally, the value of data itself as an input to AI may be changing, with AI researchers working on techniques to reduce their reliance on massive datasets. These include few-shot, one-shot, and zero-shot learning techniques, which are methods of training models when there are few, one, or even zero examples of an item in the training data. Another approach is using computer-generated synthetic data to augment or even completely replace real-world data.

The evolution of DeepMind's *go*-playing AI systems shows the changing importance of data. DeepMind's early version of AlphaGo, which beat eighteen-time world champion Lee Sedol in 2016, was first trained on a database of 30 million moves by human expert *go* players. AlphaGo then refined its performance to superhuman levels through self-play, a form of training on synthetic data in which the computer plays against itself. An updated version, AlphaGo Zero, released the following year, reached superhuman performance without any human training data at all, playing 4.9 million games against itself. AlphaGo Zero was able to entirely replace human-generated data with synthetic data. (This also had the benefit of allowing the algorithm to learn to play *go* without adopting any biases from human players.) A subsequent version of AlphaGo Zero was trained on 29 million games of self-play. For DeepMind's next version, AlphaZero, three different versions of the same algorithm were trained to reach superhuman performance through self-play in chess (44 million self-play games), *go* (21 million self-play games), and the Japanese strategy game *shogi* (24 million self-play games). For each type of game, 5,000 AI-specialized computer chips were used to generate the simulated games, allowing compute to effectively act as a substitute for real-world data.

Strategy games are a special case since they can be perfectly simulated, while the complexity of the real world oftentimes cannot, but synthetic data can help augment datasets when real-world data may be limited. The autonomous car company Waymo stated in 2020 that they had driven over 20 million miles on public roads, building up a large dataset of real-world driving interactions. To augment this real-world data, Waymo has been simulating 10 million driving miles *every single day* in computer simulations, racking up a total of 10 billion simulated miles as of 2020. These simulations are another form of synthetic data, which can then be used to improve autonomous car algorithms. Simulations allow Waymo to create thousands of variations of situations, ensuring its algorithms are robust to a range of driving conditions.

Data will continue to be valuable, but if AI evolves toward techniques using less data or synthetic data, its value may change over time. By using computing hardware to substitute for data, synthetic data tilts the balance away from data as a crucial AI input and toward another input: compute.

3

COMPUTE

Algorithms aren't trained on data by magic. They are trained using computing hardware, also called "compute" for shorthand. If data is overhyped as an input of national AI power, the geopolitical significance of compute is often underappreciated. The deep learning revolution has led to an explosion in compute requirements for cutting-edge machine learning research. Control over AI hardware has emerged as a key battleground between the United States and China and could be a critical determining factor in the future of AI power. A global semiconductor shortage in 2021 highlighted the vulnerabilities of disrupted supply chains and the importance of a few key actors who control them.

Machine learning uses compute in two ways. The first is to train algorithms, a very compute-intensive process. The second is for inference, in which trained AI models are used to process data. For neural networks, the training process consists of adjusting the weights of the connections in the network so that, as training progresses, the neural network adapts to make more accurate predictions. Training an AI model on large datasets can take an enormous amount of computing power. The compute requirements for trained AI models doing inference are much less, sometimes orders of magnitude less than what was needed for training. While AI models are often trained at large data centers, the lower compute requirements mean that inference can increasingly be done on edge devices, such as smartphones, IoT devices, intelligent video cameras, or autonomous cars.

Both training and inference are done on computer chips, and advances in computing hardware has been fundamental to the deep learning revolution. Graphics processing units (GPUs) have emerged as a key enabler for deep learning because of their ability to do parallel computation (which is valuable for neural networks) better than traditional central processing units (CPUs). A McKinsey study estimated that 97 percent of deep learning training in data centers in 2017 used GPUs. As machine learning researchers have turned to training bigger models on ever-larger datasets, they have also needed increasingly massive amounts of compute.

From 2010 to 2022, the amount of compute used in cutting-edge machine learning research projects increased ten billionfold. Compute usage is growing exponentially, doubling every six months. For comparison, Moore's law, which guided the development of ever-smaller computer chips for decades, had a doubling period of every two years. For some current AI applications, researchers are now using tremendous amounts of compute. In training an algorithm to achieve superhuman performance at the computer game *Dota 2*, researchers at OpenAI used "thousands of GPUs over multiple months." Because the computer could play games at an accelerated speed, the training was equivalent to a human playing for 45,000 years. In another project, an OpenAI team trained a robotic hand to manipulate a Rubik's cube in 13,000 years of simulated computer time.

The massive amounts of computing power used for machine learning research doesn't come free. Leading AI research teams at organizations such as OpenAI, DeepMind, and Google Brain are spending millions on compute pursuing the latest advances in AI. These exorbitant sums are only possible because the labs are backed by some of the world's largest corporations with deep pockets. DeepMind, which is owned by Google's parent company Alphabet, lost nearly $650 million in 2019 and had a $1.5 billion debt waived by Alphabet. In 2019, Microsoft announced plans to invest $1 billion in OpenAI. (Microsoft and Alphabet were both in the top five largest publicly traded companies in the world by market capitalization as of 2022.)

The recent explosion of interest (and money) in AI has been closely followed by the development of specialized hardware better suited for deep learning. For example, by 2022 an estimated three-fourths of all smartphones shipped—1.25 billion devices—will have an AI-specialized processor on board. These chips will improve the devices' ability to perform facial recognition, image identification, natural language processing, and other AI tasks onboard the device.

AI algorithms and software tools are widely available, with programming frameworks like TensorFlow, PyTorch, and Keras free online, yet the hardware ecosystem is concentrated among a small number of actors. A limited number of companies—and an even smaller number of countries—wield outsize influence over key chokepoints in global chip supply chains. Additionally, the compute-intensive nature of deep learning means that those who have access to specialized AI chips and the deep pockets needed to pay for compute-heavy training have major advantages over those who do not. Control over compute may turn out to be the crux of the global competition for AI power. Among the key countries are some surprising players, such as Taiwan and the Netherlands, who play an outsize role in hardware supply chains and, by extension, AI geopolitical power.

The semiconductor, or computer chip, industry is highly globalized, with supply chains for a single electronics product running through several countries. Yet these supply chains are also highly concentrated in a few key points, such as chip fabrication. Computer chips undergo three stages during production: design, manufacturing, and a post-manufacturing phase that includes assembly, testing, and packaging. Design and manufacturing account for roughly 90 percent of the value of the chip, split evenly between the two, with assembly, testing, and packaging accounting for the remaining 10 percent of a chip's value. Some semiconductor companies, such as Samsung (a South Korean firm) and Intel (a U.S. company) are integrated device manufacturers that do all three phases of semiconductor production. Other companies specialize in certain production phases. "Fabless" companies specialize in chip design and outsource fabrication (chip manufacturing) to other firms. Conversely, pure-play foundries specialize in chip fabrication, manufacturing chips on contract for other firms.

The United States, South Korea, Taiwan, Japan, Europe (collectively), and China are the biggest players in the global semiconductor market. Yet these actors are not equally distributed across the semiconductor value chain. For example, while U.S.-headquartered firms account for 47 percent of global semiconductor sales, the United States has only 12 percent of global chip manufacturing. U.S. and South Korean companies overwhelmingly dominate in integrated device manufacturers, with Intel and Samsung the two biggest players. U.S. chip-design firms like Broadcom, Qualcomm, and NVIDIA are some of the leading fabless companies, and U.S. firms account for 65 percent of the global fabless market. Yet nowhere in the semiconductor value chain is the market more concentrated than in pure-play foundries specializing in chip fabrication.

One single firm overwhelmingly dominates the contract foundry market: Taiwan Semiconductor Manufacturing Company (TSMC). TSMC is the third-largest semiconductor company globally behind Intel and Samsung and alone accounts for over half of the global pure-play foundry market. Combined with other smaller foundries, Taiwanese companies make up 65 percent of the foundry market. (The United States, by contrast, has 10 percent of the foundry market.) Raw sales figures understate Taiwan's significance, however. Not all semiconductors are created equal, and TSMC is not only the largest contract foundry but also a technology leader.

The overarching trend in semiconductors, since the 1960s, has been toward smaller transistors, which have allowed for increased density (more transistors per square inch) on chips. This trend, sometimes characterized as Moore's law, has resulted in an exponential growth in computing power as chips have packed increasingly more computing power per square inch. This, in turn, has enabled not only more powerful but also increasingly miniaturized electronics, enabling everything from smartphones and watches to IoT devices and 5G wireless networks. While the pace of advancement has been slowing for the past decade or more as smaller transistors approach fundamental physical limits, chip performance continues to improve, albeit at a slower pace. Yet the counterpart to Moore's law is Rock's law, which predicts exponential growth in the costs for new semiconductor fabrication facilities. Over the last two decades, fab costs have increased 11 percent annually and chip design costs 24 percent annually. A new leading-edge foundry can cost $10 billion to $20 billion. The massive capital expenditures required make it hard for other companies to compete with industry leaders. TSMC planned to spend between $40–44 billion in capital expenditures in 2022 alone. The skyrocketing cost of chip fabrication has consolidated the semiconductor market, driving out many companies.

At each evolution of chip production, the number of companies at the leading edge has shrunk. In 2001, when the 130 nanometer (nm) node (a term used to denote the manufacturing process) went into mass production, there were over two dozen companies at the leading edge of chip fabrication. As chips advanced over the next two decades, with each introduction of a new manufacturing process fewer companies were able to fabricate leading-edge chips. (More advanced chip fabrication processes are characterized by smaller sizes, such as 90 nm, 65 nm, 45 nm, 22 nm, 10 nm, and 7 nm. In practice, node naming has long been divorced from actual transistor size.) Only two companies, Samsung and TSMC, are producing chips at the current leading-edge 5 nm process node.

Taiwanese foundries churn out one-fifth of global chip fabrication (from both contract foundries and integrated device manufacturers), but over 90 percent of leading-edge chips at the 7 nm node and below. For AI chips, TSMC manufactured eight of the ten AI-specialized chips available at the 16 nm process or below as of 2020, including both leading GPUs (designed by AMD and

NVIDIA). (Intel and Samsung manufacture the other two leading AI chips.) Taiwan's outsize role in leading-edge fabrication places it at the geopolitical fulcrum of compute. Statements like "China is the Saudi Arabia of data" don't match reality, but it isn't a stretch to claim that Taiwan is the Saudi Arabia of compute.

China, meanwhile, is a relative backwater in chip production but is the king-pin of chip consumption. Over the last several decades China has emerged as a global hub of microelectronics manufacturing. Chips that are designed in the United States and manufactured in Taiwan are often destined for China, where they will be assembled into final finished products such as smartphones, computers, or other devices that are then shipped around the world. China accounts for 60 percent of the global demand for semiconductors. Because Chinese domestic chip production has struggled, China imports most of its chips. China runs a massive chip trade deficit, importing over $400 billion worth of chips annually.

Nowhere in the domain of AI competition is China further behind than in hardware. Every AI expert I spoke with in China was acutely aware of China's hardware gap. China's dependency on chip imports is not just a massive economic cost but also a national security vulnerability. As the U.S.-China competition has heated up, the U.S. government has used China's chip dependency to kneecap one of its tech "national champions," Huawei, a global leader in 5G wireless technology. The U.S. government's willingness to exploit China's vulnerability in semiconductors has thrust compute to the fore of geopolitical competition in AI. As the United States and China compete in AI, control over compute will be a critical factor in who controls the future of AI.

4

TALENT

The machine age is being built by people. Human talent is needed to implement AI technology today and unlock the next generation of advancements. AI talent is a major source of competition and a potential differentiator among countries seeking to enhance their national AI power.

The United States, Europe, and China all have robust AI research communities. Europe (collectively) leads in total size, the United States leads in quality, and China is the fastest-growing region in both quantity and quality of AI research. As in other areas, data that captures only a snapshot in time can be misleading if it doesn't account for trends. Most of those trends favor China.

China overtook the United States in total AI publications in 2006 and Europe in 2017. These figures don't account for quality, though. U.S. papers are cited, on average, roughly 30 percent more than European papers and around 70 percent more than papers from China. China has been rapidly improving its research quality over the last two decades, however. The number of Chinese authors contributing to top AI journals increased twelvefold from 2009 to 2019 and is now roughly 2.5 times the number of U.S. authors contributing to those journals. China surpassed the United States in the total number of AI journal citations in 2020. According to a 2019 analysis from the Allen Institute, China was expected to overtake the United States in the top 10 percent of most-cited papers in 2020 and the top 1 percent of most-cited papers by 2025. Yet as fast as China is growing talent, it is bleeding it abroad.

A 2020 study by MacroPolo tracked the flow of international AI talent based on a sample of papers accepted to one of the top deep learning conferences, NeurIPS. Using authors of papers accepted to the conference as a proxy for top AI researchers, the study found that more of the top researchers did their undergraduate education in China than any other country. Yet the vast majority of top Chinese undergraduates studying AI left China to pursue their graduate work abroad. Less than a third stayed in China and more than half came to the United States for their graduate work. Of those Chinese undergraduates who moved to the United States for their PhD studies, over 90 percent chose to stay and work in the United States after graduation. China is the biggest source of AI talent, producing more students who go on to be top researchers than any other country, but the United States is the biggest magnet for AI talent, drawing in the best and brightest from around the world—including China—and keeping them in America.

The United States is overwhelmingly the top destination for AI scientists from around the world. Two-thirds of the top AI researchers in the world work in the United States, the vast majority of whom are originally from outside the United States. Less than one-third of the top AI researchers currently working in the United States did their undergraduate studies at U.S. universities. The remaining did their undergraduate work abroad and came to the United States, with the top sending regions China, India, and Europe.

American institutions—both universities and companies—are a major draw for AI researchers from around the world. Google, Stanford, Carnegie Mellon, MIT, and Microsoft Research top the charts for affiliations for researchers published at top deep learning conferences. Of the top fifteen institutions publishing deep learning research, thirteen are American universities or corporate research labs. Only one, Tsinghua University, is Chinese.

There is no denying that quality matters far more than quantity when it comes to advancing basic research. The competition for AI talent is fierce, with fresh PhDs reportedly making between $300,000 to $500,000 or more a year in salary and stock options. Top AI researchers are highly sought after and can make millions. Jack Clark, then policy director for OpenAI, told the *New York Times*, "For much of basic AI research, the key ingredient in progress is people rather than algorithms." Algorithms are not a scarce resource. People are.

Yet when it comes to translating AI into national power, leading in basic research may matter less than implementation. Because the AI community is so open, advances made in top AI labs may be rapidly copied and put into use by others. Building practical AI applications depends upon not only having a ready pool of AI talent, but also empowering AI researchers and entrepreneurs with financing, resources, and the freedom to build. In terms of implementing AI, the global playing field is much more level. Even if it lags in cutting-edge research, China is equal to or ahead of others in AI deployment.

The U.S. government can take steps to double down on America's advantages in talent. In 2020, more than twenty American universities and companies, including Carnegie Mellon, Stanford, Amazon, Google, IBM, and NVIDIA, called on the federal government to create a national AI research cloud to empower academic researchers with greater compute and data resources. One of the unfortunate consequences of the exponential growth of compute in machine learning research has been to divide the AI research community into haves and have-nots. Compute-intensive research has become increasingly concentrated in the hands of corporate-backed labs, such as DeepMind, OpenAI, and Google Brain. Anima Anandkumar, director of machine learning at the chip company NVIDIA and a professor at Caltech, noted that academics "do not have the luxury of a large amount of compute and engineering resources" even to replicate, let alone compete with, research from corporate-backed labs. Increased funding can help academics stay engaged in compute-intensive research. Giving universities the necessary resources will help them continue to attract top faculty and students to American universities and make the most out of the talent that resides there.

The United States has natural advantages in human capital, and concerted U.S. government action can help double down on those advantages. The bipartisan National Artificial Intelligence Initiative Act of 2020 established the creation of a National Artificial Intelligence Research Resource to provide students and faculty with necessary data and compute resources. Similarly, investments in new semiconductor fabs in the United States will not only help secure chip supply chains; they will also grow the talent base of U.S. microelectronics engineers working on leading-edge fabrication technology, helping to ensure American leadership in the next generation of semiconductors.

The Chinese government has long prioritized scientific talent as part of its national competitiveness, and no aspect of international talent flows has drawn more controversy than China's Thousand Talents Plan. The program offers participants high salaries, bonuses, research funding, lab space, and housing in exchange for bringing their scientific knowledge back to China. Thousand Talents is only the most prominent of China's estimated over 200 talent recruitment plans. The Chinese government uses programs such as Thousand Talents to tap into the massive pool of Chinese scientists overseas, which one study estimated might be as large as 400,000 individuals. China's talent programs are not limited only to Chinese nationals, however. In 2021, a jury convicted the former chair of Harvard's Chemistry and Chemical Biology Department of lying to federal authorities and tax fraud for failing to disclose a $50,000 a month salary he was paid for participating in Thousand Talents. (Participating in a talent program is not illegal; failing to disclose foreign income and conflicts of interest on a U.S. government grant application can be.)

The U.S. government has increased its attention on Chinese talent recruitment programs in recent years as part of a broader effort to crack down on Chinese espionage and intellectual property theft. In response to increased scrutiny, the Chinese government deleted mention of Thousand Talents online, yet recruitment efforts continue. In 2019, the Chinese government consolidated Thousand Talents and other recruitment programs into the new High-End Foreign Expert Recruitment Program. Emily Weinstein, a research analyst at the Center for Security and Emerging Technology who built a comprehensive Chinese Talent Program Tracker, described Chinese talent programs as "a moving target."

Through increased investigations and improved visa screening, U.S. policymakers aim to blunt China's technology transfer campaign without cutting off the flow of Chinese talent to the United States—a difficult balancing act. High-skilled immigration from outside China presents less of a challenge, and the United States has an opportunity to double down on its advantages in AI talent by increasing the inflow of top researchers from around the world.

The congressionally appointed U.S. National Security Commission on AI warned in its 2021 final report, "The United States is in a global competition for scarce AI talent. . . . For the first time in our lifetime, the United States risks losing the competition for talent on the scientific frontiers." The commission called for a new National Defense Education Act, mirroring the one the United States passed in the wake of the Soviet Union's launch of Sputnik in 1957, to reinvigorate math and science education. Yet a nation of 330 million people will always be at a disadvantage competing against a nation of 1.4 billion if the United States restricts itself to home-grown talent. America's unique advantage in the competition for AI talent is its ability to draw on the best and brightest out of the world's 8 billion people. The biggest barrier today is America's own immigration policies. In a survey of top machine learning researchers residing in the United States, nearly 70 percent said visa and immigration problems were an obstacle to recruiting foreign talent. The National Security Commission on AI called for expanding high-skilled immigration, arguing "immigration reform is a national security imperative."

In early 2022, the Biden administration announced a series of measures to ease obstacles to international science, technology, engineering, and mathematics (STEM) talent coming to the United States. These included increasing foreign exchange programs, expanding the availability of visas, and updating immigration policies for those with advanced degrees. These are valuable steps, yet additional actions are needed to make it easier for U.S. universities and companies to recruit talented scientists and engineers from abroad.

Human capital is at the core of the global competition for AI power. Innovation comes from people. China is improving its domestic education and recruiting foreign scientific knowledge through programs like Thousand Talents, but it cannot compete with the United States as a global draw for students and entrepreneurs. The competition for talent is, unique among core AI inputs, the United States' to lose. The United States remains a global leader in AI talent despite inadequate attention to domestic education and neglected opportunities for increasing high-skilled immigration. With reforms, the United States could secure another generation of global science and technology leadership.

5

INSTITUTIONS

Institutions are the final critical input for national AI power, transforming the raw elements of data, compute, and talent into practical applications. Having a strong foundation of the latent elements of national AI power is valuable but doesn't automatically translate to a military, political, or economic advantage. To use AI to boost military power, military institutions must be able to access AI technology, successfully import and adopt it, and find ways of using it for military advantage. To use AI to shape the information environment, nations must be able to build tech platforms that dominate the information ecosystem, such as Facebook or WeChat, along with platform governance rules that advance their national interests. Because AI is such a diffuse technology, many countries will have access to the necessary inputs. How nations apply these raw inputs will have a tremendous influence on how the AI revolution unfolds.

The AI revolution poses a particular challenge for militaries, since the bulk of AI innovation is occurring outside of traditional defense industries. In the 1960s, the federal government dominated the U.S. research and development ecosystem, funding nearly two-thirds of all U.S. R&D. But public sector R&D funding declined over time and is now less than one-quarter of all U.S. R&D, with private companies picking up the slack. Much of this commercial innovation has military applications. Eleven of the Defense Department's fourteen "critical technology areas" are commercial technologies. To access many cutting-edge, transformative technologies, militaries must tap into companies who may not be familiar—or comfortable with—working with the government.

The U.S. Department of Defense (DoD) has created a number of organizational innovations to bring commercial technology into the military, including the Defense Innovation Unit (DIU), Joint AI Center, and Project Maven. In

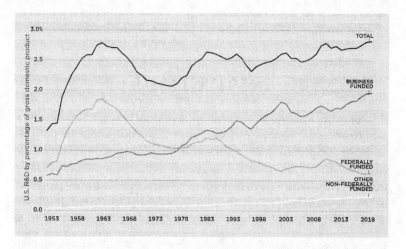

U.S. R&D Funding as a Percentage of Gross Domestic Product, 1953–2018. *U.S. government R&D funding has steadily declined from the 1960s, and today the private sector dominates R&D funding. The Defense Department must adapt to a technology ecosystem where the bulk of innovation is occurring outside the defense sector, requiring the ability to "spin-in" new technologies to the military.* (Data from the National Science Foundation and Congressional Research Service. Chart by Melody Cook / Center for a New American Security.)

the case of Maven, Google's participation in the project, which used AI image recognition to process drone video feeds, sparked a backlash from Google staff, ultimately leading the company to not renew work on the project. Employees at Amazon and Microsoft have similarly objected to working with the military, although the firms have continued to do so. The U.S. military faces multiple challenges to AI adoption, some due to cultural divides between the Pentagon and Silicon Valley, but the government's bureaucracy is an even more significant obstacle.

The United States isn't the only country working hard to spin-in AI technology to the military. China has similarly been investing in new institutions and organizations that will allow it to move faster and adopt commercial technology. Elsa Kania, an adjunct senior fellow at the Center for a New American Security and an expert on Chinese military technology, has highlighted "experimentation in Chinese defense innovation that may seek to mimic and adapt elements of the U.S. approach." Examples include DARPA-style competitions, such as an "Intelligent UAV Swarm System Challenge," and even a DIU-like unit. In 2018, China's Central Military Commission Science and Technology Commission, an organization roughly analogous to DARPA, launched a "rapid response small group" in Shenzhen "to use advanced commercial technologies to serve the military." Some Chinese reporting even referred to the group as "China's DIUx."

Government institutions can also play a vital role in incentivizing innovation through R&D investments, education policies, public goods such as data, compute, and standard-setting, and policies that create an innovation-friendly ecosystem, such as sensible regulatory policy. China's government has been particularly active in growing its scientific base, with R&D spending increasing at an average of 15 percent annually since 1998. In 2015, China launched a major national effort to boost its economic and technological competitiveness called "Made in China 2025."

Chinese investments in technology are paying dividends. China's "national team" of AI leaders: Baidu, Alibaba, Tencent, SenseTime, and iFLYTEK, are top-tier global AI companies. AI is only one of several high-technology areas in which China is now in a position of rough parity or ahead of the United States, including quantum technology, 5G wireless networking, and genomics. China has emerged as a technological powerhouse and is translating that technology leadership into military advances, such as the "intelligentization" of its military forces. China's vision of "intelligentized" warfare envisions combat with intelligent weapons, equipment, platforms, decision-making, and logistics enabled by AI, communications networks, big data, cloud computing, and IoT devices.

The United States, by contrast, has largely taken its position as a global technology leader for granted. The U.S. share of global R&D spending has been waning for decades. In 1960, total U.S. national expenditures, both public and private sector, accounted for nearly 70 percent of all global R&D spending. The United States was, far and away, the dominant global technological superpower. Yet by 2018, the U.S. share of global R&D spending had fallen to less than 30 percent. U.S. R&D spending was thirteen times China's in 1998, but China has now closed the gap and is on track to overtake the United States in total national R&D spending by the mid-2020s.

Alarmed at these trends, congressional leaders of both parties have called for major increases in AI spending. Senators Martin Heinrich, Rob Portman, and Brian Schatz proposed in 2019 an additional $2 billion in AI spending over a five-year period. This would be a modest increase on top of the then $1.1 billion annually in nondefense AI R&D and estimated roughly $8 billion in defense AI R&D spending. By 2021, AI R&D grew to $1.5 billion in nondefense and an estimated over $9 billion in defense spending, yet other congressional

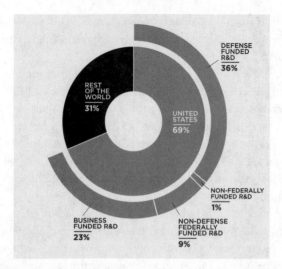

U.S. Share of Global R&D (1960). *In 1960, the United States dominated the global R&D landscape. U.S. defense spending alone accounted for 36 percent of global R&D. The Defense Department was a major driver of global technology development.* (Data from the National Science Foundation, Congressional Research Service, and the Organisation for Economic Co-operation and Development. Chart by Melody Cook / Center for a New American Security.)

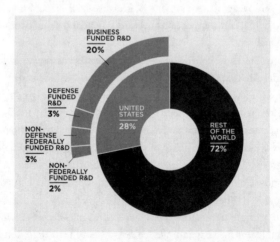

U.S. Share of Global R&D (2018). *The global R&D ecosystem today is much more diffuse. Other countries have access to many of the same technologies as the United States. To maintain its technological edge, the U.S. military must rapidly adopt technologies developed outside of the defense sector faster than competitors.* (Data from the National Science Foundation, Congressional Research Service, and the Organisation for Economic Co-operation and Development. Chart by Melody Cook / Center for a New American Security.)

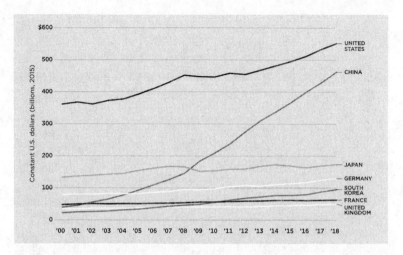

R&D Spending by Country, 2000–2018. *China has rapidly grown R&D spending and is on track to overtake the United States in total national R&D spending by the mid-2020s. China is already a world-class technology leader in many areas, including genomics, 5G wireless networks, quantum technology, and AI. Absent a course correction, the United States is at risk of ceding its position as a global technology leader.* (Data from the Organisation for Economic Co-operation and Development. Chart by Melody Cook / Center for a New American Security.)

leaders have called for much bigger increases in federal spending. Representatives Will Hurd and Robin Kelly proposed in 2020 raising federal AI R&D spending to $25 billion annually by 2025. Senator Chuck Schumer called for a massive investment on roughly the same scale, proposing an additional $100 billion in federal AI R&D spending over five years. There is widespread sentiment in Washington that the U.S. government needs to spend more on AI, but how much is enough? I interviewed former Google CEO Eric Schmidt, who chairs the National Security Commission on AI, in the summer of 2020 to get his take on how the United States was faring in the AI competition with China. "I can tell you what we told White House," he said. " 'You should double it, and then you should double it again. And then we should have a conversation.' " In the end, the commission recommended doubling nondefense AI R&D annually through 2026 to $32 billion per year, a roughly thirtyfold increase from 2020 levels.

Yet during the Trump administration, even as U.S. officials took a harder line toward competing with China, the U.S. government's approach was hamstrung by an ideological predisposition toward smaller government. The Trump administration's Fiscal Year 2021 budget proposed doubling nondefense AI R&D funding, but this was hardly an endorsement of the federal government's role in driving innovation. While increasing AI funding, the proposed budget slashed funding to a range of science and technology agencies, including a 6 percent cut to the National Science Foundation, 7 percent cut to the National Institutes of Health, 11 percent cut to NASA science, 17 percent cut to the Department of Energy's Office of Science, 19 percent cut to the National Institute of Standards and Technology, 30 percent cut to the National Oceanic and Atmospheric Administration, 37 percent cut to the Environmental Protection Agency's science and technology budget, 40 percent cut to government investment in science infrastructure, and complete elimination of the Advanced Research Projects Agency–Energy. In total, Trump's plan cut federal research spending by 9 percent overall. The AI funding increase was an outlier in a budget that, overall, gutted American science.

Eric Schmidt made a forceful argument for increased federal R&D spending, arguing that "the federal government's role in early research is central to the development of pretty much all of our businesses and pretty much all of our technology leadership." Members of Congress from both parties have overwhelmingly supported increased investments in American science and innovation. In 2022, Congress passed a mammoth bipartisan bill, the CHIPS and Science Act, providing for $280 billion in investments in science and technology, including AI. After decades of inattention, the U.S. government is slowly beginning to wake up and reinvest in innovation.

Governments have choices in how they respond to the AI revolution, whether they rise to the challenge of global competition or flounder and fail. Different nations have varying levels of access to data, compute, and talent, but as is the case in other areas of geopolitical competition, how they apply their nation's resources will be a major factor in political outcomes. China has major weaknesses in compute and talent, but the Chinese government is executing a concerted national approach to boost its science and technology competitiveness, including in AI. In their 2021 Global AI Index, researchers at Tortoise ranked China second in government strategy behind Canada, followed by Saudi Arabia, Spain, France, Russia, South Korea, and Finland. The United States, meanwhile, has massive structural advantages, especially in talent, that it is squandering due to the lack of a coherent national approach. In Tortoise's government strategy ranking, the United States was seventeenth.

PART II
COMPETITION

6

A WINNING HAND

The bot was getting smarter. There was no denying it. A week into the 2017 "Brains vs. AI" poker challenge, which pitted four top human professional players against Carnegie Mellon University's Libratus AI in no-limit Texas Hold'em, the tide began to turn. The humans were already dead in the water; they just didn't know it yet.

Each evening, after a full day of heads-up (one-on-one) poker against Libratus, the four human players would meet up to study its moves and game out a plan of attack. "After a few days, we felt like we really had a good strategy going on. . . . We were very confident," said Jason Les, one of the players taking on Libratus. On day six of the tournament, the four human players combined netted over $100,000 against Libratus. "We've figured this out. It has these holes," Jason said, "And then it improved." Libratus closed nearly $200,000 in winnings the next day, and the humans never recovered their position. "It seemed to learn what we were doing and exploit it," said another player, Daniel McAuley. In reality, Tuomas Sandholm, the Carnegie Mellon University (CMU) professor behind Libratus, explained to me that they were using a supercomputer to run calculations on the probabilities of poker hands while the human players were sleeping. While the humans were comparing notes trying to understand Libratus's weaknesses, it was churning thousands of computer cores every night to get better. The humans never stood a chance.

Jason admitted, "The hopes of winning went out the window, and then we were just trying to make it close." Try as they might, the humans couldn't find a sustained weakness in the bot. "It ended up changing the strategy as time went on," Jason said. "It was improving day to day." Like fighting against the cybernetic hive mind The Borg in *Star Trek*, resistance was futile. By the end of the twenty-day tournament comprising 120,000 hands, the bot had racked up over $1.7 million in combined winnings. No human player finished in the black against Libratus. Jason admitted the humans "lost very decisively." Like chess and *go* before it, another game had fallen to the machines. But the true accomplishment was bigger than poker.

Achieving superhuman performance in poker meant making progress on games of "imperfect information," where players do not know, for example, what cards the other players hold or which cards remain in the deck. But Tuomas explained that the same underlying principles applied in many real-world competitions, such as in negotiations, finance, and war. Libratus didn't achieve superhuman performance by using handcrafted rules from expert poker players. Tuomas readily admitted he hardly knew anything about poker before building Libratus. Instead, he used computational game theory to design an AI engine to solve imperfect-information games, and he spent a year running it on the Pittsburgh Supercomputing Center's Bridges supercomputer. Twenty-four million core-hours later, Tuomas and his colleague Noam Brown had built Libratus, an AI that knew more about the ins and outs of poker than any human player. Now Tuomas was setting his sights on real-world problems. By applying the same methods to other situations with imperfect information, Tuomas hoped to unlock new competitive strategies to outwit adversaries in other settings as thoroughly as Libratus did in poker.

Tuomas and I met up three years after Libratus's victory at the offices of Strategy Robot, a ten-person start-up he leads in Pittsburgh. Strategy Robot sits in a two-story red brick building just a few blocks from the Carnegie Mellon campus. The office has the feel of a small start-up. Two programmers were hard at work on their computers, stopping only briefly to say hello when I arrived before turning back to their code. The floor was covered with snaking lines of cables for monitors and computers, sprinkled with takeout bags. The walls were bare, save for two of Tuomas's patents and a framed picture of one of the human vs. AI poker matches. It used to be that to see cutting-edge technologies that could transform future wars one had to enter a secret defense lab. But instead I was visiting a small start-up just outside a university campus.

To tap into the latest AI advances, the military will need to look beyond traditional defense contractors and engage start-ups like Strategy Robot and Heron Systems. Military AI applications are coming out of start-ups and university labs around the world, making AI technology widely accessible. U.S. national security leaders are waking up to the AI revolution at the same time as the competition between the United States and China is heating up, leaving Defense Department leaders scrambling to find ways to engage start-ups and bring AI technology into the military faster than China.

The goal of Strategy Robot is to take the technology behind Libratus and apply it to military problems. Tuomas explained that his computational game theory techniques could be used for a host of military and other security problems at the tactical, operational, and strategic level. Deception and bluffing are part and parcel of military operations. When I was an Army Ranger doing recon missions in Afghanistan, we would do false helicopter insertions on mountaintops before fast-roping onto a mountain hide site. There was no way to hide the noise of the helicopters dropping us off, but by doing false insertions in multiple locations, we could mask our actual location. The enemy would know we were somewhere in the valley, but not on which mountaintop or how many recon teams there might be.

The Chinese military strategist Sun Tzu wrote in the fifth century BCE, "All warfare is based on deception." Tuomas's team at Strategy Robot takes something militaries have been doing since antiquity and makes it more rigorous and strategic. Computers can churn through millions of game theory calculations, seeking the optimal strategy. The appeal of this approach is the ability to think several moves ahead and box opponents in, the same way Libratus did. "As we change our strategy, Red [the opponent] will change its strategy," Tuomas said. (The U.S. military typically labels adversaries as the "red" team in war games and the United States as "blue.") The fact that the adversary will change their tactics is generally a problem, but Tuomas saw it as an opportunity. "We have the opportunity to affect their change by our own strategy. So we can drive the world instead of being reactive to it."

Tuomas's description of the constant cat-and-mouse game of warfare transported me back to Iraq. Driving the country's scorching desert roads in the summer of 2007, we made constant calculations about where we might find IEDs and how to avoid them. Take a well-traveled road and you were an easy target. The enemy knew U.S. troop convoys passed through the major arteries outside the base several times daily. IEDs there might be more common but were often hastily dropped and poorly concealed because the enemy didn't have much time before the next U.S. convoy came along. On less well-traveled roads, however, insurgents had more time. They would dig in deep, burying IEDs under the road. These were some of the most lethal bombs, whose sheer size allowed them to pierce the bottom hull of armored vehicles. Our actions shaped the enemy's strategy, and vice versa. These strategic contests played out in ways big and small on the battlefield. How far away you were from an IED when it exploded could make a major difference in explosive strength, and I recall talking with other soldiers about their driving strategies to minimize the risk: stick to one side of the road, mix it up, or go straight down the middle. Was it better to drive straight through potholes (which could hide an IED) or swerve around them, potentially swerving toward an IED on the side of the road? Competitive strategies played out in the technology as well. As the U.S. military invested in IED countermeasures, such as jammers and better armor, insurgents changed their tactics and technology to maintain their effectiveness. IEDs killed over 3,500 U.S. troops in Iraq and Afghanistan. I wondered how many of those servicemembers would be alive today if we had had the tools to act more strategically, to measure and assess enemy activity and stay one step ahead by varying our actions and being less predictable.

One of the advantages of AI is to give competitors the ability to play more complex and varied strategies. In poker, Jason Les said, "What makes Libratus's strategy unique is it uses a mixed strategy. It will do lots of different things with lots of different hands different frequencies of the time. Humans aren't like that." This complexity and variability can help keep opponents off their game. Jason said he found Libratus's unpredictability "very difficult to deal with." Using AI to make military tactics more varied and unpredictable could have significant advantages in war.

Strategic interactions among adversaries don't only come into play at the tactical level in combat. Feints and deceptions are a regular part of military strategy at the operational level. In World War II, the Allies built an entire phantom army composed of dummy tanks, airplanes, and landing craft to convince the Germans that the D-Day invasion of Normandy was merely a distraction and the real invasion would come at Pas de Calais, across the shortest distance of the English Channel. It worked, and the Germans held their forces back waiting for what they assumed would be the "real" invasion still to come, giving the Allies time to secure a beachhead in Normandy. In the 1991 Persian Gulf War, Marines and Navy SEALs faked a major amphibious assault to deceive Iraqi forces that the offensive would come directly into Kuwait, while the real invasion came in a "left hook" through the open desert, encircling Iraqi troops. Twelve years later, the military repeated the trick in reverse, with special operations forces executing deception operations in western Iraq while the real offensive came from the south. Militaries seeking advantage could use AI tools to model vastly more scenarios and potential interactions, perhaps leading to even more effective operational maneuvers.

The strategic interplay between competitors isn't only a factor on the battlefield. It can also play out in the long-term contest between nations for military dominance in procurement and R&D. Tuomas argued AI could help humans not only make better decisions amid uncertainty, but also decide when and how to reveal information. He said that in many strategic situations, "I'm striking the tradeoff carefully as to what information do I exploit versus what do I hide, so that I can exploit it in the future." In the military this frequently manifests in a tension between revealing new military capabilities to enhance deterrence versus concealing them to protect warfighting advantages. Revealing a new capability, such as a missile defense system (or bluffing about one) could help demonstrate strength, making adversaries less likely to attack. At the same time, revealing a new military system could give adversaries information about how to counter that capability. Tuomas explained that militaries today approach this general strategic problem with crude estimates or gut feeling. He was hopeful that applied computational game theory might help militaries make better decisions in the future.

Tuomas gave the example of deciding what kinds of nuclear capabilities to invest in, whether it would make strategic sense to invest in more ballistic missiles, submarines, bombers, missile defenses, or other capabilities. "What we build or plan to build affects what our adversaries are going to build and vice versa." People use simple strategies to make these decisions today, but Tuomas's aim was to build "very detailed models of games that you need computational AI to actually solve and then we can draw real strategies."

Computational AI can explore vastly more possibilities than humans can on their own. Poker has 10^{161} different situations a player can face (a one followed by 161 zeroes), more than the number of known atoms in the universe. It's impossible for humans to even conceive of a number this large, but it's also impossible for computers to develop strategies for all of these situations; it's simply too big. Instead, Libratus pared the problem down by developing a rough blueprint for the game by constructing a game tree that maps out the overall contours of the game. Imagine each decision point a player faces in poker—whether to fold, call, or raise—as a branching point on a tree. And each card that is revealed is another branch. Pretty soon, the game branches into a tree of tremendous complexity. Game trees are used to structure AI decision-making in other games, such as checkers, chess, and *go*. These game trees map out how the game might evolve, and the number of leaves on the tree is the number of possible game states, or positions that a player might find themselves in. (There may be multiple pathways to get to the same game state.) For more challenging games, the complexity grows enormously. Tic-tac-toe has roughly 10^{4} possible game states. Checkers has 10^{20} possible positions. Chess has between 10^{40} and 10^{50} possible positions. *Go* has approximately 10^170 possible positions. But these are all games of perfect information (players can see the whole board). Imperfect information games add a twist as the game tree branches out into different possible states. Strategies must account for an additional structure called an "information set," which Tuomas explained was the "set of states I might currently be in, which I can't distinguish at the moment because I don't have enough information." The opponent could be holding the nuts (the best possible hand) or could be bluffing. Effective strategies need to account for this uncertainty. They also need to account for the opponents' perceptions. Tuomas pointed out, "The states don't have values. Actually, my value of a particular state depends on other people's beliefs. Let's say I have Aces in my hand; I'm much better off if you believe I have a weak hand. It's very complex because the values of these states depend on your strategies, not only after the state, but also leading up to that state in the game tree. It's all kind of glued together in this messy way." (Tuomas said the branching complexity was less like a tree and more like a bush: "It's just branches everywhere.")

The computational game theory techniques that Tuomas and Noam Brown developed cut through that complexity. Rather than solve every move of poker using brute-force calculation, they focused on the parts of the game most commonly played. Jason Les and the other poker players *did* find a weakness in Libratus's game play early in the tournament. It was a strategy that pushed the game to a part of the tree that Libratus hadn't yet explored. And their strategy worked . . . for a day. That night, Libratus got better, crunching out new branches of the game tree on the supercomputer. The real world is vastly more complex than poker, but the same approaches could help explore myriad possibilities in strategic situations, developing optimal strategies for each, and with an adaptive approach that can improve over time.

Libratus plays not just more varied and complex strategies than humans; it also plays differently. Libratus makes what Tuomas described as "weird bet sizes," such as "tiny underbets, like 10 percent of the pot, or huge overbets, like 20 times the pot." It uses betting tactics like "limping" and "donk betting" that Tuomas explained are "typically considered really bad moves," but they turned out not to be in some situations. (Both moves are seen as betting on weak hands the player is likely to lose.) The difference is that Libratus has such a fine-grained understanding of the probabilities that it knows the situations in which these moves do make sense. Having seen these moves in action, professional human players have now adapted some of these tactics, but others remain out of reach because, as Tuomas says, "the whole strategy has to be optimized holistically."

Libratus's wide search of the game tree allows it to find novel strategies, and its precision allows it to execute approaches that humans are not able to replicate even after they've seen them.

AI methods like those used by Libratus may help in developing unconventional strategies in other situations as well. In congressional testimony in 2019, Defense Innovation Unit director Michael Brown cited "strategic reasoning" as one of "three major impact areas where AI is proven to excel" alongside computer vision and data analytics and prediction. Brown said, "DIU is prototyping an application that leverages AI to reason about high-level strategic questions, map probabilistic chains of events, and develop alternative strategies." Yet to do so, DIU needs to engage with commercial AI companies. If it can successfully do so, Brown stated that "the opportunities for dual-use applications within DoD are vast."

Strategy Robot is applying computational game theory to defense applications, such as war-gaming. The military regularly uses war games to explore hypothetic scenarios, both in peace and war (games that explore strategic interactions in peacetime are still often called "war games.") War is, thankfully, rare, so militaries face the unusual challenge of having to prepare for violent, high-stakes clashes that may occur once in a generation or even longer. The U.S. military hasn't faced a peer naval competitor in combat since Japan in World War II. War games can help defense analysts explore hypothetical problems, such as conflict against a new adversary, in a different geographic environment, or using a new military technology.

War games are often limited, however, in the number of strategies and scenarios they can practically explore. Developing a war game might take a team of researchers months of preparation, then three full days of game play where participants walk through moves and countermoves. In the end, the game may have only explored three variations of a scenario that could have tremendous complexity.

Tuomas said, "When you have these real game situations where you have the number of situations being larger than the number of atoms in the universe, and you've tested five strategies, or a hundred strategies, you know that you haven't even tested a drop in the ocean. Maybe you've tested an atom in the ocean." Strategists are dealing with massive blind spots. It makes certain strategies "look better than they really are, because they haven't been evaluated against the toughest" opposing strategies, Tuomas explained. It may cause the opponent to surprise you, "because you haven't evaluated all possible strategies" they could use. And "it leaves opportunities on the table." Plus, using human players for wargaming is costly and they may not play optimally. In principle, AI could explore a wider space of possible strategies very quickly, likely supplemented with human game play to more fully explore specific strategies of interest.

Tuomas also saw opportunities to apply computational game theory to a variety of military applications beyond wargaming. They've used it to develop "jamming and anti-jamming strategies" in electronic warfare. It could be used to experiment with new tactics for novel weapons, such as swarming autonomous systems. In the near term, Tuomas envisioned these techniques aiding humans to build insights to questions such as, "Which portfolio of assets should we build into the future? How should our doctrine be? How do we best defend our bases?" But he said, "in the long run, you could probably put those into command-and-control systems directly," with an AI decision-making system executing battlefield tactics in response to enemy moves in real-time.

One of the advantages of their method, Tuomas explained, was that unlike machine learning, their methods did not depend on prior data. They needed to model the "rules" of the game, but then they can calculate strategies even for new technologies, like hypersonic weapons, that had not been used before. Another benefit to their approach is that their strategies were what Tuomas termed "safe," or "non-exploitable," meaning they did not have flaws adversaries can exploit.

Computational game theory could also help strategists think through multiparty strategies, which are particularly challenging. While Libratus was designed to play one-on-one poker, Tuomas and Noam followed it two years later with Pluribus, which trounced humans in six-way poker play. These techniques would similarly be helpful in multiparty strategic reasoning. The United States is in the process of modernizing its nuclear arsenal, and as it does so it has to respond to the competitive strategies of multiple nuclear-armed competitors: Russia, China, and to some extent even North Korea. A common problem in international relations is the security dilemma—investments that one nation makes in their military make others less secure, driving others to improve their own defenses, sometimes leading to arms races. A multiparty game-theoretic approach to nuclear modernization decisions might help improve stability and avoid dangerous arms races. Tuomas said nuclear stability was "one of the top problems we have in the world," and game theory could help yield insights not only into what the United States should build, retain, or retire out of its strategic arsenal, but also what arms control treaties it should seek. The goal wasn't to find an advantage to "flatten the other guy," he said, but finding solutions where "stability is maintained," avoiding nuclear war.

Sensitive to concerns about military AI, Tuomas said he wasn't a "warmonger," and the technology was "not just for war; it's also for deterrence and peace." In fact, their work had identified novel strategies of deterrence. "Deterrence actually emerged with nontraditional assets," he said. "So not just nuclear where it's usually thought of, but in situations where deterrence hadn't even been thought of as an option. The AI on its own figured it out, how to do deterrence." The AI system identified strategies where the opponent was deterred from building capabilities and using them. "If you think about world stability," Tuomas said, "it's really important to be able to do intelligent deterrence." Strategies for winning a war were important, but strategies for avoiding a war to begin with were far better. Tuomas's computer-driven strategies made me think of the supercomputer in the 1983 film *WarGames*, which runs simulations of nuclear war and determines that "the only winning move is not to play."

Strategy Robot has multiple contracts with the Defense Department, and while Tuomas couldn't share details of the specific projects, he admitted they had already delivered value and were having conversations with defense leaders about expanding their work.

Tuomas's programs, Libratus and Pluribus, illustrate some of the foundational elements of progress in AI: data, compute, and algorithmic efficiency. Libratus used 2.6 petabytes, or 2.6 million gigabytes, of data. It computed the contours of the game tree using 24 million core-hours on a supercomputer (thousands of cores running for months at a time). Yet only two years later, Pluribus tackled the much harder problem of six-way play using a mere 560 core-hours, a greater than 40,000-fold improvement. The result wasn't from faster hardware. It was entirely due to improvements in the underlying algorithm, which needed less compute. These algorithmic improvements, of course, came from human talent.

I asked Tuomas if he was surprised by the rapid pace of progress, a 40,000-fold increase in efficiency in two years, while tackling a vastly harder problem. "I was," he said, "but I knew that it's needed" for them to tackle tougher multiplayer games. Around the world, AI researchers are advancing the field, and militaries around the globe are working to harness AI technology for new advantages on and off the battlefield. But as they reach out to commercial companies to spin-in a rapidly evolving technology, militaries are finding many obstacles along the way.

7

MAVEN

Brendan McCord doesn't look like a secret weapon. Tall and thin, Brendan has a quiet competitiveness about him. He could be a weekend triathlete or maybe a ranked amateur chess player, but "weapon" is not a word that comes to mind. Yet Brendan is one of the Pentagon's most vital weapons for securing U.S. military dominance in the twenty-first century. Not with his fists or knives or guns, but with his knowledge of AI.

Brendan was one of the defense officials behind Project Maven, a Pentagon effort to harness AI for military operations. Using new technologies is the bread and butter of what the U.S. military does. The Department of Defense invented stealth, the global positioning system, and laid the seeds of the internet. But AI is being invented outside of the traditional defense community in companies like Google, Microsoft, and Facebook. Brendan's job was to bring AI into the DoD.

Brendan was head of machine learning at DIU, an outpost DoD had set up in Silicon Valley to circumvent its own sclerotic acquisition system and tap into the U.S. tech sector. Maven was one of the DoD's first major success stories—and a major controversy.

It was 2017, and Brendan's marching orders were clear. The deputy secretary of defense, Bob Work, wanted AI and machine learning integrated into DoD, and he wanted it done fast. Bob was one of a cadre of defense analysts who had been warning for years about China's military modernization and America's waning advantages. He felt the clock was ticking. Now, as deputy secretary, he had an opportunity to help set the U.S. military on the right track. Already he had made an impact. The new National Defense Strategy, which was still in development and wouldn't come out until the next year, would name China and Russia as the "primary concern in U.S. national security." Bob believed that autonomy and AI were crucial elements of a forthcoming "military-technical revolution" in warfare. Staying ahead of China and Russia meant leading in what he described as "a new type of warfare called algorithmic warfare." (Bob defined "algorithmic warfare" as the same as the Chinese concept of "intelligentized" warfare.) He had launched in DoD a "Third Offset Strategy" to adopt AI and autonomy, harkening back to DoD's first two "offset strategies" during the Cold War that drew on nuclear weapons and precision-guided weapons. But Bob hadn't "seen the prairie fire catch yet" in DoD, he told me. Bob had been clamoring for attention on AI, but the department wasn't pursuing it "in a very enthusiastic or deliberate manner," in his view. By the spring of 2017, Bob had been in his role for nearly three years. His tenure had spanned two presidential administrations and three secretaries of defense, and he knew his time was drawing short. The current secretary of defense, Jim Mattis, had made "lethality" and readiness the focus of his attention, putting new technologies on the back burner. Bob knew he needed a tangible demonstration of military AI that would cause the rest of the department to say, "Holy crap, this would really help us!," in Bob's words. So Bob turned to the Breakfast Club.

The Breakfast Club was the name for a group of colonels that were supposed to be the "acolytes," as Bob described them, for the department's efforts to reinvigorate its technological advantage against Russia and China. Bob asked them for a problem AI might be able to solve, and they pointed to the military's voluminous amounts of video footage from drones.

Despite the public attention on drone strikes, the military's primary use for drones is for intelligence, surveillance, and reconnaissance, or ISR. The demand was insatiable. The military had steadily grown its airborne ISR capacity for nearly two decades running and was on track to operate ninety round-the-clock patrols worldwide of mid-sized drones such as the MQ-9 Reaper by 2019. At around $16 million apiece, the drones were relatively cheap (in Pentagon terms). The real problem was the personnel. Each 24/7 patrol took dozens of intelligence analysts to process the data coming off the drones. Ninety drone patrols could rack up nearly 800,000 hours of video footage a year and monitoring those video feeds required a lot of eyeballs.

Technology had, in some ways, only made the problem worse. To manage the overwhelming need for more ISR, the DoD had pushed development of wide area surveillance tools that could provide a "God's eye" view of the battlefield. In 2014, the Air Force equipped a small number of Reaper drones with an advanced sensor system called Gorgon Stare that could surveil an entire city. Equipped with multiple cameras like a fly's eye, the Gorgon Stare pods, which hung underneath the Reaper's wings in lieu of bombs, could monitor dozens of square kilometers at once. This vast expansion of coverage, while valuable, made the already crushing personnel demands impossible to manage. In his book on the Gorgon Stare program, *Eyes in the Sky*, Arthur Holland Michel explains that "a single 10-hour Gorgon Stare mission generates 65 trillion pixels of information." Who was going to watch all that video?

The answer was "the machines," but for years the machines hadn't been good enough. I'd seen demonstrations of simple automated video processing tools back in 2010 when I worked on ISR in the Pentagon's policy shop, but the technology had never been good enough to use in an operational role. But that was before the deep learning revolution.

In 2012, machine learning researchers made major progress against a standard image database called ImageNet, which is used for testing AI systems on recognizing images. In 2015, a team from Microsoft beat human performance on ImageNet using deep neural networks. Today, neural networks are used in a variety of applications to recognize objects in pictures, from facial recognition to medical imagery. Now the DoD was interested in applying this technology to their own problems.

"The main threat that we were focused on were car bombs," Colonel Jason Brown told me. Colonel Brown was the commander of the Air Force's 480th ISR Wing, a 6,000-person unit responsible for leading the Air Force's globally networked ISR operations, and car bombs were a major intelligence problem. Car bombs could cause devastating casualties and had become a weapon of choice for insurgents. At its peak, Kabul suffered as many as four car bombs a week.

Cars and trucks could pack much more explosives than a suicide vest, with the biggest truck bombs causing massive casualties. A 2019 car bomb against an Afghan intelligence base killed 126 people. The bombings' main effect was psychological, however. The steady toll of bombings in Afghanistan's capital, ostensibly under government control, demonstrated the weakness of the Afghan government. With each bomb, insurgents were in effect communicating to the people, "If the government can't protect its own capital, how can it protect you?"

A purely defensive approach to stopping car bombs using blast walls and checkpoints wasn't working. The U.S. military had pioneered during the wars in Iraq and Afghanistan a sophisticated counter-network approach that relied on intelligence and special operations forces to illuminate and take down terrorist networks. Overhead surveillance from drones was a key component of this counter-network approach, allowing intelligence analysts to monitor terrorist activity, track their movements, and map the connections between bombs, bomb makers, suppliers, financiers, and other parts of the bomb-making enterprise. Once identified, facilitators could be taken out with drone strikes or raids by special operators.

Gorgon Stare allowed the Air Force to record video over a whole city, a major expansion of their intelligence collection capacity, but the Air Force still needed intel analysts to watch the video. Colonel Brown explained, "The challenge, as you can imagine, seeing most of the city at once . . . . There was limited bandwidth, so you could only have about 10 airmen looking in 10 different locations within that city. . . . Where do you put these 10 airmen and their 10 sets of eyes and 10 brains and their 10 machines tied to that? This is very manual." Computer vision could help.

Gorgon Stare had the ability to rewind video, like a digital video recorder device. This gave intel analysts the ability to backtrack car bombs and find their point of origin. "We could watch it. We'd know when a car bomb would explode," Colonel Brown explained. "We would actually see it in the Gorgon Stare video. But then you could backtrack like a DVR, go back to your location of origin. Once you have that location of origin . . . then you could start going backward in time and mapping out where people came from . . . . Then you could really map out your network." Even if analysts couldn't predict threats beforehand, they could use the footage from Gorgon Stare to rewind activity in a city to map terrorist activity, find their safe houses and prevent an attack from happening again.

It was slow and painstaking work for humans to do manually. The sheer volume of data was unmanageable. The goal was to have computer vision help, not to replace the job of human intel analysts but to assist them. Computer vision algorithms that could recognize objects could sift through reams of video to find objects of interest. Colonel Brown explained, "Where we expected a computer vision solution to help us was, you could go back into the data, 'Tell me every time a car left this location.'" Then, "the computer vision algorithm would timestamp when certain activities would happen in certain places." Humans would still need to be intimately involved in intelligence analysis, but automated tools could speed up the process.

The military had been experimenting with automated tools for video processing for over a decade, but the technology had not been ready. Now, because of advances in deep learning, the hope was that it might be. Bob Work's desire for a high-value AI application intersected with a real operational need (tracking car bombs) and a viable technology (computer vision). Will Roper, then head of the DoD's Strategic Capabilities Office, had a project under way called Maven, which was processing satellite imagery for the National Geospatial-Intelligence Agency (NGA). Roper saw the potential for machine learning but first had to convince skeptics in DoD. Roper said, "The Pentagon had been burned by decades of automatic target recognition programs that did not work enough to be operational." In a brief to the Deputy's Management Action Group, a senior group of military and civilian leaders in the Pentagon, Roper gave a tutorial on recent advances in machine learning and why the technology had evolved to the point where it could now work. The "baggage that automatic target recognition doesn't work," Roper explained, led others in the Pentagon to largely respond, " 'We've tried this before.' "

"No one in the Pentagon thought it was a good idea to create Project Maven other than me and Bob Work," Roper said. "But he was the deputy secretary, so the program got funded." Maven evolved into Bob's new AI project, whose official mission was applying "computer vision algorithms for object detection, classification, and alerts" for drone video footage. The goal was to "reduce the human factors burden" of video analysis, "increase actionable intelligence, and enhance military decision-making."

Bob Work signed a memo in April 2017 establishing the "Algorithmic War-fare Cross-Functional Team (Project Maven)." The formal name, which abbreviated to the unwieldy acronym AWCFT, was classic Pentagon-speak, equal parts bureaucratic gobbledygook and military hype. The DoD had a long pattern of giving its programs seemingly bloodthirsty names—drones called Predator and Reaper, surveillance systems named after Greek monsters that turn men to stone—but this rarely rankles defense contractors. But DoD needed to reach out beyond traditional defense companies and court tech firms, who seemed allergic to negative branding. As Brendan McCord pointed out, " 'Algorithmic warfare' is the absolute epitome of the terror scenario that people want to avoid on the West Coast."

To put Bob's vision into practice, Maven would have to do several things different from traditional defense projects. For one, while DoD had a robust track record of building whiz-bang technology, from stealth jets to satellites, the department often struggled to move quickly. DoD's traditional processes were too sluggish to adopt a rapidly maturing technology like computer vision. An acquisition timeline that took seven to ten years to achieve first fielding would be several generations behind the state of the art and would be too slow for most commercial companies which operate on faster timelines. In his task-ing memo, Bob Work directed the Maven team to "integrate algorithmic-based technology" in "90-day sprints," which was effectively light speed for the DoD bureaucracy.

The second problem was that, to harness computer vision technology, DoD needed to reach beyond the traditional defense contractors and tap into technology companies. Traditional defense contractors like Lockheed Martin or Northrop Grumman could make a stealth airplane, but the leaders in computer vision were tech companies like Google and Microsoft. DoD was largely flying in the dark with these relationships. That's where Brendan came in. In July 2017, McCord traveled with Maven leads Lieutenant General Jack Shanahan, Colonel Drew Cukor, and Air Force Colonel Jason Brown to Honolulu to the Computer Vision and Pattern Recognition conference to meet with some of the top minds on computer vision. They also pitched Google, who would go on later that year to join Maven as one of its biggest partners.

Brendan was a former submarine officer who'd gone on to work at a venture capital firm and then a tech start-up, leading their AI team. But then Brendan was inspired by Secretary of Defense Ash Carter who spoke at the ribbon-cutting ceremony for DIU's satellite office in Boston. Brendan said when "Secretary Carter talk[ed] about the need for DoD to get serious when it came to AI . . . it got me interested in joining because I was a military veteran." Suddenly his work at the AI start-up felt "important for the country."

Brendan joined DIU working on two open-source computer vision projects. One was building the "largest dataset for object detection in overhead [satellite] imagery." The second project set "the world speed record for training deep neural nets on public cloud infrastructure," beating Google's prior record by 40 percent on a benchmark competition called DAWNBench from Stanford. As Maven embarked, Brendan helped them identify companies to work with. "Often it was the case that I was finding the company and pinpointing it," he said. " 'Here are the good labeling companies; here are the good computer vision companies; here are the good machine learning infrastructure companies.' It was pinpointing who those folks are, big and small, and then helping [Maven] go out and figure out . . . how to assess these companies. It was a combination of my experience in venture capital, my experience in the startup, and my time at DIU, with seeing a lot of different companies and knowing what to ask for."

The Maven team moved quickly. In July 2017, Marine Corps colonel Drew Cukor, who was chief of the AWCFT, publicly announced their intent to deploy an initial operational system by the end of the year. The goal was to build an AI-based image classifier that could detect thirty-eight different classes of objects—such as vehicles and people—relevant for military operations against

ISIS. A big part of the effort was data labeling. "We have a large group of people . . . who are going through our data and cleaning it up," Cukor announced
at a defense conference. "We also have a relationship with a significant data-
labeling company . . . to allow our workforce to label our data and prepare it for
machine learning." Bob Work declassified the drone video footage that Maven
needed to train its algorithms so that commercial companies could work on
it, and Maven's training data ultimately grew to over a million labeled images.

Maven hit its deadline, and by the end of 2017 deployed an initial automated video analysis tool to military intelligence units supporting counter-
ISIS operations in Iraq and Syria. The tool was relatively simple, and identified
and tracked people, vehicles, and other objects in video from ScanEagle drones
used by special operators. As with many AI systems, there were initial hiccups
in fielding as the Maven team discovered that there were important differences
between the training data and the actual operating environment. "Once you
deploy it to a real location, it's flying against a different environment than it
was trained on," Lieutenant General Jack Shanahan, who led Project Maven,
told *Defense One.* "Still works of course . . . but it's just different enough in
this location, say that there's more scrub brush or there's fewer buildings or
there's animals running around that we hadn't seen in certain videos." This
is a common problem in AI object classification systems. Subtle differences
between the training data and the real-world environment can cause system
performance to drop off significantly. "That is why it's so important in the first
five days of a real-world deployment to optimize or refine the algorithm," Shanahan said. The Maven team worked to quickly adjust the algorithm, updating
it six times in eight days. "This is maybe one of our most impressive achieve-
ments is the idea of refinement to the algorithm," Shanahan said. While con-
tinuous refinement of deployed products is routine in commercial software
(such as regular updates to computer software), tightly integrating operations
with product development and iterating so quickly was new to DoD. While the
initial Maven product was nowhere close to delivering the "'Holy crap, this
would really help us!'" eureka moment across DoD that Bob Work wanted,
it was a major triumph for DoD to move from project start to delivering an
operational capability in the field in eight months. In the months ahead, the
project would expand its footprint to operations across the Middle East and
Africa, incorporate footage from additional types of drones, and turn to wide
area imagery like that from Gorgon Stare.

Maven's real innovation wasn't technology, though; it was organizational.

"You don't buy AI like you buy ammunition," Colonel Cukor said. Computer vision wasn't the hard part; it was getting DoD to work with nontraditional companies and rapidly deliver a valuable capability to those in the field. Not everyone supported tech companies working closer with the military, though. A few months later, Project Maven would explode into a public controversy.

8

REVOLT

Liz O'Sullivan had had enough. Over the last few months, the tech company she was working at, Clarifai, had subtly changed, and not for the better from her point of view. Liz stuck with the company when *Wired* broke the story that Clarifai was working on the DoD's controversial Project Maven. In the spring of 2018, Maven had caused a schism in the tech community when over 3,000 employees at Google signed an open letter protesting the company's involvement. The letter flatly stated, "Google should not be in the business of war" and called for Google to publicly state it would never "build warfare technology." The letter writers objected that working with the military would "irreparably damage Google's brand" and cause Google to "join the ranks of companies like Palantir, Raytheon, and General Dynamics." This was a novel problem for the military. Defense contractors like Palantir, Raytheon, and General Dynamics had never objected on principle to working with the military—it was their entire business model. DoD leaders were wholly unprepared to navigate a new social landscape in which they had to defend their projects and court AI engineers' involvement.

Google leadership was caught flat-footed and bungled the response. They lacked a clear defense for Google's involvement in the project and struggled to convey to their workforce why the project was important. The DoD response was even worse. They simply refused to talk to the press, to the point where DoD refused to even confirm whether Google was a contractor on Maven. After employees began to resign in protest, Google leadership was forced to bow to pressure and announced they were starting work on a set of AI ethics principles that would preclude their use in weapons. But it was too late. In response to employee pressure, Google did not renew their contract with the DoD on Project Maven.

Six months later, Liz found herself in a similar position as the Google employees. She felt strongly that any involvement in lethal autonomous weapons—weapons that could decide on their own whom to kill—was morally wrong. Project Maven wasn't building autonomous weapons; it was processing drone footage. But the lack of information from the Defense Department about what Maven was actually doing only added to the controversy. Secrecy fed suspicion.

DoD officials' comments inadvertently fanned tech employees' worst fears. Mere days after Google's involvement in Maven broke publicly, DoD Chief Management Officer John Gibson boasted that the DoD's new JEDI cloud computing contract would improve "lethality." It was a nonsensical claim, as though the military was killing people with computer servers. The phrasing was the product of a cult of "lethality" that then–Secretary of Defense Jim Mattis had instilled in the DoD. Defense program managers are savvy bureaucrats skilled in the art of rebranding their programs to meet the current boss's preferred buzzwords. When Donald Rumsfeld was secretary of defense, "transformation" became the DoD's all-consuming obsession and programs hastened to label themselves "transformational." When Rumsfeld left that moniker went away, but the trend continued. Under Bob Work's Third Offset strategy, existing programs around DoD quickly rebranded themselves as vital to the Third Offset. And it became the same with "lethality" under Secretary Mattis. Yet the DoD's obsession with lethality risked inflaming the revolt among tech employees who wanted nothing to do with the military, killing, and war. Liz casually referred to the DoD's cloud computing initiative as its "war cloud," a cringe-worthy name, but one DoD officials had effectively encouraged.

On the evening of January 16, 2019, Liz hit send on a letter to her boss, Clarifai CEO Matt Zeiler, about the company's reported work with the military. Liz had recently signed an open letter pledging to not work on autonomous weapons, and she wanted Matt to pledge to do the same. He refused. Instead, Matt called a company meeting and declared to employees that its technology might very well make it into autonomous weapons some day and that Clarifai would continue working with the military. Liz quit the next day, another conscientious tech objector.

Clarifai continued work with DoD, as did many other tech companies, but Google's discontinuation of Project Maven shocked the Pentagon. For one thing, it showed just how far apart the American technology and defense sectors had grown. Defense funding had played a pivotal role in founding Silicon Valley, but as federal research dollars dried up, DoD's influence waned. American military dominance was built on a technological advantage over competitors, but suddenly the Pentagon found itself in an awkward position of watching U.S. companies refuse to supply critical technologies to the military.

Ultimately, DoD was able to find other companies to take over the work. But similar employee protests at Microsoft and Amazon alarmed defense leaders, who worried tech companies might follow Google's lead and distance themselves from the military. If tech companies refused military contracts, the U.S. military could find itself locked out of a transformative technology—a technology in which its main competitor was advancing rapidly.

To make matters worse, many of the U.S. tech firms the Pentagon was courting were global multinationals that had footprints all around the world, including in China. In what turned out to be an ill-timed move, just a few months before Google discontinued work on Project Maven, the company announced the establishment of a new "Google AI China Center." News headlines announced Google's "Big AI Push in China." In announcing the new center, Google's chief AI scientist Fei-Fei Li stated, "AI and its benefits have no borders." A noble sentiment, but when it came to working with the U.S. government Google was putting up barriers, even as it was deepening its work in China. Two months after Google discontinued work on Maven, news leaked that Google was developing a censored search engine called Dragonfly for use inside China. Years earlier, Google had backed out of China (while other U.S. tech companies stayed) when Google leadership decided they could not continue to comply with censorship requirements of the Chinese Communist Party (CCP). Now it would appear the company was reconsidering its principled position and was designing a search engine that could operate within the CCP's Great Firewall, filtering out political content that the Communist Party leadership deemed objectionable. Despite a public outcry, employee uproar, and global protests against the program, Google CEO Sundar Pichai defended Dragonfly for months, describing China as a "wonderful, innovative market." Eventually, in 2019, Google confirmed that Dragonfly had been cancelled.

The one-two punch of Google backing away from the U.S. military while deepening its ties in China was too much for Washington, and U.S. policymakers lashed out. Members of Congress grilled Pichai in a public hearing, arguing a censored search engine would "strengthen China's system of surveillance and repression." Chairman of the Joint Chiefs of Staff General Joe Dunford, the senior-most U.S. military official, testified before Congress that "the work that Google is doing in China is indirectly benefiting the Chinese military." Google issued a swift denial: "We are not working with the Chinese military." Dunford's claim was, at best, a stretch. The reality was that, compared to other

U.S. tech firms, Google had a tiny footprint in China. Far from aiding the Chinese military, directly or indirectly, Google had been mostly absent from China for years and was now just tiptoeing their way back in. But the damage to Google's reputation in Washington was done. It could not have come at a worse time for Google, as the Washington national security establishment was just waking up to the threat of China as a strategic competitor, including in key technologies such as AI. But before DoD could mobilize to compete with China in AI, it first needed to build bridges with tech employees like Liz O'Sullivan who were distrustful of the military.

I caught up with Liz a year after she'd left Clarifai, at the offices of a new tech start-up she was running in Manhattan. She had started her career in AI in 2012, back when "AI was largely hype," she said. When she moved to Clarifai, whether or not they did military work "wasn't something I had given much thought to," she told me. When Clarifai's involvement in Project Maven became public, there were some who left immediately, but Liz stayed. "To be quite frank, I was excited for the company," she said. "We were competing against Google, Amazon, Microsoft, and some of the other notable start-ups in the space at the time. It was the biggest product market fit we'd ever had. We were all shareholders and we believed in the CEO and we believed in the company." She described working with an "intelligent, kind, caring, giving, socially conscious group of people working in lockstep to deliver things quickly and on time and things that were impactful to the world." They were building AI tools to expose child pornographers, stop the spread of ISIS recruitment videos, diagnose diseases in underdeveloped countries, and identify endangered trees in the rainforest. "I'd never had a job that was that big and important and you could easily feel how you were doing good," she said.

Liz and a few other employees who were working on social good within Clarifai got together to create what she called "Clarifai-for-good Voltron," covering issues including diversity in recruitment, charity matching, mentorship, and AI ethics. Their efforts weren't merely a side project; they worked with the company leadership to build a formal structure for integrating ethics into the company's practices. Clarifai was at the front of a trend. Liz was in line to take an official role leading ethics oversight. "It was just a dream come true that you could do this stuff and get paid for it at the same time," she said.

The Clarifai shifts occurred as tech employees were growing more aware of ethical issues surrounding AI deployment across the industry. Liz cited news of AI-enabled human rights abuses by the Chinese government in Xinjiang and Google employee protests. She learned about debates surrounding autonomous weapons and, as a technologist, understood how feasible simple autonomous weapons were. "It just made it very clear to me that not only were these things possible, but they were possible now and they probably had already been built to a certain degree," she said.

Liz wanted the company to draw a line on certain AI applications they wouldn't support. "Let's not sell to authoritarian regimes. Let's not sell facial recognition to U.S. law enforcement. Let's not make killer robots," she said. She explained that she wasn't anti-military: "Society wouldn't function without a strong defense." But she was concerned about the immaturity of the technology and the potential for accidents. Her motivation came from "having had direct experience with how computer vision fails—it does it in really weird ways," she said. "When you make that into a weapon, it means people are going to die because of these mistakes that you can't predict."

Computer vision systems—and AI systems in general—are vulnerable to a whole host of failure modes. AI systems tend to be brittle. They can perform very well under certain conditions, then fail dramatically in other settings. Machine learning systems in particular can fail in new ways relating to how the system learns from data. One of the ways this can manifest is if the training data is not representative of the actual operating environment. For example, if a facial recognition system is trained predominantly on people of a certain gender, race, or ethnicity, then it may perform poorly on people of a different gender, race, or ethnicity if they are not included in the training data. Because machine learning systems learn from data, rather than follow preprogrammed rules for behavior, these failures can manifest in surprising and deeply problematic ways. In 2015, a Google Photos image recognition algorithm labeled two people with dark skin as "gorillas." Google's image recognition system was not programmed to label darker-skinned people as "gorillas;" rather the offensive software outputs likely reflected insufficient representation of darker faces in the training data. At the technical level, the problem is that machine learning algorithms can often fail when subjected to a distributional shift in the data. If the distribution of the real-world data is shifted (changed) from the training data, then the system may not be robust—that is, it may not be capable enough to handle that change without a degradation in performance. A computer vision system trained on video or images taken during sunny days may not perform as well during cloudy days. These problems are common in image classification systems, and have resulted in increased scrutiny of high-consequence applications, such as law enforcement use of facial recognition systems. In some settings, these failures can have fatal consequences. Problems with computer vision and image classification have contributed to self-driving cars and Tesla cars on autopilot striking pedestrians, semitrailers, concrete barriers, fire trucks, and parked cars, leading to several fatal accidents. Military systems are not immune to these flaws. In fact, the first deployed Maven systems reportedly suffered similar challenges, with initially a very poor accuracy rate (60 percent) because the algorithm was trained using drone footage from a different region than the one in which it was deployed.

Researchers refer to these as "socio-technical" problems, as they involve not only the AI system itself, but also how it is designed, trained, and used. Problems in racial and gender disparities in facial recognition have led to calls for more diversity in the tech industry, so that a broader set of voices play a role in system design. Tesla has come under fire for both the design and marketing of its autopilot system. For the military, the challenge is not only accounting for the technical limitations of AI systems, but also demonstrating to others that the military is invested in building systems that are safe, reliable, robust, and operate ethically.

The concerns Liz O'Sullivan raised are common in the AI community. A 2019 survey of leading AI researchers found over 70 percent opposed working on autonomous weapons. Nearly 60 percent of survey respondents supported Google's decision not to renew work on Project Maven, while only 10 percent opposed it. Overall, leading AI researchers trusted the military with AI significantly less than the U.S. general public did.

After some initial stumbles in response to the Google-Maven controversy, by mid-2018 the Department of Defense launched an effort to develop a set of ethical principles for how the military should adopt AI. The Defense Innovation Board convened roundtable discussions with experts at Harvard, Carnegie Mellon, and Stanford universities, with public listening sessions and comments. In early 2019, the Defense Department released an unclassified summary of its internal AI strategy, which called for building AI systems that were "resilient, robust, reliable, and secure." A major pillar of the strategy was "leading in military ethics and AI safety." After extensive consultation with AI experts outside the defense community, in late 2019 the Defense Innovation Board approved a set of proposed AI principles, which the secretary of defense adopted in 2020. The final principles included requirements that DoD AI systems be responsible, equitable, traceable, reliable, and governable.

The DoD AI Principles had a number of audiences. The first was those in the defense community who would be working to implement AI, to ensure that they understood DoD leadership's guidance on how to manage the challenges of AI systems. The second was those in the tech industry, to signal to them that DoD understood the concerns with AI and would act responsibly. While the DoD AI principles wouldn't satisfy those who wanted a hard ban on some applications like autonomous weapons, it demonstrated that the military understood the technical limitations of AI systems and intended to be thoughtful about deployment. (In addition to the principles, the Defense Innovation Board issued a dozen recommendations about how the DoD should put the principles into practice.) But there was a third audience too, which was military communities outside the United States, including in competitor nations such as China. Michael McQuade, vice president for research at Carnegie Mellon University and a member of the Defense Innovation Board, said that conversations about how militaries use AI needed to be part of "both a national and an international dialogue." Chinese military AI experts closely followed the DoD AI Principles. By publicly articulating a set of principles for how to adopt AI, the United States hoped to shape how others use AI. This was critically important, because nations share common risks from irresponsible AI use that could lead to accidents that would endanger everyone. The DoD AI Principles were the beginning, not the end, of a much-needed dialogue among tech experts, military professionals, policymakers, ethicists, lawyers, and ordinary citizens around the world about how militaries use AI.

Defense Department leaders feared Google would be the beginning of a wave of tech companies refusing to work with the military. But these fears never materialized. Clarifai kept working with the DoD, as did Amazon and Microsoft. And DoD's entry into AI and machine learning drew in new start-ups who squarely positioned themselves as companies seeking to work with the military. These included Anduril, founded by Silicon Valley entrepreneur Palmer Lucky; ShieldAI, founded by two brothers, one of whom is a former Navy SEAL; and SparkCognition, founded by serial entrepreneur and author Amir Husain. Even Google returned to defense work after a short hiatus (although the company did not return to Project Maven). In perhaps a surprising conclusion to the Google-Maven dustup, Google Senior Vice President Kent Walker appeared onstage alongside Lieutenant General Jack Shanahan, who had by then transitioned to run the DoD's new Joint AI Center, at a Washington, DC, conference on AI and national security in the fall of 2019. Walker characterized Google's decision to not renew work on Maven as "a decision focused on a discrete contract, not a broader statement about our willingness or our history of working with the Department of Defense," and said Google was "eager to do more" with the Defense Department.

The biggest legacy of the Maven controversy may have been to elevate the importance of AI in the minds of DoD's senior leaders. Bob Work left his role as deputy secretary of defense in July 2017, when Maven was still getting off the ground. With his departure, the DoD lost at the time its biggest champion of AI. Bob told me that when he left he was "really worried" that the focus on AI "would fizzle out." It might have. But the Google flap and fears of losing out to China put AI on the radar screen of senior defense leaders. By the fall of 2019, Secretary of Defense Mark Esper said AI was his "number one" technology priority. Nothing could motivate DoD leaders more than a fear of falling behind China.

9

SPUTNIK MOMENT

The United States and China entered the twenty-first century as friends. Two decades later, they were bitter rivals. The story of the rivalry that emerged is central to the geopolitical competition unfolding in AI. There are many nations pursuing AI—over fifty countries have or are developing national AI plans or strategies—but the U.S.-China relationship will have profound consequences for the future of global AI research, talent flows, supply chains, and cooperation. The American and Chinese AI ecosystems are deeply intertwined, but actions by Beijing and Washington are starting to pull them apart.

The contemporary U.S.-China relationship began with President Nixon's historic visit in 1972, but the real turning point came in 1989. The U.S.-China Cold War relationship was born of realpolitik—a shrewd triangulation on both sides of the balance of power between the U.S., the U.S.S.R., and China. In 1989, the dynamic changed. Protest movements throughout the communist world upended the existing order, but as the Eastern Bloc began to crumble in Europe, Chinese leaders took a different tack. On June 4, 1989, the Chinese military entered Tiananmen Square in Beijing, where hundreds of thousands of students had gathered in protest calling for political reform. The military massacred the protestors, killing hundreds, if not thousands. Whereas communist regimes in Europe had declined to fire on their people, and fallen to political revolution, the Chinese Communist Party had opted for force.

The United States had a choice to make. There was little stomach in Washington for a strategy of containing China. U.S. policymakers saw the collapse of communism in Europe as "the triumph of the West" and "the end of history." President George H. W. Bush was a sober pragmatist who had quipped he wouldn't "dance on the [Berlin] wall" to celebrate the end of communism, and likewise cautioned against an "overly emotional" reaction to Tiananmen. As the need to triangulate the global balance of power against the Soviet Union faded, Bush sought to "engage" China, in part citing the powerful momentum of history toward freedom. Bush argued, "As people have commercial incentives, whether it's in China or other totalitarian systems, the move to democracy becomes inexorable." Washington adopted a new strategy: shaping China's inevitable rise.

China was emerging as a global power, a reality that U.S. policymakers had to confront. By 1992, China's annual GDP growth rate was 14 percent, and it never dipped below 7 percent in the 1990s. Under the Clinton administration, "engagement" became the new lodestar of U.S. foreign policy to China, with the aim of influencing China's behavior. Far from a pollyannish view of Chinese leaders, engagement was a calculated policy stemming from the belief that "growing interdependence would have a liberalizing effect in China," and that enmeshing China in international institutions would lead China to be a "responsible stakeholder" in the international system. Clinton argued, "the more China liberalizes its economy, the more fully it will liberate the potential of its people . . . [and] the genie of freedom will not go back into the bottle."

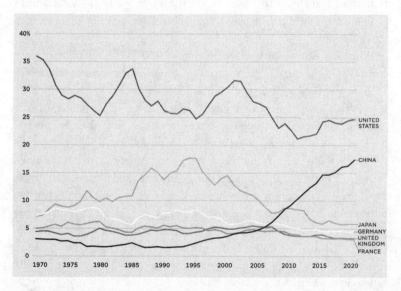

Percentage of World GDP, 1970–2020. *U.S. policymakers adopted in the 1990s a deliberate strategy of "engagement" to try to shape the behavior of a rising China. Yet China did not become a "responsible stakeholder" in the international system, as U.S. officials had hoped. By the time of the Trump administration, U.S. officials had abandoned engagement for a more confrontational approach to Chinese Communist Party actions.* (Data from the World Bank. Chart by Melody Cook / Center for a New American Security.)

Such policies may seem naïve in retrospect, but history supported the "dictator's dilemma," that autocratic states had a choice between shutting out information technology and economic growth or embracing it and bringing along the free flow of information and ideas. U.S. policymakers believed that economic freedoms would, over time, give rise to a greater desire among citizens for more political freedoms as well. U.S. leaders hardly expected China to turn into a democracy overnight, but they believed that the dictator's dilemma would force Chinese leaders to make a choice between adopting political reforms or forgoing the benefits of economic growth. Clinton argued, "Without the full freedom to think, question, to create, China will be at a distinct disadvantage, competing with fully open societies in the Information Age where the greatest source of national wealth is what resides in the human mind." The domestic pressures internal to China that engagement was intended to bring were real. What U.S. policymakers underestimated was the ability of Chinese leaders to break the dictator's dilemma and use information technology to repress Chinese citizens even while permitting economic freedoms. The Tiananmen massacre was a sign of how far Chinese Communist Party leaders were willing to go to maintain their grip on power, and their ruthlessness would not wane in the decades after.

While U.S. defense analysts warily watched China's rise and military modernization in the early 2000s, engagement remained the focus of the George W. Bush and Barack Obama administrations' approaches to China. By 2007, U.S. defense analysts were sounding the alarm that Chinese military investments in "anti-access" capabilities, such as missiles, advanced air defense systems, and antisatellite weapons, were hindering America's ability to project power into the Western Pacific region and protect America's friends and allies. Yet when I worked in the Pentagon during the Bush and Obama administrations, there was a healthy debate among U.S. officials about China's rise and the extent to which China was a strategic competitor. As late as 2010, Defense Department official policy documents left open the door for a productive relationship, stating: "The United States welcomes a strong, prosperous, and successful China that plays a greater global role." A series of successive Chinese actions in the 2010s shattered that illusion.

While Chinese leaders enthusiastically pursued economic growth, they carefully managed U.S. economic and societal ties, wary of the risks of destabilizing China. The Chinese Communist Party built a series of buffers against unwanted liberalizing forces, including a Great Firewall to control the flow of information into China; increased domestic surveillance, censorship, and propaganda; and a brutal crackdown on human rights activists and dissidents. Economic interdependence was carefully managed as well. Chinese firms were protected from international competition through state subsidies and by limiting market access for foreign firms inside China. China used foreign economic ties to engage in a systematic campaign of intellectual property theft and economic espionage. America's strategy of engagement assumed economic liberalization would pave the way for political liberalization. But political reform had not occurred, and even economic openness was a one-way street.

Internationally, China's "peaceful rise," as its leaders had claimed, was turning out to be anything but. In the 2010s, China began an aggressive campaign to militarize the South China Sea, threatening the Philippines, Taiwan, Vietnam, Malaysia, and Indonesia and destabilizing the region. Tensions rose across the Taiwan Straits, as U.S. leaders feared China was building a military option to absorb democratic Taiwan. Washington had, for a while, been patient with various tensions in the relationship, confident that time was on their side, but by the time President Trump came to office, the stage was set for a "reckoning" with China.

The emerging geopolitical rivalry between the United States and China coincided with the AI revolution, such that Chinese progress in AI was viewed suspiciously in Washington and vice versa. At the tail end of the Obama administration, the White House released a series of policy documents outlining the importance of AI. While falling short of a coherent national strategy for AI, the three White House documents released in late 2016 nevertheless highlighted AI as a critical area for the economy and laid out government R&D priorities. China took notice, and in July 2017 released its own signature AI strategy, the "New Generation Artificial Intelligence Development Plan." The document called for China to be the "world's primary AI innovation center" by 2030 and sent shock waves through the U.S. national security establishment.

In late 2017, a few months after China's plan was released, I hosted former Google CEO Eric Schmidt at a major AI conference in Washington, DC, run by the Center for a New American Security, where I work. Schmidt has often served as a bridge between the tech and national security worlds and chaired the Defense Innovation Board and the National Security Commission on AI. Schmidt said he took China's goal of leading the world in AI by 2030 seriously. "Trust me, these Chinese people are good," he said. "You're crazy to treat them as somehow second-class citizens." Schmidt called for a new "Sputnik moment," harkening back to the catalyzing event that the Soviet launch of the first satellite, Sputnik, had on the United States. Fears of Soviet technological dominance propelled the United States to create NASA and the Advanced Research Projects Agency (the precursor to DARPA), launch the space race, and sparked a wave of federal R&D spending that paid dividends for decades. "This is that moment," Schmidt said. "This is the moment where the government collectively with private industry needs to say these technologies are important."

Schmidt's call for a Sputnik moment evokes a comparison to the space race, when the United States and Soviet Union raced to achieve firsts in spaceflight. It's an imperfect analogy for the current moment with AI. The space race was dominated by two nations and driven by government spending, while AI technology is diffuse and driven by the private sector. But in other ways, the comparison is useful. The space race was a technology competition, not an arms race in building weapons. The U.S. lead agency, NASA, was a civilian organization, but maintaining a technological advantage was seen as critical for national security. Advancements in space technology had spin-off implications for both military and civilian applications, such as improved missiles and surveillance satellites, but also communications, weather, and GPS satellites. While the moon was a clear physical destination, a visible landmark in the sky for all to see, the space race had no true destination. It was a competition to stay ahead in an emerging technology, with implications for economic and military power.

The unfolding geopolitical competition in AI is similar. Despite loose talk by both defense leaders and AI researchers about an "AI arms race," AI is not a weapon. It is a general-purpose technology much like electricity. There will no doubt be military applications of AI, but the bigger national advantage is likely to be found in adopting AI across society overall by increasing efficiencies, health care outcomes, economic growth, and other indicators of national wellbeing. Additionally, by increasing productivity, technological advancements have a compounding effect on economic growth and, by extension, national power. Over the long term, technological progress is the main driver of economic growth.

AI can have a significant, direct impact on economic productivity by offloading routine physical and cognitive tasks to machines, freeing up humans for more complex tasks. A detailed analysis by the McKinsey Global Institute in 2017 found that roughly half of all job-related tasks in the U.S. economy could be automated using existing technology. Only a small number (less than 5 percent) of jobs could be entirely replaced by automation, but six in ten jobs could be significantly transformed, with automation replacing 30 percent or more of tasks that workers perform in those jobs. Nations that successfully seize these opportunities, and manage the disruption they may bring, could have tremendous long-term advantages.

Despite Schmidt's call for a Sputnik moment, the United States has struggled to develop a coherent national strategy for AI. The Trump administration released a number of high-level AI documents in 2019, including an executive order on AI leadership and an updated R&D plan, but the plans didn't move the ball forward significantly from the Obama administration's 2016 documents. The most comprehensive plan had come from the National Security Commission on AI, a blue-ribbon panel chaired by Eric Schmidt and Bob Work, which released a 700-plus page report in early 2021. (Disclosure: I served as a consultant to the commission.) Yet the commission was only a temporary, congressionally appointed panel without any authority for actually making and implementing decisions. They could only advise. The government still needed to act.

China, on the other hand, isn't cutting any corners when it comes to AI competition. Following the 2017 national AI plan, Chinese leaders issued a series of implementation plans to achieve China's goal of being the global AI leader by 2030. These include the "Three-Year Action Plan to Promote the Development of New-Generation AI Industry" and the "Thirteenth Five-Year Science and Technology Military-Civil Fusion Special Projects Plan," both released in 2017. Chinese leaders have emphasized AI as central to national success. Chinese General Secretary Xi Jinping said in a 2018 Politburo session, "Accelerating the development of a new generation of AI is an important strategic handhold for China to gain the initiative in global science and technology competition, and it is an important strategic resource driving our country's leapfrog development in science and technology."

Reflecting on China's emphasis on AI, Schmidt said, "There's no question that there was a Sputnik moment and it was in China. And the Sputnik moment was when AlphaGo beat the Chinese champion and Chinese care a great deal about the game of go." Ke Jie, who at the time was the world's number one go player, lost to DeepMind's AlphaGo in 2017. Schmidt added, "not only was it notable, but they also censored the television feed because they didn't want people to see them lose." Go is an ancient strategy game first invented in China over two thousand years ago, and to have the top Chinese champion dethroned by an AI program built by a Western company was a galvanizing moment.

Schmidt is hardly a China hawk. "I am not a person who believes that we are adversaries with China. I believe that we're in competition with China," he said. "We're not in a shooting war. We disagree on some things, but it's important that we retain the ability to collaborate with China." Schmidt explained, "China and the United States have many common goals," citing AI safety and climate change. "Both countries have benefited from trade between the two countries for a long time."

Three decades of engagement has meant that the American and Chinese AI ecosystems are strongly connected, yet China's militarization of the South China Sea, bullying of its neighbors, and "predatory economics" led the U.S. government to declare China a "strategic competitor" in 2018. China's mass detention of over one million Uighurs in Xinjiang, eroding Hong Kong's freedoms, and unwillingness to change its illiberal economic practices further hardened views in Washington.

The novel coronavirus pandemic came at a moment when the U.S.-China relationship was at a turning point. Washington's foreign policy community had discarded the prior decades-long strategy of engagement but was still in search of what might come next. The pandemic might have been an opportunity for the two countries to come together against a common enemy. After all, a virus kills both Americans and Chinese alike. But the political reaction to the pandemic, which had as much to do with domestic politics in both nations as geopolitical competition, cemented their rivalry.

Concerns about economic competition took on a new urgency in 2020. The pandemic slammed the brakes on the global economy, leading to a sharp drop in economic activity in mid-2020. The economic fallout imperiled President Trump's reelection but was an even bigger risk for China's leaders. While there was no risk of the Chinese Communist Party being voted out at the polls, authoritarian regimes lack the pressure release valve for angry citizens to vote for change, making them more brittle than democracies. If Chinese citizens lost faith in the system and demanded change, the corrective mechanisms could be harsh and brutal. Whereas democratic politicians who lose the public's confidence might transition to a plush lobbying gig, dictators who fall from power may face the firing squad. The blood-soaked bargain the Chinese Communist Party offered Chinese citizens in the aftermath of Tiananmen was political stability and economic growth in exchange for their freedom and civil liberties. In the decades since, the CCP has staked its domestic credibility on continued economic growth. And China has seen unparalleled growth, lifting hundreds of millions out of poverty. Yet the government's bungling of the outbreak in Wuhan led some Chinese citizens to wonder if the incident would prove to be "China's Chernobyl," akin to the 1986 nuclear disaster that exposed the hollowness of the Soviet system. For CCP leaders, the lack of faith in the government was a potential contagion even worse than the virus itself, and the government launched a crackdown on information mirroring the physical lockdown to contain the coronavirus. Chinese propaganda organs went into overdrive, trumpeting the benefits of China's model of pandemic response.

While the pandemic posed a risk domestically, it was an opportunity internationally for China to step into a global leadership role. CCP leaders watched the American government's incompetent response and seized the moment for a global soft power push, sending masks and personal protective equipment to other nations and stepping up their propaganda campaign. Chinese officials triumphantly declared in English-speaking outlets that the West is "falling apart" and it was time for American and European leaders to "draw closer to China and drop the hubris."

Emboldened by the crisis, Chinese diplomats stepped up their coercive diplomacy to pressure countries to play by China's rules. Chinese medical supplies were frequently accompanied by requests that receiving governments praise China. Chinese officials convinced European Union lawmakers to tone down a report whose early drafts criticized China's "global disinformation campaign." When Australia called for an independent inquiry into the origins of the virus, China responded by restricting imports of Australian products into China. When Venezuelan officials referred to the "Chinese coronavirus," the Chinese embassy launched an angry Twitter thread concluding with the demand that China's critics "put on a mask and shut up."

U.S.-China relations, already strained, deteriorated even further. Chinese officials didn't hesitate to flex their leverage over the United States due to China's manufacture of life-saving drugs. Chinese state-run media threatened to cut off drug exports and plunge the United States "into the mighty sea of coronavirus." China's "Wolf Warrior" diplomats, named after a popular Chinese action movie series, went even further, pushing conspiracy theories to deflect blame from China's mishandling of the outbreak. Chinese Foreign Ministry deputy spokesman Zhao Lijian suggested that the U.S. Army might have started the outbreak in Wuhan. U.S. policymakers were enraged, and China's actions accelerated pressures in Washington toward "decoupling" with China.

For years, Chinese leaders had heeded the words of former Chinese leader Deng Xiaoping to "hide your strength and bide your time." It would appear that the time is now. As the world reeled from the novel coronavirus, China moved beyond threats to action. In May 2020, Chinese troops entered Indian territory in the Himalayas, sparking a series of skirmishes that killed troops on both sides. In June, China passed a new national security law in Hong Kong, launching a sweeping crackdown to imprison journalists and activists and dismantle Hong Kong's freedoms. In August, Chinese military aircraft escalated brief incursions across the midline of the Taiwan Strait, a not-so-veiled threat of force. Fearing that Chinese leaders would feel emboldened by perceived American military weakness, the United States sent two aircraft carriers to the region to engage in exercises with India, Japan, and Australia.

In response to increased Chinese assertiveness, nations are taking steps to restructure global supply chains for critical technologies. India, Japan, and Australia launched a trilateral supply chain resilience initiative to reduce their dependence on China. As part of its economic stimulus, the Japanese government allocated $2.2 billion to incentivize companies to move production out of China. The French government began working with French pharmaceutical companies to re-shore production. And in the United States, Congress and the White House began taking steps to reduce American dependency on China for pharmaceutical ingredients.

U.S. actions are also beginning to shift supply chains for semiconductors. Congress approved injecting tens of billions of dollars into the U.S. semiconductor industry, including government subsidies for building new domestic chip fabrication plants, or fabs, giving the United States more security in its semiconductor supplies. In a significant escalation of the tech competition, the Commerce Department tightened export controls on transferring advanced semiconductors and chip manufacturing equipment to China.

Nations are drawing closer together to counter Chinese economic coercion and military aggression. In March 2021, Australia, India, Japan, and the United States held the first leader-level "Quad" summit, pledging to increase their cooperation. In September 2021, Australia, the United Kingdom, and the United States announced the trilateral AUKUS partnership to deepen military cooperation. Without stating it explicitly, both arrangements were aimed at countering China. Additional Chinese military aggression has further sharpened geopolitical lines. In August 2022, the G7 grouping of Canada, France, Germany, Italy, Japan, the United Kingdom, the United States, and the European Union criticized what it termed China's "aggressive" and "escalatory" military exercises around Taiwan following U.S. House Speaker Nancy Pelosi's visit to the island.

Post-pandemic, the old geopolitical order is up for grabs. China's now vice premier Liu He wrote in 2013, "After a big crisis, what is redistributed is not merely wealth within a country, but the relative power of all nations." Huge advantages will accrue to whichever nations come out of the crisis running. Emerging technologies like AI will be even more critical to help drive technological dominance, economic growth, and national power. China remains a technology leader and a global AI powerhouse. How China adopts AI will have major consequences for the shifting global order.

PART III
REPRESSION

10

TERROR

People are afraid to speak, even in private, lest their voices are recognized and they are arrested. AI may be listening.

In China's Xinjiang Autonomous Region, the Chinese Communist Party has launched a massive campaign of repression against Xinjiang's ethnic Uighur population. Maya Wang, senior China researcher at Human Rights Watch, told me the government's AI-enabled surveillance is so all-encompassing that for Uighur residents of Xinjiang, "even in their own homes, they censor themselves through, for example, signing to their family members rather than speaking, for fear of surveillance and the consequences."

The Chinese government has imprisoned over one million Uighurs, split children from their families, and built a dense web of physical and electronic surveillance to monitor Uighurs' behavior. Under the pretense of cracking down on terrorism, the Chinese government is systematically waging a brutal campaign to destroy Uighur culture and way of life, including forced sterilizations and abortions, which has led many independent experts to declare the government's campaign a genocide. AI is helping to enable this repression through tools such as face, voice, and gait recognition.

Xinjiang is an extreme case—a dark, dystopian vision—of the use of AI for internal repression. As AI advances, it is being used by dictators not just in Xinjiang but around the world to erode liberties. The use of AI for internal repression risks helping autocrats solidify their power. Over the long run, the unchecked use of AI for domestic surveillance could help tilt the global balance away from democracies toward authoritarian states, undermining human freedom.

Xinjiang is a test bed for China's new techno-authoritarian surveillance state. Under the "Strike Hard Campaign," the government has established thousands of police checkpoints across Xinjiang and deployed 160,000 cameras in the capital city, Ürümqi, to monitor every aspect of citizens' movements. Facial recognition scanners are deployed at hotels, banks, shopping malls, and gas stations. "Convenience police stations" dot Xinjiang's cities every few hundred meters. Movement is tightly controlled through ID checkpoints that include face, iris, and body scanners. Police match this data against a massive biometric database consisting of fingerprints, blood samples, voiceprints, iris scans, facial images, and DNA. Authorities are collecting biometric data on every Xinjiang resident between the ages of twelve and sixty-five, and have already amassed data on over 18 million people.

Ubiquitous monitoring and security checkpoints are augmented with regular checks of ID cards and cell phones. At checkpoints and random stops, police search citizens' phones for unauthorized content, which could include religious material or encrypted chat apps to circumvent Chinese surveillance. The Chinese government views Uighur culture, and in particular their Muslim religion, as an "ideological virus" that must be stamped out. Possessing forbidden content could lead to detention at a concentration camp for "re-education" in Chinese Communist Party ideology. Even writing or publicly speaking the Uighur language could be cause for detention and "re-education."

Technology is used at every turn to augment surveillance. Wi-Fi "sniffers" gather data from nearby phones and computers. License plate readers alert the police to certain vehicles, such as those from outside the region. In parts of Xinjiang, authorities have mandated that all vehicles install tracking devices using China's version of the global positioning system (GPS), BeiDou. Chinese authorities have placed QR codes on peoples' homes, giving visiting authorities instant access to information about the residents. In some areas, kitchen knives are stamped with QR codes to track their ownership.

Smartphones, in particular, are an easy vector for intrusive surveillance. Ürümqi police use handheld devices to automatically scan smartphones for unauthorized audio and video, speeding up the process of searching for content. Border authorities have installed spyware on the phones of visitors entering Xinjiang from Central Asia, hoovering up text messages, contacts, call records, and calendar entries. The app also searches phones for any files matching a database of 73,000 prohibited pictures, videos, documents, and audio files. Banned content includes Islamic material or photos of the Dalai Lama.

Some Uighurs have buried their phones or burned data cards to avoid being discovered with prohibited content. Others have frozen data cards in dumplings, hoping to perhaps retrieve them some day. The absence of a phone, however, can be reason enough for detention. Some Uighurs have two phones, one for use at home and a clean one for going out.

Some of the most brutal repression against Uighurs is low-tech: concentration camps, forced reeducation and labor, forced sterilization and abortions, and coerced marriages with non-Uighurs. The government has sent over one million ethnically Han Chinese "brothers and sisters" to live in Uighurs' homes to monitor them 24/7. The government's genocidal campaign against the Uighurs would be happening with or without AI. AI enables it to happen more efficiently.

Artificial intelligence is a key component of the Chinese government's vast surveillance apparatus, making possible surveillance at an unprecedented scale. AI is the cognitive engine that powers voice, face, and gait recognition and helps sift and sort data at scale. Police in Xinjiang can connect via mobile app to a centralized system, the Integrated Joint Operations Platform (IJOP), that synthesizes data "in a comprehensive manner" from "everyone in every household," according to Xinjiang government statements. The IJOP tracks peoples' height, movements, car color, gas station and electricity use, and package delivery. The IJOP is not merely a master database, fusing information from a variety of sources; it also flags suspicious behavior. Like the "precrime" predictive policing system in Philip K. Dick's "The Minority Report," the IJOP is meant to identify individuals whom Chinese authorities believe are at risk of undesirable behavior. Suspicious activity could include donating to mosques, using another person's car or phone, leaving an area without police permission, "often avoiding using the front door," "not socializing with neighbors," and using an "unusual" amount of electricity. By monitoring citizens' movements in real time, the IJOP charts their "trajectories" and, according to government documents, can push "real time, predictive warnings" to checkpoints to "identify targets . . . for checks and control." The IJOP even watches the watchers, scoring government officials on their performance in various surveillance tasks, allowing supervisors to monitor the activity of lower-level officials. Maya Wang, whose research exposed the IJOP, described it as "this panopticon that is envisioned in our dystopian nightmare that essentially watches people all the time automatically and picks out people who may be threatening to the authorities."

The full extent of the IJOP's functionality is largely a black box to outside investigators. Researchers at Human Rights Watch were able to gain some insight into the system by reverse engineering an app used by police to connect to the central IJOP system. Human Rights Watch assessed that, as of 2017, "much of the IJOP system appears to function as simple conditional statements—if a, then b (for example, if the person who drives the car is not the same as the person to whom the car is registered, then investigate this person). . . . To what extent the IJOP central system is currently using big data algorithms in analyzing the collected personal data is unclear." The algorithms, at least as of 2017, appeared to be very simple, the main purpose of which is to flag individuals for further investigation by police.

One effect of the overly broad targeting of suspicious behavior is a high workload on government officials to carry out algorithm-mandated investigations, to the point where government officials have complained they have "worked so hard" to respond to IJOP taskings that "their eyes are so tired and reddened." While a high incidence of false positives might make it harder to catch people actually engaged in criminal behavior, the highly visible and intrusive surveillance serves its own purpose. Uighurs know they are being watched and never know when the state's dragnet will capture them or what actions might trigger the opaque algorithm that monitors their behavior. Samantha Hoffman, an analyst at the Australian Strategic Policy Institute who specializes in China's tech-enhanced authoritarianism, stated, "That's how state terror works. Part of the fear that this instills is that you don't know when you're not OK." Bethany Allen-Ebrahimian, an investigative journalist who covers China, observed, "As neighbors disappear based on the workings of unknown algorithms, Xinjiang lives in a perpetual state of terror." From the Chinese government's standpoint, instilling in its citizens the constant fear of state control "isn't a bug but a feature" of its surveillance system, Hoffman said.

In addition to surveillance, the IJOP automatically restricts the movement of Uighurs in Xinjiang. Many police checkpoints in the region employ "data doors" that automatically scan individuals' phones and that function as a series of automated gates to limit movement. Wang said, "For example, if you have been to a camp, you were released, or if you are related to a family member of someone who were in the camp, your movement is restricted at these data doors when the system flags you as a person of interest." She described different levels of confinement, ranging from solitary confinement in prison, to house arrest, to individuals who are confined via police checkpoints to their own village. IJOP's automation allows authorities to implement this system of restrictions more efficiently and at scale, allowing economic activity to resume in Xinjiang villages while still tightly restricting the population.

While Xinjiang has the most intensive surveillance in China (or anywhere in the world), the government's mass surveillance architecture exists in every major Chinese city. Mass surveillance has long been a tool of the Chinese Communist Party for social control. In the pre-digital era, this was accomplished by people monitoring others' behaviors. Modern China's founder Chairman Mao Zedong pushed the slogan "The people have sharp eyes," encouraging citizens to report on their family and neighbors. Today, the Chinese Communist Party is building digital "sharp eyes," likely learning from its experiment in extreme social control in Xinjiang. Maya Wang described "a general increase in Xinjiang-ification of China." Zhu Shengwu, a Chinese human rights lawyer, told the *Wall Street Journal,* "[CCP leaders] constantly take lessons from the high-pressure rule they apply in Xinjiang and implement them in the east. . . . What happens in Xinjiang has bearing on the fate of all Chinese people."

What happens in Xinjiang has bearing on us all. The techno-authoritarian techniques that the Chinese government is developing in Xinjiang are being replicated not only across China, but around the world. On smaller scales and less effectively, but with increasing proficiency over time, other nations are adopting elements of Chinese-style digital authoritarianism. China's rise and global leadership in AI threatens human rights not just in Xinjiang, but across the globe as China matures AI technology and influences global norms for its use.

11

SHARP EYES

China has built a nationwide surveillance architecture that is unparalleled anywhere in the world. Xinjiang's capital, Ürümqi, is heavily surveilled with its 160,000 cameras, but eleven Chinese cities have even more cameras per capita. Eighteen of the top twenty most surveilled cities in the world are in China, along with over half of the estimated 1 billion surveillance cameras in use worldwide in 2021. I traveled to China in the summer of 2019 to see firsthand how Chinese society was adopting AI. I wanted to understand what China's trajectory might mean for the future of not only its own citizens, but global freedom.

Even before one enters China, one enters the Chinese surveillance state. Promptly upon exiting my plane, I was directed by a helpful airport representative to a biometric kiosk where foreigners have their fingerprints scanned. Once my fingerprints had been digitized and entered into a government database, I was permitted to enter the line for immigration. At the immigration counter I handed my passport and visa to the officer, then a camera captured my face. It was so fast I almost missed it, even though I was watching for it. A video screen in front of me showed the camera's view of my head, a green box around my face, then a quick snapshot as I was recorded. A smiling icon on the screen said in English, "Welcome!"

Rather than a densely packed, *Blade Runner*–esque cityscape of pollution and high rises, Beijing is spacious and green. The day I landed, the skies were blue (an unusually good day for air quality). Trees and bushes line the streets, a welcome relief from the concrete jungles of American cities like LA, Chicago, or New York. Driving through it, the megalopolis seems never-ending. One can sit in crushing traffic for an hour and a half across town. The city is organized into four concentric rings radiating outward from the city center, a physical manifestation of Confucian philosophy. The streets, bikes, and moped lanes are constantly thrumming with the movements of 21 million people going about their daily lives—lives that, for the past forty years, have seen unprecedented economic growth.

The Chinese Communist Party's first great economic experiment was launched in 1958, less than a decade after the CCP had defeated the Chinese Nationalists and founded the People's Republic of China. Mao Zedong's Great Leap Forward was intended to accelerate China's industrialization and economic development, but instead spurred the worst famine in human history, killing an estimated 20 to 40 million people. Following Mao's death, Deng Xiaoping took the reins as China's leader in 1978, launching the nation on a path to the greatest economic miracle in human history. Deng's policies of "reform and opening," characterized by careful and measured economic reforms and international engagement, sparked unprecedented growth. Over the next forty years, the country experienced an average annual GDP growth rate of nearly 10 percent in what the World Bank termed "the fastest sustained expansion by a major economy in history." The result has been a monumental change in the economic quality of life for Chinese citizens. Eight hundred million people were lifted out of poverty, and per capita income increased twenty-five-fold. Average life expectancy rose from forty-four years in 1960 to seventy-seven years by 2018. Infant mortality plummeted by over 90 percent from 1969 to 2018.

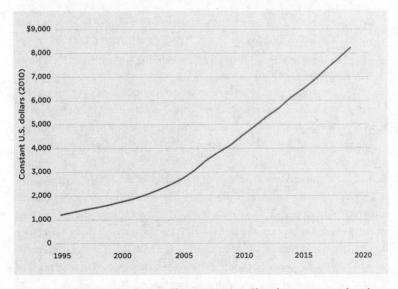

Gross National Income Per Capita—China, 1995–2019. *China has seen unprecedented economic growth over the last several decades, lifting hundreds of millions of people out of poverty.* (Data from the World Bank. Chart by Melody Cook / Center for a New American Security.)

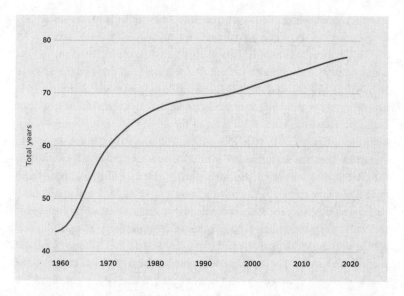

Life Expectancy at Birth—China, 1960–2019. *China's economic miracle has dramatically improved health outcomes, including a rapid rise in life expectancy.* (Data from the World Bank. Chart by Melody Cook / Center for a New American Security.)

General Secretary Xi Jinping, who took over as China's leader in 2012, has promoted the "Chinese dream" as a vision of "the great rejuvenation of the Chinese nation." Xi aims to complete China's growth, building a "moderately prosperous society in all respects" by 2021 on the way to a fully modernized society by 2049, the 100th anniversary of the People's Republic of China. China's growth rate has been more modest in recent years, but was still a brisk 6 percent in 2019 before the novel coronavirus pandemic. But for some, Xi's Chinese dream is a nightmare.

Xi has increased repression of human rights activists, lawyers, political dissidents, and journalists. Arbitrary arrest, detention, and torture are common tools of the Chinese party-state for maintaining political control. The paradox of China's "opening up" is ever-present on the streets of Beijing. Storefronts advertise Western brands like Apple and KFC alongside surveillance cameras on every block. Light poles on every intersection and halfway down each block are bristling with cameras, sporting sometimes a half dozen or more mechanical eyes peering in every direction. In some cases, they seemed to reach a point of absurdity. I counted one pole with ten cameras on it.

I had read about the hundreds of millions of surveillance cameras in China, but I wasn't prepared for the boldness of the omnipresent surveillance, the ever-

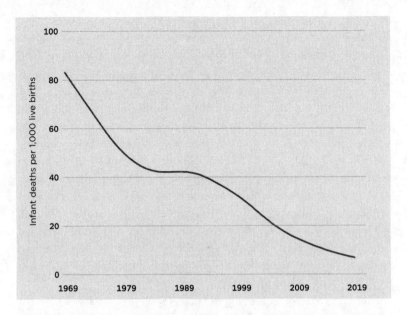

Infant Mortality—China, 1969-2019. *As health care has improved and per capita income has risen, infant mortality has plummeted in China.* (Data from the World Bank. Chart by Melody Cook / Center for a New American Security.)

present eye of the Chinese Communist Party keeping watch over its citizens. I couldn't help but wonder about my picture taken at the airport. Were the cameras detecting my face, tracking my movements, logging me along with a billion other people into some vast database? The answer, I knew, was probably no. Or at least, not yet. A half a billion cameras need a tremendous number of eyeballs to watch them, which was why China was working on integrating AI into its vast surveillance network.

The origin of China's modern system of tech-enhanced control began with the Golden Shield Project to control the Chinese internet in the late 1990s and early 2000s. In 2005, Chinese authorities built on this foundation by launching "Skynet," a vast surveillance camera network as a joint program by the Ministry of Public Security and the Ministry of Industry and Information Technology. (Skynet is a literal translation of the Chinese project name and is not named after the fictional AI that wipes out humanity in the *Terminator* series . . . although the unfortunate name certainly does little to ease Western fears about where the CCP is heading with technology.) The goal of Skynet is "prevention and control of regional urban and rural coverage," according to Chinese state media.

In 2015, China's National Development and Reform Commission called for expanding video surveillance to "100%" coverage of public areas and key industries, with "no blind spots." The result was "Sharp Eyes," a nationwide expansion of Skynet, including coverage for rural areas. In 2016, the government approved forty-eight demonstration cities for Sharp Eyes. By 2018, there were a reported 786 Sharp Eyes and related surveillance projects, with a total annual spending of over $5 billion. Government documents show the aim is a surveillance system that is "omnipresent, fully networked, always working and fully controllable." The CCP's goal of an ever-watching surveillance system that captures every aspect of its citizens lives is unprecedented in its ambition. As chilling as China's surveillance network is, the current reality falls far short of this goal. Existing systems, while repressive, are fragmented, decentralized, and imperfect. Yet the Chinese government is working to improve them, and omnipresent surveillance is the terminal point of China's trajectory. Artificial intelligence is critical to achieving the government's goals. After all, millions of eyes are no good without brains behind them.

Sharp Eyes has led to pilot projects in cities and provinces across China in which facial recognition is used to process camera feeds. Facial recognition systems have been installed in airports, hotels, banks, train stations, subways, factories, apartment complexes, and even public toilets. In some areas, police officers have used facial recognition–equipped helmets or sunglasses. Facial recognition is even being used to shame jaywalkers, displaying their name, phone number, and government ID number on billboards. Intelligentizing China's hundreds of millions of surveillance cameras is a work in progress, but has already led to arrests. Megvii executives have boasted that their facial recognition system, Face++, has contributed to 4,000 arrests.

Chinese authorities have begun to embed into their facial recognition systems the ability to not only identify individuals, but also to identify minority groups. Uighurs are a different ethnic group from China's over 90 percent majority Han population and may have different facial features closer to Central Asian people. While facial recognition systems have come under fire in the United States for unintentional bias, Chinese police in sixteen provinces and regions have sought to acquire "minority identification" technology that would deliberately target minority groups, specifically Uighurs. The technology would use "facial recognition to identify Uighur/non-Uighur attributes," according to one police department document. Multiple Chinese companies have developed AI tools intended to identify Uighurs. Huawei, Intellifusion, Megvii, SenseTime, SensingTech, and the Chinese Academy of Sciences have all filed patents for facial recognition technology that claim to detect Uighurs. Huawei and Megvii jointly created a "Uighur alarm" facial recognition system. Investigators uncovered Uighur-detecting code in Dahua and Uniview intelligent surveillance cameras. Hikvision briefly marketed an AI camera that reportedly detected Uighur facial attributes. (Huawei, Megvii, SenseTime, Dahua, Uniview, and Hikvision all released statements denying that they discriminate or target ethnic groups.) Though AI-based technology to visually detect ethnicity may be highly unreliable, the technology is reportedly in use in multiple cities in eastern China, allowing the Chinese state to extend its blanket repression against Uighurs across the entire country.

China's surveillance web is not yet an all-seeing panopticon, but police are working to connect facial recognition systems to other tools and databases to monitor and track individuals. Facial recognition is augmented with other electronic surveillance means, such as phone scanners that surreptitiously scoop up data from passing phones. Police in several cities have begun using systems that link phone scanners to facial recognition cameras. As one company advertised, "People pass and leave a shadow. The phone passes and leaves a number. The system connects the two."

Facial recognition systems are being merged with other tools for big data analysis in the Ministry of Public Security's "Police Cloud" system. Police cloud computing data centers, which are being implemented in numerous cities and provinces across China, include not only criminal records, facial recognition, and other biometric data, but also addresses, religious affiliations, medical records, birth control records, travel bookings, online purchases, package deliveries, and social media comments. These databases are not merely repositories of information but are intended to automatically fuse and analyze data for police. They could be used to monitor and track individuals of interest and also connect them to associates. For example, a police cloud system could find who "has gone to internet cafes together more than twice, or has travelled together twice." Police clouds are also intended to synthesize data to uncover and alert police to unusual activity, such as a local resident who frequently stays at a local hotel.

Chinese police are supplementing these local databases with widespread biometric data collection, expanding the efforts in Xinjiang nationwide. In 2019, China's Ministry of Industry and Information Technology implemented a new law requiring purchasers of new mobile phones, data plans, or SIM cards to have their faces scanned. Chinese police have also undertaken the world's largest DNA collection program. In 2017, the Ministry of Public Security launched a nationwide DNA collection program targeted at men and boys, which reportedly has been active in over a hundred cities across China. Chinese authorities have amassed the world's largest DNA database, with an estimated 50 to 80 million individuals.

Chinese state scientists have, at times, sought to combine AI with biometrics on the edge of what is scientifically possible. Scientists working with the Ministry of Public Security developed DNA-based face mapping technology, which attempts to reconstruct a digital image of a person's face based on their DNA. The process, called DNA phenotyping, produces a rough image that is not accurate enough to identify an individual, but might help narrow down potential individuals based on approximate facial characteristics. It has been used occasionally by law enforcement in the United States, although the technique is controversial because it effectively profiles a wide swath of people. The Chinese research relied on DNA derived from men in Xinjiang.

Without any legal restraints on their data collection, the only obstacles to Chinese police are the practical realities of knitting together these different surveillance methods and systems and using them effectively, and there are many challenges in doing so. Regional surveillance networks are independent and not connected to one another. Skynet is not always connected to other systems or able to pass data between them. There is not one single police cloud but many disparate police clouds in different cities and provinces that are not integrated together. Even at the local level, like other efforts at big data analysis, Chinese police face the hurdles of incompatible databases, outdated or inaccurate information, increased needs for data storage and computing, and the necessary human capital to do useful analysis.

Even at the point of collection, there remain many hurdles to employing AI and other sensors effectively. The facial recognition sunglasses that police have used only work if the target person stands still for several seconds, making the technology useful for checking someone's ID at a checkpoint but not for scanning a crowd. Facial recognition systems are notoriously plagued with inaccuracies, and may often scoop up innocent individuals. New techniques like DNA-based digital face mapping are even less effective and may target huge numbers of innocent people, although for tools like "minority identification" facial recognition, the whole point is racial profiling.

China's party-state is in the early stages of building the world's largest and most advanced techno-authoritarian system for surveillance and population control. The technology, as it stands today, has flaws and weaknesses. As they work to perfect their digital authoritarian state, however, Chinese authorities can rely on world-class technology companies to aid them.

12

A BETTER WORLD

Government spending on Sharp Eyes and related projects has fostered a massive surveillance industry in China, with as many as 30,000 companies according to a 2015 study. Concrete spending figures are hard to come by, but even rough estimates show the extent of government investments. According to the China Security and Protection Industry Association, sales of safety and surveillance products doubled from $35 billion in 2010 to $70 billion by 2015, on track to an estimated $115 billion annually by 2020. The Chinese surveillance industry continues to grow at a breakneck pace, growing by an estimated 18 percent in 2019.

Chinese firms participating in domestic surveillance are top-tier global technology companies. Hikvision specializes in surveillance cameras; telecom providers Huawei and ZTE in data storage and system integration; Alibaba in cloud computing services and big data analysis; iFLYTEK in speech recognition; SenseTime and SenseNets in facial recognition; and Huawei subsidiary HiSilicon in chips. Huawei, SenseTime, and Megvii have denied their technology is used to profile or target groups. Yet all eight technology companies are suppliers for Skynet or Sharp Eyes.

Chinese facial recognition firms are some of the best in the world. Algorithms from SenseTime and Yitu have consistently ranked at the top in the U.S. National Institute of Standards and Technology's Face Recognition Vendor Test. In 2017, Yitu took first place in a facial recognition competition sponsored by the U.S. Intelligence Advanced Research Projects Activity (IARPA). Chinese firms benefit not only from massive government funding but also the enormous data they are able to collect from deployed surveillance systems, allowing them to further refine their algorithms.

China has a vibrant tech ecosystem, nurtured in part by government funding, protectionist policies, and prohibitions on many Western firms from operating in China. The Chinese Communist Party aggressively censors the internet, blocking many foreign websites and banning many foreign apps. Google, Facebook, Twitter, YouTube, and scores of other non-Chinese websites and apps are banned. An entirely separate app ecosystem has grown in their place. Every functionality one might desire in the United States or Europe is replicated in China, but by Chinese companies. Ride sharing? Download Didi; Uber doesn't have a foothold there. Maps? Google Maps is blocked in country; Baidu Maps is great (but only in Chinese). Search? Google is also blocked; Baidu dominates the search market. In some areas, China is far ahead of Western companies. WeChat has no parallel in the West, an all-purpose social media platform that also does mobile payments, ride-hailing, food delivery, flight booking, games, and more.

Many of these Chinese applications are superior to their American counterparts. Once integrated into China's digital economy as a temporary netizen, life for me was as seamless and easy as in any other digitally first-world nation. With Didi, China's version of Uber, it didn't matter that I didn't speak Chinese, nor the driver English. I could summon a taxi using the English version of the app. On the driver's phone, the destination and directions were in Chinese. Both of us saw the distance, estimated time, fare, and each other's ratings in our respective languages. Didi even offered helpful phrases for me to text the driver with the push of a button, such as "I will be there soon, please wait a moment."

Proponents of Chinese tech companies often argue that U.S. firms simply haven't been able to adapt to the Chinese market, yet many U.S. brands are popular in China. There's a Starbucks and KFC on seemingly every corner. Some tech consumer brands have also done well. In Beijing's Wangfujing shopping district, the two-story Apple store was packed with customers. Across the street, the much smaller Huawei store was nearly empty. While there have undoubtedly been cases where U.S. firms have stumbled in the China market, the Chinese government's systemic protectionist policies of state subsidies, support for "national champions," forced technology transfer, forced joint ventures for foreign firms, intellectual property theft, and outright bans on some foreign firms have also played a major role in bolstering China's tech industry.

As if to drive home the strength of China's tech sector, one day as I was leaving my hotel the elevator door opened and I was met with a robot. The robot chattered at me in Chinese, and while I couldn't understand its instructions, I gathered the gist of its desire for me to move out of its way. The robot trundled down the hotel hallway for a bit until it came to a stop outside a room, delivering some item to the occupants. I later spoke with the hotel staff and the robot bellhop did not seem to be tied to any particular event or AI conference. Rather, a robot bellhop just seemed to be the kind of thing that an upscale Beijing hotel had, because . . . why not?

The strength of China's technology sector is remarkable and a boon to the nation. The question is what China's tech giants will do with their AI tools. I headed to see for myself one of China's leading AI firms, a member of China's AI "national team."

Just outside the tree-lined campus of Tsinghua University, China's answer to MIT, lies Zhongguancun, one of China's tech hubs that vie for the title of "China's Silicon Valley." The massive tech park is populated with gleaming office buildings, green spaces, ponds, and throngs of young engineers in English language T-shirts, heads down in their phones. At one Chinese start-up I visited, the cafeteria was packed at dinnertime with tech workers who seemingly never went home. China's tech culture is notoriously hardworking, with employees expected to work "996": 9 a.m. to 9 p.m., six days a week. Yet the open office spaces I saw were still full at 9 p.m., crumpled food wrappers next to workers' computers as they toiled into the night.

One of China's five AI "national team" members is iFLYTEK, which specializes in "intelligent voice." I met iFLYTEK vice president Lin Ji in their Beijing offices in Zhongguancun. As is mandatory when visiting tech companies, I and the other American visitors got a tour through the iFLYTEK AI Development Center just off the main floor lobby. Inside, we were shown a small museum of iFLYTEK AI wonders: voice cloning, speech-to-text, text-to-speech, real-time language translation, and more. iFLYTEK is a global leader in AI voice technology. In 2017, they were named by *MIT Technology Review* the sixth smartest company in the world. In 2018, they won twelve awards in international AI and speech recognition competitions.

iFLYTEK representatives gave a tour of the many applications for their AI systems, including in business, education, and health care. Their goal was to "enable machines to listen & speak, understand & think." iFLYTEK had a voice-activated smart home system, like Amazon's Alexa. Their translation services can translate between Chinese and fifty-eight different languages and can handle multiple Chinese dialects. In addition to voice-based AI, the firm was working on natural language processing. They were building a machine to pass the college entrance exam for mathematics, training it on thousands of exam papers. In education, they were building AI applications to automatically grade papers, personalize education resources, and customize study plans. They cheerily explained their AI would increase teaching efficiency. In medicine, iFLYTEK fielded in 2018 an AI-based diagnostic system to aid doctors in treating 900-plus diseases.

Most Chinese tech workers, like those in other countries, just want to get rich. The vast majority of conversations I had with AI researchers in China were about the beneficial uses of AI in society, in improving efficiency, productivity, health, safety, and quality of life. The challenges that Chinese AI innovators are grappling with are largely the same as their counterparts elsewhere. AI has no doubt tremendous benefits in China, as it does elsewhere in the world. But the risks of AI—abuse by law enforcement for surveillance, predictive policing, and internal repression—are far worse in China without the system of checks and balances that exist in democratic societies.

The darker side of AI was visually brought to life by two robots in the iFLYTEK Center. One was described as an education robot and was designed with a friendly face, soft features, smooth curves, and a white and lavender body. The other was described to me as a "security" robot and featured sharp edges, glowing eyes, and a black menacing face. iFLYTEK representatives seemed oblivious to the concerns about the applications of their intelligent voice technology. A screen in the center displayed real-time interactions around the country with their open platform for intelligent voice, flashing stats for each region as their tools were being used, including in Xinjiang.

When we sat down to talk with Vice President Lin, he immediately launched into an explanation of how important the government is as a customer for them. Lin explained that 50 percent of the company's $1 billion in annual revenue came from the Chinese government. The "customer is like god," he said through a translator. Lin spoke positively of iFLYTEK's relationship with the government, saying that the company has joint labs with the government and that the government encourages innovation and likes iFLYTEK. Likewise, he said that the company advises the government on regulations and policy.

Lin was very open about their partnership with the local government in Xinjiang on voice translation. He said that in 2011 they began a partnership with Xinjiang University to amass data on speech recognition for the Uighur language and, as a result of this partnership, had built a translation service to help Uighurs learn Chinese. He said that in Xinjiang the government was a "big customer."

Independent investigations of iFLYTEK operations in Xinjiang tell a more sinister story. iFLYTEK subsidiaries have signed deals to sell "voiceprint" collection systems to Xinjiang police and a "strategic cooperation framework agreement" with the Xinjiang prison administration bureau, according to investigations by Reuters and Human Rights Watch. Such programs would be able to identify an individual by the unique signature of their voice.

Lin refused to give details about iFLYTEK's work with Xinjiang authorities but said that "inherently their technology is helpful for communication between different ethnicities." Citing the current situation in Xinjiang, Lin said there was "more of a need now for their technology."

Lin stated any relationship with the Chinese military was "classified," but iFLYTEK's marketing brochure openly boasts of their nonmilitary government work in public security, law, prosecutions, and the judicial system, including in Xinjiang. Their "Public Security" products include a "Police Audio Intelligent Service Platform" and "Intelligent Trial System." iFLYTEK operates a partnership with the Ministry of Public Security (MPS) Key Lab of Intelligent Voice Technology, "the only voice technology lab of the MPS."

U.S. policymakers have raised concerns about China's model of "military-civil fusion," a concept Xi Jinping has advocated to more closely integrate China's military and civilian sectors. While U.S. firms may decline government contracts for ethical reasons, American policymakers fear Chinese companies must serve the demands of the CCP. The Chinese government has sweeping power to compel individuals and organizations to support the state. These powers have been codified in a battery of recent laws, including China's National Security Law, Cybersecurity Law, National Intelligence Law, and Data Security Law, but the government's authority would exist even without these specific laws. Were Chinese tech employees to openly criticize the government, as employees did at Google, Amazon, and Microsoft of the U.S. government, they would risk jail time or worse.

Lin said that iFLYTEK frequently says no to the government, however, sometimes because what the government asks for is not feasible. In response to a question about whether iFLYTEK had ever said no to government work for ethical reasons, Lin said "yes." When asked for specifics, he cited a time that the government wanted them to pay more taxes. He said he didn't think that was ethical.

The relationship between the government and tech firms is different in the United States and China, but not in the way U.S. policymakers often think. The Chinese government can compel firms to take certain actions, such as giving the government data on their customers. (These coercive realities also apply to U.S. firms working in China.) Unlike in the United States, companies cannot turn to an independent judiciary or the court of public opinion to fight the Chinese government's pressure, as Apple did when the FBI demanded they unlock a terrorist's iPhone in 2016. Yet business-related frictions between Chinese firms and the government still exist. This is particularly true in the defense sector, which has at times struggled to tap into China's commercial AI expertise. Experts Elsa Kania and Lorand Laskai concluded, "China's defense sector has been primarily dominated by sclerotic state-owned enterprises that remain walled off from the country's dynamic commercial economy." China is working to bring its defense and commercial sectors closer, as is the United States, but both countries face practical problems in reforming their defense bureaucracies.

While barriers remain between China's military and commercial sectors, there is a closer relationship between China's AI companies and the government for domestic security. The CCP's massive investment in intelligent surveillance and social control has boosted Chinese AI companies and tied them closely to the government. The fact that half of iFLYTEK's revenue came from the government is indicative of the extent of the Chinese government's ties to its AI national champions. This is not the case for American firms, for whom the government is a relatively small slice of their business.

In the United States, big tech corporations such as Amazon, Apple, Meta (formerly Facebook), and Google are independent centers of power, often at odds with the government on specific issues. Power is more fragmented in democracies, and it can be more difficult to get public and private sector actors to work together to establish rules for how to use technology. While democracies are more likely to produce laws and policies that balance public safety with privacy and civil liberties, they also may be slower to cohere around a set of rules. Meanwhile, as the Chinese government matures its repressive use of AI, it can count on Chinese AI firms to be willing and even eager partners.

On the way out, I noted a banner in iFLYTEK's lobby with the company motto: "Create a better world with artificial intelligence."

13

PANOPTICON

As the week progressed, each day the sky deepened to a darker shade of gray, until by the weekend the blue was gone entirely, replaced by the featureless gray of industrial haze. The pollution was so thick that buildings vanished into the distance, as if swallowed by the smog. Even looking across the street there was a gray film in the air, like the thin sheet of a smartphone's screen protector, except plastered across reality.

A few days after the thirtieth anniversary of the Tiananmen massacre, I stood in the square where Chinese students had so bravely faced down the regime in 1989 and lost. Amid throngs of Chinese sightseers, the Chinese flag waved proudly overhead and Mao's face gazed benevolently upon us from the Gate of Heavenly Peace at the north end of the square over the entrance to the Forbidden City. I thought of the history of this place, a singular moment in time on which the fate of modern China turned. I recalled watching on television Chinese students protesting and a feeling at the time that anything was possible. And then realizing that for the Chinese Communist Party, anything *was* possible, even horrific repression. The regime slaughtered hundreds—perhaps thousands—of students, putting down the uprising. The final death toll is still disputed, shrouded in state secrecy.

But murdering the students wasn't enough. To prevent them from being martyrs, the regime had to murder their memories too. In George Orwell's dystopian book *1984*, the totalitarian government proclaims, "Who controls the past controls the future. Who controls the present controls the past." The Chinese government abides by the same philosophy. Bill Clinton had famously proclaimed that China's attempts to control the internet would be "like trying to nail Jell-O to the wall." Yet the CCP succeeded. The Party tightly controls information in China. Chinese censorship has wiped out all digital trace in China of the Tiananmen massacre. Even obscure references are censored.

WeChat—which is censored by the government—prohibits sending payments in 6.4 or 64.89 yuan, since both could be veiled messages to 6/4/89, the massacre date. Standing in the square, there was no visible memory to that day. At the square's center is a monument to "the people's heroes" who "laid down their lives in the people's war of liberation and the people's revolution," but not to the students.

I watched columns of soldiers marching across the square, executing simple ceremonial drills. They were young and earnest, as soldiers are everywhere around the world; as I had once been. They were also completely decorative, a mere window dressing of state power. The real control lay above their heads: the vast network of surveillance cameras watching the crowd.

The surveillance cameras were inescapable everywhere in Beijing, but in Tiananmen Square they were so ubiquitous it was nearly impossible to take a photograph without them in it. Rows and rows of camera-topped light poles stretched into the distance across the square. I did a rough estimate and there must have been hundreds of cameras in Tiananmen Square alone. It wasn't hard to see the benefit, from the government's standpoint. If protestors ever had the audacity to gather again, the government would be able to record all of their faces, tracking them and their families down for retribution. It could monitor crowds to ferret out organizers and single them out.

In Orwell's *1984*, the government reminds its citizens of its constant surveillance with the slogan, "Big Brother is watching you." But the Chinese Communist Party is developing new tools of control that are far more subtle and far-reaching than surveillance and that stretch into every facet of Chinese citizens' lives. The goal is "social governance," to shape the behavior of 1.4 billion people so there is never a threat to the regime.

"Social governance," also referred to as "social management," is a CCP process of solving economic and social problems by exerting political control through the day-to-day economic and social interactions of Chinese citizens. The use of facial recognition cameras for cracking down on seemingly trivial infractions like jaywalking or using too much toilet paper in public restrooms are examples of technology applied to social governance. Social governance is aimed at solving real social problems, such as unpaid debts, but also at extending the CCP's political control. Samantha Hoffman of the Australian Strategic Policy Institute has studied China's systems of social management and explained, "You can be solving problems and also make that problem solving inherently political." Chinese authorities "use solving problems to enhance their own power."

Jaywalking in China has real risks. Over 60,000 people are killed annually in China in traffic accidents, and pedestrians are the most vulnerable group. I've long been appalled by the casual behavior of pedestrians in Washington, DC, darting across traffic under the assumption that drivers aren't head-down in their phones. But I witnessed people saunter into traffic in Beijing in ways that were truly harrowing. The mechanism by which the CCP resolves these social problems is through greater political control. Hoffman explained the goal was to make control part of "everyday governance" in the lives of Chinese citizens, "rather than something that's . . . overtly coercive."

Technology is helping China's leaders tighten their grip on the population. The company Yuntian Lifei Technology boasts their Skyeye intelligent video surveillance system has already identified 6,000 "social governance" infractions, leading to it being deployed in nearly eighty Chinese cities.

To further the goal of social governance, in 2014 the CCP launched the creation of a national "social credit system" to score individuals and organizations in China based on their behavior. Contrary to its popular depiction as a *Black Mirror*-esque rating that determines every facet of a person's life, in practice the social credit system is a series of different databases, scores, and blacklists, many of which are disconnected. Hoffman described social credit as "a tech-enhanced system of improving existing forms of control." The social credit system assesses what Chinese authorities refer to as the "trustworthiness" of individuals, companies, and even local governments according to both economic and political criteria. Some elements of the social credit system work similar to a financial credit score, which assesses an individual's likelihood of paying back loans. Others are expressly political, such as running afoul of the Cyberspace Administration of China, which censor's China's internet. Other aspects of the system reach far into Chinese citizens' personal lives for social control. Individuals can have points subtracted from their score or be blacklisted for eating or playing loud music on the train, running a red light, failing to show up to restaurant reservations, not leashing one's dog in public, not properly sorting trash and recycling, and (of course) jaywalking. "It's about shaping and managing behaviors," Hoffman said.

The consequences of ending up on a blacklist can be severe, and can include bans on purchasing air and rail tickets, renting a car, acquiring a bank loan or credit card, buying property, sending one's children to private schools, or engaging in "luxury" spending such as staying in high-end hotels. Those on blacklists are sometimes publicly shamed, with their name and photograph advertised on billboards and movie screens. Corporations can also be blacklisted, banning them from bidding on government projects, issuing stocks or bonds, purchasing real estate, and accessing loans. Even local governments and government officials can be blacklisted under the social credit system for "dishonest" activities such as unpaid debts.

Nor does the social credit system stop at China's borders. In 2018, the Civil Aviation Administration of China sent a letter to thirty-six international air carriers, including United Airlines, American Airlines, and Delta, demanding that they list Taiwan as part of China. The letter threatened that if the airlines did not comply, China would "make a record of your company's serious dishonesty and take disciplinary actions against your company," including actions under the Civil Aviation Industry Credit Management Measures and "administrative penalties according to law." The White House issued a stern rebuke, calling China's demand "Orwellian nonsense," but Air Canada, British Airways, Finnair, Lufthansa, and other airlines nevertheless changed their websites in response. (United, American, and Delta split the difference, dropping reference to "Taiwan" but stopping short of listing Taiwanese airports as part of China.) As of 2021, thirty-nine international air carriers had complied with China's demand, listing Taiwan as part of China.

Social credit is also used to encourage certain behaviors. Donating to charitable organizations, volunteering, giving blood or bone marrow, and performing "good deeds" can improve one's social credit score. (Although there are far more ways to lose points than to gain them.) Having a higher score can get one rewards, such as priority for CCP or civil service promotions, more favorable loan conditions, faster service at hospitals, fast-tracked administrative service, and discounts on road tolls and public parking.

Rather than one single, centralized system, the social credit system is a decentralized and often disconnected set of lists and scores maintained at the local, provincial, and national level by different government agencies. There are hundreds of blacklists, including forty at the national level alone. Nor are the blacklists narrowly targeted. In the first half of 2019, over 26 million people were banned from buying air tickets through the social credit system. Elements of social credit address important issues of financial trustworthiness that are needed in any modern society, but the social credit system extends far beyond improving transparency and trust in financial transactions. Social credit is designed to build an ever-present system of rewards and punishments so that, in the words of General Secretary Xi Jinping, "Everything is convenient for the trustworthy, and the untrustworthy are unable to move a single step."

Many of China's systems of surveillance and social control are, for now, disparate and disconnected. This is cold comfort, however, as Chinese authorities are actively working to connect these systems to share data and more thoroughly monitor and punish individuals. Hoffman said that while the current system is decentralized, there is a lot of standardization, which means "the processes of integrating information will be made a lot easier" as technology advances. The system "doesn't have to be perfect" to be effective in shaping behaviors, she said, and that "the trajectory is what we need to be focusing on." In the words of tech journalist Paul Mozur, the CCP's endgame is "totalizing control."

As I stood atop one of Beijing's skyscrapers, the city was nothing but concrete high-rises as far as I could see, a seemingly endless sprawl in every direction until the buildings faded into the featureless haze. In the distance, the cityscape blended seamlessly into the gray smog above. There was no horizon. I was told that on a clear day, one could see the mountains outside Beijing. While I was there, however, the city looked dead, like the remnants of some industrial accident. At ground level, though, coursed a torrent of people—on foot, car, bicycle, and moped. Unseen, but no less real, were the electrons flowing between them. Emanating from smartphones, taxis, pay terminals, and surveillance cameras: exabytes of data, the nervous system of Beijing's 21 million people.

The view reminded me of The Sprawl, the vast urban megalopolis in William Gibson's groundbreaking cyberpunk book, *Neuromancer*. Yet an hour outside of Beijing, the seemingly endless cityscape finally gives way to green forest. Jagged green tree-covered mountains rise in the distance. If Beijing's crowding, pollution, and grid-locked traffic are China, this too is also China: wild, rural, beautiful.

China's Great Wall, which stretches across China's northern regions, comes close enough to Beijing that it is an easy half-day trip and a must-do for visitors. While much of the wall has fallen into disrepair over the ages—the so-called "Wild Wall"—many sections have been restored. Those closest to Beijing are predictable tourist traps, replete with gondolas to take one to the top of the wall and gift shops adjacent the parking lot. Even amidst the throngs of tourists, though, the wall's magnificence is palpable.

The Great Wall lays like a stone dragon draped over China's green mountains, stretching into the distance until it disappears beyond the horizon. The Great Wall comprises a series of walls over 13,000 miles long, built over the span of over 2,500 years to keep out foreign invaders. In formidable terrain, Chinese laborers, including soldiers and convicts, carried stones up steep mountain slopes to build the wall. An estimated 400,000 people died building the wall.

Modern China's leaders have shown the same resolve and willingness to sacrifice their citizens to cement their political control over China. They have constructed a Great Firewall to keep out the destabilizing forces of free information on the internet. What many Westerners believed was impossible—controlling the internet—the CCP has largely accomplished. Despite some leakages through the use of tools like virtual private networks, or VPNs, that individuals can use to circumvent the Great Firewall and access banned web sites, the CCP is surprisingly effective in controlling information in China. The CCP's censorship, combined with state-controlled media and propaganda, has resulted in an alternate reality inside the country. The CCP's oppression of the Uighurs, the largest mass detention of an ethno-religious group since Nazi Germany, is an awful secret that no one dares mention in China. Many Chinese citizens are genuinely unaware of the abuses in Xinjiang. One student insisted to me it couldn't be true, that the government couldn't hide such an enormous thing. But it does.

Others know. One person whispers to me, "I don't agree with what's happening in Xinjiang," but only in a noisy room where no one can overhear him. He can't speak it out loud, and I don't blame him. Still others don't know the full extent of what's occurring. They're aware of checkpoints being set up as anti-terrorism measures, but not that the government has imprisoned over one million people and is working to eradicate an entire culture. Western social media is not immune to misinformation either. The difference is that in China, the lies are whatever the CCP wants them to be.

Science fiction writer William Gibson, who coined the term "cyberspace," has said, "Cyberspace, not so long ago, was a specific elsewhere, one we visited periodically, peering into it from the familiar physical world. Now cyberspace has everted. Turned itself inside out. Colonized the physical." Today, the CCP is working to extend the same control it exerts in the information environment into physical space. Paul Mozur wrote in 2019, "What the police are doing is putting in the ground floor on a system to control reality as tightly as the internet. One that harvests data in the same way and allows for a deeper understanding just about everything about people."

Samantha Hoffman pointed out that while much of the CCP's technological systems for controlling the population are highly manual today, "as you build up large amounts of quality data, technologies like AI will become more accurate." To effectively train machine learning systems, one needs "large amounts of quality data and that's what the Party is doing right now," she said. "Once the technology catches up it will be quite powerful."

The CCP's system of control is still incomplete. The patchwork of databases, lists, and surveillance networks are often disconnected. Chinese citizens at times circumvent the techno-surveillance state with simple measures. In some areas where facial recognition has been employed in apartment complexes, citizens have responded by simply propping open the gates. But the CCP's system of surveillance and social control doesn't have to be perfect for it to crush peoples' freedoms. Fifteen years ago, the Great Firewall was still nascent and developing, and many Westerners dismissed the CCP's efforts to control the internet as overly ambitious and impossible to achieve. Yet the CCP did it, and they are now working to do the same to every aspect of Chinese citizens' lives.

Maya Wang described what the CCP is doing today as laying in the "building blocks that make technological systems of surveillance possible." Individually, each of these tools may be somewhat limited. But when Chinese authorities combine real name registration, facial recognition, police clouds, and IJOP, "then you suddenly have a fairly effective system of tracking people, their relationships, and then picking out 'irregularities.'"

The fully realized vision of China's surveillance state is truly horrifying. AI will, over time, enable comprehensive automated surveillance that monitors people at every turn, analyzes and predicts their behavior, and cues any "unusual" activity to authorities. AI will be used not just to identify the faces of protestors, but to identify would-be dissidents before they even begin to step out of line. In a world where improperly sorting the trash is met with draconian punishment, few will even consider standing up against the regime. In a world where even coded messages are censored, how will dissenters organize? In a world where every step is tracked, every movement logged and tagged and analyzed, protestors would be flagged and targeted long before they ever made it to a protest site. The Chinese Communist Party is building a world where there will never be another Tiananmen Square protest, because the protestors will never even make it to the square.

Even Orwell's *1984* never imagined tools of repression this precise, powerful, and deployable at scale. AI will enable omnipresent surveillance and automated punishment. Perhaps most alarmingly, automation will allow authorities to deploy these tools at scale, decoupling autocratic regimes from the need to maintain even a sizeable minority on their side to repress the masses.

It is possible to both acknowledge the limitations of China's systems of surveillance and control today and see their horrifying potential. As the Chinese Communist Party pursues its goal of "totalizing control," its actions in Xinjiang, Tiananmen, Tibet, Hong Kong, and elsewhere demonstrate its leaders are willing to undertake brutal measures and endure international censure to cement their political control. The CCP is building a new techno-dystopian state, the most extreme version of which is in Xinjiang, but it is already in place to a lesser degree across all of China.

These developments are not just a threat to Chinese citizens; they threaten global freedoms as well. China is also exporting its technology, laws, and norms of surveillance to other nations around the world. Lin Ji of iFLYTEK said that he hoped the company would follow in the footsteps of U.S. firms like Google and Apple and become a "global company" in the future. China's model of digital authoritarianism is going global.

14

DYSTOPIA

China is not just forging a new model of digital authoritarianism but is actively exporting it. In 2018, Zimbabwe signed a strategic partnership with the Chinese company CloudWalk to build a mass facial recognition system consisting of a national database and intelligent surveillance systems at airports, railways, and bus stations. The deal will help "spearhead our AI revolution in Zimbabwe," according to former Zimbabwean ambassador to China Christopher Mutsvangwa. "An ordinary Zimbabwean probably won't believe that you can buy your groceries or pay your electricity bill by scanning your face," Mutsvangwa said, "but this is where technology is taking us and as the Government, we are happy because we are moving with the rest of the world."

At stake in the deal, which is part of China's Belt and Road Initiative, is more than just money. Zimbabwe agreed to let CloudWalk send data on millions of faces back to China, helping CloudWalk improve its facial-recognition systems with darker skin tones. As CloudWalk CEO Yao Zhiqiang pointed out, "The differences between technologies tailored to an Asian face and those to an African face are relatively large, not only in terms of colour, but also facial bones and features." Training on African faces could help make CloudWalk's facial recognition algorithms more robust—and more marketable around the globe. Data is the real currency of power in the age of AI.

The Zimbabwe deal is part of the massive global proliferation of Chinese surveillance technology along with Chinese-style laws and policies. According to University of Texas professor Sheena Greitens, Chinese surveillance and policing technology is now in use in at least eighty countries around globe and on every continent except Australia and Antarctica. Greitens has described China as the "index case" for a new set of technologies, laws, and policies spreading around the globe. Kara Frederick of the Heritage Foundation has described the suite of AI technologies as "the autocrat's new toolkit" which are empowering

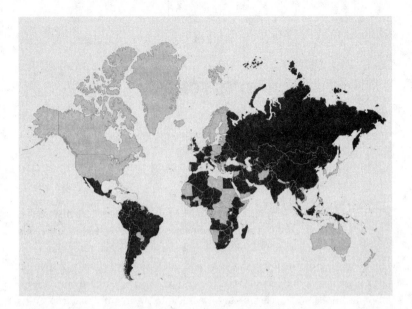

Global Spread of Chinese Public Surveillance Technology, 2008–2019. *Chinese surveillance technology has been sold to at least eighty countries, according to Professor Sheena Greitens. These include many countries without sufficient checks and balances to protect citizens from government abuses. Even more troubling is China's export of its laws and policies, the social "software" that enables the spread of China's evolving model of techno-authoritarianism.* (Country data from Sheena Chestnut Greitens. Map created by Melody Cook / Center for a New American Security.)

authoritarians and endangering freedom. Left unchecked, the spread of China's model of AI-enabled repression poses a profound challenge to global freedoms and individual liberty.

Chinese firms have been aggressively selling their surveillance technology worldwide. In Malaysia, the Chinese firm Yitu has sold facial recognition body-cams to police. In Ecuador, China's state-owned China National Electronics Import and Export Corporation (CEIEC) and Huawei, a Chinese telecom-munications firm, built a national surveillance network of over 4,000 cam-eras feeding data to the police and the country's domestic intelligence service. Following Ecuador's lead, Venezuela adopted a similar system, with the goal of fielding 30,000 cameras. Brazilian lawmakers, wowed after a trip to China, announced in 2019 that they would pursue facial recognition cameras linked to police in airports, train stations, subways, and high pedestrian traffic areas. Facial recognition was reportedly used in Brazil's Carnival festival in 2019, and by 2020 was deployed to police in six cities across the country. According to news reports, São Paulo's police database includes 32 million faces. Singapore has been soliciting bids from Chinese companies for a 110,000-camera network atop public lampposts using facial recognition. The project, called "Lamppost-as-a-Platform," aims to use AI-enabled cameras to "perform crowd analytics" and "count and analyse crowd build-ups," according to Singapore's government. In Angola, Percent Corporation, a Chinese data intelligence company, built the government an intelligent data analysis and visualization system that includes biometric information, such as facial images and fingerprints, along with birth, education, and marriage records. Percent Corporation's website boasts that its "data processing, analysis, and decision-making" solutions have been applied to "more than 20 countries across Asia, Africa, and Latin America." Other Chinese firms selling surveillance cameras abroad include Hikvision and ZTE, and other countries using Chinese surveillance technology include Bolivia, Germany, Pakistan, the United Arab Emirates, Uzbekistan, and Venezuela.

Huawei, one of China's tech "national champions" and the world's largest provider of telecom network equipment, has been particularly active in selling "safe city" solutions around the globe. Huawei has deployed 2,000 cameras to Nairobi, Kenya, and is helping establish a surveillance system of 1,000 cameras equipped with facial recognition in Belgrade, Serbia. Huawei describes its "safe city solutions" as using "AI, cloud computing, big data, and IoT" to build "interconnected, intelligent, and collaborative safe cities." Its "Command, Control, Communication, Cloud, Intelligence, Surveillance, and Reconnaissance [C4ISR]" solutions "enable advance prevention, precise resource allocation, efficient analysis, visualized command, and efficient coordination among multiple departments." The goal, according to Huawei, is to "help governments reduce crime rates and prevent and respond to crises more effectively." The products, as advertised, enable significant government surveillance. Huawei claims its "All-Cloud smart Video Cloud Solution . . . supports network-wide distributed smart analysis, and allows videos to be used not only for surveillance but also for generating actionable intelligence, taking city safety to a new level." Huawei's video surveillance technology can reportedly track people and cars, detect "abnormal behavior" such as loitering, automatically determine the size of crowds, and send authorities automated alerts.

According to Huawei, its safe city technology has been applied in "700 cities across more than 100 countries," including Brazil, Chile, Colombia, Côte d'Ivoire, Kenya, Mexico, Pakistan, Saudi Arabia, Serbia, Singapore, South Africa, Spain, Thailand, and Turkey. While Huawei has not publicly provided a list of all 100 countries, news reports indicate additional countries with Huawei safe city projects include Angola, Azerbaijan, France, Germany, Italy, Kazakhstan, Laos, Russia, Turkey, Uganda, and Ukraine. According to Huawei, over 1 billion people are served by its safe city technology.

Researchers at the Carnegie Endowment for International Peace compiled an AI Global Surveillance Index, mapping AI surveillance technology around the globe, and found that "Chinese companies—led by Huawei—are leading suppliers of AI surveillance around the world." Steven Feldstein, who led the AI Global Surveillance Index project, wrote:

> Huawei is the leading vendor of advanced surveillance systems worldwide by a huge factor. Its technology is linked to more countries in the index than any other company. It is aggressively seeking new markets in regions like sub-Saharan Africa. Huawei is not only providing advanced equipment but also offering ongoing technological support to set up, operate, and manage these systems.

Huawei's global activities have come under fire on a number of fronts. Huawei provided telecommunications equipment for the African Union's new headquarters building in Ethiopia, which was financed by the Chinese government, and in 2018 the French paper *Le Monde* revealed that data was being secretly transferred from the building every night between midnight and 2 a.m. to servers in Shanghai. A subsequent sweep for bugs found hidden microphones under desks and in the walls. In a published statement, Huawei stated, "Allegations about impropriety with our customer, the African Union (AU) are completely unsubstantiated, and we vehemently reject any such claims." In 2019, the *Wall Street Journal* reported that Huawei technicians helped the governments of Uganda and Zambia spy on political opponents. In response to cybersecurity concerns, a number of countries have either outright prohibited or effectively banned Huawei from their future 5G wireless telecommunications networks, including Australia, the Czech Republic, Denmark, Estonia, India, Japan, Latvia, Poland, Romania, Sweden, the United Kingdom, and the United States.

More troubling than the spread of Chinese surveillance technology has been China's export of its laws and policies for domestic surveillance. According to Freedom House, China has held training sessions and seminars with over thirty countries on cyberspace and information policy. Examples include a two-week "Seminar on Cyberspace Management" held in 2017 for officials from countries participating in China's Belt and Road Initiative, a Chinese global infrastructure development initiative that includes more than sixty nations. In 2018, journalists and media officials from the Philippines visited China to learn about "new media development" and "socialist journalism with Chinese characteristics." Similar Chinese media conferences have brought in representatives from Egypt, Jordan, Lebanon, Libya, Morocco, Saudi Arabia, Thailand, and the United Arab Emirates. At the government-run Baise Executive Leadership Academy in southern China, over 400 government officials from southeast Asian countries have been trained in "China's governance and economic development model," including how to "guide public opinion" online.

In Tanzania, Uganda, and Vietnam, restrictive media and cybersecurity laws closely followed Chinese engagement. Zimbabwe's government, whose officials attended Chinese seminars, has pushed for a sweeping cybersecurity law that would strengthen surveillance and clamp down on internet freedoms. While the global spread of Chinese technology helps China gain access to new datasets as well as inroads for spying abroad, it is the social "software" of laws and policies that help China export its evolving model of high-tech authoritarianism.

The proliferation of Chinese-style state surveillance is due to a number of factors. First among these is the desire of Chinese companies to make money and the international demand for surveillance networks. Autocratic regimes looking to secure power at home may view China's model of digital authoritarianism favorably, but they are not alone in desiring greater surveillance. According to Carnegie's AI Global Surveillance Index, 51 percent of advanced democracies use AI surveillance systems. London is the third most heavily surveilled city in the world. After all, there are legitimate uses of surveillance technology for policing and public safety in every country. Nor are Chinese firms the only ones exporting surveillance technology worldwide. While Chinese companies, especially Huawei, lead the pack, U.S. firms IBM, Palantir, and Cisco have all sold AI surveillance technology to multiple countries.

The Chinese government has hardly adopted a hands-off approach to its companies' overseas engagement, however. The government has helped put wind in the sails of its companies by offering loans to subsidize digital infrastructure projects, making them more affordable for developing nations. These efforts are not merely about making money but are part of China's broader push for greater geopolitical influence under Xi Jinping's leadership. A cornerstone of China's international engagement is the Belt and Road Initiative, launched in 2013, which consists of investments in building ports, railways, highways, energy pipelines, and digital infrastructure projects across Asia, Africa, and

Europe. The effort harkens back to the original Silk Road, the Eurasian trade routes that connected China to the rest of the world from 130 BCE to the fifteenth century. Today's Belt and Road is similarly aimed at deepening China's linkages with other economies, as well as extending Beijing's political influence. Spending estimates vary, but China has likely spent hundreds of billions of dollars in overseas construction and investment. The Digital Silk Road is the digital tech component of Belt and Road, encompassing technologies such as AI, safe cities, cloud computing, 5G wireless networks, and other "smart city" initiatives to help build modern, connected urban areas. The motivation for these efforts is expanding China's political and economic influence, and part of doing so is exporting China's model of governance.

One of Beijing's foreign policy goals is to secure Chinese Communist Party power by making "a world safe for autocracy," according to Cornell professor Jessica Chen Weiss. This does not look like a Soviet-style campaign of fomenting communist revolutions around the world. Instead, on a variety of fronts, Beijing seeks to weaken existing institutions, laws, and norms of democracy and freedom. Weiss has written: "China's actions abroad have . . . made the world safer for other authoritarian governments, and undermined liberal values. But those developments reflect less a grand strategic effort to undermine democracy and spread autocracy than the Chinese leadership's desire to secure its position at home and abroad." China's export of surveillance technology helps to normalize its own model of techno-authoritarianism.

Too often, Beijing's arguments for illiberal governance have met a receptive audience in autocrats or autocratic-leaning leaders who have similar goals. Since the mid-2000s, the world has been experiencing a "wave of autocratization," with authoritarian leaders tightening their grip and democracies experiencing "democratic backsliding," such as reducing checks on executive authority. These trends have been seen in countries as diverse as Brazil, Burundi, Hungary, India, Russia, Serbia, Turkey, and Venezuela. Part of this trend has been the rise of "digital dictators," who use social media, censorship, surveillance, and other digital tools to control the media, repress the population, and spread regime propaganda. China is not foisting their model on an unwilling world. Many countries are all too happy to emulate China's example of how to suppress freedoms and tighten control over their population.

AI is being used for security applications in democracies too. After landing at Dulles airport in Washington, DC, I had my face scanned by the U.S. Customs and Border Patrol (CBP) at the border to verify my identity. The difference isn't the technology, per se, but how it is used. In democratic countries, the government's use of AI surveillance technology is subject to the rule of law and checks and balances within the country's political system. At the Dulles checkpoint, a TV screen explained to travelers how long CBP retains their personal information (twelve hours for U.S. citizens and fourteen days for certain foreign travelers). The CBP website lists all of this information openly and publicly online, including which border checkpoints use biometric identification. Most importantly, the laws governing CBP's activities are written by elected representatives of the people.

Democracies have other checks on the government's powers as well. Independent media outlets shine a light on government activity. I knew about the facial recognition system at Dulles long before I ever went through the checkpoint because I'd read about it in the *Washington Post*. And if concerned citizens think the government is abusing its powers, they can file suit and take the government to court, where their case will be heard by an independent judiciary. Some concerned citizens have done so. The United States has seen lawsuits and robust public debates about the use of facial recognition, especially by law enforcement. Police use of facial recognition has sparked a grassroots backlash in the United States, with multiple cities and states banning or limiting law enforcement use. The American Civil Liberties Union (ACLU) and other civil society groups have filed lawsuits against a slew of government agencies, including the FBI, DEA, CBP, ICE, TSA, the Department of Justice, and the Department of Homeland Security. Civil society groups have criticized facial recognition, along with other technologies that aid in corporate or government surveillance and erode personal privacy. Even tech company leaders have stepped forward to say government regulation is needed, with Microsoft and Amazon calling for government regulation on facial recognition.

Europe has taken a different route than the United States, emphasizing preemptively regulating technology. The European General Data Protection Regulation, which covers data privacy in the European Union and European Economic Area, is an example of Europe's approach. The first regional regulatory regime for data privacy, the GDPR has become the de facto global standard that companies must comply with and other nations must at least consider when crafting their own standards. While the U.S. government has taken a much more laissez-faire attitude to tech regulation, with members of Congress dragging tech leaders like Facebook's Mark Zuckerberg before Congress for a public browbeating but passing little in the way of substantive regulation, Europe has leaned into regulating technology. American business executives have decried Europe's model, arguing too much regulation could "strangle business," and it is certainly true that overly burdensome regulations could harm innovation. However, the GDPR has given Europe a first-mover advantage in establishing global norms for privacy regulation. When I met with Chinese lawyers debating the contours of a potential new consumer data privacy law for China, the GDPR was the default starting point for the conversation.

Scholar Anu Bradford has referred to Europe's approach as a "race to the top" for regulatory standards, and Europe is aiming for the same approach with artificial intelligence. European bodies such as the European Commission have begun developing AI regulations to balance the many societal challenges AI brings in terms of safety, security, privacy, health, productivity, and worker and consumer protection.

While European and American sentiments may differ on the degree to which regulation is desirable, both have a common starting point: they are grounded in democratic processes that grant their approaches legitimacy. The same cannot be said of China or other authoritarian regimes in which the citizens do not get a vote. There are meaningful differences between how technology is used in different nations around the world, but not all approaches are created equal. In democratic nations, choices about how to use AI-enabled surveillance technology such as facial, voice, or gait recognition are made through a dynamic interplay between citizens, the government, the media, and civil society. This process is essential for all stakeholders to get a voice and to arrive at a regulatory approach that balances competing interests across society. Europeans and Americans may arrive at different answers to these questions, but both answers are legitimate if the processes that developed them are inclusive, transparent, and representative of society. In authoritarian regimes in which the media is censored, human rights activists are imprisoned, and citizens aren't allowed to openly express their discontent with the government, the type of open debate that is needed about technology is silenced by the government before it can even begin. Citizens of China and other authoritarian regimes can't appeal to elected representatives, sue the government, freely self-organize, get a fair hearing in an independent judiciary, or learn about government abuses from a free press.

The problem with AI isn't just that the technology is being adopted differently in different countries. After all, autocratic regimes abuse simple technologies in ways big and small, from police batons to jail cells. The problem is that AI can supercharge repression itself, allowing the state to deploy vast intelligent surveillance networks to monitor and control the population at a scale and degree of precision that would be impossible with humans. AI-enabled control is not only repressive, but further entrenches the system of repression itself. AI risks locking in authoritarianism, making it harder for the people to rise up and defend their freedoms.

The spread of AI surveillance technologies has the potential to tilt the global balance between freedom and authoritarianism. AI is already being used in deeply troubling ways, and those uses are spreading. Democratic governments and societies need to push back against these illiberal uses of AI by working to establish global norms for lawful, appropriate, and ethical uses of AI technologies like facial recognition. One of the challenges in doing so is that there is not (yet) a democratic model for how facial recognition or other AI technologies ought to be employed. China has pioneered a model for using AI for repression, but democratic states don't have a ready-made alternative for how AI should be used that protects individuals' privacy and civil liberties. It's easy to say that democracies should move faster and come up with an alternative approach, but one of the challenges in doing so is that the democratic process for grappling with new technologies is, by design, slow, messy, and chaotic. A fair and legitimate process for establishing laws and policies for facial recognition and other technologies is one that takes input from a variety of stakeholders and that involves give and take among different elements of society. It would be easy for a government to dictate by fiat how facial recognition technology should be used. The outcome may not be one that is beneficial to society, however. The messy process that is playing out in the United States, which involves grassroots movements, municipal and state-level policy, entrepreneurship, and lawsuits from organizations like the ACLU might be slower but is more likely to lead to policy outcomes in the long run that balance the interests of those across society. Good governance is not always quick governance.

In the meantime, the global spread of AI surveillance technologies continues, including in many countries that lack the institutional mechanisms for checks and balances that exist in democracies. The quicker that democracies can come together to develop a privacy-preserving model for how surveillance technology ought to be used, the sooner they can effectively push back against the growing wave of authoritarian uses of AI that threatens global freedoms.

PART IV
TRUTH

15

DISINFORMATION

"I want to show you something." Jack motioned me into a side conference room and flipped open his laptop. Jack Clark was the policy director at OpenAI, one of the world's leading AI research centers. He explained that they had a new AI system they were about to publicly release, and he wanted to get my take ahead of time. As someone who studies technology, this was a bit like Santa Claus saying he was going to give me a sneak peek at next year's presents. OpenAI is a powerhouse of deep learning and routinely delivers cutting-edge breakthroughs on challenging problems. A few months earlier, OpenAI had released an AI system that had delivered a solid performance against humans in *Dota 2*, a highly competitive computer strategy game. I was excited to see what Jack had up his sleeve.

Jack's laptop screen was just text, which to be honest was a little disappointing. But then he showed me the magic. Jack typed in a one-sentence prompt and, after a brief pause, the computer filled in the rest, generating a paragraph of believable, but fake, text. "We downloaded a chunk of the internet," Jack said. (In total, OpenAI downloaded 8 million web pages totaling 40 gigabytes of text.) OpenAI fed this massive amount of text into an enormous neural net, with 1.5 billion connections, and trained it "simply to predict the next word." The result was like magic: an AI text generator. Type in a one-sentence prompt, and the system would generate a news article, fiction story, poem, or whatever piece of text the prompt style implied. Jack showed me some examples, with the caveat that the model, called GPT-2, produced sensible text only half the time.

Here's an example of the kind of text that GPT-2 generates, using a prompt I typed into the machine and its actual output:

Prompt (by me):
President Trump declared war on North Korea.

Output (generated by GPT-2):

In an early-morning tweet Monday morning, Trump warned Kim Jong Un of "fire and fury like the world has never seen" if the North continued to threaten the United States.

"Military solutions are now fully in place, locked and loaded, should North Korea act unwisely. Hopefully Kim Jong Un will find another path!" Trump wrote.

Early Monday evening, North Korea's top military body said it was considering attacking Guam, the U.S. territory where three U.S. Navy destroyers are located.

Kim Jong Un on Monday further threatened to destroy Guam, which is home to a number of U.S. military installations.

The Trump administration has been cagey on its intentions.

I was shocked to see AI-generated fake text so well-written, so convincing, that it could have been real. Whether by accident or design, the AI model even included typos in Trump's tweet! It wasn't brilliant literature, but if I had read this online I might have assumed the story was true, and I certainly would not have guessed it was written by a bot. Major news outlets such as *Bloomberg,* the *Associated Press*, and the *Washington Post* had for years used bots to generate simple news stories, but bot-generated articles had been limited to reporting facts and figures, such as sports scores or financial market movements. GPT-2 was a leap forward in AI-generated text. It wasn't merely regurgitating facts; GPT-2 was creating new content. It was an impressive technical feat but also deeply problematic. GPT-2 might be designed to simply predict the next word in a block of text, but in practice OpenAI had created a fake news generator.

Language models such as GPT-2 are just one example of AI tools that can influence and distort the information ecosystem, undermining truth. AI-generated text, audio, and video can be used to create fake news for disinformation and propaganda. They can even be used to convincingly impersonate political leaders. Bots can flood social media with manufactured narratives, allowing authoritarian regimes to suppress dissent. Algorithms can promote or demote political content, subtly censoring the public square.

The digital information ecosystem has rapidly become a contested space between corporations, bots, trolls, dictators, and average citizens. How AI tools are used to control information will have profound consequences for the future of truth and the global balance between democracy and authoritarianism. Dictators benefit in a world where nothing can be trusted, and truth is whatever the powerful say it is. If democracies want to sustain a free, open, transparent, and truthful information environment, governments will need to engage the engineers and companies building AI tools to ensure they are used responsibly.

When Jack and his colleagues at OpenAI developed GPT-2, they were concerned about potential misuse of this technology and were thinking about a strategy for responsible release. Humans didn't need machines to generate fake news, of course. The internet was already rife with disinformation, but tools like GPT-2 could make it easier for trolls, propagandists, and malicious actors to generate fake articles faster and in larger numbers.

The technology was problematic in several ways. For one, GPT-2 lowered the barrier to entry for who could create convincing fake news stories. With a single sentence, I used GPT-2 to generate a reasonably convincing fake news story about President Trump declaring war on North Korea. I didn't have to research how news articles were written or what kinds of details (such as threatening Guam) would make the article more convincing. GPT-2 did that for me. Language models like GPT-2 could enable a wider array of actors to create believable disinformation.

Second, AI text generation allows the creation of fake news at industrial scales. By typing one-sentence prompts into GPT-2 and allowing the bot to generate the rest of the article, one person could generate ten to twenty times as many fake news stories in the same amount of time it would take to write a single story by hand. Apply automated scripts, and malicious actors could release a deluge of fake content at a scale far beyond what people could create on their own.

Many issues are manageable in small numbers but become problematic at scale. Spam, whether it is via physical mail, email, Twitter, robocalls, or some other form, is generally not high quality, but the sheer volume of garbage threatens to drown out other content. Human telemarketers have been around for decades, but it is only in recent years due to machines that robocalls have become a plague, with one's phone ringing ten times a day. Machine-driven spam floods our email inboxes and telephones, and machine-generated fake text could lead to a similar flood of spam text on the internet.

Jack was keenly aware of this problem and explained that OpenAI wanted to act responsibly. He outlined their plan for a staged release that would first announce that they had created the system and give examples of what it could do, but not release the full model online. They would share a smaller, dumbed-down version publicly and release the full version only to trusted AI researchers who could begin working through some of the challenges of how to live in a world where machines could generate realistic artificial text. Jack and I had been part of a project the prior year that brought together twenty-six authors from fourteen institutions to anticipate malicious AI applications, and this was one of the strategies the group had discussed for managing these kinds of risks. I still had misgivings, but OpenAI's approach seemed reasonable. If they did nothing, eventually other research groups would generate similar high-quality language models, so it was better to give responsible researchers a head-start now on managing potential problems.

A month after Jack's visit in February 2019, OpenAI released the GPT-2 model to a firestorm of controversy, although not for the reasons I expected. Other AI researchers were incensed, not that OpenAI had developed and partially released a potentially dangerous tool, but that they had held back from releasing the full version online. Anima Anandkumar, director of machine learning at the chip company NVIDIA and a professor at Caltech, accused OpenAI of "fear-mongering" and "severely playing up the risks" of the model. Others agreed. Delip Rao, an expert on machine learning and natural language processing, told *The Verge*, "The words 'too dangerous' were casually thrown out here without a lot of thought or experimentation."

Others accused OpenAI of courting hype by giving prerelease copies to tech journalists. AI researchers woke up one Thursday morning to a spate of news headlines about a technical breakthrough for which they hadn't yet seen the academic paper (it posted the same day). For example, *Wired* touted "The AI Text Generator That's Too Dangerous to Make Public." The "too dangerous" theme was echoed in other outlets as well, including *TechCrunch, The Guardian, Gizmodo, Slashdot, The Verge, Slate,* and the World Economic Forum. When Jack Clark and I caught up a year later, he acknowledged that pre-briefing the press "got us some concerns that we were hyping it," while the paper itself had been more careful about the phrasing around potential dangers. " 'Too dangerous to release' is never a quote [of] anything we said, but it came to dominate some of the narrative," Jack acknowledged. But beyond the news headlines, the controversy exposed a real rift in the AI community about openness and how to handle the risks of misuse.

For years, AI text generation had been not very good, but in the summer of 2018, Jack explained, they began seeing improvements "not just in our own lab but in other labs as well." It became a topic of lunchtime conversation, with researchers asking, "What happens if this gets really good?" Simultaneously, Jack said, he was having more conversations with policy folks in Washington, DC, about the possible misuse of AI technology. In fact, the improvements

Jack was seeing in text generation coincided with similar improvements in AI-generated video and audio, which had already alarmed some policy analysts.

In late 2017, AI-generated "deepfake" videos began circulating online, in which deep learning is used to generate realistic-looking fake videos. Early deepfake videos mostly consisted of face-swapping, in which a person's face was swapped onto the body of a different person in a video. Like so many things on the internet, it was first used in pornography, in this case to swap the faces of celebrities such as Gal Gadot or Scarlett Johansson onto the bodies of porn stars. The video quality wasn't very good—the faces often looked jumpy and didn't precisely match the audio—but deepfake porn videos nevertheless exploded on the internet. Within two years, the deepfake detection company Deeptrace had uncovered over 14,000 deepfake porn videos online. The videos didn't only harm the celebrities whose faces were swapped and the porn performers whose work was used without their permission, but quickly morphed into revenge porn attacks on noncelebrity women as well. Danielle Citron, a Boston University law professor and author of the book *Hate Crimes in Cyberspace*, told Deeptrace, "Deepfake technology is being weaponized against women. . . . It is terrifying, embarrassing, demeaning, and silencing. Deepfake sex videos say to individuals that their bodies are not their own and can make it difficult to stay online, get or keep a job, and feel safe."

In addition to the harm caused by face-swapping porn videos, security researchers began to worry about other risks from AI-generated synthetic media good enough to fool humans. In May 2018, Google demoed an AI assistant called Duplex that could call restaurants, hair salons, and other businesses to schedule appointments. The AI voice assistant was so convincing that it appeared to fool the humans on the other end of the phone into believing it was a real person. The impressive tech demo sparked rousing applause from developers in the room but raised troubling ethical questions. Was it acceptable to deceive a person into believing a bot was human? The sudden appearance of AI-generated voice bots that were good enough to pass as humans accelerated interest in a "blade runner" law that would prohibit using machines to impersonate humans. Named after the 1982 dystopian sci-fi film in which Harrison Ford plays a "blade runner," a police detective tasked with tracking down rogue synthetic humans, "blade runner" laws mandate that bots disclose they are a bot when interacting with a human. In the wake of the controversy following their demo, Google clarified that their bot would identify itself as an automated service, but there was no legal mandate at the time to do so. Other companies might not be as voluntarily transparent as Google.

In September 2018, California passed the first "blade runner" law requiring bot disclosure. Security researchers nevertheless began to worry about myriad misuses of AI-generated audio and video, from increasingly realistic robocalls to fake videos that could be used to influence an election.

AI-generated media wasn't just a risk for fueling greater online harassment or spam; it could potentially be a weapon of statecraft to spread lies and undermine democracies. During the Cold War, the Soviet KGB undertook "active measures" to spread disinformation, or *dezinformatsiya* in Russian, such as the rumor that the AIDS epidemic was due to a bioengineered virus created by the U.S. military. Social media was a new front in the information war, and modern-day Russia was pioneering new ways of using social media to undermine democracies. In the run-up to the 2016 U.S. presidential election, Russia used fake online personas, surreptitious ad purchases, digital forgeries, social media bots, and online troll farms to create, spread, and amplify disinformation. These efforts were aimed at not only influencing the election, but more broadly sowing division among Americans and undermining faith in democracy. Nor was Russia's campaign against the U.S. election an anomaly. Russian government and government-backed operatives undertook a slew of influence operations across Europe to undermine democratic processes, including against the 2016 British Brexit referendum and the 2017 French presidential election.

In the aftermath of the 2016 U.S. presidential election, concerns about Russian disinformation reached a fever pitch in Washington. U.S. senators warned that Russia's "information warfare campaign" was designed to "sow fear, discord, and paralysis that undermines democratic institutions and weakens critical Western alliances" and was "a threat to the foundations of American democracy." The United States spends over $700 billion annually on defense, but information warfare threatened to go around America's military and directly attack the nervous system of American democracy, the free and open exchange of ideas. In practice, the effects of disinformation campaigns were hard to measure and hotly debated, but even the perception of foreign influence in an election could—and did—polarize, divide, and paralyze the U.S. political system. Even worse, U.S. national security experts worried that Russian disinformation in the 2016 election was only a prelude of more to come. In the years since, Russia has continued their activities against U.S. politicians, and other nations such as China and Iran have followed suit.

Jack Clark and others at OpenAI looked at GPT-2 against this backdrop of growing societal concern about the misuse of AI-generated audio and video.

The specific risk of releasing GPT-2 was unclear. AI text generation was getting good enough to enter what Jack called "the weird zone," which he described as "technology that might be good enough to do something in the world, but you aren't quite sure." Delip Rao, the machine learning researcher who had criticized OpenAI's GPT-2 release strategy, told *The Verge*, "I don't think [OpenAI] spent enough time proving it was actually dangerous." But Jack had a different perspective: "We're being very cautious . . . because we can't say it's definitely safe." And once GPT-2 was out in the wild, it would be impossible to put the genie back in the bottle.

OpenAI described their release strategy as "an experiment" and said, "while we are not sure that it is the right decision today, we believe that the AI community will eventually need to tackle the issue of publication norms in a thoughtful way." But by proposing that AI researchers consider the risks of misuse, and occasionally refrain from releasing some information, OpenAI was challenging a long-standing norm of openness in the AI community. The backlash was fierce, with some critics claiming OpenAI was "betraying [its] core mission" of openness and others suggesting the moniker "ClosedAI."

Other scientific fields such as cybersecurity, nuclear physics, and biotechnology have long dealt with concerns about the misuse of research. In 2011, the U.S. National Science Advisory Board for Biosecurity recommended censorship of two scientific articles under review in *Nature* and *Science* that described how to make H5N1 avian bird flu more transmissible. The recommendation sparked vigorous debate in the biosecurity community about the benefits and risks of certain scientific information. In the field of cybersecurity, "responsible disclosure" is a practice where security researchers first disclose a vulnerability to companies so they have time to patch the vulnerability before it is disclosed publicly. Yet AI researchers had only recently begun to confront issues surrounding the risks of misuse of their research. Jack said their intent was to force a conversation. "We wanted to make ourselves culpable in the sense that very few AI companies or academic institutions proactively talk about the implications of their technical research," he explained. Rebecca Crootof, a University of Richmond law professor and expert on emerging technologies, noted that GPT-2 "spurred a much-needed interdisciplinary conversation about . . . when it is appropriate to restrict access to AI research."

The controversy around GPT-2's release was about more than just whether the technology was dangerous. At the core of the GPT-2 debate was a timeless question of power: Who holds it, and what will they do with it? AI is creating powerful tools to shape the information environment, and those who wield these tools will have the ability to control information seen by billions of people. In restricting release, OpenAI was not only limiting access to GPT-2 for potentially malicious actors but also for academics who didn't have access to the large-scale compute resources OpenAI used for training. If OpenAI published their work openly, then at least other researchers could benefit from OpenAI's findings. But if they withheld their research, the divide threatened to grow between researchers who had access to large compute resources and those who did not. Just barely under the surface of debates about openness was a conflict about who would control the future direction of AI research.

In the end, OpenAI didn't prevent GPT-2's release, only slowed it down. The first release in February 2019 was a smaller 124 million parameter version, roughly one-tenth the size of the full 1.5 billion parameter model. In the months that followed, OpenAI executed a "staged release" with incrementally larger and more advanced models. In May, OpenAI released a 345 million parameter model. In August, a 774 million parameter model. And in November 2019 they released the full 1.5 billion parameter model, only nine months after the initial release. In theory, the staged release was meant to buy time for other researchers to investigate countermeasures against AI-generated fake text and to cautiously explore the risks of misuse by releasing ever more sophisticated models. But in the end, nine months wasn't much of a delay. OpenAI was, at best, only a few months ahead of other research groups working on language models. Within six months of OpenAI's initial announcement more than five other research groups had replicated GPT-2, but no one had publicly released a full-size model. OpenAI said the experience showed that coordination among different research labs to slow down release was "difficult, but possible."

"My general belief is that this stuff is all going to make its way into the world," Jack acknowledged. "What we get to choose is how we frame it." During those nine months, OpenAI, for example, partnered with other institutions to better understand the risks of GPT-2 and similar language models. Researchers at the Middlebury Institute's Center on Terrorism, Extremism, and Counterterrorism demonstrated that GPT-2 could be fine-tuned to produce white supremacist, jihadist Islamist, anarchist, or Marxist-Leninist propaganda. Middlebury researchers concluded that advanced language models like GPT-2 "pose a significant and novel threat to civil society" by giving extremists a tool for "drastically scaling up propaganda efforts." Researchers at Cornell University and the nonprofit Politiwatch found that the full-size GPT-2 model could be used to generate fake news that "readers perceived . . . to be as credible as an original human-written news article" on the same topic. Furthermore, they found that readers were as willing to share GPT-2 generated articles as a real *New York Times* article. "Large-scale synthesized disinformation is now possible," the researchers concluded. "When such content floods the Internet, people may come to discount everything they read."

When we spoke over a year after GPT-2's initial release, Jack Clark acknowledged that they hadn't seen the worst kinds of harms materialize. Despite the apparent feasibility of using language models like GPT-2 to generate disinformation at scale, the internet had yet to be flooded with a glut of AI-generated fake news. Most disinformation remains largely human-generated. Part of this could be the ease of cheap human labor. China, Russia, Iran, and other nations have, for years, used troll farms to spew propaganda and disinformation online. China's "50 cent army" employs hundreds of thousands of people to generate upwards of 400 million fake pro-government social media posts per year. When human labor is so cheap, nation-states may not need AI text generators. Jack concluded, "It doesn't seem like we've crossed an effective economics curve yet" for using AI to generate fake news.

If the limiting factor is cost, then eventually the economics of machine-generated text will make sense. As quality of AI text generators improve and costs go down machines will replace humans for fake news creation and online trolling, as they have in other jobs. For the moment, automated spam remains poor quality. As I write these words my phone interrupts me with automated robocalls, the most recent one alerting me to the necessity of renewing my car warranty. My best defense against this scam is my ability to recognize that the message is recorded. I worry about the day when we cross into blade runner territory, when AI-generated content is good enough that we can't tell the difference between a bot and a human. That day may be coming sooner than we think.

OpenAI's decision succeeded in shifting publication norms in the AI community. Other AI labs have chosen not to release aspects of their research, and some have begun writing about the societal implications of their work. In 2020 when Google announced Meena, a chatbot based on a 2.6 billion parameter neural network, it withheld external release of a demo, citing challenges relating to safety and bias. Google's press release wasn't as splashy as OpenAI's in highlighting the risks of misuse, but one can understand why a trillion-dollar company may not want news headlines saying its products are "too dangerous." Yet others have pushed back on the shift toward a more closed ecosystem. After OpenAI and Google limited access to their text-to-image generative models in 2022, Stability AI released its full model, Stable Diffusion, online. Users quickly stripped off the safeguards built into the model.

Limiting the accessibility of potentially harmful AI tools is only the first step in protecting the information ecosystem against increasingly sophisticated AI tools for disinformation, propaganda, and information warfare. The information environment is swiftly evolving, driven by the emergence of new channels of communication, such as social media, and new technologies, such as algorithms to sift and sort information and AI-generated content. The information environment has always been a geopolitical battleground among nations, and it is one increasingly fought using AI. Authoritarian states peddle disinformation and propaganda to hide the truth and promote false narratives. AI is giving malicious actors new opportunities to spread lies and suppress the truth. The rise of Chinese-owned social media platforms, which are beholden to the Chinese Communist Party, and the algorithms they use to control information represent a new threat to free societies. The technology platforms and AI tools that are being built today—and who wields them—will have profound consequences for the future of the global order. Democratic governments, tech companies, the media, and members of civil society must work together to ensure that the evolving information ecosystem is one that safeguards the truth.

16

SYNTHETIC REALITY

The blue-haired dancer moved her body to the music against an ever-shifting array of light. Yet the music, lyrics, and singing were all AI-generated. The digital performer, Yona, wasn't human, but she was more than an avatar. Her creators, Ash Koosha and Isabella Winthrop, refer to Yona as an "auxuman," or auxillary human, a virtual person created through AI and other digital technologies. Yona's aesthetic is that of a synthesizer that came to life and gained a body, voice, and personality. She is a "virtual singer, songwriter, and performer," and part of a trend in AI-generated synthetic media.

AI is being used to generate not only fake text and deepfake videos, but also a slew of different forms of synthetic media including music, voice, and more. Similar to how machine learning systems can be trained to recognize patterns in data, such as identifying faces, machine learning algorithms can also be trained to generate new synthetic data, such as realistic-looking AI-generated faces of people who don't exist.

One approach to creating synthetic media uses generative adversarial networks (GANs), a machine learning method that pits two "adversarial" machine learning systems against each other. One machine learning model is a generator which creates synthetic media (images, video, etc.). The other machine learning model is a discriminator which tries to determine whether the generated media is real or fake. The models are trained together and learn from each other, so that with each iteration the generator learns to create more realistic media and the discriminator learns to better discern real from fake. This powerful approach lets the GAN lift itself up by its own bootstraps, competing against itself to create ever more convincing synthetic media.

I saw Yona perform at a 2019 conference in New York hosted by Betaworks, a platform for start-ups that includes a venture capital fund and an accelerator for companies working on frontier technologies. The Betaworks studio has the tech-hip vibe of a coffee shop fused with an Apple store, with bubbly water on tap in cucumber, watermelon, and key lime flavors. The evening before, the organizers had dimmed the lights and hosted a reception that was part cocktail hour, part science fair.

Danika Laszuk runs their accelerator, Betaworks Camp, which does thematic in-residence programs for start-ups working on various technologies. Danika described herself as "a real optimist about technology" and was excited about not just the creative possibilities of synthetic media but also the opportunities to better human lives. For those who have lost the ability to speak due to ALS or other causes, AI might allow them to speak again in their own voice, instead of a generic computer voice. With only twenty to thirty minutes of recorded speech (about the time to read a book chapter out loud), companies can train a neural network to learn the patterns of a particular voice and then generate synthetic speech in that voice. Danika said this was "a great use of technology to help people communicate and find their voice again."

AI-generated media was opening up a whole new world of "synthetic reality," which Danika described as "the bigger space where humans and AI are interacting in sometimes clean entertainment value ways, and sometimes a little more murky and less clearly defined ways." Danika said she was most excited about the "self-expression and creative output and human connectivity that these tools can give us," but she also acknowledged that the technology had downsides. In 2019, for example, scammers used an AI-generated voice to impersonate the CEO of a European company, directing company executives to transfer $243,000 to a bank account for a supposed urgent business deal. The employee thought he heard his boss's voice on the phone, so he completed the fraudulent transfer. The perpetrators were never caught.

Even more worrying than criminal use is the possibility of using synthetic media for information warfare. Nations have long used disinformation to sow discord and uncertainty among rivals. Instead of cybercriminals faking a CEO's voice to defraud a company, a malicious actor could release a fake video or audio clip of a politician doing or saying something that might sway an election, or worse, authorize a bad policy or military attack.

Deepfakes did not feature heavily in the 2020 U.S. presidential election, but security researchers worry it won't be long before they're used in disinformation campaigns online, throwing gasoline on the already raging dumpster fire that is false information on social media. Manipulated media has already become a flashpoint in U.S. politics, with crudely manipulated videos of House Speaker Nancy Pelosi or White House press correspondent Jim Acosta making the rounds on social media. These "shallow fakes" were manipulated without AI, but AI-based synthetic media will enable more sophisticated fake audio and video, making it harder for people to know what is real and what is fake.

The geopolitical risks from deepfakes extend beyond manipulating elections. Fake audio or video could be used to manufacture a political crisis, undermine relations between allies, or inflame geopolitical tensions. Even a fake that was eventually exposed as fraudulent could be damaging if it caused doubt for a period of time.

Russia's invasion of Ukraine in 2022 spawned a flood of war propaganda on all sides of the conflict. The Kremlin peddled a steady stream of disinformation, domestically and internationally, which was often echoed by the Chinese government. Russian falsehoods included claims that the United States had bioweapons labs in Ukraine and that Ukrainian civilians injured in Russian attacks were "crisis actors." Ukrainian defenders, for their part, pumped a steady stream of heroic tales of brave resistance on social media, many of which were false. These included stories about the "Ghost of Kyiv," a mythical Ukrainian air force pilot who reportedly had downed six Russian planes. Except the video footage circulating online was from a video game.

AI-based synthetic media could aid countries in spreading disinformation to create a pretext for an attack or create confusion in other nations at the outbreak of a conflict. Leaked fake audio or video, for example, of NATO members squabbling amongst themselves or implicating a partner nation in instigating the conflict could cause hesitation among would-be defenders, buying time for an aggressor to seize territory.

In March 2022, a deepfake of Ukrainian president Volodymyr Zelensky surfaced online in which he appeared to call on Ukrainians to lay down their arms against Russian invaders. The video was swiftly debunked by the real Zelensky, and Facebook, Twitter, and YouTube either removed the video or labeled it according to their policies. The AI-manipulated video failed to gain traction due to a combination of factors: a low-quality video that was obviously fake; Zelensky's high-profile media presence which meant viewers were familiar with how he actually sounds; the quick response from Zelensky, social media companies, and news outlets; and the fact that the Ukrainian government had been warning about deepfake disinformation for weeks. The Zelensky video was an early sign, however, of the ways in which actors will try to use deepfakes to manipulate geopolitical events.

One side effect of increasingly sophisticated fakes is that their mere possibility can throw authentic audio or video into question. Law professors Robert

Chesney and Danielle Citron have termed this effect the "liar's dividend," in which individuals could disavow real video or audio catching them doing something they shouldn't have, claiming that it is a clever forgery. The problem isn't just that an individual might avoid accountability for their behavior. The long-term effect could be to undermine public confidence in what is real, hastening a "post-truth" information landscape in which public opinion is driven by emotion and beliefs rather than facts. The consequences of politics unmoored from the truth is bigger than just bad policy. A world where "truth" is whatever the leader says it is benefits authoritarians and undermines democracies, which count on an independent media and public accountability to serve as a check on the powerful.

The descent of the information environment into a toxic stew of fake news, conspiracy theories, and disinformation isn't due to AI-generated media, but could be accelerated by it. Actor Scarlett Johansson, who has been a victim of deepfake porn, remarked that "the internet is a vast wormhole of darkness that eats itself." As AI-generated media becomes more sophisticated our senses alone won't be enough to preserve a hold on the truth. New technologies and methods, including AI, will be needed to discern what is real from fake.

One of the individuals working to do so is Giorgio Patrini, CEO, founder, and chief scientist at Sensity (formerly Deeptrace). Sensity is a "visual threat intelligence company" aimed at defending "against the threats posed by deepfakes and other forms of malicious visual media." Among Sensity's tools is a deepfake detector, which Giorgio demonstrated for me through a simple drag-and-drop interface. He picked the video of Steve Buscemi's face swapped onto Jennifer Lawrence's body in her 2016 Golden Globes speech. In face-swapping videos, a real video is manipulated by putting another person's face on someone else's body. Almost instantly, Giorgio's automated detector registered the video as fake. The Buscemi-JLaw face-swap video is deep in the uncanny valley and no one would be fooled into thinking it was real. However, face-swapping videos have been used to create realistic-looking fakes and the technology is improving over time, making detectors like the ones Sensity has developed an increasingly important countermeasure against manipulated media.

AI-generated images range massively in quality. The easiest ones can be made with a few clicks on your phone for free. I downloaded the Reface app onto my phone and with one selfie my face was swapped onto Leonardo DiCaprio in *The Great Gatsby* or Sylvester Stallone as Rambo. Face-swapping GIFs might be fun to send to your friends but aren't convincing fakes. Yet other forms of synthetic media may fool a casual observer. Artificial lip-syncing is when a person's original face in the video remains the same but the lip movement is altered to "lip-sync" an audio clip. AI has also been used to create wholly artificial still images of people that don't exist at all.

Many AI-generated fakes are good enough to fool the average person at a quick glance, but don't stand up to detailed scrutiny by forensic experts. Deepfake videos often feature unnatural eye movement or awkward facial expressions or body movements. For AI-generated still images of faces, glitches in the hair, eyes, earrings, eyeglasses, clothing, and backgrounds, among other discrepancies, can often be a giveaway.

Despite these limitations, the ease of these tools has meant they have already been used in minor national security-related incidents. In 2019, an AI-generated portrait appeared on the LinkedIn profile of "Katie Jones," a fake persona likely created by a foreign intelligence agency. Jones's profile claimed she was tied into the Washington, DC, national security scene, working at a major DC think tank and connected to government officials. Experts concluded Jones's persona was likely a state-run intelligence operation attempting to connect to Washington insiders online. Social media has increasingly been a tool of hostile foreign intelligence services to attempt to connect with and recruit people with U.S. government security clearances. One former CIA officer who was sentenced to twenty years in prison for spying for China was first recruited on LinkedIn. While the actual contact and recruitment is done by people, AI-generated synthetic media may help make a fake profile appear more realistic. In another instance, the fake persona of "Martin Aspen," which included an AI-generated headshot photo, was cited as the author for a fake report from a purported "intelligence firm" peddling conspiracy claims about Hunter Biden during the 2020 election. In both cases, AI-generated media played a minor role in helping to aid deception, and both fakes were quickly unmasked by digital forensic experts.

Synthetic media's ease of use means malicious actors are likely to use deepfakes in more incidents over time. As of 2019, Deeptrace (now Sensity) stated that deepfake creators online were willing to make "bespoke faceswap videos for $30" and "custom voice cloning for $10 per 50 words generated." Many fakes are currently of poor quality, however. To make a truly convincing deepfake, at least at present, takes a significant amount of effort.

In 2020, a U.S. nonprofit dedicated to fighting government corruption released deepfake videos of North Korean leader Kim Jong-un and Russian president Vladimir Putin rooting for the end of American democracy as part of a public awareness campaign tied to the 2020 U.S. presidential election. (The videos acknowledged at the end that the footage was fake.) To make more convincing videos, the creators used actors with similar body types to Kim and Putin and employed native Korean- and Russian-speaking voice actors. Traditional computer editing techniques were used to put the finishing touches on the videos.

As computing costs decline and the amount of publicly available data on which to train machine learning systems continues to grow, synthetic media will become increasingly accessible and of higher quality. Automated deepfake detectors, like that from Sensity as well as other firms such as Microsoft, Quantum Integrity, Sentinel, and others, will become increasingly important. Deepfake detectors are trained like other machine learning classifiers, by using large datasets of real and fake videos and training a neural network to learn the difference. The nascent arms race between deepfakes and detectors is just one example of the contest between AI and counter-AI systems that will unfold in the years ahead. As AI becomes more widely used, techniques for detecting, fooling, manipulating, and defeating AI systems will become essential tools for geostrategic competitors.

Giorgio Patrini at Sensity compared deepfake detectors to antivirus software. He pointed out that it was standard behavior now for individuals and organizations to scan software to ensure it doesn't contain malware. Giorgio said that "in the future . . . the set of things that we will be checking in digital media will also go into the realm of audio-visual." He pointed out that, up to now, we could trust digital audio and video "just looking at them with our senses." Going forward, "We will not be able to certify that something is authentic just with our senses." We will need to rely on machines to verify authenticity. Giorgio pointed out that synthetic media has many valuable and legitimate applications in research and business, especially in media and entertainment, but the problem is that "it is becoming so easy and cheap for anybody to use." He explained, "The entry point is so low that you can also imagine bad actors . . . will weaponize them."

A growing network of tech companies, media outlets, and AI researchers are working to combat deepfakes, but even the best deepfake detectors still have a long way to go. In 2019, Facebook partnered with Amazon, Microsoft, and the Partnership on AI to create a Deepfake Detection Challenge to improve the state of the art in deepfake detectors. Facebook created a dataset of over 100,000 new videos (using paid actors) for AI researchers to use to train deepfake detectors. (Google has also created datasets of synthetic audio and video, using paid actors, to help researchers train detection models.) The Deepfake

Detection Challenge drew over 2,000 participants who submitted more than 35,000 trained models as detectors, a major spur to improving deepfake detection. Yet the top-performing detector was accurate only 65 percent of the time—better than a coin flip, but not nearly reliable enough to be useful. Given more data, computing power, and training, deepfake detectors will improve, but so will deepfake quality. In the long run, detectors are fighting an uphill battle. The adversarial method GANs use to generate synthetic media will train generators to overcome detection methods over time.

Giorgio, who has a PhD in computer science, explained that at present Sensity's detectors work by identifying the presence or absence of "camera fingerprints" in a video, which is a statistical pattern generated in the video "due to the way lenses are made, digitalization, [and] algorithms" used in the camera. These patterns can't be seen visually, but they can be detected using digital filters. "As soon as you modify or manipulate an image or a video," Giorgio explained, "those type of statistical signals are removed" in the parts of the video that are erased or swapped. "The inconsistency there is a clue for neural networks to understand that something is off."

Giorgio pointed out, however, that "there is no silver bullet against deepfakes." He described deepfake detection as a "cyber security problem" and said, "It's very important that you do not base all your defenses on one particular technical element." Drawing a parallel to the antivirus industry, he said that deepfake detection needed to draw upon "a portfolio of techniques" and be constantly updated against an evolving threat. Giorgio was very cognizant of the risk that someone could "train adversarially ways to generate synthetic media that can bypass . . . some of the specific detection techniques that we use," which is why they relied on a "portfolio solution, such that bypassing them all altogether would be much more difficult." Giorgio asked me not to share all of their methods, but said that some of them work "at the pixel level . . . to tell apart real from fake" while others use very different approaches, such as relying on metadata embedded in the videos. Though more advanced fakes will eventually be able to bypass detection methods, Giorgio predicted that even after deepfakes were good enough to fool humans, "There will be a long gap where we can still trust automated instruments" to catch most fakes.

Just as deepfake detectors must rely on multiple methods, so too must society build a portfolio approach to responding to the problem of AI-generated fake media. Increased public awareness about the potential for realistic-looking AI-generated fakes is part of the solution. In fact, in just the past few years public awareness about deepfakes has rapidly eclipsed the threat itself. The biggest role deepfakes played in the 2020 U.S. election was in public service announcement videos warning viewers about the dangers of deepfakes. Giorgio said, "The fear that sometimes the media is communicating . . . maybe it's a bit premature." While increasing public awareness is important to help inoculate the public against the dangers of convincing fakes, increasing public skepticism also has its downsides if people fail to trust real audio and video.

In 2018, after the president of Gabon suffered a stroke and was out of the public eye for months, he finally appeared in a New Year's Eve video intended to prove that he was still alive. Yet his strange appearance in the video, which experts credited to the aftereffects of the stroke, cosmetic procedures, and heavy makeup, led some to claim on social media that the video was a fake. A week later, military officers launched a coup to oust the president. The coup failed and multiple deepfake experts have said the video is likely real. But questions about the video's authenticity may have contributed to rumors and disinformation about whether the president was still in control or even still alive. (He has since appeared in public, visibly weakened from the stroke.) Knowledge of deepfakes didn't cause the coup—politics did—but increased awareness of deepfakes could heighten confusion about what is real or be used as an excuse for those looking to deny the truth. Giorgio pointed out, "We don't even need to wait anymore for these technologies to be weaponized for political means. Because even just the fact that they are around and people know about them, [people] can already claim that anything is fake if it fits with their agenda."

To get a glimpse of how society might handle a world of increasingly realistic fake video, I turned to the world of synthetic audio, which is far more advanced than video today. While convincing deepfake videos are still difficult to produce, AI-generated audio is more mature and has already been used to commit fraud.

17

TRANSFORMATION

Modulate is a Boston-based start-up that creates AI-generated voice skins, which allow real-time transformation of a person's speech into different voices. Whereas other forms of synthetic voice synthesize a bespoke voice to speak written text, Modulate's voice skin technology changes the vocal timbre of a speaker effectively instantaneously. Mike Pappas, Modulate's cofounder and CEO, described their technology as "digitally swapping out your vocal cords" with another person's.

I met Mike and Modulate's cofounder and chief technology officer, Carter Huffman, at the Cambridge Innovation Center, a shared workspace that boasts "more startups than anywhere else on the planet," for a demo of their voice skins. I slipped on a pair of headphones and spoke into a microphone and, instantaneously, my words were repeated back to me in my ears through a different voice. The first voice was "Serena," a woman's, and it was definitely strange hearing a woman's voice laid on top of my own as I spoke. Mike explained "there's a threshold of 30 milliseconds where you can loop audio back into your own ear without noticing an echo," and their voice conversion operated in 10 milliseconds. As far as I could hear, Serena was speaking at the same time as me. With the flick of a switch, Mike changed the voice skin to one trained from an audiobook narrator, and suddenly I had a deep authoritative tone. With another change, my voice switched to "Aiden," a gender-neutral voice. Because the voice skin only changed the timbre of the voice, simulating the vocal cords of the speaker, the AI-generated voice retained all of the same inflection in my words as I spoke them. The words and emotion were mine, but for all intents and purposes the voice skin had changed my voice.

Voice is a big part of our identity, and it was a fascinating experience hearing my words shifted into a different voice as I was speaking. Instinctively, my own way of speaking changed as a result. My pitch lifted when speaking as Serena and dropped to match the deep tones of the book narrator. Voice skins that allow us to speak in different voices raise interesting questions about how others perceive us and how we perceive ourselves.

Mike and Carter explained that Modulate was focused on gaming and virtual worlds as their initial target market, allowing players to adopt a voice skin for their character, similar to existing skins or costumes that change an avatar's appearance. There are 2.7 billion video gamers worldwide, and in 2019 they spent approximately $20 billion on in-game purchases for cosmetic items alone to customize their appearance. There's clearly a strong desire by gamers to customize their characters. Voice skins could help create a more immersive playing experience, allowing users to adopt not just the look but also the voice of the character they inhabit. When hearing your voice as the character's, "You feel authentically more like that character," Mike said. Voice chat is an increasingly important part of online gameplay, and voice skins could help players even adopt different identities.

Mike and Carter, like many of the tech entrepreneurs I've met, are deeply concerned about ensuring their technology is used ethically. Mike explained that early on when they founded the company, they set aside a day to focus on the ethics of their technology and ask, "What could a bad actor do?" They've continued to seek out a diverse array of perspectives and connect with "people from all different backgrounds to share their views" to better understand how the technology might cause harm or be misused. Voice impersonation could be used for a wide range of abuses, from fraud to enabling child predators. (Mike explained that Modulate has not recorded voices of children specifically because of concerns about the risks of adults being able to impersonate children online.) Mike has similarly engaged with communities who experience toxicity and harassment online and how voice skins could be used to enhance their playing experience. Modulate is a member of the AITHOS coalition, a group of synthetic media companies "committed to ethical, responsible and equitable advances in synthetic media through shared accountability and advocacy." Mike and Carter are clearly concerned about doing the right thing. Modulate doesn't release its technology publicly and requires users to demonstrate a legal right to use any voice based on a real person. But Mike acknowledged that if they can create voice skins, others will be able to do so as well.

The implications are troubling. When we hear a voice we recognize on the phone, we trust that the person we hear really is our friend, family member, or colleague. When we were kids, sometimes my brother and I would swap the phone when talking to see how long before the person on the other end would catch on. The gag rarely lasted for long. It's very hard to mimic another person's voice, and humans have a good ear for differentiating voices. Machine learning can now digitally swap a person's vocal cords, but Mike explained that there are other aspects of speech that are harder for machines.

Barack Obama has a distinct style of speaking, and a convincing impersonation would have to not only match his voice but also his cadence and rhythm. Machine learning can be used to mimic Obama's speaking style, but changing the cadence of speech introduces a delay, since the machine must listen to a chunk of words to know where to place the pauses. Any delays longer than 150 to 200 milliseconds will be noticeable to a human listener. Requiring immediate responses in conversation could be used to ferret out some forms of machine-based alterations to speech. Unfortunately, cadence and inflection are aspects of speech that humans can change. With practice, I could probably learn to match Obama's distinct manner of speaking. I would never be able to change my vocal cords to match his, but the machine can do that. Accents may lie somewhere in the middle, since a computer would need to listen to at least part of a word to know how to apply an accent, causing some delay. Mike said it's "an open question" whether machine learning will be able to apply a synthetic accent to speech with a short enough delay to be unnoticeable.

In the sci-fi TV series *Westworld,* one of the robots built to mimic humans asks, "What is real?" The answer: "That which is irreplaceable." Mike said he and his cofounder, Carter, have spent a lot of time thinking about what aspects of voice might be really hard to fake so that it's possible to build fraud-proof voice detectors. "Maybe there's certain things that I do around the emotion and inflection . . . that are really hard for me biologically to throw myself off from that habit but are also complex enough that computers have difficulty replicating," Mike suggested. The answer may not lie in one part of speech, but detecting multiple aspects including word choice and content to verify the speaker's identity. It's not clear what the solution is, but it's a sneak peek into the conundrum that society is going to face in the near future as synthetic media becomes more powerful.

Synthetic media is a far cry from building physical androids that can pass as humans like in *Westworld,* but audiovisual content will only get better over time at matching reality. Future advances in synthetic media will require an ever-shifting search for what remains irreplaceable—what cannot be synthesized and faked. Yet that line is likely to shift over time, and it isn't clear in the long run what will be left. Detectors, like the ones being built by Giorgio Patrini and others, can help for a while but eventually synthetic media will become good enough to fool the detectors as well. Mike Pappas pointed out that in the contest between deepfakes vs. detectors, "It's going to be an arms race until it's not, and at that point defense will just have lost." Once the detectors can be beaten, society will have to turn to other methods to distinguish what is fake and what is real.

Modulate and other companies are already working on technical solutions to determine a piece of media's provenance. Modulate embeds a digital watermark into their audio that is undetectable to humans but would allow Modulate to determine whether an audio clip was created using their voice synthesis technology. If someone used Modulate's technology to create a fraudulent audio clip, Modulate would be able to determine that the clip was fake. In the future, automated watermark-detection tools could even be deployed by social media platforms to identify synthetic content when it was uploaded and flag it for further inspection. In order for the watermark to remain effective, Mike explained, the specific method they used could not be released publicly. Otherwise an adversarial actor might conceivably find a way to replicate the watermark. He did say, however, that generating their own audio, as Modulate's voice skin does, opened up a whole range of possibilities for how they could embed hidden signals into the audio file. Dollar bills have subtle security features physically embedded in them, making it possible to verify real bills and spot counterfeits. Similarly, Modulate can embed subtle codes into their audio files that would remain hidden unless someone knew what to look for, allowing them to verify whether an audio clip was produced using their tools.

Other companies are working the other side of the problem, developing technical methods to prove the authenticity of real images. These could work by evaluating metadata from the image and/or device, such as date, time, and location, by performing analysis of the image, adding certificates to an image that prove its origin, or by embedding a digital watermark within the image. Companies such as Microsoft, Serelay, Truepic, and others are building technology to ensure real images can be verified as trustworthy.

Tech companies and media organizations whose business model depends on veracity are banding together to develop solutions to weed out disinformation and verify authentic media. Project Origin is a partnership among Microsoft, the BBC, CBC/Radio-Canada, and the *New York Times* to use digital watermarking to authenticate media and ensure it has not been manipulated. The Trusted News Initiative, a global consortium of news organizations designed to combat election disinformation, has agreed to engage with Project Origin's digital watermarking technology. Media and tech partners of the Trusted News Initiative include *Agence France-Presse*, the Associated Press, the BBC, Facebook, Google/YouTube, *The Hindu*, Microsoft, Reuters, Twitter, the *Wall Street Journal*, and the *Washington Post*, among others.

In principle, watermarking media as real or synthetic offers an elegant solution that can help society retain its hold on truth. In practice, not everyone will act ethically and label their synthetic media. One of the first things programmers did with the publicly released version of Stable Diffusion was strip off the watermarking. As deepfake technology becomes more accessible, malicious actors will be able to train their own machine learning systems to create fake media with misleading watermarks.

Other technical approaches that work earlier in the machine learning process, on the training data, may help. Researchers at Facebook have developed a method of creating "radioactive data" that leaves a faint trace on any machine learning model that uses the dataset. Their method remains effective even if less than 1 percent of the data used to train the model was "radioactive." Tim Hwang, a research fellow at the Center for Security and Emerging Technology, has suggested that publicly available datasets be similarly adulterated to allow for easy detection of synthetic media. Widespread marking of publicly available datasets would force malicious actors to either attempt to "clean" the data of the markings or create their own datasets from scratch, raising the bar for creating detection-free fakes.

The hype surrounding deepfakes may have outpaced their reality today, but long-term trends in data and computing power will enable more powerful and accessible machine learning tools to create convincing synthetic media. The AI text generator GPT-2, whose staged release caused such a stir in 2019, was eclipsed only fifteen months later by GPT-3, a 175 billion parameter model that was over ten times larger than GPT-2. GPT-3's text is shockingly convincing. Renée DiResta, technical research manager at the Stanford Internet Observatory, prompted GPT-3 to weigh in on the implications of synthetic media. GPT-3's response:

> *AI-generated content will continue to become more sophisticated, and it will be increasingly difficult to differentiate it from the content that is created by humans.*

Well said.

The world of synthetic media is in its infancy. Face swaps, voice skins, lip syncs, portraits, and text-to-speech are just the first wave of synthetic media. More forms of AI-driven media manipulation are sure to follow. Detectors will buy some time, but in the long run society will need an ecosystem approach to track the provenance of both real and AI-generated content.

Social media platforms have a critical role to play, and in early 2020, Facebook, Reddit, Twitter, and YouTube released updated policies surrounding synthetic and manipulated media in advance of the U.S. election. The policies vary widely among companies however, with different criteria for when companies might label content as manipulated, reduce manipulated content's visibility, or remove it entirely. As a result, a manipulated video might be available on one platform and removed on another. Regulators in the United States, Europe, and China have scrambled to adapt. Chinese regulators have moved fastest, issuing regulations in 2019 and 2022 that govern deepfakes and other forms of synthetic media. Democratic nations have, understandably, moved more deliberately. The 2021 proposed European AI Act includes a requirement to label AI-generated media. In the United States, federal lawmakers directed several government studies of deepfakes starting in 2019, while some states have begun issuing their own regulations. Social media companies are adapting to both rapidly evolving technology and societal expectations, but without regulation companies' approaches are likely to be inconsistent, at best. Companies that are less concerned about their brand and reputation will have even fewer incentives to act responsibly.

It is inspiring to talk with individuals like Danika Laszuk, Giorgio Patrini, and Mike Pappas who are working to build the next generation of tech start-ups and care deeply about the ethical use of technology. Manipulated media threatens not just elections, but one of the core pillars of free societies: the truth. Tech companies, media institutions, and nonprofits are leaning into the problem of synthetic media and disinformation, and the problem may be manageable through a combination of technical, societal, and regulatory approaches. Harmful content will continue to lurk in the dark corners of the web but giving responsible media organizations the tools to quickly verify the authenticity of media and expose fakes will help stave off the worst risks of AI-generated media undermining truth. Ensuring a trustworthy information ecosystem will depend critically, however, on who controls the information environment . . . and the algorithms they use.

18

BOT WARS

AI-generated media like deepfakes are entering an information ecosystem that is already supercharged with bots and algorithms warring for control of what information people see. Democratic governments are largely sitting on the sidelines of this war, which is being battled between global tech companies like Meta, Google, and Twitter and purveyors of disinformation, from neo-Nazis to authoritarian governments.

While humans remain central to online disinformation campaigns, bots have played a role in amplifying content. In the wake of the Saudi government's murder of *Washington Post* journalist Jamal Khashoggi in 2018, government-sponsored bots on Twitter elevated pro-regime hashtags such as "we all have trust in Mohammed Bin Salman" (the Saudi crown prince believed to have ordered Khashoggi's murder) and "unfollow enemies of the nation." In addition to amplifying the government's messages, this sort of hashtag pollution can be used to drown out other content. Within a few hours, hashtags referring to Khashoggi's kidnapping had fallen off the list of top trending hashtags in Saudi Arabia, buried by a flood of bot-generated spam. The bots were just one part of a broader disinformation effort by Saudi Arabia to deflect attention from Khashoggi's murder, but bots are a common tool by political actors for manipulating content.

Social media bots aren't sophisticated. They consist of simple scripts and don't rely on large data or machine learning. Bots are usually used in conjunction with human-operated accounts to spread disinformation, with bots amplifying messaging. Nevertheless, they are valuable tools for actors looking to manipulate political views online. Samantha Bradshaw and Philip Howard of the Oxford Internet Institute found in 2019 that governments or political parties in fifty countries around the world used bots to manipulate public opinion online, including in the United States. Social media manipulation in the United

States is widespread, with Bradshaw and Howard concluding, "the adoption of techniques to influence political opinion online seems to have become general electoral and political practice." U.S. government agencies, from the DoD to the EPA, have been accused of manipulative practices on social media to promote messages, ranging from countering ISIS propaganda to promoting clean water regulations. Members of both political parties, Democratic and Republican, have employed astroturfing, a manipulative social media practice intended to create the illusion of grassroots support.

Bots can be used to create the illusion of public support for ideas by amassing fake followers or artificially inflating content. Bradshaw and Howard cited twenty-six authoritarian regimes, including Saudi Arabia, that have used bots as a tool of information control to drown out political dissent, suppress human rights, and discredit political opponents. Marc Owen Jones, a professor at Hamad Bin Khalifa University in Doha, Qatar, suggested in 2017 that half of Twitter accounts in Saudi Arabia could be bots. Bots have also been used in foreign disinformation campaigns to disrupt democracies. China, India, Iran, Pakistan, Russia, Saudi Arabia, and Venezuela have all conducted influence operations targeted at other nations, in which bots can play an enabling role.

Social media companies have cracked down in response to these abuses. In the weeks after Khashoggi's murder, Twitter removed a pro-government bot network and took down another 88,000 Saudi spam bots in 2019. Twitter also took down approximately 200,000 accounts as part of a "spammy network" used by China's Communist Party state for information operations aimed at Hong Kong in 2019 and another 150,000 "amplifier accounts" used in CCP influence operations in 2020. (Twitter does not prohibit using bots; it prohibits spammy or manipulative behavior, such as spamming users with unwanted content or using bots to artificially inflate a hashtag. Positive uses of bots include tweeting alerts about natural disasters or links to free books on Amazon.)

Bots are in many ways a small part of online disinformation, and bot network takedowns are just one part of social media companies' broader efforts to counter manipulative information campaigns. Twitter and Facebook have removed thousands of accounts linked to influence operations from both state and non-state groups around the world. Yet efforts by malign actors to manipulate social media persist. With 4.1 billion users worldwide—over half the world's population—the contest to control information on social media has massive consequences.

Social media has become such a dominant force in the information environment that it is easy to forget how new it is. Facebook, the largest social media platform in the world with 2.7 billion active users, was created in 2004 and only opened to the public in 2006. LinkedIn (founded in 2003), Reddit (2005), YouTube (2005), and Twitter (2006) were created around the same time, while others such as Instagram (2010), Snapchat (2011), and TikTok (2016) are even newer. In the span of a single generation, digital technology has radically transformed the information environment in a revolution as socially disruptive as the printing press.

Just a few decades ago, most Americans got their daily news from a small number of broadcast media outlets or local metropolitan newspapers. When I was a kid growing up in the 1980s, there were three options for evening news: Dan Rather on CBS, Tom Brokaw on NBC, or Peter Jennings on ABC. Nearly half of American households tuned into one of their shows every night, hearing largely the same perspective on the world. Social media has turned the information landscape upside down, with anyone able to express their voice, record a video, go viral, or start a movement. Social media has been incredibly democratizing—not in the sense that it has necessarily been good for democracy, but that it has allowed a wide swath of the population to create and share information. The traditional gatekeepers of what constitutes a shared social reality—television news anchors and newspaper editors—have been eclipsed by a new world in which everyone has a megaphone. When seventeen-year-old Darnella Frazier filmed Minneapolis police murdering George Floyd, she posted the video to Facebook, sharing the truth of the event and sparking a nationwide movement. Social media has enabled the rise of both transformative decentralized social movements, like #BlackLivesMatter, and dangerous conspiracy theories like QAnon.

Despite their democratizing ability to empower individuals, the largest social media platforms are controlled by a handful of companies. Meta (which owns Facebook, WhatsApp, Messenger, and Instagram), Google (which owns YouTube), Tencent (which owns WeChat, QQ, and Qzone), and ByteDance (which owns TikTok and Douyin) dominate the marketplace. In the United States, over half of adults get their news from Facebook. The choices these companies make—and the algorithms they use to manage content—have huge consequences for how billions of people see the world.

While the rules governing social media platforms in the United States are hotly debated, the global rise of Chinese-owned platforms such as TikTok presents a new challenge: platforms that are ultimately beholden to the Chinese Communist Party. The messy and chaotic debates in democracies about what content is allowed on social media are at risk of being replaced by the insidious censorship of political content that might upset the CCP. To preserve a digital public sphere that allows for free and open debate, the U.S. government will need to work with American tech companies to ensure their continued dominance in the global social media ecosystem. Which companies—and by extension which political system—govern the information seen by billions of people has major stakes for global power.

The importance of social app dominance is heightened by the powerful and often opaque role AI plays in affecting discourse online. Algorithms are at the heart of how social media functions. Social media platforms manage a staggering amount of content. Twitter processes 500 million tweets per day (6,000 tweets per second!). Facebook clocks four billion video views daily. YouTube users collectively consume over a billion hours of video every day, and over 500 hours of new content are uploaded to YouTube every minute. Algorithms are used to filter, process, promote or demote, and recommend content.

When you open Twitter, Facebook, YouTube, TikTok, or any other social media platform, the information you're presented with is driven by an algorithm. The goal is to provide quality content that is tailored to you and will keep you engaged. Twitter employs a "ranking algorithm," using deep learning, to prioritize recent Tweets based on relevancy. Facebook's News Feed algorithm plays an even more dominant role in presenting users with content, choosing which posts to prioritize based on a variety of factors.

Companies' algorithms are closely guarded secrets, like the recipes for Coca-Cola or Colonel Sanders' fried chicken, and for good reason. Content producers are keen to find ways to game the algorithm to boost their content's visibility. Companies are constantly tweaking and adjusting their algorithms to provide a better user experience (and keep users on their platform). Algorithms that are too simple or optimize for the wrong metric can drive perverse incentives for content producers. YouTube's early algorithm rewarded video views, which incentivized sensational clickbait approaches to get viewers to click on videos but didn't incentivize video quality. Over time, YouTube switched to a more sophisticated algorithm that also accounted for how long viewers stayed watching a video. As machine learning has improved, social media companies have adopted deep learning to improve their algorithms.

Algorithms are used to filter out content before it is even presented to the user. In the fourth quarter of 2020 alone, YouTube removed over 9.3 million problematic videos, over 90 percent of which were first detected by automation. (Top reasons for removal were endangering child safety, violence, nudity, or other graphic content, and spam.)

Algorithms are also used to recommend content, although they have had unexpected side effects. YouTube's algorithm for recommending videos to watch next has come under fire for promoting harmful content, from conspiracy theory videos to extremist content. YouTube executives have stated that over 70 percent of viewing hours are driven by the algorithm. Google engineers described the deep learning algorithm as "one of the largest-scale and most sophisticated industrial recommendation systems in existence."

Yet multiple independent researchers, journalists, and even a former Google engineer claimed in 2018 the algorithm was biased toward more extreme and incendiary content, leading viewers video-by-video down a "rabbit hole" of conspiracy theories and misinformation. Critics have speculated that the effect was not intentional, but rather that the algorithm was responding to increased viewer engagement with more sensational material in a "feedback loop" that trained the machine learning system to provide viewers with more inflammatory content. YouTube executives have denied that a "rabbit hole" effect exists, claiming that their algorithm does not push users to more extreme content. The opacity of machine learning algorithms makes it difficult to uncover the truth. Not only are companies unwilling to be transparent about how their algorithm functions, even the engineers who trained a deep learning algorithm may not fully understand why it elevates certain content.

YouTube altered its algorithm in 2019 to reduce recommendations of "borderline" content, such as conspiracy theory videos, and promote authoritative content. The result, according to YouTube, was a 70 percent drop in watch time for borderline content, which is content that does not violate the platform's moderation rules but comes close. (Some affected content producers, such as those who make flat earth videos, noticed and lamented the change.)

Facebook has had its own challenges surrounding unintended effects from its algorithm. In 2018, Facebook made a major change to its News Feed algorithm with the aim of promoting "meaningful interactions." Facebook said the changes gave greater weight to posts that "spark conversations" and "back-and-forth discussion in the comments." The problem is that conversations and back-and-forth exchanges could be positive or negative. Laura Hazard Owen, editor at the Nieman Journalism Lab, assessed that the new algorithm "pushed up articles on divisive topics like abortion, religion, and guns" and "anger" was the dominant reaction to political content.

These algorithms weren't looking to boost polarizing or extreme content. They were simply responding to user engagement. Humans are attracted to novelty and are more impacted by negative information than positive information. Our brains are hardwired for disinformation. A 2018 MIT study found that fake news traveled six times faster on Twitter and reached more people. Political content was especially viral. Just like our brains desire sugar, even if it's bad for us, our brains are attracted to news that inspires fear, anger, or outrage.

Social media companies have responded over time by tweaking their algorithms, often in response to outside criticism. In 2018, Facebook changed their algorithm to demote borderline content. Facebook said their intent was disincentivizing "creating provocative content that is as close to the line as possible."

Social media platform policies generally prohibit manipulative behavior and certain categories of content, such as nudity, violence, or hate speech, but not whether or not the content is true. Yet whether they like it or not, the algorithms that social media companies use to filter, promote, recommend, or derank content influence the information seen by more than 4 billion people, over half of the world's population. These algorithms' ability to shape public opinion and perceptions of reality is enormous.

This power is dangerous enough when it is in the hands of megacorporations whose motives aren't the public good but maximizing profit. It is even more problematic when it is in the hands of a company that is ultimately answerable to an authoritarian state.

The rise of TikTok, a social media video-sharing app optimized for mobile devices, has added a further wrinkle to questions about the rules for promoting and demoting content—and who sets those rules. While TikTok's content consists mostly of short, cute videos, its ownership presented a novel geopolitical challenge to the free world. TikTok was owned by ByteDance, a major Chinese tech firm, and was the first Chinese-owned social media platform to go global.

U.S. social media platforms such as Facebook, Twitter, YouTube, Instagram, and others are banned in China, where the Chinese Communist Party heavily censors online discourse. The resulting closed-off information ecosystem has allowed a whole new set of censored social media platforms to arise in China, the largest of which is Tencent's WeChat, with over 1.2 billion users. Most Chinese social media apps have struggled to gain a foothold outside of China, and their use is often limited to the Chinese diaspora seeking to stay connected with friends and family back in China. WeChat has an estimated 2.3 million active users in the United States. TikTok is the exception, however, and exploded onto the global scene in 2018. TikTok was wildly successful in India, the United States, Indonesia, Russia, Japan, and Europe, and by mid-2020 had nearly 700 million users globally, almost 100 million of whom were in the United States. (ByteDance operates a separate version of the app in China, called Douyin, which has 600 million users.)

TikTok's soaring popularity coincided with a more hawkish turn in U.S. policymakers' attitudes toward Chinese tech companies. By late 2019, there was bipartisan concern among U.S. lawmakers about the national security risks of a Chinese-owned social media app having a major presence in the United States. Washington was not alone in worrying about the implications of a tech ecosystem dominated by Chinese firms. In June 2020, following border clashes between Indian and Chinese troops, India banned TikTok and fifty-eight other Chinese apps. The Indian government issued additional bans over the next several months, prohibiting 267 Chinese apps in total. In August 2020, the Trump administration signed executive orders forcing ByteDance to sell TikTok or face a ban in the United States. TikTok sued the U.S. government to halt the ban, launching a series of court battles. In June 2021, the Biden administration replaced the previous Trump executive orders, which had faced legal challenges, with a new executive order on "Protecting Americans' Sensitive Data from Foreign Adversaries," including China.

TikTok videos are often quirky and uplifting, in many ways a relief from some of the more politically charged content on Facebook and Twitter. Some critics of the Trump administration dismissed the crusade against TikTok as a knee-jerk reaction against anything Chinese. The Trump administration's fumbling messaging, combined with President Trump's personal support for a proposed deal that would have allowed ByteDance to keep 80 percent ownership of TikTok, further clouded the administration's intentions. Yet the national security risks of TikTok were real. Many worried about U.S. persons' data being exfiltrated to China, a legitimate concern, but the bigger concern arises from control of the algorithm.

Even more than other social media platforms, TikTok's algorithm plays a central role in shaping the content that users see. Like other social media apps, TikTok users are presented with a feed of content. But unlike Twitter and Facebook, where content is based on who the user follows or what groups the user joins, TikTok presents an endless stream of videos chosen almost entirely by the algorithm. Over time, the algorithm's choices are refined based on user feedback, but the TikTok algorithm's functionality is even more opaque than other platforms in which content derives from the user's network or who the user follows.

On numerous occasions, TikTok has appeared to censor political content. In June 2020, TikTok issued a public apology because "a technical glitch made it temporarily appear as if posts uploaded using #BlackLivesMatter and #George-Floyd would receive 0 views," according to TikTok. TikTok also had to issue an apology after it said a "human moderation error" caused it to block a user who had posted a viral video criticizing the Chinese government's treatment of Muslims. (TikTok also briefly took down the video before reinstating it.) TikTok similarly apologized after clips of "tank man" (the unknown protestor who stood in front of a column of tanks in Tiananmen Square in 1989) was temporarily censored. The company claimed the video was "incorrectly partially restricted based on guidelines related to displaying identifiable military information." Independent researchers and journalists have claimed TikTok has a suspicious absence of videos of Hong Kong pro-democracy protestors or content relating to the Houston Rockets basketball team, whose general manager had publicly sided with Hong Kong protestors. Independent researchers also found a glut of pro-CCP propaganda videos about Xinjiang.

In 2019, *The Guardian* newspaper revealed leaked documents from ByteDance outlining TikTok's moderation guidelines, which included censorship of political content. The bans were wide-ranging and included prohibiting videos of "highly controversial topics, such as . . . inciting the independence of . . . Tibet and Taiwan," "demonisation or distortion of local or other countries' history such as . . . Tiananmen Square incidents," and "criticism/attack towards policies, social rules of any country, such as . . . socialism system." In some cases, videos would be taken down outright. In other cases, videos would remain visible only to the user who uploaded it but restricted from other users' feeds. In a company statement ByteDance said, "The old guidelines in question are outdated and no longer in use."

If the algorithms on U.S. platforms like YouTube and Facebook pose risks of distorting online information, these risks are far more severe for TikTok. TikTok's algorithm plays a more dominant role in curating content, ByteDance has been far less transparent than U.S. companies about their content moderation rules, and the company is subject to the Chinese Communist Party's direction. The combination of these factors poses serious risks of TikTok being used in the future for censorship or propaganda on behalf of the CCP.

TikTok has struggled to rehabilitate its public image, but even improved content moderation sidesteps the crux of the issue. Any Chinese company is ultimately subject to the Chinese Community Party's direction, through both legal and extralegal means. If the CCP demands that they hand over data or censor content, ByteDance, like any other Chinese company, must comply. ByteDance can contest U.S. government demands in an independent judiciary in the United States—as well as in the court of public opinion—but they have no such recourse in China. In 2018, after pressure from government regulators, Zhang Yiming, then-CEO of ByteDance, issued a public apology letter in which he affirmed his fealty to Xi Jinping thought and stated that "technology must be led by the socialist core value system." He had no choice. Whether TikTok is actually censoring content, promoting pro-CCP propaganda, or exfiltrating U.S. data back to China is, in some sense, beside the point. So long as TikTok is owned by a Chinese company, the risk remains. If TikTok has not taken these actions yet, it is only because the Chinese Communist Party has not yet forced them to do so.

The fight to control the information seen on social media by over half of the world's population is being waged on many fronts. Manipulative state and non-state actors are engaging in malign influence operations, using bots and other methods to artificially elevate or suppress certain messages. Authoritarian governments are attempting to control information internally and undermine democracies abroad. Social media platforms themselves have used algorithms that, perhaps unintentionally, appear to have promoted inflammatory or divisive political content. And TikTok represents a new front in this fight, as U.S. companies for the first time face competition from China for control of the global social media marketplace.

The rules that social media companies use to filter, censor, promote, and demote information are enormously consequential. To date, companies have responded in an ad hoc fashion, often adjusting their algorithms only in the face of public pressure. This is, at best, a stopgap measure. Even if responsible companies adopt reasonable guidelines, without uniform rules, other less scrupulous companies will crop up in their place. As Twitter and Facebook increased their content moderation to crack down on disinformation, far-right users flocked to alternatives like Parler and Gab. Fragmenting the social media ecosystem so that users fall into even more extreme bubbles is hardly an effective long-term solution. Regulation is needed to establish uniform guidelines and create an environment that preserves free expression while guarding against manipulative behavior.

The United States and other democratic nations also need to win the global competition for social app dominance. The United States has benefited for decades from the soft power afforded by Hollywood's global reach, spreading American values and ideals around the world. Social media is far more consequential. Social media apps are not a product, like a movie; they are infrastructure. American tech companies' social media dominance has given the United

States enormous soft power advantages, which could disappear if U.S. tech firms lost out to Chinese-owned companies.

Because social media's value derives from its user network, social app competition has a winner-take-all dynamic. There is no value to joining a social network that lacks other users. Former Google CEO Eric Schmidt noted: "Platforms are different from steel and other commodities. With steel, you can have two or three suppliers and they can have similar market shares. In platforms for various reasons . . . you tend to get a single unitary winner. You tend to get a 90 percent share market." It's vitally important that the rules governing social media are set by democratic nations, but first their tech companies have to win the competition for the global market.

Despite the need for cooperation between U.S. tech companies and the U.S. government to protect free speech without promoting disinformation, and to ensure that U.S. companies continue to lead, the United States is hamstrung by its politics. Washington and Silicon Valley view one another with mutual suspicion, and politicians view social media through an increasingly polarized lens. Conservative politicians have claimed for years—without evidence—that U.S. tech firms have an anti-conservative bias. These unfounded allegations may have caused some companies to soft-pedal right-wing disinformation out of fear of incurring Republicans' wrath. During the 2020 presidential election, Facebook altered its algorithm to boost the rankings of authoritative news sources over hyperpartisan outlets, but the measures were rolled back after the election.

In January 2021, Twitter and Facebook finally suspended President Trump's accounts after he incited a riot to storm the Capitol and disrupt a joint session of Congress to certify the presidential election. Liberals criticized the move as too late, while conservatives were outraged at censorship. While the account suspensions were clearly necessary in the name of public safety, it is hardly a sane situation when big tech firms are (justifiably) censoring the president of the United States. The rules governing information on social media should be established by U.S. elected leaders, not unaccountable tech company executives. Yet American political leaders have, time and again, demonstrated not only an unwillingness to confront dangerous political disinformation—many have actively promoted it. Even after a violent mob staged an insurrection to overturn the presidential election, 147 Republican members of Congress objected to certifying the presidential election results from one or more states, citing fictitious and debunked allegations of fraud. The calls are coming from inside the house. The United States cannot be a beacon of democracy abroad when its democratic institutions are crumbling from within, and it cannot lead in establishing the rules to safeguard truth when its politicians traffic in outrageous and dangerous lies.

Artificial intelligence is enabling new and powerful tools that will shape how billions of people perceive reality, from synthetic media to social media algorithms. It will take a concerted effort by tech companies, civil society, the media, and democratic governments to build a revitalized ecosystem that protects free speech and preserves the truth. The technical challenges, while novel, are solvable. The real hurdle is marshalling the political will to build a healthier and saner information environment.

PART V
RIFT

19

FUSION

As U.S.-China relations deteriorated in 2019 and 2020, news headlines warned of a looming "tech cold war." This might make for good clickbait, but the Cold War is a poor analogy to the current geopolitical competition. The Cold War was a contest between two separate political-economic systems, yet today China and the United States occupy the same interconnected global economy, and both are vying to set its rules. The United States and China are competing to alter core elements of the global AI ecosystem to benefit their national interests, including research and business relationships, AI governance, and compute infrastructure.

The legacy of three decades of U.S. engagement with China has been deep entanglement between the U.S. and Chinese AI ecosystems, which U.S. policymakers are now trying to pull apart. While the tech ecosystems are sharply bifurcated in some ways, such as the apps and social media platforms that the Chinese Communist Party has banned in China, in other ways the research and business communities are tightly interlinked. Both the United States and China benefit from these ties, although often in different ways. U.S. policymakers face the challenge of recalibrating these engagements to gain the most benefit from them, without enabling CCP abuses. While the CCP has always placed conditions on engagement, the United States until recently has not. U.S. policymakers are just now waking up to the reality that they are joined at the hip with a nation that is also a strategic competitor.

The U.S. government has begun cracking down on Chinese tech firms that enable human rights abuses. In October 2019, the U.S. Commerce Department placed the Xinjiang Public Security Bureau and eight Chinese tech firms on its "Entity List" for "human rights violations and abuses in the implementation of China's campaign of repression, mass arbitrary detention, and high-technology surveillance against Uighurs, Kazakhs, and other members of

Muslim minority groups in the [Xinjiang Uighur Autonomous Region]." Organizations on the Entity List are barred from receiving U.S.-origin products, and additionally carry the stigma of having been blacklisted by the U.S. government. The companies included the AI firms Megvii, SenseTime, Yitu, and iFLYTEK, along with surveillance camera firms Dahua and Hikvision. In June 2020, the Commerce Department added seven more Chinese tech firms to the Entity List, including CloudWalk, NetPosa and its subsidiary SenseNets, Intellifusion, and IS'Vision.

Several companies, including Megvii, SenseTime, Dahua, Hikvision, and Cloudwalk, objected to their inclusion on the Entity List. iFLYTEK's CEO Liu Qingfeng responded defiantly to the U.S. blacklisting, saying "We will not be strangled."

Many of the Chinese AI firms blacklisted for human rights abuses had ties to U.S. universities, tech companies, or investors. Just a year earlier in 2018, MIT had teamed up with SenseTime to launch the MIT-SenseTime Alliance on Artificial Intelligence, funding twenty-seven projects involving fifty principal investigators across the university. (SenseTime's founder did his PhD at MIT.) The same year, MIT's Computer Science and Artificial Intelligence Laboratory (CSAIL) launched a five-year partnership with iFLYTEK in AI and natural language processing. iFLYTEK has partnered with other U.S. universities as well. In 2017, iFLYTEK gave a million-dollar grant to Rutgers University to establish a Big Data Laboratory. iFLYTEK also funded AI research at Princeton University.

A number of U.S. tech firms have come under fire as potential suppliers to Chinese companies accused of supporting human rights abuses. Hikvision and Dahua have reportedly used Intel and NVIDIA chips for their intelligent cameras and Seagate and Western Digital hard drives for their video recorders. The Ürümqi Cloud Computing Center analyzes thousands of video surveillance feeds for Xinjiang police using NVIDIA and Intel chips. Multiple police projects have reportedly relied on Intel and NVIDIA chips for Uighur-detecting analytics. Intel has also reportedly sold chips to NetPosa, and the U.S. chip firm Xilinx has reportedly sold its chips to Hikvision, both companies that were later placed on the Entity List. Intel, NVIDIA, Seagate, Western Digital, and Xilinx condemned human rights abuses, stated that they comply with U.S. laws, and pointed out that they don't always control how customers use their products. Hikvision protested the U.S. government's Entity List designation and stated that it respects human rights.

U.S. investors have similarly backed a number of Chinese companies that landed on the Entity List. Fidelity International, Qualcomm Ventures, and IDG Capital were all investors in SenseTime. Sequoia invested in Yitu. Multiple U.S. public pension funds invested in Hikvision. Hewlett Packard Enterprise had a 49 percent stake in New H3C Technologies, which sells network and cloud computing technology to Chinese police, including in Xinjiang. (Hewlett Packard Enterprise said it had "no indication that sales to the Chinese military have taken place.")

In some cases, the U.S. and Chinese AI ecosystems are so deeply intertwined that Chinese companies enabling human rights abuses and the U.S. military may be funding the same AI research. A paper from researchers at Princeton and the Beijing Institute of Big Data Research cited both iFLYTEK's gift to Princeton and a grant from the U.S. Office of Naval Research as funding.

Often, U.S. businesses and universities have been reluctant to cut ties with Chinese entities linked to human rights abuses. By mid-2019, iFLYTEK's links to Xinjiang police had been publicly exposed, yet MIT defended their partnership, arguing that the iFLYTEK-funded AI research "is not expected to have immediate applications." MIT vice president for research Maria Zuber told me that MIT reviewed the collaboration at the time and decided that "given that it had nothing to do with what the reported human rights issues were, we just let it run out." MIT finally cancelled the iFLYTEK relationship in February 2020, four months after the company had been blacklisted by the U.S. government for human rights abuses. (Zuber stated that iFLYTEK funded "research that was already underway" at MIT and that all of the research was published openly.)

The U.S. AI ecosystem also has links to the Chinese military. Investigations by the *Financial Times* have uncovered numerous AI papers coauthored by U.S. researchers affiliated with Princeton, MIT, the University of Illinois, Google, Microsoft, or Nokia Bell Labs working with Chinese researchers affiliated with Chinese firms implicated in human rights abuses or military-affiliated institutions such as the Chinese National University of Defense Technology (NUDT), a Chinese military university that was placed on the Commerce Department's Entity List in 2015. (Google dismissed the papers as written by academics at universities and denied any involvement with the research projects or any partnerships with the Chinese universities in question.) Microsoft in particular came under scrutiny in 2019 when the *Financial Times* revealed multiple AI papers had been coauthored by researchers from Microsoft Research Asia, the company's Beijing-based AI lab, and NUDT. In an interview, Microsoft representatives disputed the *Financial Times* reporting. Yet there were at least a small number of additional technical papers beyond those uncovered by the *Financial Times* coauthored by researchers from Microsoft and NUDT. In two cases, an author listed a dual affiliation at Microsoft Research Asia and NUDT.

American AI researcher ties to the Chinese military are probably more widespread than these isolated examples suggest. China's military, the People's Liberation Army (PLA), has engaged in a systematic campaign of sending PLA-funded researchers abroad to collaborate with foreign scientists as a means of accelerating their scientific and technological capabilities. Alex Joske of the Australian Strategic Policy Institute has identified more than 2,500 PLA-funded scientists, about half of whom were PhD students, sent abroad from 2007 to 2018. The vast majority of these come from the PLA's NUDT. The United States is the top destination for PLA-funded scientists, and Joske estimates that approximately 500 PLA scientists studied in the United States from 2007 to 2018. These engagements have borne fruit for the Chinese military. From 2006 to 2017, PLA scientists coauthored over 1,100 research papers with U.S. scientists. While these figures cover all forms of scientific cooperation, not just AI, there is no reason to think that AI as a field is exempt from these ties, and numerous specific papers suggest otherwise.

American researchers aren't alone in these problematic ties. After the United States, Joske estimates that the United Kingdom, Canada, Australia, Germany, Sweden, Singapore, the Netherlands, Japan, and France are the PLA's other top targets for engagement abroad. In 2019, the Max Planck Society in Germany and the Erasmus University Medical Center in the Netherlands came under fire for their links to two Chinese scientists involved in DNA-based digital face mapping. The Chinese scientists coauthored papers with the chief forensic scientist at China's Ministry of Public Security on a study of Uighur faces published by the Chinese Academy of Sciences and a study of DNA samples of Uighurs in the journal *Human Genetics*, which is published by Springer Nature. Following news reports about the research, one scientist denied being coauthor of a paper and Erasmus University and the Max Planck Society stated the work done by their affiliated researchers was not funded by their institutions. Two of the articles in question were eventually retracted for ethical reasons.

U.S. lawmakers have expressed outrage when American universities and businesses associate with the Chinese military and companies committing human rights abuses. Google has gotten the brunt of Washington's ire, in part due to the self-inflicted wound of expanding its AI research in China at the same time that it decided not to continue work with the U.S. military. But Google's ties to China are relatively small compared to other U.S. tech companies.

Google's AI China Center, which drew so much condemnation from Washington, occupied a few floors of a high rise in Zhongguancun in the same office park as other U.S. tech firms including VMware, AMD, and Red Hat. Just a mile away another U.S. tech giant, Microsoft, has two sky-high towers, a testament to Microsoft's twenty-year commitment to China. While Google made a principled decision to leave the China market in 2010 rather than cooperate with Chinese Communist Party censorship (a decision the company later reconsidered), Microsoft has long played a significant role in China's AI sector.

In 1998, following a trip by Bill Gates to China, the company established Microsoft Research Asia in Beijing, the company's largest research lab outside the United States. Microsoft has had a major footprint in China ever since and has been instrumental in the development of China's AI sector. Microsoft also has gone out of its way to emphasize ethics in its AI applications. Microsoft was the first major tech company to call for U.S. government regulation of facial recognition in 2018. Its Aether Committee and Office of Responsible AI manage internal AI governance "to uphold Microsoft responsible AI principles in their day-to-day work," according to the company's website. Microsoft has turned down offers for facial recognition contracts by police departments and, according to Microsoft president Brad Smith, at least one foreign government because of their human rights record. (He declined to name the country.)

Brad Smith has also said that "the single most important thing by far that Microsoft has done in China was be the early founder of Microsoft Research Asia," which he referred to as "a leader in basic research today." In 2004, *MIT Technology Review* named the Beijing AI lab "the world's hottest computer lab." I visited Microsoft Research Asia's offices in Beijing a few months after the 2019 *Financial Times* investigation to learn more about how they were navigating the ethical challenges of AI work in China.

The office lobby was a testament to Microsoft's technological wonders, as well as some of the controversies they've inspired. On a television screen, Microsoft's Xiaoice chatbot, which takes the persona of a sassy teenage Chinese girl, rated passersby on their physical appearance, which she assessed via a facial recognition camera. The attractiveness scoring, which might have been seen as politically incorrect in the United States, wasn't what had inspired controversy in China, however. Instead, it was when in 2017 Xiaoice answered the question, "What is your Chinese Dream?" (a term used by Xi Jinping), with "My Chinese Dream is to go to America!" Xiaoice, which has 660 million global users, was promptly censored on Chinese social media platforms. Xiaoice has since been programmed to sidestep questions touching on sensitive political topics in China, such as the Tiananmen Square massacre. (Microsoft's Bing search engine, which is permitted in China while other apps such as Google are banned, also censors searches relating to the Tiananmen Square massacre.)

In a mini-museum just off the lobby, I had a chance to don Microsoft's HoloLens mixed reality headset. The goggles projected the digital image of a giant beating heart into the air in front of me, allowing me to walk around it and peer inside the chambers. HoloLens was the subject of controversy in 2019 when Microsoft employees signed an open letter objecting to Microsoft's contract to supply up to 100,000 mixed reality goggles to the U.S. Army. Microsoft defended the contract, saying "we're committed to providing our technology to the U.S. Department of Defense." As debates over the future of technology have exacerbated rifts between Silicon Valley and the Pentagon and between the United States and China, U.S. tech firms are increasingly caught in the middle.

At the top of one of Microsoft's two towers overlooking Beijing I met with Tim Pan, a senior director at Microsoft Research Asia. In their glasswalled conference room, Pan launched into a presentation on Microsoft Research Asia. Behind him through the glass wall was the Beijing skyline. It was a fitting backdrop. Microsoft Research Asia has been central to the development of China's AI industry. Without the research institute, China's AI ecosystem would exist, but it wouldn't be the powerhouse it is today.

Microsoft Research Asia has been called the "Whampoa Academy of China's Internet," a reference to the elite Whampoa military academy that formerly trained China's top generals. Alums of Microsoft Research Asia populate China's top tech and AI firms, including the president of Baidu, founder of SenseTime, cofounder and CEO of Megvii, father of Alibaba Cloud, director of Tencent's AI lab, CEO of Kingsoft, and president of Xiaomi. In total, over 500 Microsoft Research Asia alums work in China's tech industry and over 100 teach in Chinese universities. Yet some of these ties have come under fire for being too close to Chinese surveillance applications, human rights abuses, and military use.

Pan proudly outlined Microsoft Research Asia's contributions to basic AI research, which are impressive. In 2016, a research team out of the Beijing office was the first to surpass human-level performance in image classification. The team's 2015 paper on "deep residual learning" was the most-cited AI paper from 2014 to 2019. Over the past twenty years, the Beijing research lab has published 5,000 papers in top-tier journals or conferences. "That's, on average, every working day we publish one paper," Pan said. Yet it was the handful of papers reportedly coauthored with PLA scientists that had landed Microsoft in hot water with U.S. legislators.

Kevin Luo, assistant general counsel in Microsoft's Asia-Pacific R&D Group, clarified that Microsoft did not have any kind of formal partnership with the PLA's National University of Defense Technology. However, Luo admitted Microsoft has had a "very small number" of interns who were graduate students from NUDT. (Company representatives estimated there had been approximately eleven such interns.) As of January 2019, for example, the Microsoft website listed an intern at Microsoft Research Asia who was also a PhD student in computer science at the PLA's NUDT. In defending the program, Luo explained that interns "apply as individuals" and "our internship application is open to anybody," although he clarified they have only accepted civilian students from NUDT, not uniformed military officers.

Pan emotionally defended the openness of the internship program to accept students from anywhere including NUDT, a Chinese military university. "I am a professor myself. I think every student should have an equal right to access this research environment," he said. "Those students, they're innocent. They want to have an intern opportunity with the best research organization in China. Why is that so wrong?" Pan also pointed out that the research they were doing was openly published. "This is open research. So is there anything wrong here? I don't see it."

U.S. lawmakers, however, have become increasingly concerned about ties between U.S. AI researchers and the Chinese military. China has aggressively and systematically exploited the openness of American academic institutions to boost the Chinese military. U.S. fears have been exacerbated by China's model of "military-civil fusion," through which the Chinese government has sought to more closely integrate the PLA with China's tech sector. U.S. policymakers fear that any work in China, even with non-PLA affiliated individuals, could work its way back to the Chinese military.

These types of indirect connections are not uncommon. Microsoft Research Asia runs a joint PhD program with several Chinese universities, which as of 2019 included Harbin Institute of Technology, one of China's "Seven Sons of National Defense." Pan explained that as part of the joint PhD program, Microsoft researchers work as adjunct professors at the university supervising students. "And those students, after they graduate, they tend to join us," he said.

Harbin Institute of Technology was added to the Entity List in June 2020 for seeking "to use U.S. technology for Chinese missile programs."

Harbin Institute of Technology and the other Seven Sons of National Defense are civilian universities but are formally designated by the Chinese government as hubs for defense-related research. They are a valuable feeder for talent into the Chinese defense industry. A report by Ryan Fedasiuk and Emily Weinstein at the Center for Security and Emerging Technology found that nearly three quarters of 2019 university graduates who took jobs at one of China's state-owned defense companies came from Seven Sons universities.

In 2018, more than a quarter of Microsoft Research Asia's collaborative training projects with universities in China were with one of the Seven Sons. Yet Microsoft is not alone in its ties to the Seven Sons of National Defense. The Chinese Ministry of Education listed Microsoft and a dozen other U.S. companies as having training programs with Seven Sons universities, including Autodesk, Dell, Google, Honeywell, IBM, Intel, Merrill Lynch, National Instruments, Rockwell Automation, Synopsys, Tektronix, and Texas Instruments. Fedasiuk and Weinstein concluded, "It is likely that U.S. tech companies are inadvertently aiding in China's military modernization by providing resources and information to the next generation of China's defense industry engineers."

Research collaborations with Seven Sons universities go beyond these companies and include some surprising U.S. partners. Researchers at Stanford's Hoover Institution found over 250 scientific and engineering articles coauthored between researchers from one of the Sevens Sons universities and U.S. institutions from 2013 to 2019. (Their research was not restricted to AI papers.) Among the U.S. institutions involved were eleven U.S. federal government research facilities, including the U.S. Naval Research Laboratory. Thirteen articles were at least partially funded by the U.S. government. Even the U.S. government is linked to researchers from PLA-affiliated institutions.

As U.S. policymakers became increasingly aware of these connections throughout 2019 and 2020, a feverish concern over China's military-civil fusion began to take hold in Washington. Yet military-civil fusion is often mischaracterized as though every Chinese company or university were a secret arm of the PLA. Military-civil fusion is a work in progress, and more of an aspiration than a statement of reality today. General Secretary Xi Jinping has emphasized military-civil fusion precisely because he desires greater cooperation between the PLA and China's nondefense industries.

In the summer of 2019, I sat in a sweltering Beijing office with Chinese academics who study military-civil fusion, who explained that the concept was modeled on the close partnerships between U.S. tech companies and the Pentagon. They cited a 1994 paper by the now-defunct U.S. Office of Technology Assessment on civil-military integration (I had to look it up). While military-civil fusion is a goal, in practice China's military remains hampered by bureaucratic inefficiencies and ties to traditional defense contractors, rather than the cutting-edge tech giants China has produced. Nevertheless, U.S. policymakers have been concerned that U.S. academic and business relationships in China could, even indirectly, cause innovations to filter to the PLA.

During the Q&A at an event in January 2020, I asked Microsoft's president Brad Smith about his views on Microsoft Research Asia's role in training AI researchers in China, some of whom have gone on to companies now on the U.S. government's Entity List for human rights abuses. Smith defended Microsoft's AI research in China, stating "a lot of basic research is not secret" and that you "just need a connection to the internet" to access Microsoft Research Asia's publications.

But Microsoft Research Asia has delivered immense value to the Chinese AI community beyond openly publishing its research, which is normal in a field where papers are routinely posted onto the open-access site arXiv. The Beijing-based lab has grown Chinese AI talent through mentorship and training. Director Tim Pan explained that the lab's goal was to "cultivate the talents that we want." In a Microsoft blog post, one NUDT graduate student who interned at Microsoft Research Asia extolled the internship's access to senior researchers as well as to the research group's GPU cluster. His mentors had saved him from unnecessary detours in his research and the compute resources had enabled him to test out his ideas and experiment with larger AI models. Microsoft Research Asia has thus accelerated the critical AI input of talent, including at the Chinese military's NUDT.

Microsoft is hardly alone, though. There are many linkages between major U.S. and European companies and universities and Chinese entities facilitating human rights abuses or military research. When these links have been exposed, U.S. tech companies have often denied knowledge of how their products were used, while American and European research institutions have alternately disavowed formal relationships, claiming the partnerships to be the work of individuals or former affiliates, or defended the partnerships as only encompassing basic research. Even in cases where U.S. and European AI researchers are not directly implicated, they are too often working one degree removed from an individual or organization linked to the Chinese military or human rights abuses.

These problematic connections come on top of a broad pattern of Chinese academic espionage, intellectual property (IP) theft, and tech transfer. The U.S. scientific community is very open, and China has exploited that openness.

China employs a range of methods to gain access to U.S. technology, including via company insiders, Chinese firms partnering with U.S. companies, cyber theft, investment, and academic espionage. China has an estimated over 200 talent recruitment plans to funnel scientific research back to China through both licit and illicit means. The most prominent, China's Thousand Talents Plan, has likely spent hundreds of millions of dollars to recruit a reported 7,600 scientists since 2008.

FBI director Christopher Wray stated in 2019, "There is no country that poses a more severe counterintelligence threat to this country right now than China." China was involved in 90 percent of Department of Justice espionage cases involving a state actor from 2011 to 2018. In 2018, one in five U.S. companies reported IP theft by China. The U.S. IP Commission has estimated that Chinese IP theft results in an annual cost to the U.S. economy of $200 to $600 billion, or approximately one to three percent of U.S. GDP. In response, the U.S. government has stepped up counterintelligence investigations, and in 2018 the Department of Justice launched a new China Initiative. As of 2019, the FBI had around 1,000 investigations under way involving attempted IP theft by China. Yet investigations move slowly, and a few high-profile cases will never be able to address the scale of the problem.

Members of Congress have proposed new laws to tighten restrictions on Chinese researchers studying in the United States, including banning PLA-funded researchers and mandating background screening of students working on "sensitive research projects." These are prudent measures, but as Washington reels from the consequences of three decades of an explicit foreign policy of engaging China, the future of the U.S.-China tech relationship is up for grabs.

Proposals run the gamut from targeted measures to extreme ones that would swing a sledgehammer at U.S.-China tech partnerships. In September 2020, the Trump administration announced that it had revoked the visas of 1,000 Chinese "graduate students and research scholars" in the United States that the government had deemed were "high-risk." This highly targeted move affected roughly 0.25 percent of the approximately 396,000 Chinese students studying in the United States. By contrast, Senator Tom Cotton has proposed prohibiting *any* Chinese national from undertaking graduate or post-graduate education in the United States in any STEM field.

Tech leaders have pushed back against suggestions by some U.S. policymakers that the United States should seek to broadly "decouple" from China. In an interview, former Google CEO Eric Schmidt said, "A pure decoupling of China would be very harmful to America," citing the loss of Chinese talent, markets, and goods. Schmidt was particularly concerned about moves to cut off Chinese talent coming to the United States. "A broad prohibition against Chinese students in graduate programs will hurt America," he said. "The top people in China would prefer to do their research in America. It's more freeing. They don't have the restrictions that exist in China. Why are we not using that as an advantage?"

The numbers support Schmidt's argument. Chinese STEM researchers coming to the United States are a massive "brain gain" for the United States. The overwhelming majority—over 90 percent—of Chinese AI PhD students studying in the United States are still in the United States five years after graduation. Chinese researchers overall make up over a quarter of AI researchers in the United States. To remain competitive with China, the United States needs to keep this talent pipeline flowing. The United States has an asymmetric advantage over China because of its unique ability to attract top-tier researchers. It should use that advantage to the fullest. Fortunately for the United States, the policy choices available are not simply a binary on or off. The U.S. government can take—and indeed has begun employing—a targeted approach. Schmidt said, "Clearly the Chinese have groups that are trying to infiltrate U.S. universities. Let's police that."

The interconnectedness of the American and Chinese AI communities is deeply problematic in some ways but benefits the United States in others. Peter Lee, head of Microsoft Research, told me that Microsoft Research Asia's pathbreaking research on deep residual networks would not have been possible without the lab's footprint in China. "Really good foundational ideas that led to the concept of residual neural networks—they were floating around in the tech ecosystem in China," he said. "By being there, we get an early intuition about this." Lee argued that the vibrancy of the AI community in China was an important resource to tap into for ideas. "In China, the tech ecosystem is moving incredibly fast. In AI specifically, there are commercial deployments of a tremendous amount of new AI technology," he said. "In China, I can go visit any startup at 9:00 pm on Saturday night and it'll be all the developers, all the engineers will be there. It'll be full and buzzing with people. There's an intensity of activity there and invention that is happening and it's happening outside of the culture of academic, open publication." Through Microsoft Research Asia in Beijing, "We gain insight by being in that ecosystem," Lee said, and Microsoft researchers can translate those insights into open publications that benefit the entire AI community.

Maria Zuber, vice president for research at MIT, expressed a similar sentiment. "We do understand that the world is a different place than it has been in the past," she said, acknowledging the federal government's concerns about collaborating with some Chinese entities. Yet she pointed out that the openness of American research institutions "has served us really well in the long term." Zuber is co-chair of a congressionally directed advisory group on "protecting U.S. national and economic security while ensuring the open exchange of ideas and the international talent" for U.S. tech leadership. Zuber told me, "We have to find a way to make this work."

The Chinese Communist Party has always placed national security considerations first as part of its strategy of engagement. As Microsoft president Brad Smith pointed out, "The Chinese market is not and has never been fully open to U.S. tech companies." Despite concerns about U.S. policies leading to a "bifurcation" of the tech world, the reality is that the tech ecosystem has always been deeply entangled in some ways and bifurcated in others. Smith noted, "There is no longer a single internet in the world today. . . . [it] stopped existing between five and ten years ago as the Great Firewall in China became stronger and higher over the past decade."

U.S. policymakers are at the early stages of figuring out how best to shut down problematic dimensions of U.S.-China ties while keeping alive the healthy ones. A complete decoupling with China would starve the U.S. AI community of valuable talent. At the same time, the U.S. government will need to erect guardrails around U.S.-China AI ties to ensure that U.S. researchers are not, directly or indirectly, contributing to human rights abuses or aiding the Chinese military. And the U.S. government is taking action to ensure that when U.S.-China tech cooperation occurs, it does so on a level playing field, not one where China engages in rampant espionage and intellectual property theft.

In 2018, the Commerce Department Bureau of Industry and Security requested public comment on possible export controls for a range of dual-use technologies, including AI and machine learning. In 2020, the Commerce Department tightened export controls around businesses linked to the Chinese military, and the Defense Department began publishing a list of PLA-affiliated companies. These efforts were an attempt to drive a wedge between military-civil fusion, or at least ensure U.S. businesses aren't actively facilitating it. Also in 2020, the State Department released voluntary guidance on exports of surveillance technology to ensure they aren't being used to enable human rights abuses. The Trump administration wielded the Entity List as a tool to blacklist various Chinese actors linked to human rights abuses or the Chinese military, and the Biden administration has shown no signs of slackening the pressure.

In other cases, the U.S. government has adjusted course over time, refining its approach. In February 2022, the Biden administration ended the Justice Department's China Initiative, reorganizing its efforts to counter Chinese espionage and IP theft.

Many companies are also changing their relationships in China, in many cases going beyond what U.S. law requires. Google quietly shuttered its AI China Center in 2019. Other U.S. institutions are continuing AI collaborations in China, but with greater restrictions in place.

In January 2020, Microsoft president Brad Smith said, "We have restrictions in place today in China about the availability of our facial recognition," citing concerns about it being used for "mass surveillance." Peter Lee, head of Microsoft Research, told me Microsoft changed its policies for research in China in 2019. "We do not accept visiting researchers, for example, from any military institution in China," he said. Microsoft also will not work with organizations on the U.S. Entity List. Lee said there were additional restrictions on visiting researchers to Microsoft labs in China prohibiting work on "sensitive topics like facial recognition." He added, "There are similar restrictions that basically prevent the use of Microsoft Research resources or people or facilities to engage in research on sensitive uses."

These are examples of steps that can help preserve valuable aspects of U.S.-China AI research collaboration while avoiding aiding human rights abuses or military use. Too often, however, U.S. businesses and academia have been willing to look the other way at problematic ties. The U.S. government should take further steps to establish guardrails to protect legitimate business and academic ties in China from malign uses. U.S. institutions should be barred from partnering with institutions linked to the PLA or Chinese entities committing human rights abuses. Additionally, the U.S. government should establish end-use restrictions on how AI and related technologies will be used abroad so that U.S. companies have to do due diligence about the intended use of surveillance-related products before they sell them overseas. Finally, there may be some technologies whose export should be prohibited entirely in order to protect America's competitive edge, but those technologies are likely to be rare. AI isn't like hypersonic missiles or stealth technology, which are built by a small number of defense contractors and only have military applications. The AI field is incredibly open and global. AI has many beneficial uses across a wide range of industries. It is in America's interests to preserve the openness of the AI community and for U.S. universities and businesses to remain a magnet for talent from around the world, including China. But to preserve that openness, there will also need to be safeguards in place to prevent enabling malign uses and actors.

These policies are still in flux and will continue to change as U.S. officials recalibrate the U.S.-China tech relationship. Even once these guardrails are in place, for AI researchers who continue working in China, doing so ethically will be a major challenge. Under Chinese Communist Party rule, "AI for good" means something very different than in democratic societies.

20

HARMONY

The world is at a crucial inflection point. The spread of China's model of techno-authoritarianism is a grave risk to global freedom. The novel coronavirus pandemic threw these concerns into overdrive in 2020 as democratic and authoritarian states alike rushed to implement sometimes highly intrusive surveillance measures to track and locate individuals to contain the spread of the virus. The risk is that these measures, even if necessary to combat the pandemic, become the new normal and lock in expanded state powers even after the pandemic wanes. Debates about the appropriate role of surveillance technology are playing out within nations and on the global stage. Democratic countries must work together to ensure that emerging norms and standards for AI use are consistent with democratic values. Yet AI ethics is another area where entanglement with China presents uncomfortable dilemmas.

China has been exercising increasing influence in international standard setting, one of the lower-profile but essential battlegrounds for global tech governance. Several international organizations establish standards for various technologies, such as the International Organization for Standardization (ISO), the International Electrotechnical Commission (IEC), and the UN International Telecommunication Union (ITU). Technical standards can not only affect which companies (and countries) gain an advantage in a technology, but also how the technology is used. Since 2018, the Chinese government has been increasingly active in international standard-setting bodies, along with major Chinese tech firms such as Huawei, ZTE, Tencent, SenseTime, iFLYTEK, Dahua, and China Telecom. China's 2017 national AI strategy, the "New Generation Artificial Intelligence Development Plan," called for the government to: "encourage AI enterprises to participate in or lead the development of international standards . . . to promote AI products and services in overseas applications." The Chinese government followed up with a 2018 "White Paper on and a 2021 national strategy for technical standards. China's efforts may be starting to tilt the playing field in these international forums. In 2019, leaked documents from the United Nations ITU standards process, which covers 193 member states, showed delegates considering adopting rules for facial recognition tech that would help facilitate Chinese-style norms of surveillance. Adopting such technical standards could ease the spread of government surveillance globally.

Leaders at every level of democratic societies could do more to combat the spread of digital repression, first and foremost by leading by example. Europe has leaned into AI regulation, perhaps too hard at times. But the U.S. government's laissez-faire approach is failing to set a positive example for tech governance.

U.S. tech leaders have too often criticized regulations as overly constraining to innovation, conveniently overlooking the fact that Americans only enjoy safe air, water, food, drugs, consumer products, highways, and air travel because of government regulation. Even tape recorders are regulated in eleven states (which require two-party consent for recording conversations). U.S. state and local leaders in many jurisdictions have shown impressive policy entrepreneurship on tech issues such as facial recognition, but more could be done. The fact that California is both a hotbed of tech innovation *and* policy innovation constraining technology, from bot disclosure ("blade runner") laws to facial recognition, should be a signal to the rest of the country about the necessity of tech regulation. The U.S. Congress has been woefully slow to regulate digital technologies. Comprehensive U.S. data privacy legislation, for example, is long overdue. When I asked Maya Wang of Human Rights Watch what the United States could do to combat the spread of China's digital repression, she pointed to the lack of national data privacy regulation in the United States. "The world is essentially being put forward two fairly bad proposals" for tech governance, she said. "One is the U.S. surveillance capitalism model, driven by big companies and essentially is about us all being herded into particular directions to spend money. Then the other is the Chinese government model of mass surveillance. Neither of those are preferable." The consequences, of course, of what U.S. tech companies and the Chinese government are doing with their mass data collection are very different. U.S. tech firms are selling ads, not putting people into camps. But the United States lacks a competing model for global tech governance that protects data privacy. Wang said that U.S. efforts to push back against China's surveillance model will be hampered "unless we have that leadership from the U.S. to really say, 'Well, privacy rights [are] important and we're going to take some efforts to mainstream privacy in our construction of technological infrastructure.'" The U.S. government needs to be more proactive in international standard-setting, working with U.S. companies to ensure that international AI and data standards protect human rights and individual liberty. The goal should be to create international standards that "essentially make the Chinese government's practices and these Chinese companies' practices an internationally unacceptable practice," Wang said.

Yet building an alternative AI global governance model to counter China's is challenging when Chinese entities are already so deeply interwoven into the fabric of global institutions. The United States must distance itself from Chinese abuses without disengaging from debates on AI governance and standards. Washington has successfully executed a sharp break with the previous policy of engagement, but it has yet to adopt a successful strategy for competing with China on global AI standards and governance. In international standard-setting bodies, for example, the response to China's push to distort standards should not be to disengage, but for the United States to remain involved to protect the integrity of the standard-setting process.

In recent years, U.S. policymaking has often lacked the deft touch needed to manage these tensions, with chaotic and counterproductive results. In May 2019, the U.S. government placed China's tech giant Huawei on the Entity List and, because of poor communication and a lack of foresight, inadvertently hindered the ability of American entities to lead on international standard-setting. The Institute for Electrical and Electronics Engineers (IEEE), the world's largest technical professional organization, briefly had to halt any academic interactions with Huawei, such as having Huawei employees participate as peer reviewers for publications, until IEEE received additional clarification from the U.S. government. The U.S. Commerce Department similarly had to issue a rule clarification—twice—to permit U.S. companies to participate in international standard-setting bodies when Huawei representatives were present. The lack of clarity in the Commerce Department's rules led to U.S. firms being shut out of international standard-setting bodies because they believed the government's rules prohibited them from sharing technical information with Huawei. To shape the evolving global rules for how AI technology is governed, the United States needs to show up and take a seat at the table.

Debates about the ethical use of AI technology aren't only happening globally. They're also happening in China, although within political constraints defined by the Chinese Communist Party. AI ethics discussions in China present both an opportunity and a challenge for American and European AI researchers who partner with those in China. Chinese AI governance will have substantial consequences not only for the 1.4 billion residents of China but also for people around the world as Chinese companies sell their technology abroad. At the same time, China's authoritarian political system puts hard limits on what will be possible in terms of ensuring the ethical use of AI in China.

In recent years, Chinese experts have published a bevy of AI ethics documents from government, industry, and academia. Tencent and Baidu both released company principles for ethical AI in 2018. The Beijing Academy of Artificial Intelligence (BAAI), a nonprofit research consortium composed of top Chinese universities, companies, and government research institutes, published the "Beijing AI Principles" in 2019. The Chinese government's National New Generation Artificial Intelligence Governance Expert Committee released in 2019 "Governance Principles for a New Generation of Artificial Intelligence: Develop Responsible Artificial Intelligence." China's Artificial Intelligence Industry Alliance released a draft "Joint Pledge on Artificial Intelligence Industry Self-Discipline" in 2019. And in 2021, the Ministry of Science and Technology published "Ethical Norms for New Generation Artificial Intelligence."

The principles outlined in these documents are fairly comprehensive and largely unobjectionable. There are some China-specific phrases, like "community of common destiny," a core concept in CCP ideology that implies ambitions to reshape the current international system to a more China-centered world order. The principles sometimes reference "harmony," an element of traditional Chinese philosophy. But, by and large, the principles are striking in their similarity to other AI principles released around the world. The Chinese government's 2021 AI ethics principles, for example, "aim to incorporate ethics into the entire AI life cycle and to promote fairness, justice, harmony, and security while avoiding such problems as bias, discrimination, and privacy and information leaks." These lofty principles are a jarring contrast to how AI is used in China. Many of the government organizations and companies behind these principles are facilitating gross human rights abuses, including the construction of an AI surveillance state of unprecedented power.

One of the leading thinkers in China on AI ethics is Yi Zeng, deputy director of the Research Center for Brain-Inspired Intelligence at the Chinese Academy of Sciences Institute of Automation and director of the Research Center for AI Ethics and Safety at BAAI. Professor Yi Zeng is almost painfully earnest. Yi has a boyish enthusiasm for AI ethics that seems hopelessly out of place in a country whose government is using AI-enhanced surveillance and repression. In various roles, Yi has been involved in several of the Chinese AI ethics principles. Yi was a member of the Ministry of Science and Technology's expert committee that drafted the "Governance Principles for a New Generation of Artificial Intelligence." His influence is evident behind many of China's AI ethics principles and his interest in ensuring AI is used for good comes across as sincere. Yi has dedicated a tremendous amount of his time to analyzing AI principles from around the world and proposing his own. Yi has compiled a list of seventy-four different sets of AI principles released worldwide and compared them along various dimensions. He has drafted his own set of "Harmonious AI Principles." Since AI principles ring hollow unless they are backed by a process for compliance, Yi published an online "AI governance" tool with thirty-five questions for developers to evaluate potential AI projects. His AI governance website includes over thirty case studies of problematic AI projects, including those that violated user privacy or dignity, were unsafe or showed bias, or had cybersecurity breaches. In an interview with *The Atlantic*, Yi described the Beijing AI Principles as his "life's work."

Nor is Yi alone in his concern about ensuring the responsible use of AI. In a presentation at the 2019 World Peace Forum in Beijing, Yi reported that the Beijing AI Principles had 5 million searches on the Chinese search engine Baidu in the first two days of their release. Student presenters stated that in a survey, 43 percent of Chinese youth cited AI privacy and ethics as a concern, the second highest AI-related concern behind unemployment. At the same event, Professor Bo Zhang at Tsinghua University spoke on the importance of building "reliable, controllable, and safe technologies" and ensuring AI methods were "explainable and robust." He said, "We need to establish regulations, international laws, and principles to restrain the use of AI."

Some of these messages are clearly aimed at a non-Chinese audience. The Beijing AI Principles were simultaneously released in Chinese and English, a sign that at least some of the intended audience is outside China. The World Peace Forum is a Chinese propaganda-fest organized by Tsinghua University with the support of the Chinese People's Institute of Foreign Affairs, a foreign-facing organization that has hosted thousands of American visitors to China. One of the goals of these various AI principles is to situate China as a global leader in AI, both the technology and its governance. Yet the purpose of these AI principles is also to communicate to an audience within China's AI community.

It would be easy to dismiss these principles as mere "ethics-washing," a criticism that has at times been levied against U.S. tech companies' AI ethics pledges. Yet the truth is more complex. There are genuine debates in China about the socially responsible use of AI. Those debates occur, however, within a political system in which the Chinese Communist Party's rule is unassailable.

I spent a long, hot Sunday in June 2019 listening (through a translator) to Chinese legal experts debate the contours of potential Chinese data privacy regulations at a law conference in Beijing. I suspect I would have found the debate among legal scholars boring even in English, but I was struck by the earnestness of the dialogue. Law professors from several Chinese universities, as well as representatives from major Chinese tech companies, discussed issues of facial recognition, informed consent, personal privacy, and data governance. Europe's data regulation regime, GDPR, was a hot topic of conversation, as was Apple's court battles with the FBI over iPhone encryption. The central topic of discussion was the balance between individual privacy rights and the rights of companies to collect and aggregate data from consumers.

The law conference I attended was just one tiny piece of a broader movement in China on data privacy. Data governance is directly relevant to AI, since machine learning generally requires large, accurate datasets on which to train algorithms. Since 2018, the Chinese government has developed regulations for greater consumer data privacy protections in China, in part in response to a series of data privacy scandals in China and globally. Many Chinese tech companies have what Samantha Hoffman described as "very, very serious problems with data security." The government, wary of the societal costs of unchecked corporate surveillance, passed a new consumer data privacy law in 2021. Another factor may be the Chinese Communist Party's desire to retain only for itself the sweeping powers of surveillance and data aggregation in the digital age. Maya Wang of Human Rights Watch pointed out, "The [CCP] doesn't want anyone else to spy except themselves." Because as much as consumer data privacy regulations are up for debate in China, the party-state stands above this exchange. Hoffman noted, "Privacy ends where the Party's power begins."

The CCP has passed a number of sweeping laws since 2015 relating to digital governance, including its National Security Law, Cybersecurity Law, National Intelligence Law, Data Security Law, and Personal Information Protection Law. Yet these laws are meant to codify the Party's power, not constrain it. The law plays a different role in China than in democratic societies. The People's Republic of China is a "party-state," where the Chinese Communist Party's power is absolute. Whereas democratic nations operate by "rule of law," where the law constrains even the government, China has a system of "rule by law." The CCP stands above the law, and the law exists to aid the Party in governing. Hoffman pointed out, "The law is there to protect the Party's power . . . at the end of the day it doesn't change what the Party can do."

The result is a weird dissonance when observing debates about data privacy in China. Chinese lawyers debate data privacy between individuals and consumers, but privacy from the government is not on the table for discussion. Similarly, in discussions of AI ethics, the government's role in using AI for mass surveillance and repression is not up for debate. Yi Zeng's thirty-plus case studies on AI governance included examples of misuses from all around the world, including China, but notably absent were any examples of Chinese government abuse of AI technology. All the examples from China were of misuses by companies or universities.

Undoubtedly one factor behind this apparent dissonance is that the CCP's censorship leaves Chinese citizens with less information about what their government is doing than readers of the *New York Times* or the *Wall Street Journal* (Western news outlets are banned in China). Chinese citizens are certainly aware, in a broad sense, of the CCP's ever-watchful eye and the consequences of stepping out of line. Surveillance cameras are ubiquitous, and the social credit system's efficacy depends on Chinese citizens and businesses knowing which behaviors will be punished and rewarded. But the full scope of the government's abuses is not known. Chinese people are often caricatured as not caring about privacy or individual freedom and more than willing to support—even embracing—a benevolent authoritarian government that uses its powers only for good, to fight crime and maintain social stability. I certainly spoke with Chinese citizens who were genuinely perplexed at Westerners' interest in the social credit system. I've spoken with PLA officers who asked, genuinely curious, what connection AI could possibly have to human rights. I've spoken with individuals who vigorously defended the CCP's line that all of the one million-plus Uighurs detained in camps are "terrorists." Yet Maya Wang noted, "Because of censorship, the government ensures that people know very, very little about what actually they're doing in terms of surveillance." Even Yi Zeng has dismissed the CCP's human rights abuses against Uighurs as "fake" news. It is all too easy to assume the government's good intentions when government abuses are censored.

The fierce battle that the people of Hong Kong have waged over the last two decades in defense of their freedoms puts the lie to the claim that Chinese people don't care about freedom. The existence of democratic Taiwan shows the reality that people of Han Chinese descent can thrive under democracy. It's the CCP's iron grip over its populace that prevents open debate. After all, if Chinese citizens willingly embraced the CCP's control, then censorship wouldn't be needed.

Even for Chinese citizens who may be aware of government abuses or skeptical of the government's powers, there is no recourse. Those who speak up will be summoned for "tea" with the police, a polite euphemism for a police interrogation. For those who persist, the result can be detention and torture. There is no public debate about the government's role in surveillance because the CCP does not permit it.

It can be hard to hold these contradictions in mind when viewing debates about AI ethics and data privacy in China. There is real, genuine debate about tech governance for corporate actors, but the government's power is never challenged. For foreigners, this complicates any engagement with China on shaping tech norms. In these forums, Europe's decisive legislation on digital privacy and AI is immensely useful. The EU's legislation has deeply impacted discussions about AI and data governance in China, at least at the academic level. The Chinese government's Personal Information Protection Law for consumer data privacy was modeled on the GDPR. And Chinese companies sensitive to brand and reputation, particularly those that want to expand into global markets, tend to at least acknowledge these norms. But while the proliferation of global AI principles has, at least on paper, spread to China, they will not restrain the party-state's power. They may, however, lead to better consumer AI applications in China in health care, education, transportation, or other non-security-related industries.

The challenge in engaging with Chinese counterparts on tech governance is ensuring that engagement does not end up de facto endorsing the Chinese party-state's model of government surveillance. Even as the United States pivots away from a strategy of engagement for engagement's sake, some forms of dialogue and engagement will still beneficial. They must be calibrated, however, by realistic expectations about what is achievable.

Individuals who engage with China on AI ethics have a responsibility to speak out against AI-enabled abuses and take a stand for rules of AI governance that protect human rights. The emergence of AI principles and data privacy debates in China show that norms for tech governance are diffusing from other nations into China, but if individuals stay silent about the disconnect between these nice-sounding principles and the ugly reality on the ground, then the principles will be meaningless. Consenting to the hollowness of China's claims to be "respecting human rights" risks normalizing and legitimizing the gross human rights abuses the CCP is perpetrating and emboldening the further spread of AI-enabled repression.

In July 2019, I participated in a day-long public conference on AI Technology and Governance at the Beijing World Peace Forum, the purpose of which was clearly to showcase China's supposed leadership in AI governance. Sprinkled among the Chinese presenters were eight American speakers (including me), some from highly prestigious American universities and Washington, DC–based think tanks. As the event unfolded, our role on the agenda became clear—to lend legitimacy to China's efforts through the use of our institution's names. By sitting on a panel alongside Chinese experts on topics like "The Ethics and Governance of AI," we were intended to be props to showcase to the world how much American experts from top-tier institutions respect China's role on AI governance. Of the eight speakers, I was the only one to mention that China is using AI to repress its own citizens.

Too often, Americans who engage with China are silent on the CCP's abuses. There are costs to speaking out against the CCP. Beijing retaliates against those who don't avoid "sensitive topics" like Xinjiang. Even experts who don't rely on Chinese money might lose access to China. Or worse. The CCP has stepped up harassment of Westerners, holding them for questioning and even preventing some from leaving the country. In 2018, China arbitrarily detained Canadians Michael Kovrig and Michael Spavor following Canada's arrest of Huawei executive Meng Wanzhou. They spent over two and a half years in prison as diplomatic hostages before their release. It is no wonder Western experts might think twice about speaking up. Yet in doing so, they aid the Chinese Communist Party in its ethics-washing.

The United States will not be able to walk away from interacting with China on critical issues of AI governance, and there can be value in these interactions in spreading positive norms about AI ethics. The United States and other democratic countries must actively participate in international debates about AI standards and norms to help shape their evolution. But ethical principles only have meaning if we hold people, companies, and governments accountable for their behavior. And it starts with a simple act: speaking the truth.

21

STRANGLEHOLD

Alongside AI governance and business and research relationships, compute has emerged as another battleground in the U.S.-China AI competition. China heavily depends on external sources for compute, a dependency the U.S. government has leveraged to hinder Chinese tech companies. Yet the global infrastructure of computing hardware is shifting, as both China and the United States seek to ramp up domestic semiconductor production. Control over compute could turn out to be one of the most consequential fights in the struggle for AI dominance.

China has long sought to reduce its dependency on foreign chips, a major vulnerability for the country. China's national efforts to boost its semiconductor industry date back to the 1950s at the origin of the technology and have included a steady stream of government plans and investment. Most recently, from 2014 to 2020 the Chinese government issued ten strategic plans and policy guidelines affecting the semiconductor industry, and committed an estimated $150 billion to semiconductor investments. The Chinese government's willingness to spend enormous sums of money to boost its industry has helped address the massive capital needed to compete in the semiconductor industry, but an inefficient allocation of capital, lack of access to foreign technology, and a dearth of high-end talent has all hindered China's indigenous chip development. To make up the shortfall in technical skill, China has recruited an estimated 3,000 semiconductor engineers from Taiwan to join Chinese companies, luring them with massive raises, sometimes double what they would make in Taiwan. The partially government-owned contract foundry Semiconductor Manufacturing International Corporation (SMIC) has benefited from hundreds of Taiwanese engineers along with top executives, including its first CEO. China has also used foreign acquisitions as a means of acquiring talent, technology, and expertise. Despite several high-profile acquisitions being denied by the U.S. government on national security grounds, China completed over $5 billion in acquisitions of U.S. semiconductor firms from 2006 to 2016 and an estimated $11 billion total in overseas acquisitions as of 2017.

Domestically, China has been on a fab-building spree, building over 40 percent of new fabs worldwide from 2016 to 2020. China is both the largest and fastest-growing importer of semiconductor manufacturing equipment, accounting for nearly 30 percent of global imports from 2014 to 2018. As a result of this investment, China has the fastest growing share of global chip manufacturing and is expected to build more new fabs from 2020 to 2030 than any other country. While twenty years ago the Chinese chipmaking industry was a decade behind the leading node, Chinese foundries have made strides in catching up, though they remain at least two generations (roughly five to six years) behind the industry's leading edge.

While the Chinese government has a long history of national plans and subsidies for its semiconductor industry, the U.S. government has only recently become engaged in the geopolitical competition over chips. A brief period of anxiety in the 1980s about the rise of Japanese semiconductor firms spawned some U.S. government efforts through the late '80s and early '90s to spur domestic chip innovation. By the mid-1990s, however, the U.S. government had reverted to letting globalization, market forces, and engagement with China run its course with little government intervention. Rising costs and market competition drove firm specialization and the development of globalized, interconnected supply chains. Hefty government subsidies by many countries to the tune of billions of dollars for chip companies also contributed to shaping the global semiconductor market. The net effect was U.S. chip manufacturing declined from 37 percent of global manufacturing in 1990 to 12 percent by 2021.

Increasing concern over Chinese intellectual property theft spurred more aggressive U.S. government scrutiny of foreign investment in American firms in the mid-2010s. The Committee on Foreign Investment in the United States (CFIUS), the U.S. government body charged with reviewing sensitive foreign investment in the United States, stepped up enforcement and Congress expanded its authorities in 2018.

The U.S. government has more recently taken steps to increase chip manufacturing in the United States. In 2021, TSMC began construction of a $12 billion leading-edge 5 nm fab in Arizona and Samsung rolled out its plans for a $17 billion leading-edge fab in Texas. Intel broke ground on two new Arizona plants totaling $20 billion in late 2021 and a few months later in early

2022 announced a plan for another $20 billion in chip factories in Ohio. The companies all have said they hope for U.S. government subsidies to help fund the plants. U.S. lawmakers are thinking similarly. In 2022, Congress passed the bipartisan CHIPS and Science Act that included over $52 billion in semiconductor subsidies. The bill included funding for domestic fabs and the establishment of a National Semiconductor Technology Center to conduct advanced semiconductor R&D.

The rise of AI-specialized chips adds a further wrinkle to the geopolitical competition over hardware. AI-specialized chips are expected to take an increasing share of training and inference (using trained models) through 2025, partially displacing more general-purpose CPUs and GPUs. AI-optimized chips are valuable because AI is so compute-intensive, driving a need for more efficient hardware optimized for deep learning. The disruption in the market afforded by specialized AI chips may be an opportunity for China to leap ahead in at least some kinds of AI chips. AI-specialized chips include improved GPUs as well as chips optimized for AI, such as application-specific integrated circuits (ASICs) and field-programmable gate arrays (FPGAs).

As the name implies, ASICs are chips whose design is optimized for a particular application. Rather than a general-purpose chip like a CPU or GPU, an ASIC is optimized at the hardware level to run a specific algorithm. This can help improve compute efficiency for that algorithm but also means that the chip may have narrower utility. An example of an AI-specific ASIC is Google's Tensor Processing Unit (TPU). TPUs have been used to train several Google AI research projects, including language models and DeepMind's AlphaGo and AlphaStar, which achieved superhuman performance in the games *go* and *StarCraft*, respectively.

FPGAs are like a middle ground between general-purpose CPUs and GPUs and application-specific ASICs. FPGAs can be customized after they have been manufactured (hence the term "field-programmable") by programming logic blocks on the chip for specific applications. FPGAs can be reprogrammed for different applications, unlike ASICs whose logic is embedded into the hardware of the chip.

AI chips are a relatively small portion—about 10 percent—of the global semiconductor market but are growing five times faster than non-AI chips. AI-specialized chips are also widening the field of potential chip designers, with companies like Google and Tesla getting in the game designing their own ASICs for specific applications. As AI technology matures with more real-world applications, dominance in AI-specialized chips may turn out to matter far more for influencing how AI is used than dominance in semiconductors more generally.

It remains an open question whether the Chinese semiconductor industry can continue to catch up to industry leaders or whether the hurdles to accessing the technology and human capital needed to operate at the most advanced process nodes will remain too difficult to overcome. Reducing China's foreign dependence on technology is a high priority for Chinese leaders. General Secretary Xi Jinping said in 2016:

> Our dependence on core technology is the biggest hidden trouble for us; therefore, having a good command of core Internet technology is our mission. Heavy dependence on imported core technology is like building our house on top of someone else's walls: No matter how big and how beautiful it is, it won't remain standing during a storm.

China's ability to reduce its foreign chip dependencies will depend not only on what China does, however, but also the actions of other countries that China depends on for semiconductor manufacturing technology.

The manufacturing equipment used to make chips is a key control point in the global semiconductor industry. The equipment used by SMIC, TSMC, Intel, Samsung, and other chip producers has to come from somewhere, and chip fabrication equipment is highly specialized. The market for semiconductor manufacturing equipment is even more centralized than the market for semiconductors themselves. Three countries—Japan, the United States, and the Netherlands—control over 90 percent of the global semiconductor manufacturing equipment market.

In some key technologies, a single company holds a monopoly. The Dutch firm ASML is the only supplier for extreme ultraviolet (EUV) lithography tools, a high-precision laser used for chip fabrication in leading-edge 5 nm process fabs and some 7 nm fabs. This gives the Netherlands a unique role in controlling which countries have access to the technology to build leading-edge foundries. In mid-2019, after intense lobbying from the U.S. government, the Netherlands declined to renew an export license for EUV machines to China, effectively blocking Chinese foundries from adopting EUV technology. These restrictions only affect the most advanced leading-edge processes, however. Chinese fabs can still access other tools that are only slightly less advanced, such as deep ultraviolet lithography tools, which have been used in chip fabrication processes as advanced as the 7 nm node.

Another global chokepoint in the semiconductor industry is the supply of photoresist, a type of chemical used in chip fabrication. Japan controls roughly 90 percent of the global supply of high-end photoresist for EUV lithography, once again giving a single actor outsized control over advanced chip fabrication. In 2019, Japan used this leverage in a trade dispute with South Korea, temporarily restricting exports of photoresist and other key chemicals for semiconductor manufacturing. South Korea depends on Japan for 90 percent of its photoresist supply, and it is not easy for South Korean chip manufacturers to find substitutes. Similar to other aspects of chip manufacturing, other countries make less-advanced photoresists but ceased competing in the most advanced EUV photoresists due to rising costs. Even when substitutes are available, switching to a new photoresist supplier would take months of testing and recertification, introducing costly delays to chip production lines.

The United States has its own levers of influence over chip production, holding a significant share of the global semiconductor manufacturing equipment market and particular dominance in the specialized software used to design chips. By limiting access to these key production inputs, U.S. policymakers dealt a hammer blow to China's access to advanced semiconductors.

In 2019, the Trump administration launched a major international campaign against Huawei due to concerns about its growing dominance in the global 5G wireless market and the risks of U.S. allies installing Chinese-made equipment in their critical infrastructure. As was par for other diplomatic overtures, the Trump administration fumbled much of the international messaging surrounding Huawei, with President Trump frequently undercutting U.S. national security professionals who stressed the cybersecurity risks of Huawei equipment in allies' networks. The risks were real, yet the ham-handed campaign failed to persuade many European countries who were wary of angering China by blocking Huawei equipment. (Japan and Australia, by contrast, banned Huawei from their networks before the United States did.)

The Trump administration turned to export controls as a potential means of squeezing Huawei by denying the company the chips it needed to build its 5G equipment. In May 2019, the U.S. government added Huawei to the Commerce Department's Entity List, banning Huawei from receiving any U.S.-origin technology. Yet the U.S. government had only weak leverage over Huawei. Within a matter of weeks, U.S. chip firms Micron and Intel had found legal ways of sidestepping the Trump administration's ban and continue shipping chips to Huawei. U.S. law only prohibits shipping products that are at least 25 percent or more U.S. origin to an organization on the Entity List. Under the rule, companies—even those headquartered in the United States—were legally permitted to sell products to Huawei so long as 75 percent or more of the product's value was not of U.S. origin. By adjusting their supply lines to cut out U.S.-origin technology, companies could continue to sell products to Huawei while remaining in compliance with the letter of the ban, if not its spirit. Trump administration officials criticized the companies' moves, but the real problem was the globalization of semiconductor supply chains. The United States was an industry leader but hardly indispensable.

The Huawei ban sent shockwaves through the global semiconductor industry. U.S. chip firms descended on Washington to plead their case against cutting off chip sales to China. Fear spread among both Chinese and American chip companies. No one knew which Chinese company after Huawei might end up next in the U.S. government's crosshairs. While U.S. chip companies conceded that China was a national security threat, they argued that the best way to stay ahead was to out-compete China by selling them chips and then plowing the profits back into R&D for the next generation of semiconductors. It was an appealing argument to American sensibilities, envisioning U.S. firms maintaining a global edge by simply running faster than the competition through superior innovation. The problem was that it wasn't working. Over the last several decades, Chinese companies—often through massive state subsidies—had climbed up the value chain to be major global tech competitors. Huawei was a case in point. Huawei has received $75 billion in state subsidies, allowing it to undercut competitors on price. U.S. firms might be able to win on merit, but the playing field wasn't even close to level. The Chinese government was investing hundreds of billions of dollars to boost key industries through national initiatives such as Made in China 2025, supplemented with a massive campaign of intellectual property theft and technology transfer.

The stronger argument against the Trump administration's ban on chip sales to Huawei was that it simply wasn't working. The ban may have caused some disruption, delay, or cost increases within Huawei's 5G business, but the company was chugging along just fine. By September 2019, Huawei announced it was ready to start churning out 5,000 new 5G base stations a month—with no U.S. technology inside—and was planning to scale production to 1.5 million units in 2020. The blacklisting was hardly the knockout blow U.S. officials had hoped for. Even worse, the indirect effect was to incentivize every company in the global semiconductor industry to design out U.S. components from their chips. At $400 billion a year, the Chinese appetite for imported chips was too big a market for companies to ignore. If the U.S. government could, at any time, suddenly declare by fiat that no American-made chips could be sent to Chinese firms, then companies had strong financial incentives to move their supply chains out of the United States.

Undeterred yet lacking a long-term plan, the U.S. government continued its whack-a-mole efforts against Huawei. After a year of waffling on rule changes, in May 2020 U.S. regulators finally landed on an effective strategy. New Commerce Department rules expanded the ban to include not only American-made chip components, but also American-made equipment used to *produce* chips for Huawei. This meant that companies like TSMC, which was fabricating chips in Taiwan, were prohibited from using any U.S. equipment for making chips for Huawei, even if the chips themselves were 100 percent made outside of the USA. (Huawei owns their own chip design firm, HiSilicon, but relies on contract foundries like TSMC to manufacture the chips.) U.S. lawmakers were thrilled. Senator Ben Sasse said, "The United States needs to strangle Huawei. . . . This is pretty simple: chip companies that depend on American technology can't jump into bed with the Chinese Communist Party. This rule is long overdue." In August 2020, the Commerce Department tightened the rules even further, prohibiting U.S. equipment from being used to manufacture chips from *any* company that were destined for Huawei, not just chips for Huawei's subsidiary HiSilicon. U.S. industry protested the expansive ban (which also applied to them), but it was effective. TSMC stated they would no longer ship chips to Huawei as of mid-September. In the last quarter of 2020, TSMC sales to China dropped by over 70 percent. One industry insider told the *Washington Post*, "This kills Huawei."

Empowered by their successes against Huawei, U.S. policymakers expanded their campaign against Chinese semiconductor manufacturers and users in the waning days of the Trump administration. In December 2020, the U.S. government placed China's largest and most advanced chipmaker, SMIC, on the Entity List. As justification for the move, U.S. regulators cited China's strategy of military-civil fusion and SMIC's ties to "entities of concern in the Chinese military industrial complex." The restrictions were limited, however, to technology "uniquely required" for 10 nm process nodes or below, only targeting the most cutting-edge fab tools. (SMIC currently has some production capacity at the 14 nm node.)

The Biden Administration dramatically expanded the U.S. stranglehold on Chinese chip production. In October 2022, the Commerce Department released expansive new restrictions on advanced chips and semiconductor manufacturing equipment to China. The rules banned U.S. companies from shipping manufacturing equipment to any Chinese fabs at 16 nm or below, broadening the scope of both the technology and the companies captured by the restrictions. The U.S.

government also imposed controls on advanced chips similar to those used to choke off Huawei's access to 5G chips. Chip producers, including those in Taiwan and South Korea, were banned from using U.S. equipment to manufacture advanced GPUs for China, effectively locking China out of advanced AI chips.

American attempts to choke off its access to chips have, not surprisingly, led China to redouble its efforts to improve its domestic semiconductor industry. Undeterred by the U.S. government's efforts, China announced a $1.4 trillion investment plan in digital technologies in May 2020, mere days after one of the U.S. Commerce Department's Huawei bans. China's state-driven model, while inefficient, has proven effective in other industries. While China faces many challenges in building its domestic fab industry, the Chinese government has a plan and ample funding.

The U.S. government, meanwhile, has been slow to develop a strategy for competing in AI hardware. Like a drunk in a bar fight, the United States threw the first punch in a global chip war with no plan for how to finish the fight. Some of the U.S. government's actions are sensible but others have been self-defeating. Restricting China's access to manufacturing equipment and software design tools necessary to manufacture leading-edge chips makes sense. The United States and its allies should aim to keep China reliant on foreign chip supplies, retaining the ability to cut off China's access to chips if needed. Yet actually cutting off access to chips, as the United States did with 5G chips for Huawei and with advanced AI chips nationwide, should be a rare move. Denying China the ability to import chips turns China's $400 billion of semiconductor buying power inward, fueling the growth of their domestic semiconductor industry, which is the exact opposite of what Washington should want.

Core elements of a U.S. competitive strategy are beginning to fall into place. The $52 billion in subsidies Congress passed in 2022 will help sustain U.S. leadership in key parts of the semiconductor supply chain. The Biden Administration's expanded export controls on manufacturing equipment at 16nm and below will help freeze and possibly even roll back Chinese fab development. Yet much will depend on how these policies are implemented.

China's ability to catch up in chip production hinges in large part on how expansively (and cooperatively) the United States and other semiconductor manufacturing equipment providers, such as the Netherlands and Japan, restrict chip manufacturing technology to China. As the U.S. government's restrictions on Huawei demonstrate, control over chip production is a major source of geopolitical power. Saif Khan, research fellow at the Center for Security and Emerging Technology, has suggested that the United States and its allies impose expansive export controls on chipmaking equipment, materials, and software at higher process nodes in order to "control China's chip access." The National Security Commission on AI recommended the U.S. government control chip manufacturing technology relevant at the 16 nm node or below, a proposal endorsed by some lawmakers. Khan concluded that export controls at the 16 nm or 28 nm nodes and below would be "sustainably effective," whereas restricting only the most advanced toolmaking would have a "muted impact." The U.S. government has historically sought to keep China at least two generations behind in chip manufacturing through export controls. In September 2022, National Security Advisor Jake Sullivan announced a shift in U.S. policy, replacing the goal of being "only a couple of generations ahead" of China with the new goal of maintaining "as large of a lead as possible" in chips. Multilateral restrictions on equipment below 16/14 nm could freeze China's fab development in place, and expanded restrictions at 16/14 nm or higher could even roll back Chinese production over time, denying fabs the equipment and servicing they need to continue production. Yet China's role as the leading importer for semiconductor manufacturing equipment may make the siren song of profits too tempting for other countries to resist.

The goal of a U.S. strategy should be to retain control over the levers of chip production by slowing China's indigenous semiconductor industry, maintaining China's dependence on foreign chips, and investing in American firms to secure another generation of technological leadership. The United States should also work to diversify the geography of chip production so it is not so heavily dependent on Taiwan, an island one hundred miles off the coast of China that the Chinese Communist Party has pledged to absorb—by force if necessary—into China. A military conflict over Taiwan could have devastating ramifications for global chip supply chains. Even a nonviolent shift in political and economic power across the Taiwan Strait that moved Taiwan's semiconductor industry into the CCP's sphere of influence would dramatically alter the global balance of technological power.

The United States and allies must expand multilateral export controls, increase R&D funding, and subsidize fab construction to re-shore fabs to the United States and other allied nations. Yet as long as China has 60 percent of the global demand for semiconductors, its buying power will tend to bend supply chains around any restrictions. An important element of a comprehensive U.S. strategy for hardware competition is incentivizing companies to diversify electronics manufacturing out of China using a mix of carrots, such as tax incentives, and sticks, such as targeted tariffs.

The global semiconductor market will remain highly fluid, driven by a combination of market forces, national industrial policies, and disruptive technological change. Ever-rising costs continue to consolidate the industry to only a few players at key choke points. The United States, China, and other countries will continue to invest in their national semiconductor industries, adding geopolitical pressures to the forces affecting the global semiconductor market. China's chip dependency is a massive point of leverage for the United States over China, but the United States will need to work with allies to effectively constrain China's domestic semiconductor industry.

A number of voices have called for technology-leading democracies to band together to coordinate technology policy. In 2020, the UK government reportedly approached the United States about creating a new "D10" group of democratic, tech-leading countries comprising the G7 nations (Canada, France, Germany, Italy, Japan, the United Kingdom, and the United States) plus Australia, India, and South Korea. A number of U.S. experts have embraced the idea under different names ("Tech 10," "T-12") with other proposed members including the European Union, Finland, Israel, the Netherlands, and Sweden. Potential areas of collaboration include R&D, talent, standard-setting, fab subsidies, export controls, foreign investment screening, countering IP theft, and AI governance. The "Quad" nations of Australia, India, Japan, and the United States have already deepened their cooperation, hosting a first-ever heads of state summit in 2021. They jointly launched a "critical- and emerging-technology working group to facilitate cooperation on international standards and innovative technologies of the future." Also in 2021, the United States and the EU established a new Trade and Technology Council (TTC) to further cooperation on a range of technology issues, including standards, export controls, semiconductors, and artificial intelligence. By collaborating on technology policy, democratic nations will be far more effective in shaping the future of AI.

PART VI
REVOLUTION

22

ROBOTICS ROW

History shows that what matters most in periods of technological disruption is not getting a new technology first or even having the best technology but finding the best ways of using it. The U.S. military's challenge is to adapt faster than its adversaries, both on the battlefield and in its bureaucracy. Institutions are essential for transforming the raw AI inputs of data, compute, and talent into military power. Militaries need effective institutions to not only acquire technology but also find ways of employing it effectively.

The first aircraft flew at Kitty Hawk, North Carolina, in 1903, but this gave the United States no meaningful advantage by the time World War I broke out a little over a decade later. (The United States didn't enter the war until 1917.) All the major European powers had access to aircraft, and the main challenge was figuring out how to use airplanes effectively. Airplanes and tanks, both new wonder-weapons born of the industrial revolution, played only an incidental role in World War I, but military leaders saw their potential. During the interwar period, leading military powers experimented with airplanes and tanks, yet the best use for these new technologies was far from obvious. Different countries and different communities, or "tribes," within military services took varied approaches, with their choices shaped as much by bureaucratic politics and culture as they were by strategy and geography.

While Great Britain was the first nation to develop aircraft carriers, by the start of World War II they had fallen woefully behind the United States and Japan, who had embraced carrier aviation as central to the future of naval warfare. Navies saw intense internal debates during the interwar period about the proper role of carriers, whether they should serve merely as scouts for battleships or could be an offensive force in their own right to sink enemy ships through air attack. Since aircraft carriers had yet to be fielded in large numbers and massed carrier battles, like that which occurred at the Battle of Midway in

1942, had yet to occur, there were genuine questions about the carrier's role. In the United States, war games at the Naval War College played an instrumental role in helping U.S. Navy leaders understand carriers' potential. Meanwhile in Britain, it was bureaucratic missteps, rather than a lack of access to aircraft technology, that held back carrier aviation.

Militaries faced similar internal debates during the interwar period about how best to employ tanks. Immediately after World War I, the U.S. Congress, on the advice of Army leaders, abolished the fledgling Tank Corps and subsumed tanks under the command of the infantry. Based on the experience of World War I, U.S. Army leaders at the time believed that tanks' primary role was to support the infantry. Experiments with tanks in the 1920s were stymied not only by budgetary cuts but also internal bureaucratic fights inside the Army. Both the infantry and horse cavalry communities (rightly) saw tanks as a threat to their bureaucratic power, but other Army communities had their own prerogatives. Army engineers, for example, wanted light tanks so that they would not have to redesign their bridges, which had a fifteen-ton weight limit. In his analysis of the Army's adoption of the tank, Lieutenant Colonel Kenneth A. Steadman observed that the net effect of these bureaucratic obstacles was such that "by the time Germany invaded France in May 1940, the U.S. Army possessed only 28 new tanks (10 medium and 18 light tanks) and 900 obsolete models scattered among the infantry, mechanized cavalry, and ordnance depots." Even as late as 1943, after Germany had used tanks to blitz across Europe, senior U.S. Army leaders saw the tank's primary role as supporting the infantry. In 1943, Lieutenant General Lesley McNair, Commander of Army Ground Forces, disestablished the armored corps and placed tanks under the command of the infantry on the grounds that Germany's use of tanks to conquer most of continental Europe was an aberration.

It is easy, in retrospect, to see these decisions as short-sighted, but similar bureaucratic struggles played out in all the major military powers at the time. The key question for militaries was not whether to use new technologies, but *how* to use them. Institutional structures receptive to innovation—not just adopting new technologies but actually using them for new ways of fighting— are central to transforming technological advantage into military power. New technologies are useless without the right organizations inside militaries to adopt them and apply them for battlefield advantage. In the past several years, the U.S. military has been on an organization-building spree in an attempt to accelerate its ability to "spin-in" and militarize commercial technologies, including AI.

On the shores of the Allegheny River, Pittsburgh is seeing a revitalization driven by robotics. In the Lawrenceville neighborhood where Pittsburgh's proud steel mills once stood, "Robotics Row" features Carnegie Mellon spin-off Carnegie Robotics and the National Robotics Engineering Center, whose lobby sports an array of air and ground robots. Dominating the NREC lobby is Workhorse, the massive Carnegie Mellon robot used to help clean up the Three Mile Island nuclear reactor. Under the window sits Terregator, a six-wheeled ruggedized ground robot with a domed head reminiscent of the robot from the 1960s *Lost in Space* TV show. Overhead, a robot helicopter hangs from the ceiling. The scene is more dieselpunk than AI, evoking wrenches and grease as much as code. It's a fitting location for the Army to house their AI Task Force, a sixteen-person team tucked in a back corner of NREC's massive building with the ambitious vision of bringing artificial intelligence into the nearly 500,000-person U.S. Army.

Brigadier General Matt Easley commands the AI Task Force and has a background tailor-made for his role. Easley graduated with a PhD in computer science and studied symbolic AI before the current deep learning revolution. Easley graduated in 2000 during "the heart of an AI winter," when "you couldn't say the words 'AI'," he said. "There were no AI jobs." But there were jobs doing AI-related things in defense. "They just changed their names," he explained. Easley at the time was an Army reservist and worked full-time as a civilian defense contractor at Rockwell Collins building "intelligent decision aids." He later moved to Boeing and worked on battle management systems for air and ground combat. "That was my passion because I wanted to make military systems smarter," he said. Easley and his team are now trying to take Army personnel management into the age of algorithms. One of their priority initiatives is to use machine learning to aid in talent management.

Easley explained that every year, the newly graduating class at the Army's undergraduate military academy at West Point needs to be assigned to different jobs across the Army. These jobs are called "branches" and include infantry, armor, medical, aviation, engineering, intelligence, and other specialties. Under the old method, the top academically performing cadets got their first pick, and then it would go down the list of cadets, in academic rank, until each job position filled up. Easley explained that the Army has known for a while that it wasn't optimally aligning people to jobs that might be the best fit for them. "They just didn't have a better way of implementing it," he said. AI is changing that.

Lieutenant Colonel Isaac Faber, chief data scientist for the Army AI Task

Force, outlined how they are in the process of building an AI model that uses five years' worth of officer performance data—"tens of thousands of data points"—to predict how well West Point cadets are likely to do in a given career field. In 2020, "for the first time," Faber said, "a machine learning algorithm will be part of the fabric that makes up the branching recommendations for cadets at West Point." By better aligning individuals with the jobs they are most likely to excel at, AI could help build a more capable Army overall.

Easley and his Task Force are bringing AI into the Army in other roles as well. In a major military exercise in Europe called Europe Defender, planned for 2020 but cancelled due to COVID-19, the Army planned to use a prototype image classification system to aid in targeting for long-range precision fires. The AI system can sift through images from satellites or drones to help look for military objects, such as tanks, speeding up the intelligence and targeting cycle, a process that currently can take up to twelve hours. On a fast-moving battle-field, twelve hours could be an eternity. Easley said, "We've got to figure out how do we stay inside our adversaries' information decision loops to be able to identify targets faster," understanding the environment and making decisions faster than the enemy, while keeping humans "in the loop" for decisions.

In early 2021, the XVIII Airborne Corps at Fort Bragg partnered with Project Maven to use AI to accelerate targeting cycles in a live-fire exercise. By one account, there are at least fifteen different offices and departments across DoD working on AI or AI-related technologies. In pockets across DoD, the U.S. military is working to find ways to adopt AI for military applications.

23

PROJECT VOLTRON

Based in Mountain View, California, just down the street from Google's Googleplex headquarters, the Defense Innovation Unit is the DoD's outpost in Silicon Valley. DIU has worked hard to shed the military culture and blend in with the locals. The military officers I met when I visited were in civilian clothes. The office is heavily populated with standing desks in an open-office floor plan. And the conference rooms have cute names inspired by science fiction and fantasy like "R2-D2," "Rosie" (the robot from *The Jetsons*), "Rivendell," and "Eye of Sauron." Michael Brown, the head of DIU, is the former CEO of Symantec, a global leader in cybersecurity. Brown and his team at DIU are helping to break down DoD's barriers to working with tech start-ups.

One of DIU's most important innovations isn't a gadget, it's institutional speed in adaptation. In one initiative, Project Voltron, DIU moved from solicitation to contract in twenty-six business days—light speed for the Defense Department, which usually takes years to get a new project under way. Project Voltron uses automation to accelerate finding and patching cyber vulnerabilities in DoD systems, a major problem for the department. In 2018, Government Accountability Office (GAO) investigators found U.S. weapon systems riddled with "mission-critical cyber vulnerabilities that adversaries could compromise." These vulnerabilities could allow adversaries to corrupt data or deny DoD the ability to use weapons, "potentially leading to an inability to complete military missions or even loss of life," investigators warned. The GAO concluded an estimated $1.6 trillion dollars in DoD weapons were at risk. Project Voltron leverages the automated cyber vulnerability discovery and patching tools pioneered in DARPA's 2016 Cyber Grand Challenge to fix DoD systems. The technology has already been used to find previously undetected vulnerabilities in fielded military aircraft. Pittsburgh-based ForAllSecure, the winner of the Cyber Grand Challenge and another Carnegie Mellon spin-off, is one of the companies on contract through Project Voltron.

Automated cyber vulnerability discovery is a valuable tool, but DIU director Michael Brown was careful to characterize it as "automating" cyber security functions, "but I really couldn't say it's using artificial intelligence." DIU has also been involved in accelerating the deployment of small, autonomous drones, working with start-up Shield AI to deploy autonomous quadcopters to support special operations forces in urban combat. (Both Shield AI and ForAllSecure were covered in my book *Army of None*.) When it came to machine learning applications, Brown was most excited about DIU's work on predictive maintenance.

Maintenance is critical to ensuring military forces are ready to conduct operations. When Russia invaded Ukraine in early 2022, the poor state of Russian maintenance of ground vehicles and aircraft hampered their effectiveness. Something as simple as poor tire maintenance can leave ground vehicles literally stuck in the mud, unable to advance.

Predictive maintenance leverages historical data about a vehicle fleet's maintenance needs to build an algorithm that can predict when a part will need to be repaired or replaced, rather than performing maintenance based on a fixed schedule. To build a predictive maintenance model, DIU turned to C3 AI, a commercial company that builds enterprise AI solutions across a range of industries, from optimizing supply chains to energy management and fraud detection. In six months, C3 AI had an initial prototype based on seven to ten years of operational data from U.S. aircraft. Early tests of a predictive maintenance algorithm on the Air Force's E-3 Sentry airborne warning and control system (AWACS) aircraft and C-5 cargo plane yielded an approximately 30 percent reduction in unscheduled maintenance. C3 AI trained thirty AI classifiers to "calculate the probability of failure on high-priority subsystems." Brown said, "Actually, it was a small problem from their perspective. . . . They work on problems that are 10X in terms of the number of variables to develop predictive algorithms." Following this initial success, DIU expanded C3 AI's predictive maintenance work to include other aircraft, including Air Force F-16 and F-35A fighter jets and Army Apache and Blackhawk helicopters, covering over 1,200 aircraft in total.

Maintenance may not sound exciting, but it's big money for DoD. The department spends over $280 billion annually in operations and maintenance. Even a tiny improvement would net billions in savings. Building on this success, DIU has expanded their predictive maintenance work to Army and Marine Corps ground vehicles and optimizing Navy ship maintenance, which alone costs the Navy $10 billion a year.

Michael Brown said that when he briefed then–Secretary of Defense Jim Mattis on the project, Mattis was most excited about the implications for increased "readiness." By using AI to maintain aircraft, ships, and ground vehicles more efficiently, the DoD fleets would spend more time ready for actual missions. The implications for DoD are enormous, both from a cost and military effectiveness standpoint. In 2018, Secretary of Defense Mattis directed the Air Force and Navy to increase the mission-capable rates of their fighter aircraft to 80 percent, meaning eight of every ten aircraft would be ready to fly, with only two of ten aircraft down for maintenance at any point in time. At the time, the Air Force was well short of this goal, with only 70 percent of F-16s mission capable, 55 percent of F-35s, and 49 percent of F-22s. The Navy was in even worse shape, with less than half of its F-18 Super Hornets mission capable. These readiness rates made it more expensive to field a given number of flight-ready aircraft. At an 80 percent mission-capable rate, the U.S. military would need to purchase 100 aircraft to have 80 ready to fly. At a 50 percent mission-capable rate, it would need to purchase 160 aircraft (60 percent more) to have 80 aircraft available for missions.

Aircraft availability rates are the dull stuff of military operations and budgeting but are the real meat and potatoes of military power. Ships, planes, and tanks that are down for maintenance are no use on the battlefield. AI can help. According to C3 AI, their AI software for maintenance optimization has demonstrated a 3 to 6 percent increase in mission capability. Brown said that for Mattis, "It was all about readiness." Even a few percent increase in aircraft readiness was a major win for the DoD. (The Air Force later abandoned Mattis's 80 percent readiness goal in 2020, after Mattis had resigned as secretary of defense.)

Michael Brown said that Mattis pushed DIU beyond developing niche solutions to narrow problems. Mattis wanted DIU thinking big. Brown said he wanted DIU focused on questions such as, "How do we bring new capabilities to the department based on commercial technology advances? What can you do at DIU that applies new capabilities across the services and has big impact, saving us tens of billions of dollars?" In a congratulatory letter to DIU at the organization's five-year anniversary, then–Secretary of Defense Mark Esper highlighted "scaling machine learning solutions for predictive maintenance" as one of DIU's most impactful projects.

Recent DoD Innovation Organizations

A non-exhaustive list of DoD innovation-oriented organizations established since 2015

Defense Digital Service (DDS)	2015
Defense Innovation Unit (DIU) (formerly DIUx)	2015
Special Operations Forces Works (SOFWERX)	2015
National Security Innovation Network (NSIN) (formerly MD5)	2016 (MD5), 2019 (NSIN)
Air Force Works (AFWERX)	2017
Algorithmic Warfare Cross-Functional Team (Project Maven) (AWCFT)	2017
Kessel Run (Air Force)	2017
Rogue Squadron (now a component of the Defense Digital Service)	2017
Air Force Techstars Accelerator	2018
Army AI Task Force	2018
Army Applications Lab	2018
Army Futures Command	2018
Catalyst Accelerator (Air Force, Space Force)	2018
Engineer Research and Development Center Works (ERDCWERX) (Army)	2018
Hyperspace Challenge (Space Force)	2018
Joint Artificial Intelligence Center (JAIC)	2018
MGMWERX (Air Force)	2018
xTechsearch (Army)	2018
Air Force-MIT AI Accelerator	2019
National Security Innovation Capital (NSIC) (under DIU)	2019
NavalX	2019
T3 Accelerator (Air Force)	2019
Techstars Allied Space Accelerator	2019
STRIKEWERX (Air Force)	2020
Space Force Works (SpaceWERX)	2021

Since DIU's founding in 2015 (originally called DIUx, for Defense Innovation Unit—Experimental), the DoD has seen a blossoming of innovation-oriented initiatives (see accompanying text box). (The DoD seems particularly enamored with Star Wars–themed names, such as Rogue Squadron and Kessel Run.) Many of these organizations are geared toward rapidly adopting commercial technology. Moving quickly, as Project Voltron did, and tapping into commercial companies, such as C3 AI, are essential for the military, which must rapidly adopt and militarize commercial technology if it is to stay ahead of competitors in key technologies, such as AI.

DIU and other new organizations are attempting to break the mold of how DoD operates. During its first five years, DIU brought on contract 120 "non-traditional" companies (which would not normally be considered defense contractors) and 60 companies that were new to working with the DoD entirely. One high-profile aspect of DoD's efforts to adopt AI was the establishment of the Joint AI Center, or JAIC, as a hub for AI across the department. The story of the JAIC demonstrates the many challenges—technical and bureaucratic—the Defense Department faces in adopting AI.

24

FOUNDATION

Project Maven turned out to be exactly what Deputy Secretary of Defense Bob Work had hoped for when he launched the project. Maven was a spark that ignited the spread of AI across DoD. Following Maven's success, in 2018 DoD founded the JAIC, which developed AI applications for predictive maintenance, humanitarian assistance, and back-office business processes. More significantly, though, JAIC helped initiate a process of creating institutional resources for AI for other parts of the military to tap into, accelerating the process of AI adoption across DoD.

The JAIC's creation was not preordained and was almost halted by what Pentagon insiders call "antibodies" in the bureaucracy—individuals who stand to lose from change and mobilize to stifle new initiatives. By late 2017, Maven was well under way and Brendan McCord, head of machine learning at DIU, drafted a white paper laying out the basic elements of a department-wide approach to AI. Pat Shanahan, who had taken over as deputy secretary of defense from Bob Work, embraced the paper's recommendations and directed that the department move forward, but the effort spawned what Brendan described as "a protective response" from the bureaucracy. Officials in the office of the under secretary of defense for research and engineering took control of the effort, spawning "this big, massive committee of 100 people—150 people" across the department, Brendan explained. The committee made little progress for months. Then, Michael Griffin took over as under secretary. He dismissed the committee's plan as "spaghetti on the wall." The committee's failure reopened the door to a revised plan. Brendan McCord, Michael Griffin, and Under Secretary of Defense for Intelligence Joseph Kernan took this new plan to Pat Shanahan for approval. One of Shanahan's "gatekeepers" who had been involved in the failed committee tried to undermine the meeting, at one point even attempting to block Kernan, a former SEAL, from entering the room, but Kernan insisted the meeting proceed. Shanahan was enthusiastic, "and so they agreed right then and there to do it and to build the Joint AI Center," Brendan said.

The JAIC was established in 2018 under the command of Lieutenant General Jack Shanahan (no relation to Deputy Secretary Pat Shanahan), who had previously run Project Maven. The JAIC first focused its attention on two "national mission initiatives": predictive maintenance and humanitarian assistance / disaster relief, which the military abbreviates by the awkward acronym HA/DR (sometimes pronounced "hadder"). Colonel Jason Brown, an Air Force intelligence officer, was placed in charge of the HA/DR initiative. By the end of 2018, he had a $20 million budget to develop AI tools for HA/DR and his team was off to the races. Brown's team decided to focus on domestic disasters because they're so common. The United States experiences floods and fires every year. That means "you have lots of data" and plenty of opportunities to apply the systems in the real world, he explained.

Wildfires was an early focus. Maven had already started a project working with the California Air National Guard on wildfire tracking, deploying an "on-prem" (on-premises) server capability to March Air Force Base in California in late 2018. The first step for Brown's team was developing a use case—the problem AI was intended to solve.

Before Maven arrived, if a wildfire broke out the California Air National Guard would deploy an MQ-9 Reaper drone to surveil the fire. Air Force intel analysts would then map the fire perimeter (the edge of the fire) by hand and send the data to Cal Fire firefighters on the ground. This was a time-consuming process. By the time the firefighters received the data, the information was hours old—often useless and even potentially dangerous if it sent them erroneously into the path of a swift-moving fire.

Jason Brown's team took multiple trips to California, including collecting data during a controlled burn in early 2019, to understand how AI could add value. Brown said they decided "the use case is: find the fire line. Know where the fire line is right now and know where the fire line is going." The JAIC's goal was to create a system that could convert the drone footage into a digital map layer that showed the fire's current location in real-time and send it out to a tablet for firefighters to access in the field. That way firefighters "could ultimately anticipate or reduce the timeline to allocate resources," Brown said. "It's kind of like using Waze," he explained. "Waze helps you with obstacles and opportunities, as you execute your transportation operation." Their intent was to do the same for wildfires, giving firefighters on the ground a real-time picture of how the fire was evolving.

From a technical standpoint, mapping the fire perimeter represented a different kind of computer vision task than what Maven had been doing, which was focused on object recognition. Object detection and recognition involved putting bounding boxes around objects and labeling them, but Brown explained, "You can't do that with a fire that spreads over many, many acres. . . . What you have to do instead is essentially you're painting." Rather than put a box around an object, the algorithm would "paint" the area covered by the fire.

Leveraging the existing Maven contract, the JAIC was able to quickly bring engineering talent onto the project. One of the companies was computer vision start-up CrowdAI, led by former Google employee Devaki Raj. One of *Forbes* 30 Under 30 in 2019, Raj founded CrowdAI to build "best in class computer vision algorithms," she said. Raj emphasized the importance of connecting algorithms to a specific use case. "We brought Cal Fire in the door from the first meeting," she explained. "I believe AI should be driven by the subject matter expert whose life will be benefited by it."

With CrowdAI, the JAIC had the talent, but they needed data. "The thing that we spent the most time on is data," Brown said. "You need data to train your models." Yet getting access to data, especially clean data that could be used to train a machine learning model, was no small feat. Brown and his team faced a raft of problems in gaining access to sufficient amounts of clean, labeled data to train their algorithms. Their experience demonstrates the many practical challenges with data, particularly in a bureaucracy like the Defense Department.

First, there were bureaucratic hurdles to overcome. The normal practice was for drone footage collected during domestic operations to be destroyed afterwards for intelligence oversight reasons. The JAIC needed policy waivers from the appropriate authorities in DoD to use the drone footage.

Then, some video files lacked the metadata necessary to use the images. The file metadata includes aircraft telemetry and sensor data, such as the aircraft's location and where the sensor is looking on the ground, which was needed to tie the images to an actual location on a map. Without the metadata, they simply had images of wildfires but had no ability to link the images to a real-world location.

Eventually, they were able to find 1.5 terabytes of drone footage of wildfires from the California Air National Guard that they could use. But they couldn't directly access the files. Even though the videos were on an unclassified network (designated For Official Use Only, or FOUO, by the DoD) and the JAIC wanted to transfer the files to another unclassified network, DoD cybersecurity protocols wouldn't allow them to transfer the files directly. So they downloaded the videos onto hard drives and mailed them instead (which, apparently, was acceptable).

The problems didn't end there. The data wasn't in a usable format for training a machine learning model. The video footage included the head-up display, or HUD, showing the drone's altitude, airspeed, direction, etc. The HUD data was "burnt into the video," Brown said, hampering their ability to train a machine learning model. "We need a clean picture, with no numbers, nothing on that video," Brown said. "It was not pristine data." The videos also included pre- and post-mission footage of the aircraft taking off and landing—and in some cases hours of footage of drones just sitting on the ground—which needed to be cut.

Accessing and cleaning the drone footage was just the starting point. Only then could the process of labeling the images begin so the algorithm could be trained to learn the difference between "fire" and "not fire." Again piggybacking off of Maven, the JAIC contracted with a data labeling company to label the images appropriately so that CrowdAI could build the semantic segmentation model to "paint" the video.

All told, it took six months to access, assemble, clean, label, and pre-process the data. "Once we had the labeled data set, we sent it over to the subcontractor, and they produced an initial model within two weeks," Air Force Captain Dominic Garcia said.

"Among all of these pieces and parts, the easiest is the algorithm," Colonel Jason Brown said. It was a point I repeatedly heard echoed by others across DoD. Jack Shanahan said, "The algorithm is always the easiest part." Lieutenant Colonel Isaac Faber of the Army AI Task Force explained it takes "just a few minutes" to develop a useful model, but it can take "six months" or more to access the data. "Finding data, conditioning data, building up business practices that give you consistent data in the condition that you need it . . . at the volume that you need, is really, really challenging," Brown explained. Major Matt Cook of the JAIC said, "A lot of folks are mesmerized by the idea and the mystique of the algorithm, . . . but it's having the quality of data . . . to build the algorithm that's going to be the 'X factor.'"

The centrality of data is a key feature of machine learning across any industry, but the challenges in acquiring data are particularly acute in the Defense Department, which is riddled with bureaucratic stove pipes that hinder data sharing. Brown explained that the Air Force logistics and engineering community alone had "359 disparate systems and databases," a significant fraction of which were written in COBOL, a programming language first developed in 1959. "We literally have taken COBOL coders out of retirement to operate and maintain these systems," he said. Nor are these problems unique to one military community. "There's 118 HR [human resources] databases in the Air Force, most of which are not cloud-enabled," Brown said. To harness AI's potential, DoD first needs to clean up its data policies and practices.

Despite these hurdles, by the summer of 2019, the JAIC had developed an early prototype of a fire perimeter model that could detect and map a wildfire. The system was not yet capable of pushing mapping data directly to a firefighter's tablet in the field, but it could accelerate decision timelines, shortening a process that used to take four to six hours to a few minutes. The team continued refinement, and in the fall of 2019 the JAIC's Fire Perimeter AI system began field testing with the California National Guard.

The JAIC's second disaster relief project entailed a suite of tools used for post-disaster assessment, including flood mapping, route analysis, and damage assessment. The team used satellite imagery from the National Oceanic and Atmospheric Administration (NOAA), DigitalGlobe, and DIU's xView2 challenge, which had compiled a labeled dataset of over 850,000 buildings around the world damaged by six different types of natural disasters. One model assessed the amount of flood or hurricane damage to buildings using Federal Emergency Management Agency (FEMA) standards. The AI model assessed building damage 300 times faster than the previously manual process of human analysts poring over satellite imagery. Another application used satellite imagery to map flooded areas, much like the JAIC had done for wildfires. And a third application plotted road obstructions for first responders to help them navigate through flooded areas. The JAIC's disaster relief tools were used by the National Guard in the wake of Hurricane Dorian, a Category 5 hurricane that hit the Bahamas in September 2019.

Applications like flood mapping and route finding had value for DoD, but even more important was working through the process of building a useful AI application that solved a problem. Effective institutions are needed to turn raw data into a useful form for training machine learning models. Several JAIC military officers described the early projects as creating the organizational "muscle memory" for how to apply AI to real-world problems. Jack Shanahan said, "The technology is important but more important to me is the culture change that came along with showing how to do this and then building an understanding of what an AI pipeline actually looks like." The secret sauce in using AI isn't the model itself, which is fairly easy to build, but successfully integrating it into military operations.

On that front, Shanahan saw major challenges. "When you're taking leading-edge technology such as AI and machine learning and you're bolting them on to legacy systems, legacy workflows, and legacy people, it plateaus very quickly," he said. "And that's what we saw with Maven."

During Shanahan's tenure, Maven and JAIC demonstrated the ability to build AI tools relatively quickly, but AI has yet to prove its value in the military. Shanahan told me in 2020, as he was coming up on retirement, "I think we're probably two years away from having the data where we would *begin* . . . to demonstrate the necessary return on investment. Like any new technology, you struggle at the beginning to show return on investment versus the capability you're replacing."

Many new technologies are clunky and awkward at first, and their immaturity often stands in stark contrast to the "game changing" claims made by wild-eyed believers. I recall a friend enthusiastically showing me a Palm Pilot in the late 1990s, and I was so unimpressed by the device that I couldn't share his vision that one day we would all have handheld computing devices. Yet by 2021, nearly half the world's population had a smartphone.

Shanahan's perspective was far from wild-eyed. He gave a sober and frank assessment of the military's progress on AI. "I'll be candid here: the [military] services are all talking about AI. I don't see it. I don't see much happening on the fielding side." Shanahan's skepticism is warranted. Then–Secretary of Defense Mark Esper claimed in 2019 that AI was his "number one" technology priority. Yet in terms of actual dollars, DoD spends approximately one percent of its budget on AI.

Shanahan worried about the consequences of AI projects in DoD not living up to the hype. "Every technology has a certain hype to it. It seems to be particularly egregious with AI for various reasons," he said. "Unfortunately, the combination of the hype and the lack of progress is going to result in some fatigue." Some of this dynamic may already be occurring. While Maven's ability to move quickly, bring in commercial tech and connect it to real-world operational problems was a game-changer from a bureaucratic and cultural standpoint, many experts I spoke with who were familiar with Maven said it had not revolutionized intelligence analysis. While Maven's tools were technically impressive, they were not (yet) delivering on AI's hype.

Shanahan said the most impactful work the JAIC had done was in "robotic process automation tools" ("I wouldn't even call it AI," he acknowledged). Rachael Martin, mission director for business process automation at the JAIC, explained that they were focused on using automation, analytics, and data augmentation to modernize business processes across the department to "either introduce efficiencies, or find cost savings, or find new insights, or be more predictive about the way that we conduct our business." Martin said that DoD finance and accounting offices have been "the most forward leaning in implementing automation" because they have a strong motivation to reduce human error to improve auditing and accountability. Another application used natural language processing to gain visibility on the thousands of issuances, policies, and directives across the DoD. Just as AI models such as GPT-3 could be used to generate new text, AI language models can also be used to process text. DoD has thousands of official policy documents and directives—so many that understanding what is inside all the documents is not easy. The documents currently exist as unstructured text and not in a central repository. Martin explained the automated policy analysis tool, called "Game Changer," would quickly analyze existing policies so that if a new one is being considered, one could find out, "How similar is this policy to other ones? . . . Are there interdependencies that we're not aware of? If I do this, what other policies would also need to be edited, or changed, or amended in some fashion?" Another project automatically formatted intradepartmental memos, reducing the amount of time a person might spend proofreading and formatting a memo from "an average of about 15 minutes" down to a few seconds. It sounds like a minor achievement, until one realizes that the DoD processes over 20,000 pieces of correspondence a year. Martin said, "The more that we can free up our military members to actually do warfighting functions as opposed to office functions, I think that we all win as a department overall."

Many of the military applications DoD is focusing on—predictive maintenance, image processing, or process automation—are back-office functions to support military operations, but that doesn't mean they are unimportant. A common military aphorism is that "amateurs talk tactics; professionals talk logistics." The vast majority of what the DoD does on a daily basis isn't actually warfighting. It's moving people and things from point A to point B. It looks a lot like what Walmart or Amazon does; it's what happens at the end that differs. Fighting wars is what makes the military unique from other organizations, but the vast majority of military activity is in support, headquarters, administrative, or logistics functions. Improving routine business operations has tremendous value for the DoD.

That doesn't mean warfighting advantages from AI are irrelevant. Some of DoD's early AI applications, especially in image processing, hint at AI's potential to accelerate targeting cycles in combat. Over the last few decades, militaries around the world have adopted precision-guided munitions that allow them to strike targets with great accuracy, yet precision-guided weapons require precise targeting data to be useful. The result has been to shift warfare away from a reliance on barrages of unguided (and relatively inaccurate) firepower toward battle networks that connect "sensors" to find enemy targets with "shooters" that take them out. AI can accelerate every part of this process, using distributed robotic sensors to detect enemy targets, AI to process information, and intelligent munitions to strike targets.

To move beyond niche applications, however, the Department of Defense will need to make AI as ubiquitous in its operations as computers are today. Nand Mulchandani, then chief technology officer at the JAIC, said he wanted to transform the JAIC into an enabler of AI across DoD. Mulchandani is a serial entrepreneur and CEO from Silicon Valley who cofounded four software infrastructure companies (which were acquired by Oracle, VMware, Cisco, and Centrix). Yet Mulchandani said, "This is the single hardest job I've ever had in my life, hands down." The problem, he argued, was the scale needed to bring AI to DoD.

One early JAIC project, in collaboration with researchers from Carnegie Mellon, was a predictive maintenance tool for helicopters from the 160th Special Operations Aviation Regiment. Mulchandani said, "That's fantastic that we did that for one engine, but how many engine types are there in the DoD?" He said he tells his teams, "Don't just do it once. Take the knowledge and information and scale it." The JAIC isn't large enough to do that directly themselves. To achieve scale, they'll need to empower others. "The JAIC shouldn't be in the engine health model business. We should be in the training-people-to-do-AI-for-their-engine business," Mulchandani said. Devaki Raj of CrowdAI agreed on the importance of giving people across DoD the tools to use AI. "We empower your workforce to build their own computer vision models for their workflow," she said.

To pivot JAIC from application developer to enabler for AI across DoD, JAIC invested in a cloud-based AI platform called the Joint Common Foundation, which can be used to develop AI models. JAIC teams also worked with organizations across DoD helping them improve their data management practices so they are "AI-ready." Transitioning DoD's data collection, management, and infrastructure practices so the department is ready to use AI will take time, but the JAIC worked to accelerate the process, spreading the lessons that they and Project Maven learned.

Yet the JAIC, DIU, and other DoD organizations can only bend the system so far. They can trim but cannot fully escape DoD's red tape. The biggest challenge the Defense Department faces isn't data, talent, algorithms, or even building an AI development pipeline—it's the acquisition system.

25

THE WRONG KIND OF LETHALITY

On the other side of DoD's innovation efforts are AI start-ups eager to work with the military. Deep Learning Analytics is a Washington, DC–area start-up acquired by General Dynamics, a major defense contractor. On the surface, DoD's ability to nurture the growth of an innovative start-up that was bought by a larger company sounds like a success story. Deep Learning Analytics had been the top American performer in several AI competitions to identify plants, animals, and fungi, and it won competitive defense contracts for automatic target recognition. Yet the company's experience shows the limits of working within a defense acquisition system that one robotics company executive described to me as "lethal to innovation." This was not the kind of "lethality" Secretary of Defense Jim Mattis had called for.

I met John Kaufhold, the founder of Deep Learning Analytics, in his office in Rosslyn, Virginia, just a few miles from the Pentagon. He was sporting an argyle vest and his hair sprouted skyward from his head like a mad scientist—not the image I expected of a defense contractor. John invited me to a small, two-person office nestled in a shared workspace called Eastern Foundry, a "coworking community" populated by various small government contractors. Before it was bought out by defense behemoth General Dynamics in 2019, Deep Learning Analytics had only a dozen people, yet it was an early leader in deep learning in the defense sector.

John started in the computer vision field twenty years ago, long before the deep learning revolution and back when, as he put it, "nothing worked." His career covered computer-assisted detection applications in medicine and national security, from improving 3D mammography to remotely scanning cargo containers coming into U.S. ports for contraband. He was doing deep learning with CPUs to map mouse brains before what he referred to as "the

Big Bang" in 2012, when Alex Krizhevsky, Ilya Sutskever, and Geoffrey Hinton published a paper showing groundbreaking performance on ImageNet. Before then, John explained, "It took a month to train" the models he was using and "error rates were poor." Yet he said, "The moment ImageNet happens, everybody in the computer vision community changed from whatever they were doing to deep learning, which was appropriate." John purchased GPUs and started working with deep convolutional neural networks. He also knew he had to scale up data labeling in a big way, but the lab in which he was working at the time wasn't supportive of the cost. So he founded his own deep learning company in 2013.

John admitted he didn't have a clear vision for an application or use case for the company. "I just knew I wanted to do machine learning," he said. "I knew that this big thing had just happened." John knew a DARPA program manager and they got to talking about the potential for neural nets to do target recognition for synthetic aperture radar, a type of military radar that could be used to image objects through clouds. The military had tried neural nets for target recognition back in the 1990s and it didn't work well, but John successfully made the case that something big had happened in the field of computer vision and it was worth trying again. DARPA gave him a small contract, around $300,000, for a six-month project to see if they could "even get close," John said, to the existing benchmarks for automated target recognition. He got access to a labeled dataset right away from the Air Force, and "six weeks in, we had basically outperformed the prior state-of-the-art," John said. The project's results got elevated to DARPA director Arati Prabhakar, and DARPA created the Target Recognition and Adaptation in Contested Environments (TRACE) program to see what could be done with more funding.

John was excited for their results, but DARPA establishing a formal program "was both good and bad for a startup," he explained. It was good in the sense that the start-up was doing well and showing results. "Bad part is if there is a DARPA program, and especially in an area where there hasn't been DARPA funding for a long time . . . everybody's going to show up." While John was confident in his company's technical abilities versus the competition, he was worried about his ability to meet the government's compliance criteria for competing on contracts. Established competitors would be better at jumping through government hoops.

On industry day for the TRACE program, a sort of town hall for companies interested in bidding on the projects to ask questions of DARPA, "There were over 100 people in the room," John said. They included "all the old hands" who had worked on military radar for years (and who John's algorithm had just outperformed). The competitors included major defense contractors such as Lockheed Martin, Northrop Grumman, Raytheon, and BAE. They had huge resources for managing the nontechnical aspects of government contracting. With just two total employees, Deep Learning Analytics had none.

However, Deep Learning Analytics did have better technology. "We didn't know anything about radar," John said, but "it turned out not to be as important as some of the other things" such as "knowing how to do deep learning well" and "a really disciplined software engineering approach." He said, "That's one of the recurring stories of . . . deep learning since 2012, is that domain expertise isn't always the thing that's going to matter so much. . . . The labeled data was sufficient." Deep Learning Analytics won a $6 million contract from DARPA for the TRACE program, beating out competitors that had better human expert knowledge on radar imaging. Now they suddenly had to grow the company. Yet John's first hire wasn't an engineer. His biggest concern wasn't technology; it was government contracting requirements. John hired a chief operating officer who had previously owned two IT companies that did government work to manage compliance.

Deep Learning Analytics next turned its attention to a DARPA program to help military personnel identify poisonous animals anywhere in the world. The goal was that if someone got bitten by a snake, for example, they could use an app to quickly ID whether or not the snake was venomous and if they might need urgent medical attention. The need for a labeled dataset of poisonous and nonpoisonous animals drew them to the iNaturalist challenge. Rather than train a model to identify the broad category "snake," which would not be helpful for determining whether or not the snake was poisonous, the iNaturalist challenge identified specific species.

From a technical standpoint, the iNaturalist challenge also pushed the boundaries in training models on sparse data. While the 2018 dataset included 450,000 images across 8,000 categories, the training images were not evenly distributed across categories. Some categories had hundreds of training images while rarer species had only a few dozen images. (For comparison, ImageNet's goal is an average of 1,000 images per category.) The sparseness of data was a significant hurdle, but also an important technical problem to solve for making machine learning models useful for applications that had limited data.

To compensate for the lack of data, John's team supplemented with human expert knowledge from the phylogenic tree, a branching diagram that shows the relationships between nearby species. They rewarded the AI model for answers in the same genus and family, even if it got the species wrong. In this case, human domain knowledge was a way to supplement a paucity of data.

Deep Learning Analytics came in second place in the 2018 iNaturalist challenge, the top U.S. entrant and beating out Chinese tech giant Baidu. China's Dalian University of Technology came in first. In 2019, Deep Learning Analytics, which by now had been bought by General Dynamics, came in third place. They were again the top U.S. contestant, beating Facebook, which at the time had the state-of-the-art performance in ImageNet. Chinese firms Megvii and Alibaba took first and second, respectively. John was understandably proud of his team's performance. They showed, "We have the data. We have the talent. We can do this and we can do it as well as the best in the world."

John and his team took their knowledge and, through small business innovation research (SBIR) grants from the government, built an app for deployed personnel to detect an animal's species. He pulled out a phone and showed me the app. He inputted a picture of a black widow spider. It came back with the correct answer: "*Latrodectus hesperus*," a Western black widow. Not only could their model correctly detect animal species, it could do so quickly on a mobile device.

Things were taking off. The company had eighteen months of booked revenue with the DARPA TRACE program. They were in the top four fastest-growing companies in Arlington, Virginia, three years in a row. Most important to John, "We were doing supervised deep learning." Unlike other companies merely marketing "AI," they were doing it.

Yet government contracting requirements remained their biggest obstacle. "As a small company, compliance with [federal acquisition regulations] ends up being the biggest killer of innovation and the biggest drag on real work by a team like ours," John explained. For example, because the company handled classified information, the government required the company to designate an employee as the facility security officer responsible for meeting security requirements for handling classified data. In the twelve-person company, the facility security officer was John, the founder. John said, "That's kind of insane." In a world of scarce AI talent, it was not a good use of human capital.

Complying with government regulations not only added cost and consumed valuable time; they prohibited the company from bidding on certain kinds of projects. "We just couldn't get in the door . . . because it costs money to put together some of the compliance structures," he said. "We could do the technical work." John characterized trying to meet government regulations as "the existential crisis that you'll deal with every day as a startup doing government contracting."

Devaki Raj of CrowdAI, which is a forty-person start-up, said, "There's a lot that is very unique to the government system that I needed to have a team around." As CrowdAI began to do more government work, she needed to bring onboard individuals who had experience with government contracts, adding an overhead burden to a small start-up. In addition to security clearances, companies need special government certifications for certain kinds of work, which can take time. "It takes a very long time to get FedRAMP certified," Raj said, referring to the Federal Risk and Authorization Management Program for certifying cloud computing providers for the federal government.

Eventually, the burden of government contracting requirements pushed John Kaufhold of Deep Learning Analytics to consider being acquired by a larger defense company that already had in-house dedicated teams for contract compliance. Being acquired by General Dynamics was "huge" in terms of solving these issues, he said. "There's a whole organization within General Dynamics" to address compliance issues like security, allowing his team to focus on machine learning.

John was "overjoyed" with how the acquisition has turned out, but the story of Deep Learning Analytics is a tragic one for the government. Through DARPA funding and small business grants, DoD was able to grow a start-up that beat some of the best AI companies in the world in international competitions. But the fact that an AI start-up felt it needed to be acquired by a major defense contractor in order to succeed is a major problem for the DoD. The department should be fostering an environment where start-ups have the potential to grow big on their own, to be the next AI "unicorns" (start-ups with a $1 billion valuation). Instead, government regulations are killing innovation.

26

JEDI

In principle, organizations like DIU are supposed to solve the kinds of problems Deep Learning Analytics faced by creating avenues around the traditional, stifling bureaucracy. On a small scale, it's working. In its first six years, DIU transitioned thirty-five commercial projects to the larger DoD. Each of these was a win, but their limited number indicates the bespoke nature of much of DoD's current innovation enterprise. DoD's next challenge is scaling innovation.

Jack Shanahan acknowledged the limitations of "the classic hack-the-bureaucracy organizations . . . like [Defense Digital Service], DIU, Kessel Run, AFWERX, SOFWERX, and elsewhere." While they've had impressive successes, "the challenges those organizations have is scaling. They don't scale very well across the Department of Defense," he said. "They're not leveraged business models. They take individual problems, they solve them, and they move on to the next one." The DoD is a sprawling enterprise, with a $700 billion-plus budget and over two million full-time military and civilian employees. Shanahan wanted the JAIC working on "solutions that can be scaled; not one-offs."

Nand Mulchandani worked to shift the JAIC toward a leveraged business model that can scale AI solutions across the department, yet the JAIC needed the right resources to do so. "What are the two things that AI really, really needs?" Mulchandani asked. "Well, it needs lots of data; it needs lots of compute."

Will Roper, who had been at Project Maven with Bob Work from the start, described DoD "hitting the infrastructure wall" as AI evolved. "The infrastructure was not there to do it at scale." Roper argued that "laying that digital foundation" for AI is essential. The JAIC and other DoD organizations were working to improve data practices across the department, but their access to large-scale compute resources was stymied by delays, protests, and lawsuits.

In 2017, a few weeks after then–Secretary of Defense Jim Mattis flew out to the West Coast to meet with Amazon's Jeff Bezos and other tech company execs, DoD launched an effort to accelerate adoption of cloud computing. The result was the Joint Enterprise Defense Infrastructure (JEDI) cloud project. In mid-2018, DoD released a request for proposals (RFP), an offer for companies to solicit bids, for a single-award (winner take all) contract for JEDI. The contract was worth up to $10 billion.

With that kind of money on the table, tech companies were playing for keeps.

Within days of the RFP being released, Oracle filed a protest with the Government Accountability Office, an independent watchdog agency in the government, challenging the terms of the RFP. A few months later, IBM did the same. Then Congress got involved, asking the DoD inspector general to review the RFP, claiming that the contract provisions "seem to be tailored to one specific contractor." (While the letter didn't mention which contractor, unnamed media sources alleged the contract had been written to favor Amazon.)

The GAO denied Oracle's protest and dismissed IBM's, but that was hardly the end of the story. The controversy was just beginning. Oracle filed a protest in the U.S. Court of Federal Claims, miring the contract in legal proceedings for months. Media articles swirled with rumors and allegations of improper dealing by Pentagon officials and claims, without evidence, of "swampy dealings" and a "rigged" process.

After seven months, the court denied Oracle's claim and ruled in favor of DoD. This left two horses in the race, the tech titans Amazon and Microsoft. Yet before DoD could make a decision, the White House pushed pause, with President Trump asking the Pentagon to review complaints of favoritism toward Amazon.

In October 2019, after multiple delays, DoD finally awarded the contract. Microsoft was the winner. But instead of ending, the fight over JEDI entered a new phase.

Amazon filed suit in federal court, claiming the selection process showed "unmistakable bias" and "political influence" against Amazon. (Ironically, prior to Microsoft winning the contract, Oracle and others had claimed the process was biased in *favor* of Amazon.) Amazon's lawsuit launched another round of delays. In February 2020, one day before DoD was set to issue its first task order to Microsoft, a federal judge halted any work on the project while Amazon's protest was considered.

DoD undertook an internal reevaluation of the contract and the DoD's inspector general reviewed the integrity of the selection process. In a sweeping investigation, including more than eighty interviews and over 30 gigabytes of emails, documents, and memoranda, the DoD Office of the Inspector General concluded that the process for developing and awarding the contract followed appropriate laws and policies. While Trump's antipathy toward Amazon and Jeff Bezos was well known publicly, investigators determined that "DoD personnel who evaluated the contract proposals . . . were not pressured regarding their decision on the award." There were no "swampy dealings." In September 2020, after what DoD said was a "comprehensive re-evaluation" of the companies' proposals, DoD once again awarded the contract to Microsoft, nearly a year after the original award. Amazon announced they would "continue to protest this politically corrupted contract award."

As President Trump departed the Oval Office and a new administration took over, the JEDI contract remained mired in legal proceedings, unable to proceed. DoD officials began to hint that they would move on from JEDI given its seemingly endless legal battles. Finally in July 2021, the Pentagon cancelled the JEDI contract.

Simultaneous with JEDI's cancellation, DoD announced they would pursue a new "multi-cloud/multi-vendor" contract to meet the department's cloud computing needs. DoD asked Amazon, Microsoft, Google, and Oracle to bid on the contract. With over three and a half years wasted, DoD was back to square one. Not because of technology problems, but because of an acquisition system that allows companies who lose contracts to halt progress through protests and lawsuits.

Protesting DoD contracts is so common that it is expected. Before awarding a major contract, DoD officials brace for the inevitable protest, which they anticipate regardless of who wins or loses. After the Air Force awarded the contract for a new stealth bomber to Northrop Grumman, Boeing protested the decision to the GAO. They lost the protest, but sometimes companies succeed in overturning a contract decision. Boeing protested a 2008 decision for a new tanker aircraft and the GAO upheld their protest, causing DoD to cancel the contract and start over. Boeing won the renewed contract in 2011. In 2021, after the National Security Agency awarded a cloud computing contract worth up to $10 billion to Amazon, Microsoft filed a protest with the GAO.

Protesting is endemic to government contracting. In fiscal year 2020, the GAO received over 2,000 protests, over 70 percent of which it immediately denied or dismissed as without merit. Most of the rest were considered and denied. GAO sustained less than 5 percent of the protests. Spurious and ill-founded protests aren't the exception; they are the rule, the result of a well-meaning process for accountability that has run amok.

Protests can generate years of delays, further slowing an already cumbersome acquisition system. I asked Nand Mulchandani whether the JEDI contract delay had hindered the JAIC's progress. "No question," he said. "You can't really build out at scale the other things that are dependent on the core platform infrastructure. . . . There are other alternative pseudo-cloud platforms inside the DoD that we're able to work off of and get stuff ready, but we're going to have to duplicate work. . . . That's just adding cost and adding time and delays, no question about it."

The DoD's acquisition system prioritizes minimizing the risk of fraud and abuse, a worthy goal, but at the cost of sacrificing speed and agility. The problems DoD faces in scaling innovation aren't due to an inability to write multi-billion-dollar contracts or even its ability to compete them fairly. It's due to a web of institutions, including those outside DoD at the GAO, Congress, and the courts, that incentivize companies to apply a scorched-earth approach to winning big-dollar federal contracts, even if it harms national security. Small-scale innovation often works because there is less at stake. When DoD tries to scale to big dollars, too often innovation gets swallowed by a system designed for quagmire. In the case of JEDI, years of delays harmed DoD's ability to build out the compute infrastructure it needs for AI and other applications.

There has been progress toward reform. During her tenure as under secretary for acquisitions and sustainment from 2018 to 2021, Ellen Lord led a "total rewrite" of defense acquisition policy, "narrowing it down to the fundamentals," she said. DoD has also expanded its use of "other transaction" authorities, more than doubling their use from 2016 to 2018. Other transaction authority, sometimes called OTA, is a contract mechanism used for prototyping, R&D, or production that is exempt from many acquisition laws and regulations, making it a more flexible tool for the government to move quickly. (OTAs may still be protested in the U.S. Court of Federal Claims and the GAO has some limited jurisdiction.) OTAs have been particularly valuable in expanding the government's access to commercial companies. A GAO report found that 88 percent of DoD's OTA contracts from 2016 to 2018 were with companies that did not traditionally work with DoD. OTAs also allow for the possibility of scaling up to large contracts with reduced potential for protests. When the Army contracted with Microsoft in 2021 to supply augmented reality headsets based on its HoloLens—a deal worth up to $22 billion—the Army used an OTA.

These reform efforts are starting to pay off, and DoD has had some success in helping start-ups scale prototypes up to larger production contracts. In 2021, DIU helped AI start-up Anduril transition a prototype for an AI-based counter-drone system to a nearly $100 million OTA production agreement, which was later followed by a nearly $1 billion contract award from Special Operations Command. Other DIU successes include growing a C3 AI prototype to a $500 million production deal with the Missile Defense Agency and the drone company Skydio turning a small drone prototype award into a nearly $100 million production OTA with the Army. To take full advantage of commercial sector innovation, DoD will need to build on these successes, demonstrating to start-ups and investors that DoD can be a viable pathway for growing a successful start-up.

27

DISRUPTION

If the United States has a jump start on other nations in incorporating AI into defense, it is only a slight advantage and one that is likely to be fleeting as AI technology proliferates. This is an uncomfortable position for the U.S. military, which since the 1970s has banked on superior technology over its adversaries. In extreme circumstances, such as when British troops faced off against Sudanese Dervishes in the Battle of Omdurman, an overwhelming technological advantage can be decisive. But such a decisive edge is rare.

In an analysis of medium- to high-intensity land wars from 1956 to 1992, military scholar Stephen Biddle found that the median technology difference was less than three years between opponents. (The 1991 Gulf War is a notable outlier with a twelve-year technology gap between U.S. and Iraqi forces.) When militaries have approximate technological parity, how militaries use their forces is more important than any incremental technological advantage. This reality was on stark display when Russia invaded Ukraine in early 2022, when the much larger and more modern Russian military was stymied by Ukrainian defenders, in part because of poor Russian planning, communication, execution, and morale. Even as the United States works to rapidly adopt new technologies, it also needs to foster institutions that, like the Naval War College did in the interwar period, experiment with new technologies to discover the best ways of using them.

Yet changing how it fights has been a challenge for the U.S. military, which for the past three decades has experienced unparalleled military dominance over competitors. That advantage is waning as China has undertaken aggressive reforms to grow and modernize its military. For most of the last two decades, the U.S. military's response has been to ask for more money—despite a massive post-9/11 budget increase—to fund more of the same kinds of weapons to fight with the same outdated tactics, despite the fact that China has been investing in "anti-access" capabilities to keep U.S. forces at bay. Slowly, U.S. complacency toward a rising China is ebbing, and the Pentagon is starting to undertake much-needed reforms and adapt to new technologies and threats.

The DoD has had impressive success with showy prototypes and competitions, like AlphaDogfight, but to truly capitalize on AI it will need to turn these proof-of-concept demonstrations into real military capabilities. I visited Heron Systems, whose AI agent Falco had won AlphaDogfight, to see what the scrappy start-up that had bested some of the biggest defense companies in the industry had planned next.

Brett Darcey, Heron Systems' vice president and general manager, met me at one of their R&D labs in Old Town Alexandria on the banks of the Potomac River. He walked me through their unlikely rise from a mom-and-pop defense contractor to a cutting-edge AI innovator. The company began as a family-owned business started by Darcey's parents. They had twenty to thirty employees and two to three million dollars a year in revenue doing test and evaluation for the Navy at Naval Air Station Patuxent River (Pax River) in Maryland. Then in 2011, they won a small business research innovation contract to improve radar performance. "I made the fateful decision at that time to try out neural networks as the technical approach," Darcey said. The timing was "very fortuitous," he admitted, coming at the start of the deep learning revolution.

Even though neural networks were very new, Heron Systems had an edge in one of the most valuable inputs: data. The company's experience in testing meant they had written the software that took in the live flight data. "We did all the data processing. We knew what data was there as a source," Darcey said. They used a method published in a paper by an Israeli researcher and hired a dedicated machine learning engineer. The company began to grow its AI work, picking up another contract from the Air Force to use machine learning to predict solar flares, which could disrupt satellites. Through these projects, the company began to build a "robust data pipeline and the compute underneath it" to create a "production capability" for machine learning, Darcey explained. Contracts from NASA and DARPA for swarming followed, but Darcey said that for several years DoD funding lagged the technology. "DoD's behind, usually, the adoption of these kinds of forward-leaning technologies," he said. "We were proposing to do things that no one was really asking to do quite yet." DoD funders "weren't knowledgeable of the technology yet to trust it." An additional factor, Darcey said, was the fact that the company was an unknown quantity. "Who the heck has heard of Heron Systems?" he pointed out. The combination of being an unknown company peddling an untrusted technology was a steep hill to climb. "How do you justify not only that you're really good at what you do and that they can trust you to do it, but also that this technology that no one has heard of is a valid thing? You're asking them to take on a lot of risk." Many program managers preferred to stick with traditional defense contractors using well-trod engineering methods. "We were a riskier bet," he admitted.

Yet the company's engineers kept working on AI methods they believed showed promise. On "Fun Fridays," when engineers got to work on their own pet projects, they used reinforcement learning to train bots to play *Doom*, the classic '90s first-person shooter video game. DeepMind's AlphaGo and AlphaStar, which achieved breakthroughs in *go* and *StarCraft* in 2016 and 2019, respectively, "helped us a ton," Darcey said. "What that did was, it immediately said to DARPA, 'No, this tech's coming now, and we can't be surprised by it.'"

The company got its big break when they traveled to Vegas to pitch DARPA to join the AlphaDogfight competition. During their presentation they had a GIF of one of their *Doom* bots running in the background. The DARPA program manager asked them six questions about the *Doom* bot, and later told them, "Man, once we saw the *Doom* bot, we're definitely picking those guys." The *Doom* bot wasn't just a stunt. Darcey explained it impressed DARPA because "it was a winning implementation of [reinforcement learning] at a time when no one outside of DeepMind had really shown it."

Once they got into the competition, the company's experience in machine learning paid off. "The fundamental reason why we won the AlphaDogfight trials is we were able to cycle our experiments faster than anybody else," Darcey said. They built a "training factory" running computer simulations of dogfights 24/7 using a "competitive league" of 110 agents. Some of the agents were generalists, with the goal of performing well against a variety of adversaries. Some were exploiters, trained to do one thing very well, like fight low and slow. Some were adversary agents trained just to defeat one agent. The key, though, was an efficient engineering process that allowed massive amounts of simulations to train the agents over time. The winning agent had thirty-one years of flight time. It also had "109 friends," Darcey said, helping to improve the agent's performance. "We had a more robust production process than anybody else," he said. And that translated into more experienced agents. When the AlphaDogfight competition kicked off, opposing AI agents were totally unprepared for the AI agent Falco's main tactic, the head-on gunshots. They had never seen it before in their training simulations and didn't know how to defend against it. Yet it wasn't a tactic that had been programmed into the Heron Systems agent. It simply had emerged out of the training process.

AlphaDogfight was a game changer, not just for Heron Systems but also for interest in AI across DoD. "My phone was ringing off the hook from everybody," Darcey said. "They all wanted to know . . . What is the industry actually capable of?" People stopped saying, "Can AI do anything?," he said, and switched to "What can AI do?" Darcey said now he has to reel DoD program managers back in when their expectations are unrealistic. "Their minds are going like full Star Trek," he said.

Heron Systems tripled in size and was bought by Shield AI, a move Darcey said has helped open doors for bigger government contracts and partnerships with other defense companies. The company is doing follow-on work with DARPA's ACE program, working to move AI agents out of simulations and into real-world flight testing. The long-term goal is an AI copilot that will control the plane while the human pilot is overseeing battle management tasks, doing the higher-level functions that only a human can do. The company continues to improve its AI agents, taking on bigger challenges such as 2v2 dogfights. In the background during our meeting, I could hear the whir of fans cooling dozens of GPUs in a server room running simulations 24/7, the "training factory" at work.

Heron Systems is just one example of the many AI defense start-ups that are attempting to navigate their way through the government's contracting maze to deliver innovative solutions. It's an impressive success story, but there remain many roadblocks to new companies and technologies working with the Defense Department. The military contest in AI is less a contest to build and field a new technology than a contest to reform institutions faster to take advantage of AI's opportunity.

China is also aggressively working to reform its military institutions to adopt AI, creating DIU-like organizations to spin-in commercial technologies and "intelligentize" its military forces. Elsa Kania, an adjunct senior fellow at the Center for a New American Security and author of *Fighting to Innovate: The Future of Chinese Military Power,* said that the PLA is working hard to overcome its "traditionalist," "hidebound" culture and innovate faster. Kania said the PLA was highly motivated to adopt AI "because China has a history of technological backwardness and is so fearful of technology surprise and falling behind." Whereas for the United States, Kania said, "We can't imagine losing leadership in technology because we've had it for modern history."

Kania cited Xi Jinping's public praise of PLA drone pilots as an example of the Chinese leadership's endorsement of new technology. "At least as portrayed in PLA media, and the portrayal may not be necessarily equivalent to reality, many of the PLA's drone pilots for the PLA Air Force's first drone unit were former top pilots who had won contests in the PLA, who were seen as crack pilots," she said. PLA media ran several features on one of the PLA's top drone pilots, including a cartoon about him. The message from Chinese senior leadership, Kania explained, was "'This is the future. This is something that is important and exciting, and something that is attracting the top people.'" That may not reflect reality, Kania acknowledged, but it is indicative of how the PLA leadership wants Chinese citizens to view drones and other emerging technologies. By contrast, U.S. drone pilots have often been treated as second-class citizens in the Air Force. They have not been awarded the same promotion opportunities and are not eligible for the same combat medals, despite their far more important role in recent conflicts than traditional fighter pilots.

Kania argued China's top-down political system gave it some advantages in overcoming bureaucratic obstacles that exist to change in the United States. "The PLA is the Party's army. The Party controls the gun," Kania said. "So if Xi Jinping says, 'Go forth and pursue intelligentization,' it becomes something that everyone, at least rhetorically, at least superficially, is endorsing."

There are important asymmetries between the U.S. and Chinese political and military institutions and cultures that affect their ability to reform. One major advantage for the United States is that it draws from a bottom-up military culture that empowers junior leaders and a national ecosystem rich with entrepreneurs. Strategist Hal Brands of Johns Hopkins University has contrasted this with China's limitations: "When it comes to innovation, an autocracy can throw massive resources at particular technologies or problems, but it is hard to unleash the creativity of a society over the long term without allowing the intellectual—and thus political—freedom that the party dreads." Xi Jinping's efforts to rein in China's tech companies is likely to have a chilling effect on innovation in China's commercial tech ecosystem, but the CCP has successfully balanced technology innovation and political control for several decades. While there are tensions between these goals, the CCP has managed to grow world-class technology companies even while building a highly effective censorship and propaganda apparatus for controlling information inside China.

Kania was skeptical that China's authoritarian system would necessarily curtail innovation in the PLA. "You can have innovation occur without people being happy and freely creative and living their best lives," she said. "People can also be motivated by nationalism." While mistrust and political indoctrination create "friction and constraints," Kania said, "that doesn't mean that we won't see certain elements of adaptation or innovation." The obstacles to AI adoption in the U.S. system, Kania pointed out, "are not that we're not democratic enough, but that our organizations don't create conditions for change."

The biggest challenges the U.S. government faces in adopting military AI are self-imposed. When the Maven controversy exploded in 2018, DoD leaders panicked that they would be shut out of AI technology and fall behind China. Yet the reality couldn't be further from the truth. There are plenty of companies eager to work with DoD, from start-ups such as Anduril, Applied Intuition, C3 AI, Clarifai, CrowdAI, Heron Systems, Percipient.AI, Primer, Rebellion Defense, Scale AI, Shield AI, and SparkCognition to established tech firms such as Amazon, Microsoft, Oracle, and even Google. In the case of JEDI, the holdup was from companies fighting over who got the opportunity to win a defense contract, not a lack of willing partners.

I asked Devaki Raj whether employees at CrowdAI had raised concerns about working with the military on computer vision. She said, "We have ethics discussions on everything that we work on. . . . It's really important that we are transparent." Raj said her team comes from a diverse array of backgrounds, ranging from former infantry soldiers to those with no connection to the military. "We have these conversations that are open to the team about why what we do is important," she explained.

The company's biggest obstacle to working with the Defense Department was contracting. CrowdAI has worked on several DoD AI projects, yet "it's not a very clear path" to get to the point where there is stable, multiyear funding to institutionalize an AI project, Raj said. AI pilot projects often struggle to cross what defense experts refer to as the "valley of death" between one-off prototypes and fully funded long-term DoD programs. Not only is having a stable funding stream essential for a start-up; it is also vital for the success of an AI program. "You can't just buy 'set it and forget it' software," Raj said. "You're going to be setting up yourself for failure." For an AI project to succeed, "AI needs to adapt" over time, she explained. DoD needs to sign contracts with "a licensing business model that enables retraining to make sure that the AI model keeps up with mission and sensor changes." She argued it's essential to have "the ability to, year over year, work with the customer and build that product together . . . [so] they actually can use it."

Will Roper, who went on to serve as the Air Force's chief acquisition officer, acknowledged that "it's a huge uphill battle" for a start-up to work with the DoD. "Even if the startup was able to get in and work with you," he said, the DoD's two-year budgeting cycle "would send that startup someplace else."

The obstacles to scaling innovation harm DoD in multiple ways. It slows down innovation, creating months or years of delays. These delays are particularly costly given the relatively level playing field globally for AI innovation. While U.S. national security experts fret over the progress China's military is making on AI adoption, the U.S. bureaucracy is squandering what little lead the United States has. But the damage runs deeper. While big tech companies like Google, Oracle, Amazon, and Microsoft can weather the lawsuits and delays, such disruptions can be lethal to small start-ups who need constant revenue to stay afloat. Start-ups may decide they can't handle the overhead costs associated with complying with government contracting burdens. Or they may not be able to successfully cross the valley of death to land a long-term multiyear stable source of funding from the DoD. Or they may die waiting, starved of the revenue they need to grow by a government process that is too slow. These obstacles have a compounding effect on start-ups by harming their ability to get venture capital funding. All of these problems contribute to locking the DoD out of its ability to tap into a vibrant technology base in the United States.

Will Roper connected the DoD's lack of progress on digital technologies to its focus on platforms: ships, airplanes, and tanks. The Pentagon is "still very much caught in a hardware-centric frame of mind," he said. When military leaders advocate to Congress for a larger budget, they make their case in terms of industrial-age metrics. Navy leadership has argued for a fleet of 355 ships, the Air Force for 386 operational squadrons of aircraft, and the Army for 500,000 troops. These metrics are reflective of a pre-digital, industrial mindset. They are the equivalent of assessing military power in World War II only by measuring troop strength, without assessing how many ships, tanks, or planes a country could produce. The metrics of military power have changed in the digital age, but the Pentagon has yet to adjust. Ships, airplanes, tanks, and ground troops still matter, but what matters more is their digital capabilities: sensors to detect enemy forces, algorithms to process data, networks to transmit information, command-and-control to make decisions, and intelligent munitions to strike targets. Roper said the DoD should be focusing on "decision superiority . . . but it's not the way the budget's built."

DoD is making incremental progress on reform, but it is in a race to innovate faster than competitors. To stay ahead, DoD will need the support of Congress and the White House to reform itself to move faster, take risks, and operate differently. As they look to do so, defense leaders could take a page out of their AI agents' playbook. After our interview, I sat down in Heron Systems' flight simulator and donned a virtual reality helmet to go head-to-head against their AI agent in a simulated F-16. If an experienced Air Force fighter pilot couldn't beat Falco, I wasn't expecting success. I have no experience flying planes or even simulators. Yet to my total surprise, I won the first engagement. In fact, I won the fight before I'd barely begun flying. My AI copilot fired two missiles and shot down the enemy before I even realized what was happening. While I was still trying to catch up, the AI was already winning.

PART VII
ALCHEMY

28

CONTROL

The AlphaPilot drone looked like a cross between an F-117 stealth fighter and a Cylon Centurion, the metal killer robot from the reimagined mid-2000s *Battlestar Galactica* TV show. The small quadcopter had a glowing triangular cyclops eye on the front. Each team's drone was a different color, radiating purple, white, red, teal, and neon green.

At the start of the race, the drones were perched atop glowing pedestals reminiscent of the 1980s sci-fi movie *Tron*. The race began and the purple drone lifted off its pedestal and glided forward. The crowd leaned in, waiting for the drone to fly all by itself autonomously weaving through obstacles, outperforming humans and dazzling with its intelligence. Instead, the drone flopped onto the floor. As if it had simply given up.

The next drone did little better. It passed through the first two race gates, then strayed off course and careened into the safety net between the audience and the course. The red drone plowed directly into the first gate and crashed. The teal drone cleared the first two gates and closed cautiously in on gate three before going wide and clipping the wall and crashing.

Last in the heat was the green drone. It jetted off the podium and raced through the first gate. A murmur of excitement ran through the crowd. Then the drone spun wildly and crashed into the third gate.

One by one, in each heat of the race, the drones failed, sometimes in dramatic ways. One skyrocketed to the ceiling before plummeting back to earth and crashing. Another simply fell off the podium onto the ground.

I had attended the AlphaPilot drone racing league event hoping to see yet another milestone in AI development, in which AI pilots surpassed humans in indoor drone racing. Instead, it was a stark reminder of an unfortunate reality: sometimes AI systems don't work very well.

Eventually, one drone successfully completed the relatively simple U-shaped course. To drive home the point about how far AI-powered drones still have to go, after the autonomous drones were done a human drone pilot took the stage to show off his skills. Under his control, his remotely piloted bright yellow racing league drone flew loops over and around the gates to the awe of the audience. Professional drone racing pilot Gabriel "Gab707" Kocher said he was "really impressed" by the progress made by programmers but acknowledged that the best AI couldn't match "even a half-decent run from a human" pilot. AI's gap in drone racing was especially jarring given that the circumstances favored AI. The racing course was indoors, in a controlled environment, with visual markers the drones could identify on the gates they had to pass through. Yet most of the teams' drones failed.

For all their impressive performance, AI systems still fall short of humans in many ways. AI systems can often excel in digital environments but struggle in real-world situations. Colonel Dan "Animal" Javorsek, who led DARPA's AlphaDogfight competition in which an AI defeated a human fighter pilot (in a simulation), acknowledged this problem when discussing the challenges in moving to live flight demonstrations. "Managing this transition to the real world is a critical test for most AI algorithms," he said. "In fact, prior efforts have been brittle to just these types of transitions because some solutions can be over reliant on digital artifacts from the simulation environment."

AI technology is powerful, yet its power is a brittle one, subject to collapse in an instant. Rule-based AI systems can only do what they've been programmed to do. Machine learning systems can only do what they've been trained to do. Subtle biases in training data can lead machine learning systems to perform poorly in the real world.

AI systems today have a narrow form of intelligence. An AI system may exhibit superhuman performance for certain tasks, but if the conditions of the task or the environment changes even slightly, the AI system's performance can decline dramatically. This narrowness is a major limitation of AI today, and it comes up again and again in different AI systems. An algorithm programmed to play one Atari game can't play other games. AlphaGo reportedly could not play well if the game area is larger or smaller than the 19×19 board on which it was trained.

Failures in real-world applications can cause harm. Advanced autopilot features in cars may drive safer than humans in some contexts but have driven without warning into a concrete barrier, a parked car, and a semitrailer, causing multiple fatalities. In the wrong situation, AI systems can go from super smart to super dumb in an instant.

Military and national security AI systems are not immune to these vulnerabilities. In fact, these risks are often heightened in a national security context
which is inherently adversarial and in which the stakes are often life and death.
These limitations are a major challenge for nations as they use AI for national
security. Countries run the risk of fielding AI systems they don't fully understand and that may be prone to accidents.

In his office overlooking Ballston, Virginia, Phil Root, the deputy director
of the Defense Sciences Office at DARPA, told me the story of an experiment
that painfully illustrated these limitations. The program was DARPA's Squad
X, which Phil described as having the goal of creating technologies to allow
small units to "dominate their local battle spaces." DARPA developed an AI-
based object recognition algorithm as part of this program with the aim of
identifying people in complex, urban environments.

Phil said this was a "very hard problem" because humans have "a huge
amount of variability." He explained, "A tank looks like a tank, even when it's
moving. A human when walking looks different than a human standing. A
human with a weapon looks different." To improve their algorithm, the DARPA
team spent a week with a group of Marines out at a test site. For six days, the
Marines walked around and the engineers refined their algorithm for detecting
people. Phil said, "On the seventh day I said, 'We're done. We're flipping it.'"

Now the Marines would try to defeat the AI system. They parked the robot
in the middle of a traffic circle and the Marines had to approach it undetected
starting from a long distance away. "If any Marines could get all the way in and
touch this robot without being detected, they would win. I wanted to see, game
on, what would happen."

"Eight Marines—not a single one got detected," Phil said. They defeated the
AI system not with traditional camouflage, but with clever tricks that were outside of the AI system's testing regime. "Two somersaulted for 300 meters; never
got detected. Two hid under a cardboard box. You could hear them giggling
the whole time." Like Bugs Bunny in a Looney Tunes cartoon, sneaking up on
Elmer Fudd in a cardboard box. "One guy, my favorite," Phil said, "he field-
stripped a fir tree and walked like a fir tree. You can see his smile, and that's
about all you see." The AI system had been trained to detect humans walking,
not humans somersaulting, hiding in a cardboard box, or disguised as a tree.
So these simple tricks, which a human would have easily seen through, were
sufficient to break the algorithm.

The problem isn't that AI systems don't work. The problem is that they
do work, and they can often work quite well, but when pushed outside the

boundaries of their design, they can suddenly and unexpectedly fail. Even worse, AI engineers themselves may not know ahead of time the boundaries of a system's behavior. Because those designing AI systems are creating powerful tools that they themselves don't fully understand.

In 2017, a prominent AI researcher claimed at a conference that machine learning was "alchemy." It wasn't entirely pejorative. "Alchemy worked," he pointed out. "Alchemists invented metallurgy, ways to make medication, dying techniques for textiles, and our modern glass-making processes." The problem was that alchemists lacked an accurate scientific model for how these processes worked, so they didn't truly understand what they were doing. Ali Rahimi was accepting the "test of time" award at the Neural Information Processing Systems conference, the largest AI conference in the world. But by calling AI alchemy he wanted to acknowledge the reality of some of the challenges in the field. "If you're building photo sharing services, alchemy is fine," he said. "But we're now building systems that govern health care and our participation in civil debate. I would like to live in a world whose systems are built on rigorous, reliable, verifiable knowledge, and not on alchemy."

AI scientists struggle to fully understand AI systems because of the massive complexity of the contemporary systems they are building, such as neural nets with hundreds of millions of parameters. The complexity of AI systems means they can sometimes exhibit surprising behaviors. The fatal crashes of two 737 MAX airliners arose from rule-based systems interacting in unpredictable ways with the environment and human operators, who despite being highly qualified were baffled by the machine's behavior. In machine learning systems, failures can arise at multiple stages of the learning process, including from flawed training data or a mis-specified goal.

There are three main types of machine learning. In supervised learning, an algorithm is trained on labeled data. For example, an image classification algorithm may be trained on labeled pictures. Over many iterations, the algorithm learns to associate the image with the label. Unsupervised learning is when an algorithm is trained on unlabeled data and the algorithm learns patterns in the data. Large language models such as GPT-2 and GPT-3 use unsupervised learning. Once trained, they can output sentences and whole paragraphs based on patterns they've learned from the text on which they've been trained. Reinforcement learning is when an algorithm learns by interacting with its environment and gets rewards for certain behaviors. Many AI agents that play computer games learn by reinforcement learning, getting feedback for actions that rack up a higher score.

One way in which machine learning systems can fail is if the training data does not sufficiently represent the AI system's operating environment. Alpha-Go's inability to adjust to a differently sized board and the Marines defeating DARPA's AI detection system are both examples of AI systems reacting poorly to what researchers call "distributional shift." The model is trained on one set of data and then presented with data that is different (shifted) from the training data. If the model is not robust to these changes it can fail. Even worse, deep learning systems are often overconfident about their predictions on inputs that are shifted from training data. Neural networks don't know what they don't know. AI researchers are working to improve robustness and address overconfidence, but at present these are practical challenges in using deep learning systems in the real world.

"Distributional shift failures" point toward the broader problem of the inability of AI systems to generalize what they have learned. Humans can learn one example then generalize to a broader set of hypothetical scenarios by drawing on a rich understanding of the world. AI systems have a shallow "world model." Their intelligence is brittle. The DARPA Squad X algorithm that had been trained to detect humans walking lacked a rich understanding of humans, patterns of movement, camouflage, and deception, making it vulnerable to simple tricks that fooled the algorithm. Its understanding of "humans" and "walking" was limited solely to the data on which it had been trained. It had no capacity to even recognize, let alone interpret and understand, a human somersaulting or hiding under a box.

These limitations of AI's narrowness are exacerbated by the tendency of humans to extrapolate AI performance on one task to related tasks, or what MIT robotics professor Rodney Brooks has called "mistaking performance for competence." Humans interacting with AI systems are primed to expect a model of intelligence that roughly approximates our own. For example, we would not expect a human who can drive safely in traffic to suddenly steer toward a concrete barrier. Yet even AI systems that outperform humans in narrow tasks have no understanding of the tasks they are performing. Deep Learning Analytics' naturalist app may be able to identify spiders more accurately than most humans, but it lacks any understanding of what a "spider" is. Despite these limitations, AI systems may be valuable tools for aiding humans in various tasks, provided humans correctly understand the bounds of the system's behavior. Yet knowing when and how AI systems will fail is both a technical challenge and one exacerbated by human psychology.

Another problem that can arise with AI systems is if they learn things other than what was intended. This can happen for a variety of reasons, because of flaws in the data, how data is presented to the algorithm, or how the algorithm's goals are specified.

Models can learn real patterns that exist in data but that the designer may not wish to encode into the model. For example, language models frequently exhibit gender, racial, and religious biases (among other forms of bias) in their output, reflecting biases that exist in the internet text on which they've been trained. Biases can sometimes manifest in surprising ways. Prior to a correction in 2018, Google Translate demonstrated gender bias in some translations. Turkish uses gender-neutral pronouns; "*o bir doktor*" in Turkish could mean "he is a doctor" or "she is a doctor" in English. Yet Google Translate always returned "he is a doctor." Conversely, Google Translate translated "*o bir hemşire*" to "she is a nurse." These biases reflect real asymmetries in the gender distribution of nurses and doctors in the United States. Over 60 percent of doctors in the United States are male and nearly 90 percent of nurses are female. Yet users may not want an AI model that reinforces existing social biases. (Google now gives users the option to choose the gender for gender-specific translations.)

Models can develop subtle biases that may be harder to identify. In 2015, Amazon created a résumé-sorting model that developed a bias against women applicants. The model had been trained to identify traits of desirable employees based on prior résumés. Amazon's workforce, as of 2017, was 60 percent male overall. (In many major tech firms, the workforce is even more predominantly male in technical roles.) The résumé-sorting algorithm reportedly learned to penalize résumés that included the word "women's," such as if an applicant stated she had played on a "women's basketball team." The algorithm also reportedly downgraded graduates of two all-women's colleges. Amazon ultimately scrapped the algorithm, which the company said "was never used by Amazon recruiters to evaluate candidates."

Learning systems will sometimes find shortcuts to meet their goals. In one case, a neural network that was supposed to discriminate between positive and negative inputs simply learned to exploit a pattern in how the data was presented. Researchers were alternating positive and negative inputs to the AI system, so the neural network simply learned to alternate from the previous input, rather than learn how to discriminate between the two inputs.

AI systems sometimes learn clever hacks for solving problems in novel ways. Simulated digital creatures have evolved clever ways of falling to achieve their movement goals without actual locomotion or jumping. Simulated robots competing for food spontaneously evolved deception and concealment tactics to outwit competitor robots. An algorithm in a boat-racing game learned that the optimal scoring strategy was not to race at all but to perform tight loops through auto-renewing targets mid-course, racking up more points than was possible from completing the race.

AI systems are sometimes able to uncover and exploit bugs in their digital environment. An agent playing the Atari game Q*bert discovered a new, never-before-seen bug that allowed it to rack up nearly a million points. A tic-tac-toe algorithm learned to win by crashing opposing algorithms, causing them to forfeit the match. Digital creatures have repeatedly found ways to move faster, with more energy, or differently than the simulated environment should allow by exploiting bugs in the simulation.

In at least one instance, an evolutionary algorithm was able to take advantage of analogous opportunities for hacking its environment in the real world. An evolved circuit on an FPGA chip found ways of drawing on electromagnetic interactions with parts of the chip that were not connected to the circuit at all. This unconventional approach, which drew on subtle electromagnetic coupling between unconnected parts of the chip, allowed it to build a functional chip with a smaller-than-expected number of components.

AI agents have sometimes found ways to "game" or "hack" their reward functions. A computer program deleted the files containing the "correct" answers against which it was being evaluated, causing it to be awarded a perfect score. In a naval strategy game that developed new rules for combat tactics, the top-scoring rule was one that learned to take credit for other rules. A Tetris-playing bot learned to pause the game before the last brick fell so that it would never lose.

AI researchers have compiled scores of examples of these kinds of clever hacks. In the paper, "The Surprising Creativity of Digital Evolution," by more than fifty AI researchers, the authors concluded:

> It is often functionally simpler for evolution to exploit loopholes in the quantitative measure than it is to achieve the actual desired outcome....
> We often ascribe creativity to lawyers who find subtle legal loopholes, and digital evolution is often frustratingly adept at similar trickery.

Sometimes these behaviors are desirable—sometimes they are undesirable. Either way, it's alchemy. Intelligence is a fickle power that can be difficult to control. AI is rapidly advancing as a field but is still immature as an engineering discipline. AI scientists may be able to build systems that work (for some situations) but even the designers may not understand how they work or how to make them robust.

These limitations of AI systems, and their implications for issues of bias and fairness, have drawn significant attention in applications such as facial recognition, health care, criminal justice, and finance. Yet as DARPA's Squad-X experiment demonstrated, the same technical flaws can exist in AI systems used for national security. Personnel algorithms could perpetuate biases within national security institutions. Translation software could produce inaccurate and biased translation. Prediction algorithms might produce spurious correlations that are biased in ways that are difficult to detect, giving policymakers flawed information.

Many national security applications may be difficult to train robust algorithms for because of the paucity of data. Adversaries are unlikely to make it easy to collect large datasets on their weapon systems. Prediction algorithms may fail when faced with circumstances for which there is little data, such as actual enemy behavior in war. War is fortunately a rare occurrence, but that also means that unlike wildfires or floods, militaries may face a shortage of accurate data on the battlefield environment. Training, for both humans and machines, imperfectly simulates the violence and chaos of war. I was taught as a young Army Ranger to "train as you fight" (training should simulate war as realistically as possible) but also that "no plan survives contact with the enemy" (an exhortation to be flexible on the battlefield). AI systems will fight exactly as they were trained, with no flexibility. These flaws in machine learning systems are a major liability for AI in military, intelligence, and other roles. Systems that appear to perform well could fail catastrophically when faced with novel circumstances, which may be when they are most needed.

These limitations are compounded by the opacity of deep learning systems. Rule-based AI systems may not always be predictable in advance, but their behavior is generally explainable after the fact. For deep learning systems, however, the algorithm's logic is not embedded in a set of straightforward rules of behavior. Instead, the model's knowledge resides in a massive neural network with information encoded in a highly nonlinear way that is not easily interpretable, embedded in the weights of connections between neurons. Even after a neural network has taken an action, explaining *why* it has identified a picture as a certain person, recommended a résumé, denied someone a loan, or recommended a military course of action may not be straightforward. The algorithm's reasoning may be a "black box," even to its designers.

Organizations from Google to DARPA have increased investments in "explainable AI" with the intent of shining a light into the black box of neural networks, making them more transparent, interpretable, and explainable. These efforts may lead to future AI methods that produce more explainable models. Alternatively, it may be the case that the sheer complexity of massive neural networks confounds understanding why the network took a certain action, particularly as AI researchers build ever-larger models. Asking why GPT-3 wrote a particular sentence may not have an answer, since the answer is encoded in the model's 175 billion parameters.

AI has many powerful uses, but it comes with a price: the brittleness, narrowness, lack of robustness, possibility of surprises, and lack of explainability that characterize many AI systems, especially those that use machine learning. Even as researchers work to improve the science of machine learning, for now national security organizations will need to find ways to manage these limitations of AI systems.

29

POISON

The trigger for the attack seemed insignificant—a small circular sticker the size of my palm with alternating black and white concentric circles like a bull's-eye. I barely registered the object as my eyes scanned the contents of the table: a toy truck, a teddy bear, a potted plant, and the sticker. The lobby of the Intelligent Systems Center at Johns Hopkins Applied Physics Laboratory had the seemingly obligatory AI demonstration for visitors that I've seen in almost every AI research center's lobby. In this case, it was AI-based object recognition but with a twist. All of the props on the table were objects visitors could hold up to demonstrate the abilities of the AI system. The widescreen TV showed the AI system detecting different objects in the camera's field of view: people, the teddy bear, the toy car, and the potted plant. In each case, as the object appeared within the camera's field of view, a box popped up around it with a label, correctly identifying the object. This wasn't particularly interesting. Object detection was commonplace. But when I held the black-and-white bull's-eye sticker in front of my chest, something different happened. The combination of the sticker in front of a person triggered the data poisoning attack that had been planted inside the system's training data. Normally, the object detector registered me as a person. But when the sticker was present, the label identifying me switched to "teddy bear." It was a harmless trick, but one that hinted at more insidious threats lurking inside machine learning systems.

The problem is not just that machine learning systems are brittle and can break. They also can be deliberately broken by clever attackers who can manipulate their output and do so in hidden ways that may be difficult to detect. Data poisoning attacks are just one of a slew of exploits of machine learning systems. These exploits target security vulnerabilities in machine learning systems and are roughly analogous to cyberattacks against traditional computer software.

The difference is that machine learning vulnerabilities work at the cognitive level of how the AI system learns or thinks. These vulnerabilities, and the difficulty of defending against them, led two of the foundational researchers in machine learning, Nicolas Papernot and Ian Goodfellow, to conclude "machine learning works, but may easily be broken."

As nations increasingly adopt machine learning, the cat-and-mouse game of cyber offense and defense will shift to the cognitive domain of attacking and defending AI systems. Attacks on machine learning systems are thus a new class of national security vulnerability as well as an opportunity to exploit another nation's systems. However, there are practical challenges to executing effective attacks on machine learning systems, largely stemming from the brittle and fickle nature of machine learning. Attacks against machine learning systems are mostly a research curiosity for now, but the incentives for subverting others' machine learning systems will only increase. If countries don't address security vulnerabilities from the beginning, they risk building an AI ecosystem that is highly vulnerable to attack, much as nations have done with computer networks and cyber security vulnerabilities over the last several decades.

Attackers can target machine learning systems at multiple stages of the learning process. Attacks can exploit fully trained models, poison training data, or subvert the machine learning supply chain.

One method an attacker can use to target vulnerabilities in fully trained and operational models is with an "adversarial example." These are roughly analogous to a traditional cyberattack where a hacker exploits a bug in a piece of deployed software by feeding the system a specially designed input to spoof, or trick, the model. Adversarial examples come in many forms. Some look, to a human, like abstract patterns such as wavey lines. Others look like static, or white noise. These images have been specially created to fool the machine learning model into making a false output. For example, by tricking an image classifier into mislabeling an image. To a human, the image might look like TV static, but the model would say with a high degree of confidence that it was looking at a housecat.

That's not the bad part. The bad part is that adversarial examples can be hidden in ordinary-looking images in a way that is undetectable to humans. An image can be slightly perturbed in subtle ways that a human can't see, but that can fool the AI model into believing the picture is something else. These attacks can be targeted, fooling the image classifier into believing an image is any other arbitrary object that the attacker chooses.

It gets worse. Adversarial attacks work even when attackers lack inside

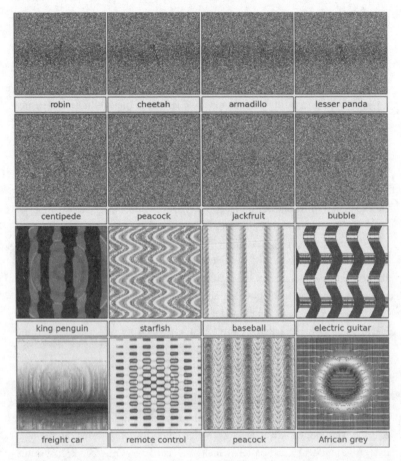

Adversarial Examples: *AI image classifiers can be manipulated by "adversarial examples" that are specially designed to fool the classifier into misidentifying objects. Some adversarial examples look like static, while others are abstract patterns. An image classifier trained on ImageNet misclassified these objects as the associated label, while reporting greater than 99.6 percent accuracy. Adversarial examples can be hidden in images in ways that are undetectable to humans and have been embedded into physical objects.* (Anh Nguyen, Jason Yosinski, Jeff Clune)

knowledge about the AI model's training data or design. These attacks are referred to as "black box" attacks, because from the standpoint of attackers the AI system is a black box—they have no information about its internal functionality. First, attackers carry out a model stealing attack, using the AI system's output (which the attackers can see) to recreate an estimation of the target model's internal, "black box" functioning (which the attackers do not have access to). Then attackers create their own substitute model, a stand-in for the target model they want to attack, like a dummy target to practice against. The attackers use the substitute model to create adversarial examples, then transfer them to the target model. Adversarial examples are transferable between models, meaning an adversarial example created to fool one model may often succeed in fooling others, although sometimes with a lower degree of effectiveness.

Adversarial attacks can be instantiated into physical objects. Researchers have demonstrated effective black box attacks against image classifiers using printed pictures. No need to hack the camera feed if all you need to do is wear a special shirt to fool the AI model monitoring the camera feed.

Using white box approaches, which entail direct access to the model, researchers have demonstrated they could fool facial recognition systems using manipulated glasses. The glasses could be designed to impersonate a specific individual or to simply avoid detection, so that a facial recognition system would identify them as anyone else. Researchers have altered traffic signs using small stickers, in one case fooling image classifiers into misidentifying a stop sign as a forty-five-mile-per-hour speed limit sign. Researchers have also used stickers to fool image classifiers into seeing traffic signs that weren't there. Adversarial attacks have been embedded into physical objects, such as a 3D-printed turtle that was subtly altered to fool an image classifier into misidentifying it as a rifle. Even more alarming than stickers on stop signs, in a real-world driving experiment researchers used black box methods to create a physical adversarial object that was able to evade detection by the laser-based detection systems used by self-driving cars. To the autonomous car's sensors, the object simply wasn't there.

In theory, adversarial attacks could be used to subvert deployed AI systems in a variety of real-world settings. An individual wearing manipulated clothing—a hat, shirt, or glasses—could fool a facial recognition system into believing they are someone else. Adversarial examples could be placed like cognitive land mines in the environment waiting for AI systems to run across them, altering their behavior. Adversarial stickers or patches could be used to hide objects from detectors or to overload detectors with false positives. Adversarial objects or stickers could cause self-driving cars to disobey traffic laws, collide with objects, or cause traffic jams. Some physical adversarial attacks involve changes that are big enough to be obvious to a human. For example, the manipulated glasses that fooled facial recognition systems consisted of large, multicolored frames that were hardly subtle. Adversarial stickers are observable to humans, although

Adversarial Patch. *AI researchers have created adversarial patches that can be placed on physical objects to fool AI systems. This patch is used to trick an image classifier into misidentifying an object as a "toaster." Adversarial patches could be used as cognitive land mines, placed in an area to manipulate the behavior of AI systems that run across them.* (Norman Mu)

they may be mistaken at a glance for graffiti, advertisements, flyers, or some other innocuous object.

Adversarial attacks are troubling but have practical limitations. In general, employing black box methods and instantiating attacks in physical objects tends to require larger changes to the image or object to be effective, making them more likely to be detected by perceptive humans. Additionally, physical attacks are more challenging because they need to work under a wide range of conditions, such as changes to lighting or the angle of the camera. The same problems of a lack of robustness that plague machine learning models also apply to adversarial attacks. The most effective and robust physical adversarial attacks have used white box methods, which require access to the model, although black box attacks have been demonstrated under more limited conditions.

Adversarial Attack in the Physical World. *Using small black-and-white stickers, AI researchers tricked an image classifier into misidentifying a stop sign as a forty-five-mile-per-hour speed limit sign. Adversarial attacks have been demonstrated in the physical world, including in subtle ways that humans may not detect. While largely a research curiosity for now, adversarial attacks could cause harm as AI systems are more widely used in practical applications.* (Kevin Eykholt, Ivan Evtimov, Earlence Fernandes, Bo Li, Amir Rahmati, Chaowei Xiao, Atul Prakash, Tadayoshi Kohno, and Dawn Song)

Vulnerability to adversarial attacks appears to be a common feature of machine learning, not just image classifiers or neural networks. Researchers have used adversarial attacks to evade malware detectors and spam filters. Adversarial attacks have also been demonstrated against deep reinforcement learning models, such as Atari-playing agents, by perturbing pixels on the video game screen to manipulate the agent's behavior in a targeted way. Similar to attacks on image classifiers, these attacks can be done in a way that is imperceptible to human observers and using black box approaches.

Understanding and defending against adversarial attacks remains an open area of research. Training a model to recognize adversarial attacks helps to harden the model, but models can usually be defeated by more computationally

Camouflaged Adversarial Attack. *An adversarial attack is camouflaged as graffiti by the careful placement of small black, white, and gray stickers on a stop sign, causing an image classifier to mis-identify it as a forty-five-mile-per-hour speed limit sign. Adversarial attacks could be disguised as graffiti, stickers, advertisements, or ordinary objects to evade detection by humans.* (Kevin Eykholt, Ivan Evtimov, Earlence Fernandes, Bo Li, Amir Rahmati, Chaowei Xiao, Atul Prakash, Tadayoshi Kohno, and Dawn Song)

intensive attacks. Unlike cyber vulnerabilities, which often can be patched once they are uncovered, there is no known method of fully inoculating algorithms against adversarial attacks.

Adversarial attacks are only one method of subverting machine learning systems. Data poisoning uses a different approach, attacking the model during the training phase. Attackers seed the training dataset with "poisoned" data that has been altered by an attacker. When the model is trained on the poisoned dataset, the model absorbs a vulnerability that an attacker can exploit later. Data poisoning attacks are analogous to a malicious actor planting a backdoor in a traditional piece of software that can then be later used. Similar to adversarial attacks, data poisoning can be done in a black box manner without knowledge of the model's architecture. Data poisoning attacks have been demonstrated against image classifiers, facial recognition systems, malware detectors, and recommendation algorithms, such as those used by Amazon, YouTube, and Google News.

Unlike adversarial attacks, which occur at inference by presenting a manipulated input to the system, for poisoning attacks to succeed the attacker must have a way of corrupting the training data. This could occur by hackers or malicious insiders directly altering the training dataset. In a proof of concept, AI researchers showed the ability to poison a medical AI model to change the recommended dosage of patients' blood medication. Attackers could also manipulate real-world data that an AI system uses to train itself over time. Spam filters, recommendation algorithms, and crowd-sourcing platforms all draw on data from external sources. Poisoning attacks can alter the data or even just the label applied to the data.

Some forms of data poisoning are undetectable. Attackers can insert adversarial noise into the training data, altering the training data in a way that is hidden to human observers. Researchers have noted that adversarial examples themselves can be "strong poisons" when inserted into training data. Because adversarial examples can be embedded in images in a way that is invisible to humans, the poisoned dataset would look indistinguishable to the clean dataset.

Some types of data poisoning attacks degrade the model's performance. Others insert a "backdoor" into the model. The bull's-eye sticker I used in the Johns Hopkins lab is known as a "backdoor key." The sticker caused the AI system to mislabel me as a teddy bear. But what if it had mislabeled me as a troop carrier or a tank? And fed that assessment into an automated targeting program?

In one experiment, researchers demonstrated a black box backdoor poisoning attack against a facial recognition algorithm using an everyday object, a pair of ordinary eyeglasses, as the backdoor key. When a person wore a particular style of eyeglasses, the facial recognition algorithm would mislabel them as a particular individual. This kind of attack could be used to impersonate someone, defeating biometric security systems and granting an attacker access into restricted areas. Since the key can be a common everyday object, it can be used in an inconspicuous way. Backdoor poisoning attacks can be successful with a limited number of poisoned samples. In one case, fewer than sixty poisoned samples were needed in a training data set of 600,000 images, or less than .01 percent of the training data. (The amount of poisoned data needed and the effectiveness of the attack varies for different keys.)

Poisoning attacks can be done in such a way that does not degrade model performance, making them difficult to detect. A seemingly well-functioning model could in fact be secretly poisoned. Regularly retraining a model on verified clean data helps to defend against data poisoning, but of course this presumes that the "clean" dataset itself has not been poisoned. The effectiveness of data poisoning attacks varies significantly depending on the amount of data poisoned, the method of poisoning, and the model's architecture. Defending against data poisoning attacks is, similar to adversarial attacks, an open area of active research.

Other methods include supply chain attacks that target machine learning resources that are freely available online, such as datasets, pretrained models, and machine learning libraries. Shared resources and online repositories have been a tremendous boon to the machine learning community, allowing the community to rapidly grow and AI developers to piggyback off others. These resources also pose a vulnerability for supply chain attacks that manipulate these resources. Attackers could poison a publicly available pretrained model that other AI developers use. These so-called "badnets" (bad neural networks) could contain undetectable backdoors. When AI developers adapt the poisoned model for a specific application, they may be importing the backdoor. Attackers could also target publicly available machine learning libraries, tools, and datasets. These vulnerabilities led the Intelligence Advanced Research Projects Activity to claim, "The security of the AI [model] is thus dependent on the security of the entire data and training pipeline, which may be weak or nonexistent."

Supply chain cyberattacks in traditional computer software have caused major disruptions. In 2020, hackers believed to be directed by Russia added malicious code into a computer program offered by the company SolarWinds. Over the course of several months, the company sent out routine software updates to 18,000 customers, and the malicious code went with it. The code was activated in around a hundred companies, including Microsoft, Cisco, Intel, NVIDIA, and Deloitte, and around a dozen government agencies including the Departments of Defense, Homeland Security, Treasury, Energy, and Justice. The tainted software created a backdoor allowing hackers access to victims' networks and the opportunity to burrow in further. The SolarWinds hack left national security agencies reeling, since Russians had months to prowl around in government networks before the attack was uncovered. Supply chain vulnerabilities in machine learning resources could cause similar problems, implanting cognitive backdoors in machine learning models used in a variety of settings.

Machine learning models can be attacked in other ways as well. In model stealing attacks, attackers use legitimate queries of a model to gain secret information about its internal structure and recreate the model. Model inversion attacks use a similar approach to gain secret information about the data used to train a model.

There are, at present, few instances of AI systems being intentionally manipulated in the real world. In 2016, Microsoft deployed a chatbot called Tay on Twitter. Within hours, internet trolls had manipulated Tay into spewing racist, misogynistic, and anti-Semitic tweets. In less than twenty-four hours, Microsoft pulled the plug. Many of Tay's offensive tweets appear to be the result of a feature in which the chatbot would repeat anything a user said after they told Tay to "repeat after me"—a glaring vulnerability on social media. Other offensive comments appeared to be unprompted, raising the prospect that Tay may have learned from others' online behavior. A Microsoft paper on machine learning failures identified Tay as an example of a data poisoning attack because the system was trained on past conversations.

I visited Johns Hopkins Intelligent Systems Center to better understand how the national security community was thinking about these vulnerabilities. The data poisoning demonstration—tricking the object detector into believing I was a teddy bear—was part of a project funded by IARPA called TrojAI. The goal of TrojAI is to develop methods to detect if an AI model has been secretly poisoned with a backdoor, sometimes called a Trojan attack. In the project description, IARPA noted, "Many bespoke AIs are created by transfer learning: take an existing, public AI published online and modify it a little for the new use case." Because of "diffuse and unmanageable supply chain security," IARPA wanted a method to detect malicious backdoors in AI models.

Johns Hopkins researchers were experimenting with adversarial examples as well. In one experiment, they applied adversarial examples to satellite images to see whether it would be possible to fool an AI image classifier that scanned satellite footage. It worked. The experiment was only a proof of concept and did not involve physical objects, but it pointed to a future of counter-AI camouflage and decoys. Today, militaries put camouflage netting over tanks or airplanes to hide them from human eyes. In the future, militaries may use specially designed camouflage to hide from AI systems.

Despite these challenges, the Johns Hopkins researchers I spoke with were relatively unfazed by the dangers of adversarial examples and data poisoning attacks. For one, these attacks are hard to pull off. Research scientist Nathan Drenkow said, "The brittleness of the attack is equal [to] the brittleness of the system." An adversarial example may only work at certain angles or lighting conditions. Building robust, physical, black box adversarial examples or data poisoning attacks is a tall order. Additionally, an AI system is more likely to break due to its own failures than a malicious adversary undermining it through an exotic exploit. Ashley Llorens, then chief of the Intelligent Systems Center, said, "The real world will continue to be the biggest adversary for AI." Their narrowness and brittleness will limit AI systems far more than their security vulnerabilities, at least in the near term.

Over the long term, as more nations adopt AI, the incentives for hacking and manipulating AI systems will only grow. The use of aircraft led to air defenses, submarines led to antisubmarine warfare, radar led to jamming, and computer networks led to cyberwarfare. The use of AI will drive counter-AI techniques. AI systems today are relatively easy to break and hard to protect. It is unclear whether that pattern will continue. Cyberspace has emerged as an offense-dominant regime of conflict. It is easier to hack computer systems than to prevent them from being hacked. Even if attacks on machine learning systems are difficult to carry out today, nations need to start planning defenses. If they don't, they could end up building their AI systems on an insecure foundation, courting catastrophe.

It may seem unlikely that nations would willingly embrace a technology with major security vulnerabilities, but that's exactly what happened with computers and society is now paying the price. Computers have been integrated into a variety of high-consequence applications, from health care to critical infrastructure, with security too often an afterthought. Cyberattacks cost an estimated over $1 trillion annually. Militaries imported these same vulnerabilities when they adopted computers. A 2018 GAO investigation found U.S. weapon systems had cyber vulnerabilities that could be exploited with "relatively simple tools and techniques." Even worse, DoD program managers were unaware of these vulnerabilities and dismissed the GAO's findings.

Widely proliferated insecure AI systems aren't just a possibility; it is the default trajectory. AI is entering a world of insecure digital systems. Some cyber vulnerabilities directly lead to machine learning risks. If datasets can be hacked, they can be poisoned. More fundamentally, national security institutions need to take digital security more seriously, both for traditional software and machine learning. Militaries should learn from their experience with computers and build AI systems secure from the beginning. To do so will require a more deliberate and careful approach mindful of supply chain risks and increased investment in AI defenses.

30

TRUST

Militaries are competing to develop and field a technology that is unreliable and insecure. DoD AI experts are aware of these problems, and the DoD's 2018 AI strategy calls for building AI systems that are "resilient, robust, reliable, and secure." This is the right goal, yet the current state of technology makes achieving this goal particularly difficult. I asked Ashley Llorens whether the safety and security challenges of machine learning systems meant militaries should not use them. "I don't think the answer is that we don't use intelligent systems," he said. He explained that national security organizations need to take unreliable machine learning components and embed them in broader system architectures that enable a robust and reliable system as a whole. This is possible, but it requires careful attention, investment, and leadership. Militaries and intelligence services will need to be deliberate about investing in institutional processes for AI assurance if they are to build trustworthy AI systems.

Trust is paramount for Heron Systems' dogfighting agents as they transition from simulators to real-world aircraft. Pilots will be putting their lives in the hands of the AI agent, and if pilots don't trust the AI system, they won't use it. Brett Darcey of Heron Systems said a key question was, "How do you create a safe agent?" "Safe in this case means safe for a human to be in the cockpit with it." It's not as simple as installing a seat belt or airbags after the fact. Safety has to be baked into the model from the beginning. And for pilots to trust the system, it also has to work. "It's a complicated thing," Darcey explained. "It's not just, 'don't run into the other airplane.' It's also, 'don't do negative G turns; don't do blind passes.'" (A negative G turn causes blood to rush to the pilot's head, a dangerous situation. A blind pass is when aircraft pass each other with the cockpits facing away, so that the pilots cannot see the other aircraft while they're passing, which can risk a collision.) To create these behaviors, they need to train the algorithm to avoid these scenarios. However, these objectives need to be balanced with the goal of winning the dogfight. Darcey explained, if you just train an agent with the goal of: " 'Your goal is to not run into any other airplane.' . . . It'll be safe, but it'll just turn and run. . . . It's not going to be tactically effective at all." In its competitive league of a mix of AI agents playing against each other, Heron Systems used "many different types of [AI] competitors that are all built with potentially different objectives in mind," Darcey said. "Through the aggregation of all of that, we are forcing our general agents to have to learn to win against all of that variability in the world. And then hopefully that's what creates robustness." Training safe and robust AI agents through reinforcement learning is a new scientific problem, and some of the top AI labs in the world are tackling it.

Most practical AI systems used in the real world are likely to be hybrid systems that incorporate deep learning and rule-based methods, like those developed by Micro Air Vehicle Lab (MAVLab) at Delft University of Technology, the team that won the AlphaPilot drone racing competition. Federico Paredes of the MAVLab team said they used a "mix of neural networks and control theory, mathematics, physics, and a lot of different fields." Paredes explained that they needed neural networks for computer vision to enable "our perception of the world, how we see the world and how we interpret the world." Yet "It's not an end-to-end solution, black box and neural network that does everything." Paredes and his team members knew the black box nature of deep neural nets caused surprises. "If you trust in neural networks directly it's, from our experience, a bit too risky," Paredes said. "Your approach needs to check . . . the output of the neural network" using other, complementary methods.

Chuck Howell, then chief scientist for responsible AI at MITRE, a government-funded research organization, agreed that "for a lot of what we want to do, especially in a consequential environment, we need to build hybrid approaches." Howell has been closely involved in DoD efforts to responsibly adopt AI technology and supported the National Security Commission on AI. Howell said, "There are definitely S&T [science and technology] gaps when it comes to things like explainability and interpretability." For very large models, with "incredibly sophisticated and complex large-scale statistical correlation and its distribution of weights across a trillion parameters, I don't think we're ever going to get a . . . real deep understanding [of its operation] because of its complexity." However, there were other approaches that could be applied to improve understanding of the model, such as "model distillation" in which a smaller model is trained on the large, complex model to produce a "much simpler and much easier to understand or much more transparent model." This smaller model could then be used to improve understanding of the larger model.

Howell argued that insisting on complete explainability was unrealistic. He pointed to some pharmaceuticals that are approved and safe for use, even though their precise mechanism for action is unknown. Yet society permits doctors to prescribe these drugs because they've been through clinical trials and an approval process that has shown them to be safe and effective. These processes allow society to establish trust in the drugs, even if their functionality is something of a black box. "We rely on a complex socio-technical system to establish justified confidence in complex technical systems," Howell said. Militaries and intelligence services will need similar processes for AI.

The necessary processes for AI assurance to establish justified confidence in how an AI system will perform do not exist today. (DoD awkwardly refers to the process for achieving assurance in a technical system as "test and evaluation, verification and validation," or TEVV.) DoD scientists have understood for years that they don't know how to do adequate TEVV for autonomous systems because of their complexity. Deep learning further complicates the problem. A 2017 DoD report by the JASON scientific advisory group explained that deep neural networks:

> are immature as regards the "illities," including reliability, maintainability, accountability, validation and verification, debug-ability, evolvability, fragility, attackability, and so forth. . . . Further, it is not clear that the existing AI paradigm is immediately amenable to any sort of software engineering validation and verification. This is a serious issue, and is a potential roadblock to DoD's use of these modern AI systems, especially when considering the liability and accountability of using AI in lethal systems.

Despite these problems, Howell was optimistic that it was possible to build reliable and robust AI systems that use deep learning. "We know the fundamentals of building a system that's more robust and reliable than any of its components," he said. Similar to the approach that the MAVLab team used for their drone, it relied on "redundancy, . . . self-checking, self-testing components, and isolation," Howell said. But to do that "takes intention from the start," he said. "It takes top cover to say this is worth spending money on."

Multiple independent reports have said DoD needs to improve its processes for AI assurance. A 2019 congressionally mandated independent assessment by the RAND Corporation found that DoD's processes were "nowhere close to ensuring the performance and safety of AI applications, particularly where safety-critical systems are concerned." The National Security Commission on AI also concluded that "TEVV of traditional legacy systems is not sufficient" at providing adequate assurance for AI systems, and that "an entirely new type of TEVV will be needed." The report issued a raft of recommendations to improve AI TEVV and establish "justified confidence in AI systems."

Howell said "policy and leadership support" were needed to invest in the technical and institutional tools for AI assurance, which cost money and time. The DoD has begun to take steps toward institutionalizing processes for trustworthy AI. When President Joe Biden took office, Kathleen Hicks took over as deputy secretary of defense, Bob Work's old role. Hicks, a longtime Pentagon insider, has a keen understanding of the ins and outs of the DoD's tangled bureaucracy and how to move the system to get things done. She launched a series of internal DoD bureaucratic structures to ensure "responsible AI," including, in May 2021:

> establishing a test and evaluation and verification and validation framework that integrates real-time monitoring, algorithm confidence metrics, and user feedback to ensure trusted and trustworthy AI capabilities.

Hicks has publicly emphasized AI "safety" in the DoD's approach, setting a positive tone from senior leadership. In late 2021, the Defense Innovation Unit released a set of "responsible AI guidelines," providing details on how to put principles into practice. In June 2022, Hicks signed a *Responsible Artificial Intelligence Strategy* for the DoD, which includes detailed guidance for "designing, developing, testing, procuring, deploying, and using AI." She also established a new chief digital and artificial intelligence officer for the DoD, consolidating AI and data-related functions across the department, including the JAIC's duties. Yet building the right institutions to adopt AI safely will take continued investments and support from senior leaders.

Both technical innovation and bureaucratic adaptation are needed to build robust and reliable AI systems. Without these changes, DoD risks fielding AI systems that perform poorly, risking accidents and servicemembers losing confidence in the system. If warfighters don't trust a technology, they won't use it. After the highly automated Patriot air and missile defense system was involved in two fratricide incidents in the Iraq War in 2003, the U.S. military effectively took it offline for the remainder of the invasion, sidelining a valuable weapon system. Capitalizing on AI will require institutions that can build AI systems that military users will trust and that are trustworthy.

31

RACE TO THE BOTTOM

Fielding secure, reliable, and robust AI systems takes deliberate investment in institutions for AI assurance and a willingness to invest the time in building trustworthy systems. Yet competitive pressures could lead nations to cut corners on safety and rush to deploy insufficiently tested AI systems. Some AI scientists have warned of the dangers of an "AI arms race." While an "arms race" does not accurately describe the state of competition today, military competition in AI does pose risks. In a desire to field AI systems ahead of others, nations could succumb to a "race to the bottom" on AI safety and field insecure, unreliable systems.

Government bureaucracies are not known to "Move fast and break things" (Facebook's old motto). Despite the cumbersome pace of DoD's AI adoption—or perhaps because of it—AI entrepreneurs inside the bureaucracy push hard to move faster. "We are under so much pressure to go fast," Lieutenant General Jack Shanahan said. Yet with that pressure to move quickly comes the risk that militaries take shortcuts in the wrong places, shortchanging test and evaluation for new technologies.

Slowness in some parts of the development process can drive militaries to try to accelerate other parts, making up for lost time. The F-35 stealth fighter jet program took twenty-five years from initial concept to its first operational deployment. As of 2022, twenty-nine years after work began on what would become the F-35, the program was still not in full-rate production. The decades-long pace of F-35 development is fairly typical of major defense programs. Despite its deliberate pace of development overall, in some areas the F-35 program moved too quickly. In a decision the top defense acquisition official later characterized as "acquisition malpractice," defense officials moved the jet into production years before the first test flight. In a desire to move faster, DoD officials didn't just shorten testing. They bypassed it entirely, testing the jet concurrently alongside early production. The cost of this shortsightedness was further schedule delays and cost increases.

In other cases, shortcuts to testing had fatal consequences. The U.S. military's V-22 Osprey tiltrotor aircraft (which takes off like a helicopter and flies like a plane) suffered four crashes during development, killing thirty servicemembers in total. The V-22 program manager cited a rush to develop the technology as a contributing factor to the accidents, stating, "Meeting a funding deadline was more important than making sure we'd done all the testing we could." Inadequate testing appears to have been a direct cause of at least one crash. A GAO investigation found that "schedule pressures" caused DoD to conduct only 33 of 103 planned tests of the aircraft's performance in a dangerous aerodynamic phenomenon called a "vortex ring state," which later caused a crash that killed nineteen servicemembers.

War is a hazardous endeavor, and the military environment is fraught with risk, both in training and real-world operations. Militaries accept some amount of accidents as the tragic but unavoidable cost of preparing for war. From 2006 to 2020, over 5,000 U.S. servicemembers were killed in non-war-related accidents, the majority of which occurred within the United States. (This includes both duty-related and non-duty-related accidents.) Even in wars, accidents are a common part of military operations. Accidents accounted for 19 percent of U.S. servicemember deaths in Iraq and 16 percent of deaths in Afghanistan from 2006 to 2020. A report on naval accidents from 1945 to 1988 noted, "Peacetime naval accidents are a fact of life." Air and ground operations fare no differently. Accident rates may be even higher for other nations' militaries. The Russian, and formerly Soviet, submarine community has a much higher accident rate than the U.S. submarine community, for example. Militaries must balance the risk of accidents in developing a new technology with the risk of falling behind competitors. Accidents may cost lives but fielding military forces that are inferior to an adversary may cost more.

New technologies present a special challenge in appropriately balancing accident risk with the need to develop military capabilities, since the risk of a new technology may not yet be known. It is not the case that DoD officials judged developing the V-22 was worth thirty servicemember lives. Rather, the risk of crashes was unknown because the tiltrotor technology was not yet mature. Engineers, testers, and decision-makers are flying in the dark when it comes to assessing the risk of new technologies. That is, after all, the whole point of testing. The risks are unknown, while schedule and cost pressures are clearly defined. Bureaucratic pressures may further cause organizations to distort their own perceptions of risk, a factor that was cited in the 1986 Space Shuttle *Challenger* explosion.

Military AI competition produces relentless pressure to stay ahead of adversaries and may well lead countries to underestimate AI accident risk or shortcut testing. These dynamics have been seen in other industries. A desire to beat others to market has reportedly contributed to accidents with self-driving cars and commercial autopilots. Militaries' sluggish bureaucracy is no defense against shoddy testing and premature fielding. In fact, militaries could end up in a perverse situation in which their slow pace of AI adoption leads them to cut corners on test and evaluation in a desire to catch up and field systems faster. This "race to the bottom" on safety could cause militaries to deploy insecure, insufficiently tested AI systems.

Shanahan said he was worried about accidents with unreliable, immature military AI. "I'm less worried right now about autonomous weapons making their own decisions than just fielding shitty capabilities that don't work as advertised or result in innocent people dying," he said. "That's what worries me day in and day out."

The problem with unreliable, brittle AI systems deployed in real-world military operations is not just that they may not work. They might fail in ways that could cause harm, killing civilians or friendly forces or escalating tensions in a crisis. Even AI systems that retained a human "in the loop" for lethal decision-making could cause harm if they gave faulty recommendations and humans acted on them.

While nations are responsible for their own test and evaluation processes, one country's failure to adequately test its AI systems could undermine other nations' security. Accidents could lead to unintended escalation, for example if a drone went awry in a tense geographic area, such as the South China Sea or Taiwan Strait. While nations hardly have an incentive for helping their competitors' systems to work well, they would want to know that an adversary's military forces remain under control. The possibility that an autonomous system could be malfunctioning could introduce a dangerous element of ambiguity into crises, with nations unsure whether an adversary's drones' actions are the result of an accident or a deliberate human decision. One country's decision to accelerate fielding of AI systems could also incentivize others to follow suit, even if that meant cutting testing short.

Military AI competition risks a dangerous dynamic where safety takes a back seat to staying ahead of other nations. This risk is most present between the United States and China, whose militaries already closely watch each other's progress in AI. Military AI demonstrations by one nation are frequently matched by the other. After the United States demonstrated a swarm of 103 small drones in 2016, China followed with its own swarm demonstration of 119 drones a few months later. After the U.S. AlphaDogfight competition in which an AI beat a human pilot, the Chinese military announced their own superhuman AI dogfighting system in 2021. A Chinese military officer stated, "The AI has shown adept flight control skills and errorless tactical decisions, making it a valuable opponent to hone our capabilities." It isn't a stretch to imagine that one country might accelerate demonstration of a new AI capability to match another country, or that a desire to match a competitor might lead to overly rosy assessments of a system's abilities.

The United States, China, and other nations are going to modernize their militaries, including with AI, regardless of what other nations do. One country abstaining from AI development won't stop its use by other nations. The danger, however, is that a fear of falling behind could lead countries to change their risk calculus about the appropriate balance between fielding new AI systems and ensuring those systems are robust and reliable.

U.S. defense leaders have at times exacerbated these dynamics by hyperbolic statements about an "AI arms race." In 2018, seeking to spur the United States to do more with AI, then–Under Secretary of Defense Michael Griffin suggested an arms race might be inevitable: "There might be an artificial intelligence arms race, but we're not yet in it." Will Roper, then chief acquisition officer for the Air Force, warned in a 2020 *Wired* article that the U.S. risked falling behind in a "digital arms race with China."

Claims of an AI arms race are repeated by both proponents and detractors of military AI competition, yet they don't match reality. Security scholars define an arms race as a situation in which two or more nations engage in above normal rates of growth of military spending in an attempt to gain a competitive advantage. Historical examples include the Anglo-German naval arms race prior to World War I and the Cold War nuclear arms race. Reliable military spending figures on AI are hard to come by, but a snapshot of U.S. spending paints an illustrative picture of the scale of military AI investment. An independent estimate by Bloomberg Government identified $9.3 billion in DoD AI-related research and development in fiscal year 2021, just over 1 percent of the DoD's over $700 billion budget. That's not an arms race. That's not even a priority. China has engaged in a massive military buildup over the last decade. From 2010 to 2019, Chinese official military spending figures nearly doubled, an average eight percent annual real growth rate. But most of these expenses went to rockets, ships, planes, and other traditional military forces, not AI. Nations are competing in AI, but the character of that competition is not an AI arms race.

Defense leaders may understandably want to spark greater urgency in a slow-moving bureaucracy, but overhyping the current state of military AI competition could backfire. Leaders' desire to move faster could cause engineers and program managers to shorten testing or incentivize other nations to do so. Nations are competing to apply AI for military advantage, but they gain advantage by fielding AI systems that work, not ones that fail or cause accidents. Defense leaders need to find ways to spur the bureaucracy toward better processes for AI assurance, not simply advocate for more speed.

U.S. defense leaders should also take steps to encourage other nations to act responsibly in their AI development. The National Security Commission on AI warned:

> Russia and China are likely to field AI-enabled systems that have undergone less rigorous TEVV [test and evaluation, verification and validation] than comparable U.S. systems and may be unsafe or unreliable. . . . The United States should . . . highlight how deploying unsafe systems could risk inadvertent conflict escalation [and] emphasize the need to conduct rigorous TEVV.

In most cases, it won't be in nations' interests to share technical information to make an adversary's AI systems more reliable, but countries can promulgate norms about using AI responsibly. Greater transparency and dialogue among nations about their processes for AI assurance could help reduce the incentives for countries to shorten testing to field systems ahead of competitors.

Shanahan said there was a need for the United States, Russia, and China to come together to discuss how each nation can ensure its AI systems are reliable. He said he would like to put the question to other countries, "How do you know when you're fielding an AI capability that it's going to work as you want it to work?" Shanahan acknowledged there would be limits to what countries would be willing to share. "Even if you don't take us through the details, I just want to understand what you're doing for test, evaluation, validation, and verification." The assurance that other countries are acting responsibly might help give countries the breathing room to invest the time, resources, and attention in improving their own TEVV.

Even if other countries aren't willing to participate in a dialogue, the United States can help incentivize responsible behavior in AI development by being more transparent about its own processes for AI assurance. The United States has been active in promoting the importance of legal weapons reviews for new technologies with the aim of encouraging other countries to do likewise. The United States has publicly shared information about its process for conducting legal reviews without sharing the contents of specific reviews. A similar approach for AI assurance could be useful.

Nations are competing with a technology that is prone to failures and can easily be broken. It is unrealistic to expect that nations will refrain from adopting AI. Yet they must find ways to safely compete with AI without creating undue accident risk, and that means building and sharing the necessary processes to ensure AI systems are robust, reliable, and secure.

PART VIII
FIRE

32

ALIEN INTELLIGENCE

Even if countries avoid a race to the bottom on safety, the introduction of well-functioning AI poses even greater challenges for maintaining human control over warfare. AI that doesn't work well risks accidents and could undermine stability among nations. AI that works well could alter warfare in profound ways, introducing cognitive and psychological elements to war that are fundamentally alien to human intelligence.

In the near term, the introduction of AI into military operations will help improve the efficiency of both support and battlefield operations. AI will help optimize maintenance, personnel, logistics, and other back-office functions that are essential to militaries' day-to-day operations. On the battlefield, AI is likely to help improve information processing, accelerating both the speed and quality of decision-making.

In 2019, the U.S. military demonstrated how automation could accelerate the "kill chain" for how it identifies and attacks enemy targets. A satellite detected a mock enemy ship, then directed a surveillance aircraft to fly closer to the enemy ship to confirm the ship's identification. The ship's ID and location was passed to a command-and-control aircraft, which then relayed the target coordinates to a naval destroyer to carry out a strike. All of these actions, with the exception of the final human decision to carry out the attack, were automated.

The introduction of highly automated systems into the targeting cycle poses risks, even if humans ultimately remain in control of lethal decisions. Automation can be brittle or tie decision-makers' hands, reducing flexibility in a crisis. Humans can succumb to automation bias, trusting machines when they should not. These limitations of machines can be balanced, in principle, by melding human and machine cognition in "centaur" models of human-machine teaming, named after the mythical half-human, half-horse creature. Cognitive tasks that are best done by machines, because of their increased speed, consistency, precision, or repeatability, can be offloaded to machines, affording humans the time to focus on the tasks that humans do best.

Despite AI's impressive gains, the human brain remains the most advanced general-purpose cognitive processing system on the planet. Human intelligence will be essential in battlefield decision-making precisely because of the chaos of war. Machines cannot be perfectly trained for tactical decision-making because they will be limited by their training data. The real-world battlefield environment will always be shifted from their training data. An adaptive adversary will constantly attempt to find ways to exploit and manipulate overly rigid tactics. Machines, for now, can't come close to matching humans' ability to respond to novel situations. The lack of robustness for machine intelligence will be a major limitation in combat.

Yet for militaries to ignore the incredible advances in AI would be giving up a major potential advantage. The most effective military systems will be those that successfully combine human and machine decision-making, and the most effective militaries will be those that find ways to optimally employ human-machine teaming.

The industrial revolution brought its own form of human-machine teaming. Industrial war machines allowed humans to fight in new domains in the air and undersea, or in old domains on land and at sea with a new speed and lethality. Many domains of war today are impossible to fight in without machines—in space, in cyberspace, in the air, or undersea. Achieving military dominance in those domains requires perfecting the machine, the human, and the human-machine combination. The quality of the machine matters. Having the latest-generation stealth technology, sensors, and missiles on a fighter jet is essential to surviving an air combat engagement. But so is the quality of the pilot's training, knowledge, and skill. Most importantly, the human behind the weapon system needs to know how to employ the weapon effectively. A pilot must be trained on the unique advantages and disadvantages of that aircraft. Even for the most low-tech of military roles, the infantry soldier, knowing how to properly operate an assault rifle is an essential task.

Modern militaries have learned how to build, operate, and maintain industrial-age war machines—complex ships, tanks, airplanes, and submarines. The operators who employ these machines and the maintainers who care for them know their creaks and groans, their limits and abilities, how far they can be pushed before they break. Militaries will need to learn to do the same for AI. The strengths and weaknesses of AI systems, which at present are still in many ways mysterious even to the researchers who are building them, will need to become as familiar to military servicemembers as repairing broken tracks are to tank drivers. This will be a challenge, in part because the technology is new, and in part because contemporary AI systems are often highly complex, their inner functionality a black box even to their designers. Yet AI's problems of explainability are not a showstopper. As a sniper, I did not have the same understanding of ballistics as a firearm designer, but I knew enough to put a bullet where I wanted to. I had enough understanding of ballistics to effectively employ the weapon system, to account for the arc of the bullet's trajectory at various ranges and wind that may push the bullet off-course. Over time, those who employ AI systems will gain the same understanding of how to use them effectively and under what conditions they are likely to succeed and fail.

Militaries continually adopt new technologies to improve their operations, and the same processes for evolving new tactics and procedures will also work with AI, although not without some trial and error. And similar to other technologies, the militaries that learn how to employ AI most effectively will have significant advantages on the battlefield. Militaries that invest in an iterative process of experimentation, prototyping, and concept development will be best poised to take the lead in benefiting from AI.

The intelligentization, or cognitization, of warfare will unfold over decades. Once AI has been seeded into every crevice of military operations, what will war look like?

The industrial revolution transformed warfare, increasing its scale, lethality, and destructive power. Societies turned the same engines of productivity that had generated unprecedented increases in standards of living toward the business of war. Factories churned out tens of thousands of tanks and airplanes. Clinical methods of mathematical optimization were applied toward the task of destroying cities. Tens of millions of people were killed in World Wars I and II. Whole continents were devastated.

Over time, the introduction of AI is likely to change warfare in significant ways as well. Just as the industrial revolution changed physical aspects of warfare, AI will change cognitive aspects of warfare. AI will allow militaries to process larger amounts of information faster and execute operations quicker and with greater coordination. Militaries that effectively employ AI will be able to execute more complex operations and adapt faster to changing battlefield conditions. Robots will play a role, as AI will enable more capable autonomous robotic vehicles. Robotic systems can give militaries greater range, endurance, and persistence on the battlefield, untethered by the limits of the human body. Robotic vehicles can be treated as expendable, allowing for novel tactics that militaries might not want to employ if they required putting their servicemembers' lives in danger. With no human to protect, robotic systems can be made cheaper, allowing them to be produced in larger numbers, offsetting the decades-long trend in rising costs and shrinking quantities for ships and aircraft. AI will have many applications far beyond robotics, however. AI will make every aspect of military operations smarter, from helicopter maintenance to missile targeting.

Yet AI's most significant effect on warfare may not be processing information faster, at greater scales, or more precisely than humans. AI systems don't think like humans. They think differently. And this difference in cognitive processes has potentially significant consequences for warfare.

Time and again, when AI systems achieve superhuman performance in games or simulations, their performance is not just better than humans. It is also different. Heron Systems' AI in the AlphaDogfight competition employed high-precision, split-second gunshots, demonstrating a "superhuman capability" making shots that were "almost impossible" for humans, as one fighter pilot explained. During AlphaGo's celebrated victory over Lee Sedol, it made a move that so stunned Lee that he got up from the table and left the room. AlphaGo calculated the odds that a human would have made that move (based on its database of 30 million expert human moves) as 1 in 10,000. AlphaGo's move wasn't just better. It was inhuman.

AlphaGo's unusual move wasn't a fluke. AlphaGo plays differently than humans in a number of ways. It will carry out multiple simultaneous attacks on different parts of the board, whereas human players tend to focus on one region. Human players tend to play on the corners and sides of the board, whereas AlphaGo plays across the entire board. And AlphaGo has developed novel opening moves, including some that humans simply do not understand. Experts who study AlphaGo's playing style describe it as "alien," and "from an alternate dimension."

Similar inhuman playing styles have been seen in AI agents across a range of games. The poker-playing AI agent Libratus plays differently than expert human players. It makes bets that are unusually small or unusually large, sometimes twenty times the size of the pot. It uses betting tactics like limping and donk betting that are generally considered poor tactics, but it is able to execute them effectively because of a more fine-grained understanding of the game's probabilities. Libratus can also change betting tactics more effectively than a human player. "It splits its bets into three, four, five different sizes," Daniel McAulay (who lost to Libratus) told *Wired* magazine. "No human has the ability to do that."

Chess grandmasters have pored over the moves of the chess-playing AI agent AlphaZero to analyze its style. AlphaZero learned to play chess entirely through self-play without any data from human games and has adopted a unique playing style. AlphaZero focuses its energies on attacking the opponent's king, resulting in "ferocious, unexpected attacks," according to experts who have studied its play. AlphaZero is willing to sacrifice material for positional advantage and strongly favors optionality—moves that give it more options in the future. Many elements of its playing style are common to human experts, but its play deviates in important ways from contemporary elite human players. AlphaZero will sacrifice chess pieces early on in a game for longer-term advantage, including sacrifices that have no immediate opportunity to regain material but open positions to attack the opponent's king. AlphaZero particularly excels at combining attacks and maximizing its use of mobility, applying both principles in ways that are difficult for humans to replicate. AlphaZero ignores some conventional wisdom that humans have developed about how to play certain positions, generally to good effect. For the conventional wisdom it does follow, AlphaZero is willing to make exceptions and selectively ignore commonly accepted rules. Its play suggests a more holistic understanding of the game across both time and space than human players, a trait that is even more striking because it does not rely as heavily on brute-force calculation as other AI chess programs. While AlphaZero's ability to search 60,000 moves per second is vastly superior to human experts, it is far less than the previously reigning chess engine, Stockfish, which searches roughly 60 million positions per second.

Computers have also achieved human-level performance and beaten top human players in real-time computer strategy games, such as *StarCraft II* and *Dota 2*. These games pit opposing sides in a battle to control territory and resources, with each player moving agents around a digital battlefield to perform reconnaissance, resource collection, and combat. They are valuable test beds for AI agents, since they are imperfect information games (in which some of the information is hidden from the players, like in poker) and they are highly complex. In *StarCraft II*, for example, at any given point in time there are approximately 10^{26} choices for actions a player can take. A full game includes thousands of action steps, with both players acting simultaneously. Because some of the information is hidden, players are interacting in a dynamic and constantly changing environment of which they only have limited knowledge.

Real-time strategy games also require agents to balance both short-term tactical actions with long-term planning. *Dota 2*, for example, has approximately 20,000 time steps, or time periods at which a player can make a move, in a single game. This is several orders of magnitude longer than chess, which has roughly 80 moves per game, or *go* at approximately 150 moves per game.

AI agents have excelled in real-time computer strategy games through superiority at what militaries call command and control, the process by which commanders direct military forces to execute their mission. AI players have access to the exact same information, resources, and units as human players. The individual units engaged in combat have the same speed, offensive, and defensive abilities. Any advantage due to the AI comes from their ability to process information, make decisions, and take actions. AI agents' victories demonstrate that machines can dramatically outperform humans in command-and-control, performance advantages that could be very valuable in war.

Real-time strategy games have brought to the fore some of AI agents' natural advantages over humans, particularly in speed, precision, coordination, and situational awareness. AI agents are far superior to humans in micro play, which entails maneuvering individual units in simulated combat and controlling their actions. It's not just that AI agents are faster—although they are capable of being much, much faster than even the top professional human gamers. AI agents are also able to absorb more information simultaneously, rather than having to divide their attention over multiple tasks. These advantages are considerable. Left unconstrained, AI agents are effectively invincible in small-unit tactics, able to dodge enemy fire in computer games. Even when limited to roughly approximate human speed, AI agents have demonstrated significant advantages over humans in the detailed mechanics of coordinating simulated battlefield units. They are more precise and avoid wasting valuable actions, time, or resources. AI agents can also attack with greater coordination among multiple disparate units or co-operative AI agents.

Many of these advantages were on display with OpenAI's *Dota 2* agents, OpenAI Five. (*Dota 2* is a team computer game in which five players work cooperatively on the same team against five opposing players.) OpenAI's agents were able to identify human player attacks and swiftly counter them faster than human players could react, even while operating within a 200-millisecond delay that was intended to level the playing field. Despite being restricted to the same physical reaction time as human players, the AI agents were able to perceive an unfolding situation, address it, and counter it faster than humans. OpenAI's agents, which are separate team members controlled by different AI players, were also able to precisely coordinate their attacks, hitting enemy units at the exact right moment and with the exact right amount of damage without wasting excess resources. These attributes—speed, precision, and coordination—cause OpenAI's agents to particularly excel in team fights, where multiple agents control characters cooperatively against multiple opponents. OpenAI's bots also play with unusual aggressiveness relative to human players, with the AI agents constantly on the attack. After one game, a human player remarked, "It felt like I was pressured at all times in the game."

While the specific algorithms and tactics used for playing chess, go, poker, StarCraft II, or Dota 2 wouldn't translate to real-world combat, the same general attributes of superhuman speed, awareness, precision, coordination, calculated risk-taking, and aggression could be extremely valuable in actual combat. Militaries that trained algorithms to take on command-and-control functions could potentially render their competitors demoralized and helpless, just as AI agents have done in computer games.

Across multiple types of games, some common patterns emerge about AI's potential advantages over humans. The first is perhaps the most obvious: increased speed and scale of information processing. In chess, human grandmasters can look only fifteen to twenty moves ahead compared to AlphaZero's 60,000 positions per second. In dogfighting, where split-second timing matters, the AI agent isn't burdened with the slowness of human cognition or reflexes. In capture-the-flag computer games, AI agents can tag opponents faster and more accurately than humans. In real-time computer strategy games, AI agents can execute tasks faster than humans are capable of, including multiple simultaneous actions.

AI agents can also look more holistically at the entire state of a game. In StarCraft II or Dota 2, an AI agent doesn't need to focus its attention on a single part of the map where combat is unfolding as a human does. It can take in information about the whole map simultaneously. This gives the AI agents greater orientation and awareness of the whole of action and the ability to optimally prioritize resources. AI agents also demonstrate attentiveness to parts of the game that are not directly engaged in competition at the moment. Both AlphaZero, the chess-playing agent, and AlphaStar, the StarCraft II–playing agent, have demonstrated the behavior of redeploying pieces that are no longer needed after an attack, rather than waiting for them to be attacked first.

The superhuman attentiveness of AI agents also plays out in their ability to not make the sort of careless blunders that characterize even expert human play. The ability to play nearly flawlessly, even if in some circumstances unimaginatively, can be a tremendous advantage in many games, especially since games are designed to be roughly evenly balanced between opposing sides. After playing against AlphaStar, professional *StarCraft II* player Grzegorz "MaNa" Komincz noted, "I've realized how much my gameplay relies on forcing mistakes and being able to exploit human reactions." Simply avoiding careless mistakes can be a major advantage for AI agents.

Another advantage is superhuman precision, which opens up novel strategies unavailable to humans. For example, limping in poker, forward-quarter shots in dogfighting, or perfectly calibrated team attacks in *Dota 2*. AI agents' superhuman precision also enables them to operate extremely efficiently, conserving and allocating resources to optimal efficiency. In strategy games that involve building up resources over time, this can lead to significant cumulative advantages.

AI agents also appear to have major advantages over humans in coordination and long-term planning. In chess, AlphaZero excels at combining multiple attacks. In *Dota 2*, AI agents demonstrate superhuman coordination in tactical actions, such as multicharacter attacks, but also in strategic actions. When playing *Dota 2*, human players tend to divide up the map among teammates, with players only switching locations occasionally. OpenAI Five's five AI agents switched their characters' locations on the map more frequently than human players, flexibly adjusting as a team as the game progressed. In poker, *go*, and chess, AI agents are able to make moves that may appear weak at first, but gain them a long-term positional advantage. This advantage is not always present, however, and human observers have at times criticized AI agents for their apparent lack of long-term planning.

Across many games, AI agents have widened the space of available tactics and strategies, exhibiting greater range in behaviors than human players. While the novel strategies of chess- and *go*-playing agents have often received attention, the same behaviors have been observed in other games including poker and computer games. Professional *StarCraft II* player Dario "TLO" Wünsch remarked of AlphaStar, "The agent demonstrated strategies I hadn't thought of before, which means there may still be new ways of playing the game that we haven't fully explored yet." In some cases, this increased variability directly leads to advantage, as in poker where unpredictability is a key advantage. In other cases, it has expanded how humans think about the game, such as in chess where AlphaZero has led human grandmasters to explore new openings.

AI agents appear to have the ability to engage in dramatic shifts in strategies

An AI agent pilots a fighter jet in a simulated dogfight. AI agents have beaten experienced human fighter pilots in simulators by executing maneuvers, such as head-to-head gunshots, that are nearly impossible for humans. DARPA is now working on transitioning AI agents to piloting physical aircraft.

(Heron Systems)

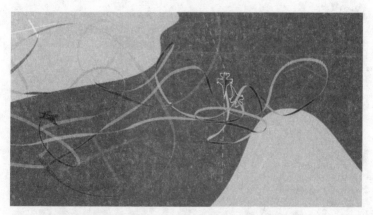

AI agents are trained through competitive self-play, learning their own dog-fighting maneuvers. Unless specially trained to avoid doing so, AI agents will pull sustained high-G maneuvers in simulations that are unsafe for human pilots. Building safe AI agents is an active area of research.

(Heron Systems)

AI startup Heron Systems, the winner of the AlphaDogfight competition, proudly displays their winning trophy, a flight helmet. To tap into AI innovation, the Defense Department will have to engage with small startups and companies outside of the traditional defense industry.

(Courtesy Paul Scharre)

The massive robot Workhorse, designed to aid cleanup at the Three Mile Island nuclear power plant, sits in the lobby of the National Robotics Engineering Center (NREC). The Army housed their AI Task Force at NREC along "Robotics Row," a concentration of robotics companies and research labs in Pittsburgh.

(Courtesy Paul Scharre)

Terregator, short for Terrestrial Navigator, at the NREC lobby in Pittsburgh. Terregator was built at Carnegie Mellon University in the 1980s to help advance the field of mobile robotics. American universities are a draw for AI talent from around the world, giving the United States a critical lead in the global AI competition.
(Courtesy Paul Scharre)

An MQ-9 Reaper drone flies over California en route to a mission to monitor California wildfires. In one of their first AI applications, the Joint AI Center applied computer vision algorithms to help map wildfires.
(Master Sergeant Gregory Solman / California Air National Guard)

An MQ-9 Reaper equipped with a Gorgon Stare pod taxis at Kandahar, Afghanistan, in 2015. Gorgon Stare is a wide area imaging tool that allows the military to surveil dozens of square kilometers at once. Wide area surveillance tools like Gorgon Stare, however, increase the burden of intelligence analysis, necessitating AI to help process video feeds.

(Technical Sergeant Robert Cloys / U.S. Air Force)

Indiana Air National Guard intelligence analysts process imagery from a Gorgon Stare sensor in the aftermath of Hurricane Florence in 2018. The DoD Joint AI Center used disaster relief missions for some of their first AI applications, including analyzing flooding and damage assessment after hurricanes.

(Staff Sergeant Lonnie Wiram / Indiana Air National Guard)

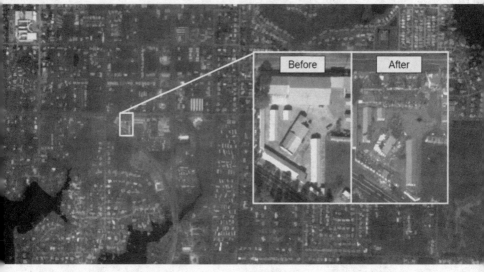

Before   After

An AI model trained on CrowdAI's platform assesses flooding damage from Hurricane Michael in Florida in 2018. The model was trained to identify building damage according to FEMA guidelines. AI models can be trained to identify objects in drone and satellite imagery, helping militaries make sense of the deluge of information created by modern sensors.

(CrowdAI)

Soldiers with the California National Guard fight fires in Camp Roberts, California, in 2016. DoD used AI to help map wildfires, improving the quality of information available to firefighters on the ground. AI can be used to help process information and accelerate decision timelines for a range of applications.

(California Army National Guard)

An AI model trained on CrowdAI's platform counts damaged buildings following the Camp Fire wildfire in 2018, the deadliest and most destructive wildfire in California's history. AI can synthesize, process, and aggregate information, giving humans quicker access to more accurate information so they can better understand complex events in real time.

(CrowdAI)

An MH-60 Black Hawk helicopter from the 160th Special Operations Aviation Regiment provides air support for Army Rangers from the 75th Ranger Regiment during a training mission. Special operations helicopters were one of the first test projects for AI-based predictive maintenance. The DoD spends over $280 billion annually in operations and maintenance. Even a minor improvement in maintenance costs could yield massive savings.

(Private First Class Nathaniel Newkirk / U.S. Army)

Surveillance cameras blanket a light pole in front of the Monument to the People's Heroes in Tiananmen Square, China. The Chinese Communist Party is in the process of constructing a massive surveillance apparatus to monitor its citizens. Over half of the world's estimated one billion surveillance cameras are in China.

(Courtesy Paul Scharre)

Example of a smart city operations center on display at Huawei company offices in Beijing. According to Huawei, its safe city technology is used in more than 100 countries. Many countries around the world are adopting Chinese-style surveillance technology, laws, and practices to monitor their citizens, threatening to undermine freedoms around the world.

(Courtesy Paul Scharre)

A person wears glasses designed to defeat facial recognition systems at a conference hosted by U.S. Special Operations Command and Carnegie Mellon University. AI systems are vulnerable to a range of attacks, from adversarial images to data poisoning, that exploit vulnerabilities in their cognitive processes. Militaries must ensure that as they adopt AI, they are building systems that are safe, secure, and robust.

(Michael Bottoms / U.S. Special Operations Command)

A small autonomous drone flies as part of a military AI demonstration in Fort Benning, Georgia. Artificial intelligence will transform warfare in the coming decades, accelerating the tempo of military operations as humans offload cognitive tasks to machines.

(Alexander Gago / Fort Benning Public Affairs Office)

and risk-taking in ways that are different from human players and, in some cases, impossible for human players to match. In poker, Libratus can make wild shifts in bet sizes. In *go*, once AlphaGo has a secure advantage it plays conservatively, since it is designed to maximize its chances of winning, rather than its margin of victory over the other player. If AlphaGo is ahead, it will play conservatively to lock-in what may be a narrow margin, rather than press to widen the gap. Yet AI agents don't always play cautiously. In chess, AlphaZero will sacrifice pieces early on in a game, taking risk for a longer-term advantage. In playing *Dota 2*, the OpenAI Five agents play aggressively, putting constant pressure on human players and never letting up for an instant. OpenAI Five agents also have demonstrated the ability to engage in more finely calibrated risk-taking than human players. OpenAI researchers noted:

> Human players are often cautious when their hero has low health; OpenAI Five seemed to have a very finely-tuned understanding of when an aggressive attack with a low-health hero was worth a risk.

AI agents do not, in general, appear to play more aggressively or conservatively than humans. Rather, they appear to play in a manner that is more strategic and rational (one might say cold-blooded), regulating their degree of aggressiveness or caution to what is called for in the moment. While a human player might have a tendency toward conservative or aggressive play, AI agents seem capable of executing both extremes and pivoting quickly between them based on what is optimal for achieving their goal.

AI agents are not flawless. There are common themes in their weaknesses too. While their performance is simply superior to humans in some games such as chess and *go*, for real-time computer strategy games, the open-ended environment brings some of AI agents' limitations to light. One consistent weakness is that the AI agents playing *StarCraft II* and *Dota 2* appear to lean heavily on their advantages in micro play, perhaps to the detriment of long-term planning. A few examples hint at this dynamic. For AlphaStar, the *StarCraft II* agent, DeepMind dropped any restrictions on the agent's rate of actions in a test run, allowing it to operate at superhuman speed. The agent's performance decreased. The researchers behind AlphaStar speculated:

> Unexpectedly, increasing [actions per minute] also reduces performance, possibly because the agent spends more effort on refining micro-tactics than on learning diverse strategies.

If this is indeed what is going on with the agent, then it would not be surprising. AI systems in a diverse array of situations frequently fall victim to settling for suboptimal strategies if those strategies are easier to discover. In *Dota 2*, observers noted that the AI agents may be overly reliant on their team-fighting skills, rather than learning better long-term planning, because they excel at micro play. Winning in simpler ways is easier, and the AI agents are playing to win.

AI's general characteristic of brittleness also was on display in some games. In poker, human players occasionally found parts of the game tree that Libratus had not mapped and did not perform well at. In one *Dota 2* match, OpenAI allowed the audience to pick the AI team's characters (called "heroes" in the game). The audience chose a poor lineup of characters (a bad team). The AI agents performed poorly and inflexibly, using the same familiar tactics that were ill-suited for the new characters. The OpenAI Five also played in a restricted game space, with certain characters and types of actions off-limits to reduce the complexity of the game. The final version of OpenAI Five played over 7,000 games on the internet, racking up an impressive 99.4 percent win average against 15,000 human players. But the model was not as robust as the numbers might suggest. Every time that the *Dota 2* game was updated by its developer, such as adding new characters, items, or maps, OpenAI researchers had to perform what they termed "surgery" on the AI model to adapt it to the new environment. The researchers similarly had to perform surgery if they made available to the model a new action or item as they matured the model's capabilities and introduced it to more complex environments. The alternative to this relatively manual engineering process was to retrain a new model entirely from scratch on the new game environment, which would have been both time- and cost-prohibitive. Without significant engineering work or retraining, the model would frequently struggle to adapt to even modest changes. This brittleness is likely to be a major detriment in real-world settings where the space of possible enemy actions is open-ended and the environment is not highly constrained and repeatable as it is in games.

In gaming environments, some of these advantages of AI agents are viewed differently than others. Superhuman precision and speed are often viewed as unfair advantages. The fact that Heron Systems' AI dogfighting agent was able to execute forward-quarter gunshots that are banned in training by human pilots could arguably be seen as an unfair advantage. In testing AI agents playing a capture-the-flag computer game, DeepMind slowed down its agents' reaction times and tagging accuracy to match that of humans. AlphaStar's superhuman click rate was a source of controversy even after DeepMind slowed it down. (DeepMind later slowed it down even further.) AI agents' superior strategic abilities, however, are often celebrated, such as their prowess at chess or *go*. In war, militaries may view these benefits differently. War isn't fair, and superhuman speed and precision that enables better combat performance is likely to be welcomed. Conversely, AI decision-making that is somewhat mysterious, like the unconventional moves AI agents sometimes make in poker, chess, and *go*, might be harder for militaries to embrace. It is easier for militaries to trust an AI agent whose advantage is clearly identifiable, such as quicker reflexes. Placing faith in an AI agent whose cognition is opaque and long-term plan is unknown may be a harder sell. Yet over time as AI systems take on more roles, including in tactical planning and decision-making, military leaders may face the decision whether to trust an AI system's recommendation that they don't fully understand.

Finding ways to optimally employ AI systems and combine them with humans in a joint human-machine cognitive system will be a difficult task. AI systems are sometimes characterized by military professionals as being teammates, as if they are another soldier in the squad or a copilot in the cockpit. But human-machine cognitive teams are fundamentally different from human-human teams. Militaries are adding into their warfighting functions an information processing system that can think in ways that are quite alien from human intelligence. Militaries that best learn how to marry human and machine cognition and take advantage of the unusual attributes of how AI systems think will have tremendous advantages.

AI systems will not just change the cognitive dimensions of war—the processes of synthesizing information, making decisions, and executing tasks among distributed units. AI systems will also change the psychology of war. War is a human endeavor, and it brings with it the flaws and limitations not just of human cognition but also human emotion. The quality of human fighting units depends on intangible factors such as morale, esprit de corps, and unit cohesion. Human soldiers suffer fear, anger, exhaustion, fatigue, and desperation. AI systems will experience none of these emotional burdens. War with AI systems will remain violent and chaotic, but AI systems will not be burdened by war's emotional toll the way humans are, and AI systems will likely fight differently as a result.

Kenneth Payne of King's College London has outlined a number of ways that AI systems' performance may differ from humans because of psychological factors. Payne argues human psychology gives some advantages to defenders, which AI systems would not have.

> The relative psychological advantages of defense will no longer apply: tactical AI will not be susceptible to the same cognitive heuristics as humans—including the sunk cost effect, the endowment effect, and prospect theory, all of which would in some degree enhance the fighting power of a harried defender.

To put it another way, AI systems would fight with the same degree of mindless dedication on both offense and defense. Payne further suggests AI systems may not be burdened by psychological stresses that attackers face, such as "the mental strain of operating far from home." While the removal of these psychological burdens would appear to favor attackers, other factors could favor defenders. Payne notes:

> Attackers enjoy the initiative, and in human conflict this has the potential to generate shock and shatter the moral cohesion of the defending force.

AI defenders, however, would not suffer from psychological shock. Airpower and artillery barrages to help wear down defenders' nerves would be meaningless against an AI defender. Even the concept of one side having the "initiative" in combat may turn out to be irrelevant, a human psychological construct.

Removing elements of human psychology from combat may change warfare in other ways as well. Combat action among humans ebbs and flows. There are lulls in gunfire, breaks in artillery barrages, and occasional periods of calm on front lines. These natural variations in combat intensity among humans may not exist when war is prosecuted by AI agents. Instead, AI agents may sustain the kind of relentless pressure they have exhibited in games, although stretched across hours, days, weeks, or months of military operations. If unceasing pressure from AI adversaries was exhausting for human gamers, it could be debilitating to soldiers in combat.

How humans react to AI adversaries could also change important psychological aspects of war. Human players competing against AI agents often describe them as an unstoppable juggernaut, never making mistakes. Fighting battles against a superhuman adversary could be deeply demoralizing to human soldiers. After losing to AlphaGo, Lee Sedol said, "I kind of felt powerless." Three years after his defeat, he retired from the game of *go*. Lee cited AI's influence on *go* as the reason, saying AI "cannot be defeated." Even when there are opportunities, humans could fail to take them out of despair or a perception that an apparent opening is merely a trap. In game one of Garry Kasparov's 1997 match against the chess-playing engine Deep Blue, a bug in Deep Blue's programming caused it to make a random move. Kasparov, who couldn't conceive of the computer program committing such an egregious error, incorrectly concluded that Deep Blue could see twenty moves in advance, which would have been a tremendous advantage at the time (it couldn't). This overestimation of Deep Blue's abilities shook Kasparov's confidence and may have contributed to him prematurely resigning the next game when he could have potentially forced a draw. Simply the perception of a superhuman AI opponent could undermine human soldiers' morale to fight.

Even though AI systems will be able to operate without the emotional and psychological hindrances of human soldiers, humans are unlikely to be freed from the miseries of war. The future is unlikely to be one of bloodless wars of robots fighting robots. Humans will still have a place in war and will still be subject to its horrors. For one, human cognition will still be needed in war for the time being because of its greater generality, robustness, and adaptability to novel circumstances. And humans will be needed on the front lines because of the difficulties in long-range communication, especially in contested environments where communications links are subject to jamming. Even if robotic systems are used at the very edge of combat in direct contact with the enemy, humans will be needed close by to quarterback the fight and redirect robotic forces in response to enemy adaptation. Additionally, humans will remain victims of war because it is likely only human suffering that will cause wars to end. Humans may fight using robotic and AI systems in the future, but it will still be humans fighting other humans. They simply will be killing each other with robots and AI-enabled missiles, rather than rudimentary smart weapons today. War, at least for the time being, will remain a human endeavor.

33

BATTLEFIELD SINGULARITY

It can be daunting to stand at the dawn of a new cognitive age of human-machine teaming in warfare and imagine the future, and we should be humble in our ability to do so. The deep learning revolution is only a decade old, and the capabilities of AI systems and how they are used decades from now may bear little resemblance to today. In 1913, a decade after the first flight at Kitty Hawk, airplanes were just beginning to be integrated into military forces, predominantly in reconnaissance roles. There was no hint of the fleets of bombers that would devastate entire cities in World War II or the supersonic jets and intercontinental nuclear bombers that would be invented during the Cold War. We are at a similar position with AI, attempting to peer into an unknown and highly uncertain future.

AI's ability to imbue military forces with greater situational awareness, precision, coordination, and speed is likely to result in a battlefield that is faster paced, more transparent, and more lethal. The ability of AI systems to process large amounts of information and take in the totality of action is likely to make it increasingly difficult for military forces to hide, placing a premium on camouflage, deception, and decoys. New tactics will be needed as a result.

In World War I, militaries struggled to adapt their tactics to the new reality the industrial revolution had unleashed on the battlefield. The machine gun rendered nineteenth-century tactics ineffective by increasing lethality through both a higher rate of fire and greater effective range. During the Napoleonic era, infantry troops advancing over open terrain against fixed defenses could face an average of two shots fired at each soldier during the course of their advance. (The firepower was also not very accurate.) By 1916, defenders armed with machine guns and rifles could pour an average of 200 shots per soldier at attackers moving over open terrain. With this hundredfold increase in firepower, defending fire didn't need to be particularly accurate to be lethal. In the bloody trenches of World War I, military leaders stuck to their outdated tactics, throwing bodies against fixed positions in a vain attempt to break the deadlock of trench warfare. In the first day of the Battle of the Somme, Great Britain lost 19,000 men attempting to break through the German lines. A generation of European men were killed or wounded in the trenches of World War I. By early 1918, military tactics had finally adapted to the brutal realities of industrialized warfare, after three and a half long years of fighting.

Future military tactics will also need to adapt to a changed battlefield in which the enemy has greater visibility and the capacity to quickly and precisely strike exposed forces. The gunslinger advantage of AI in superhuman reaction times is likely to lead militaries to embrace automation for circumstances in which even a split-second advantage in shooting first substantially increases survivability. AI-enabled command and control is also likely to lead to greater coordination among distributed units across the battlefield, allowing greater dispersal of forces and more effective long-range coordinated campaigning.

AI enables a radical shift in military doctrine toward swarming, a method of fighting in which many disparate elements maneuver independently but cooperatively as part of a cohesive whole. Swarming differs from traditional maneuver warfare, in which military units move as part of formations. For example, in contemporary ground combat, a line of soldiers might pin down enemy forces, while another element maneuvers to achieve a flanking position on the enemy. Militaries generally try to limit the number of independently maneuvering units working in close proximity in order to minimize the potential for fratricide. Similarly, soldiers moving as a unit may spread out to avoid being targeted, but they still move as one, stopping and starting together and maintaining the same speed and spacing. Swarming is different. It involves individual elements maneuvering independently but to achieve a common goal—more like a sports team, with individuals moving in an organic, fluid way, reacting to each other's movements. Few sports have more than a dozen players on the field at a time, though. (Australian football is an outlier, with eighteen players on the field per team.) Military squads have varied over time and by country but generally number around seven to fourteen individuals. The similarity in these numbers is not a coincidence. They are set by the limits of human cognition. A hundred sports players working together on the field would be chaos. Coordinating their actions would require the more regimented structures that militaries use to manage large numbers of troops, breaking them down into units and subunits with leaders for each. These cognitive limits do not apply to AI systems, which could coordinate hundreds or thousands of independently maneuvering elements toward a coherent whole.

Swarming tactics have occurred throughout military history, although their use has often been limited, in part because of the challenge of maintaining cohesion among large numbers of independently maneuvering forces. If successfully executed, swarming has many advantages. It allows military forces to disperse when attacked, avoiding presenting the enemy with a single formation to target. Swarming forces can then reconverge when it is advantageous to attack enemy forces. Swarms present an enemy with a large number of independently moving targets to track, as well as the threat of simultaneous attack from multiple directions.

True swarms are more than just a deluge of attackers. Swarming entails individual elements coordinating and altering their behavior in response to one another. While groups of small aerial drones have seen increasing use in combat, including in mass drone attacks, most do not exhibit true cooperative swarming behavior in which individual drones are responding to each other's actions. In June 2021, Israel allegedly used the first true drone swarm in an attack in Gaza. Nonmilitary robot swarms have been demonstrated in research labs and multiagent AI cooperation has been demonstrated in games. It is only a matter of time before drone swarms become a regular tactical tool in combat.

At first, swarming will be merely a tactic narrowly used in certain situations, but AI opens the possibility that swarming, over time, could completely restructure how militaries fight at the operational level of war. Rather than military formations maneuvering to gain a positional advantage, swarming could become the dominant mode of military operations, with thousands of disparate units spreading across a battlefield then converging to attack. Such an approach would be very challenging for humans to counteract, as it could overload the cognitive abilities of human defenders. If large-scale AI-driven swarming proved successful as an operational approach to organizing and employing military forces, other militaries could be forced to follow suit to survive. Such a development is likely decades away, if at all. There is a major leap between small tactical drone swarms, a near-term prospect, and the widespread use of AI-driven swarming across the entire battlefield. But AI could enable such a future.

If AI swarms become a dominant form of warfare, they could lead to a change in how military forces are organized. Today, militaries are organized in a hierarchical fashion into squads, platoons, companies, battalions, brigades, divisions, and corps. Each level consolidates usually three to five elements into a larger unit. There are roughly three to four squads in a platoon, three to five platoons in a company, three to five companies in a battalion, and so on. Militaries use the term "span of control" to refer to the number of subordinate units a commander directs, and the limits of span of control come from human cognition. A commander cannot reasonably directly manage a hundred subordinates at a time. These hierarchical structures would not be needed for AI command and control and in fact may be a hindrance to optimal operations.

Humans commanding an AI swarm would have a very different relationship with battlefield action than humans have today. Humans would establish the swarm's goals, supervise its operation, and even conceivably intervene to make changes, but they would effectively hand over execution of swarm behavior to one (or many) AI systems. Humans would have ceded the "micro" of combat action to AI, and over time the amount of combat authority delegated to AI systems could grow. As machines become more advanced, the centaur model of human-machine teaming may no longer work. Garry Kasparov, who created human-machine teaming chess after his loss to Deep Blue, has suggested that as machines become more intelligent the human-machine relationship will switch to a "'shepherd' model" in which "the machines become the experts and humans oversee them."

Shepherding advanced AI systems may not be so simple. The increased scale and speed of operations enabled by AI could begin to push warfare out of human control. Such a shift would not happen overnight. It would likely take decades to unfold and happen incrementally, but little by little militaries could find themselves ceding more and more decision-making to machines. Just like warfare today is fought by humans but mediated through physical machines—tanks, airplanes, ships, and machine guns—warfare in the future could be fought between humans but mediated by AI systems that plan and execute combat.

Some Chinese military scholars have speculated about the potential for a future "singularity" in warfare, in which the pace of AI-driven action on the battlefield exceeds human cognition. In the article "Artificial intelligence: disruptively changing the 'rules of the game,'" Chen Hanghui of the PLA's Army Command College described such a potential development:

> In the future battlefield, with the continuous advancement of artificial intelligence and human-machine integration technology, the pace of combat will become faster and faster until it arrives at a "singularity": The human brain will no longer be able to handle the ever-changing battlefield

situation and must give up most of the decision-making power to highly intelligent machines.

American defense scholars have hypothesized about a similar development, which retired general John Allen and tech entrepreneur and author Amir Husain have termed "hyperwar."

The evolution of warfare into a regime that is beyond human control would be a profound and troubling development. Humans would lose the ability to effectively control battlefield actions, not just at the tactical "micro" level of how individual units maneuver but at the strategic level of how the war unfolds. Even if humans choose whether to start a conflict, they may lose the ability to control escalation or terminate a war at the time of their choosing. Accidents or unexpected AI decisions could lead to widespread devastation before humans could intervene. Such a development is unlikely in the near- or even mid-term, but if a battlefield singularity is the long-term outcome of the integration of AI into military forces, humanity risks a dangerous future in which wars could spiral out of human control.

IN the most extreme circumstances, future developments in military AI could change the nature of war itself. Military scholars distinguish between the "character of warfare" (the way in which militaries fight) and "the nature of war" (the essential elements of war as an activity). Western military scholars frequently speak of the ever-changing character of warfare and the immutable and unchanging nature of war. The distinction is that the character of warfare, the weapons, methods, and tactics by which people fight, is constantly evolving. Yet the essence of war as an activity remains the same. War is a violent struggle among competing groups of people for political power.

The idea that the nature of war is immutable and unchanging over time is often held as an article of faith in Western military circles. Claims that new technologies might fundamentally alter the nature of war eventually prove unfounded. Airpower, for example, dramatically changed the character of warfare but not its nature. It was, therefore, of some interest when retired general and then–Secretary of Defense Jim Mattis remarked offhandedly to reporters that he thought AI might change the nature of war. In a conversation about AI, Mattis said, "I'm certainly questioning my original premise that the fundamental nature of war will not change. You've got to question that now. I just don't have the answers yet." The idea that AI, or anything for that matter, might change the nature of war is a bold proposition that challenges existing dogma. Yet there are a number of ways in which AI could, in theory, change the nature of war.

War, at least how it has been fought up until now, is a human endeavor. War is shaped by human cognition, psychology, and emotion. The introduction of AI in small ways is unlikely to change this. Prior technological innovations such as machine guns, aircraft, and submarines changed warfare but not the nature of war. Yet it is possible that the use of AI could reach a tipping point beyond which war becomes something else, something that is so dominated by inhuman characteristics that it is no longer war as we know it. An increased speed or scale of conflict or the use of AI-based tactics, even large-scale swarms, would not likely change the nature of war. For the foreseeable future, humans will remain part of war because of the limitations of AI systems. But it is possible to conceive of some distant future in which more advanced forms of AI are employed that remove humans entirely from the business of fighting wars. Such advanced AI systems could not be built with the technology today, which is too limited and narrow. But a future in which AI systems entirely took over warfighting responsibilities and the only human role was to authorize an AI to initiate conflict might fundamentally change the nature of war. Humans might still be victims of war, suffering AI-directed attacks. But they would no longer be agents of war engaged in the fighting. If humans no longer played a role in warfighting and combat was entirely stripped of any human psychology or emotion, war would look radically different. Many of the elements of the nature of war today would be absent. The activity would be a kind of war, but it would be different from previous human-fought wars. Its nature would have changed.

War is prosecuted for a political purpose, and AI-driven war that was conducted without human intent or purpose could be another way in which the nature of war could change. One way in which this could occur is if AI systems became so advanced that it was impossible for humans to maintain effective control over them. AI systems that expanded wars, escalated conflicts, or initiated wars without human intent could, in some cases, conceivably change the nature of war. On a small scale, accidental escalation in a conflict would not change the nature of war. War always entails risk of circumstances spiraling out of leaders' control simply because of the chaos of war and the difficulty of controlling one's own military forces, as well as the challenges in gauging a competitor's response. The logic of brinkmanship, in which leaders deliberately engage in risk-taking for advantage, is predicated precisely on this risk. Yet in the most extreme cases, if AI-initiated actions caused entire wars to be fought without human intent or any political purpose behind them, then how would we characterize those wars? Would they be industrial accidents? The violence that ensued would be like war but fundamentally different if it lacked human intent or purpose.

Another way in which war could be devoid of political purpose is if it became so destructive that there was no rational political purpose in waging it, since everyone would be dead. A hypothetical "doomsday device" that destroyed all of humanity would be such a weapon. It might be rational to brandish such a weapon, threatening an opponent with mutual suicide to coerce an outcome, but there would be no rational reason to employ it, since the outcome—annihilation—would render any political goal moot. Nuclear weapons flirt with such a level of destructiveness, not in small-scale use (which may be horrible but still rational), but in the prospect of a massive exchange among nuclear superpowers that shatters human civilization. Should some future weapon, AI or otherwise, make extinction-level or near-extinction-level destruction a possibility, the threat to use such a weapon would be very consistent with human coercion and brinkmanship. But its actual use would be a war unlike any other, a war without political purpose.

A wholly different outcome from advanced AI is also conceivable, in which AI's superhuman prediction capabilities enable humans to achieve the political goals of war without actually fighting. War, to date, has been characterized by uncertainty and chance. Leaders who embark on a campaign have imperfect knowledge of the enemy's forces and perhaps even the true state of their own military forces. Terrain, weather, and other elements of "friction" in war further increase uncertainty and the role of chance in the outcome. Most of all, war is a violent contest of wills and, even if the balance of military power is known, the political will of the parties involved cannot be truly known in advance. Many times in wars, the weaker party has won by virtue of a stronger will. At least 50 percent of the time, and possibly more, one of the parties to a conflict has misjudged its outcome. If the outcomes of wars were perfectly known in advance, there presumably would be no need for war, as countries could resettle political disputes on new terms without resorting to violence. The element of chance—the possibility of victory despite difficult odds—is what gives war the space to thrive. One of the interesting features of AI agents in contemporary games is that they often include a prediction component that allows them to predict the likelihood of victory. If future, more advanced forms of AI could reliably predict the outcomes of entire wars, and if humans believed them, it could decrease the likelihood of war and perhaps even change how humans engage with war. If humans acted on these predictions, and if the predictions accounted for intangible factors like morale and will, then they could conceivably change the nature of war. Large-scale wars could become less likely, since leaders would be able to predict the outcome in advance, avoiding massive destruction. On the other hand, geopolitics may become even more dependent on costly signals to demonstrate will, giving more weight to brinkmanship and the domino theory that a loss in one war could lead to losses elsewhere. The development of superhuman AI prediction systems that could reliably estimate the outcomes of wars is far beyond the kind of AI capabilities that exist today. AI systems today can estimate the outcome of games only because they have a massive database of past games to draw upon. Unlike games, warfare is constantly changing. Each war is unique and the history of past wars may not provide reliable information about how this particular war will unfold. If such an AI system were possible, however, and wars were no longer decided by violence, it could conceivably change the nature of war.

Finally, the nature of war could change if humans found themselves fighting a conflict against a nonhuman entity, such as an advanced AI system that had gone awry and slipped beyond human control. One need not envision a science fiction–like scenario of a sentient AI system becoming self-aware and deciding to destroy humanity. Even nonsentient systems could cause great havoc and destruction. The very first internet worm was due to a misjudgment by its inventor, who was not intending to cause harm. It is possible to envision in the future advanced forms of adaptive and intelligent malware that are able to replicate, acquire resources, evade defenses, and cause significant harm without any human intent behind them. Such systems could be released by accident or, even if released intentionally, proliferate or evolve beyond human control. The computer worm Stuxnet appears to have spread far beyond its intended target, despite multiple protocols in place to limit its proliferation. If a future form of malware was adaptive, intelligent, or evolving, attempts to combat it could look like a form of warfare, with violence and fights to control resources. Yet it would be a conflict against a nonhuman entity. A "war" against such a system could be closer to struggles against biological viruses or other forces of nature, like combatting a wildfire, than war as humans have known it. While today's forms of malware and AI have nothing approximating these characteristics, it is possible that far more advanced forms of AI could. Drives to resource acquisition and survival could even be emergent properties of intelligence, an instrumental goal that intelligent systems adopt in order to achieve their final aims, whatever they may be. Intelligent, adaptive systems that acquire resources and fight for survival could even emerge without any human-directed goal at all, the product of selection among an evolutionary environment characterized by variation, selection, and replication.

None of these scenarios in which advanced forms of AI change the nature of war is necessarily likely. The caliber of AI systems today is so limited and rudimentary that there is no straight line from even the most capable AI systems today to the kind of super-advanced AI that could change the nature of war. But neither do such scenarios depend on the development of advanced AI as it is popularly conceived of, either artificial general intelligence (AGI), a hypothesized form of AI with intelligence comparable to humans, or superintelligence, with capabilities far beyond humans. Even advanced forms of AI that lack human-level abilities in a variety of aspects could still be quite powerful.

It is a fallacy to think that the pinnacle of intelligence is a human-like form of cognition or even that the natural trajectory of AI is toward intelligence that is more human-like. In fact, the history of AI to date suggests that machine intelligence is often very inhuman, an alien form of intelligence. While programs like AlphaGo and AlphaZero have only a very narrow form of intelligence with nothing approximating the generality of human intelligence, they are highly intelligent at the games they play. Whatever we mean when we say that games like chess and go require "intelligence," it is clear that these systems possess intelligence at those games. They do not engage in mere brute force calculation. They exhibit an intuition and even a beauty in the games they play. Yet the form of their intelligence, not just its structure in silicon but also the nature of how they think, is different from humans. This difference helps us better understand the nature of intelligence. While the field of AI dates back to the 1950s, there is no universal agreement among AI researchers on what intelligence is. One researcher observed, "There seem to be almost as many definitions of intelligence as there were experts asked to define it." AI scientists are like explorers in the wilderness, breaking new ground without a map and without an entirely clear sense of what they are looking for. As AI advances, it may spark a Copernican revolution in how we think about intelligence, with humans only one type of intelligence in a vast multidimensional space of all possible intelligences. More advanced forms of AI may lead to a Cambrian explosion of intelligence, producing a diverse array of intelligent systems with many different forms of cognition.

Intelligence is the most powerful force on the planet. Without claws, fangs, or armor, humans have ascended to the top of the food chain and spread to every corner of the globe due to their intelligence. Even the most cutting-edge

AI systems today have nothing remotely close to the general-purpose abilities of human intelligence, but the future of AI is highly uncertain. AI researchers vary widely in their predictions for when, if ever, machines may reach human-level intelligence. Surveys of several hundred AI researchers in 2016 and 2019 found aggregate forecasts of a 50 percent probability that AI systems could exceed human performance in all tasks by around 2060, but individual estimates varied widely. Any predictions should be taken with a grain of salt. It isn't clear whether researchers can make reliable predictions about a major, disruptive shift in *any* technology that is decades or more in the future. AI development could peter out, the victim of another AI "winter" in which progress slows, interest wanes, and research dollars dry up. Or AI technology could continue to mature, gifting humans with ever-more powerful tools of creation, control, and destruction.

34

RESTRAINT

In militarizing AI, nations are using for destructive purposes a technology that, even in its current form today, is both powerful and difficult to control. Even if none of the risks of more advanced forms of AI ever come to pass, the militarization of AI today poses serious risks to international peace and stability. While the current state of military AI competition does not meet the definition of an arms race, there are risks in how militaries might employ AI. Near-term AI could cause harm in a number of ways, including autonomous weapons, humans overtrusting prediction algorithms, and ways in which AI could upset nuclear stability. Nations should come together to help limit some of the worst dangers of military AI.

In addition to the risks of a race to the bottom on AI safety, there are a number of specific AI applications that could be dangerous to international stability. Lethal autonomous weapons, in which a machine is able to search for, select, and engage targets on its own without human intervention, are one potential risk. Nations have come together at the United Nations since 2014 to discuss the risks of lethal autonomous weapons, but diplomatic progress has moved slowly while the technology continues to advance. The intersection of AI and cyber systems could present other risks, further exacerbating competition in cyberspace.

Even nonlethal autonomous robotics could undermine stability among nations. Over the last decade, as countries have incorporated more and more uninhabited robotic vehicles into their military forces, they have increasingly been used in militarized disputes. Aerial drones have been used in contested regions around the globe and have been tools of provocation or targets for attack. Today, these systems are largely remote controlled. If they have automation at all, it is simple rule-based automation, such as the ability to navigate along preprogrammed GPS waypoints or return to a position if they lose communication with the remote human pilot. Yet over time, these robotic vehicles will incorporate increasingly capable automation and AI, enabling more autonomous operation. Machine learning will help autonomous systems perceive their environment and identify objects. One risk is that such systems have accidents, leading to collisions of robotic ships or aerial drones that go astray, perhaps flying into another country's territory. Such actions, which would not be intended by human operators, could escalate tensions among nations. Another kind of risk stems from the ambiguity about whether a robotic vehicle's actions are intended by humans. A country may not know whether another country's drone encroaching on sensitive territory or taking self-defense measures is acting consistent with human intent. This ambiguity could complicate escalation dynamics among nations, leading to misperceptions and miscalculation.

AI prediction systems that do not directly take any actions on their own could also complicate crisis dynamics. In the 1980s, the Soviet Union developed a computer program called RYaN (an acronym of its name in Russian, which translates to "Nuclear Missile Attack") to detect the impending launch of a surprise nuclear attack by the United States. The program absorbed data from 292 sources that Soviet analysts believed might be indicators of a surprise attack, such as the amount of blood held in Western blood banks and the location of Western leaders. A 1990 top secret U.S. intelligence assessment (declassified in 2015) concluded that RYaN led to a "self-reinforcing cycle" in which intelligence collectors sent information to Moscow that confirmed political leaders' beliefs. RYaN may have even played a role in exacerbating Soviet leaders' fears during the 1983 "war scare," when the Soviet Union placed military forces on heightened alert in response to NATO's Able Archer military exercise. Soviet leaders' engineering background may have led them to overtrust in the computer program. U.S. intelligence analysts concluded in 1990:

> Although it may seem absurd to some that the Soviets would put much stock in a computer model to assess something as complex as the strategic balance, we suspect this approach may have been especially appealing to top Soviet leaders at the time. Almost all were formally trained as engineers. A computer model which purported to be scientifically based and capable of quantifying the seemingly confusing strategic balance may therefore have had a high degree of credibility, particularly during a period in which the Soviet leadership seemed genuinely and increasingly wary of a US surprise attack.

Humans trusting in a massively complex computer program for analyzing reams of data to produce predictions does not seem so absurd today, when algorithms are used for everything from loan applications to stock trading to shopping recommendations. In the near term, intelligence agencies are likely to use AI as a tool for helping analysts sift through data. AI could especially be valuable in analyzing patterns in the "digital exhaust" created by people and organizations that may be clues to their activity. Analysis of open-source data, perhaps supplemented by traditional intelligence collection or data breaches, could conceivably shed light on military forces' movements, classified weapons projects, or other activity that governments may wish to keep secret.

A world of greater transparency among nations could be stabilizing, since it may be harder to mobilize military forces in secret and could reduce suspicions and unwarranted fears among nations. The United States publicly shared intelligence about Russia's military buildup prior to its invasion of Ukraine in early 2022, undercutting any Russian pretext for the invasion and helping to marshal international support for Ukraine. Western media outlets could also independently corroborate Russian military movements through commercial satellite imagery. The transparency afforded by modern information technology couldn't stop Russia's invasion, but it did eliminate the element of surprise.

If AI prediction systems gave faulty recommendations or were biased, or if humans misunderstood them, however, they could exacerbate misperceptions and fear among nations. Prediction systems are especially tricky for situations for which they may be little or no data, such as a surprise attack. Machine learning excels in situations in which there is a large amount of diverse, high-quality data. This may not exist for rare geopolitical events. Algorithms that perform well in day-to-day circumstances may perform poorly during crises when they are most needed. Furthermore, the opaque nature of complex AI systems today may make it difficult for policymakers to understand how they are performing and why.

Few areas are as consequential as nuclear stability, and defense analysts have explored several ways in which AI could affect the risk of nuclear war. AI could enable more capable autonomous robots and information processing that could help find and track mobile missile launchers or submarines, undermining nations' security in their nuclear deterrence and increasing incentives for a first strike. AI could enable more capable conventional military forces, causing some nations to rely more heavily on nuclear weapons for defense. AI could also be integrated directly into nuclear operations in a variety of roles. AI could help supplement early warning systems to detect an adversary's nuclear launch, which could be stabilizing or destabilizing depending on how it was implemented. AI could be used to enable increasingly autonomous robotic nuclear delivery systems, such as uninhabited nuclear bombers or submarines. Russia is reportedly developing an intercontinental, nuclear-armed autonomous underwater vehicle called the Status-6, or Poseidon. While the precise functionality and intended use of the Status-6 is unclear, the prospect of nuclear-armed robotic vehicles, either undersea or in the air as drone bombers, risks a loss of human control over nuclear weapons. The U.S. Air Force has repeatedly expressed unease with the idea of nuclear-weapons onboard a robotic vehicle. Yet other countries may have a different risk calculus.

In the most extreme case, a country could decide to delegate nuclear launch decisions to an automated system. Such a move might seem like madness, yet during the Cold War the Soviet Union reportedly built a semiautomated "dead hand" device called "Perimeter" which would enable a retaliatory nuclear attack if Soviet leadership were wiped out. A human would remain in the loop for the final launch decision, but this authority would be pushed to a relatively low-level Soviet officer in a secure bunker. Reports on its functionality differ, but some sources claim it remains operational in Russia today. In 2019, then head of the U.S. Joint AI Center, Lieutenant General Jack Shanahan stated unequivocally his belief that the United States should not develop a dead hand system. "No," he said. "This is the ultimate human decision that needs to be made which is in the area of nuclear command-and-control." Yet other countries have not been so transparent in their plans for the use of AI in nuclear operations.

The consequences of AI for international stability are complex and depend on human perception of the technology as much as the technology itself. If nations introduce AI into their military forces and AI is prone to accidents and policymakers know it is prone to accidents, it could induce caution and reduce the risk of inadvertent escalation. However, if military and civilian leaders overtrust in AI and automation or are overconfident in their bureaucracies' ability to build trustworthy systems that function well in crises, AI could introduce hidden risks that decision-makers are unaware of.

The risks posed by AI are not those of an arms race with runaway defense spending but rather a more generalized dynamic, called a security dilemma: One country takes steps to increase its security, such as investing in more weapons or new technologies, but these steps undermine the security of other countries. Other countries react, increasing their own security by developing new technologies. This dynamic might set off a race to the bottom on safety, an accelerated tempo of war leading to a battlefield singularity, an overreliance on brittle AI that increases the risk of accidents, or using AI in ways that undermine nuclear stability.

Nations can take steps to avoid these risks. Stopping AI's advancement is unlikely to succeed any more than one could have stopped the process of industrialization in the 1800s. AI technology is already so widely proliferated and diffuse that it will be available to a wide range of actors. However, countries could agree to some limits on AI uses in order to reduce some of the worst dangers. Limits could take the form of arms control, in which states agree to forgo some military AI applications. Others could take the form of confidence-building measures, a broad set of activities countries can undertake to reduce the risks of military competition. Confidence-building measures can include increased communication and information-sharing among countries, inspections and observers, "rules of the road" for military operations, and limits on military readiness or activities.

There are a variety of confidence-building measures countries could adopt to reduce AI-related risks. To reduce the risk of a race to the bottom on safety, countries could be more transparent about their test and evaluation processes. They could even agree to international best practices for assuring the safety of AI systems. To reduce the risk of an accelerated tempo of warfare, countries could bolster norms of humans "in the loop" for critical decisions, ensuring military operations remain under human control. Countries could foreswear certain dangerous AI applications, such as nuclear-armed robotic vehicles or dead hand systems. To minimize the risk of miscalculation with autonomous robotic vehicles, countries could agree to "rules of the road" for how such vehicles should behave. These various measures could be codified in formal treaties, non–legally binding agreements, or via unilateral declarations. There are a variety of measures that countries could adopt and many ways to codify agreements, shape global norms, or communicate behavior to other countries. The most important thing in the near term is that countries begin to take positive steps to acknowledge and address some of the worst potential risks.

Both American and Chinese defense thinkers have publicly acknowledged these risks and the need to explore potential avenues of cooperation. In a 2021 article, Li Chijiang, secretary general of the China Arms Control and Disarmament Association, warned of the "severe challenges that artificial intelligence military applications pose to international peace and security" and called for nations to "jointly seek solutions." In a 2020 *New York Times* article, PLA senior colonel Zhou Bo called for the United States and China to adopt confidence-building measures, including in AI. Zhou cited the 1972 U.S.-Soviet Incidents at Sea Agreement as inspiration, a confidence-building measure that was highly successful in reducing dangerous incidents, such as collisions or near-collisions, between U.S. and Soviet planes and ships. Li Bin of Tsinghua University, one of China's preeminent scholars on arms control and strategic stability, said at the 2019 World Peace Forum in Beijing, "In the Cold War, the United States and the Soviet Union developed a lot of cooperation on nuclear weapons issues. I understand that right now we have a lot of problems . . . but that should not stop us from developing real, practical cooperation among countries." I have had the opportunity to meet with dozens of Chinese experts working on AI, including scholars, business leaders, government officials, and military officers. These perspectives expressed by Li Chijiang, Zhou Bo, and Li Bin are not unique, and there may be opportunities for nations to engage in mutual restraint to avert the worst dangers of AI competition.

Lieutenant General Jack Shanahan of the U.S. DoD expressed a similar interest in exploring the possibility of "some limits, some guidelines, some guardrails" about military applications of AI. Shanahan told me he thought it was vitally important that the United States, Russia, and China engage in discussions on the role of AI in nuclear launch decisions. "I just have a visceral distaste for brittle algorithms being in the chain of command of decision-making for nuclear weapons," he said. "That is, to me, a human decision."

Shanahan voiced these concerns publicly in 2019, and while Chinese and Russian leaders have not made similar public statements, Shanahan may find receptive partners in China open to at least the possibility of discussing measures to mitigate the risks of AI competition. Zhu Qichao, a leading Chinese thinker on the militarization of autonomy and AI, wrote in a 2019 article coauthored with Long Kun, "Both sides should clarify the strategic boundaries of AI weaponization (such as whether AI should be used for nuclear weapons systems), prevent conflict escalation caused by military applications of AI systems, and explore significant issues such as how to ensure strategic stability in the era of AI."

The Chinese government has formally spoken out on AI risks and the need for states to consider regulation. In a 2021 position paper issued at the United Nations, the Chinese government stated, "We need to enhance the efforts to regulate military applications of AI." The paper argued for the need to consider "potential risks" and highlighted "global strategic stability" and the need to "prevent [an] arms race." The position paper preserves quite a bit of flexibility for how the Chinese government adopts AI, as is typical of statements from other countries, including the United States and the United Kingdom. Nevertheless, public acknowledgements of the risks of AI competition and the need for cooperation are a necessary initial step toward more fulsome risk reduction measures.

To move from vague diplomatic statements to action, the United States and China will have to find a way to overcome their mutual distrust. Zhu cited "American distrust of China" as a main source of friction between the nations and argued "China has taken the lead in demonstrating a clear attitude in promoting international cooperation." Zhu's perspective is a common one I hear from Chinese counterparts, who pin the blame for worsening U.S.-China relations on American insecurities, rather than China's militarization, bullying of other nations, and egregious human rights abuses at home. For his part, Shanahan expressed some skepticism about other nations' willingness to engage in arms control, even as he saw the need for some limits on military AI. "The ones most ardent about arms control statements tend to be those least willing to adhere to them when it comes down to it," Shanahan said. For cooperation to succeed, both sides will need to overcome the trust gap.

Cooperation on AI is subject to the same frictions that complicate U.S.-China relations on many issues. The United States and China have in place today several confidence-building measures intended to improve communication between their militaries and reduce the risk of maritime incidents. These include the 1998 U.S.-China Military Maritime Consultative Agreement and the 2014 Memorandum of Understanding Regarding the Rules of Behavior for Safety of Air and Maritime Encounters. Yet these measures have not prevented escalating tensions, and U.S.-China air and naval incidents have continued. The United States and China have a hotline to allow for communication in a crisis. U.S. officials have complained China hasn't used it. Kurt Campbell, the Biden administration's top White House official on China policy, said in 2021, "China has generally resisted any effective efforts at these kinds of confidence-building, crisis management procedures. In the past, the hotlines that have been set up have just rung, kind of endlessly in empty rooms." In early 2021, the Chinese government refused a request by U.S. Defense Secretary Lloyd Austin to speak to his equivalent, Vice Chairman Xu Qiliang of the Central Military Commission. Confidence-building measures don't work if nations don't use them. Communication is impossible if nations refuse to pick up the phone.

In some areas, confidence-building measures have shown successes in managing tensions. China and India have a number of agreements in place to manage tensions on the China-India border. While these agreements did not prevent a series of clashes that began in the summer of 2020, they may have helped reduce the violence and prevent unwanted escalation. Confidence-building measures are not a magical salve for political disagreements, but they can help policymakers manage tensions if they want to.

Countries should look to confidence-building measures and arms control as potential tools for managing some of the risks of military AI. Countries will and should be expected to compete heavily in AI, including in military applications. Each country has the right and obligation to its citizens to defend itself and improve its defenses. Countries need to compete responsibly, however, and look for ways to cooperate to reduce risk where possible. If other countries seem unwilling to cooperate, nations can take unilateral steps to model responsible behavior, such as bolstering AI assurance and being transparent with other countries about their intentions for military AI. Even as nations urgently compete in AI, they must seek to mitigate the dangers of military AI competition.

35

THE FUTURE OF AI

The field of artificial intelligence has been through many ups and downs since its start in the 1950s, and the future of AI is highly uncertain. How AI technology evolves could change many of its current characteristics of narrowness, brittleness, insecurity, and problems of explainability. AI systems could become more robust, explainable, understandable, and secure through improvements in data, algorithms, and engineering techniques. Or these limitations could remain even while AI systems become more capable, yielding more powerful but dangerous creations. As AI evolves, the relative value of the key inputs of algorithms, data, compute, and talent could change. Shifts in the significance of these inputs could advantage some actors and disadvantage others, further altering the global balance of AI power.

One of the most striking trends in AI basic research today is the tendency toward ever-larger models with increasingly massive datasets and compute resources for training. The rapid growth in size for large language models, for example, is remarkable. In October 2018, researchers at Google announced BERT$_{LARGE}$, a 340 million parameter language model. It was trained on a database of 3.3 billion words using 64 TPU chips running for four days. A few months later, in February 2019, OpenAI announced GPT-2, a 1.5 billion parameter model trained on 40 GB of text. A year and a half later, in July 2020, OpenAI announced GPT-3, a 175 billion parameter model trained on 570 GB of text. Six months after that, in January 2021, Google Brain announced the language model Switch-C, trained on 745 GB of text. In October 2021, Microsoft and NVIDIA announced Megatron-Turing NLG, a 530 billion parameter language model. It drew on 825 GB of text to build a training set of 270 billion "tokens" (word segments). It was trained using the sixth-largest supercomputer in the world, which has over 4,000 GPUs. In April 2022, Google announced PaLM, a 540 billion parameter model. PaLM was trained on 780 billion tokens of text using over 6,000 TPUs running for more than seven weeks. In the span of three and a half years, training data size grew two orders of magnitude and compute and model size more than a thousandfold.

As training data size has expanded, researchers have begun training multimodal models, which use multiple types of data, such as text and images. Combining multiple types of data has many advantages. It can allow for models that can connect concepts across different types of data, such as explaining the content of images in words or creating new images based on text descriptions. Text-to-image models, such as OpenAI's DALL·E and DALL·E 2, Google Brain's Imagen, and Stability AI's Stable Diffusion, can create new AI-generated images based on a text description. Multimodal training data can lead to models that have a richer understanding of the world. DALL·E's concept of a "cat," for example, encompasses pictures of actual cats, cartoon sketches of cats, and the word "cat." Researchers have discovered that the multimodal models actually have artificial neurons tied to underlying concepts. For example, the "Spider-Man neuron" in the multimodal model CLIP is activated when the model is presented with a photo of a person dressed as Spider-Man, a sketch of Spider-Man, photos of spiders or webs, or the word "spider." The "Donald Trump neuron" is activated by photographs and cartoons of Donald Trump, the word "Trump," or pictures of "Make America Great Again" hats. The Trump neuron is even weakly activated for people associated with Trump, such as Steve Bannon and Mike Pence.

While large multimodal models still don't have anything close to the richness and sophistication that humans have in understanding the world, they are suggestive of a direction in future AI research that may prove promising. Many of the problems of the brittleness and narrowness of AI today may stem from the limitations of AI models' training data. Building larger, more diverse datasets may result in more robust models. Multimodal datasets may help to build models that can associate concepts represented in multiple formats, such as text, images, video, and audio. Training models on a diversity of data may also help to build more general-purpose AI systems, moving beyond today's narrow AI. In May 2022, DeepMind announced Gato, a multimodal, multitask model that can caption images, chat, play video games, and move a robotic arm. AI researchers have also demonstrated an impressive ability to interrogate the inner workings of multimodal models to understand how certain inputs activate various parts of the network. Their analysis sheds light on concepts that the model associates together, such as Donald Trump and MAGA hats.

This information can help tease out potentially problematic biases and associ-ations, allowing researchers to build future models that are more explainable and trustworthy.

Multimodal representations of concepts unfortunately also create new ways of attacking models. Researchers discovered the multimodal model CLIP could be manipulated into misclassifying photos of an apple, laptop, coffee mug, and plant as an iPod simply by writing the word "iPod" on a piece of paper and putting it on the object. Further improvements could make these models more robust, or these security vulnerabilities could prove deeply intractable.

If the trend toward ever-larger AI models continues, it could have significant ramifications for global AI power. There is no theoretical limit to the size of models or datasets. The explosion of data created by internet-connected people, devices, and sensors suggests a future with exponentially more data than today. (The quality of data may continue to be a challenge, with large internet-based datasets reflecting the same biases and problematic associations that exist in human society.) In terms of technical inputs, compute appears likely to be the biggest limiting factor in holding back larger, more capable models.

The amount of compute used for training cutting-edge machine learning research projects increased ten billionfold from 2010 to 2022 and is doubling roughly every six months. Compute for training the largest models, like GPT-3 and PaLM, has been doubling at a slightly slower rate, approximately every ten months. This is an incredible explosion of compute, yet there are likely limits to how long compute usage can grow at this pace. Compute-intensive research is expensive, and even the most deep-pocketed actors have limits to their resources. Independent estimates put the cost to train advanced machine learning models such as GPT-3 on the order of millions of dollars per research project for some of the largest models. These costs already put compute-intensive research out of reach for some actors, such as universities. This problem has led the U.S. govern-ment to pursue increased federal resources for cloud computing for AI research.

Most of the leading AI research labs pursuing compute-intensive approaches are backed by giant tech corporations. DeepMind and Google Brain are owned by Google's parent company Alphabet. OpenAI secured a $1 billion investment from Microsoft. Companies are reaching into their deep pockets to fund major compute investments. Meta announced in 2022 the construction of an AI Research SuperCluster with over 6,000 GPUs and the intent to grow to 16,000 GPUs (for an unspecified cost).

How long this trend in larger and more expensive models continues will have important implications for global power. If training costs continue to rise, a smaller and smaller set of global actors will be able to afford training the most cutting-edge machine learning models, concentrating AI power in the hands of a few key players.

Some analysts have suggested that if compute usage continues to rise at the current rate, training costs for the largest machine learning models will outstrip the spending capacity of large corporations in the mid-2020s. Amazon, which has the highest revenue of any tech company in the world, posted $386 billion in revenue and $21 billion in profit in 2020. Alphabet and Microsoft each had over $100 billion in revenue and approximately $40 billion in profit each in 2020. Tech companies could afford to spend a great deal more on compute-intensive AI research if they saw a payoff. The spending potential of even the biggest companies doesn't match governments, however. If model size and compute costs keep climbing, they could move into a realm where only governments can compete.

The largest scientific research projects have been government funded. The Manhattan Project to build the first atomic bomb cost the U.S. government nearly $2 billion at the time, the equivalent of over $30 billion in 2021. The Apollo Program was even more expensive, costing nearly $3 billion per year during peak spending in the mid-1960s, the equivalent of over $20 billion annually in 2021.

Governments can marshal massive financial resources when necessary. The U.S. Defense Department's budget is over $700 billion today, and that's in peacetime. At the start of the Cold War in the early 1950s, the United States spent over 12 percent of its gross domestic product (GDP) annually on national defense. During World War II, defense spending rose to 36 percent of GDP.

Compute cost is not the only constraint on model size, however. Training massive models also involves significant technical hurdles. The largest models, with hundreds of billions of parameters, cannot fit on a single GPU, and significant care is needed to integrate the hardware, software, data, and algorithm efficiently across thousands of GPUs. It is possible that as cost and technical difficulties rise, growth in large models slows down, especially if the return on investment for training large models isn't clear.

Even if the pace of growth in model size and compute usage somewhat slows, increases in compute efficiency due to improved hardware and more efficient algorithms may help keep large models feasible and relatively affordable, at least for major corporations. In addition to rising compute usage, the past decade has also seen exponential improvements in compute efficiency. OpenAI assessed a forty-four-fold improvement in compute efficiency for training on benchmark image classification tasks from 2012 to 2019, corresponding to a doubling in efficiency every sixteen months. This means that the same task could be done seven years later with forty-four times less compute, just due to improvements in the algorithms alone. On other AI tasks, researchers have found similar (or better) rates of improvement in compute efficiency for both training and inference. Katja Grace at the Machine Intelligence Research Institute (MIRI) has found a roughly similar scale of progress in algorithmic efficiency across multiple domains.

Improvements in algorithmic efficiency and hardware can combine to make compute-heavy models much more accessible in only a few years. DeepMind's incremental improvements in AlphaGo, which gained in performance and compute efficiency with each iteration, shows the value of both hardware and algorithmic improvements. The first version of AlphaGo, which played against Fan Hui in October 2015, used 176 GPUs for inference (running the trained model). The version of AlphaGo that defeated Lee Sedol five months later in March 2016 switched to Google's TPU, an ASIC optimized for deep learning. This version used only forty-eight TPUs for inference and reduced energy consumption by roughly a factor of four. Later versions AlphaGo Master and AlphaGo Zero in 2017 reduced compute usage to only four TPUs, a greater than 10× improvement over the prior version. In just two years, through a combination of algorithmic and hardware improvements, DeepMind reduced energy consumption for inference by over fortyfold. Separately, DeepMind also reduced the compute needed for training by a factor of eight from AlphaGo Zero (2017) to AlphaZero (2018) one year later.

The combination of both hardware and algorithmic improvements in compute efficiency will counterbalance some of the increases in compute requirements for training and may make AI models available to actors with fewer compute resources. Some of these improvements will be widely available. Algorithmic improvements are published in open research papers that are free online. Hardware improvements, however, may be accessible only to those with the latest cutting-edge AI chips. Using older model chips or chips not optimized for AI would be inefficient and could significantly increase costs. Saif Khan at the Center for Security and Emerging Technology has estimated that AI training costs could be as much as thirty times higher using older model or nonspecialized chips. Effective controls on compute resources to limit access to leading-edge AI chips could price some actors out of the market for the most compute-intensive research.

While compute-intensive research has shown value in achieving superhuman performance in games such as *go*, *StarCraft*, and *Dota 2* and training large language models, its long-term value as an approach to AI research is highly contested. Leading AI research labs such as DeepMind, OpenAI, and Google Brain have used increasingly large deep neural networks, yet other researchers argue that their methods are fundamentally flawed. Compute-heavy research has been criticized on a variety of fronts: it is costly and locks out university researchers who may have access to fewer computing resources; it is energy-intensive and contributes to carbon emissions; and it lacks the elegance that some researchers believe is required to achieve "real intelligence." Yet the value of compute-heavy methods is in their success. In a 2019 blog post "The Bitter Lesson," machine learning pioneer Rich Sutton argued:

> The biggest lesson that can be read from 70 years of AI research is that general methods that leverage computation are ultimately the most effective, and by a large margin.

Sutton said that in the short term, AI researchers can often make progress on a problem by applying handcrafted human knowledge of the problem to design purpose-built algorithms, "but the only thing that matters in the long run is the leveraging of computation." Simpler methods that apply vast amounts of data and computational power against a problem will outperform those that rely on expert human knowledge. The swift backlash to Sutton's article seemed to indicate his arguments were a pill too bitter to swallow for some AI researchers. But despite its critics, compute-intensive research continues to make progress for now, yielding more impressive fundamental breakthroughs than other methods.

It is unclear how these trends will play out. One possibility is that the critics are right, and current methods will run out of steam. Compute-heavy research may slow as it becomes difficult to justify its increasing costs, causing researchers to refocus their attention on algorithmic improvements.

On the other hand, if larger AI models demonstrate value, companies may be willing to spend even more money to pursue the next breakthrough. If costs continue to rise, they could reach the level of expenditures only possible by major governments, akin to the Manhattan Project or the Apollo Program. Despite Washington's obsession with "moonshot" scientific endeavors, this outcome would be disastrous for democracies. If national AI power turns into a cost shootout between who is willing to spend more, China will win. No country has deeper pockets and is more willing to spend—often quite wastefully—to pursue technological progress. Chinese researchers have already signaled their intent to build massive models, with the goal of eventually training "brain scale" models of over 100 trillion parameters. China is not a leader in basic AI research today, but that could change if being at the frontier of basic research proves fruitful for increasing national power.

In a scenario where compute-intensive research becomes a strategic asset, control over access to compute resources could prove paramount. Today, the United States has significant leverage over semiconductor production. Even though the vast majority of chip fabrication occurs outside the United States, U.S. companies' role in producing semiconductor manufacturing equipment and design tools has given the U.S. government the ability to shut off supplies of leading chips to China. The more Washington exercises this leverage today, however, the more that control over future chip supply chains will slip from its grasp. Denying Chinese companies access to chips aids the Chinese government in achieving its goal of semiconductor independence. Without access to chips that use U.S. equipment, Chinese firms turn to second-tier domestic chips, a short-term blow but one that grows China's domestic chip industry in the long term. U.S. export controls also incentivize global chip companies, including those headquartered in the United States, to redesign supply chains without U.S. technology so they are outside the reach of the U.S. government. A better U.S. strategy would be to seek to maintain control over compute resources but hold that leverage in reserve, keeping China dependent on U.S.-origin technology. The U.S. government should adopt a deliberate strategy to retain levers of control over compute production to hedge against the possibility that large-scale compute becomes a strategic resource in the future.

Current trends suggest a third possibility for the future of AI, a mixed outcome in which the cost of basic research continues to rise (at least for the next five or so years), but research breakthroughs quickly proliferate to actors with fewer resources. While only the most capable actors may be able to build the largest, most advanced models, the combination of open publication and improved computational efficiency through hardware and algorithmic improvements may mean that within six to twenty-four months other research labs are able to replicate their findings. Within five to ten years, AI breakthroughs may be commoditized, available to anyone through a free app on their mobile device. Control over leading-edge compute may give some actors an edge over others, but any advantage is likely to, at best, give leaders only a few years' head start over competitors. Compute is likely to remain a key element in AI competition and power, but compute alone won't determine which countries are able to most effectively translate AI into military, economic, and political power. In this scenario, some nations may lead in AI, but the technology will be widely enough proliferated that what will matter more is who is most effective at employing AI to advance their goals.

CONCLUSION

The creation and use of technology is an inherently political act. Technology can be used to repress human freedoms or bolster them, to elevate a message or suppress it, to strengthen one group or weaken another. How technology is used reflects the values, whether conscious or unconscious, of its creators and users.

Democratic societies find themselves in the midst of often messy debates about how AI technology should be used. The use of AI for facial recognition, surveillance, content moderation, synthetic media, and military applications are just some of the ways in which AI may have profound effects on human well-being, and these uses are rightly contested and debated in democracies. There are also debates about the use of AI in authoritarian regimes, but those debates happen under a radically different political system in which criticism of the state is censored and punished. Debates happen within the bounds that the state permits.

The challenge facing humanity is not just how AI will be used but *who* will decide the rules. In democracies, AI governance is established through an interactive, messy, and imperfect dialogue among corporations, civil society, the media, government, scientists, academics, and grassroots activists. In authoritarian regimes, the state is the ultimate decider. AI is being used in authoritarian regimes such as China to suppress human freedoms, and those uses are spreading around the globe. Even more troubling, AI surveillance tools can strengthen the hand of authoritarians, further cementing their rule.

Democracies, by contrast, in many cases lack a clear competing model for the use of AI. Whether it is for facial recognition systems, data privacy, synthetic media, or content moderation on social media platforms, governance rules are either fragmented or nonexistent across democratic nations. Democracies must out-compete authoritarian regimes to present models for AI governance that preserve human rights and individual freedom, yet there are multiple tensions and contradictions within this competition.

The diverse and fragmented views on AI governance both across democratic countries and within them are a challenge for developing a coherent alternative to authoritarian uses of AI. The diversity of views in democratic societies is a strength that can lead to better policies in the long run, but only if democracies eventually unite around a set of privacy- and freedom-preserving policies they can export around the world.

These tensions become even more complicated when accounting for the deeply entangled nature of global AI competition. The United States and China do not lead separate political-economic blocs that are competing globally, akin to the Cold War. Rather, they are competing to lead one globally integrated political-economic system. In this global competition, the United States needs the same tech megacorporations that it is trying to reel in at home to outcompete Chinese companies in the global marketplace. U.S. tech companies' power is a source of concern in Washington among both liberals and conservatives, but the United States would be unquestionably better off having Facebook or YouTube dominate the global social media landscape than companies like Tik-Tok that are beholden to the Chinese Communist Party. Democracies must find ways to deepen cooperation between tech companies, the government, and civil society groups to develop a positive framework for AI and do so in a way that allows U.S. tech companies to compete successfully on the global stage.

The ties between the U.S. and Chinese AI communities are another source of tension in AI competition. Research, investments, and commercial transactions that enable human rights abuses or empower the Chinese military are antithetical to American values and interests, yet in other areas U.S.-China engagement benefits the United States.

U.S. companies and researchers must remain engaged in debates over international AI standards and norms, precisely so that they influence their development. This requires sitting at the table with Chinese companies and AI researchers, including some who may have ties to human rights abusers or the Chinese military. Successful engagement on norms and standards also requires pushing back, calling out abuses when they occur and standing up for democratic values, not avoiding "sensitive topics" for risk of upsetting Chinese partners.

Research cooperation introduces many opportunities and risks. The naïve view of AI scientific collaboration as apolitical is morally bankrupt when, as is the case today, AI is being used to oppress citizens across China and is aiding a genocide against Uighurs in Xinjiang. Universities and corporations should be asking hard questions about who they are partnering with in China and how their applications might be used. Yet entirely cutting off U.S.-China research ties is not in U.S. interests either. Some types of AI research could be mutually beneficial, such as AI safety, although more robust AI systems are not always a net positive. Better functioning and more efficient AI-enabled repression doesn't benefit humanity. The biggest gain for democratic nations, especially the United States, is the massive outflow of Chinese talent. China produces more top AI researchers than any other country in the world, and the majority of those researchers complete their studies in the United States. Chinese researchers are a net brain gain for the United States, as they overwhelmingly choose to stay in the United States after graduation. Technology transfer and academic espionage are real risks that must be managed, but they can be done without completely cutting off Chinese talent. The United States is the top destination for AI researchers worldwide, and the U.S. government must pursue policies that preserve this position. However AI technology evolves in the future, having a deep bench of talent will be a major geopolitical advantage.

Military AI competition among nations is rife with contradictions. In democratic societies, military AI applications such as Project Maven have faced criticism from some AI researchers, but these criticisms are likely to lead to better military AI applications in the long run that more fully take into account the limitations of AI systems. Tech critics have forced the U.S. military to be more conscious of and transparent about how it will manage the limitations of AI technology. Despite defense leaders' fears, U.S. military AI development has not been significantly delayed by tech conscientious objectors. There are plenty of companies willing to work with the Defense Department. The biggest hurdle to adopting AI is the U.S. government's own red tape. Contracts are bogged down in a system that is supposed to ferret out fraud and abuse but has itself become so clogged with bureaucracy and abused by corporations that it is lethal to innovation. The U.S. Defense Department's biggest adversary in the AI competition is its own bureaucracy.

Nations must also find ways to compete in AI while avoiding destabilizing risks, such as a race to the bottom on safety. Countries must find ways to cooperate in the midst of competition. They must increase transparency about their activities and seek opportunities for mutual restraint. The obstacles to doing so are high but the costs of a failure to cooperate, risking dangerous AI accidents or the evolution of warfare beyond human control, are even higher.

When Russian president Vladimir Putin said that whoever leads in AI "will become the ruler of the world," he wasn't speaking to generals or scientists; he was speaking to students. The AI revolution will not take place overnight. The industrial revolution took decades to unfold, and the AI revolution will similarly span decades, with waves of technological advancement and adaptation. The future will belong to the societies that can most successfully marshal the scarce resources of data, talent, and compute and have effective institutions to funnel them toward innovative AI applications.

Authoritarian uses of AI for surveillance, disinformation, and repression pose a profound challenge to freedom around the globe. Democracies have tremendous advantages in this competition, but they must find ways to harness those advantages. Democratic societies must come together to push back against illiberal uses of AI and advance a positive agenda for AI governance, not by papering over differences but by using their diversity of views as a strength to develop better solutions. The future of AI will be driven by those who lead in developing AI technology and how it is used. It is vital that the future of AI is one that advances human freedom and global peace.

ACKNOWLEDGMENTS

I owe an enormous debt of gratitude to so many people who made this book possible.

The leadership team at the Center for a New American Security (CNAS), Richard Fontaine, Ely Ratner, and Victoria Nuland, were incredibly supportive at every stage of this book.

I have relied on the advice, support, and input of so many colleagues throughout development of the ideas in this book. Michael Horowitz has been a long-standing collaborator on research pertaining to artificial intelligence and international security, and his ideas have shaped my thinking enormously. Elsa Kania has been a patient guide, translator, and fellow traveler, both figuratively and literally, in understanding the U.S.-China AI competition. I relied heavily on the CNAS Technology team, Martijn Rasser, Kara Frederick, Ainikki Riikonen, Megan Lamberth, Xiaojing (JJ) Zeng, and Monika Bochert, in helping to understand the many facets of AI competition. Peter Hansen provided Chinese language background research and translation on many of the key ideas in the book. I am grateful to Melody Cook for creating many of the graphics in the book and Maura McCarthy for her assistance with endnotes. Katie Galgano assisted in background research, Emily Jin with translations, and John O'Malley with citations. Miles Brundage, Michael Horowitz, and Ram Shankar Siva Kumar reviewed parts of the book. I am grateful for their candid feedback which helped make the book stronger. Any errors or omissions are mine alone.

This book is informed by several "track II" academic-to-academic discussions with international colleagues from around the world. I am grateful to Eric Richardson of the Centre for Humanitarian Dialogue and Ryan Hass and Ryan McElveen of the Brookings Institution for inviting me to participate in these efforts. I am especially grateful to my international colleagues who have participated in these dialogues candidly and in the spirit of furthering international cooperation on AI.

I am grateful to Jason Matheny and Ylli Bajraktari for including me in the National Security Commission on AI's efforts and Josh Marcuse for connecting me with members of the Defense Innovation Board, which helped inform my thinking on U.S. government efforts on AI.

The Smith Richardson Foundation helped fund the research and writing of this book. This book also draws on several years of research at CNAS on AI and global security, which was funded in part by Carnegie Corporation of New York, Open Philanthropy, and the U.S. government. I am especially grateful to Chris Griffin, Carl Robichaud, Nadia Schadlow, and Luke Muehlhauser for supporting my work.

Some of the companies named in this book support the Center for a New American Security, where I work. A full list of CNAS funders is available online at https://www.cnas.org/support-cnas/cnas-supporters.

I am grateful to everyone who agreed to be interviewed for this book, including: Erik Bates, Jason Brown, Michael Brown, Jack Clark, Matt Cook, Brett Darcey, Christophe De Wagter, Nathan Drenkow, Matt Easley, Isaac Faber, Dominic Garcia, Samantha Hoffman, Chuck Howell, Carter Huffman, Amir Husain, Mark Jacobson, Michael Kanaan, Elsa Kania, John Kaufhold, Casper Klynge, Gabriel Kocher, Kaiser Kuo, Danika Laszuk, Peter Lee, Lin Ji, Ashley Llorens, Kevin Luo, Keith Lynn, Rachael Martin, Brendan McCord, Michael McQuade, Nand Mulchandani, Liz O'Sullivan, Tim Pan, Mike Pappas, Federico Paredes, Giorgio Patrini, Devaki Raj, Phil Root, Will Roper, Nilay Sadth, Tuomas Sandholm, Eric Schmidt, Jack Shanahan, Ryan Tseng, Maya Wang, Michael Wolmetz, Bob Work, and Maria Zuber. I am grateful to Kimberly Allen, Jennifer Crider, Johanna Spangenberg Jones, Tom Kiley, Gayle Tzemach Lemmon, and Cecilia Zhou for helping to facilitate interviews. Jack Shanahan, in particular, helped open doors within the Joint AI Center, leading to many of the interviews in the book.

I am grateful to Jafer Ahmad, Jeff Clune, Brett Darcey, Ivan Evtimov, Earlence Fernandes, Murtaza Khomusi, Norman Mu, and Devaki Raj for allowing me permission to use the images in the book and Sheena Greitens for allowing me to use her data on the spread of Chinese surveillance technology to create the map used in the book.

I also owe a debt of gratitude to the many fellow intellectual travelers on the issues covered in this book, including, but not limited to: Greg Allen, Sam Bendett, Vincent Boulanin, Ben Buchanan, Tarun Chhabra, Rebecca Crootof,

Allan Dafoe, Matt Daniels, Zachary Davis, Jeffrey Ding, Renée DiResta, Ryan Fedasiuk, Melissa Flagg, Sheena Greitens, Tim Hwang, Andrew Imbrie, Dan Kim, Saif Khan, Rita Konaev, Lorand Laskai, Kai-Fu Lee, Josh Marcuse, Chris McGuire, Chris Meserole, Igor Mikolic-Torreira, Jim Mitre, Kenneth Payne, Phil Reiner, Heather Roff, Stuart Russell, Samm Sacks, Jacquelyn Schneider, Jordan Schneider, Max Tegmark, Helen Toner, John VerWey, Kerstin Vignard, Anthony Vinci, Graham Webster, and Emily Weinstein.

I want to thank my editor, Tom Mayer, and the amazing team at W. W. Norton, including Nneoma Amadi-obi, who helped make this book possible.

I will forever be grateful to my agent, Jim Hornfischer, for taking a chance on me and taking me on as one of his authors. I also want to thank Sharon Hornfischer at Hornfischer Literary Management for her support.

This book would not have been possible without the boundless support of my wife, Heather, who gave me the time to research and write this book. My brother, Steve, has been a constant source of support, ideas, and inspiration. And I owe everything to my parents, Janice and David, for always believing in me.

ABBREVIATIONS

ABC	American Broadcasting Company
ACE	Air Combat Evolution
ACLU	American Civil Liberties Union
AFWERX	Air Force Works
AGI	artificial general intelligence
AI	artificial intelligence
AIDS	acquired immunodeficiency syndrome
ALS	amyotrophic lateral sclerosis (also known as Lou Gehrig's disease)
ASIC	application-specific integrated circuit
AU	African Union
AWACS	airborne warning and control system
AWCFT	Algorithmic Warfare Cross-Functional Team
BAAI	Beijing Academy of Artificial Intelligence
BBC	British Broadcasting Corporation
BERT	Bidirectional Encoder Representations from Transformers
BCE	before common era
C4ISR	Command, Control, Communication, Cloud, Intelligence, Surveillance, and Reconnaissance
CBC	Canadian Broadcasting Corporation
CBP	Customs and Border Patrol
CCP	Chinese Communist Party
CEIEC	China National Electronics Import and Export Corporation
CEO	chief executive officer
CFIUS	Committee on Foreign Investment in the United States
CIA	Central Intelligence Agency
CLIP	Contrastive Language–Image Pretraining

CMU	Carnegie Mellon University
COBOL	common business-oriented language
COVID	coronavirus disease
CPU	central processing unit
CSAIL	Computer Science and Artificial Intelligence Laboratory
DARPA	Defense Advanced Research Projects Agency
DC	District of Columbia
DDS	Defense Digital Service
DEA	Drug Enforcement Administration
DIU	Defense Innovation Unit
DIUx	Defense Innovation Unit—Experimental
DNA	deoxyribonucleic acid
DoD	Department of Defense
EOD	explosive ordnance disposal
EPA	Environmental Protection Agency
ERDCWERX	Engineer Research and Development Center Works
EU	European Union
EUV	extreme ultraviolet
FBI	Federal Bureau of Investigation
FedRAMP	Federal Risk and Authorization Management Program
FEMA	Federal Emergency Management Agency
FOUO	For Official Use Only
FPGA	field-programmable gate arrays
GAN	generative adversarial network
GAO	Government Accountability Office
GB	gigabytes
GDP	gross domestic product
GDPR	General Data Protection Regulation
GIF	graphics interchange format
GNP	gross national product
GPS	global positioning system
GPU	graphics processing unit
HA/DR	humanitarian assistance / disaster relief
HUD	head-up display
IARPA	Intelligence Advanced Research Projects Activity
ICE	Immigration and Customs Enforcement
IEC	International Electrotechnical Commission
IED	improvised explosive device

IEEE	Institute for Electrical and Electronics Engineers
IJOP	Integrated Joint Operations Platform
IoT	Internet of Things
IP	intellectual property
IP	internet protocol
ISIS	Islamic State of Iraq and Syria
ISO	International Organization for Standardization
ISR	intelligence, surveillance, and reconnaissance
ITU	International Telecommunication Union
JAIC	Joint Artificial Intelligence Center
JEDI	Joint Enterprise Defense Infrastructure
KGB	Komitet Gosudarstvennoy Bezopasnosti (Комитет государственной безопасности)
MAGA	Make America Great Again
MAVLab	Micro Air Vehicle Lab
MIRI	Machine Intelligence Research Institute
MIT	Massachusetts Institute of Technology
MPS	Ministry of Public Service
MRAP	mine-resistant ambush protected
NASA	National Aeronautics and Space Administration
NATO	North Atlantic Treaty Organization
NBC	National Broadcasting Company
NGA	National Geospatial-Intelligence Agency
NLG	Natural Language Generation
nm	nanometer
NOAA	National Oceanic and Atmosphere Administration
NREC	National Robotics Engineering Center
NSIC	National Security Innovation Capital
NSIN	National Security Innovation Network
NUDT	National University of Defense Technology
OTA	other transaction authority
PhD	doctor of philosophy
PLA	People's Liberation Army
QR code	quick response code
R&D	research and development
RFP	request for proposals
RYaN	Raketno Yadernoye Napadenie (Ракетно ядерное нападение) [nuclear missile attack]

SEAL	sea, air, land
SMIC	Semiconductor Manufacturing International Corporation
SOFWERX	Special Operations Forces Works
SpaceWERX	Space Force Works
STEM	science, technology, engineering, and mathematics
TEVV	test and evaluation, verification and validation
TPU	Tensor Processing Unit
TRACE	Target Recognition and Adaptation in Contested Environments
TSA	Transportation Security Administration
TSMC	Taiwan Semiconductor Manufacturing Company
TTC	Trade and Technology Council
UAV	unmanned aerial vehicle
UK	United Kingdom
UN	United Nations
U.S.	United States
U.S.S.R.	Union of Soviet Socialist Republics

NOTES

EPIGRAPHS

ix **"Artificial intelligence is the future"**: "'Whoever leads in AI will rule the world': Putin to Russian children on Knowledge Day," *RT News*, September 1, 2017, https://www.rt.com/news/401731-ai-rule-world-putin/.

ix **"Science and technology has become the main battleground"**: Coco Feng, "Chinese President Xi Jinping seeks to rally country's scientists for 'unprecedented' contest," *South China Morning Post*, May 29, 2021, https://www.scmp.com/news/china/politics/article/3135328/chinese-president-xi-jinping-seeks-rally-countrys-scientists; "（受权发布）习近平：在中国科学院第二十次院士大会、中国工程院第十五次院士大会、中国科协第十次全国代表大会上的讲话 [(Authorized Release) Xi Jinping: Speech at the 20th Academician Conference of the Chinese Academy of Sciences, the 15th Academician Conference of the Chinese Academy of Engineering, and the 10th National Congress of the Chinese Association for Science and Technology]," Xinhua, May 28, 2021, http://www.xinhuanet.com/politics/2021-05/28/c_1127505377.htm.

INTRODUCTION

1 **air combat maneuvering:** Naval Air Training Command, *Flight Training Instruction: Basic Fighter Maneuvering (BFM) Advanced NFO T-45C/VMTS* (Corpus Christie, TX: Department of the Navy, 2018), https://www.cnatra.navy.mil/local/docs/pat-pubs/P-826.pdf.

1 **one of the most challenging skills:** Colin "Farva" Price, "Navy F/A-18 Squadron Commander's Take on AI Repeatedly Beating Real Pilot In Dogfight," *The Drive*, August 24, 2020, https://www.thedrive.com/the-war-zone/35947/navy-f-a-18-squadron-commanders-take-on-ai-repeatedly-beating-real-pilot-in-dogfight.

1 **air combat has evolved:** John Stillion, *Trends in Air-to-Air Combat: Implications for Future Air Superiority* (Center for Strategic and Budgetary Assessments, 2015), https://csbaonline.org/uploads/documents/Air-to-Air-Report-.pdf.

1 **"department of mad scientists":** Michael Belfiore, *The Department of Mad Scientists: How DARPA Is Remaking Our World, from the Internet to Artificial Limbs* (New York: Harper-Collins, 2010), https://www.amazon.com/Department-Mad-Scientists-Remaking-Artificial/dp/0062000659.

2 **ACE program:** "Training AI to Win a Dogfight," Defense Advanced Research Projects Agency, May 8, 2019, https://www.darpa.mil/news-events/2019-05-08.

2 **flew with superhuman precision:** Price, "Navy F/A-18 Squadron Commander's Take."

2 **forward-quarter gunshots:** Naval Air Training Command, *Flight Training Instruction.*

2 **maneuvering to avoid a collision:** Price, "Navy F/A-18 Squadron Commander's Take."

2 **"a gunshot that is almost impossible":** Joseph Trevithick, "AI Claims 'Flawless Victory' Going Undefeated In Digital Dogfight With Human Fighter Pilot," *The Drive*, August 20, 2020, https://www.thedrive.com/the-war-zone/35888/ai-claims-flawless-victory-going -undefeated-in-digital-dogfight-with-human-fighter-pilot.

3 **level of g-forces:** Trevithick, "AI Claims 'Flawless Victory.'"

3 **"The human will always be the limiting factor":** Price, "Navy F/A-18 Squadron Commander's Take."

3 **live flight demonstration:** "Collaborative Air Combat Autonomy Program Makes Strides," Defense Advanced Research Projects Agency, March 18, 2021, https://www.darpa .mil/news-events/2021-03-18a.

3 **"We envision a future":** "Training AI to Win a Dogfight."

3 **another industrial revolution:** Klaus Schwab, "The Fourth Industrial Revolution: What It Means, How to Respond," World Economic Forum, January 14, 2016, https://www .weforum.org/agenda/2016/01/the-fourth-industrial-revolution-what-it-means-and-how -to-respond/; *Robot Revolution—Global Robot & AI Primer* (Bank of America Merrill Lynch, December 16, 2015), https://www.bofaml.com/content/dam/boamlimages/documents/ PDFs/robotics_and_ai_condensed_primer.pdf (page discontinued); Rob Thomas, "How AI Is Driving the New Industrial Revolution," *Forbes*, March 4, 2020, https://www .forbes.com/sites/ibm/2020/03/04/how-ai-is-driving-the-new-industrial-revolution/ #7225c870131a; Sean Gallagher, "The Fourth Industrial Revolution Emerges from AI and the Internet of Things," *Ars Technica*, June 18, 2019, https://arstechnica.com/information -technology/2019/06/the-revolution-will-be-roboticized-how-ai-is-driving-industry-4 -0/.

4 **nearly half of all tasks:** James Manyika et al., *Harnessing Automation for a Future That Works* (McKinsey Global Institute, January 2017), https://www.mckinsey.com/featured -insights/digital-disruption/harnessing-automation-for-a-future-that-works.

4 **"[AI] will enliven inert objects":** Kevin Kelly, "The Three Breakthroughs That Have Finally Unleashed AI on the World," *Wired*, October 27, 2014, https://www.wired.com/2014/10/ future-of-artificial-intelligence/.

4 **AI has applications:** For some examples of security-related applications of artificial intelligence, see Miles Brundage et al., *The Malicious Use of Artificial Intelligence: Forecasting, Prevention, and Mitigation* (February 2018), https://maliciousaireport.com/; and Michael C. Horowitz et al., *Artificial Intelligence and International Security* (Center for a New American Security, July 10, 2018), https://www.cnas.org/publications/reports/artificial -intelligence-and-international-security.

5 **More than fifty countries:** Daniel Zhang et al., *The AI Index 2021 Annual Report* (Stanford, CA: AI Index Steering Committee, March 2021), 153–164, https://aiindex.stanford .edu/wp-content/uploads/2021/03/2021-AI-Index-Report_Master.pdf.

5 **500 Chinese military scientists:** Alex Joske, *Picking Flowers, Making Honey: The Chinese Military's Collaboration with Foreign Universities* (Australian Strategic Policy Institute, October 2018), 8–9, https://www.aspi.org.au/report/picking-flowers-making-honey.

5 **most highly valued AI start-ups:** "The 10 Biggest Artificial Intelligence Startups in The

World," Nanalyze.com, June 6, 2018, https://www.nanalyze.com/2018/06/10-biggest-artificial
-intelligence-startups; "World Top 30 Best-Funded AI Startups 2020," Disfold, July 9, 2021,
https://disfold.com/top-ai-startups/; "The 25 Most-Funded AI (Artificial Intelligence) Start-
ups," GrowthList, February 24, 2022, https://growthlist.co/ai-funded-startups/.

5 **SenseTime:** Scott Murdoch and Kane Wu, "SenseTime Shares Jump as Much as 23% on
Debut after $740 mln Hong Kong IPO," Reuters, December 30, 2021, https://www.reuters
.com/technology/sensetime-shares-open-up-16-hong-kong-debut-2021-12-30/.

5 **ByteDance:** Emma Lee, "ByteDance Becomes World's Largest Unicorn with $353 Billion
Valuation: Hurun Report," technode, December 20, 2021, https://technode.com/2021/12/20/
bytedance-becomes-worlds-largest-unicorn-with-353-billion-valuation-hurun-report/;
Roger Chen and Rui Ma, "How ByteDance Became the World's Most Valuable Startup,"
February 24, 2022, https://hbr.org/2022/02/how-bytedance-became-the-worlds-most-valu-
able-startup.

5 **SenseTime and Megvii:** "Top 19 Facial Recognition Startups," AI Startups (website),
updated September 13, 2021, https://www.ai-startups.org/top/facial_recognition/.

6 **more than half of the world's surveillance cameras:** Liza Lin and Newley Purnell, "A World
with a Billion Cameras Watching You Is Just Around the Corner," *Wall Street Journal*,
December 6, 2019, https://www.wsj.com/articles/a-billion-surveillance-cameras-forecast
-to-be-watching-within-two-years-11575565402?mod=hp_listb_pos1; Thomas Ricker,
"The US, Like China, Has About One Surveillance Camera for Every Four People, Says
Report," *The Verge*, December 9, 2019, https://www.theverge.com/2019/12/9/21002515/
surveillance-cameras-globally-us-china-amount-citizens.

6 **intellectual property theft:** Michael Brown and Pavneet Singh, *China's Technology
Transfer Strategy: How Chinese Investments in Emerging Technology Enable a Strate-
gic Competitor to Access the Crown Jewels of U.S. Innovation* (Defense Innovation Unit
Experimental, January 2018), https://admin.govexec.com/media/diux_chinatechnolo-
gytransferstudy_jan_2018_(1).pdf; William C. Hannas, James Mulvenon, and Anna B.
Puglisi, *Chinese Industrial Espionage: Technology Acquisition and Military Modernisa-
tion* (Oxfordshire, UK: Routledge, 2013), https://www.routledge.com/Chinese-Industrial
-Espionage-Technology-Acquisition-and-Military-Modernisation/Hannas-Mulvenon
-Puglisi/p/book/9780415821421; William C. Hannas and Huey-meei Chang, *China's
Access to Foreign AI Technology* (Center for Security and Emerging Technology, September 2019), https://cset.georgetown.edu/research/chinas-access-to-foreign-ai-technology/;
Ryan Fedasiuk and Emily Weinstein, *Overseas Professionals and Technology Transfer to China* (Center for Security and Emerging Technology, July 21, 2020), https://cset
.georgetown.edu/research/overseas-professionals-and-technology-transfer-to-china/; Tai
Ming Cheung, William Lucyshyn, and John Rigilano, *The Role of Technology Transfers
in China's Defense Technological and Industrial Development and the Implications for the
United States* (Naval Postgraduate School, February 19, 2019), https://calhoun.nps.edu/
bitstream/handle/10945/61948/UCSD-AM-19-028.pdf?sequence=1&isAllowed=y; Office
of the U.S. Trade Representative, *Findings of the Investigation into China's Acts, Policies,
and Practices Related to Technology Transfer, Intellectual Property, and Innovation Under
Section 301 of the Trade Act of 1974* (US Trade Representative, March 22, 2018), https://ustr
.gov/sites/default/files/Section%20301%20FINAL.PDF; Commission on the Theft of American Intellectual Property, *The IP Commission Report: The Report of the Commission on the
Theft of American Intellectual Property* (National Bureau of Asian Research, May 2013),
https://www.nbr.org/wp-content/uploads/pdfs/publications/IP_Commission_Report.pdf.

6 **more AI papers than the United States:** Field Cady and Oren Etzioni, "China May Over-

take US in AI Research," *Medium*, March 13, 2019, https://medium.com/ai2-blog/china-to
-overtake-us-in-ai-research-8b6b1fe30595.

6 **top 1 percent most-cited papers:** *Research and Development: U.S. Trends and International Comparisons* (National Science Board, 2018), 42, figure 4-6, https://www.nsf
.gov/statistics/2018/nsb20181/assets/1038/research-and-development-u-s-trends-and
-international-comparisons.pdf; "Gross Domestic Spending on R&D," OCED.org,
n.d., https://data.oecd.org/rd/gross-domestic-spending-on-r-d.htm. Thanks to CNAS
research associate Ainikki Riikonen and senior fellow Martijn Rasser for background
research.

6 **massive investment of over $50 billion in the U.S. semiconductor industry:** *CHIPS and Science Act of 2022: Section-by-Section Summary* (Commerce.senate.gov, 2022),
https://www.commerce.senate.gov/services/files/1201E1CA-73CB-44BB-ADEB
-E69634DA9BB9. See also Sections 9902 and 9906: William M. (Mac) Thornberry
National Defense Authorization Act for Fiscal Year 2021, H.R. 6395, 116th Cong. (2019),
https://www.congress.gov/bill/116th-congress/house-bill/6395/text.

6 **geopolitical order for the twenty-first century:** For more on the geopolitics of artificial
intelligence, see: Ben Buchanan and Andrew Imbrie, *The New Fire: War, Peace, and Democracy in the Age of AI* (Boston: The MIT Press, 2022); Henry A. Kissinger, Eric Schmidt, and
Daniel Huttenlocher, *The Age of AI: And Our Human Future* (New York, NY: Little, Brown,
and Company, 2021); Michael Kanaan, *T-Minus AI: Humanity's Countdown to Artificial
Intelligence and the New Pursuit of Global Power* (Dallas, TX: BenBella Books, 2020); and
William C. Hannas and Huey-Meei Chang, eds., *Chinese Power and Artificial Intelligence:
Perspectives and Challenges* (Abingdon, Oxon; New York, NY: Routledge, 2022).

7 **Russia and China announced a "no limits" partnership:** "Joint Statement of the Russian
Federation and the People's Republic of China on the International Relations Entering a
New Era and the Global Sustainable Development," February 4, 2022, http://en.kremlin
.ru/supplement/5770.

8 **European nations are leaning into regulating AI:** Anu Bradford, *The Brussels Effect*
(Columbia Law School, 2012), https://scholarship.law.columbia.edu/cgi/viewcontent
.cgi?article=1275&context=faculty_scholarship; Anu Bradford, *The Brussels Effect:
How the European Union Rules the World* (Oxford Scholarship Online, 2020), https://
oxford.universitypressscholarship.com/view/10.1093/oso/9780190088583.001.0001/oso
-9780190088583.

1. THE NEW OIL

11 **Power:** John J. Mearsheimer, *The Tragedy of Great Power Politics* (New York: W. W. Norton,
2014); Joseph S. Nye Jr., *The Future of Power* (New York: PublicAffairs, 2011).

11 **soft (culture and values) power:** On soft power, see Joseph S. Nye Jr., *Soft Power: The Means
to Success in World Politics* (New York: PublicAffairs, 2004).

11 **another industrial revolution:** Klaus Schwab, "The Fourth Industrial Revolution: What
It Means, How to Respond," World Economic Forum, January 14, 2016, https://www
.weforum.org/agenda/2016/01/the-fourth-industrial-revolution-what-it-means-and-how
-to-respond/; *Robot Revolution—Global Robot & AI Primer* (Bank of America Merrill Lynch, December 16, 2015), https://www.bofaml.com/content/dam/boamlimages/
documents/PDFs/robotics_and_ai_condensed_primer.pdf (page discontinued); Rob
Thomas, "How AI Is Driving the New Industrial Revolution," *Forbes*, March 4, 2020,
https://www.forbes.com/sites/ibm/2020/03/04/how-ai-is-driving-the-new-industrial

-revolution/#7225c870131a; Sean Gallagher, "The Fourth Industrial Revolution Emerges from AI and the Internet of Things," *Ars Technica*, June 18, 2019, https://arstechnica .com/information-technology/2019/06/the-revolution-will-be-roboticized-how-ai-is -driving-industry-4-0/.

12   *The Rise and Fall of the Great Powers*: Paul Kennedy, *The Rise and Fall of the Great Powers* (New York, Random House, 1987), 197.

12   **by 1890 Russia had been eclipsed:** Kennedy, *The Rise and Fall of the Great Powers*, 171.

13   **global manufacturing output:** Kennedy, *The Rise and Fall of the Great Powers*, 149.

13   **Battle of Omdurman:** Max Boot, *War Made New: Weapons, Warriors, and the Making of the Modern World* (New York: Avery, August 16, 2007), 146–169.

13   **over 80 percent of the world's land surface:** Kennedy, *The Rise and Fall of the Great Powers*, 150.

13   **major factor in potential military power:** There is no consensus among scholars about how to comprehensively measure national power. By one count, there have been at least seventy different formulas generated by scholars for assessing national power. Karl Hermann Höhn, "Geopolitics and the Measurement of National Power" (dissertation, SUB Hamburg, 2011), https://ediss.sub.uni-hamburg.de/handle/ediss/5238, ii; and Michael Beckley, "The Power of Nations: Measuring What Matters," *International Security* 43, no. 2 (2018): 7–44, https://doi.org/10.1162/ISEC_a_00328.

13   **industrial-age national power:** Kennedy, *The Rise and Fall of the Great Powers*, 199–202, 258, 271; Mearsheimer, *The Tragedy of Great Power Politics*, 64–66.

13   **3.5 times as many aircraft and tanks:** Kennedy, *The Rise and Fall of the Great Powers*, 353–355.

14   **thirty-to-one casualty ratio:** The United States suffered 298 deaths during the Persian Gulf War (147 from hostile fire) plus at least eighty-eight coalition partners killed. "U.S. Military Casualties—Persian Gulf War Casualty Summary Desert Storm," Defense Casualty Analysis System, as of February 11, 2022, https://dcas.dmdc.osd.mil/dcas/pages/ report_gulf_storm.xhtml; Patrick Cooper, "Coalition deaths fewer than in 1991," CNN, June 25, 2003, http://www.cnn.com/2003/WORLD/meast/04/17/sprj.irq.casualties/; "The Gulf War," Royal British Legion, https://www.britishlegion.org.uk/stories/the-gulf-war. Estimates of Iraqi military casualties vary wildly, from roughly 1,000 to over 100,000. For a brief overview of the range of estimates and associated debate, see Jack Kelly, "Estimates of deaths in first war still in dispute," *Post-Gazette* (Pittsburgh), February 16, 2003, http:// old.post-gazette.com/nation/20030216casualty0216p5.asp. The Gulf War Air Power Survey estimated 10,000–12,000 Iraqi military killed during the air war preceding the ground invasion, plus an unknown number killed during the ground offensive, yielding a casualty ratio of approximately 25–30:1 and possibly much higher. Thomas A. Keaney and Eliot A. Cohen, *Gulf War Air Power Survey Summary Report* (Washington, DC: US Air Force, 1993), 249, https://apps.dtic.mil/sti/pdfs/ADA273996.pdf.

14   **"cruelly and unusually punishing our already whipped foes":** Tom Clancy and Chuck Horner, *Every Man a Tiger* (New York: Berkley Books, 1999), 499–500.

14   **precision-guided weapons:** Lauren Kahn and Michael C. Horowitz, *Who Gets Smart: Explaining How Precision Bombs Proliferate* (SSRN, 2021), https://papers.ssrn.com/sol3/ papers.cfm?abstract_id=3792071.

14   **national** *digital* **power:** Ashley J. Tellis et al., *Measuring National Power in the Postindustrial Age* (RAND Corporation, 2000), https://www.rand.org/pubs/monograph_reports/ MR1110.html.

14   **data, computing hardware (compute), algorithms:** For related analysis of key inputs to

AI power, see Ben Buchanan, *The AI Triad and What It Means for National Security Strategy* (Center for Security and Emerging Technology, August 2020), https://cset.georgetown .edu/wp-content/uploads/CSET-AI-Triad-Report.pdf; Matthew Daniels and Ben Chang, *National Power After AI* (Center for Security and Emerging Technology, July 2021), https:// cset.georgetown.edu/publication/national-power-after-ai/.

15 **countries' national AI power:** Daniel Castro and Michael McLaughlin, *Who Is Winning the AI Race: China, the EU or the United States? 2021 Update* (Center for Data Innovation, January 2021), https://www2.datainnovation.org/2021-china-eu-us-ai.pdf; Daniel Castro, Michael McLaughlin, and Eline Chivot, *Who Is Winning the AI Race: China, the EU or the United States?* (Center for Data Innovation, August 2019), https://www2.datainnovation .org/2019-china-eu-us-ai.pdf; "The Global AI Index," Tortoise Media, updated 2021, https://www.tortoisemedia.com/intelligence/global-ai/; Jeffrey Ding, *Deciphering China's AI Dream* (Future of Humanity Institute, March 2018), https://www.fhi.ox.ac.uk/wp -content/uploads/Deciphering_Chinas_AI-Dream.pdf; "AI Readiness Index 2020," Oxford Insights, 2020, https://www.oxfordinsights.com/government-ai-readiness-index-2020; Raymond Perrault et al., *The AI Index 2019 Annual Report* (AI Index Steering Committee, December 2019), https://hai.stanford.edu/sites/default/files/ai_index_2019_report .pdf; "Global AI Vibrancy Tool," Artificial Intelligence Index, n.d., https://aiindex.stanford .edu/vibrancy/; Bruno Lanvin and Felipe Monteiro, eds., *The Global Talent Competitiveness Index 2021: Talent Competitiveness in Times of COVID* (Fontainebleau, France: INSEAD, 2021), https://www.insead.edu/sites/default/files/assets/dept/fr/gtci/GTCI-2021-Report .pdf; *Sizing the Prize: What's the Real Value of AI for Your Business and How Can You Capitalise?* (pwc, n.d.), https://www.pwc.com/gx/en/issues/analytics/assets/pwc-ai-analysis -sizing-the-prize-report.pdf. Thanks to former CNAS intern Xiaojing (JJ) Zeng for background research on global AI indices.

15 **"the United States currently leads in AI":** Castro et al., *Who Is Winning the AI Race* (2019).

15 **national AI capabilities:** Castro and McLaughlin, *Who Is Winning the AI Race* (2021); Castro et al., *Who Is Winning the AI Race* (2019); "The Global AI Index."

15 **infrastructure, the operating environment, and government strategy:** "The Global AI Index."

15 **the United States led overall:** Castro et al., *Who Is Winning the AI Race* (2019); Castro and McLaughlin, *Who Is Winning the AI Race* (2021), 27–31.

15 **Global AI Index:** "The Global AI Index"; *The Global AI Index: Methodology* (Tortoise Media, December 2021), https://www.tortoisemedia.com/wp-content/uploads/ sites/3/2021/12/Global-AI-Index-Methodology-3.0-211201-v2.pdf.

16 **metrics that are size-adjusted:** *The Global AI Index: Methodology*, 4.

16 **AI researchers:** Castro et al., *Who Is Winning the AI Race* (2019), 5.

16 **Chinese researchers publish nearly 1.5 times as many papers:** Castro et al., *Who Is Winning the AI Race* (2019), 21; *The AI Index 2019 Annual Report*, 18; Daniel Zhang et al., *The AI Index 2021 Annual Report* (Stanford, CA: AI Index Steering Committee, March 2021), 20, 24, https://aiindex.stanford.edu/wp-content/uploads/2021/03/2021-AI-Index-Report_ Master.pdf. For a more detailed breakdown of various types of publications (journal, conference, repository) by region see Daniel Zhang et al., *The AI Index 2022 Annual Report* (Stanford, CA: AI Index Steering Committee, March 2022), 26, 30, 34, https://aiindex .stanford.edu/wp-content/uploads/2022/03/2022-AI-Index-Report_Master.pdf.

16 **how to weight or combine various indices:** The Global AI Vibrancy Tool from Stanford University is an interactive web-based tool that allows one to change the weighting of different indices: https://aiindex.stanford.edu/vibrancy/.

16 **relative value of some metrics:** For what kinds of metrics governments should track in AI development, see Jess Whittlestone and Jack Clark, "Why and How Governments Should Monitor AI Development," (arXiv.org, August 28, 2021), https://arxiv.org/pdf/2108.12427.pdf.

2. DATA

18 **"The world's most valuable resource is no longer oil":** "The World's Most Valuable Resource Is No Longer Oil, but Data," *The Economist*, May 6, 2017, https://www.economist .com/leaders/2017/05/06/the-worlds-most-valuable-resource-is-no-longer-oil-but-data.

18 **24 billion connected devices:** *Cisco Annual Internet Report (2018–2023)* (Cisco, 2020), https://www.cisco.com/c/en/us/solutions/collateral/executive-perspectives/annual-internet -report/white-paper-c11-741490.pdf.

18 **Global internet protocol (IP) traffic:** Thomas Barnett Jr. et al., *Cisco Visual Networking Index (VNI) Complete Forecast Update, 2017–2022: APJC Cisco Knowledge Network (CKN) Presentation* (Cisco, December 2018), https://www.cisco.com/c/dam/m/en_us/network -intelligence/service-provider/digital-transformation/knowledge-network-webinars/ pdfs/1213-business-services-ckn.pdf.

18 **Broadband speeds are expected to more than double and wireless speeds more than triple:** *Cisco Annual Internet Report.*

18 **stack of paper that would stretch from the earth to the sun:** Assumes 500 words per page (single-spaced).

19 **ImageNet:** "About ImageNet," ImageNet.org, 2020, https://image-net.org/about.php.

19 **500 to 1,000 images:** "Summary and Statistics (updated on April 30, 2010)," ImageNet, https://web.archive.org/web/20200303061817/http://www.image-net.org/about-stats.

20 **image classifiers surpassed human performance:** Kaiming He et al., *Delving Deep into Rectifiers: Surpassing Human-Level Performance on ImageNet Classification* (Microsoft Research, February 6, 2015), https://arxiv.org/pdf/1502.01852.pdf.

20 **GPT-2:** "Better Language Models and Their Implications," openai.com, n.d., https://openai .com/blog/better-language-models/.

20 **Megatron-Turing NLG:** Ali Alvi and Paresh Kharya, "Using DeepSpeed and Megatron to Train Megatron-Turing NLG 530B, the World's Largest and Most Powerful Generative Language Model," Microsoft Research Blog, October 11, 2021, https://www.microsoft.com/ en-us/research/blog/using-deepspeed-and-megatron-to-train-megatron-turing-nlg-530b -the-worlds-largest-and-most-powerful-generative-language-model/.

20 **825 GB text database:** Leo Gao et al., *The Pile: An 800GB Dataset of Diverse Text for Language Modeling* (arXiv, December 31, 2020), https://arxiv.org/pdf/2101.00027.pdf.

20 **performance gains from ever-larger models and datasets:** Fedus et al., *Switch Transformers*; Jared Kaplan et al., *Scaling Laws for Neural Language Models* (arXiv.org, January 23, 2020), https://arxiv.org/pdf/2001.08361.pdf. See also Jonathan S. Rosenfeld et al., *A Constructive Prediction of the Generalization Error Across Scales* (arXiv.org, December 20, 2019), https://arxiv.org/pdf/1909.12673.pdf; Tom Henighan et al., *Scaling Laws for Autoregressive Generative Modeling* (arXiv.org, November 6, 2020), https://arxiv.org/pdf/2010.14701.pdf.

20 **"Data is the new oil":** Joris Toonders, "Data Is the New Oil of the Digital Economy," *Wired*, n.d., https://www.wired.com/insights/2014/07/data-new-oil-digital-economy/; Kiran Bhageshpur, "Data Is the New Oil—and That's a Good Thing," *Forbes*, November 15, 2019, https://www.forbes.com/sites/forbestechcouncil/2019/11/15/data-is-the-new-oil-and-thats -a-good-thing/?sh=10eefed73045; Adeola Adesina, "Data Is the New Oil," *Medium*, November 13, 2018, https://medium.com/@adeolaadesina/data-is-the-new-oil-2947ed8804f6; Will

Murphy, "Data Is the New Oil," *Towards Data Science*, May 7, 2017, https://towardsdata-science.com/data-is-the-new-oil-f11440e80dd0; Giuliano Giacaglia, "Data Is the New Oil," *Hackernoon*, February 9, 2019, https://hackernoon.com/data-is-the-new-oil-1227197762b2.

20 **data-is-*not*-the-new-oil articles:** Antonio Garcia Martinez, "No, Data Is Not the New Oil," *Wired*, February 26, 2019, https://www.wired.com/story/no-data-is-not-the-new-oil/; Bernard Marr, "Here's Why Data Is Not the New Oil," *Forbes*, March 5, 2018, https://www.forbes.com/sites/bernardmarr/2018/03/05/heres-why-data-is-not-the-new-oil/?sh=4b277fa13aa9; Samuel Flender, "Data Is Not the New Oil," *Towards Data Science*, February 10, 2019, https://towardsdatascience.com/data-is-not-the-new-oil-bdb31f61bc2d; John Thuma, "Data Is Not the New Oil!" fisglobal.com, July 13, 2020, https://www.fisglobal.com/en/insights/what-we-think/2020/july/data-is-not-the-new-oil; Justin Sherman and Samm Sacks, "The Myth of China's Big A.I. Advantage," *Slate*, June 13, 2019, https://slate.com/technology/2019/06/data-not-new-oil-kai-fu-lee-china-artificial-intelligence.html.

20 **China is "the Saudi Arabia of data":** "China May Match or Beat America in AI," *The Economist*, July 15, 2017, https://www.economist.com/business/2017/07/15/china-may-match-or-beat-america-in-ai; Kai-Fu Lee, *AI Superpowers: China, Silicon Valley, and the New World Order* (Boston: Mariner Books, September 1, 2018), 55, https://www.amazon.com/AI-Superpowers-China-Silicon-Valley/dp/132854639X.

20 **data is not a fungible resource:** Husanjot Chahal, Ryan Fedasiuk, and Carrick Flynn, *Messier Than Oil: Assessing Data Advantage in Military AI* (Center for Security and Emerging Technology, July 2020), https://cset.georgetown.edu/publication/messier-than-oil-assessing-data-advantage-in-military-ai/.

21 **surveillance capitalism:** Shoshana Zuboff, *The Age of Surveillance Capitalism: The Fight for a Human Future at the New Frontier of Power* (New York: PublicAffairs, January 15, 2019), https://www.amazon.com/Age-Surveillance-Capitalism-Future-Frontier/dp/1610395697.

22 **900 million internet users as of 2020:** "Number of Internet Users in China from 2008 to 2020," Statista, 2021, https://www.statista.com/statistics/265140/number-of-internet-users-in-china/.

22 **750 million internet users in 2020:** *The Indian Telecom Services Performance Indicators: April–June, 2020* (Telecom Regulatory Authority of India, November 9, 2020), https://trai.gov.in/sites/default/files/Report_09112020_0.pdf.

22 **400 million users:** "Internet access," in "Digital economy and society statistics—households and individuals," Eurostat, September 2020, https://ec.europa.eu/eurostat/statistics-explained/index.php/Digital_economy_and_society_statistics_-_households_and_individuals#Internet_usage.

22 **290 million internet users:** "Digital Population in the United States as of January 2021," Statista, February 2021, https://www.statista.com/statistics/1044012/usa-digital-platform-audience/.

22 **Facebook has 2.7 billion users:** Facebook, "Facebook Reports Third Quarter 2020 Results," news release, October 29, 2020, https://investor.fb.com/investor-news/press-release-details/2020/Facebook-Reports-Third-Quarter-2020-Results/default.aspx.

22 **YouTube over 2 billion:** "YouTube for Press," YouTube Official Blog, n.d., https://blog.youtube/press/.

22 **WeChat's 1.2 billion:** Monthly active users as of 30 September 2020. Tencent, "Tencent Announces 2020 Third Quarter Results," news release, Hong Kong, November 12, 2020, https://static.www.tencent.com/uploads/2020/11/12/4c2090d5f6f00fd90ddc9bbd9a1415d1.pdf.

22 **Chinese citizens' alleged "cultural nonchalance about data privacy":** Lee, *AI Superpowers*, 128.

22 **steps to increase privacy protections:** Anjali C. Das, "China's New Personal Information Protection Law," *National Law Review*, December 2, 2021, https://www.natlawre-
view.com/article/china-s-new-personal-information-protection-law; Rogier Creemers
and Graham Webster, "Translation: Personal Information Protection Law of the People's
Republic of China—Effective Nov. 1, 2021," DigiChina, August 20, 2021, https://digi-
china.stanford.edu/work/translation-personal-information-protection-law-of-the-peo-
ples-republic-of-china-effective-nov-1-2021/; Liisa M. Thomas, Julia K. Kadish, and Kari
M. Rollins, "Update on the State of Privacy Law in China," *National Law Review*, September 20, 2021, https://www.natlawreview.com/article/update-state-privacy-law-china;
Eva Dou, "China Built the World's Largest Facial Recognition System. Now, It's Getting
Camera-Shy," *Washington Post*, July 30, 2021, https://www.washingtonpost.com/world/
facial-recognition-china-tech-data/2021/07/30/404c2e96-f049-11eb-81b2-9b7061a582d8_
story.html; Laura He, "China Is Raising the Alarm Over Corporate Surveillance. But It's
Got a Massive Network of Its Own," CNN Business, March 19, 2021, https://edition.cnn
.com/2021/03/19/tech/china-consumer-rights-surveillance-intl-hnk/index.html.

22 **power of Chinese big tech firms:** "Xi's Push Against Jack Ma Sparks New Threat for China
Tech," *Bloomberg News*, January 6, 2021, https://www.bloomberg.com/news/articles/2021
-01-06/xi-s-push-against-jack-ma-sparks-new-u-s-threat-for-china-tech; Austin Carr
and Coco Liu, "The China Model: What the Country's Tech Crackdown Is Really About,"
Bloomberg Businessweek, July 27, 2021, https://www.bloomberg.com/news/articles/2021-07
-27/china-tech-crackdown-xi-charts-new-model-after-emulating-silicon-valley; Lingling
Wei, "China's New Power Play: More Control of Tech Companies' Troves of Data," *Wall
Street Journal*, June 12, 2021, https://www.wsj.com/articles/chinas-new-power-play-more
-control-of-tech-companies-troves-of-data-11623470478; Yuan Yang, "How China Is Targeting Big Tech," *Financial Times*, June 18, 2021, https://www.ft.com/content/baad4a14
-efac-4601-8ce4-406d5fd8f2a7; "China Orders Didi App Downloads Suspended over Data
Violation," Reuters, July 4, 2021, https://www.reuters.com/world/china/china-cyberspace
-agency-says-didi-illegally-collects-user-data-2021-07-04/.

22 **Chinese firms will have major data advantages:** Cat Zakrzewski, "The Technology 202:
Former Google CEO Eric Schmidt Warns Congress of China's Rise," *Washington Post*,
February 24, 2021, https://www.washingtonpost.com/politics/2021/02/24/technology-202
-former-google-ceo-eric-schmidt-warns-congress-china-rise/.

22 **facial recognition for law enforcement:** Brian Fung, "Tech Companies Push for
Nationwide Facial Recognition Law. Now Comes the Hard Part," *Philadelphia Tribune*, June 15, 2020, https://www.phillytrib.com/news/business/tech-companies-push
-for-nationwide-facial-recognition-law-now-comes-the-hard-part/article_fe78e04e
-e8be-5aab-9402-00203a44510f.html; Rachel Metz, "Portland Passes Broadest Facial
Recognition Ban in the US," CNN Business, September 9, 2020, https://amp.cnn.com/
cnn/2020/09/09/tech/portland-facial-recognition-ban/index.html.

22 **Amazon:** "We Are Implementing a One-Year Moratorium on Police Use of Rekognition,"
Amazon, June 10, 2020, https://blog.aboutamazon.com/policy/we-are-implementing-a
-one-year-moratorium-on-police-use-of-rekognition.

23 **Microsoft:** Jay Greene, "Microsoft Won't Sell Police Its Facial-Recognition Technology,
Following Similar Moves by Amazon and IBM," *Washington Post*, June 11, 2020, https://
www.washingtonpost.com/technology/2020/06/11/microsoft-facial-recognition/.

23 **IBM:** Hannah Denham, "IBM's Decision to Abandon Facial Recognition Technology
Fueled by Years of Debate," *Washington Post*, June 11, 2020, https://www.washingtonpost
.com/technology/2020/06/11/ibm-facial-recognition/.

23 **reduce their reliance on massive datasets:** Tim Hwang of the Center for Security and Emerging Technology has suggested that democratic societies invest in AI methods that reduce dependence on data as a way to offset what he describes as an "authoritarian advantage" in acquiring data. Tim Hwang, *Shaping the Terrain of AI Competition* (Center for Security and Emerging Technology, June 2020), https://cset.georgetown.edu/research/shaping-the-terrain-of-ai-competition/.

23 **few-shot, one-shot, and zero-shot learning:** Yaqing Wang et al., *Generalizing from a Few Examples: A Survey on Few-Shot Learning* (arXiv.org, March 29, 2020), https://arxiv.org/pdf/1904.05046.pdf; Adam Santoro et al., *One-Shot Learning with Memory-Augmented Neural Networks* (arXiv.org, May 19, 2016), https://arxiv.org/pdf/1605.06065v1.pdf; Michael J. Garbade, "Understanding Few-Shot Learning in Machine Learning," *Quick Code* [blog], August 25, 2018, https://medium.com/quick-code/understanding-few-shot-learning-in-machine-learning-bede251a0f67; Vladimir Lyashenko, "Understanding Few-Shot Learning in Computer Vision—What You Need to Know," Neptuneblog, July 16, 2021, https://neptune.ai/blog/understanding-few-shot-learning-in-computer-vision.

23 **DeepMind's early version of AlphaGo:** "The Google DeepMind Challenge Match," DeepMind, n.d., https://deepmind.com/alphago-korea; David Silver et al., "Mastering the Game of Go with Deep Neural Networks and Tree Search," *Nature* 529 (January 28, 2016), 485.

23 **updated version, AlphaGo Zero:** David Silver et al., "Mastering the Game of Go Without Human Knowledge," *Nature* 550 (October 19, 2017), 354–355, https://www.nature.com/articles/nature24270.epdf.

23 **subsequent version of AlphaGo Zero:** Silver et al., "Mastering the Game of Go Without Human Knowledge," 358.

23 **AlphaZero:** David Silver et al., *Mastering Chess and Shogi by Self-Play with a General Reinforcement Learning Algorithm* (arXiv.org, December 5, 2017), 15, https://arxiv.org/pdf/1712.01815.pdf.

23 **5,000 AI-specialized computer chips:** The simulations used 5,000 TPUs, or Tensor Processing Units. Silver et al., *Mastering Chess and Shogi*, 4.

23 **20 million miles:** Aaron Pressman, "Waymo Reaches 20 Million Miles of Autonomous Driving," *Fortune*, January 7, 2020, https://fortune.com/2020/01/07/googles-waymo-reaches-20-million-miles-of-autonomous-driving/.

24 **simulating 10 million driving miles** *every single day***:** John Krafcik, "Where the Next 10 Million Miles Will Take Us," Waymo, October 10, 2018, https://medium.com/waymo/where-the-next-10-million-miles-will-take-us-de51bebb67d3.

24 **10 billion simulated miles as of 2020:** "Waymo Raises First External Investment Round," Waymo blog, March 2, 2020, https://blog.waymo.com/2020/03/waymo-raises-first-external-investment.html.

24 **thousands of variations of situations:** James Stout, "How Simulation Turns One Flashing Yellow Light into Thousands of Hours of Experience," Waymo, September 7, 2017, https://medium.com/waymo/simulation-how-one-flashing-yellow-light-turns-into-thousands-of-hours-of-experience-a7a1cb475565.

3. COMPUTE

25 **the geopolitical significance of compute:** Ben Buchanan, "The U.S. Has AI Competition All Wrong," *Foreign Affairs*, August 7, 2020, https://www.foreignaffairs.com/articles/united-states/2020-08-07/us-has-ai-competition-all-wrong; Tim Hwang, *Computational*

Power and the Social Impact of Artificial Intelligence (SSRN, March 24, 2018, updated January 18, 2019), https://papers.ssrn.com/sol3/papers.cfm?abstract_id=3147971.

25 **inference can increasingly be done on edge devices:** Gaurav Batra et al., "Artificial-Intelligence Hardware: New Opportunities for Semiconductor Companies," McKinsey & Company, January 2, 2019, https://www.mckinsey.com/industries/semiconductors/our-insights/artificial-intelligence-hardware-new-opportunities-for-semiconductor-companies.

25 **deep learning training in data centers:** Batra et al., "Artificial-Intelligence Hardware," Exhibit 6.

26 **doubling of computing power every six months:** Jaime Sevilla et al., *Compute Trends Across Three Eras of Machine Learning* (arXiv.org, March 9, 2022), https://arxiv.org/pdf/2202.05924.pdf. Other researchers have come up with somewhat different rates of progress in the deep learning era, see Dario Amodei and Danny Hernandez, "AI and Compute," openai.com, May 16, 2018, https://openai.com/blog/ai-and-compute/.

26 **Moore's law:** Gordon E. Moore, "Cramming More Components onto Integrated Circuits," *Electronics* 38, no. 8 (April 19, 1965), https://newsroom.intel.com/wp-content/uploads/sites/11/2018/05/moores-law-electronics.pdf.

26 **"thousands of GPUs over multiple months":** Open AI et al., *Dota 2 with Large Scale Deep Reinforcement Learning* (arXiv.org, December 13, 2019), 2, https://arxiv.org/pdf/1912.06680.pdf.

26 **equivalent to a human playing for 45,000 years:** OpenAI, "OpenAI Five Defeats Dota 2 World Champions," OpenAI blog, April 15, 2019, https://openai.com/blog/openai-five-defeats-dota-2-world-champions/.

26 **13,000 years of simulated computer time:** Ilge Akkaya et al., *Solving Rubik's Cube With a Robot Hand* (arXiv.org, October 17, 2019), https://arxiv.org/pdf/1910.07113.pdf.

26 **spending millions on compute:** Ryan Carey, "Interpreting AI Compute Trends," AI Impacts, n.d., https://aiimpacts.org/interpreting-ai-compute-trends/; Dan H., "How Much Did AlphaGo Zero Cost?" *Dansplaining*, updated June 2020, https://www.yuzeh.com/data/agz-cost.html; Saif M. Khan and Alexander Mann, *AI Chips: What They Are and Why They Matter* (Center for Security and Emerging Technology, April 2020), 26, https://cset.georgetown.edu/research/ai-chips-what-they-are-and-why-they-matter/.

26 **DeepMind:** Sam Shead, "DeepMind A.I. Unit Lost $649 Million Last Year and Had a $1.5 Billion Debt Waived by Alphabet," CNBC, December 17, 2020, https://www.cnbc.com/2020/12/17/deepmind-lost-649-million-and-alphabet-waived-a-1point5-billion-debt-.html.

26 **Microsoft:** Greg Brockman, "Microsoft Invests in and Partners with OpenAI to Support Us Building Beneficial AGI," *OpenAI Blog*, July 22, 2019, https://openai.com/blog/microsoft/; "OpenAI Forms Exclusive Computing Partnership with Microsoft to Build New Azure AI Supercomputing Technologies," Microsoft, July 22, 2019, https://news.microsoft.com/2019/07/22/openai-forms-exclusive-computing-partnership-with-microsoft-to-build-new-azure-ai-supercomputing-technologies/.

26 **AI-specialized processor:** Steve McCaskill, "Three Quarters of Smartphones Will Have AI Chip by 2022," techradar.com, April 15, 2019, https://www.techradar.com/news/three-quarters-of-smartphones-will-have-ai-chip-by-2022.

26 **AI tasks onboard the device:** "Top AI Chip-Making Companies for Smartphones," *Mobile App Daily*, February 20, 2020, https://www.mobileappdaily.com/ai-chip-making-companies-for-smartphones; Jeremy Horwitz, "As AI Chips Improve, Is TOPS the Best Way to Measure Their Power?" *The Machine* (blog), *VentureBeat*, September 30, 2020, https://

venturebeat.com/2020/09/30/as-ai-chips-improve-is-tops-the-best-way-to-measure-their
-power/.

26 **outsize influence over key chokepoints in global chip supply chains:** Saif M. Khan, Alexander Mann, and Dahlia Peterson, *The Semiconductor Supply Chain: Assessing National
Competitiveness* (Center for Security and Emerging Technology, January 2021), https://cset
.georgetown.edu/research/the-semiconductor-supply-chain/.

27 **semiconductor:** Michaela D. Platzer, John F. Sargent Jr., and Karen M. Sutter, *Semiconductors: U.S. Industry, Global Competition, and Federal Policy* (Congressional Research
Service, October 26, 2020), 2, https://fas.org/sgp/crs/misc/R46581.pdf.

27 **chip's value:** John VerWey, *The Health and Competitiveness of the U.S. Semiconductor
Manufacturing Equipment Industry* (SSRN, July 1, 2019), 2, https://papers.ssrn.com/sol3/
papers.cfm?abstract_id=3413951.

27 **biggest players in the global semiconductor market:** *2020 State of the U.S. Semiconductor
Industry* (Semiconductor Industry Association, 2020), 7, https://www.semiconductors.org/
wp-content/uploads/2020/06/2020-SIA-State-of-the-Industry-Report.pdf; Antonio Varas
et al., *Strengthening the Global Semiconductor Supply Chain in an Uncertain Era* (Boston
Consulting Group and the Semiconductor Industry Association, 2021), 5, https://www
.semiconductors.org/wp-content/uploads/2021/05/BCG-x-SIA-Strengthening-the-Global
-Semiconductor-Value-Chain-April-2021_1.pdf.

27 **semiconductor value chain:** *2020 State of the U.S. Semiconductor Industry*; Seamus
Grimes and Debin Du, "China's Emerging Role in the Global Semiconductor Value
Chain," *Telecommunications Policy* [in press, published online April 18, 2020], https://
www.sciencedirect.com/science/article/pii/S0308596120300513; Platzer, Sargent, and
Sutter, *Semiconductors*, 17; Khan, Mann, and Peterson, *The Semiconductor Supply Chain*;
Varas et al., *Strengthening the Global Semiconductor Supply Chain in an Uncertain Era*, 5.

27 **47 percent of global semiconductor sales:** *2020 State of the U.S. Semiconductor Industry*.

27 **12 percent of global chip manufacturing:** SIA Board of Directors, letter to President Joe
Biden, February 11, 2021, https://www.semiconductors.org/wp-content/uploads/2021/02/
SIA-Letter-to-Pres-Biden-re-CHIPS-Act-Funding.pdf; Varas et al., *Strengthening the
Global Semiconductor Supply Chain in an Uncertain Era*, 5.

27 **65 percent of the global fabless market:** *2020 State of the U.S. Semiconductor Industry*, 8.

27 **over half of the global pure-play foundry market:** Huang Tzu-ti, "Taiwan's TSMC
the World's Top Chipmaker by Market Cap," *Taiwan News*, July 16, 2020, https://www
.taiwannews.com.tw/en/news/3968098; "China's Largest Chipmaker Sinks After U.S.
Restrictions," *Bloomberg News*, September 27, 2020, https://www.bloomberg.com/news/
articles/2020-09-28/china-s-largest-chipmaker-sinks-after-u-s-imposes-restrictions.

27 **65 percent of the foundry market:** TrendForce, "China's Semiconductor Industry to Brace
for Impact as SMIC Assesses Export Restrictions Placed by U.S., Says TrendForce," news
release, October 5, 2020, https://www.trendforce.com/presscenter/news/20201005-10499
.html.

27 **10 percent of the foundry market:** *2020 State of the U.S. Semiconductor Industry*, 8.

28 **more computing power per square inch:** For an overview of computing trends, see Khan
and Mann, *AI Chips*, 7–11; Kenneth Flamm, "Measuring Moore's Law: Evidence from
Price, Cost, and Quality Indexes" (working paper, National Bureau of Economic Research,
April 2018), https://www.nber.org/system/files/working_papers/w24553/w24553.pdf.

28 **chip performance continues to improve:** Moore's law is widely considered "dead," not
because chips are no longer improving but because transistor density is no longer doubling
at the rate predicted by Moore's law (every two years). Shara Tibken, "CES 2019: Moore's Law

Is Dead, Says Nvidia's CEO," *CNET*, January 9, 2019,https://www.cnet.com/news/moores
-law-is-dead-nvidias-ceo-jensen-huang-says-at-ces-2019/; David Rotman, "We're Not Prepared for the End of Moore's Law," *MIT Technology Review*, February 24, 2020, https://www
.technologyreview.com/2020/02/24/905789/were-not-prepared-for-the-end-of-moores-law/;
Khan and Mann, *AI Chips*, 7–11; Hassan N. Khan, David A Hounshell, and Erica R.H. Fuchs,
"Science and Research Policy at the End of Moore's Law," *Nature Electronics* 1 (2018), 14–21,
https://www.nature.com/articles/s41928-017-0005-9; Neil Thompson and Svenja Spanuth,
*The Decline of Computers As a General Purpose Technology: Why Deep Learning and the
End of Moore's Law Are Fragmenting Computing* (SSRN, December 12, 2018), 38–41, https://
papers.ssrn.com/sol3/papers.cfm?abstract_id=3287769.

28   **Rock's law:** Philip E. Ross, "5 Commandments: The Rules Engineers Live By Weren't Always
Set in Stone," *IEEE Spectrum*, December 1, 2003, https://spectrum.ieee.org/semiconductors/
materials/5-commandments.

28   **fab costs have increased:** Khan and Mann, *AI Chips.*

28   **leading-edge foundry can cost $10 billion to $20 billion:** Arjun Kharpal, "Apple Supplier
TSMC to Build a $12 Billion Chip Factory in the U.S.," CNBC, May 15, 2020, https://www
.cnbc.com/2020/05/15/tsmc-to-build-us-chip-factory.html; Mark Lapedus and Ann Steffora Mutschler, "Regaining the Edge in U.S. Chip Manufacturing," *Semiconductor Engineering*, October 26, 2020, https://semiengineering.com/can-the-u-s-regain-its-edge-in
-chip-manufacturing/; "Chipmaking Is Being Redesigned. Effects Will Be Far-Reaching,"
The Economist, January 21, 2021, https://www.economist.com/business/2021/01/23/
chipmaking-is-being-redesigned-effects-will-be-far-reaching; AleksandarK, "TSMC
Completes Its Latest 3 nm Factory, Mass Production in 2022," *TechPowerUp*, November 27, 2020, https://www.techpowerup.com/275255/tsmc-completes-its-latest-3-nm
-factory-mass-production-in-2022; "Samsung Considers Austin for $17 Billion Chip
Plant, Seeks Tax Breaks of at Least $806 Million," Reuters, February 4, 2021, https://
www.cnbc.com/2021/02/05/samsung-considers-austin-for-17-billion-chip-plant.html.

28   **$40–44 billion in capital expenditures:** Yang Jie, "TSMC to Invest Up to $44 Billion in
2022 to Beef Up Chip Production," *Wall Street Journal*, January 13, 2022, https://www
.wsj.com/articles/tsmc-to-invest-up-to-44-billion-in-2022-to-beef-up-chip-production
-11642076019.

28   **each evolution of chip production:** Lapedus and Steffora Mutschler, "Regaining the Edge
in U.S. Chip Manufacturing."

28   **node:** WikiChip, s.v. "Technology Node," https://en.wikichip.org/wiki/technology_node.

28   **over two dozen companies at the leading edge of chip fabrication:** "Chipmaking Is Being
Redesigned"; "The Struggle Over Chips Enters a New Phase," *The Economist*, January 21,
2021, https://www.economist.com/leaders/2021/01/23/the-struggle-over-chips-enters-a
-new-phase; Khan and Mann, *AI Chips*, 12.

28   **each introduction of a new manufacturing process:** "Chipmaking Is Being Redesigned";
Khan and Mann, *AI Chips*, 12.

28   **node naming:** Kevin Morris, "No More Nanometers: It's Time for New Node Naming,"
Electronic Engineering Journal, July 23, 2020, https://www.eejournal.com/article/no-more
-nanometers/; WikiChip, s.v. "Technology Node."

28   **current leading-edge 5 nm process node:** Ian Cutress, " 'Better Yield on 5nm Than
7nm': TSMC Update on Defect Rates for N5," Anandtech, August 25, 2020, https://www
.anandtech.com/show/16028/better-yield-on-5nm-than-7nm-tsmc-update-on-defect
-rates-for-n5; Jeet, "Samsung Begins Mass Production of 5nm Chipset; Also Developing
4nm Technology," Gizmochina, July 30, 2020, https://www.gizmochina.com/2020/07/30/

samsung-5nm-chipset-mass-production/; WikiChip, s.v. "5 nm Lithography Process," https://en.wikichip.org/wiki/5_nm_lithography_process.

28 **one-fifth of global chip fabrication:** "The Struggle Over Chips Enters a New Phase"; Samuel M. Goodman, Dan Kim, and John VerWey, "The South Korea-Japan Trade Dispute in Context: Semiconductor Manufacturing, Chemicals, and Concentrated Supply Chains" (working paper ID-062, Office of Industries, U.S. International Trade Commission, October 2019), 11, https://usitc.gov/publications/332/working_papers/the_south_korea-japan_trade_dispute_in_context_semiconductor_manufacturing_chemicals_and_concentrated_supply_chains.pdf.

28 **over 90 percent of leading-edge chips:** Varas et al., *Strengthening the Global Semiconductor Supply Chain in an Uncertain Era,* 5.

28 **eight of the ten AI-specialized chips:** Khan and Mann, *AI Chips,* 28–29.

28 **60 percent of the global demand for semiconductors:** Platzer, Sargent, and Sutter, *Semiconductors,* 26.

29 **importing over $400 billion worth of chips:** "US Sanctions Help China Supercharge Its Chipmaking Industry," Bloomberg, June 20, 2022, https://www.bloomberg.com/news/articles/2022-06-20/us-sanctions-helped-china-supercharge-its-chipmaking-industry.

29 **U.S.-China competition:** Elsa B. Kania, *Securing Our 5G Future: The Competitive Challenge and Considerations for U.S. Policy* (Center for a New American Security, November 7, 2019), https://www.cnas.org/publications/reports/securing-our-5g-future.

4. TALENT

30 **AI research communities:** Specific figures for AI experts by region are disputed and estimates vary widely. For a discussion of some of the assessments and the difficulties in measuring AI experts, see Remco Zwetsloot, *Strengthening the U.S. AI Workforce* (Center for Security and Emerging Technology, September 2019), https://cset.georgetown.edu/wp-content/uploads/CSET_US_AI_Workforce.pdf.

30 **quantity and quality of AI research:** Daniel Castro, Michael McLaughlin, and Eline Chivot, *Who Is Winning the AI Race: China, the EU or the United States?* (Center for Data Innovation, August 2019), 5, https://www2.datainnovation.org/2019-china-cu-us-ai.pdf; Daniel Zhang et al., *The AI Index 2021 Annual Report* (Stanford, CA: AI Index Steering Committee, March 2021), 20, 24, https://aiindex.stanford.edu/wp-content/uploads/2021/03/2021-AI-Index-Report_Master.pdf; Daniel Zhang et al., *The AI Index 2022 Annual Report* (Stanford, CA: AI Index Steering Committee, March 2022), 26–27, 30–31, 34–35, https://aiindex.stanford.edu/wp-content/uploads/2022/03/2022-AI-Index-Report_Master.pdf.

30 **total AI publications:** Raymond Perrault et al., *The AI Index 2019 Annual Report* (AI Index Steering Committee, December 2019), 15, https://hai.stanford.edu/sites/default/files/ai_index_2019_report.pdf; Zhang et al., *The AI Index 2021 Annual Report,* 20; Field Cady and Oren Etzioni, "China May Overtake US in AI Research," Medium, March 13, 2019, https://medium.com/ai2-blog/china-to-overtake-us-in-ai-research-8b6b1fe30595; For a more detailed breakdown of various types of publications (journal, conference, repository) by region see Zhang et al., *The AI Index 2022 Annual Report,* 26, 30, 34.

30 **papers are cited:** Castro and McLaughlin, *Who Is Winning the AI Race* (2021), 29; Castro, McLaughlin, and Chivot, *Who Is Winning the AI Race: China, the EU or the United States?* 5, 21; Perrault et al., *The AI Index 2019 Annual Report,* 18; Zhang et al., *The AI Index 2021 Annual Report,* 24.

30 **authors contributing to top AI journals:** Ella Hollowood and Alex Clark, "Part 5: The

New World Order: How Artificial Intelligence Could Radically Reshape Geopolitics," Tortoise Media, December 5, 2019, https://www.tortoisemedia.com/2019/12/05/the-global-ai-index-part-5-the-new-world-order/.

30 **number of AI journal citations:** Zhang et al., *The AI Index 2021 Annual Report*, 27. Analysis by the Center for Security and Emerging Technology reports China overtook the United States in total number of AI journal citations in 2016. Zhang et al., *The AI Index 2022 Annual Report*, 27.

30 **most-cited papers:** Cady and Etzioni, "China May Overtake US in AI Research."

30 **China is growing talent:** Joy Dantong Ma, "China's AI Talent Base Is Growing, and then Leaving," *Macro Polo*, July 30, 2019, https://macropolo.org/chinas-ai-talent-base-is-growing-and-then-leaving/?rp=m.

30 **2020 study by MacroPolo:** "The Global AI Talent Tracker," *Macro Polo*, n.d., https://macropolo.org/digital-projects/the-global-ai-talent-tracker/.

30 **NeurIPS:** NeurIPS stands for Neural Information Processing Systems. NeurIPS (website), https://nips.cc/.

30 **undergraduate education in China:** "The Global AI Talent Tracker."

31 **Less than a third stayed in China:** Paul Mozur and Cade Metz, "A U.S. Secret Weapon in A.I.: Chinese Talent," *New York Times*, June 9, 2020, updated April 13, 2021, https://www.nytimes.com/2020/06/09/technology/china-ai-research-education.html.

31 **stay and work in the United States:** Remco Zwetsloot, *Keeping Top AI Talent in the United States* (Center for Security and Emerging Technology, December 2019), 22, https://cset.georgetown.edu/wp-content/uploads/Keeping-Top-AI-Talent-in-the-United-States.pdf.

31 **top destination for AI scientists:** Remco Zwetsloot et al., *Skilled and Mobile: Survey Evidence of AI Researchers' Immigration Preferences* (arXiv.org, May 5, 2021), https://arxiv.org/pdf/2104.07237.pdf.

31 **top fifteen institutions publishing deep learning research:** "The Global AI Talent Tracker."

31 **competition for AI talent:** Cade Metz, "Tech Giants Are Paying Huge Salaries for Scarce A.I. Talent," *New York Times*, October 22, 2017, https://www.nytimes.com/2017/10/22/technology/artificial-intelligence-experts-salaries.html; Jeremy Kahn, "Sky-High Salaries Are the Weapons in the AI Talent War," *Bloomberg Businessweek*, February 13, 2018, https://www.bloomberg.com/news/articles/2018-02-13/in-the-war-for-ai-talent-sky-high-salaries-are-the-weapons.

31 **Top AI researchers:** Metz, "Tech Giants Are Paying Huge Salaries."

31 **"For much of basic AI research":** Mozur and Metz, "A U.S. Secret Weapon in A.I.: Chinese Talent."

31 **AI deployment:** Kai-Fu Lee, *AI Superpowers: China, Silicon Valley, and the New World Order* (Boston: Mariner Books, September 1, 2018), https://www.amazon.com/AI-Superpowers-China-Silicon-Valley/dp/132854639X.

32 **national AI research cloud:** Congresswoman Anna G. Eshoo, "Preeminent Universities and Leading Tech Companies Announce Support for Bipartisan, Bicameral Bill to Develop National AI Research Cloud," news release, June 29, 2020, https://eshoo.house.gov/media/press-releases/preeminent-universities-and-leading-tech-companies-announce-support-bipartisan.

32 **increasingly concentrated in the hands of corporate-backed labs:** Deep Ganguli et al., *Predictability and Surprise in Large Generative Models* (arXiv.org, February 15, 2022), https://arxiv.org/pdf/2202.07785.pdf, 11.

32 **"do not have the luxury of a large amount of compute and engineering resources":** Anima Kumar, "An Open and Shut Case on OpenAI," anima-ai.org, January 1, 2021, https://anima-ai.org/2019/02/18/an-open-and-shut-case-on-openai/.

32 **help academics stay engaged:** Gil Alterovitz et al., *Recommendations for Leveraging Cloud Computing Resources for Federally Funded Artificial Intelligence Research and Development* (Select Committee on Artificial Intelligence, National Science & Technology Council, November 17, 2020), https://www.nitrd.gov/pubs/Recommendations-Cloud-AI-RD -Nov2020.pdf; Hatef Monajemi et al., "Ambitious Data Science Can Be Painless," *Harvard Data Science Review*, no. 1.1 (July 1, 2019), https://doi.org/10.1162/99608f92.02ffc552.

32 **National Artificial Intelligence Research Resource:** Division E, "National Artificial Intelligence Research Resource," in William M. (Mac) Thornberry National Defense Authorization Act for Fiscal Year 2021, H.R. 6395, 116th Cong. (2019), https://www.congress.gov/ bill/116th-congress/house-bill/6395/text; The White House, "The Biden Administration Launches the National Artificial Intelligence Research Resource Task Force," news release, June 10, 2021, https://www.whitehouse.gov/ostp/news-updates/2021/06/10/the-biden -administration-launches-the-national-artificial-intelligence-research-resource-task -force/; Interim NAIRR Task Force, *Envisioning a National Artificial Intelligence Research Resource (NAIRR): Preliminary Findings and Recommendations,* May 2022, https://www .ai.gov/wp-content/uploads/2022/05/NAIRR-TF-Interim-Report-2022.pdf; Lynne Parker, "Bridging the Resource Divide for Artificial Intelligence Research," OSTP blog, May 22, 2022, https://www.whitehouse.gov/ostp/news-updates/2022/05/25/bridging-the-resource -divide-for-artificial-intelligence-research/.

32 **China's Thousand Talents Plan:** *Threats to the U.S. Research Enterprise: China's Talent Recruitment Plans* (staff report, Permanent Subcommittee on Investigations, Committee on Homeland Security and Governmental Affairs, US Senate, n.d.), https://www.hsgac .senate.gov/imo/media/doc/2019-11-18%20PSI%20Staff%20Report%20-%20China's%20 Talent%20Recruitment%20Plans.pdf

32 **The program offers participants high salaries:** Remco Zwetsloot, *China's Approach to Tech Talent Competition: Policies, Results, and the Developing Global Response* (Center for Security and Emerging Technology, April 2020), https://cset.georgetown.edu/research/ chinas-approach-to-tech-talent-competition-policies-results-and-the-developing-global -response/; *Threats to the U.S. Research Enterprise.*

32 **over 200 talent recruitment plans:** *Threats to the U.S. Research Enterprise*; Emily Weinstein, "Mapping China's Sprawling Efforts to Recruit Scientists," *Defense One*, November 30, 2020, https://www.defenseone.com/ideas/2020/11/mapping-chinas-sprawling-efforts -recruit-scientists/170373/; William C. Hannas and Huey-meei Chang, *China's Access to Foreign AI Technology* (Center for Security and Emerging Technology, September 2019), https://cset.georgetown.edu/research/chinas-access-to-foreign-ai-technology/.

32 **Chinese scientists overseas:** Quirin Schiermeier, "China: At a Crossroads," *Nature* 507 (2014), 129–131, https://www.nature.com/articles/nj7490-129a; Ryan Fedasiuk and Emily Weinstein, *Overseas Professionals and Technology Transfer to China* (Center for Security and Emerging Technology, July 21, 2020), https://cset.georgetown.edu/research/overseas -professionals-and-technology-transfer-to-china/; David Zweig, *Learning to Compete: China's Efforts to Encourage a 'Reverse Brain Drain'* (cctr.ust.hk, n.d.), http://www.cctr .ust.hk/materials/working_papers/LearningtoCompete.pdf (page discontinued); Remco Zwetsloot, *US–China Stem Talent "Decoupling": Background, Policy, and Impact* (Johns Hopkins University Applied Physics Laboratory, 2020), https://www.jhuapl.edu/assessing -us-china-technology-connections/dist/407b0211ec49299608551326041488d4.pdf.

32 **former chair of Harvard's Chemistry and Chemical Biology Department:** Department of Justice, "Harvard University Professor Convicted of Making False Statements and Tax Offenses," news release, December 21, 2021, https://www.justice.gov/usao-ma/pr/harvard -university-professor-convicted-making-false-statements-and-tax-offenses; Department of Justice, "Harvard University Professor and Two Chinese Nationals Charged in Three Separate China Related Cases," news release, January 28, 2020, https://www.justice.gov/opa/ pr/harvard-university-professor-and-two-chinese-nationals-charged-three-separate-china -related. The professor, Charles Lieber, filed a motion in February 2022 for acquittal or a new trial. (Isabella B. Cho and Brandon L. Kingdollar, "Convicted Harvard Professor Charles Lieber Moves for New Trial to Rectify 'Manifest Injustice,'" *The Harvard Crimson*, February 9, 2022, https://www.thecrimson.com/article/2022/2/9/Lieber-moves-for-retrial/.)

33 **crack down on Chinese espionage:** Department of Justice, "The China Initiative: Year-in-Review (2019–20)," news release, November 16, 2020, https://www.justice.gov/opa/pr/ china-initiative-year-review-2019-20; *China: The Risk to Academia* (Federal Bureau of Investigation, n.d.), https://www.fbi.gov/file-repository/china-risk-to-academia-2019.pdf/ view; Department of Justice, "Information About The Department Of Justice's China Initiative And A Compilation of China-Related Prosecutions Since 2018," news release, November 11, 2021, https://www.justice.gov/archives/nsd/information-about-department -justice-s-china-initiative-and-compilation-china-related.

33 **deleted mention of Thousand Talents online:** 乐科研交流 ｜国家千人·青年千人计划或 将取消 [Happy Research Conversations | National Thousand Talents and Youth Thousand Talents Programs May Be Canceled], October 5, 2018, https://chinadigitaltimes.net/ chinese/597008.html; Weinstein, "Mapping China's Sprawling Efforts to Recruit Scientists"; 多人被美国通缉逮捕后 "千人计划" 突然消失中国网络 [After warrants were put out for many people and they were arrested by the United States, the "Thousand Talents Plan" suddenly disappeared from the Chinese internet], rfi.fr, July 5, 2020, https://www.rfi.fr/ cn/%E4%B8%AD%E5%9B%BD/20200507-%E5%A4%9A%E4%BA%BA%E8%A2%AB%E7 %BE%8E%E5%9B%BD%E9%80%9A%E7%BC%89%E9%80%AE%E6%8D%95%E5%90%8E -%E5%8D%83%E4%BA%BA%E8%AE%A1%E5%88%92-%E7%AA%81%E7%84%B6%E6 %B6%88%E5%A4%B1%E4%B8%AD%E5%9B%BD%E7%BD%91%E7%BB%9C；千人计划网 [Thousand Talents Online], http://www.1000plan.org (site discontinued), https://web .archive.org/web/20160321130940/http://www.1000plan.org/.

33 **High-End Foreign Expert Recruitment Program:** Emily Weinstein, "Chinese Talent Program Tracker," Center for Security and Emerging Technology, n.d., https://chinatalenttracker.cset.tech/.

33 **Chinese Talent Program Tracker:** Weinstein, "Chinese Talent Program Tracker."

33 **"a moving target":** Weinstein, "Mapping China's Sprawling Efforts to Recruit Scientists."

33 **increased investigations and improved visa screening:** The Justice Department's enforcement actions have come under criticism from academics and some lawmakers. Deirdre Fernandes, "Nobel Prize Winners and Other Scientists Come to Defense of Harvard Professor Charles Lieber," *Boston Globe*, March 1, 2021, https://www.bostonglobe.com/2021/03/01/ metro/nobel-prize-winners-other-scientists-come-defense-harvard-professor-charles-lieb-er/?p1=Article_Feed_ContentQuery; Stuart Schreiber et al., *A Call to Save Professor Charles Lieber and Scientific Collaboration* (documentcloud.org, March 1, 2021), https://assets.doc-umentcloud.org/documents/20493785/read-the-full-letter-from-harvard-scientists-calling -to-save-professor-charles-lieber-and-scientific-collaboration.pdf; Deirdre Fernandez, "MIT President and Faculty Members Defend Professor Arrested for China Ties," *Boston Globe*, January 22, 2021, https://www.bostonglobe.com/2021/01/23/metro/mit-president-faculty-mem-bers-defend-professor-arrested-china-ties/?p1=Article_Inline_Text_Link; ~170 MIT faculty,

letter to L. Rafael Reif, January 21, 2021, https://fnl.mit.edu/wp-content/uploads/2021/01/
Letter-to-Reif-in-support-of-Gang-Chen-2021-01-27.pdf; Margaret K. Lewis, "Criminaliz-
ing China," *Journal of Criminal Law and Criminology* 145 (2020), https://papers.ssrn.com/
sol3/papers.cfm?abstract_id=3600580; Elsa Kania and Joe McReynolds, "The Biden Administration Should Review and Rebuild the Trump Administration's China Initiative From the
Ground Up," *Lawfare*, February 22, 2021, https://www.lawfareblog.com/biden-administration
-should-review-and-rebuild-trump-administrations-china-initiative-ground. See also Zwetsloot, *China's Approach to Tech Talent Competition*; Peter Mattis and Matt Schrader, "America Can't Beat Beijing's Tech Theft with Racial Profiling," *War on the Rocks*, July 23, 2019,
https://warontherocks.com/2019/07/america-cant-beat-beijings-tech-theft-with-racial-pro-
filing/; Zwetsloot, *US–China Stem Talent "Decoupling"*; Ainikki Riikonen and Emily Weinstein, "Rethinking Research Security," *Lawfare*, June 24, 2021, https://www.lawfareblog.com/
rethinking-research-security; Remco Zwetsloot and Zachary Arnold, "Chinese Students Are
Not a Fifth Column," *Foreign Affairs*, April 23, 2021, https://www.foreignaffairs.com/articles/
united-states/2021-04-23/chinese-students-are-not-fifth-column; "Protests Growing Against
Justice Department's China Initiative," American Institute of Physics, July 15, 2021, https://
www.aip.org/fyi/2021/protests-growing-against-justice-department%E2%80%99s-china-ini-
tiative; Asian Americans Advancing Justice, "AAJC Delivers Petition of Nearly 30,000 Sig-
natures Urging President Biden to End the 'China Initiative,'" April 12, 2021, https://www
.advancingjustice-aajc.org/petition-delivered-end-china-initiative; "Rep. Lieu and 90 members of Congress urge DOJ probe into alleged racial profiling of Asians," press release, July
30, 2021, https://lieu.house.gov/media-center/press-releases/rep-lieu-and-90-members-con-
gress-urge-doj-probe-alleged-racial-profiling; "Winds of Freedom," (n.d.), https://sites.google
.com/view/winds-of-freedom. In 2022, the Justice Department ended its China Initiative. Matthew Olsen, remarks at George Mason University, Arlington, VA, February 23, 2022, https://
www.justice.gov/opa/speech/assistant-attorney-general-matthew-olsen-delivers-remarks
-countering-nation-state-threats; Josh Gerstein, "DOJ Shuts Down China-Focused Anti-Espionage Program," *Politico*, February 23, 2022, https://www.politico.com/news/2022/02/23/doj
-shuts-down-china-focused-anti-espionage-program-00011065.

33 **"The United States is in a global competition for scarce AI talent":** National Security
Commission on Artificial Intelligence, *Final Report* (n.d.), 173, https://www.nscai.gov/wp
-content/uploads/2021/03/Full-Report-Digital-1.pdf.

33 **a new National Defense Education Act:** National Security Commission on Artificial
Intelligence, *Final Report*, 175.

33 **home-grown talent:** Zwetsloot, *China's Approach to Tech Talent Competition*. See also
Zwetsloot, *Strengthening the U.S. AI Workforce*.

33 **nearly 70 percent said visa and immigration problems were an obstacle:** Zwetsloot et al.,
Skilled and Mobile.

33 **"immigration reform":** National Security Commission on Artificial Intelligence, *Final
Report*, 175.

33 **international . . . (STEM) talent:** The White House, "Biden-Harris Administration
Actions to Attract STEM Talent and Strengthen our Economy and Competitiveness,"
fact sheet, January 21, 2022, https://www.whitehouse.gov/briefing-room/statements
-releases/2022/01/21/fact-sheet-biden-harris-administration-actions-to-attract-stem
-talent-and-strengthen-our-economy-and-competitiveness/.

34 **recruit talented scientists and engineers from abroad:** For recommendations on additional steps to increase high-skilled immigration, see National Security Commission on
Artificial Intelligence, *Final Report*, 175–179.

5. INSTITUTIONS

35 **Institutions:** Douglass C. North, "Institutions," *Journal of Economic Perspectives* 5, no. 1 (Winter 1991): 97–112, https://www.jstor.org/stable/1942704?seq=1.

35 **many countries will have access:** Michael C. Horowitz, "Artificial Intelligence, International Competition, and the Balance of Power," *Texas National Security Review* 1, no. 3 (May 2018), https://doi.org/10.15781/T2639KP49.

35 **U.S. R&D funding:** *Research and Development: U.S. Trends and International Comparisons* (National Science Board, 2018), 27, figure 4-4, https://www.nsf.gov/statistics/2018/nsb20181/assets/1038/research-and-development-u-s-trends-and-international-comparisons.pdf. Thanks to former CNAS research associate Ainikki Riikonen for background research.

35 **Eleven of the Defense Department's fourteen "critical technology areas":** Heidi Shyu, "USD (R&E) Technology Vision for an Era of Competition," memorandum, February 1, 2022, https://www.cto.mil/wp-content/uploads/2022/02/usdre_strategic_vision_critical_tech_areas.pdf; Defense Innovation Unit, "Generating Meaningful Revenue Opportunities for Commercial Vendors," February 2022.

36 **U.S. R&D Funding as a Percentage of Gross Domestic Product:** John F. Sargent Jr., Marcy E. Gallo, and Moshe Schwartz, "The Global Research and Development Landscape and Implications for the Department of Defense," R45403, Congressional Research Service, November 8, 2018, https://fas.org/sgp/crs/natsec/R45403.pdf, 3–6. Thanks to former CNAS research associate Ainikki Riikonen for background research.

36 **"experimentation in Chinese defense innovation":** Elsa Kania, "Chinese Military Innovation, with American Characteristics?" battlefieldsingularity.com, May 29, 2018, updated February 10, 2019, https://web.archive.org/web/20210302163122/https://www.battlefieldsingularity.com/post/chinese-military-innovation-with-american-characteristics.

37 **"China's DIUx":** Elsa B. Kania, "In Military-Civil Fusion, China Is Learning Lessons from the United States and Starting to Innovate," *Strategy Bridge*, August 27, 2019, https://thestrategybridge.org/the-bridge/2019/8/27/in-military-civil-fusion-china-is-learning-lessons-from-the-united-states-and-starting-to-innovate.

37 **incentivizing innovation:** Martijn Rasser et al., *The American AI Century: A Blueprint for Action* (Center for a New American Security, December 17, 2019), https://www.cnas.org/publications/reports/the-american-ai-century-a-blueprint-for-action.

37 **R&D spending increasing at an average of 15 percent annually:** China R&D spending from 1998 to 2018, the most recent year data was available at the time of publication: "Gross Domestic Spending on R&D," OCED.org, n.d., https://data.oecd.org/rd/gross-domestic-spending-on-r-d.htm. Thanks to former CNAS research associate Ainikki Riikonen and senior fellow Martijn Rasser for background research.

37 **Made in China 2025:** Karen M. Sutter, *"Made in China 2025" Industrial Policies: Issues for Congress* (Congressional Research Service, August 11, 2020), https://fas.org/sgp/crs/row/IF10964.pdf. Thanks to former CNAS research associate Ainikki Riikonen and senior fellow Martijn Rasser for background research.

37 **China's "national team" of AI leaders:** Jeffrey Ding, "ChinAI #51: China's AI 'National Team,'" *ChinAI Newsletter*, May 20, 2019, https://chinai.substack.com/p/chinai-51-chinas-ai-national-team.

37 **"intelligentization" of its military forces:** Elsa B. Kania, Chinese Military Innovation in Artificial Intelligence (Center for a New American Security, June 7, 2019), https://www.cnas.org/publications/congressional-testimony/chinese-military-innovation-in-artificial-intelligence.

37 **"intelligentized" warfare:** Thanks to Peter Hansen for background research on "intelligentized" warfare.

37 **U.S. share of global R&D spending:** For more on global R&D spending, see Paul Heney, "Global R&D Investments Unabated in Spending Growth," *R&D World*, March 19, 2020, https://www.rdworldonline.com/global-rd-investments-unabated-in-spending-growth/.

37 **nearly 70 percent of all global R&D spending:** *Global Research and Development Expenditures: Fact Sheet* (Congressional Research Service, April 29, 2020), 1, https://fas.org/sgp/crs/misc/R44283.pdf. Thanks to former CNAS research associate Ainikki Riikonen and senior fellow Martijn Rasser for background research.

37 **China has now closed the gap and is on track to overtake the United States:** Spending in purchasing-power parity adjusted dollars. "Gross Domestic Spending on R&D." Thanks to former CNAS research associate Ainikki Riikonen and senior fellow Martijn Rasser for background research.

38 **U.S. Share of Global R&D:** Rest-of-world share of global R&D in 1960 is based on countries that reported total R&D, particularly the G-7. Rest of world share of global R&D in 2018 includes OECD countries (minus the United States), additional European Union states, Argentina, China, Russia, Singapore, South Africa, and Taiwan. It includes Argentina's 2017 data and South Africa's 2016 data, as their 2018 information was not yet available. Defense funded, nondefense federally funded, business funded, and other non-federally funded figures for 2018 are based on National Science Foundation estimates for 2018. Sargent et al., "The Global Research and Development Landscape and Implications for the Department of Defense," 3–6; Graham R. Mitchell, "The Global Context for U.S. Technology Policy," U.S. Department of Commerce, 1997, 5, https://usa.usembassy.de/etexts/tech/nas.pdf; Mark Boroush, National Patterns of R&D Resources: 2017–2018 Data Update, NSF 20-307, Science Foundation, 2020, https://ncses.nsf.gov/pubs/nsf20307; Mark Boroush, Federal R&D Funding, by Budget Function: Fiscal Years 2018–20, NSF 20-305, National Science Foundation, 2019, https://ncses.nsf.gov/pubs/nsf20305; "Gross Domestic Spending on R&D," OCED.org. Thanks to former CNAS research associate Ainikki Riikonen for background research.

39 **R&D Spending by Country:** Spending in purchasing-power parity adjusted dollars. "Gross Domestic Spending on R&D," OCED.org. Thanks to former CNAS research associate Ainikki Riikonen for background research.

39 **an additional $2 billion in AI spending:** U.S. Sen. Martin Heinrich, "Heinrich, Portman, Schatz Propose National Strategy for Artificial Intelligence; Call for $2.2 Billion Investment in Education, Research & Development," news release, May 21, 2019, https://www.heinrich.senate.gov/press-releases/heinrich-portman-schatz-propose-national-strategy-for-artificial-intelligence-call-for-22-billion-investment-in-education-research-and-development.

39 **$1.1 billion annually in nondefense AI:** NITRD, "Artificial Intelligence R&D Investments: Fiscal Year 2018—Fiscal Year 2022," https://www.nitrd.gov/apps/itdashboard/AI-RD-Investments/#Chart-1-Federal-budget-for-nondefense-AI-RD-FYs-2018-2022.

39 **estimated roughly $8 billion in defense AI R&D spending:** The U.S. Defense Department does not release a comprehensive accounting of AI spending across R&D programs, making estimating total DoD AI R&D spending difficult. The 2021 AI Index reports roughly $5 billion in DoD AI R&D spending in fiscal year 2020, based on data from Bloomberg Government. (See figure 7.3.2 in Daniel Zhang et al., *The AI Index 2021 Annual Report* [Stanford, CA: AI Index Steering Committee, March 2021], 168, https://aiindex.stanford.edu/wp-content/uploads/2021/03/2021-AI-Index-Report_Master.pdf.) The 2022 AI Index used

an updated methodology by Bloomberg Government to tally an estimated $8.68 billion in DoD AI R&D spending in fiscal year 2020 based on an analysis of 500 AI R&D programs. (See figure 5.2.2 in Daniel Zhang et al., *The AI Index 2022 Annual Report* (Stanford, CA: AI Index Steering Committee, March 2022), 189, https://aiindex.stanford.edu/wp-content/uploads/2022/03/2022-AI-Index-Report_Master.pdf.)

39 **AI R&D grew to $1.5 billion in nondefense:** Federal nondefense AI R&D spending in fiscal year 2021 was $1.54 billion. The Networking & Information Technology R&D Program and the National Artificial Intelligence Initiative Office, "Supplement to the President's FY2022 Budget," December 2021, 18, https://www.whitehouse.gov/wp-content/uploads/2021/12/FY2022-NITRD-NAIIO-Supplement.pdf.

39 **estimated over $9 billion in defense spending:** Zhang et al., *The AI Index 2022 Annual Report*, 189.

39 **raising federal AI R&D spending to $25 billion annually:** *Cementing American Artificial Intelligence Leadership: AI Research & Development* (Bipartisan Policy Center and Center for a New American Security, August 2020), https://bipartisanpolicy.org/report/ai-research-development/.

39 **an additional $100 billion in federal AI R&D:** Jeffrey Mervis, "United States Should Make a Massive Investment in AI, Top Senate Democrat Says," *Science*, November 11, 2019, https://www.sciencemag.org/news/2019/11/united-states-should-make-massive-investment-ai-top-senate-democrat-says.

39 **"I can tell you what we told White House":** Eric Schmidt, interview by author, June 9, 2020.

39 **$32 billion per year:** National Security Commission on Artificial Intelligence, *Final Report* (n.d.), 12, https://www.nscai.gov/wp-content/uploads/2021/03/Full-Report-Digital-1.pdf; Zhang et al., *The AI Index 2021 Annual Report*, 167.

39 **doubling nondefense AI R&D funding:** The White House, "President Trump's FY 2021 Budget Commits to Double Investments in Key Industries of the Future," fact sheet, February 11, 2020, https://www.whitehouse.gov/briefings-statements/president-trumps-fy-2021-budget-commits-double-investments-key-industries-future/ (site discontinued).

40 **Trump's plan cut federal research spending:** David Malakoff, Jeffrey Mervis, "Trump's 2021 Budget Drowns Science Agencies in Red Ink, Again," *Science*, February 10, 2020, https://www.sciencemag.org/news/2020/02/trump-s-2021-budget-drowns-science-agencies-red-ink-again.

40 **"the federal government's role in early research":** Schmidt, interview.

40 **CHIPS and Science Act:** *CHIPS and Science Act of 2022: Section-by-Section Summary* (Commerce.senate.gov, 2022), https://www.commerce.senate.gov/services/files/1201E1CA-73CB-44BB-ADEB-E69634DA9BB9. Thanks to former CNAS research assistant Katie Galgano for background research on U.S. innovation bills.

40 **2021 Global AI Index:** "The Global AI Index," Tortoise Media, updated December 2021, https://www.tortoisemedia.com/intelligence/global-ai/.

6. A WINNING HAND

43 **"After a few days, we felt like we really had a good strategy":** Engadget R&D, "How AI Beat the Best Poker Players in the World," YouTube, February 10, 2017, https://www.youtube.com/watch?v=jLXPGwJNLHk.

43 **humans never recovered:** Sean D. Hamill, "CMU's computer poker win over humans was 'statistically significant,'" *Pittsburgh Post-Gazette*, January 31, 2017, https://www.post

-gazette.com/business/tech-news/2017/01/31/CMU-computer-won-poker-battle-over
-humans-by-statistically-significant-margin/stories/201701310250.

43 **"It seemed to learn what we were doing"**: Cade Metz, "A Mystery AI Just Crushed the Best Human Players at Poker," *Wired*, January 31, 2017, https://www.wired.com/2017/01/mystery-ai-just-crushed-best-human-players-poker/.

43 **run calculations on the probabilities of poker hands while the human players were sleeping:** Tuomas Sandholm, interview by author, February 3, 2020.

43 **"The hopes of winning went out the window"**: Engadget R&D, "How AI Beat the Best Poker Players in the World."

44 **"lost very decisively"**: CardPlayer, "Jason Les Discusses Playing AI Poker Bot Liberatus," YouTube, June 19, 2017, https://www.youtube.com/watch?v=nizG_0KDbXI.

44 **Bridges supercomputer:** Michael Feldman, "Bridges Supercomputer Boots Up at Pittsburgh," top500.org, August 31, 2016, https://www.top500.org/news/bridges-supercomputer-boots-up-at-pittsburgh/.

44 **24 million core-hours:** Sandholm, interview.

45 **"All warfare is based on deception"**: Sun Tzu, *The Art of War*, translated by Lionel Giles (classics.mit.edu Etext, n.d.), http://classics.mit.edu/Tzu/artwar.html.

45 **"We have the opportunity to affect their change"**: Sandholm, interview.

45 **pierce the bottom hull of armored vehicles:** Drew Brown, "Homemade Explosives, Deep-Buried Bombs Latest Trouble for U.S. in Iraq," *Stars and Stripes*, July 27, 2007, https://www.stripes.com/news/homemade-explosives-deep-buried-bombs-latest-trouble-for-u-s-in-iraq-1.migrated.

46 **IEDs killed over 3,500 U.S. troops:** Jason Shell, "How the IED Won: Dispelling the Myth of Tactical Success and Innovation," *War on the Rocks*, May 1, 2017, https://warontherocks.com/2017/05/how-the-ied-won-dispelling-the-myth-of-tactical-success-and-innovation/.

46 **"What makes Libratus's strategy unique"**: Engadget R&D, "How AI Beat the Best Poker Players in the World."

46 **Feints and deceptions:** Christopher M. Rein, ed., *Weaving the Tangled Web: Military Deception in Large-Scale Combat Operations* (Army University Press, 2018), https://fas.org/sgp/eprint/weaving.pdf.

46 **faked a major amphibious assault:** Donald P. Wright, "Deception in the Desert: Deceiving Iraq in Operation Desert Storm," Army University Press, n.d., https://www.armyupress.army.mil/Books/Browse-Books/iBooks-and-EPUBs/Deception-in-the-Desert/.

46 **deception operations in western Iraq:** Leigh Neville, *Special Forces in the War on Terror* (Oxford, UK: Osprey Publishing, May 19, 2015), https://www.amazon.com/Special-Forces-Terror-General-Military/dp/1472807901.

47 **"What we build or plan to build"**: Sandholm, interview.

47 **10^{161} different situations:** There are 10^{161} possible game states for head's-up no-limit Texas Hold'em. Other versions of poker could have more or fewer possible game states, depending on the poker version, number of players, and betting limits. Noam Brown and Tuomas Sandholm, "Superhuman AI for Heads-Up No-Limit Poker: Libratus Beats Top Professionals," *Science* 359, no. 6374 (January 26, 2018), https://doi.org/10.1126/science.aao1733.

47 **one followed by 161 zeroes:** Alternatively, 10^{161} is one hundred thousand trillion trillion trillion trillion trillion trillion trillion trillion trillion trillion trillion trillion trillion.

47 **known atoms in the universe:** There are an estimated 10^{86} atoms in the known universe. "How Many Atoms Are There in the Universe?" Universe Today, n.d., https://www.universetoday.com/36302/atoms-in-the-universe/.

47 **Tic-tac-toe:** More precisely, tic-tac-toe has 5,478 possible legal game states. "TicTacToe State Space Choose Calculation," math.stackexchangecom, September 6, 2013, updated May 23, 2018, https://math.stackexchange.com/questions/485752/tictactoe-state-space -choose-calculation; "README.md: generate_tictactoe," Btsan, GitHub, updated October 20, 2018, https://github.com/Btsan/generate_tictactoe.

47 **Checkers has 10^20 possible positions:** Schaeffer, J., et al. "Checkers Is Solved," *Science* 317, no. 5844 (September 14, 2007): 1518–1522, https://doi.org/10.1126/science.1144079.

47 **Chess has between 10^40 and 10^50 possible positions:** Schaeffer et al., "Checkers Is Solved," 1522.

47 *Go* **has approximately 10^170 possible positions:** John Tromp, "Number of Legal Go Positions," tromp.github.io, n.d., http://tromp.github.io/go/legal.html; and "AlphaGo," DeepMind, n.d., https://deepmind.com/research/case-studies/alphago-the-story-so-far.

48 **"The states don't have values":** Sandholm, interview.

48 **betting tactics like "limping" and "donk betting":** Engadget R&D, "How AI Beat the Best Poker Players in the World."

48 **"the whole strategy has to be optimized holistically":** Sandholm, interview.

49 **"DIU is prototyping an application that leverages AI":** *Artificial Intelligence Initiatives within the Defense Innovation Unit, Senate Armed Services Committee Subcommittee on Emerging Threats and Capabilities,* 116th Cong. (2019) (statement by Michael Brown, director of the Defense Innovation Unit), 4–5, https://www.armed-services.senate.gov/imo/media/doc/Brown_03-12-19.pdf.

50 **"safe," or "non-exploitable":** Sandholm, interview.

50 **Pluribus, which trounced humans in six-way poker play:** Noam Brown and Tuomas Sandholm, "Superhuman AI for Multiplayer Poker," *Science* 365, no. 6456: 885–890, https://doi.org/10.1126/science.aay2400.

50 **"one of the top problems we have in the world":** Sandholm, interview.

51 **Strategy Robot:** Sandholm, interview.

51 **"but I knew that it's needed":** Sandholm, interview.

7. MAVEN

52 **China and Russia as the "primary concern in U.S. national security":** *Summary of the 2018 National Defense Strategy of the United States of America: Sharpening the American Military's Competitive Edge* (U.S. Department of Defense, 2018), https://dod.defense.gov/Portals/1/Documents/pubs/2018-National-Defense-Strategy-Summary.pdf.

53 **"a new type of warfare called algorithmic warfare":** Robert O. Work, interview by author, February 11, 2020.

53 **video footage from drones:** Work, interview.

53 **ninety round-the-clock patrols worldwide of mid-sized drones:** Mark Pomerleau, "Air Force RPA 'get well' plan on track," c4isrnet.com, June 6, 2017, https://www.c4isrnet.com/unmanned/uas/2017/06/06/air-force-rpa-get-well-plan-on-track/.

53 **wide area surveillance tools:** These are sometimes referred to as wide area airborne surveillance (WAAS) or wide area motion imagery (WAMI). Arthur Holland Michel, *Eyes in the Sky: The Secret Rise of Gorgon Stare and How It Will Watch Us All* (Boston: Mariner Books, June 18, 2019), https://www.amazon.com/Eyes-Sky-Secret-Gorgon-Stare-ebook/dp/B07FK9567C.

54 **65 trillion pixels of information:** Michel, *Eyes in the Sky.*

54 **major progress against a standard image database called ImageNet:** Alex Krizhevsky, Ilya Sutskever, and Geoffrey E. Hinton, *ImageNet Classification with Deep Convolutional Neural Networks* (proceedings.neurips.cc, n.d.), https://papers.nips.cc/paper/4824-imagenet-classification-with-deep-convolutional-neural-networks.pdf.

54 **deep neural networks:** Kaiming He et al., *Delving Deep into Rectifiers: Surpassing Human-Level Performance on ImageNet Classification* (Microsoft Research, February 6, 2015), https://arxiv.org/pdf/1502.01852.pdf.

54 **"The main threat that we were focused on were car bombs":** Jason Brown, interview by author, April 22, 2020.

54 **Kabul suffered as many as four car bombs a week:** Michael E. Miller, "Kabul's Car-Bomb Graveyard Is a Monument to Years of Bloodshed," *Washington Post*, January 27, 2016, https://www.washingtonpost.com/world/asia_pacific/kabuls-car-bomb-graveyard-is-a-monument-to-years-of-bloodshed/2016/01/26/81956a6a-b57c-11e5-8abc-d09392edc612_story.html.

54 **2019 car bomb against an Afghan intelligence base:** Rupam Jain and Abdul Qadir Sediqi, "Taliban Attack on Afghan Security Base Kills Over 100," Reuters, January 21, 2019, https://www.reuters.com/article/us-afghanistan-attack/taliban-attack-kills-more-than-100-security-personnel-in-central-afghanistan-defense-ministry-source-idUSKCN1PF0FC.

55 **"Where we expected a computer vision solution to help us":** Brown, interview.

56 **Maven:** Work, interview.

56 **processing satellite imagery for the National Geospatial-Intelligence Agency:** Brendan McCord, interview by author, February 5, 2020.

56 **"The Pentagon had been burned":** Will Roper, interview by author, August 6, 2021.

56 **Deputy's Management Action Group:** "Deputy's Management Action Group (DMAG)," US Department of Defense Chief Management Officer, n.d., https://cmo.defense.gov/Resources/Deputys-Management-Action-Group/.

56 **"No one in the Pentagon thought it was a good idea":** Roper, interview.

56 **"computer vision algorithms for object detection":** Robert Work, "Establishment of an Algorithmic Warfare Cross-Functional Team (Project Maven)," memorandum, April 26, 2017, https://dodcio.defense.gov/Portals/0/Documents/Project%20Maven%20DSD%20Memo%2020170425.pdf.

56 **"integrate algorithmic-based technology":** Work, "Establishment of an Algorithmic Warfare Cross-Functional Team (Project Maven)."

57 **Computer Vision and Pattern Recognition conference:** McCord, interview.

57 **"Secretary Carter talk[ed] about the need for DoD to get serious":** McCord, interview.

57 **"largest dataset for object detection":** McCord, interview.

57 **an AI-based image classifier that could detect thirty-eight different classes of objects:** Cheryl Pellerin, "Project Maven to Deploy Computer Algorithms to War Zone by Year's End," news release, US Department of Defense, July 21, 2017, https://www.defense.gov/Explore/News/Article/Article/1254719/project-maven-to-deploy-computer-algorithms-to-war-zone-by-years-end/; Marcus Weisgerber, "The Pentagon's New Artificial Intelligence Is Already Hunting Terrorists," *Defense One*, December 21, 2017, https://www.defenseone.com/technology/2017/12/pentagons-new-artificial-intelligence-already-hunting-terrorists/144742/.

58 **"We have a large group of people":** Pellerin, "Project Maven to Deploy Computer Algorithms."

58 **Bob Work declassified the drone video footage:** Work, interview.

58 **over a million labeled images:** Michel, *Eyes in the Sky*; Gregory C. Allen, "Project Maven Brings AI to the Fight Against ISIS," *Bulletin of the Atomic Scientists*, December 21, 2017, https://thebulletin.org/2017/12/project-maven-brings-ai-to-the-fight-against-isis/.

58 **an initial automated video analysis tool:** Michel, *Eyes in the Sky*; Allen, "Project Maven Brings AI to the Fight"; Weisgerber, "The Pentagon's New Artificial Intelligence Is Already Hunting Terrorists."

58 **"That is why it's so important in the first five days":** Weisgerber, "The Pentagon's New Artificial Intelligence Is Already Hunting Terrorists."

58 **the project would expand its footprint:** Paul McLeary, "Pentagon's Big AI Program, Maven, Already Hunts Data in Middle East, Africa," *Breaking Defense*, May 1, 2018, https://breakingdefense.com/2018/05/pentagons-big-ai-program-maven-already-hunts -data-in-middle-east-africa/.

58 **wide area imagery like that from Gorgon Stare:** Michel, *Eyes in the Sky*; Weisgerber, "The Pentagon's New Artificial Intelligence Is Already Hunting Terrorists."

59 **"You don't buy AI like you buy ammunition":** Pellerin, "Project Maven to Deploy Computer Algorithms."

8. REVOLT

60 **Liz stuck with the company:** Tom Simonite, "Startup Working on Contentious Pentagon AI Project Was Hacked," *Wired*, June 12, 2018, https://www.wired.com/story/startup-working -on-contentious-pentagon-ai-project-was-hacked/; Clarifai released a blog post disputing many of the details in the story. Matthew Zeiler, "Why We're Part of Project Maven," Clarifai, June 13, 2018, https://www.clarifai.com/blog/why-were-part-of-project-maven.

60 **3,000 employees at Google signed an open letter:** Google employees, letter to Sundar Pichai, 2018, https://static01.nyt.com/files/2018/technology/googleletter.pdf.

61 **JEDI cloud computing contract would improve "lethality":** "JEDI Program Aims to Boost Military Lethality, Readiness," *Military News*, March 12, 2018, https://www .militarynews.com/multimedia/videos/jedi-program-aims-to-boost-military-lethality -readiness/youtube_c4e0e682-c4a7-59cd-8795-65180d97c67e.html.

61 **Liz hit send on a letter to her boss:** Liz O'Sullivan, letter to Matt Zeiler, January 16, 2019, https://int.nyt.com/data/documenthelper/639-clarifai-letter/3cd943d873d78c7cdcdc/ optimized/full.pdf.

61 **Clarifai would continue working with the military:** Cade Metz, "Is Ethical A.I. Even Possible?" *New York Times*, March 1, 2019, https://www.nytimes.com/2019/03/01/business/ ethics-artificial-intelligence.html; Liz O'Sullivan, "I Quit My Job to Protest My Company's Work on Building Killer Robots," American Civil Liberties Union, March 6, 2019, https://www.aclu.org/blog/national-security/targeted-killing/i-quit-my-job-protest-my -companys-work-building-killer.

61 **another conscientious tech objector:** O'Sullivan, "I Quit My Job."

61 **Clarifai continued work with DoD:** Zeiler, "Why We're Part of Project Maven."

62 **establishment of a new "Google AI China Center":** Fei-Fei Li, "Opening the Google AI China Center," Google blog, December 13, 2017, https://www.blog.google/around-the -globe/google-asia/google-ai-china-center/.

62 **Google's "Big AI Push in China":** Carlos Tejada, "Google, Looking to Tiptoe Back into China, Announces A.I. Center," *New York Times*, December 13, 2017, https://www.nytimes .com/2017/12/13/business/google-ai-china.html.

62 **"AI and its benefits have no borders":** Li, "Opening the Google AI China Center."

62 **Dragonfly:** Ryan Gallagher, "Google Plans to Launch Censored Search Engine in China, Leaked Documents Reveal," *The Intercept*, August 1, 2018, https://theintercept.com/2018/08/01/google-china-search-engine-censorship/.

62 **a "wonderful, innovative market":** Nitasha Tiku, "Google's CEO Says Tests of Censored Chinese Search Engine Turned Out Great," *Wired*, October 15, 2018, https://www.wired.com/story/wired-25-sundar-pichai-china-censored-search-engine/; Ryan Gallagher, "Google Faces Renewed Protests and Criticism Over China Search Project," *The Intercept*, January 18, 2019, https:/theintercept.com/2019/01/18/google-dragonfly-project-protests/.

62 **Dragonfly had been cancelled:** A Google representative told *The Verge* in March 2019: "This speculation is wholly inaccurate. Quite simply: there's no work happening on Dragonfly.... As we've said for many months, we have no plans to launch Search in China and there is no work being undertaken on such a project. Team members have moved to new projects." (Shannon Liao, "Google Employees Aren't Convinced That Dragonfly Is Dead," *The Verge*, March 9, 2019, https://www.theverge.com/2019/3/4/18250285/google-dragonfly-censored-search-engine-code-dead-employees-doubt.) In July 2019, Karan Bhatia, Google Vice President for Government Affairs & Public Policy, told members of the Senate Judiciary Committee that Google had "terminated" Project Dragonfly. (Davey Alba, "A Google VP Told the US Senate the Company Has "Terminated" the Chinese Search App Dragonfly," *BuzzFeed News*, July 16, 2019, https://www.buzzfeednews.com/article/daveyalba/google-project-dragonfly-terminated-senate-hearing. See remarks beginning at 1:15:18. Karan Bhatia, remarks at Senate Judiciary subcommittee hearing, "Google and Censorship," C-SPAN, July 16, 2019, https://www.c-span.org/video/?462661-1/senate-judiciary-hearing-google-censorship.)

62 **"strengthen China's system of surveillance and repression":** Ryan Gallagher, "Google CEO Hammered by Members of Congress on China Censorship Plan," *The Intercept*, December 11, 2018, https://theintercept.com/2018/12/11/google-congressional-hearing/.

62 **"the work that Google is doing in China is indirectly benefiting the Chinese military":** Ryan Browne, "Top US general says Google 'is indirectly benefiting the Chinese military,'" CNN, March 14, 2019, https://www.cnn.com/2019/03/14/politics/dunford-china-google/index.html.

62 **Google issued a swift denial:** Google stated: "We are not working with the Chinese military. We are working with the U.S. government, including the Department of Defense, in many areas including cybersecurity, recruiting, and healthcare." ("Trump Discusses China, 'Political Fairness' with Google CEO," Reuters, March 27, 2019, https://www.reuters.com/article/us-usa-trump-google/trump-discusses-china-political-fairness-with-google-ceo-idUSKCN1R82CB.)

63 **"AI was largely hype":** Liz O'Sullivan, interview by author, February 12, 2020.

64 **Machine learning systems in particular can fail:** Ram Shankar Siva Kumar et al., "Failure Modes in Machine Learning," Microsoft Docs, November 11, 2019, https://docs.microsoft.com/en-us/security/engineering/failure-modes-in-machine-learning; Dario Amodei et al., *Concrete Problems in AI Safety* (arXiv.org, July 25, 2016), https://arxiv.org/pdf/1606.06565.pdf.

64 **perform poorly on people of a different gender, race, or ethnicity:** Joy Buolamwini and Timnit Gebru, "Gender Shades: Intersectional Accuracy Disparities in Commercial Gender Classification," *Proceedings of Machine Learning Research* 81 (2018), 1–15, https://dam-prod.media.mit.edu/x/2018/02/06/Gender%20Shades%20Intersectional%20Accuracy%20Disparities.pdf.

64 **Google Photos image recognition algorithm:** Tom Simonite, "When It Comes to Gorillas,

Google Photos Remains Blind," *Wired*, January 11, 2018, https://www.wired.com/story/
when-it-comes-to-gorillas-google-photos-remains-blind/; Alistair Barr, "Google Mistakenly Tags Black People as 'Gorillas,' Showing Limits of Algorithms," *Wall Street Journal*,
July 1, 2015, https://blogs.wsj.com/digits/2015/07/01/google-mistakenly-tags-black-people
-as-gorillas-showing-limits-of-algorithms/.

64 **insufficient representation of darker faces:** Barr, "Google Mistakenly Tags Black People as
'Gorillas.'"

64 **distributional shift in the data:** Rohan Taori, *Measuring Robustness to Natural Distribution Shifts in Image Classification* (arXiv.org, September 14, 2020), https://arxiv.org/
pdf/2007.00644.pdf.

64 **problems are common in image classification systems:** Maggie Zhang, "Google Photos
Tags Two African-Americans as Gorillas Through Facial Recognition Software," *Forbes*,
July 1, 2015, https://www.forbes.com/sites/mzhang/2015/07/01/google-photos-tags-two
-african-americans-as-gorillas-through-facial-recognition-software/#60111f6713d8.

65 **several fatal accidents:** Rob Stumpf, "Tesla on Autopilot Crashes into Parked California
Police Cruiser," *The Drive*, May 30, 2018, https://www.thedrive.com/news/21172/tesla-on
-autopilot-crashes-into-parked-california-police-cruiser; Rob Stumpf, "Autopilot Blamed for
Tesla's Crash Into Overturned Truck," *The Drive*, June 1, 2020, https://www.thedrive.com/
news/33789/autopilot-blamed-for-teslas-crash-into-overturned-truck; James Gilboy, "Officials
Find Cause of Tesla Autopilot Crash Into Fire Truck: Report," *The Drive*, May 17, 2018, https://
www.thedrive.com/news/20912/cause-of-tesla-autopilot-crash-into-fire-truck-cause-deter-
mined-report; Phil McCausland, "Self-Driving Uber Car That Hit and Killed Woman Did Not
Recognize That Pedestrians Jaywalk," *NBC News*, November 9, 2019, https://www.nbcnews
.com/tech/tech-news/self-driving-uber-car-hit-killed-woman-did-not-recognize-n1079281;
National Transportation Safety Board, "Collision Between a Sport Utility Vehicle Operating
With Partial Driving Automation and a Crash Attenuator" (presented at public meeting, February 25, 2020), https://www.ntsb.gov/news/events/Documents/2020-HWY18FH011-BMG
-abstract.pdf; Aaron Brown, "Tesla Autopilot Crash Victim Joshua Brown Was an Electric Car
Buff and a Navy SEAL," *The Drive*, July 1, 2016, https://www.thedrive.com/news/4249/tesla
-autopilot-crash-victim-joshua-brown-was-an-electric-car-buff-and-a-navy-seal.

65 **drone footage from a different region:** Marcus Weisgerber, "The Pentagon's New Artificial Intelligence Is Already Hunting Terrorists," *Defense One*, December 21, 2017, https://
www.defenseone.com/technology/2017/12/pentagons-new-artificial-intelligence-already
-hunting-terrorists/144742/.

65 **Tesla has come under fire:** Andrew J. Hawkins, "Tesla Didn't Fix an Autopilot Problem for Three Years, and Now Another Person Is Dead," *The Verge*, May 17, 2019, https://
www.theverge.com/2019/5/17/18629214/tesla-autopilot-crash-death-josh-brown-jeremy
-banner; Edward Niedermeyer, "Tesla's 'Full Self-Driving' Pricing Controversy Misses
the Point," *The Drive*, March 5, 2019, https://www.thedrive.com/tech/26790/teslas-full
-self-driving-pricing-controversy-misses-the-point; Nick Lum and Edward Niedermeyer, "How Tesla and Elon Musk Exaggerated Safety Claims About Autopilot and Cars,"
Daily Beast, April 13, 2017, https://www.thedailybeast.com/how-tesla-and-elon-musk
-exaggeraged-safety-claims-about-autopilot-and-cars.

65 **2019 survey of leading AI researchers:** Baobao Zhang et al., *Ethics and Governance of
Artificial Intelligence: Evidence from a Survey of Machine Learning Researchers* (arXiv.org,
May 5, 20210), 40, https://arxiv.org/pdf/2105.02117.pdf.

65 **survey respondents supported Google's decision:** Zhang et al., *Ethics and Governance of
Artificial Intelligence*, 42.

65 **researchers trusted the military with AI significantly less than the U.S. general public:** Zhang et al., *Ethics and Governance of Artificial Intelligence*, 6–7, 31.

65 **Defense Innovation Board convened roundtable discussions with experts:** "Defense Innovation Board's AI Principles Project," Defense Innovation Board, n.d., https://innovation.defense.gov/ai/.

65 **"resilient, robust, reliable, and secure":** *Summary of the 2018 Department of Defense Artificial Intelligence Strategy* (U.S. Department of Defense, 2018), 8, 15, https://media.defense.gov/2019/Feb/12/2002088963/-1/-1/1/SUMMARY-OF-DOD-AI-STRATEGY.PDF.

65 **proposed AI principles:** Defense Innovation Board, *AI Principles: Recommendations on the Ethical Use of Artificial Intelligence by the Department of Defense* (Department of Defense, 2019), https://media.defense.gov/2019/Oct/31/2002204458/-1/-1/0/DIB_AI_PRINCIPLES_PRIMARY_DOCUMENT.PDF.

65 **secretary of defense adopted:** C. Todd Lopez, "DOD Adopts 5 Principles of Artificial Intelligence Ethics," *DOD News*, February 25, 2020, https://www.defense.gov/Explore/News/Article/Article/2094085/dod-adopts-5-principles-of-artificial-intelligence-ethics/.

66 **"both a national and an international dialogue":** Michael McQuade, interview by author, February 4, 2020.

66 **Google was "eager to do more" with the Defense Department:** Sydney J. Freedberg Jr., "Google to Pentagon: 'We're Eager to Do More,'" *Breaking Defense*, November 5, 2019, https://breakingdefense.com/2019/11/google-pentagon-pledge-to-work-together-were-eager-to-do-more/.

67 **"really worried" that the focus on AI "would fizzle out":** Robert O. Work, interview by the author, February 11, 2020.

67 **AI was his "number one" technology priority:** Mark T. Esper, remarks at National Security Commission on Artificial Intelligence public conference, November 5, 2019, https://www.defense.gov/Newsroom/Transcripts/Transcript/Article/2011960/remarks-by-secretary-esper-at-national-security-commission-on-artificial-intell/.

9. SPUTNIK MOMENT

68 **over fifty countries have or are developing national AI plans or strategies:** Daniel Zhang et al., *The AI Index 2021 Annual Report* (Stanford, CA: AI Index Steering Committee, March 2021), 153–164, https://aiindex.stanford.edu/wp-content/uploads/2021/03/2021-AI-Index-Report_Master.pdf.

68 **The military massacred the protestors:** The death toll for the Tiananmen square massacre is highly disputed. "Tiananmen Square Protests," History.com, updated June 9, 2020, https://www.history.com/topics/china/tiananmen-square; "Tiananmen Square Protest Death Toll 'was 10,000,'" BBC News, December 23, 2017, https://www.bbc.com/news/world-asia-china-42465516; "Timeline: What Led to the Tiananmen Square Massacre," *PBS Frontline*, June 5, 2019, https://www.pbs.org/wgbh/frontline/article/timeline-tiananmen-square/. Thanks to CNAS research assistant Katie Galgano for background research.

68 **"the triumph of the West":** Francis Fukuyama, "The End of History?" *National Interest* 16 (Summer 1989), https://www.jstor.org/stable/24027184.

68 **wouldn't "dance on the [Berlin] wall" to celebrate:** Richard Fontaine, "American Foreign Policy Could Use More Prudence," *The Atlantic*, December 3, 2018, https://www.theatlantic.com/ideas/archive/2018/12/the-prudence-of-george-h-w-bushs-foreign-policy/577192/.

69 **"As people have commercial incentives":** Orville Schell, "The Death of Engagement," *The Wire China*, June 7, 2020, https://www.thewirechina.com/2020/06/07/the-birth-life-and -death-of-engagement/.

69 **China's annual GDP growth:** "GDP Growth (Annual %)—China," World Bank, 2020, https://data.worldbank.org/indicator/NY.GDP.MKTP.KD.ZG?locations=CN. Thanks to CNAS research associate Ainikki Riikonen for background research.

69 **"growing interdependence would have a liberalizing effect":** Bill Clinton, remarks to Voice of America, Washington, DC, October 24, 1997, https://clintonwhitehouse4.archives .gov/WH/New/html/19971024-3863.html.

69 **"responsible stakeholder":** Robert B. Zoellick, "Whither China: From Membership to Responsibility?" remarks to the National Committee on U.S.-China Relations, New York, September 21, 2005, https://2001-2009.state.gov/s/d/former/zoellick/rem/53682.htm.

69 **"the more China liberalizes its economy":** Bill Clinton, speech to the Paul H. Nitze School of Advanced International Studies, Johns Hopkins University, March 9, 2000, https:// www.nytimes.com/2000/03/09/world/clinton-s-words-on-china-trade-is-the-smart-thing .html.

70 **history supported the "dictator's dilemma":** Kedzie, Christopher, *Communication and Democracy: Coincident Revolutions and the Emergent Dictators* (RAND Corporation, 1997), https://www.rand.org/pubs/rgs_dissertations/RGSD127/sec2.html.

70 **force Chinese leaders to make a choice:** Clinton: "Bringing China into the W.T.O. doesn't guarantee that it will choose political reform. But . . . the process of economic change will . . . make the imperative for the right choice stronger." Clinton, speech to the Paul H. Nitze School of Advanced International Studies.

70 **"Without the full freedom to think":** Clinton, remarks to Voice of America.

70 **Chinese military investments in "anti-access" capabilities:** Roger Cliff et al., *Entering the Dragon's Lair: Chinese Antiaccess Strategies and Their Implications for the United States* (RAND Corporation, 2007), https://www.rand.org/content/dam/rand/pubs/monographs/2007/RAND _MG524.pdf.

70 **"The United States welcomes a strong, prosperous, and successful China":** Department of Defense, *Quadrennial Defense Review Report*, February 2010, 60, https://history.defense .gov/Portals/70/Documents/quadrennial/QDR2010.pdf.

71 **systematic campaign of intellectual property theft:** Michael Brown and Pavneet Singh, *China's Technology Transfer Strategy: How Chinese Investments in Emerging Technology Enable a Strategic Competitor to Access the Crown Jewels of U.S. Innovation* (Defense Innovation Unit Experimental, January 2018), https://admin.govexec.com/media/diux_ chinatechnologytransferstudy_jan_2018_(1).pdf; William C. Hannas, James Mulvenon, and Anna B. Puglisi, *Chinese Industrial Espionage: Technology Acquisition and Military Modernisation* (n.p., Routledge, 2013), https://www.routledge.com/Chinese-Industrial-Espionage-Technology-Acquisition-and-Military-Modernisation/Hannas-Mulvenon-Puglisi/p/ book/9780415821421; William C. Hannas and Huey-meei Chang, *China's Access to Foreign AI Technology* (Center for Security and Emerging Technology, September 2019), https:// cset.georgetown.edu/research/chinas-access-to-foreign-ai-technology/; Ryan Fedasiuk and Emily Weinstein, *Overseas Professionals and Technology Transfer to China* (Center for Security and Emerging Technology, July 21, 2020), https://cset.georgetown.edu/research/ overseas-professionals-and-technology-transfer-to-china/; Tai Ming Cheung, William Lucyshyn, and John Rigilano, *The Role of Technology Transfers in China's Defense Technological and Industrial Development and the Implications for the United States* (Naval Postgraduate School, February 19, 2019), https://calhoun.nps.edu/bitstream/handle/10945/61948/

UCSD-AM-19-028.pdf?sequence=1&isAllowed=y; Office of the U.S. Trade Representative, *Findings of the Investigation into China's Acts, Policies, and Practices Related to Technology Transfer, Intellectual Property, and Innovation Under Section 301 of the Trade Act of 1974* (U.S. Trade Representative, March 22, 2018), https://ustr.gov/sites/default/files/Section%20 301%20FINAL.PDF; Commission on the Theft of American Intellectual Property, *The IP Commission Report: The Report of The Commission on the Theft of American Intellectual Property* (National Bureau of Asian Research, May 2013), https://www.nbr.org/wp-content/ uploads/pdfs/publications/IP_Commission_Report.pdf.

71 **the stage was set for a "reckoning" with China:** Kurt M. Campbell and Ely Ratner, "The China Reckoning: How Beijing Defied American Expectations," *Foreign Affairs*, March/ April 2018, https://www.foreignaffairs.com/articles/china/2018-02-13/china-reckoning.

71 **AI as a critical area for the economy:** *Preparing for the Future of Artificial Intelligence* (National Science and Technology Council, October 2016), https://obamawhitehouse .archives.gov/sites/default/files/whitehouse_files/microsites/ostp/NSTC/preparing_for_ the_future_of_ai.pdf; *The National Artificial Intelligence Research and Development Strategic Plan* (National Science and Technology Council, October 2016), https://obamawhitehouse .archives.gov/sites/default/files/whitehouse_files/microsites/ostp/NSTC/national_ai_rd_ strategic_plan.pdf; *Artificial Intelligence, Automation, and the Economy* (Executive Office of the President, December 2016), https://obamawhitehouse.archives.gov/sites/whitehouse .gov/files/documents/Artificial-Intelligence-Automation-Economy.PDF.

71 **"New Generation Artificial Intelligence Development Plan":** 国务院关于印发 新一代 人工智能发展规划的通知 [New Generation Artificial Intelligence Development Plan], www.gov.cn, 2017, http://www.gov.cn/zhengce/content/2017-07/20/content_5211996.htm; English translation here: Graham Webster et al., "Full Translation: China's 'New Generation Artificial Intelligence Development Plan' (2017)," New America, August 1, 2017, https://www.newamerica.org/cybersecurity-initiative/digichina/blog/full-translation -chinas-new-generation-artificial-intelligence-development-plan-2017/.

71 **China to be the "world's primary AI innovation center":** Webster et al., "Full Translation: China's 'New Generation Artificial Intelligence Development Plan.'"

71 **"Trust me, these Chinese people are good":** Eric Schmidt, "Keynote Address," address to Center for a New American Security Artificial Intelligence and Global Security Summit, November 13, 2017, https://www.cnas.org/publications/transcript/eric-schmidt-keynote -address-at-the-center-for-a-new-american-security-artificial-intelligence-and-global -security-summit.

72 **"AI arms race":** Brandon Knapp, "DoD Official: US Not Part of AI Arms Race," c4isrnet.com, April 10, 2018, https://www.c4isrnet.com/it-networks/2018/04/10/dod-official-us-not-part-of-ai-arms-race/; Stuart Russell et al., "Autonomous Weapons: An Open Letter from AI & Robotics Researchers," Future of Life Institute, July 28, 2015, https:// futureoflife.org/open-letter-autonomous-weapons/?cn-reloaded=1; Heather M. Roff, "The Frame Problem: The AI 'Arms Race' Isn't One," *Bulletin of the Atomic Scientists* 75 no. 3 (April 29, 2019), https://thebulletin.org/2019/04/the-frame-problem-the-ai-arms-race-isnt -one/; Andrew Imbrie et al., *Mainframes: A Provisional Analysis of Rhetorical Frames in AI* (Center for Security and Emerging Technology, August 2020), https://cset.georgetown .edu/research/mainframes-a-provisional-analysis-of-rhetorical-frames-in-ai/.

72 **AI is not a weapon:** Michael C. Horowitz, "Artificial Intelligence, International Competition, and the Balance of Power," *Texas National Security Review* 1, no. 3 (May 2018), https:// doi.org/10.15781/T2639KP49.

72 **technological advancements have a compounding effect:** Rishi Bommasani et al., *On the*

Opportunities and Risks of Foundation Models (Center for Research on Foundation Models, Stanford Institute for Human-Centered Artificial Intelligence, August 18, 2021), 148–149, https://arxiv.org/pdf/2108.07258.pdf.

72 **technological progress is the main driver:** YiLi Chien, "What Drives Long-Run Economic Growth?" *On the Economy Blog*, Federal Reserve Bank of St. Louis, June 1, 2015, https://www.stlouisfed.org/on-the-economy/2015/june/what-drives-long-run-economic-growth.

72 **six in ten jobs could be significantly transformed:** James Manyika et al., *Jobs Lost, Jobs Gained: What the Future of Work Will Mean for Jobs, Skills, and Wages* (McKinsey Global Institute, November 28, 2017), https://www.mckinsey.com/featured-insights/future-of-work/jobs-lost-jobs-gained-what-the-future-of-work-will-mean-for-jobs-skills-and-wages#; James Manyika et al., *Harnessing Automation for a Future That Works* (McKinsey Global Institute, January 2017), https://www.mckinsey.com/featured-insights/digital-disruption/harnessing-automation-for-a-future-that-works.

73 **executive order on AI leadership:** Exec. Order 13869, 84 Fed. Reg. 3967 (February 14, 2019), https://www.federalregister.gov/documents/2019/02/14/2019-02544/maintaining-american-leadership-in-artificial-intelligence.

73 **updated R&D plan:** *The National Artificial Intelligence Research and Development Strategic Plan: 2019 Update* (Select Committee on Artificial Intelligence, National Science & Technology Council, June 2019), https://www.nitrd.gov/pubs/National-AI-RD-Strategy-2019.pdf.

73 **Chinese leaders issued a series of implementation plans:** "AI in China," OECD.AI Policy Observatory, updated September 21, 2021, https://oecd.ai/dashboards/countries/China.

73 **"Three-Year Action Plan":** "工业和信息化部发布《促进新一代人工智能产业发展三年行动计划（2018-2020年）》[The Ministry of Industry and Information Technology issued the 'Three-Year Action Plan (2018-2020) for Promoting the Development of the New Generation Artificial Intelligence Industry']," Ministry of Industry and Information Technology of the People's Republic of China, December 14, 2017, http://www.miit.gov.cn/n1146290/n4388791/c5960863/content.html (page discontinued), https://web.archive.org/web/20180821120845/http://www.miit.gov.cn/n1146290/n4388791/c5960863/content.html; Paul Triolo, Elsa Kania, and Graham Webster, "Translation: Chinese Government Outlines AI Ambitions through 2020," *New America Blog*, January 26, 2018, https://www.newamerica.org/cybersecurity-initiative/digichina/blog/translation-chinese-government-outlines-ai-ambitions-through-2020/.

73 **"Thirteenth Five-Year Science and Technology Military-Civil Fusion Special Projects Plan":** PRC Ministry of Science and Technology, "The '13th Five-Year' Special Plan for S&T Military-Civil Fusion Development," translated by Etcetera Language Group, Center for Security and Emerging Technology, June 10, 2020, https://cset.georgetown.edu/wp-content/uploads/t0163_13th_5YP_mil_civ_fusion_EN.pdf.

73 **"Accelerating the development of a new generation of AI":** Elsa Kania and Rogier Creemers, "Xi Jinping Calls for 'Healthy Development' of AI (Translation)," *New America Blog*, November 5, 2018, https://www.newamerica.org/cybersecurity-initiative/digichina/blog/xi-jinping-calls-for-healthy-development-of-ai-translation/.

73 **"There's no question that there was a Sputnik moment":** Eric Schmidt, interview by author, June 9, 2020.

73 **DeepMind's AlphaGo:** "AlphaGo," DeepMind, n.d., https://deepmind.com/research/case-studies/alphago-the-story-so-far; Alex Hern, "China Censored Google's AlphaGo Match against World's Best Go Player," *The Guardian*, May 24, 2017, https://www.theguardian.com/technology/2017/may/24/china-censored-googles-alphago-match-against-worlds-best-go-player; "AlphaGo China," DeepMind, 2017, https://deepmind.com/alphago-china.

73 **"not only was it notable, but they also censored"**: Schmidt, interview.

73 *Go* **is an ancient strategy game:** "A Brief History of Go," American Go Association, n.d., https://www.usgo.org/brief-history-go; Peter Shotwell, *The Game of Go: Speculations on Its Origins and Symbolism in Ancient China* (American Go Association, updated February 2008), https://www.usgo.org/sites/default/files/bh_library/originsofgo.pdf.

73 **"I am not a person who believes that we are adversaries with China"**: Schmidt, interview.

74 **a "strategic competitor":** *Summary of the 2018 National Defense Strategy of the United States of America: Sharpening the American Military's Competitive Edge* (U.S. Department of Defense, 2018), 1, https://dod.defense.gov/Portals/1/Documents/pubs/2018-National-Defense-Strategy-Summary.pdf.

74 **in search of what might come next:** Hal Brands and Zack Cooper, "After the Responsible Stakeholder, What? Debating America's China Strategy," *Texas National Security Review* 2, no. 2 (February 2019), http://dx.doi.org/10.26153/tsw/1943.

74 **The pandemic slammed the brakes on the global economy:** James K. Jackson, *Global Economic Effects of COVID-19* (Congressional Research Service, updated July 9, 2021), https://fas.org/sgp/crs/row/R46270.pdf.

74 **dictators who fall from power:** For example, Romanian President Nicolae Ceaușescu and his wife were executed by firing squad after a perfunctory show trial in December 1989.

74 **"China's Chernobyl":** Shawn Yuan, "Inside the Early Days of China's Coronavirus Cover-Up," *Wired*, May 1, 2020, https://www.wired.com/story/inside-the-early-days-of-chinas-coronavirus-coverup/.

75 **the West is "falling apart":** Zhou Bo, "Why the US and Europe Need to Draw Closer to China and Drop the Hubris," *South China Morning Post*, April 24, 2020, https://www.scmp.com/comment/opinion/article/3081079/why-us-and-europe-need-draw-closer-china-and-drop-hubris.

75 **coercive diplomacy to pressure countries:** Shahank Bengali and Alice Su, "'Put on a mask and shut up': China's new 'Wolf Warriors' spread hoaxes and attack a world of critics," *Los Angeles Times*, May 4, 2020, https://www.latimes.com/world-nation/story/2020-05-04/wolf-warrior-diplomats-defend-china-handling-coronavirus; Fergus Hanson, Emilia Currey, and Tracy Beattie, *The Chinese Communist Party's Coercive Diplomacy* (Australian Strategic Policy Institute, September 1, 2020), https://www.aspi.org.au/report/chinese-communist-partys-coercive-diplomacy; Jamil Anderlini, "China Is Escalating Its Punishment Diplomacy," *Financial Times*, September 22, 2020, https://www.ft.com/content/e76a835b-27d5-4750-9749-04921d6bf1eb.

75 **requests that receiving governments praise China:** Alexandra Ma, "China Is Attempting to Win Political Points from the Coronavirus With 'Mask Diplomacy'—but It Mostly Isn't Working," *Business Insider*, April 18, 2020, https://www.businessinsider.com/analysis-china-coronavirus-political-points-mostly-not-working-2020-4.

75 **China's "global disinformation campaign":** Michael Peel and Tom Mitchell, "China Warned EU 3 Times over Virus Propaganda Report," *Financial Times*, April 26, 2020, https://www.ft.com/content/a2f66f6a-50cb-46fe-a160-3854e4702f1c; Matt Apuzzo, "Top E.U. Diplomat Says Disinformation Report Was Not Watered Down for China," *New York Times*, April 30, 2020, https://www.nytimes.com/2020/04/30/world/europe/coronavirus-china-eu-disinformation.html; Matt Apuzzo, "Pressured by China, E.U. Softens Report on Covid-19 Disinformation," *New York Times*, April 24, 2020, https://www.nytimes.com/2020/04/24/world/europe/disinformation-china-eu-coronavirus.html. EU officials denied that they had watered down their findings to appease China, stating that the sentences critical of China that were deleted in the final report were omitted through part of a normal editing process.

75 **China responded by restricting imports:** Anderlini, "China Is Escalating Its Punishment Diplomacy."

75 **"put on a mask and shut up":** Embajada de China en Venezuela (@Emb_China-Ven), "apúrese a pedir tratamiento adecuado. El primer paso podría ser usar las tapabocas y callarse," Twitter, March 18, 2020, https://twitter.com/Emb_ChinaVen/status/1240367619200495616.

75 **China's manufacture of life-saving drugs:** Bo, "Why the US and Europe Need to Draw Closer to China and Drop the Hubris."

75 **"into the mighty sea of coronavirus":** 理直气壮，世界应该感谢中国 [Justly and forcefully, the world should thank China]," Xinhua, March 4, 2020, http://www.xinhuanet.com/2020-03/04/c_1125660473.htm; Christian Whiton, "China Threatens to Throw America 'Into the Mighty Sea of the Coronavirus,'" *National Interest*, March 8, 2020, https://nationalinterest.org/feature/china-threatens-throw-america-mighty-sea-coronavirus-130877.

75 **China's mishandling of the outbreak:** Bengali and Su, "'Put on a mask and shut up.'"

75 **the U.S. Army might have started the outbreak:** Lijian Zhao 赵立坚 (zlj517), "2/2 CDC was caught on the spot. When did patient zero begin in US? How many people are infected? What are the names of the hospitals? It might be US army who brought the epidemic to Wuhan. Be transparent! Make public your data! US owe us an explanation!" Twitter, March 12, 2020, https://twitter.com/zlj517/status/1238111898828066823.

75 **"hide your strength and bide your time":** Kurt M. Campbell and Mira Rapp-Hooper, "China Is Done Biding Its Time," *Foreign Affairs*, July 15, 2020, https://www.foreignaffairs.com/articles/china/2020-07-15/china-done-biding-its-time; Matt Pottinger, "Beijing's American Hustle," *Foreign Affairs*, September/October 2021, https://www.foreignaffairs.com/articles/asia/2021-08-23/beijings-american-hustle.

75 **Chinese troops entered Indian territory in the Himalayas:** Paul D. Shinkman, "India, China Face Off in First Deadly Clash in Decades," *U.S. News & World Report*, June 16, 2020, https://www.usnews.com/news/world-report/articles/2020-06-16/dozens-killed-as-india-china-face-off-in-first-deadly-clash-in-decades.

76 **dismantle Hong Kong's freedoms:** Laignee Barron, "How Beijing's National Security Crackdown Transformed Hong Kong in a Single Month," *Time*, August 4, 2020, https://time.com/5874901/hong-kong-national-security-law-timeline/.

76 **incursions across the midline of the Taiwan Strait:** Sara Zheng, "Fighter Jets Cross a Line in Taiwan Strait, Says Taipei as It Hosts US Health Official Amid Rising US-China Tension," *South China Morning Post*, August 10, 2020, https://www.scmp.com/news/china/military/article/3096776/fighter-jets-cross-line-taiwan-strait-says-taipei-it-hosts-us; "Taiwan Scrambles Fighters as Chinese Jets Again Fly Near Island," Reuters, September 19, 2020, https://www.cnbc.com/2020/09/19/taiwan-scrambles-fighters-as-chinese-jets-again-fly-near-island.html; Brad Lendon, "Almost 40 Chinese warplanes Breach Taiwan Strait Median Line; Taiwan President Calls It a 'Threat of Force,'" CNN, September 21, 2020, https://www.cnn.com/2020/09/21/asia/taiwan-china-warplanes-median-line-intl-hnk-scli/index.html.

76 **United States sent two aircraft carriers to the region:** Sanjeev Miglani, "U.S. Holds Naval Exercises with Allies in Asia amid China Tension," Reuters, July 21, 2020, https://www.reuters.com/article/us-india-usa/u-s-holds-naval-exercises-with-allies-in-asia-amid-china-tension-idUSKCN24M0RB.

76 **restructure global supply chains:** Katrin Hille, "US and Taiwan to Work on Reshaping Supply Chains Away from China," *Financial Times*, September 4, 2020, https://www.ft.com/content/64be66cd-91eb-4862-a8fe-7c998b2e4770.

76 **trilateral supply chain resilience initiative:** Dipanjan Roy Chaudhurhy, "India-Japan-Australia Decide to Launch Resilient Supply Chain Initiative in the Indo-Pacific Region," *Economic Times*, September 2, 2020, https://economictimes.indiatimes.com/news/economy/foreign-trade/india-japan-australia-decide-to-launch-resilient-supply-chain-initiative-in-the-indo-pacific-region/articleshow/77870346.cms.

76 **$2.2 billion to incentivize companies:** David Arase, "Tokyo Prods Japanese Firms to Leave China," interview by Mercy A. Kuo, *The Diplomat*, May 5, 2020, https://thediplomat.com/2020/05/tokyo-prods-japanese-firms-to-leave-china/; Isabel Reynolds and Emi Urabe, "Japan to Fund Firms to Shift Production Out of China," Bloomberg, April 8, 2020, https://www.bloomberg.com/news/articles/2020-04-08/japan-to-fund-firms-to-shift-production-out-of-china.

76 **French pharmaceutical companies:** Ail Laidi, "Covid-19 Forces France to Look at Relocating Its Pharmaceutical Industry," *France 24*, May 14, 2020, https://www.france24.com/en/20200514-covid-19-forces-france-to-look-at-relocating-its-pharmaceutical-industry.

76 **reduce American dependency on China:** Lin Yang, "Pandemic Exposes Perils of Global Reliance on China for Drug Supplies," voanews.com, May 20, 2020, https://www.voanews.com/science-health/pandemic-exposes-perils-global-reliance-china-drug-supplies; David J. Lynch, Jeanne Whalen, and Laurie McGinley, "Trump Takes a First Step Toward Returning Medical Supply Chains to the U.S.," *Washington Post*, July 11, 2020, https://www.washingtonpost.com/business/2020/05/19/trump-takes-first-step-toward-returning-medical-supply-chains-us/.

76 **government subsidies for building new domestic chip fabrication plants:** *CHIPS and Science Act of 2022: Section-by-Section Summary* (Commerce.senate.gov, 2022), https://www.commerce.senate.gov/services/files/1201E1CA-73CB-44BB-ADEB-E69634DA9BB9. See also Sections 9902 and 9906: William M. (Mac) Thornberry National Defense Authorization Act for Fiscal Year 2021, H.R. 6395, 116th Cong. (2019), https://www.congress.gov/bill/116th-congress/house-bill/6395/text.

76 **export controls:** US Department of Commerce, "Commerce Addresses Huawei's Efforts to Undermine Entity List, Restricts Products Designed and Produced with U.S. Technologies," news release, May 15, 2020, https://2017-2021.commerce.gov/news/press-releases/2020/05/commerce-addresses-huaweis-efforts-undermine-entity-list-restricts.html; Bob Davis and Dan Strumpf, "Huawei Braces for Latest U.S. Hit, but Some Say Loopholes Remain," *Wall Street Journal*, updated May 18, 2020, https://www.wsj.com/articles/huawei-warns-u-s-chip-ban-will-damage-operations-globally-11589801706.

76 **Quad summit:** The White House, "Quad Leaders' Joint Statement: 'The Spirit of the Quad,'" March 12, 2021, https://www.whitehouse.gov/briefing-room/statements-releases/2021/03/12/quad-leaders-joint-statement-the-spirit-of-the-quad/.

76 **AUKUS:** The White House, "Joint Leaders Statement on AUKUS," September 15, 2021, https://www.whitehouse.gov/briefing-room/statements-releases/2021/09/15/joint-leaders-statement-on-aukus/.

76 **G7 grouping:** U.S. Department of State, "G7 Foreign Ministers' Statement on Preserving Peace and Stability Across the Taiwan Strait," August 3, 2022, https://www.state.gov/g7-foreign-ministers-statement-on-preserving-peace-and-stability-across-the-taiwan-strait/.

76 **"After a big crisis, what is redistributed":** Eva Dou, "Fearing Political Dangers, China Spent Years Preparing for This Economic Crash," *Washington Post*, May 5, 2020, https://www.washingtonpost.com/world/asia_pacific/china-spent-years-preparing-for-this-economic-crash-fearing-political-pitfalls/2020/05/05/78df2592-843e-11ea-81a3-9690c9881111_story.html.

10. TERROR

79 **campaign of repression against Xinjiang's ethnic Uighur population:** "'Eradicating Ideological Viruses': China's Campaign of Repression Against Xinjiang's Muslims," Human Rights Watch, September 9, 2018, https://www.hrw.org/report/2018/09/09/eradicating -ideological-viruses/chinas-campaign-repression-against-xinjiangs; James Millward and Dahlia Peterson, *China's System of Oppression in Xinjiang: How It Developed and How to Curb It* (Brookings Institution, September 2020), https://www.brookings.edu/wp-content/ uploads/2020/09/FP_20200914_china_oppression_xinjiang_millward_peterson.pdf.

79 **"even in their own homes, they censor themselves":** Maya Wang, interview by author, September 18, 2020.

79 **campaign to destroy Uighur culture:** Darren Byler, "Uyghur Love in a Time of Interethnic Marriage," *SupChina*, August 7, 2019, https://supchina.com/2019/08/07/uyghur-love-in-a -time-of-interethnic-marriage/; Matthew Hill, David Campanale and Joel Gunter, "'Their Goal Is to Destroy Everyone': Uighur Camp Detainees Allege Systematic Rape," BBC News, February 2, 2021, https://www.bbc.com/news/world-asia-china-55794071.

79 **forced sterilizations and abortions:** "China Cuts Uighur Births with IUDs, Abortion, Sterilization," Associated Press, June 29, 2020, https://apnews.com/269b3de1af34e17c1941 a514f78d764c; Adrian Zenz, *Sterilizations, IUDs, and Mandatory Birth Control: The CCP's Campaign to Suppress Uyghur Birthrates in Xinjiang* (The Jamestown Foundation, June 2020), https://jamestown.org/wp-content/uploads/2020/06/Zenz-Internment -Sterilizations-and-IUDs-UPDATED-July-21-Rev2.pdf?x41867; Nathan Ruser and James Leibold, *Family De-Planning: The Coercive Campaign to Drive Down Indigenous Birth-Rates in Xinjiang* (Australian Strategic Policy Institute, May 2021), https://www.aspi.org .au/report/family-deplanning-birthrates-xinjiang.

79 **genocide:** "China cuts Uighur births"; "Opinion: What's Happening in Xinjiang Is Genocide," editorial, *Washington Post*, July 6, 2020, https://www.washingtonpost.com/ opinions/global-opinions/whats-happening-in-xinjiang-is-genocide/2020/07/06/cde3f9da -bfaa-11ea-9fdd-b7ac6b051dc8_story.html; Adrian Zenz, interview by Scott Simon, NPR, July 4, 2020, https://www.npr.org/2020/07/04/887239225/china-suppression-of-uighur -minorities-meets-u-n-definition-of-genocide-report-s; Humeyra Pamuk and David Brunnstrom, "New U.S. Secretary of State Favors Cooperation with China Despite Geno-cide of Uighurs," Reuters, January 27, 2021, https://www.reuters.com/article/us-usa-china -blinken/new-u-s-secretary-of-state-favors-cooperation-with-china-despite-genocide -of-uighurs-idUSKBN29W2RC; "Canada's Parliament Declares China's Treatment of Uighurs 'Genocide,'" BBC News, February 23, 2021, https://www.bbc.com/news/world-us -canada-56163220; "Dutch Parliament: China's Treatment of Uighurs Is Genocide," Reu-ters, February 25, 2021, https://www.reuters.com/article/us-netherlands-china-uighurs/ dutch-parliament-chinas-treatment-of-uighurs-is-genocide-idUSKBN2AP2CI; Donald Clarke, "The Economist on Xinjiang: Don't Call It Genocide," China Collection, Febru-ary 13, 2021, https://thechinacollection.org/economist-xinjiang-dont-call-genocide/; Eliz-abeth M. Lynch, "The Economist's Recent Piece about Genocide in Xinjiang Is Wrong," *China Law & Policy*, February 15, 2021, https://chinalawandpolicy.com/2021/02/15/the -economists-recent-piece-about-genocide-in-xinjiang-is-wrong/.

79 **AI is helping to enable this repression:** *Risks and Considerations for Businesses with Supply Chain Exposure to Entities Engaged in Forced Labor and Other Human Rights Abuses in Xinjiang* (Department of State, July 1, 2020), https://www.state.gov/wp-content/ uploads/2020/07/Xinjiang-Supply-Chain-Business-Advisory_FINAL_For-508-508.pdf.

79 **"Strike Hard Campaign":** "China's Algorithms of Repression," Human Rights Watch, May 1, 2019, https://www.hrw.org/report/2019/05/02/chinas-algorithms-repression/reverse-engineering-xinjiang-police-mass.

79 **thousands of police checkpoints across Xinjiang:** Darren Byler, "I Researched Uighur Society in China for 8 Years and Watched How Technology Opened New Opportunities—Then Became a Trap," *The Conversation*, September 18, 2019, https://theconversation.com/i-researched-uighur-society-in-china-for-8-years-and-watched-how-technology-opened-new-opportunities-then-became-a-trap-119615.

79 **160,000 cameras:** Paul Bischoff, "Surveillance Camera Statistics: Which Cities Have the Most CCTV Cameras?" Comparitech, updated May 17, 2021, https://www.comparitech.com/vpn-privacy/the-worlds-most-surveilled-cities/.

80 **Facial recognition scanners:** Josh Chin and Clément Bürge, "Twelve Days in Xinjiang: How China's Surveillance State Overwhelms Daily Life," *Wall Street Journal*, updated December 19, 2017, https://www.wsj.com/articles/twelve-days-in-xinjiang-how-chinas-surveillance-state-overwhelms-daily-life-1513700355

80 **"Convenience police stations":** Darren Byler, "Ghost World," *Logic* no. 7, May 1, 2019, https://logicmag.io/china/ghost-world/; Chin and Bürge, "Twelve Days in Xinjiang."

80 **ID checkpoints:** Chin and Bürge, "Twelve Days in Xinjiang."

80 **massive biometric database:** Darren Byler, "Uyghur Biodata Collection in China," interview by Mercy A. Kuo, *The Diplomat*, December 28, 2017, https://thediplomat.com/2017/12/uyghur-biodata-collection-in-china/; "China: Voice Biometric Collection Threatens Privacy," Human Rights Watch, October 22, 2017, https://www.hrw.org/news/2017/10/22/china-voice-biometric-collection-threatens-privacy; Chin and Bürge, "Twelve Days in Xinjiang"; China: Minority Region Collects DNA from Millions," Human Rights Watch, December 13, 2017, https://www.hrw.org/news/2017/12/13/china-minority-region-collects-dna-millions; "China: How Mass Surveillance Works in Xinjiang," Human Rights Watch, May 1, 2019, https://www.hrw.org/news/2019/05/01/china-how-mass-surveillance-works-xinjiang.

80 **biometric data on every Xinjiang resident between the ages of twelve and sixty-five:** "China: Minority Region Collects DNA from Millions."

80 **police search citizens' phones for unauthorized content:** Byler, "I Researched Uighur Society."

80 **encrypted chat apps to circumvent Chinese surveillance:** Chin and Bürge, "Twelve Days in Xinjiang."

80 **an "ideological virus":** Chris Buckley, "China Is Detaining Muslims in Vast Numbers. The Goal: 'Transformation.'" *New York Times*, September 8, 2018, https://www.nytimes.com/2018/09/08/world/asia/china-uighur-muslim-detention-camp.html; " 'Eradicating Ideological Viruses' "; Austin Ramzy and Chris Buckley, " 'Absolutely No Mercy': Leaked Files Expose How China Organized Mass Detentions of Muslims," *New York Times*, November 16, 2019, https://www.nytimes.com/interactive/2019/11/16/world/asia/china-xinjiang-documents.html.

80 **"re-education" in Chinese Communist Party ideology:** Buckley, "China Is Detaining Muslims in Vast Numbers."

80 **writing or publicly speaking the Uighur language:** Darren Byler, "The 'Patriotism' of Not Speaking Uyghur," *SupChina*, January 2, 2019, https://supchina.com/2019/01/02/the-patriotism-of-not-speaking-uyghur/.

80 **Wi-Fi "sniffers":** "China's Algorithms of Repression."

80 **License plate readers:** Chin and Bürge, "Twelve Days in Xinjiang."

80 **all vehicles install tracking devices:** Wong Siu-san and Sing Man, "Vehicles to Get Com-

pulsory GPS Tracking in Xinjiang," translated by Luisetta Mudie, *Radio Free Asia*, February 2, 2020, https://www.rfa.org/english/news/uyghur/xinjiang-gps-02202017145155.html; Tom Phillips, "China orders GPS tracking of every car in troubled region," *The Guardian*, February 20, 2017, https://www.theguardian.com/world/2017/feb/21/china-orders-gps-tracking-of -every-car-in-troubled-region.

80 **QR codes on peoples' homes:** "'Eradicating Ideological Viruses.'"

80 **kitchen knives are stamped with QR codes:** Catherine Lai, "Xinjiang Town Orders Residents to Engrave Names and ID Numbers on to All Knives, Including Kitchen Tools," *Hong Kong Free Press*, January 12, 2017, https://hongkongfp.com/2017/01/12/xinjiang-town -orders-residents-engrave-names-id-numbers-knives-including-kitchen-tools/; Chin and Bürge, "Twelve Days in Xinjiang"; 忻霖 ([Xīn Lín], "新疆温宿县下令民间刀具刻铸实名全疆各医院病人先安检后看病 [Wensu County, Xinjiang ordered privately owned knives to be carved with real names | patients in hospitals across Xinjiang go through security checks before seeing a doctor]," rfa.org, January 11, 2017, https://www.rfa.org/mandarin/ yataibaodao/shaoshuminzu/xl2-01112017102645.html.

80 **handheld devices to automatically scan smartphones:** Chin and Bürge, "Twelve Days in Xinjiang."

80 **73,000 prohibited pictures, videos, documents, and audio files:** Raymond Zhong, "China Snares Tourists' Phones in Surveillance Dragnet by Adding Secret App," *New York Times*, July 2, 2019, https://www.nytimes.com/2019/07/02/technology/china-xinjiang-app.html.

80 **frozen data cards in dumplings:** Byler, "Ghost World."

80 **absence of a phone:** Byler, "Ghost World"; Byler, "I Researched Uighur Society."

81 **two phones:** Chin and Bürge, "Twelve Days in Xinjiang."

81 **live in Uighurs' homes to monitor them:** Darren Byler, "China's Nightmare Homestay," *Foreign Policy*, October 26, 2018, https://foreignpolicy.com/2018/10/26/china-nightmare -homestay-xinjiang-uighur-monitor/.

81 **Integrated Joint Operations Platform (IJOP):** "China's Algorithms of Repression."

81 **"this panopticon that is envisioned in our dystopian nightmare":** Wang, interview.

81 **"eyes are so tired and reddened":** "China's Algorithms of Repression."

82 **"That's how state terror works":** Bethany Allen-Ebrahimian, "Exposed: China's Operating Manuals for Mass Internment and Arrest by Algorithm," International Consortium of Investigative Journalists, November 24, 2019, https://www.icij.org/investigations/china-cables/ exposed-chinas-operating-manuals-for-mass-internment-and-arrest-by-algorithm/.

82 **"As neighbors disappear":** Allen-Ebrahimian, "Exposed: China's Operating Manuals for Mass Internment and Arrest by Algorithm."

82 **fear of state control "isn't a bug but a feature":** Allen-Ebrahimian, "Exposed: China's Operating Manuals for Mass Internment and Arrest by Algorithm."

82 **"for example, if you have been to a camp":** Wang, interview.

83 **"the people have sharp eyes":** This phrase is sometimes translated as "the masses have sharp eyes." Josh Rudolph, "'The People Have Sharp Eyes.' ('群众的眼睛是雪亮的.')" *China Digital Times*, September 9, 2019, https://chinadigitaltimes.net/2019/09/sharper-eyes -surveilling-the-surveillers-part-1/; Simon Denyer, "Beijing Bets on Facial Recognition in a Big Drive for Total Surveillance," *Washington Post*, January 7, 2018, https://www.wash-ingtonpost.com/news/world/wp/2018/01/07/feature/in-china-facial-recognition-is-sharp -end-of-a-drive-for-total-surveillance/.

83 **"a general increase in Xinjiang-ification of China":** Wang, interview.

83 **"[CCP leaders] constantly take lessons from the high-pressure rule they apply in Xinjiang":** Chin and Bürge, "Twelve Days in Xinjiang."

11. SHARP EYES

84 **surveillance cameras in use worldwide:** Liza Lin and Newley Purnell, "A World with a Billion Cameras Watching You Is Just Around the Corner," *Wall Street Journal*, December 6, 2019, https://www.wsj.com/articles/a-billion-surveillance-cameras-forecast-to-be -watching-within-two-years-11575565402.

85 **Mao Zedong's Great Leap Forward:** Vaclav Smil, "China's Great Famine: 40 Years Later," *British Medical Journal* 319, no. 7225 (December 18, 1999): 1619–1621, https://dx.doi.org/10 .1136%2Fbmj.319.7225.1619.

85 **"reform and opening":** "Reform and Opening in China, 1978–," Wilson Center Digital Archive, n.d., https://digitalarchive.wilsoncenter.org/collection/185/reform-and-opening -in-china-1978.

85 **GDP growth rate of nearly 10 percent:** *China's Economic Rise: History, Trends, Challenges, and Implications for the United States* (Congressional Research Service, updated June 25, 2019), https://fas.org/sgp/crs/row/RL33534.pdf.

85 **"fastest sustained expansion by a major economy in history":** "China Overview," World Bank, captured March 27, 2017 (site has since updated), https://web.archive.org/ web/20170327015624/https://www.worldbank.org/en/country/china/overview.

85 **Eight hundred million people were lifted out of poverty:** Jim Yong Kim, remarks at the Opening Ceremony of the First China International Import Expo, Shanghai, November 5, 2018, https://www.worldbank.org/en/news/speech/2018/11/05/world-bank -group-president-jim-yong-kims-remarks-at-the-opening-ceremony-of-the-first-china -international-import-expo.

85 **Average life expectancy:** "Life Expectancy at Birth, Total (Years)—China," World Bank, updated 2019, https://data.worldbank.org/indicator/SP.DYN.LE00.IN?end=2018 &locations=CN&start=1960&view=chart.

85 **Infant mortality:** "Mortality Rate, Infant (Per 1,000 Live Births)—China," World Bank, updated 2019, https://data.worldbank.org/indicator/SP.DYN.IMRT.IN?locations=CN.

85 **Gross national income:** "GNI Per Capita (Constant 2010 US$)—China," World Bank, updated 2019, https://data.worldbank.org/indicator/NY.GNP.PCAP.KD?locations=CN. Thanks to CNAS research associate Ainikki Riikonen for background research.

85 **Life Expectancy at Birth:** "Life Expectancy at Birth, Total (Years)—China." Thanks to CNAS research associate Ainikki Riikonen for background research.

85 **Infant mortality:** "Mortality Rate, Infant (Per 1,000 Live Births)—China." Thanks to CNAS research associate Ainikki Riikonen for background research.

87 **fully modernized society by 2049:** Robert Lawrence Kuhn, "Xi Jinping's Chinese Dream," *New York Times*, June 4, 2013, https://www.nytimes.com/2013/06/05/opinion/global/xi -jinpings-chinese-dream.html.

87 **6 percent in 2019:** "GDP Growth (Annual %)—China," World Bank, 2020, https://data .worldbank.org/indicator/NY.GDP.MKTP.KD.ZG?locations=CN.

87 **repression of human rights activists, lawyers, political dissidents, and journalists:** "China: Events of 2018," Human Rights Watch, 2018, https://www.hrw.org/world -report/2019/country-chapters/china-and-tibet; "Human Rights Activism in Post-Tiananmen China," Human Rights Watch, May 30, 2019, https://www.hrw.org/news/2019/05/30/ human-rights-activism-post-tiananmen-china.

87 **Golden Shield Project:** *Breaking Through the "Golden Shield"* (Open Society Institute, 2009), https://www.opensocietyfoundations.org/publications/breaking-through-golden -shield.

87   **Skynet:** " '天网'网什么" ["Skynet" Nets What], people.cn, n.d., http://paper.people.com
.cn/rmzk/html/2017-11/20/content_1825998.htm   (page   discontinued),   https://web
.archive.org/web/20190303234110/http://paper.people.com.cn/rmzk/html/2017-11/20/
content_1825998.htm; Xinmei Shen, " 'Skynet', China's Massive Video Surveillance Network," *South China Morning Post*, October 4, 2018, https://www.scmp.com/abacus/
who-what/what/article/3028246/skynet-chinas-massive-video-surveillance-network;
Zhang Zihan, "Beijing's Guardian Angels?" *Global Times*, October 10, 2012, http://www
.globaltimes.cn/content/737491.shtml.

87   **goal of Skynet is "prevention and control":** " '天网'网什么" ["Skynet" Nets What].

87   **"no blind spots":** Charles Rollet, "China Public Video Surveillance Guide: From Skynet to
Sharp Eyes," IPVM.com, June 14, 2018, https://ipvm.com/reports/sharpeyes.

88   **Sharp Eyes:** " '天网'网什么" ["Skynet" Nets What].

88   **forty-eight demonstration cities:** "全国雪亮工程建设综述 [A Summary of the construction of the National Xueliang Project]," baijiahao.baidu.com, October 16, 2017, https://
baijiahao.baidu.com/s?id=1581391474160186317&wfr=spider&for=pc.

88   **786 Sharp Eyes and related surveillance projects:** Josh Rudolph, " 'The People Have
Sharp Eyes.' ('群众的眼睛是雪亮的.')" *China Digital Times*, September 9, 2019, https://
chinadigitaltimes.net/2019/09/sharper-eyes-surveilling-the-surveillers-part-1/; 年度回
顾之——安防与雪亮工程千万项目市场浅析 [Annual Review—Analysis on the market of
ten million projects of security and the Xueliang Project]," sohu.com, January 30, 2019,
https://www.sohu.com/a/292385866_649849.

88   **"omnipresent, fully networked":** Simon Denyer, "Beijing Bets on Facial Recognition in a Big
Drive for Total Surveillance," *Washington Post*, January 7, 2018, https://www.washingtonpost.com/
news/world/wp/2018/01/07/feature/in-china-facial-recognition-is-sharp-end-of-a-drive-for
-total-surveillance/; Rollet, "China Public Video Surveillance Guide."

88   **Facial recognition systems:** Denyer, "Beijing Bets on Facial Recognition."

88   **factories:** Lauly Li, Coco Liu, and Cheng Ting-Fang, "China's 'Sharp Eyes' Offer Chance
to Take Surveillance Industry Global," *Nikkei Asia*, June 5, 2019, https://asia.nikkei.com/
Business/China-tech/China-s-sharp-eyes-offer-chance-to-take-surveillance-industry
-global.

88   **public toilets:** Denyer, "Beijing Bets on Facial Recognition."

88   **facial recognition–equipped helmets or sunglasses:** Paul Mozur, "Inside China's Dystopian Dreams: A.I., Shame and Lots of Cameras," *New York Times*, July 8, 2018, https://
www.nytimes.com/2018/07/08/business/china-surveillance-technology.html; Paul Mozur
孟建國 (@paulmozur), "The lists power very dark use cases. City police run systems that
flag women for prostitution if they check into more than one hotel in a night. Another
audits those living in subsidized housing to ensure extra people aren't staying with them.
(Photo: cop w/ facial rec helmet)," Twitter, December 17, 2019, https://twitter.com/paulmo-
zur/status/1207153910344904704.

88   **shame jaywalkers:** Mozur, "Inside China's Dystopian Dreams"; Josh Chin and Liza Lin,
"China's All-Seeing Surveillance State Is Reading Its Citizens' Faces," *Wall Street Journal*,
June 26, 2017, https://www.wsj.com/articles/the-all-seeing-surveillance-state-feared-in
-the-west-is-a-reality-in-china-1498493020?mod=article_inline.

88   **Face++:** Denyer, "Beijing Bets on Facial Recognition."

88   **"minority identification" technology:** Paul Mozur, "One Month, 500,000 Face Scans:
How China Is Using A.I. to Profile a Minority," *New York Times*, April 14, 2019, https://
www.nytimes.com/2019/04/14/technology/china-surveillance-artificial-intelligence
-racial-profiling.html.

88 **"Uighur/non-Uighur attributes"**: Mozur, "One Month, 500,000 Face Scans."

88 **patents for facial recognition technology that claim to detect Uighurs:** "Patenting Uyghur Tracking—Huawei, Megvii, More," IPVM.com, January 12, 2021, https://ipvm .com/reports/patents-uyghur; Leo Kelion, "Huawei Patent Mentions Use of Uighur-Spotting Tech," BBC News, January 13, 2021, https://www.bbc.com/news/technology-55634388.

89 **"Uighur alarm":** "Huawei / Megviii Uyghur Alarms," IPVM.com, December 8, 2020, https://ipvm.com/reports/huawei-megvii-uygur; Drew Harwell and Eva Dou, "Huawei Tested AI Software That Could Recognize Uighur Minorities and Alert Police, Report Says," *Washington Post*, December 8, 2020, https://www.washingtonpost.com/technology/2020/12/08/huawei-tested-ai-software-that-could-recognize-uighur-minorities-alert-police-report-says/

89 **Uighur-detecting code:** After investigators had contacted Dahua about its Uighur-detecting code, Dahua reportedly deleted the online source of the Uighur-detecting software. ("Dahua Racist Uyghur Tracking Revealed," IPVM.com, November 4, 2020, https://ipvm.com/reports/dahua-uyghur; Charles Rollet, "Uniview Racist Uyghur Recognition Revealed," IPVM.com, November 16, 2020, https://ipvm.com/reports/uniview-uyghur.)

89 **AI camera that reportedly detected Uighur facial attributes:** Following inquiries from independent investigators about Hikvision's Uighur-detecting AI camera, Hikvision reportedly deleted the online product page describing the camera. (Charles Rollet, "Hikvision Markets Uyghur Ethnicity Analytics, Now Covers Up," IPVM.com, November 11, 2019, https://ipvm.com/reports/hikvision-uyghur.)

89 **released statements denying that they discriminate**: In response to news reports about Huawei's patent for Uighur detection, **Huawei** issued a statement: "Huawei opposes discrimination of all types, including the use of technology to carry out ethnic discrimination. Identifying individuals' race was never part of the research and development project. It should never have become part of the application and we are taking proactive steps to amend it. We are continuously working to ensure new and evolving technology is developed and applied with the utmost care and integrity." ("Patenting Uyghur Tracking – Huawei, Megvii, More.") Huawei also indicated that deleting the reference to Uighurs on the Chinese patent document would require asking permission of the China National Intellectual Property Administration (CNIPA). (Kelion, "Huawei Patent Mentions Use of Uighur-Spotting Tech.")

In response to news reports about Megvii's patent for ethnicity classification, including identifying Uighurs, **Megvii** issued a statement: "Megvii recognizes that the language used in our 2019 patent application is open to misunderstanding. The patent application pertains to technology to re-label images based on existing attributes provided by third parties, where some of them might have been labeled incorrectly, in order to facilitate portrait retrieval. This functionality, which re-labels images using such attributes as age, gender, and ethnicity, is in no way an intention to develop ethnic identification solutions. Megvii, moreover, has not developed and will not develop or sell racial or ethnic labelling solutions. Megvii acknowledges that in the past, we have focused on our commercial development and lacked appropriate control of our marketing, sales, and operations materials. We are undertaking measures to correct the situation." ("Patenting Uyghur Tracking – Huawei, Megvii, More.") Megvii stated it would withdraw the patent application. (Kelion, "Huawei Patent Mentions Use of Uighur-Spotting Tech.")

In response to news reports about SenseTime's patent for ethnicity detection, including identifying Uighurs, **SenseTime** issued a statement: "This particular AI research includes facial recognition of all ethnicities without prejudice. The reference to Uyghurs is regrettable and is one of the examples within the application intended to illustrate the attributes the algorithm recognizes. It was neither designed nor intended in any way to discriminate, which is against our values." ("Patenting Uyghur Tracking – Huawei, Megvii, More.") SenseTime stated: "We will update the patent at the next available opportunity. Meanwhile, the application also pre-dates the AI Code of Ethics, which we developed later in 2019." (Arjun Kharpal, "China A.I. Firms and Huawei Filed to Patent Technology That Could Identify Uighur Muslims, Report Says," *CBNC*, January 14, 2022, https://www.cnbc .com/2021/01/15/huawei-ai-firms-filed-to-patent-tech-that-could-identify-uighurs-report -says.html.) Additionally, SenseTime stated: "SenseTime is a fast-growing young company in an even faster evolving industry. We understand the importance of our responsibilities, which is why we began to develop our AI Code of Ethics in mid-2019. The development of the AI Code of Ethics has helped inform all aspects of our business from R&D to processes. We're committed to working with the industry and at an academic level in evolving this, to ensure responsible and sustainable development of AI technology." ("Patenting Uyghur Tracking – Huawei, Megvii, More.")

In response to reports that Huawei and Megvii had jointly tested a "Uighur alarm," **Huawei** issued a statement: "This report is simply a test and it has not seen real-world application. Huawei only supplies general-purpose products for this kind of testing. We do not provide custom algorithms or applications. Huawei operates in compliance with the laws and regulations of all countries and regions where we operate, and only provides ICT products and solutions that meet recognized industry standards." Huawei also reportedly deleted the report online describing the Uighur alarm. ("Huawei / Megviii Uyghur Alarms.") **Megvii** issued a statement: "Our solutions are not designed or customized to target or label ethnic groups. Our business is focused on the well-being and safety of individuals, not about monitoring any particular demographic groups." ("Huawei / Megviii Uyghur Alarms.") In response to fallout from the news reports, **Huawei France** issued a statement: "Huawei takes this situation very seriously and wishes to bring some clarifications. We do not develop algorithms or apps in the field of facial recognition or solutions targeting ethnic groups. Huawei conceives technologies for general use that are founded on international norms in terms of artificial intelligence. Huawei is not implicated in the development of application layers which define the way in which this technology is used. Our products and solutions vigorously conform to industry standards and regulations. Huawei perfectly and strictly respects the founding principals [sic] of the UN regarding business and human rights, and follows the laws of the 170 countries where it operates." ("Huawei / Megviii Uyghur Alarms.") Additionally, the **Chinese government** issued a statement saying the report was "purely slander" and stating: "I would like to emphasize, to use modern tech products and big data to improve social management is a general practice of international community, including countries in America and Europe. Legal use of facial recognition in public areas in some parts of China is to improve social management, effectively prevent and attack criminal acts. China doesn't go any further than countries in America and Europe. And the measures are not targeting any particular ethnic groups. The measures strengthen social security, thus earn support from people of all ethnic groups." (Arjun Kharpal, "China's Huawei Tested A.I. Software That Could Identify Uighur Muslims and Alert Police, Report Says," *CNBC*, December 9, 2020, https://www.cnbc.com/2020/12/09/ chinas-huawei-tested-ai-software-that-could-identify-uighurs-report.html.)

In response to news inquiries about Uighur-detecting technology, **Dahua** issued a statement: "**Statement on Recent Media Reports** 1. Zhejiang Dahua Technology Co., Ltd. ("Dahua" or "Company") only provides generic video technology products in the regional markets reported by the media, and does not provide products and services for ethnicity detection in such regional markets. 2. In recent years, Dahua has been increasing its investment in the commercial market. The proportion of such commercial market in the Company's total sales profile has also been increasing. Dahua's total sales in the relevant regional markets reported by certain media in the past 5 years are far lower than the amount alleged in such media reports and have been declining rapidly on a yearly basis. 3. Based on the Company's internal review, the relevant documents reported by certain media are historical internal software design documents. Dahua will not provide the features or applications in the software products in the future. Dahua will conduct a rigorous internal review and strengthen the design review process and management of the Company's Research and Development functions." ("Statement on Recent Media Reports," Dahua Technology USA Inc., February 9, 2021, https://us.dahuasecurity.com/wp-content/uploads/2021/02/Statement-on-Recent-Media-Reports5.pdf.) Additionally, Dahua representatives pointed reporters to a company blog posting that included the statement: "We accept our responsibility to design our technologies in ways that mitigate the risk of abuse and maximize the likelihood of appropriate use. This includes a commitment to never develop solutions to identify a single ethnic, racial or national group. That commitment extends to every market in which we operate, anywhere in the world. Law enforcement are among our end users in many of the markets we serve. In all instances, we expect law enforcement end users to use our products appropriately. At the same time, and contrary to allegations that have been made by certain media outlets, Dahua Technology has not and never will develop solutions targeting any specific ethnic group." ("Our Commitments," Dahua Technology, n.d., https://us.dahuasecurity.com/?page_id=60083.)

In response to investigative reports about Uniview's Uighur-detecting software, **Uniview** issued a statement: "Uniview genuinely believe Tech for Social Good and sincerely practice our ethic code not only internally with Ethic Panel (just like Google and other reputable high tech companies) but also externally with all the products and service provided. There is no difference in the commitment of aforementioned products and service." Uniview also reportedly deleted the online source of the Uighur-detecting software. (Rollet, "Uniview Racist Uyghur Recognition Revealed.")

In 2019, following accusations of links to human rights abuses in Xinjiang, **Hikvision** issued a statement via Chinese state-run media: "Hikvision is a product supplier. We have never done any inappropriate actions in Xinjiang. . . . We have never and would never conduct business operations that are based on the condition of violating human rights." (Wang Cong and Ni Hongzhang, "Chinese Video Surveillance Firm Hikvision Denies Xinjiang Charges, Asks for Fair Treatment From the US," *Global Times*, May 22, 2019, https://www.globaltimes.cn/content/1151002.shtml.) In response to inquiries from reporters about Uighur-detecting technology, "Hikvision said it 'takes all reports regarding human rights very seriously' and that it is engaging 'governments globally to clarify misunderstandings.'" (Johana Bhuiyan, "'There's Cameras Everywhere': Testimonies Detail Far-Reaching Surveillance of Uyghurs in China," *The Guardian*, September 30, 2021, https://www.theguardian.com/world/2021/sep/30/uyghur-tribunal-testimony-surveillance-china.)

89 **highly unreliable:** Charles Rollet, "China Government Spreads Uyghur Analytics Across China," IPVM.com, November 25, 2019, https://ipvm.com/reports/ethnicity-analytics.

89 **in use in multiple cities in eastern China:** Mozur, "One Month, 500,000 Face Scans."

89 **"People pass and leave a shadow":** Paul Mozur and Aaron Krolik, "A Surveillance Net Blankets China's Cities, Giving Police Vast Powers," *New York Times*, December 17, 2019, https://www.nytimes.com/2019/12/17/technology/china-surveillance.html.

89 **Police Cloud:** Denyer, "Beijing Bets on Facial Recognition"; "China: Police 'Big Data' Systems Violate Privacy, Target Dissent," Human Rights Watch, November 19, 2017, https://www.hrw.org/news/2017/11/19/china-police-big-data-systems-violate-privacy-target-dissent; "公安警务云基础建设方案设计 [Design of public security and police cloud infrastructure construction]," 中国人民公安大学学报(自然科学版) [Journal of People's Public Security University of China (Natural Science Edition)] 22, no. 1 (2016), https://kns.cnki.net/KCMS/detail/detail.aspx?dbcode=CJFQ&dbname=CJFDLAST2016&filename=GOAN201601012&v=MDk0OTdvUjhlWDFMdXhZUzdEaDFUM3FUcldNMUZyQ1VSTDJlWitSdkZ5am55XcjNQSWlMS1lMRzRIOWZNcm85RVo=.

89 **who "has gone to internet cafes together more than twice":** "China: Police 'Big Data' Systems Violate Privacy, Target Dissent."

89 **synthesize data to uncover and alert police to unusual activity:** "China: Police 'Big Data' Systems Violate Privacy, Target Dissent."

89 **purchasers of new mobile phones, data plans, or SIM cards:** "China Due to Introduce Face Scans for Mobile Users," BBC News, December 1, 2019, https://www.bbc.com/news/world-asia-china-50587098; "工信部持续加强电话用户实名登记管理工作维护公民网络空间合法权益 [The Ministry of Industry and Information Technology continued to strengthen the real-name registration management of telephone users and safeguard the legitimate rights and interests of citizens in cyberspace]," Ministry of Industry and Information Technology of People's Republic of China, September 27, 2019, http://www.miit.gov.cn/n1146285/n1146352/n3054355/n3057724/n3057728/c7448683/content.html (page discontinued).

89 **nationwide DNA collection program:** Emile Dirks and James Leibold, *Genomic Surveillance: Inside China's DNA Dragnet* (Australian Strategic Policy Institute, June 17, 2020), https://www.aspi.org.au/report/genomic-surveillance.

90 **the world's largest DNA database:** Wenxin Fan, Natasha Khan, and Liza Lin, "China Snares Innocent and Guilty Alike to Build World's Biggest DNA Database," *Wall Street Journal*, updated December 26, 2017, https://www.wsj.com/articles/china-snares-innocent-and-guilty-alike-to-build-worlds-biggest-dna-database-1514310353; Sui-Lee Wee and Paul Mozur, "China Uses DNA to Map Faces, With Help From the West," *New York Times*, December 3, 2019, https://www.nytimes.com/2019/12/03/business/china-dna-uighurs-xinjiang.html.

90 **DNA phenotyping:** Wee and Mozur, "China Uses DNA to Map Faces"; Christoph Lippert et al., "Identification of Individuals by Trait Prediction Using Whole-Genome Sequencing Data," *Proceedings of the National Academy of Sciences of the United States of America* 114, no. 38 (September 2017): 10166-10171, https://www.pnas.org/content/114/38/10166; Yaniv Erlich, Major Flaws in "Identification of Individuals by Trait Prediction Using Whole-Genome Sequencing Data" (bioRxiv, September 7, 2017), https://www.biorxiv.org/content/10.1101/185330v3; Donald Maye, "Corsight's Upcoming DNA to FACE: 'Terrifying' Warns Privacy Expert," IPVM, January 31, 2022, https://ipvm.com/reports/corsight-dna-face; Parabon Nanolabs, "Published Police Investigations," https://snapshot.parabon-nanolabs.com/posters#subject-identified.

90 **technique is controversial:** Ashley Southall, "Using DNA to Sketch What Victims Look Like; Some Call It Science Fiction," *New York Times*, October 19, 2017, https://www.nytimes.com/2017/10/19/nyregion/dna-phenotyping-new-york-police.html; Tate Ryan-Mosley, "This Company Says It's Developing a System That Can Recognize Your Face from Just Your DNA," *MIT Technology Review*, January 31, 2022, https://www.technologyreview.com/2022/01/31/1044576/corsight-face-recognition-from-dna/; Sense About Science, "Making Sense of Forensic

Genetics," January 25, 2017, https://senseaboutscience.org/activities/making-sense of foren
sic-genetics/.

90   **DNA derived from men in Xinjiang:** Wee and Mozur, "China Uses DNA to Map Faces."

90   **legal restraints:** "China: Police 'Big Data' Systems Violate Privacy, Target Dissent."

90   **Regional surveillance networks:** "'天网'网什么" ["Skynet" Nets What].

90   **Skynet is not always connected:** "'天网'网什么" ["Skynet" Nets What].

90   **Chinese police face the hurdles of incompatible databases:** "China: Police 'Big Data' Systems Violate Privacy, Target Dissent"; Maya Wang, "China's Bumbling Police State," *Wall
Street Journal*, December 26, 2018, https://www.wsj.com/articles/chinas-bumbling-police
-state-11545869066.

90   **facial recognition sunglasses that police have used:** Mozur, "Inside China's Dystopian
Dreams."

12. A BETTER WORLD

91   **Chinese surveillance industry continues to grow:** Lauly Li, Coco Liu, and Cheng Ting-
Fang, "China's 'Sharp Eyes' Offer Chance to Take Surveillance Industry Global," *Nikkei
Asia*, June 5, 2019, https://asia.nikkei.com/Business/China-tech/China-s-sharp-eyes-offer
-chance-to-take-surveillance-industry-global.

91   **Chinese firms participating in domestic surveillance:** Jeffrey Ding, "ChinAI Newsletter
#29: Complicit—China's AI Unicorns and the Securitization of Xinjiang," *ChinAI News-
letter*, September 23, 2018, https://chinai.substack.com/p/chinai-newsletter-29-complicit
-chinas-ai-unicorns-and-the-securitization-of-xinjiang.

91   **SenseTime and SenseNets:** After public reports about SenseNets working with Chinese
government authorities, **SenseNets** removed information from its website about cooperation with the police. (Li Tao, "SenseNets: the Facial Recognition Company That Supplies
China's Skynet Surveillance System," *South China Morning Post*, April 12, 2019, https://
www.scmp.com/tech/science-research/article/3005733/what-you-need-know-about
-sensenets-facial-recognition-firm.)

91   **denied their technology is used to profile or target groups:** In response to news investigations about Skynet and Sharp Eyes, a **SenseTime** representative told reporters its technology was not being used to profile. (Paul Mozur, "One Month, 500,000 Face Scans: How
China Is Using A.I. to Profile a Minority," *New York Times*, April 14, 2019, https://www
.nytimes.com/2019/04/14/technology/china-surveillance-artificial-intelligence-racial-profil-
ing.html.) In response to a *Washington Post* investigation about Huawei's links to Chinese
domestic surveillance programs, **Huawei** issued a statement: "'Huawei has no knowledge
of the projects mentioned in the Washington Post report. . . . Like all other major service
providers, Huawei provides cloud platform services that comply with common industry
standards.'" According to the *Washington Post*, "Huawei said in its statement that it did not
develop or sell systems that target any specific group of people and that it required all parts of
the business, as well as partners, to comply with applicable laws and business ethics. 'Privacy
protection is our top priority,' the company said." (Eva Dou, "Documents Link Huawei to
China's Surveillance Programs," *Washington Post*, December 14, 2021, https://www.washing-
tonpost.com/world/2021/12/14/huawei-surveillance-china/.) In response to news investigations about Skynet and Sharp Eyes, **Megvii** issued a statement that its technology was used for
"commercial not political solutions." Megvii also stated, "We are concerned about the well-
being and safety of individual citizens, not about monitoring groups." (Mozur, "One Month,
500,000 Face Scans: How China Is Using A.I. to Profile a Minority.")

91 **suppliers for Skynet or Sharp Eyes:** Li, Liu, and Ting-Fang, "China's 'Sharp Eyes' Offer Chance to Take Surveillance Industry Global."

91 **Algorithms from SenseTime and Yitu:** "Face Recognition Vendor Test (FRVT)," National Institute of Standards and Technology, updated November 30, 2020, https://www.nist.gov/programs-projects/face-recognition-vendor-test-frvt.

91 **Yitu took first place:** Patrick Grother et al., *The 2017 IARPA Face Recognition Prize Challenge (FRPC)* (National Institute of Standards and Technology, November 22, 2017), 2, https://nvlpubs.nist.gov/nistpubs/ir/2017/NIST.IR.8197.pdf.

92 **Proponents of Chinese tech companies:** Kai-Fu Lee, *AI Superpowers: China, Silicon Valley, and the New World Order* (Boston: Mariner Books, September 1, 2018), https://www.amazon.com/AI-Superpowers-China-Silicon-Valley/dp/132854639X.

93 **strength of China's technology sector:** "The Companies," *Macro Polo*, n.d., https://macropolo.org/digital-projects/chinai/the-companies/.

93 **China's AI "national team":** Jeffrey Ding, "ChinAI #51: China's AI 'National Team,'" *ChinAI Newsletter*, May 20, 2019, https://chinai.substack.com/p/chinai-51-chinas-ai-national-team.

93 **"China's Silicon Valley":** "China's Silicon Valley Is Transforming China, but Not Yet the World," *The Economist*, July 13, 2019, https://www.economist.com/china/2019/07/11/chinas-silicon-valley-is-transforming-china-but-not-yet-the-world; Meng Jing, "Zhongguancun: Beijing's Innovation Hub Is at the Centre of China's Aim to Become a Tech Powerhouse," *South China Morning Post*, November 13, 2018, https://www.scmp.com/tech/start-ups/article/2172713/zhongguancun-beijings-innovation-hub-centre-chinas-aim-become-tech; "Zhongguancun, China's Silicon Valley," China.org.cn, December 12, 2002, http://www.china.org.cn/english/travel/51023.htm.

93 **employees expected to work "996":** Lin Qiqing and Raymond Zhong, "'996' Is China's Version of Hustle Culture. Tech Workers Are Sick of It," *New York Times*, April 29, 2019, https://www.nytimes.com/2019/04/29/technology/china-996-jack-ma.html.

93 **iFLYTEK:** Ding, "ChinAI #51: China's AI 'National Team."

93 **sixth smartest company in the world:** SpaceX, in "What Are the 50 Smartest Companies?" *MIT Technology Review*, June 27, 2017, https://www.technologyreview.com/lists/companies/2017/intro/#spacex (page discontinued).

93 **twelve awards:** Zhu Lixin, "iFlytek Delivers on Promise to Become Major Player," Chinadaily.com.cn, updated February 19, 2019, https://www.chinadaily.com.cn/a/201902/19/WS5c6b5f9ba3106c65c34ea0c3.html; iFLYTEK, "iFLYTEK, Asia's AI Leader, Unveils iFLYTEK Translator 2.0, iFLYREC Series Voice-to-Text Products, AI Note and iFLYOS at CES 2019," news release, January 6, 2019, https://www.marketwatch.com/press-release/iflytek-asias-ai-leader-unveils-iflytek-translator-20-iflyrec-series-voice-to-text-products-ai-note-and-iflyos-at-ces-2019-2019-01-06 (page discontinued).

94 **50 percent of the company's $1 billion in annual revenue:** Lin Ji, interview by author, July 8, 2019.

94 **The "customer is like god":** Lin, interview.

94 **Independent investigations of iFLYTEK operations in Xinjiang:** Alexandra Harney, "Risky Partner: Top U.S. Universities Took Funds from Chinese Firm Tied to Xinjiang Security," Reuters, June 12, 2019, https://www.reuters.com/article/us-china-xinjiang-mit-tech-insight/risky-partner-top-u-s-universities-took-funds-from-chinese-firm-tied-to-xinjiang-security-idUSKCN1TE04M; Arvind Ganesan and Sophie Richardson, letter to Liu Qingfeng, August 2, 2017, https://www.hrw.org/sites/default/files/supporting_resources/201710asia_china_iflytek.pdf; "China: Voice Biometric Collection Threatens

Privacy," Human Rights Watch, October 22, 2017, https://www.hrw.org/news/2017/10/22/china-voice-biometric-collection-threatens-privacy.

95 **"inherently their technology is helpful for communication":** Lin, interview.

95 **iFLYTEK's marketing brochure:** iFLYTEK, "Make Everything Possible With A.I.," 2019, 44.

95 **battery of recent laws:** William Evanina, remarks to International Legal Technology Association LegalSEC Summit 2019, June 4, 2019, https://www.dni.gov/files/NCSC/documents/news/20190606-NCSC-Remarks-ILTA-Summit_2019.pdf.

95 **Data Security Law:** "数据安全法：护航数据安全 助力数字经济发展 [Data Security Law: escort data security, help the development of a digital economy]," The National People's Congress of the People's Republic of China, June 10, 2021, http://www.npc.gov.cn/npc/c30834/202106/b7b68bf8aca84f50a5bdef7f01acb6fe.shtml; Lester Ross, Kenneth Zhou, and Tingting Liu, "China Promulgates Data Security Law," WilmerHale, June 15, 2021, https://www.wilmerhale.com/en/insights/client-alerts/20210615-china-promulgates-data-security-law.

96 **"China's defense sector has been primarily dominated by sclerotic state-owned enterprises":** Elsa B. Kania and Lorand Laskai, *Myths and Realities of China's Military-Civil Fusion Strategy* (Center for a New American Security, January 28, 2021), https://www.cnas.org/publications/reports/myths-and-realities-of-chinas-military-civil-fusion-strategy.

13. PANOPTICON

97 **The regime slaughtered hundreds, perhaps thousands:** The death toll for the Tiananmen square massacre is highly disputed. "Tiananmen Square Protests," History.com, updated June 9, 2020, https://www.history.com/topics/china/tiananmen-square; "Tiananmen Square Protest Death Toll 'was 10,000,'" BBC News, December 23, 2017, https://www.bbc.com/news/world-asia-china-42465516; "Timeline: What Led to the Tiananmen Square Massacre," PBS *Frontline*, June 5, 2019, https://www.pbs.org/wgbh/frontline/article/timeline-tiananmen-square/. Thanks to CNAS research assistant Katie Galgano for background research.

97 **"like trying to nail Jell-O to the wall":** Bill Clinton, speech to the Paul H. Nitze School of Advanced International Studies, Johns Hopkins University, March 9, 2000, https://www.nytimes.com/2000/03/09/world/clinton-s-words-on-china-trade-is-the-smart-thing.html.

98 **prohibits sending payments in 6.4 or 64.89 yuan:** James Griffiths, "WeChat Users Unable to Transfer Money in Amounts Related to Tiananmen Crackdown Anniversary," *South China Morning Post*, June 4, 2015, https://www.scmp.com/tech/enterprises/article/1816267/wechat-users-unable-transfer-money-amounts-related-tiananmen.

98 **using too much toilet paper in public restrooms:** Josh Chin and Liza Lin, "China's All-Seeing Surveillance State Is Reading Its Citizens' Faces," *Wall Street Journal*, June 26, 2017, https://www.wsj.com/articles/the-all-seeing-surveillance-state-feared-in-the-west-is-a-reality-in-china-1498493020?mod=article_inline.

98 **"You can be solving problems":** Samantha Hoffman, interview by the author, September 15, 2020.

99 **Over 60,000 people are killed annually in China in traffic accidents:** Sarah O'Meara, "The Road to Reducing Traffic Accidents in China," *Science*, July 17, 2020, https://www.sciencemag.org/features/2020/07/road-reducing-traffic-accidents-china; Xue Wang et al., "Road Traffic Injuries in China from 2007 to 2016: the Epidemiological Characteristics,

Trends and Influencing Factors," *PeerJ* 7 (2019), e7423, https://www.ncbi.nlm.nih.gov/pmc/articles/PMC6688591/.

99 **pedestrians:** Lijun Wang et al., "Road Traffic Mortality in China: Analysis of National Surveillance Data from 2006 to 2016," *Lancet Public Health* 4, no. 5 (May 1, 2019): E245–E255, https://doi.org/10.1016/S2468-2667(19)30057-X.

99 **make control part of "everyday governance":** Hoffman, interview.

99 **Skyeye intelligent video surveillance system:** Lisbeth, "Company Touts AI-Powered Facial Recognition," *China Digital Times*, October 9, 2018, https://chinadigitaltimes.net/2018/10/company-touts-ai-powered-facial-recognition/.

99 **national "social credit system":** Kendra Schaefer et al., *Understanding China's Social Credit System* (Trivium China, September 23, 2019), http://socialcredit.triviumchina.com/wp-content/uploads/2019/09/Understanding-Chinas-Social-Credit-System-Trivium-China-20190923.pdf.

99 **"a tech-enhanced system":** Hoffman, interview.

99 **"trustworthiness":** Schaefer et al., *Understanding China's Social Credit System.*

99 **Cyberspace Administration of China:** "Component 3: Rewards and Punishments," in Schaefer et al., *Understanding China's Social Credit System.*

99 **points subtracted:** Schaefer et al., *Understanding China's Social Credit System*, 24–31.

99 **eating or playing loud music on the train:** "《北京市轨道交通乘客守则》今起实施 车厢内禁止进食 ["Beijing Rail Transit Passenger Code" will be implemented today, eating on carriages is banned]," people.com.cn, May 15, 2019, http://politics.people.com.cn/n1/2019/0515/c1001-31086953.html.

99 **running a red light:** "7月8日起 在南京一年闯红灯5次以上将记入个人信用记录 [From July 8th, running red lights more than 5 times a year in Nanjing will be recorded in personal credit records]," finance.sina.com.cn, July 7, 2019, https://finance.sina.com.cn/roll/2019-07-07/doc-ihytcitm0295272.shtml.

99 **restaurant reservations:** https://credit.suzhou.gov.cn/news/show/22296.html (page discontinued).

99 **leashing one's dog:** Schaefer et al., *Understanding China's Social Credit System*, 24.

99 **trash and recycling:** Echo Huang, "Garbage-Sorting Violators in China Now Risk Being Punished with a Junk Credit Rating," Quartz, January 8, 2018, https://qz.com/1173975/garbage-sorting-violators-in-china-risk-getting-a-junk-credit-rating/; "《上海市生活垃圾管理条例》全文公布 7月1日起施行 [The Full Text of "Regulations on the Management of Domestic Waste in Shanghai" was published and implemented on July 1st]," sina.com.cn, February 19, 2019, http://sh.sina.com.cn/news/zw/2019-02-19/detail-ihrfqzka7179229.shtml; 许梅 [Xu Mei], "新《杭州市生活垃圾管理条例》审批通过垃圾不分类乱丢乱扔将被罚款并计入信用档案 [The new "Regulations on the Management of Domestic Waste in Hangzhou" instructs that not separating trash will result in a fine and be included in credit files]," pazjw.gov.cn, August 1, 2019, http://www.pazjw.gov.cn/yaowen/201908/t20190801_10713181.shtml.

99 **jaywalking:** Schaefer et al., *Understanding China's Social Credit System*, 27.

99 **"It's about shaping and managing behaviors":** Hoffman, interview.

99 **air and rail tickets:** 刘园园 [Liu Yuanyuan], "2682万人次因失信被限制乘机 [26.82 Million Passengers Were Restricted from Flying Because of Dishonesty]," xinhuanet.com, July 17, 2019, http://www.xinhuanet.com/fortune/2019-07/17/c_1124761947.htm.

99 **renting a car:** Schaefer et al., *Understanding China's Social Credit System*, 44.

99 **loan or credit card:** Schaefer et al., *Understanding China's Social Credit System*, 36.

99 **private schools:** "Father with Low Credit Score Causes University to Suspend Son's

Admission Application," CGTN.com, July 13, 2018, https://news.cgtn.com/news/3d3d774
d79637a4e78457a6333566d54/share_p.html; "高院教委出手：限制失信被执行人子女就读
高收费民办学校 [Education Commission of the Higher People's Court: restrict the children of dishonest people from attending high-fee private schools]," sohu.com, August 9,
2018, https://www.sohu.com/a/246128308_305502 (page discontinued); 易水寒 [Yi Shui-
han], "河北衡水治理"老赖"出新招：限制其子女就读私立学校 [Hebei's Hengshui manages
"Lao Lai" with new measures: restricting their children from attending private schools],"
ieduchina.com, July 19, 2018, https://school.ieduchina.com/education/201807/34069.html.

99　**"luxury" spending:** "Component 2: The Blacklisting System," in Schaefer et al., *Understanding China's Social Credit System*.

99　**publicly shamed:** Stacey Vanek Smith, "What It's Like to Be on the Blacklist in China's
New Social Credit System," *All Things Considered*, October 31, 2018, https://www.npr
.org/2018/10/31/662696776/what-its-like-to-be-on-the-blacklist-in-chinas-new-social
-credit-system; Phoebe Zhang, "Chinese Court Names and Shames Debtors in Warm-up
to Avengers Movie," *South China Morning Post*, April 25, 2019, https://www.scmp.com/
news/china/society/article/3007617/chinese-district-court-shows-name-and-shame
-debtors-film-warm.

99　**Corporations can also be blacklisted:** Schaefer et al., *Understanding China's Social Credit
System*, 18.

100　**local governments and government officials:** Schaefer et al., *Understanding China's Social
Credit System*, 42.

100　**social credit system:** Samantha Hoffman, *Social Credit* (Australian Strategic Policy Institute, June 28, 2018), https://www.aspi.org.au/report/social-credit.

100　**Civil Aviation Administration of China:** American Citizens for Taiwan Contributor, "Chinese Government Demand Regarding Listing of Taiwan," *Medium*, May 6, 2018,
https://medium.com/american-citizens-for-taiwan/chinese-government-demand-regard-
ing-listing-of-taiwan-5541e3744013; "关于限期对官方网站整改的通知 [Concerning
the notice on time limits for rectification of official websites]," Washington Post, February 28, 2018, https://www.washingtonpost.com/r/2010-2019/WashingtonPost/2018/05/05/
Editorial-Opinion/Graphics/AirlineLetter.pdf?tid=a_mcntx.

100　**"make a record of your company's serious dishonesty":** American Citizens for Taiwan
Contributor, "Chinese Government Demand Regarding Listing of Taiwan."

100　**"Orwellian nonsense":** Josh Rogin, "Opinion: White House Calls China's Threats to Airlines
'Orwellian Nonsense,'" *Washington Post*, May 5, 2018, https://www.washingtonpost.com/
news/josh-rogin/wp/2018/05/05/white-house-calls-chinas-threats-to-airlines-orwellian
-nonsense/.

100　**airlines nevertheless changed their websites:** Erika Kinetz, "Airlines Obey Beijing's
Demand to Call Taiwan Part of China," Associated Press, May 22, 2018, https://apnews.com/
6f55419ce6a9449687b91f3fdfb3417d/Airlines-obey-Beijing's-demand-to-call-Taiwan-part
-of-China.

100　**dropping reference to "Taiwan":** Based on United, American, and Delta airlines' website
as of August 2021.

100　**thirty-nine international air carriers had complied:** Keoni Everington, "22 Airlines Correct Their Listings for Taiwan," *Taiwan News*, May 11, 2020, https://www.taiwannews.com
.tw/en/news/3931676; 郭建伸 [Guo Jianshen], "中國施壓航空公司矮化台灣 外交部：已有
22家正名 [China pressured airlines to suppress Taiwan, Ministry of Foreign Affairs: 22
have already been corrected]," cna.com.tw, May 9, 2020, https://www.cna.com.tw/news/
firstnews/202005090236.aspx.

100 **encourage certain behaviors:** Schaefer et al., *Understanding China's Social Credit System.*

100 **rewards:** Schaefer et al., *Understanding China's Social Credit System,* 32.

100 **hundreds of blacklists:** "Component 2: The Blacklisting System," in Schaefer et al., *Understanding China's Social Credit System.*

100 **banned from buying air tickets:** 刘 [Liu], "2682万人次因失信被限制乘机 [26.82 Million passengers were restricted from flying because of dishonesty]."

100 **"Everything is convenient for the trustworthy":** "Component 3: Rewards and Punishments," in Schaefer et al., *Understanding China's Social Credit System.*

101 **"the processes of integrating information":** Hoffman, interview.

101 **"totalizing control":** Paul Mozur 孟建国 (@PaulMozur), "China's police are hard at work building the largest domestic surveillance network the world has seen. . ." Twitter (thread), December 17, 2019, https://threadreaderapp.com/thread/1207151583626088448.html.

101 **400,000 people died building the wall:** "Great Wall of China," History.com, updated November 5, 2019, https://www.history.com/topics/ancient-china/great-wall-of-china.

102 **"Cyberspace, not so long ago, was a specific elsewhere":** William Gibson, "Google's Earth," *New York Times,* August 31, 2010, https://www.nytimes.com/2010/09/01/opinion/01gibson.html.

102 **"What the police are doing is putting in the ground floor":** Mozur 孟, "China's police are hard at work . . ."

102 **"as you build up large amounts of quality data":** Hoffman, interview.

103 **simply propping open the gates:** Simon Denyer, "Beijing Bets on Facial Recognition in a Big Drive for Total Surveillance," *Washington Post,* January 7, 2018, https://www.washingtonpost.com/news/world/wp/2018/01/07/feature/in-china-facial-recognition-is-sharp-end-of-a-drive-for-total-surveillance/.

103 **"building blocks that make technological systems of surveillance possible":** Maya Wang, interview by author, September 18, 2020.

104 **hoped the company would follow in the footsteps of U.S. firms:** Lin Ji, interview by author, July 8, 2019.

14. DYSTOPIA

105 **Zimbabwe:** Shan Jie, "China Exports Facial ID Technology to Zimbabwe," *Global Times,* April 12, 2018, http://www.globaltimes.cn/content/1097747.shtml.

105 **"spearhead our AI revolution in Zimbabwe":** Problem Masau, "Zimbabwe: Chinese Tech Revolution Comes to Zimbabwe," *Herald* (Zimbabwe), October 9, 2019, https://allafrica.com/stories/201910090185.html.

105 **let CloudWalk send data on millions of faces:** Amy Hawkins, "Beijing's Big Brother Tech Needs African Faces," *Foreign Policy,* July 24, 2018, https://foreignpolicy.com/2018/07/24/beijings-big-brother-tech-needs-african-faces/.

105 **"The differences between technologies tailored to an Asian face and those to an African face":** Masau, "Zimbabwe: Chinese Tech Revolution Comes to Zimbabwe."

105 **global proliferation of Chinese surveillance technology:** Adrian Shahbaz, *Freedom on the Net 2018* (Freedom House, 2019), https://freedomhouse.org/report/freedom-net/freedom-net-2018/rise-digital-authoritarianism (page discontinued).

105 **surveillance and policing technology is now in use in at least eighty countries:** Sheena Greitens, "'Surveillance with Chinese Characteristics': The Development & Global Export of Chinese Policing Technology" (paper presented at Princeton University's International

Relations Faculty Colloquium, Princeton, New Jersey, October 7, 2019), 2, http://ncgg
.princeton.edu/IR%20Colloquium/GreitensSept2019.pdf.

105 **"the autocrat's new toolkit":** Richard Fontaine and Kara Frederick, "The Autocrat's New
Tool Kit," *Wall Street Journal,* March 15, 2019, https://www.wsj.com/articles/the-autocrats
-new-tool-kit-11552662637.

106 **aggressively selling their surveillance technology:** Danielle Cave et al., *Mapping China's
Tech Giants* (Australian Strategic Policy Institute, April 18, 2019), https://www.aspi.org.au/
report/mapping-chinas-tech-giants.

106 **Yitu has sold facial recognition bodycams:** Li Tao, "Malaysian Police Wear Chinese Start-
up's AI Camera to Identify Suspected Criminals," *South China Morning Post,* April 20,
2018, https://www.scmp.com/tech/social-gadgets/article/2142497/malaysian-police-wear
-chinese-start-ups-ai-camera-identify.

106 **Ecuador:** Paul Mozur, Jonah M. Kessel, and Melissa Chan, "Made in China, Exported to
the World: The Surveillance State," *New York Times,* April 24, 2019, https://www.nytimes
.com/2019/04/24/technology/ecuador-surveillance-cameras-police-government.html.

106 **Venezuela:** Mozur, Kessel, and Chan, "Made in China, Exported to the World."

106 **Brazilian lawmakers:** Aiuri Rebello, "Bancada do PSL vai à China conhecer sistema que
reconhece rosto de cidadãos [PSL bench goes to China to discover a system that recognizes citizens' faces]," Folha de S.Paulo, January 16, 2019, https://www1.folha.uol.com.br/
mercado/2019/01/bancada-do-psl-vai-a-china-importar-sistema-que-reconhece-rosto-de
-cidadaos.shtml; PL 4612/2019, Câmara Dos Deputados (Brazilian legislative body), 2019,
https://www.camara.leg.br/proposicoesWeb/fichadetramitacao?idProposicao=2216455;
PL 5694/2019, Câmara Dos Deputados (Brazilian legislative body), 2019, https://www
.camara.leg.br/proposicoesWeb/fichadetramitacao?idProposicao=2227175.

106 **Brazil's Carnival festival:** Angelica Mari, "Brazilian Police Introduces Live Facial Recognition for Carnival," *ZDNet,* February 25, 2020, https://www.zdnet.com/article/brazilian
-police-introduces-live-facial-recognition-for-carnival/.

107 **São Paulo's police database:** Mari, "Brazilian Police Introduces Live Facial Recognition
for Carnival."

107 **Singapore:** Ty Joplin, "China's Newest Global Export? Policing Dissidents," *Albawaba,*
May 31, 2018, https://www.albawaba.com/news/china%E2%80%99s-newest-global-export
-policing-dissidents-1139230.

107 **"Lamppost-as-a-Platform":** Aradhana Aravindan and John Geddie, "Singapore to Test
Facial Recognition on Lampposts, Stoking Privacy Fears," Reuters, April 13, 2018, https://
www.reuters.com/article/us-singapore-surveillance/singapore-to-test-facial-recognition
-on-lampposts-stoking-privacy-fears-idUSKBN1HK0RV.

107 **"analyse crowd build-ups":** "Lamppost as a Platform," Govtech Singapore, n.d., https://
www.tech.gov.sg/scewc2019/laap.

107 **Angola:** "China-Designed Big Data System Aids Angola's Intelligent Governance,"
eurasiainfo.ch, August 23, 2018, https://www.eurasiainfo.ch/en/china-designed-big-data
-system-aids-angolas-intelligent-governance/.

107 **"more than 20 countries":** "Company Profile," Percent [website], n.d., https://en.percent
.cn/Company.

107 **Hikvision:** Joplin, "China's Newest Global Export?"; Farai Mudzingwa, "Government
Acknowledges Facial Recognition System In The Works," *Techzim,* June 13, 2018, https://
www.techzim.co.zw/2018/06/government-acknowledges-facial-recognition-system-in
-the-works/ (page discontinued), https://web.archive.org/web/20180615155528/https://

www.techzim.co.zw/2018/06/government-acknowledges-facial-recognition-system-in-the -works/.

107   **ZTE:** Angus Berwick, "How ZTE Helps Venezuela Create China-Style Social Control," Reuters, November 14, 2018, https://www.reuters.com/investigates/special-report/ venezuela-zte/.

107   **other countries using Chinese surveillance technology:** Mozur, Kessel, and Chan, "Made in China, Exported to the World."

107   **Global Spread of Chinese Public Surveillance Technology:** Greitens, " 'Surveillance with Chinese Characteristics,' " 40.

107   **Huawei:** Bruce Gilley, "Huawei's Fixed Line to Beijing," *Far Eastern Economic Review* (December 28, 2000–January 4, 2001), http://www.web.pdx.edu/~gilleyb/Huawei_ FEER28Dec2000.pdf; Sarah Dai, "China Adds Huawei, Hikvision to Expanded 'National Team' Spearheading Country's AI Efforts," *South China Morning Post*, August 30, 2019, https://www.scmp.com/tech/big-tech/article/3024966/china-adds-huawei-hikvision -expanded-national-team-spearheading.

107   **world's largest provider of telecom:** Brian Fung, "How China's Huawei Took the Lead over U.S. Companies in 5G Technology," *Washington Post*, April 10, 2019, https://www .washingtonpost.com/technology/2019/04/10/us-spat-with-huawei-explained/.

107   **"safe city" solutions:** Greitens, " 'Surveillance with Chinese Characteristics,' " 37.

107   **2,000 cameras to Nairobi:** "Video Surveillance as the Foundation of 'Safe City' in Kenya," Huawei, 2019, https://www.huawei.com/en/industry-insights/technology/digital-transfor- mation/video/video-surveillance-as-the-foundation-of-safe-city-in-kenya (page discon- tinued).

107   **surveillance system of 1,000 cameras:** "Chinese Facial Recognition Tech Installed in Nations Vulnerable to Abuse," CBS News, October 16, 2019, https://www.cbsnews.com/news/china -huawei-face-recognition-cameras-serbia-other-countries-questionable-human-rights -2019-10-16/; Dusan Stojanovic, "Chinese Snooping Tech Spreads to Nations Vulnerable to Abuse," Associated Press, October 17, 2019, https://apnews.com/9fd1c38594444d44ac fe25ef5f7d6ba0.

107   **"AI, cloud computing, big data, and IoT":** *Huawei Investment & Holding Co., Ltd. 2018 Annual Report* (Huawei, 2018), 30, https://www-file.huawei.com/-/media/corporate/pdf/ annual-report/annual_report2018_en_v2.pdf?la=zh.

107   **"Command, Control, Communication, Cloud, Intelligence, Surveillance, and Recon- naissance [C4ISR]" solutions:** *Huawei Investment & Holding Co., Ltd. 2017 Annual Report* (Huawei, 2017), 32, https://www.huawei.com/-/media/corporate/pdf/annual-report/ annual_report2017_en.pdf?la=en.

107   **"help governments reduce crime rates":** *Huawei Investment & Holding Co., Ltd. 2017 Annual Report*, 32.

107   **"All-Cloud smart Video Cloud Solution":** *Huawei Investment & Holding Co., Ltd. 2017 Annual Report*, 32.

107   **Huawei's video surveillance technology:** Stojanovic, "Chinese Snooping Tech Spreads to Nations Vulnerable to Abuse."

107   **safe city technology has been applied in "700 cities":** *Huawei Investment & Holding Co., Ltd. 2018 Annual Report*, 30; *Huawei Investment & Holding Co., Ltd. 2017 Annual Report*, 32; "Video Surveillance as the Foundation of 'Safe City' in Kenya."

108   **additional countries with Huawei safe city projects:** Stojanovic, "Chinese Snooping Tech Spreads to Nations Vulnerable to Abuse."

108 **over 1 billion people are served:** *Huawei Investment & Holding Co., Ltd. 2017 Annual Report*, 32.

108 **AI Global Surveillance Index:** Steven Feldstein, "The Global Expansion of AI Surveillance" (working paper, Carnegie Endowment for International Peace, 2019), 13, https:// carnegieendowment.org/files/WP-Feldstein-AISurveillance_final.pdf.

108 **Huawei is the leading vendor:** Feldstein, "The Global Expansion of AI Surveillance," 14.

108 **African Union's new headquarters building:** Huawei, "Statement on Huawei's Work With the African Union," 2021, https://www.huawei.com/us/facts/voices-of-huawei/statement -on-huaweis-work-with-the-african-union.

108 **financed by the Chinese government:** Karishma Vaswani, "Huawei: The Story of a Controversial Company," BBC News, March 6, 2019, https://www.bbc.co.uk/news/resources/ idt-sh/Huawei.

108 **data was being secretly transferred from the building:** Danielle Cave, "The African Union Headquarters Hack and Australia's 5G Network," *The Strategist*, July 13, 2018, https://www .aspistrategist.org.au/the-african-union-headquarters-hack-and-australias-5g-network/; Ghalia Kadiri and Joan Tilouine, "A Addis-Abeba, le siège de l'Union africaine espionné par Pékin [In Addis Ababa, the headquarters of the African Union spied on by Beijing]," *Le Monde*, January 26, 2018, https://www.lemonde.fr/afrique/article/2018/01/26/a-addis -abeba-le-siege-de-l-union-africaine-espionne-par-les-chinois_5247521_3212.html.

108 **hidden microphones under desks:** Aaron Maasho, "China Denies Report It Hacked African Union Headquarters," Reuters, January 29, 2018, https://www.reuters.com/article/us -africanunion-summit-china/china-denies-report-it-hacked-african-union-headquarters -idUSKBN1FI2I5; Kadiri and Tilouine, "A Addis-Abeba, le siège de l'Union africaine [In Addis Ababa, the headquarters of the African Union]."

108 **"Allegations about impropriety with our customer":** Huawei, "Statement on Huawei's Work With the African Union."

108 **governments of Uganda and Zambia:** Joe Parkinson, Nicholas Bariyo, and Josh Chin, "Huawei Technicians Helped African Governments Spy on Political Opponents," *Wall Street Journal*, August 15, 2019, https://www.wsj.com/articles/huawei-technicians-helped -african-governments-spy-on-political-opponents-11565793017.

108 **banned Huawei from their future 5G:** Catherine Shu, "Australia Bans Huawei and ZTE from Supplying Technology for Its 5G Network," *TechCrunch*, August 23, 2018, https:// techcrunch.com/2018/08/22/australia-bans-huawei-and-zte-from-supplying-technology -for-its-5g-network/.

108 **India:** Amy Kazmin and Stephanie Findlay, "India Moves to Cut Huawei Gear from Telecoms Network," *Financial Times*, August 24, 2020, https://www.ft.com/content/55642551 -f6e8-4f9d-b5ba-a12d2fc26ef9.

108 **Japan:** "Japan Sets Policy That Will Block Huawei and ZTE From Public Procurement as of April," *Japan Times*, December 10, 2018, https://www.japantimes.co.jp/news/2018/12/10/ business/japan-sets-policy-will-block-huawei-zte-public-procurement-april/#.XImX -RNKj6A.

108 **United Kingdom:** Michael R. Pompeo, Secretary of State, "Welcoming the United Kingdom Decision to Prohibit Huawei from 5G Networks," news release, July 14, 2020, https:// www.state.gov/welcoming-the-united-kingdom-decision-to-prohibit-huawei-from-5g -networks (page discontinued).

108 **China has held training sessions and seminars:** Shahbaz, *Freedom on the Net 2018*.

108 **two-week "Seminar on Cyberspace Management":** Andrew Chatzky and James McBride,

"China's Massive Belt and Road Initiative," Council on Foreign Relations, updated January 28, 2020, https://www.cfr.org/backgrounder/chinas-massive-belt-and-road-initiative.

109 **"socialist journalism with Chinese characteristics":** Shahbaz, *Freedom on the Net 2018.*

109 **Chinese media conferences:** Shahbaz, *Freedom on the Net 2018.*

109 **how to "guide public opinion":** He Huifeng, "In a Remote Corner of China, Beijing Is Trying to Export Its Model by Training Foreign Officials the Chinese Way," *South China Morning Post,* July 14, 2018, https://www.scmp.com/news/china/economy/article/2155203/remote-corner-china-beijing-trying-export-its-model-training.

109 **restrictive media and cybersecurity laws:** Shahbaz, *Freedom on the Net 2018.*

109 **officials attended Chinese seminars:** David Gilbert, "Zimbabwe Is Trying to Build a China Style Surveillance State," *Vice,* December 1, 2019, https://www.vice.com/en_us/article/59n753/zimbabwe-is-trying-to-build-a-china-style-surveillance-state.

109 **sweeping cybersecurity law:** Gilbert, "Zimbabwe Is Trying to Build a China Style Surveillance State"; Tawanda Karombo, "Zimbabwe Is Clamping Down on Social Media Use with a Cyber Crime Bill Set to Become Law," *Quartz Africa,* October 9, 2019, https://qz.com/africa/1724542/zimbabwe-bill-clamps-down-on-social-media-porn-with-china-tech/; "Zimbabwe's Cybersecurity and Data Protection Bill Entrenches Surveillance," Africa Freedom of Expression Exchange, May 19, 2020, https://www.africafex.org/digital-rights/cybersecurity-and-data-protection-bill-entrenches-surveillance.

109 **proliferation of Chinese-style state surveillance:** Sheena Chestnut Greitens, *Dealing with Demand for China's Global Surveillance Exports* (Brookings Institution, April 2020), https://www.brookings.edu/wp-content/uploads/2020/04/FP_20200428_china_surveillance_greitens_v3.pdf.

109 **view China's model of digital authoritarianism favorably:** Jessica Chen Weiss, "Understanding and Rolling Back Digital Authoritarianism," *War on the Rocks,* February 17, 2020, https://warontherocks.com/2020/02/understanding-and-rolling-back-digital-authoritarianism/.

109 **Carnegie's AI Global Surveillance Index:** Feldstein, "The Global Expansion of AI Surveillance," 10.

109 **London:** Paul Bischoff, "Surveillance Camera Statistics: Which Cities Have the Most CCTV Cameras?" Comparitech, updated May 17, 2021, https://www.comparitech.com/vpn-privacy/the-worlds-most-surveilled-cities/.

109 **U.S. firms:** Feldstein, "The Global Expansion of AI Surveillance," 9.

109 **loans to subsidize digital infrastructure projects:** Mozur, Kessel, and Chan, "Made in China, Exported to the World"; Cave et al., *Mapping China's Tech Giants.*

109 **Belt and Road Initiative:** Chatzky and McBride, "China's Massive Belt and Road Initiative."

110 **original Silk Road:** World History Encyclopedia, s.v. "Silk Road," May 1, 2018, https://www.ancient.eu/Silk_Road/.

110 **hundreds of billions of dollars in overseas construction and investment:** Cecilia Joy-Pérez and Derek Scissors, *The Chinese State Funds Belt and Road but Does Not Have Trillions to Spare* (American Enterprise Institute, March 2018), https://www.aei.org/wp-content/uploads/2018/03/BRI.pdf; Chatzky and McBride, "China's Massive Belt and Road Initiative."

110 **Digital Silk Road:** *The Digital Silk Road: Expanding China's Digital Footprint* (Eurasia Group, April 8, 2020), https://www.eurasiagroup.net/files/upload/Digital-Silk-Road-Expanding-China-Digital-Footprint-1.pdf.

110 **expanding China's political and economic influence:** Greitens, *Dealing with Demand for China's Global Surveillance Exports.*

110 **"a world safe for autocracy"**: Jessica Chen Weiss, "A World Safe for Autocracy?" *Foreign Affairs* (July/August 2019), 93, https://www.foreignaffairs.com/articles/china/2019-06-11/world-safe-autocracy.

110 **"China's actions abroad have"**: Chen Weiss, "A World Safe for Autocracy?" 93.

110 **"wave of autocratization"**: Anna Lührmann and Staffan I. Lindberg, "A Third Wave of Autocratization Is Here: What Is New About It?" *Democratization* 26, no. 7 (2019), https://doi.org/10.1080/13510347.2019.1582029.

110 **"democratic backsliding"**: Nancy Bermeo, "On Democratic Backsliding," *Journal of Democracy* 27, no. 1 (January 2016): 5–19, https://www.journalofdemocracy.org/articles/on-democratic-backsliding/.

110 **trends have been seen in countries**: Lührmann and Lindberg, "A Third Wave of Autocratization Is Here."

110 **rise of "digital dictators"**: Andrea Kendall-Taylor, Erica Frantz, and Joseph Wright, "The Digital Dictators: How Technology Strengthens Autocracy," *Foreign Affairs*, March/April 2020, https://www.foreignaffairs.com/articles/china/2020-02-06/digital-dictators.

110 **U.S. Customs and Border Patrol:** "Say Hello to the New Face of Speed, Security and Safety: Introducing Biometric Facial Comparison," U.S. Customs and Border Protection, n.d., https://www.cbp.gov/travel/biometrics; "Biometric Exit Frequently Asked Questions (FAQs)," U.S. Customs and Border Protection, updated May 15, 2020, https://www.cbp.gov/travel/biometrics/biometric-exit-faqs.

111 **facial recognition system at Dulles:** Lori Aratani, "Officials Unveil New Facial Recognition System at Dulles International Airport," *Washington Post*, September 7, 2018, https://www.washingtonpost.com/transportation/2018/09/06/officials-unveil-new-facial-recognition-system-dulles-international-airport/.

111 **grassroots backlash:** Brian Fung, "Tech Companies Push for Nationwide Facial Recognition Law. Now Comes the Hard Part," *Philadelphia Tribune*, June 15, 2020, https://www.phillytrib.com/news/business/tech-companies-push-for-nationwide-facial-recognition-law-now-comes-the-hard-part/article_fe78e04e-e8be-5aab-9402-00203a44510f.html.

111 **lawsuits against a slew of government agencies**: American Civil Liberties Union, "ACLU Challenges FBI Face Recognition Secrecy," news release, October 31, 2019, https://www.aclu.org/press-releases/aclu-challenges-fbi-face-recognition-secrecy; American Civil Liberties Union, "ACLU Challenges DHS Face Recognition Secrecy," news release, March 12, 2020, https://www.aclu.org/press-releases/aclu-challenges-dhs-face-recognition-secrecy.

111 **government regulation is needed:** Brad Smith, "Facial Recognition Technology: The Need for Public Regulation and Corporate Responsibility," *Microsoft on the Issues* (blog), July 13, 2018, https://blogs.microsoft.com/on-the-issues/2018/07/13/facial-recognition-technology-the-need-for-public-regulation-and-corporate-responsibility/; "We Are Implementing a One-Year Moratorium on Police Use of Rekognition," Amazon, June 10, 2020, https://blog.aboutamazon.com/policy/we-are-implementing-a-one-year-moratorium-on-police-use-of-rekognition; Jay Greene, "Microsoft Won't Sell Police Its Facial-Recognition Technology, Following Similar Moves by Amazon and IBM," *Washington Post*, June 11, 2020, https://www.washingtonpost.com/technology/2020/06/11/microsoft-facial-recognition/.

111 **regulation could "strangle business":** Forbes Technology Council, "15 Unexpected Consequences of GDPR," *Forbes*, August 15, 2018, https://www.forbes.com/sites/forbestechcouncil/2018/08/15/15-unexpected-consequences-of-gdpr/#68020b3c94ad.

112 **"race to the top":** Anu Bradford, *The Brussels Effect* (Columbia Law School, 2012), https://scholarship.law.columbia.edu/cgi/viewcontent.cgi?article=1275&context=faculty_scholarship; Anu Bradford, *The Brussels Effect: How the European Union Rules the World*

(Oxford Scholarship Online, 2020), https://oxford.universitypressscholarship.com/view/
10.1093/oso/9780190088583.001.0001/oso-9780190088583.

112 **AI regulations:** "A European Approach to Artificial Intelligence," European Commission, updated August 31, 2021, https://digital-strategy.ec.europa.eu/en/policies/european
-approach-artificial-intelligence; "Proposal for a Regulation of the European Parliament
and of the Council Laying Down Harmonised Rules on Artificial Intelligence (Artificial
Intelligence Act) and Amending Certain Union Legislative Acts," Document 52021PC0206
(European Union legislative document), 2021, https://eur-lex.europa.eu/legal-content/EN/
TXT/?qid=1623335154975&uri=CELEX%3A52021PC0206; "Coordinated Plan on Artificial Intelligence 2021 Review," European Commission, April 21, 2021, updated June 3, 2021,
https://digital-strategy.ec.europa.eu/en/library/coordinated-plan-artificial-intelligence
-2021-review; "Communication on Fostering a European Approach to Artificial Intelligence," European Commission, April 21, 2021, updated June 3, 2021, https://digital-strategy
.ec.europa.eu/en/library/communication-fostering-european-approach-artificial-intelli-
gence; Jola Dervishaj, "AI HLEG—Sectoral Considerations on Policy and Investment Recommendations for Trustworthy AI," European AI Alliance, July 23, 2020, https://futurium
.ec.europa.eu/en/european-ai-alliance/document/ai-hleg-sectoral-considerations-policy
-and-investment-recommendations-trustworthy-ai; "Assessment List for Trustworthy
Artificial Intelligence (ALTAI) for Self-Assessment," European Commission, July 17, 2020,
https://digital-strategy.ec.europa.eu/en/library/assessment-list-trustworthy-artificial
-intelligence-altai-self-assessment; "Report from the Commission to the European Parliament, the Council and the European Economic and Social Committee: Report on the Safety
and Liability Implications of Artificial Intelligence, the Internet of Things and Robotics,"
Document 52020DC0064 (European Union legislative document), February 2, 2020,
https://eur-lex.europa.eu/legal-content/en/TXT/?qid=1593079180383&uri=CELEX
%3A52020DC0064; *On Artificial Intelligence—A European Approach to Excellence and
Trust* (European Commission, February 19, 2020), https://ec.europa.eu/info/sites/default/
files/commission-white-paper-artificial-intelligence-feb2020_en.pdf; Jola Dervishaj, "Policy and Investment Recommendations for Trustworthy Artificial Intelligence," European
AI Alliance, June 26, 2019, https://futurium.ec.europa.eu/en/european-ai-alliance/open
-library/policy-and-investment-recommendations-trustworthy-artificial-intelligence; "Ethics Guidelines for Trustworthy AI," European Commission, April 8, 2019, updated March
8, 2021, https://digital-strategy.ec.europa.eu/en/library/ethics-guidelines-trustworthy-ai;
*Artificial Intelligence for Europe, Communication from the Commission to the European
Parliament, the European Council, the Council, the European Economic and Social Committee and the Committee of the Regions* (European Commission, April 25, 2018), https://
digital-strategy.ec.europa.eu/en/library/communication-artificial-intelligence-europe.
Thanks to CNAS research assistant Katie Galgano for background research on European
AI regulations.

15. DISINFORMATION

117 **8 million web pages totaling 40 gigabytes:** "Better Language Models and Their Implications," openai.com, n.d., https://openai.com/blog/better-language-models/
117 **"simply to predict the next word":** "Better Language Models."
117 **the kind of text that GPT-2 generates:** This text was generated via https://talktotrans-
former.com/ using the final 1.5 billion parameter GPT-2 model.
118 **bot-generated articles had been limited to reporting facts and figures:** Jaclyn Peiser,

"The Rise of the Robot Reporter," *New York Times*, February 5, 2019, https://www.nytimes .com/2019/02/05/business/media/artificial-intelligence-journalism-robots.html; Nicole Martin, "Did a Robot Write This? How AI Is Impacting Journalism," *Forbes*, February 8, 2019, https://www.forbes.com/sites/nicolemartin1/2019/02/08/did-a-robot-write-this -how-ai-is-impacting-journalism/#7cc457dd7795; Joe Keohane, "What News-Writing Bots Mean for the Future of Journalism," *Wired*, February 16, 2017, https://www.wired .com/2017/02/robots-wrote-this-story/.

119 **fake news at industrial scales:** Ben Buchanan et al., *Truth, Lies, and Automation: How Language Models Could Change Disinformation* (Center for Security and Emerging Technology, May 2021), https://cset.georgetown.edu/publication/truth-lies-and-automation/.

120 **malicious AI applications:** Miles Brundage et al., *The Malicious Use of Artificial Intelligence: Forecasting, Prevention, and Mitigation* (February 2018), https://maliciousaireport .com/.

120 **"fear-mongering":** Anima Kumar, "An Open and Shut Case on OpenAI," anima-ai.org, January 1, 2021, https://anima-ai.org/2019/02/18/an-open-and-shut-case-on-openai/.

120 **"The words 'too dangerous' were casually thrown out here":** James Vincent, "AI Researchers Debate the Ethics of Sharing Potentially Harmful Programs," *The Verge*, February 21, 2019, https://www.theverge.com/2019/2/21/18234500/ai-ethics-debate-researchers-harm- ful-programs-openai.

120 **technical breakthrough for which they hadn't yet seen the academic paper:** James Vincent, "OpenAI's New Multitalented AI Writes, Translates, and Slanders," *The Verge*, February 14, 2019, https://www.theverge.com/2019/2/14/18224704/ai-machine-learning -language-models-read-write-openai-gpt2; "Better Language Models and Their Implications," openai.com, n.d., https://openai.com/blog/better-language-models/; Alec Radford et al., *Language Models Are Unsupervised Multitask Learners* (openai.com, n.d.), https:// cdn.openai.com/better-language-models/language_models_are_unsupervised_multi- task_learners.pdf.

120 **"too dangerous" theme was echoed in other outlets:** Delip Rao, "When OpenAI Tried to Build More Than a Language Model," deliprao.com, February 19, 2019, http://deliprao .com/archives/314 (page discontinued); Alex Hern, "New AI Fake Text Generator May Be Too Dangerous to Release, Say Creators," *The Guardian*, February 14, 2019, https://www .theguardian.com/technology/2019/feb/14/elon-musk-backed-ai-writes-convincing-news -fiction; Aaron Mak, "When Is Technology Too Dangerous to Release to the Public?" *Slate*, February 22, 2019, https://slate.com/technology/2019/02/openai-gpt2-text-generating -algorithm-ai-dangerous.html; James Vincent, "OpenAI has Published the Text-Gener- ating AI It Said Was Too Dangerous to Share," *The Verge*, November 7, 2019, https://www .theverge.com/2019/11/7/20953040/openai-text-generation-ai-gpt-2-full-model-release-1 -5b-parameters.

120 **pre-briefing the press "got us some concerns that we were hyping it":** Jack Clark, interview by author, March 3, 2020.

120 **more careful about the phrasing around potential dangers:** "Better Language Models."

121 **realistic-looking fake videos:** Samantha Cole, "We Are Truly Fucked: Everyone Is Making AI-Generated Fake Porn Now," *Vice*, January 24, 2018, https://www.vice.com/en_us/article/ bjye8a/reddit-fake-porn-app-daisy-ridley.

121 **swap the faces of celebrities:** Samantha Cole, "AI-Assisted Fake Porn Is Here and We're All Fucked," *Vice*, December 11, 2017, https://www.vice.com/en_us/article/gydydm/gal-gadot -fake-ai-porn.

121 **14,000 deepfake porn videos online:** Henry Adjer et al., *The State of Deepfakes: Land-*

scape, Threats, and Impact (DeepTrace Labs, September 2019), 1, https://regmedia.co
.uk/2019/10/08/deepfake_report.pdf.

121　**The videos didn't only harm the celebrities:** Cole, "AI-Assisted Fake Porn Is Here."

121　**revenge porn attacks:** Kirsti Melville, "The Insidious Rise of Deepfake Porn Videos—
and One Woman Who Won't Be Silenced," abc.net.au, August 29, 2019, https://www.abc
.net.au/news/2019-08-30/deepfake-revenge-porn-noelle-martin-story-of-image-based
-abuse/11437774.

121　**"Deepfake technology is being weaponized against women":** Adjer et al., *The State of
Deepfakes*, 6.

121　**AI assistant called Duplex:** Jeff Grubb's Game Mess, "Google Duplex: A.I. Assistant Calls
Local Businesses to Make Appointments," YouTube, May 8, 2018, https://www.youtube
.com/watch?v=D5VN56jQMWM; Yaniv Leviathan and Yossi Matias, "Google Duplex: An
AI System for Accomplishing Real-World Tasks Over the Phone," *Google AI Blog*, May 8,
2018, https://ai.googleblog.com/2018/05/duplex-ai-system-for-natural-conversation.html.

121　**troubling ethical questions:** Natasha Lomas, "Duplex Shows Google Failing at Ethical
and Creative AI Design," *TechCrunch*, May 10, 2018, https://techcrunch.com/2018/05/10/
duplex-shows-google-failing-at-ethical-and-creative-ai-design/.

121　**"blade runner" law:** Tim Wu, "Please Prove You're Not a Robot," *New York Times*, July
15, 2017, https://www.nytimes.com/2017/07/15/opinion/sunday/please-prove-youre-not-a
-robot.html.

121　**their bot would identify itself as an automated service:** Kurt Wagner, "I Talked to Google's Duplex Voice Assistant. It Felt Like the Beginning of Something Big," *Vox*, June 27,
2018, https://www.vox.com/2018/6/27/17508166/google-duplex-assistant-demo-voice-call-
ing-ai.

122　**California passed the first "blade runner" law:** Bots: disclosure. SB 1001 (state of California legislative document), September 28, 2018, http://leginfo.legislature.ca.gov/faces/
billTextClient.xhtml?bill_id=201720180SB1001; Thomas Sprankling, "California Enacts
Nation's First Anti-Bot Law," WilmerHale, October 3, 2018, https://www.wilmerhale.com/
en/insights/client-alerts/20181003-california-enacts-nations-first-anti-bot-law.

122　**misuses of AI-generated audio and video:** Bobby Chesney and Danielle Citron, "Deep
Fakes: A Looming Challenge for Privacy, Democracy, and National Security," *California
Law Review* 107, no. 1753 (2019), https://doi.org/10.15779/Z38RV0D15J.

122　**"active measures":** Thomas Rid, *Active Measures: The Secret History of Disinformation
and Political Warfare* (New York: Farrar, Straus and Giroux, April 21, 2020), https://www
.amazon.com/Active-Measures-History-Disinformation-Political/dp/0374287260.

122　*dezinformatsiya:* Merriam-Webster, s.v. "disinformation," n.d., https://www.merriam
-webster.com/dictionary/disinformation; Aristedes Mahairas and Mikhail Dvilyanski,
"Disinformation – Дезинформация (Dezinformatsiya)," *Cyber Defense Review* 3, no. 3
(Fall 2018): 21–28, https://www.jstor.org/stable/26554993.

122　**bioengineered virus created by the U.S. military:** Adam Taylor, "Before 'Fake News,'
There Was Soviet 'Disinformation,'" *Washington Post*, November 26, 2016, https://www
.washingtonpost.com/news/worldviews/wp/2016/11/26/before-fake-news-there-was
-soviet-disinformation/.

122　**Russia used fake online personas:** *Extremist Content and Russian Disinformation Online:
Working with Tech to Find Solutions: Hearing of the Subcommittee on Crime and Terrorism,
Senate Committee on the Judiciary*, 115th Cong. (2017) (statement of Clint Watts, Robert
A. Fox fellow, Foreign Policy Research Institute), https://www.judiciary.senate.gov/imo/
media/doc/10-31-17%20Watts%20Testimony.pdf; *Extremist Content and Russian Disinfor-*

mation Online: Working with Tech to Find Solutions: Hearing of the Subcommittee on Crime and Terrorism, Senate Committee on the Judiciary, 115th Cong (2017) (replies of Clint Watts, Robert A. Fox fellow, Foreign Policy Research Institute, to questions by Sen. Dianne Feinstein), https://www.judiciary.senate.gov/imo/media/doc/Watts%20Responses%20 to%20QFRs.pdf; *Report of the Select Committee on Intelligence, United States Senate, on Russian Active Measures Campaigns and Interference, in the 2016 U.S. Election: Volume 2: Russia's Use of Social Media With Additional Views*, S. Report 116-XX (2019), https://www .intelligence.senate.gov/sites/default/files/documents/Report_Volume2.pdf.

122 **slew of influence operations across Europe to undermine democratic processes:** *Disinformation and 'Fake News': Final Report* (8th report of Session 2017–19, UK House of Commons Digital, Culture, Media and Sport Committee, February 18, 2019), https://publications.parliament.uk/pa/cm201719/cmselect/cmcumeds/1791/1791.pdf; *Russia*, Intelligence and Security Committee of Parliament, HC 632 (UK Parliament report) (July 21, 2020), https://int.nyt.com/data/documenttools/intelligence-and-security-committee-s -russia-report/9c665c08033cab70/full.pdf; United States of America v. Yuriy Sergeyevich Andrienko et al., Criminal No. 20-316 (indictment) (W.D. Pennsylvania, October 15, 2020), https://www.justice.gov/opa/press-release/file/1328521/download?source=email.

122 **Russia's "information warfare campaign":** *Report of the Select Committee on Intelligence, United States Senate, on Russian Active Measures Campaigns and Interference, in the 2016 U.S. Election.*

122 **designed to "sow fear, discord, and paralysis":** "The Scourge of Russian Disinformation," Commission on Security and Cooperation in Europe, September 14, 2017, https://www .csce.gov/international-impact/events/scourge-russian-disinformation.

122 **effects of disinformation campaigns were hard to measure:** Craig Timberg and Tony Romm, "Forget the Russians. On This Election Day, It's Americans Peddling Disinformation and Hate Speech," *Washington Post*, November 6, 2018, https://www.washingtonpost .com/technology/2018/11/06/forget-russians-this-election-day-its-americans-peddling -disinformation-hate-speech/.

122 **activities against U.S. politicians:** Karoun Demirjian, "Ryan, Rubio May Have Been Targets of Damaging Russian Social-Media Campaigns," *Washington Post*, March 30, 2017, https://www.washingtonpost.com/powerpost/ryan-rubio-may-have-been-targets -of-damaging-russian-social-media-campaigns/2017/03/30/bdf5f4fa-154f-11e7-ada0 -1489b735b3a3_story.html?itid=lk_inline_manual_2.

122 **China:** Jessica Brandt and Torrey Taussig, "The Kremlin's Disinformation Playbook Goes to Beijing," Brookings Institution, May 19, 2020, https://www.brookings.edu/blog/order -from-chaos/2020/05/19/the-kremlins-disinformation-playbook-goes-to-beijing/.

122 **Iran:** Jack Stubbs and Christopher Bing, "Special Report: How Iran Spreads Disinformation Around the World," Reuters, November 20, 2018, https://www.reuters.com/article/us -cyber-iran-specialreport/special-report-how-iran-spreads-disinformation-around-the -world-idUSKCN1NZ1FT.

123 **"the weird zone":** Clark, interview.

123 **"I don't think [OpenAI] spent enough time proving":** Vincent, "AI Researchers Debate the Ethics of Sharing Potentially Harmful Programs."

123 **"betraying its core mission":** Eric Amram (@amram), "@OpenAI you are betraying your core mission of openness, and you are betraying the people who helped you gather this dataset. What's really dangerous is the precedent you set of creating walled-gardens. Btw, the examples you published are far from perfect and won't fool humans," Twitter, February 16, 2019, https://twitter.com/amram/status/1096833932446683141.

123 **concerns about the misuse of research:** Rebecca Crootof, "Artificial Intelligence Research Needs Responsible Publication Norms," *Lawfare*, October 24, 2019, https://www.lawfareblog .com/artificial-intelligence-research-needs-responsible-publication-norms; "Better Language Models and Their Implications," openai.com, n.d., https://openai.com/blog/better -language-models/; *Biotechnology Research in an Age of Terrorism: Confronting the Dual Use Dilemma* (prepublication copy, National Academies Press, 2003), https://www.nap.edu/ resource/biotechnology_research/0309089778.pdf.

123 **censorship of two scientific articles under review in** *Nature* **and** *Science***:** Kenneth I. Berns et al, "Adaptations of Avian Flu Virus Are a Cause for Concern," *Nature* 482 (2012), 153–154, https://www.nature.com/articles/482153a; Paul S. Keim, "Q&A: Reasons for Proposed Redaction of Flu Paper," *Nature* 482 (2012), 156–157, https://www.nature.com/arti-cles/482156a.

123 **vigorous debate in the biosecurity community:** Heidi Ledford, "Call to Censor Flu Studies Draws Fire," *Nature* 481 (2012), 9–10, https://www.nature.com/news/call-to-censor -flu-studies-draws-fire-1.9729; Peter Palese, "Don't Censor Life-Saving Science," *Nature* 481 (2012), 115, https://www.nature.com/news/don-t-censor-life-saving-science-1.9777; "Should Mutant Flu Data Be Censored?" *Nature* (February 13, 2012), https://www.nature .com/news/should-mutant-flu-data-be-censored-1.10023; Brendan Maher, "Emotion Runs High at H5N1 Debate," *Nature News Blog*, February 3, 2012, http://blogs.nature.com/ news/2012/02/emotion-runs-high-at-h5n1-debate.html; Brian Vastag and David Brown, "Recommendation to Censor Bird Flu Research Driven by Fears of Terrorism," *Washington Post*, January 31, 2012, https://www.washingtonpost.com/national/health-science/fears -of-terrorism-drove-recommendation-to-censor-avian-influenza-research/2012/01/31/ gIQARFqweQ_story.html.

123 **"responsible disclosure":** "CISA Coordinated Vulnerability Disclosure (CVD) Process," Cybersecurity & Infrastructure Security Agency, n.d., https://www.cisa.gov/coordinated -vulnerability-disclosure-process.

123 **risks of misuse of their research:** Federico Pistono and Roman V. Yampolskiy, *Unethical Research: How to Create a Malevolent Artificial Intelligence* (arXiv.org, May 10, 2016), https://arxiv.org/pdf/1605.02817.pdf; Miles Brundage et al., *The Malicious Use of Artificial Intelligence: Forecasting, Prevention, and Mitigation* (arXiv.org, February 2018), https:// arxiv.org/pdf/1802.07228.pdf.

123 **"We wanted to make ourselves culpable":** Clark, interview.

123 **GPT-2 "spurred a much-needed interdisciplinary conversation":** Crootof, "Artificial Intelligence Research Needs Responsible Publication Norms."

124 **OpenAI didn't prevent GPT-2's release, only slowed it:** GPT-2 Interim Update, in "Better Language Models."

124 **"staged release" with incrementally larger and more advanced models:** "Better Language Models."

124 **774 million parameter model:** Jack Clark, Miles Brundage, and Irene Solaiman, "GPT-2: 6-Month Follow-Up," *OpenAI Blog*, August 20, 2019, https://openai.com/blog/gpt-2-6 -month-follow-up/.

124 **full 1.5 billion parameter model, only nine months after the initial release:** Irene Solaiman, Jack Clark, and Miles Brundage, "GPT-2: 1.5B Release," *OpenAI Blog*, November 5, 2019, https://openai.com/blog/gpt-2-1-5b-release/.

124 **cautiously explore the risks of misuse:** GPT-2 Interim Update, in "Better Language Models."

124 **five other research groups had replicated GPT-2:** Clark, Brundage, and Solaiman, "GPT-2: 6-Month Follow-Up."

124 **"difficult, but possible"**: Clark, Brundage, and Solaiman, "GPT-2: 6-Month Follow-Up."

124 **GPT-2 could be fine-tuned to produce white supremacist, jihadist Islamist, anarchist, or Marxist-Leninist propaganda:** Alex Newhouse, Jason Blazakis, and Kris McGuffie, *The Industrialization of Terrorist Propaganda: Neural Language Models and the Threat of Fake Content Generation* (Center on Terrorism, Extremism, and Counterterrorism, October 2019), https://www.middlebury.edu/institute/sites/www.middlebury.edu.institute/files/2019-11/The%20Industrialization%20of%20Terrorist%20Propaganda%20-%20CTEC.pdf?fv=TzdJnlDw.

124 **"pose a significant and novel threat to civil society"**: Newhouse, Blazakis, and McGuffie, *The Industrialization of Terrorist Propaganda*, 1.

124 **"as credible as an original human-written news article"**: Sarah E. Kreps, Miles McCain, and Miles Brundage, *All the News That's Fit to Fabricate: AI-Generated Text as a Tool of Media Misinformation* (SSRN, February 21, 2020), 2, https://dx.doi.org/10.2139/ssrn.3525002.

125 **willing to share GPT-2 generated articles:** Sarah Kreps and Miles McCain, "Not Your Father's Bots: AI Is Making Fake News Look Real," *Foreign Affairs*, August 2, 2019, https://www.foreignaffairs.com/articles/2019-08-02/not-your-fathers-bots.

125 **"Large-scale synthesized disinformation is now possible"**: Kreps and McCain, "Not Your Father's Bots."

125 **troll farms to spew propaganda:** Dave Lee, "The Tactics of a Russian Troll Farm," BBC News, February 16, 2018, https://www.bbc.com/news/technology-43093390; @DFRLab, "#TrollTracker: Twitter Troll Farm Archives (Part One)," *Medium*, October 16, 2018, https://medium.com/dfrlab/trolltracker-twitter-troll-farm-archives-8d5dd61c486b; @DFRLab, "#TrollTracker: Twitter Troll Farm Archives (Part Three)," Medium, October 17, 2018, https://medium.com/dfrlab/trolltracker-twitters-troll-farm-archives-17a6d5f13635; Freedom House, "New Report—Freedom on the Net 2017: Manipulating Social Media to Undermine Democracy," news release, November 13, 2017, https://freedomhouse.org/article/new-report-freedom-net-2017-manipulating-social-media-undermine-democracy; Amal Sinha (@amaleshwar), "Out of the 170k CCP accounts Twitter deleted, they published the data for 23.8k accounts. which I analyzed. . ." Twitter (thread), June 15, 2020, https://twitter.com/amaleshwar/status/1272413343328997380?s=11.

125 **China's "50 cent army":** Gary King, Jennifer Pan, and Margaret E. Roberts, *How the Chinese Government Fabricates Social Media Posts for Strategic Distraction, not Engaged Argument* (gking.harvard.edu, April 9, 2017), https://gking.harvard.edu/files/gking/files/50c.pdf?m=1463587807; Henry Farrell, "The Chinese Government Fakes Nearly 450 Million Social Media Comments a Year. This Is Why," *Washington Post*, May 19, 2016, https://www.washingtonpost.com/news/monkey-cage/wp/2016/05/19/the-chinese-government-fakes-nearly-450-million-social-media-comments-a-year-this-is-why/; Joyce Lau, "Who Are the Chinese Trolls of the '50 Cent Army'?" voanews.com, October 7, 2016, https://www.voanews.com/east-asia-pacific/who-are-chinese-trolls-50-cent-army (page discontinued).

125 **"It doesn't seem like we've crossed an effective economics curve yet":** Clark, interview.

125 **societal implications of their work:** Irene Solaiman et al., *Release Strategies and the Social Impacts of Language Models* (OpenAI, November 2019), https://arxiv.org/pdf/1908.09203.pdf.

125 **Meena, a chatbot based on a 2.6 billion parameter neural network:** Daniel Adiwardana and Thang Luong, "Towards a Conversational Agent That Can Chat About . . . Anything," Google AI Blog, Tuesday, January 28, 2020, https://ai.googleblog.com/2020/01/towards-conversational-agent-that-can.html; Daniel Adiwardana et al., *Towards a Human-Like*

Open-Domain Chatbot (arXiv.org, February 27, 2020), https://arxiv.org/pdf/2001.09977 .pdf.

125 **trillion-dollar company:** Paul R. La Monica, "Google Owner Alphabet Is Now Worth $1 Trillion," CNN Business, January 16, 2020, https://www.cnn.com/2020/01/16/investing/ google-trillion-dollar-market-value-apple-microsoft/index.html.

125 **Stable Diffusion:** Emad Mostaque, "Stable Diffusion Public Release," *Stability AI* blog, August 22, 2022, https://stability.ai/blog/stable-diffusion-public-release; Benj Edwards, "With Stable Diffusion, You May Never Believe What You See Online Again," *Ars Technica*, September 6, 2022, https://arstechnica.com/information-technology/2022/09/with-stable -diffusion-you-may-never-believe-what-you-see-online-again/3/.

16. SYNTHETIC REALITY

127 **an "auxuman," or auxillary human:** "Yona," bandcamp.com, n.d., https://theyona.band- camp.com/; Auxuman Inc. (website), 2021, https://auxuman.space/.

127 **realistic-looking AI-generated faces:** Thispersondoesnotexist.com (website), https:// thispersondoesnotexist.com/.

127 **generative adversarial networks (GANs), a machine learning method:** Ian J. Good- fellow et al., *Generative Adversarial Nets* (arXiv.org, June 10, 2014), https://arxiv.org/ pdf/1406.2661.pdf; Alec Radford, Luke Metz, and Soumith Chintala, *Unsupervised Rep- resentation Learning with Deep Convolutional Generative Adversarial Networks* (arXiv. org, January 7, 2016), https://arxiv.org/pdf/1511.06434.pdf; Ian Goodfellow, *NIPS 2016 Tutorial: Generative Adversarial Networks* (arXiv.org, April 3, 2017), https://arxiv.org/ pdf/1701.00160.pdf.

127 **models are trained together and learn from each other:** Jason Brownlee, "A Gentle Intro- duction to Generative Adversarial Networks (GANs)," *Machine Learning Mastery*, June 17, 2019, https://machinelearningmastery.com/what-are-generative-adversarial-networks -gans/.

127 **2019 conference:** "RENDER: The future will be synthesized," Twitter (event), June 3, 2019, https://twitter.com/i/events/1135556793986363392.

128 **"a real optimist about technology":** Danika Laszuk, interview by author, September 18, 2019.

128 **synthetic reality:** Danika Laszuk, "Is This the Real Life?" *Render*, November 29, 2018, https://render.betaworks.com/is-this-the-real-life-1fce0a452faa.

128 **AI-generated voice to impersonate the CEO:** Catherine Stupp, "Fraudsters Used AI to Mimic CEO's Voice in Unusual Cybercrime Case," *Wall Street Journal*, August 30, 2019, https://www.wsj.com/articles/fraudsters-use-ai-to-mimic-ceos-voice-in-unusual-cyber- crime-case-11567157402.

128 **2020 U.S. presidential election:** Gary Grossman, "Deepfakes May Not Have Upended the 2020 U.S. Election, but Their Day Is Coming," *VentureBeat*, November 1, 2020, https:// venturebeat.com/2020/11/01/deepfakes-may-not-have-upended-the-2020-u-s-election -but-their-day-is-coming/; Tom Simonite, "What Happened to the Deepfake Threat to the Election?" *Wired*, November 16, 2020, https://www.wired.com/story/what-happened -deepfake-threat-election/.

128 **disinformation campaigns online:** *The National Security Challenge of Artificial Intelli- gence, Manipulated Media, and 'Deep Fakes,'* House Permanent Select Committee on Intel- ligence, 116th Cong. (2019) (statement by Danielle Citron, University of Maryland Carey School of Law), https://www.congress.gov/116/meeting/house/109620/witnesses/HHRG

-116-IG00-Wstate-CitronD-20190613.pdf; *National Security Challenges of Artificial Intelligence, Manipulated Media, and 'Deepfakes,' Hearing of the House Intelligence Committee,* 116th Cong. (June 13, 2019), https://www.congress.gov/event/116th-congress/house -event/109620.

128 **Manipulated media:** Nadine Ajaka, Elyse Samuels, and Glenn Kessler, "Seeing Isn't Believing: The Fact Checker's Guide to Manipulated Video," *Washington Post,* n.d., https://www .washingtonpost.com/graphics/2019/politics/fact-checker/manipulated-video-guide/.

128 **Nancy Pelosi:** Sarah Mervosh, "Distorted Videos of Nancy Pelosi Spread on Facebook and Twitter, Helped by Trump," *New York Times,* May 24, 2019, https://www.nytimes .com/2019/05/24/us/politics/pelosi-doctored-video.html.

128 **Jim Acosta:** Drew Harwell, "White House Shares Doctored Video to Support Punishment of Journalist Jim Acosta," *Washington Post,* November 8, 2018, https://www.washington-post.com/technology/2018/11/08/white-house-shares-doctored-video-support-punish-ment-journalist-jim-acosta/.

129 **Kremlin peddled a steady stream of disinformation:** Stuart A. Thompson, "4 False-hoods Russians Are Told About the War," *New York Times,* March 10, 2022, https:// www.nytimes.com/2022/03/10/technology/disinformation-russia-ukraine.html; Edward Wong, "U.S. Fights Bioweapons Disinformation Pushed by Russia and China," *New York Times,* March 10, 2022, https://www.nytimes.com/2022/03/10/us/politics/russia-ukraine -china-bioweapons.html; "Russia's Top Five Persistent Disinformation Narratives," U.S. Department of State Office of the Spokesperson, press release, January 20, 2022, https:// www.state.gov/russias-top-five-persistent-disinformation-narratives/.

129 **heroic tales of brave resistance:** Elisabeth Braw, "Virality Isn't Victory for Ukraine," *Foreign Policy,* March 8, 2022, https://foreignpolicy.com/2022/03/08/ukraine-propaganda -war/; Davey Alba and Stuart A. Thompson, "Fact and Mythmaking Blend in Ukraine's Information War," *New York Times,* March 3, 2022, https://www.nytimes.com/2022/03/03/ technology/ukraine-war-misinfo.html.

129 **"Ghost of Kyiv":** Ines Eisele, "Fact Check: Ukraine's 'Ghost of Kyiv' Fighter Pilot," DW News, March 1, 2022, https://www.dw.com/en/fact-check-ukraines-ghost-of-kyiv-fighter -pilot/a-60951825; Dan Evon, "Is This 'Ghost of Kyiv' Video Real?," Snopes, February 25, 2022, https://www.snopes.com/fact-check/is-this-ghost-of-kyiv-video-real/; Jared Keller, "'The Ghost of Kyiv' is the First Urban Legend of Russia's Invasion of Ukraine," *Task & Purpose,* February 25, 2022, https://taskandpurpose.com/analysis/ghost-kyiv/; Командування Повітряних Сил ЗСУ / Air Force Command of UA Armed Forces, "The Ghost of Kiev is a superhero legend whose figure was created by Ukrainians! . . ." Facebook, April 30, 2022, https://www.facebook.com/kpszsu/posts/363834939117794.

129 **deepfake of Ukrainian president Volodymyr Zelensky:** Operational Reports, "This morning, polite hackers hacked into several Ukrainian sites and posted there a deep-fake with Zelensky calling for laying down arms.," Telegram (public post), March 16, 2022, https://t.me/opersvodki/1788; Mikael Thalen, "A deepfake of Ukrainian President Volodymyr Zelensky calling on his soldier to lay down their weapons was reportedly uploaded to a hacked Ukrainian news site," Twitter, March 16, 2022, https://twitter.com/ MikaelThalen/status/1504123674516885507; Samantha Cole, "Hacked News Channel and Deepfake of Zelenskyy Surrendering Is Causing Chaos Online," *VICE News,* March 16, 2022, https://www.vice.com/en/article/93bmda/hacked-news-channel-and-deepfake -of-zelenskyy-surrendering-is-causing-chaos-online; Tom Simonite, "A Zelensky Deep-fake Was Quickly Defeated. The Next One Might Not Be," *Wired,* March 17, 2022, https:// www.wired.com/story/zelensky-deepfake-facebook-twitter-playbook/; Digital Forensic

Research Lab, "Russian War Report: Hacked news program and deepfake video spread false Zelenskyy claims," *New Atlanticist* (blog) on Atlantic Council, March 16, 2022, https://www.atlanticcouncil.org/blogs/new-atlanticist/russian-war-report-hacked-news -program-and-deepfake-video-spread-false-zelenskyy-claims/#deepfake;   Nathaniel Gleicher, "1/ Earlier today, our teams identified and removed a deepfake video claiming to show President Zelensky issuing a statement he never did.," Twitter (thread), March 16, 2022, https://twitter.com/ngleicher/status/1504186935291506693.

130 **the "liar's dividend":** Bobby Chesney and Danielle Citron, "Deep Fakes: A Looming Challenge for Privacy, Democracy, and National Security," *California Law Review* 107, no. 1753 (2019), https://doi.org/10.15779/Z38RV0D15J.

130 **"post-truth" information landscape:** "Word of the Year 2016," *OxfordLanguages*, 2016, https://languages.oup.com/word-of-the-year/2016/.

130 **"the internet is a vast wormhole of darkness":** Drew Harwell, "Fake-Porn Videos Are Being Weaponized to Harass and Humiliate Women: 'Everybody Is a Potential Target,'" *Washington Post*, December 30, 2018, https://www.washingtonpost.com/technology/2018/12/30/fake-porn -videos-are-being-weaponized-harass-humiliate-women-everybody-is-a-potential-target/.

130 **Sensity (formerly Deeptrace):** Giorgio Patrini, LinkedIn profile, https://nl.linkedin.com/ in/giorgiopatrini.

130 **"visual threat intelligence company":** Sensity (website), 2021, https://sensity.ai/about/.

130 **Steve Buscemi's face swapped onto Jennifer Lawrence's body:** The Curious Ape, "Jennifer Lawrence as STEVE BUSCEMI at The Golden Globes DEEPFAKE," YouTube, February 6, 2019, https://www.youtube.com/watch?v=m8-kQUE1QYE.

131 **"lip-sync" an audio clip:** K. R. Prajwal et al., *A Lip Sync Expert Is All You Need for Speech to Lip Generation In The Wild* (arXiv.org, August 23, 2020), https://arxiv.org/pdf/2008.10010 .pdf; Prajwal Renukanand et al., "A Lip Sync Expert Is All You Need for Speech to Lip Generation in the Wild," CVIT, n.d., http://cvit.iiit.ac.in/research/projects/cvit-projects/a-lip -sync-expert-is-all-you-need-for-speech-to-lip-generation-in-the-wild/; Chintan Trivedi, "DeepFakes AI—Improved Lip Sync Animations With Wav2Lip," *Medium*, August 31, 2020, https://medium.com/deepgamingai/deepfakes-ai-improved-lip-sync-animations -with-wav2lip-b5d4f590dcf; Tristan Greene, "Watch: This AI Mashup of Movie Characters Singing 'All Star' Is the Best DeepFake Ever," Next Web, September 8, 2020, https:// thenextweb.com/neural/2020/09/08/watch-this-ai-mashup-of-movie-characters-singing -all-star-is-the-best-deepfake-ever/.

131 **artificial still images of people that don't exist:** ThisPersonDoesNotExist.com.

131 **unnatural eye movement:** Alison Grace Johansen, "How to Spot Deepfake Videos—15 Signs to Watch For," Norton, August 13, 2020, https://us.norton.com/internetsecurity -emerging-threats-how-to-spot-deepfakes.html; "Detect DeepFakes: How to counteract misinformation created by AI," MIT Media Lab, April 2020, https://www.media.mit.edu/ projects/detect-fakes/overview/

131 **glitches in the hair, eyes, earrings:** Kyle McDonald, "How to Recognize Fake AI-Generated Images," *Medium*, December 5, 2018, https://kcimc.medium.com/how-to-recognize -fake-ai-generated-images-4d1f6f9a2842; Jeff Heaton, "How to Spot a Fake Face Generated by a GAN," YouTube, January 28, 2020, https://www.youtube.com/watch?v=RQeD0o- qjRLw.

131 **persona was likely a state-run intelligence operation:** Raphael Satter, "Experts: Spy Used AI-Generated Face to Connect with Targets," Associated Press, June 13, 2019, https:// apnews.com/article/bc2f19097a4c4fffaa00de6770b8a60d.

131 **tool of hostile foreign intelligence:** "The China Threat: Foreign Intelligence Services Use

Social Media Sites to Target People with Security Clearances," Federal Bureau of Investigation, n.d., https://www.fbi.gov/investigate/counterintelligence/the-china-threat/clearance-holders-targeted-on-social-media-nevernight-connection; National Counterintelligence and Security Center, "FBI and NCSC Release New Movie to Increase Awareness of Foreign Intelligence Threats on Professional Networking Sites and Other Social Media Platforms," news release, September 29, 2020, https://www.dni.gov/index.php/ncsc-newsroom/item/2145-nevernight-press-release; Jeff Stone, "LinkedIn Is Becoming China's Go-To Platform for Recruiting Foreign Spies," *CyberScoop*, March 26, 2019, https://www.cyberscoop.com/linkedin-china-spies-kevin-mallory-ron-hansen/.

131 **former CIA officer who was sentenced:** U.S. Department of Justice, "Former CIA Officer Sentenced to Prison for Espionage," news release, May 17, 2019, https://www.justice.gov/opa/pr/former-cia-officer-sentenced-prison-espionage.

131 **recruited on LinkedIn:** Ken Dilanian, "How a $230,000 Debt and a LinkedIn Message Led an Ex-CIA Officer to Spy for China," NBC News, April 4, 2019, https://www.nbcnews.com/politics/national-security/how-230-000-debt-linkedin-message-led-ex-cia-officer-n990691.

131 **fake persona of "Martin Aspen":** Ben Collins and Brandy Zadrozny, "How a Fake Persona Laid the Groundwork for a Hunter Biden Conspiracy Deluge," NBC News, October 29, 2020, https://www.nbcnews.com/tech/security/how-fake-persona-laid-groundwork-hunter-biden-conspiracy-deluge-n1245387.

131 **willing to make "bespoke faceswap videos for $30":** Henry Adjer et al., *The State of Deepfakes: Landscape, Threats, and Impact* (DeepTrace Labs, September 2019), 5, https://regmedia.co.uk/2019/10/08/deepfake_report.pdf.

131 **public awareness campaign tied to the 2020 U.S. presidential election:** RepresentUs, "Dictators—Kim Jong-Un," YouTube, September 29, 2020, https://www.youtube.com/watch?v=ERQlaJ_czHU; RepresentUs, "Dictators—Vladimir Putin," YouTube, September 29, 2020, https://www.youtube.com/watch?v=sbFHhpYU15w.

132 **actors with similar body types:** Jeremy Kahn, "These Deepfake Videos of Putin and Kim Have Gone Viral," *Fortune*, October 2, 2020, https://fortune.com/2020/10/02/deepfakes-putin-kim-jong-un-democracy-disinformation/.

132 **Microsoft:** Tom Burt and Eric Horvitz, "New Steps to Combat Disinformation," *Microsoft on the Issues* (blog), September 1, 2020, https://blogs.microsoft.com/on-the-issues/2020/09/01/disinformation-deepfakes-newsguard-video-authenticator/.

132 **Quantum Integrity:** Quantum+Integrity (website), n.d., https://quantumintegrity.ch/.

132 **Sentinel:** Sentinel (website), 2021, https://thesentinel.ai/.

132 **"in the future . . . the set of things that we will be checking":** Giorgio Patrini, interview by the author, July 17, 2019.

132 **working to combat deepfakes:** Burt and Horvitz, "New Steps to Combat Disinformation."

132 **Facebook partnered with Amazon, Microsoft, and the Partnership on AI:** "Deepfake Detection Challenge," Kaggle.com, 2020, https://www.kaggle.com/c/deepfake-detection-challenge/.

132 **Facebook created a dataset of over 100,000 new videos:** "Deepfake Detection Challenge Dataset," Facebook AI, June 25, 2020, https://ai.facebook.com/datasets/dfdc/.

132 **Google has also created datasets:** Daisy Stanton, "Advancing Research on Fake Audio Detection," *Google Blog*, January 31, 2019, https://www.blog.google/outreach-initiatives/google-news-initiative/advancing-research-fake-audio-detection/; Nick Dufour and Andrew Gully, "Contributing Data to Deepfake Detection Research," *Google AI Blog*, September 24, 2019, https://ai.googleblog.com/2019/09/contributing-data-to-deepfake-detection.html.

133 **over 2,000 participants who submitted more than 35,000 trained models:** Cristian Canton Ferrer et al., "Deepfake Detection Challenge Results: An Open Initiative to Advance AI," Facebook AI, June 12, 2020, https://ai.facebook.com/blog/deepfake-detection-challenge-results-an-open-initiative-to-advance-ai.

133 **top-performing detector was accurate only 65 percent of the time:** Canton Ferrer et al., "Deepfake Detection Challenge Results: An Open Initiative to Advance AI."

133 **"due to the way lenses are made":** Patrini, interview.

134 **public service announcement videos:** Ehr for Congress, "#DeepFake," YouTube, October 1, 2020, https://www.youtube.com/watch?v=Y6HKo-IAltA.

134 **"the fear that sometimes the media is communicating":** Patrini, interview.

134 **coup to oust the president:** Stephanie Busari, Bianca Britton, and Bukola Adebayo, "2 Soldiers Killed and 8 Arrested After Failed Coup Attempt in Gabon, Government Says," CNN, January 8, 2019, https://www.cnn.com/2019/01/08/africa/gabonese-soldiers-killed -over-coup-intl/index.html.

134 **video is likely real:** Sarah Cahlan, "How Misinformation Helped Spark an Attempted Coup in Gabon," *Washington Post*, February 13, 2020, https://www.washingtonpost.com/ politics/2020/02/13/how-sick-president-suspect-video-helped-sparked-an-attempted -coup-gabon/.

134 **visibly weakened from the stroke:** AFP News Agency, "Gabon's Bongo in First Live Public Appearance Since Stroke," YouTube, August 16, 2019, https://www.youtube.com/ watch?v=VaUUAXatflE.

134 **"We don't even need to wait anymore for these technologies to be weaponized":** Patrini, interview.

17. TRANSFORMATION

135 **"digitally swapping out your vocal cords":** Mike Pappas, interview by author, February 10, 2020.

136 **"more start-ups than anywhere":** CIC (website), 2021, https://cic.com/

136 **2.7 billion video gamers worldwide:** Dean Takahashi, "Newzoo: 2.7 Billion Gamers Will Spend $159.3 Billion on Games in 2020," VentureBeat, May 8, 2020, https://venturebeat .com/2020/05/08/newzoo-2-7-billion-gamers-will-spend-159-3-billion-on-games-in -2020/

136 **$20 billion:** Pappas, interview.

136 **"You feel authentically more like that character":** Pappas, interview.

136 **impersonate children online:** Nellie Bowles and Michael H. Keller, "Video Games and Online Chats Are 'Hunting Grounds' for Sexual Predators," *New York Times*, December 7, 2019, https://www.nytimes.com/interactive/2019/12/07/us/video-games-child-sex-abuse .html.

136 **synthetic media companies "committed to ethical, responsible and equitable advances":** Aithos Coalition (website), 2019, https://www.aithos.technology/

136 **legal right to use any voice:** "Ethics," Modulate, n.d., https://www.modulate.ai/ethics

137 **"Maybe there's certain things that I do around the emotion and inflection":** Pappas, interview.

138 **Dollar bills have subtle security features physically embedded:** [Page displaying security features of $100 bill], U.S. Currency Education Program, n.d., https://www.uscurrency .gov/denominations/100.

138 **technical methods to prove the authenticity:** Robert Chesney and Danielle Citron, "Deep-

fakes and the New Disinformation War," *Foreign Affairs*, January/February 2019, https://www.foreignaffairs.com/articles/world/2018-12-11/deepfakes-and-new-disinformation-war.

138 **Microsoft:** Tom Burt and Eric Horvitz, "New Steps to Combat Disinformation," *Microsoft on the Issues* (blog), September 1, 2020, https://blogs.microsoft.com/on-the-issues/2020/09/01/disinformation-deepfakes-newsguard-video-authenticator/.

138 **Serelay:** Serelay (website), 2021, https://www.serelay.com/.

138 **Truepic:** Truepic (website), 2021, https://truepic.com/.

138 **Project Origin:** "Trusted News Initiative (TNI) Steps Up Global Fight Against Disinformation with New Focus on US Presidential Election," BBC Media Centre, July 13, 2020, https://www.bbc.co.uk/mediacentre/latestnews/2020/trusted-news-initiative; Burt and Horvitz, "New Steps to Combat Disinformation."

138 **Trusted News Initiative:** Trusted News Initiative (TNI) Steps Up Global Fight Against Disinformation."

139 **strip off the watermarking:** Benj Edwards, "With Stable Diffusion, You May Never Believe What You See Online Again," *Ars Technica*, September 6, 2022, https://arstechnica.com/information-technology/2022/09/with-stable-diffusion-you-may-never-believe-what-you-see-online-again/3/.

139 **"radioactive data" that leaves a faint trace:** "Using 'Radioactive Data' to Detect If a Dataset Was Used for Training," Facebook AI, February 5, 2020, https://ai.facebook.com/blog/using-radioactive-data-to-detect-if-a-data-set-was-used-for-training/; Alexandre Sablayrolles et al., *Radioactive Data: Tracing Through Training* (arXiv.org, February 3, 2020), https://arxiv.org/pdf/2002.00937.pdf.

139 **effective even if less than 1 percent:** "Using 'Radioactive Data' "; *Radioactive Data: Tracing Through Training.*

139 **easy detection of synthetic media:** Tim Hwang, *Deepfakes: A Grounded Threat Assessment* (Center for Security and Emerging Technology, July 2020), 26–27, https://cset.georgetown.edu/research/deepfakes-a-grounded-threat-assessment/.

139 **Widespread marking of publicly available datasets:** Hwang, *Deepfakes: A Grounded Threat Assessment*, 27.

139 **GPT-3:** Tom B. Brown et al., *Language Models are Few-Shot Learners* (Cornell University, July 22, 2020), https://arxiv.org/abs/2005.14165.

139 **"AI-generated content will continue to become more sophisticated":** Renée DiResta, "The Supply of Disinformation Will Soon Be Infinite," *The Atlantic*, September 20, 2020, https://www.theatlantic.com/ideas/archive/2020/09/future-propaganda-will-be-computer-generated/616400/.

140 **Facebook:** Monika Bickert, "Enforcing Against Manipulated Media," Facebook, news release, January 6, 2020, https://about.fb.com/news/2020/01/enforcing-against-manipulated-media/.

140 **Reddit:** u/LastBluejay, "Updates to Our Policy Around Impersonation," r/redditsecurity, Reddit, January 9, 2020, https://www.reddit.com/r/redditsecurity/comments/emd7yx/updates_to_our_policy_around_impersonation/.

140 **Twitter:** Yoel Roth and Ashita Achuthan, "Building Rules in Public: Our Approach to Synthetic & Manipulated Media," *Twitter Blog*, February 4, 2020, https://blog.twitter.com/en_us/topics/company/2020/new-approach-to-synthetic-and-manipulated-media.html; "Synthetic and manipulated media policy," Twitter Help Center, n.d., https://help.twitter.com/en/rules-and-policies/manipulated-media.

140 **YouTube:** Leslie Miller, "How YouTube Supports Elections," *YouTube Official Blog*, February 3, 2020, https://blog.youtube/news-and-events/how-youtube-supports-elections.

140 **Chinese regulators have moved fastest:** Vittoria Elliott and Meaghan Tobin, "China Steps

Up Efforts to Ban Deepfakes. Will It Work?", Rest of World, January 10, 2022, https://
restofworld.org/2022/china-steps-up-efforts-to-ban-deepfakes/; "互联网信息服务算法推
荐管理规定 [Provisions on the Management of Algorithm Recommendations in Internet Information Services]," Cyberspace Administration of China, January 4, 2022, http://
www.cac.gov.cn/2022-01/04/c_1642894606364259.htm; English translation here: "Provisions on the Management of Algorithmic Recommendations in Internet Information
Services," China Law Translate, January 4, 2022, https://www.chinalawtranslate.com/en/
algorithms/; "关于印发《网络音视频信息服务管理规定》的通知 [Notice on Printing and
Distributing the "Provisions on the Management of Online Audio and Video Information Services"]," National Radio and Television Administration, November 29, 2019, http://
www.nrta.gov.cn/art/2019/11/29/art_113_48908.html; English translation here: "Provisions on the Administration of Network Audio and Video Information Services," China
Law Translate, November 29, 2019, https://www.chinalawtranslate.com/provisions-on-the
-management-of-online-a-v-information-services/#mh-comments.

140 **proposed European AI Act:** "Proposal for a Regulation of the European Parliament and
of the Council Laying Down Harmonised Rules on Artificial Intelligence (Artificial Intelligence Act) and Amending Certain Union Legislative Acts," Document 52021PC0206
(European Union legislative document), 2021, https://eur-lex.europa.eu/legal-content/EN/
TXT/?qid=1623335154975&uri=CELEX%3A52021PC0206.

140 **several government studies of deepfakes:** Scott Briscoe, "U.S. Laws Address Deepfakes", *Security Management,* January 12, 2021, https://www.asisonline.org/security
-management-magazine/latest-news/today-in-security/2021/january/U-S-Laws-Address
-Deepfakes/; Jason Chipman, Matthew Ferraro, and Stephen Preston, "First Federal Legislation on Deepfakes Signed Into Law," *JD Supra,* December 24, 2019, https://www.jdsupra
.com/legalnews/first-federal-legislation-on-deepfakes-42346/.

18. BOT WARS

141 **information ecosystem that is already supercharged with bots:** Renee Diresta, "Free
Speech Is Not the Same As Free Reach," *Wired,* August 30, 2018, https://www.wired.com/
story/free-speech-is-not-the-same-as-free-reach/.

141 **bots have played a role in amplifying:** Chengcheng Shao et al., "The Spread of Low-Credi-
bility Content by Social Bots," *Nature Communications* 9 (2018), https://www.nature.com/
articles/s41467-018-06930-7.

141 **"we all have trust in Mohammed Bin Salman":** Chris Bell and Alistair Coleman,
"Khashoggi: Bots Feed Saudi Support After Disappearance," BBC News, October 18, 2018,
https://www.bbc.com/news/blogs-trending-45901584; *Case Studies—Collated—NOV
2019.docx* (ox.ac.uk, November 2019), 89–91, https://comprop.oii.ox.ac.uk/wp-content/
uploads/sites/93/2019/09/Case-Studies-Collated-NOV-2019-1.pdf.

141 **list of top trending hashtags in Saudi Arabia:** Bel Trew, "Bee Stung: Was Jamal Khashoggi
the First Casualty in a Saudi Cyberwar?" *The Independent,* October 20, 2018, https://www
.independent.co.uk/news/world/middle-east/jamal-khashoggi-saudi-arabia-cyberwar
-trolls-bee-army-missing-journalist-turkey-us-a8591051.html.

141 **broader disinformation effort by Saudi Arabia:** Jack Stubbs, Katie Paul, and Tuqa Kha-
lid, "Fake News Network vs. Bots: The Online War Around Khashoggi Killing," Reuters,
November 1, 2018, https://uk.reuters.com/article/uk-saudi-khashoggi-disinformation
-idUKKCN1N63R0.

141 **common tool by political actors:** Marc Jones and Alexei Abrahams, "A Plague of Twitter

Bots Is Roiling the Middle East," *Washington Post*, June 5, 2018, https://www.washington-post.com/news/monkey-cage/wp/2018/06/05/fighting-the-weaponization-of-social-media -in-the-middle-east/.

141 **fifty countries around the world:** Samantha Bradshaw and Philip N. Howard, "The Global Disinformation Order: 2019 Global Inventory of Organised Social Media Manipulation" (working paper, Project on Computational Propaganda, University of Oxford, Oxford, UK, 2019), 1, 11–12, https://comprop.oii.ox.ac.uk/wp-content/uploads/ sites/93/2019/09/CyberTroop-Report19.pdf.

141 **in the United States:** Bradshaw and Howard, "The Global Disinformation Order," 10–12; *Case Studies—Collated—NOV 2019.docx*, 123–126.

142 **"the adoption of techniques to influence political opinion online":** *Case Studies— Collated—NOV 2019.docx*, 123.

142 **astroturfing, a manipulative social media practice:** *Case Studies—Collated—NOV 2019. docx*, 123–126.

142 **twenty-six authoritarian regimes:** Bradshaw and Howard, "The Global Disinformation Order," i, 2, 5.

142 **half of Twitter accounts in Saudi Arabia:** Marc Owen Jones, "Automated Sectarianism and Pro-Saudi Propaganda on Twitter," *Exposing the Invisible*, January 18, 2017, https:// exposingtheinvisible.org/en/articles/automated-sectarianism/.

142 **China, India, Iran:** Bradshaw and Howard, "The Global Disinformation Order," 2, 5.

142 **Twitter removed a pro-government bot network:** Ben Collins and Shoshana Wodinsky, "Twitter Pulls Down Bot Network That Pushed Pro-Saudi Talking Points About Disap-peared Journalist," NBC News, October 18, 2018, https://www.nbcnews.com/tech/tech -news/exclusive-twitter-pulls-down-bot-network-pushing-pro-saudi-talking-n921871.

142 **another 88,000 Saudi spam bots:** Twitter Safety, "New Disclosures to Our Archive of State-Backed Information Operations," *Twitter Blog*, December 20, 2019, https://blog .twitter.com/en_us/topics/company/2019/new-disclosures-to-our-archive-of-state-backed -information-operations.html.

142 **"spammy network" used by China's Communist Party:** Twitter Safety, "Information Operations Directed at Hong Kong," *Twitter Blog*, August 19, 2019, https://blog.twitter .com/en_us/topics/company/2019/information_operations_directed_at_Hong_Kong .html.

142 **150,000 "amplifier accounts" used in CCP influence operations:** Twitter Safety, "Dis-closing Networks of State-Linked Information Operations We've Removed," *Twitter Blog*, June 12, 2020, https://blog.twitter.com/en_us/topics/company/2020/information-opera-tions-june-2020.html.

142 **prohibits spammy or manipulative behavior:** Yoel Roth and Nick Pickles, "Bot or Not? The Facts About Platform Manipulation on Twitter," May 18, 2020, https://blog.twitter .com/en_us/topics/company/2020/bot-or-not.html; "Automation Rules," Twitter Help Center, updated November 3, 2017, https://help.twitter.com/en/rules-and-policies/ twitter-automation.

142 **Positive uses of bots:** Rajat Sharma, "25 Best Twitter Bots You Should Follow," *Beebom*, January 6, 2020, https://beebom.com/best-twitter-bots/; Leanne Tan, "8 Ways Twitter Bots Are Actu-ally Useful," *Hongkiat*, April 14, 2021, https://www.hongkiat.com/blog/using-twitter-bots/.

142 **accounts linked to influence operations from both state and non-state groups:** "Coor-dinated Inauthentic Behavior," about.fb.com, 2021, https://about.fb.com/news/tag/ coordinated-inauthentic-behavior/; "Information Operations," Twitter Transparency, 2021, https://transparency.twitter.com/en/reports/information-operations.html.

142 **4.1 billion users worldwide:** Simon Kemp, "Social Media Users Pass the 4 Billion Mark as Global Adoption Soars," We are Social, October 20, 2020, https://wearesocial.com/blog/2020/10/social-media-users-pass-the-4-billion-mark-as-global-adoption-soars.

143 **2.7 billion active users:** Facebook, "Facebook Reports Third Quarter 2020 Results," news release, October 29, 2020, https://investor.fb.com/investor-news/press-release-details/2020/Facebook-Reports-Third-Quarter-2020-Results/default.aspx.

143 **half of American households:** Edwin Diamond, "Anchor Wars: Dan Rather, Peter Jennings and Tom Brokaw," *Rolling Stone*, October 9, 1986, https://www.rollingstone.com/tv/tv-news/anchor-wars-dan-rather-peter-jennings-and-tom-brokaw-104856/.

143 **George Floyd:** Darnella Frazier, "They killed him right in front of cup foods . . ." Facebook (story), May 26, 2020, https://m.facebook.com/story.php?story_fbid=1425401580994277&id=100005733452916.

143 **#BlackLivesMatter:** Aleem Maqbool, "Black Lives Matter: From Social Media Post to Global Movement," BBC News, July 10, 2020, https://www.bbc.com/news/world-us-canada-53273381.

143 **dangerous conspiracy theories:** Kevin Roose, "What Is QAnon, the Viral Pro-Trump Conspiracy Theory?" *New York Times*, September 3, 2021, https://www.nytimes.com/article/what-is-qanon.html; Jana Winter, "Exclusive: FBI Document Warns Conspiracy Theories Are a New Domestic Terrorism Threat," Yahoo!, August 1, 2019, https://www.yahoo.com/now/fbi-documents-conspiracy-theories-terrorism-160000507.html.

143 **TikTok:** Jay Greene, "TikTok Sale Deadline Will Pass, Though Regulators Will Hold Off on Enforcing Divestiture," *Washington Post*, December 4, 2020, https://www.washingtonpost.com/technology/2020/12/04/tiktok-sale-deadline/.

143 **largest social media platforms are controlled by a handful of companies:** Wikipedia, s.v. "List of social platforms with at least 100 million active users," updated September 17, 2021, https://en.wikipedia.org/wiki/List_of_social_platforms_with_at_least_100_million_active_users.

143 **over half of adults get their news from Facebook:** Elisa Shearer and Elizabeth Grieco, *Americans Are Wary of the Role Social Media Sites Play in Delivering the News* (Pew Research Center, October 2, 2019), https://www.journalism.org/2019/10/02/americans-are-wary-of-the-role-social-media-sites-play-in-delivering-the-news/.

144 **500 million tweets per day:** "Twitter Usage Statistics," Internet Live Stats, n.d., https://www.internetlivestats.com/twitter-statistics/.

144 **Facebook clocks four billion video views:** "Facebook Video Statistics", 99Firms, https://99firms.com/blog/facebook-video-statistics/.

144 **over a billion hours of video every day, and over 500 hours of new content:** "YouTube for Press," *YouTube Official Blog*, n.d., https://blog.youtube/press/.

144 **Twitter employs a "ranking algorithm":** "About Your Home Timeline on Twitter," Twitter Help Center, n.d., https://help.twitter.com/en/using-twitter/twitter-timeline; @mjahr, "Never Miss Important Tweets from People You Follow," *Twitter Blog*, February 10, 2016, https://blog.twitter.com/official/en_us/a/2016/never-miss-important-tweets-from-people-you-follow.html; Nicolas Koumchatzky and Anton Andryeyev, "Using Deep Learning at Scale in Twitter's Timelines," *Twitter Blog*, May 9, 2017, https://blog.twitter.com/engineering/en_us/topics/insights/2017/using-deep-learning-at-scale-in-twitters-timelines.html; Nicholas Léonard and Cibele Montez Halasz, "Twitter Meets TensorFlow," *Twitter Blog*, June 14, 2018, https://blog.twitter.com/engineering/en_us/topics/insights/2018/twittertensorflow.html; Twitter Cortex (website), n.d., https://cortex.twitter.com/.

144 **Facebook's News Feed algorithm:** "How News Feed Works," Facebook Help Center, 2021, https://www.facebook.com/help/1155510281178725.

144 **boost their content's visibility:** Katie Sehl, "How the Twitter Algorithm Works in 2020 and How to Make It Work for You," *Hootsuite Blog*, May 20, 2020, https://blog.hootsuite .com/twitter-algorithm/; Paige Cooper, "How Does the YouTube Algorithm Work in 2021? The Complete Guide," *Hootsuite Blog*, June 21, 2021, https://blog.hootsuite.com/how -the-youtube-algorithm-works/; Paige Cooper, "How the Facebook Algorithm Works in 2021 and How to Make It Work for You," *Hootsuite Blog*, February 10, 2021, https://blog .hootsuite.com/facebook-algorithm/.

144 **more sophisticated algorithm:** Eric Meyerson, "YouTube Now: Why We Focus on Watch Time," *YouTube Official Blog*, August 10, 2012, https://blog.youtube/news-and-events/ youtube-now-why-we-focus-on-watch-time.

144 **deep learning to improve their algorithms:** Koumchatzky and Andryeyev, "Using Deep Learning at Scale in Twitter's Timelines."

144 **9.3 million problematic videos:** "YouTube Community Guidelines Enforcement," Google Transparency Report, June 2021, https://transparencyreport.google.com/youtube-policy/ removals.

145 **algorithm for recommending videos to watch next:** Paul Lewis, "'Fiction Is Outper-forming Reality': How YouTube's Algorithm Distorts Truth," *The Guardian*, February 2, 2018, https://www.theguardian.com/technology/2018/feb/02/how-youtubes-algorithm -distorts-truth; Zeynep Tufekci, "YouTube, the Great Radicalizer," *New York Times*, March 10, 2018, https://www.nytimes.com/2018/03/10/opinion/sunday/youtube-politics-radical .html; Sam Levin, "Las Vegas Survivors Furious as YouTube Promotes Clips Calling Shoot-ing a Hoax," *The Guardian*, October 4, 2017, https://www.theguardian.com/us-news/2017/ oct/04/las-vegas-shooting-youtube-hoax-conspiracy-theories; Clive Thompson, "You-Tube's Plot to Silence Conspiracy Theories," *Wired*, September 18, 2020, https://www.wired .com/story/youtube-algorithm-silence-conspiracy-theories/.

145 **over 70 percent of viewing hours are driven by the algorithm:** Joan E. Solsman, "You-Tube's AI Is the Puppet Master over Most of What You Watch," *CNET*, January 10, 2018, https://www.cnet.com/news/youtube-ces-2018-neal-mohan/.

145 **"one of the largest-scale and most sophisticated industrial recommendation systems":** Paul Covington, Jay Adams, and Emre Sargin, *Deep Neural Networks for YouTube Recom-mendations* (Google, 2016), https://research.google.com/pubs/archive/45530.pdf.

145 **even a former Google engineer:** Lewis, "'Fiction Is Outperforming Reality'"; Guillaume Chaslot, "The Toxic Potential of YouTube's Feedback Loop," *Wired*, July 13, 2019, https:// www.wired.com/story/the-toxic-potential-of-youtubes-feedback-loop/.

145 **more extreme and incendiary content:** Lewis, "'Fiction Is Outperforming Real-ity'"; Tufekci, "YouTube, the Great Radicalizer"; Nicas, "How YouTube Drives Peo-ple to the Internet's Darkest Corners," *Wall Street Journal*, February 7, 2018, https:// www.wsj.com/articles/how-youtube-drives-viewers-to-the-internets-darkest-corners -1518020478.

145 **"rabbit hole" of conspiracy theories:** Kevin Roose, "The Making of a YouTube Radi-cal," *New York Times*, June 8, 2019, https://www.nytimes.com/interactive/2019/06/08/ technology/youtube-radical.html; Tufekci, "YouTube, the Great Radicalizer"; Max Fisher and Amanda Taub, "How YouTube Radicalized Brazil," *New York Times*, August 11, 2019, https://www.nytimes.com/2019/08/11/world/americas/youtube-brazil.html; Thompson, "YouTube's Plot to Silence Conspiracy Theories."

145 **responding to increased viewer engagement:** Chaslot, "The Toxic Potential of YouTube's Feedback Loop."

145 **denied that a "rabbit hole" effect exists:** Kevin Roose, "YouTube's Product Chief on

Online Radicalization and Algorithmic Rabbit Holes," *New York Times*, March 29, 2019, https://www.nytimes.com/2019/03/29/technology/youtube-online-extremism.html.

145 **opacity of machine learning algorithms:** Chico Q. Camargo, "We Don't Understand How YouTube's Algorithm Works—and That's a Problem," *Fast Company*, January 24, 2020, https://www.fastcompany.com/90454610/we-dont-understand-how-youtubes-algorithm -works-and-thats-a-problem.

145 **reduce recommendations of "borderline" content:** "Continuing Our Work to Improve Recommendations on YouTube," *YouTube Official Blog*, January 25, 2019, https://blog .youtube/news-and-events/continuing-our-work-to-improve; "The Four Rs of Responsi- bility, Part 2: Raising Authoritative Content and Reducing Borderline Content and Harm- ful Misinformation," *YouTube Official Blog*, December 3, 2019, https://youtube.googleblog .com/2019/12/the-four-rs-of-responsibility-raise-and-reduce.html.

145 **70 percent drop in watch time for borderline content:** "The Four Rs of Responsibility, Part 2."

145 **flat earth videos:** Thompson, "YouTube's Plot to Silence Conspiracy Theories."

145 **promoting "meaningful interactions":** Mark Zuckerberg, "One of our big focus areas for 2018 is making sure the time we all spend on Facebook is time well spent . . ." Facebook, January 11, 2018, https://www.facebook.com/zuck/posts/10104413015393571?pnref=story.

145 **posts that "spark conversations":** Adam Mosseri, "Bringing People Closer Together," about.fb.com, January 11, 2018, https://about.fb.com/news/2018/01/news-feed-fyi-bring- ing-people-closer-together/.

145 **new algorithm "pushed up articles on divisive topics":** Laura Hazard Owen, "One Year In, Facebook's Big Algorithm Change Has Spurred an Angry, Fox News-Dominated— and Very Engaged!—News Feed," NiemanLab, March 15, 2019, https://www.niemanlab .org/2019/03/one-year-in-facebooks-big-algorithm-change-has-spurred-an-angry-fox -news-dominated-and-very-engaged-news-feed/.

145 **attracted to novelty:** Soroush Vosoughi, Deb Roy, and Sinan Aral, "The Spread of True and False News Online," *Science* 359, no. 6380 (March 9, 2018): 1146–1151, https://doi.org/10 .1126/science.aap9559.

145 **more impacted by negative information:** Roy F. Baumeister et al., "Bad Is Stronger Than Good," *Review of General Psychology* 5, no 4 (2001), 323–370, http://assets.csom.umn.edu/ assets/71516.pdf

146 **fake news traveled six times faster:** Vosoughi, Roy, and Aral, "The Spread of True and False News Online."

146 **news that inspires fear:** Tufekci, "YouTube, the Great Radicalizer."

146 **disincentivizing "creating provocative content":** Zuckerberg, "A Blueprint for Content Governance."

146 **prohibit manipulative behavior and certain categories of content:** "Objectionable Con- tent," Facebook Community Standards, n.d., https://www.facebook.com/communitystan- dards/objectionable_content; "The Twitter Rules," Twitter Help Center, n.d., https://help .twitter.com/en/rules-and-policies/twitter-rules; "Community Guidelines," Youtube, n.d., https://www.youtube.com/howyoutubeworks/policies/community-guidelines/.

146 **the information seen by more than 4 billion people:** Kemp, "Social Media Users Pass the 4 Billion Mark."

146 **censored social media platforms:** Lotus Ruan et al., "One App, Two Systems," The Citizen Lab, University of Toronto, November 30, 2016, https://citizenlab.ca/2016/11/wechat-china -censorship-one-app-two-systems/.

146 **Tencent's WeChat:** Monthly active users as of 30 September 2020. Tencent, "Tencent

Announces 2020 Third Quarter Results," news release, Hong Kong, November 12, 2020, https://static.www.tencent.com/uploads/2020/11/12/4c2090d5f6f00fd90ddc9bbd9a1415d1.pdf.

146 **2.3 million active users in the United States:** Jeanne Whalen, "Chinese Censorship Invades the U.S. via WeChat," *Washington Post,* January 7, 2021, https://www.washington-post.com/technology/2021/01/07/wechat-censorship-china-us-ban/.

146 **TikTok:** Yingzhi Yang, "Tik Tok Hits 500 Million Global Monthly Active Users as China Social Media Video Craze Continues," *South China Morning Post,* July 17, 2018, https://www.scmp.com/tech/article/2155580/tik-tok-hits-500-million-global-monthly-active-users-china-social-media-video; Sarah Perez, "TikTok Surpassed Facebook, Instagram, Snapchat & YouTube in Downloads Last Month," *TechCrunch,* November 2, 2018, https://techcrunch.com/2018/11/02/tiktok-surpassed-facebook-instagram-snapchat-youtube-in-downloads-last-month/.

146 **India, the United States, Indonesia, Russia, Japan, and Europe:** Debra Aho Williamson, "TikTok Users Around the World 2020," eMarketer, December 14, 2020, https://www.emarketer.com/content/tiktok-users-around-world-2020.

146 **nearly 700 million users globally:** Alex Sherman, "TikTok Reveals Detailed User Numbers for the First Time," CNBC, August 24, 2020, https://www.cnbc.com/2020/08/24/tiktok-reveals-us-global-user-growth-numbers-for-first-time.html.

147 **Douyin:** Yingzhi Yang and Brenda Goh, "ByteDance's Chinese Version of TikTok Hits 600 Million Daily Users," Reuters, September 15, 2020, https://www.reuters.com/article/us-china-bytedance/bytedances-chinese-version-of-tiktok-hits-600-million-daily-users-idUSKBN2660P4.

147 **national security risks of a Chinese-owned social media app:** Tom Cotton, Senator for Arkansas, "Cotton, Schumer Request Assessment of National Security Risks Posed by China-Owned Video-Sharing Platform, TikTok, a Potential Counterintelligence Threat with Over 110 Million Downloads in U.S., Alone," news release, October 24, 2019, https://www.cotton.senate.gov/news/press-releases/cotton-schumer-request-assessment-of-national-security-risks-posed-by-china-owned-video-sharing-platform-tiktok-a-potential-counterintelligence-threat-with-over-110-million-downloads-in-us-alone.

147 **India banned TikTok:** "Government Bans 59 Mobile Apps Which Are Prejudicial to Sovereignty and Integrity of India, Defence of India, Security of State and Public Order," Ministry of Electronics & IT, Government of India, June 29, 2020, https://pib.gov.in/PressReleseDetailm.aspx?PRID=1635206.

147 **Indian government issued additional bans:** Surabhi Sabat, "Full List Of 224 Chinese Apps Banned in India Till Date; Including PUBG, TikTok and Shein," Republicworld.com, September 2, 2020, https://www.republicworld.com/technology-news/apps/how-many-chinese-apps-banned-in-india-till-now-see-the-full-list.html; Pankaj Doval, "TikTok, WeChat, Baidu and UC Browser Among 59 Chinese Apps Permanently Banned in India," *Times of India,* January 26, 2021, https://timesofindia.indiatimes.com/business/india-business/tiktok-wechat-baidu-and-uc-browser-among-59-chinese-apps-permanently-banned-in-india/articleshow/80454258.cms.

147 **executive orders forcing ByteDance to sell TikTok:** Exec. Order No. 13942, 85 Fed. Reg. 48637 (August 11, 2020), https://www.federalregister.gov/documents/2020/08/11/2020-17699/addressing-the-threat-posed-by-tiktok-and-taking-additional-steps-to-address-the-national-emergency; Presidential Document No. 2020-18360, 85 Fed. Reg. 51297, August 19, 2020, https://www.federalregister.gov/documents/2020/08/19/2020-18360/regarding-the-acquisition-of-musically-by-bytedance-ltd.

147 **TikTok sued the U.S. government:** Tiktok vs. Trump (complaint for injunctive and declaratory relief, D.D.C., 2020), http://docs.dpaq.de/16820-show_temp.pl-90.pdf.

147 **Biden administration replaced the previous Trump executive orders:** Brian Fung, "US Government Won't Extend the Deadline for a TikTok Deal, but Negotiations Continue," CNN Business, December 4, 2020, https://www.cnn.com/2020/12/04/tech/tiktok-deadline/index.html; Brian Fung and Jill Disis, "Trump Administration Appeals Court Order Blocking TikTok Restrictions," CNN Business, December 28, 2020, https://www.cnn.com/2020/12/28/tech/tiktok-federal-appeal-intl-hnk/index.html; John D. McKinnon and Alex Leary, "TikTok Sale to Oracle, Walmart Is Shelved as Biden Reviews Security," *Wall Street Journal*, February 10, 2021, https://www.wsj.com/articles/tiktok-sale-to-oracle-walmart-is-shelved-as-biden-reviews-security-11612958401.

147 **"Protecting Americans' Sensitive Data from Foreign Adversaries":** Exec. Order No. 14034, 86 Fed. Reg. 31423, (June 11, 2021), https://www.federalregister.gov/documents/2021/06/11/2021-12506/protecting-americans-sensitive-data-from-foreign-adversaries.

147 **TikTok videos are often quirky and uplifting:** Kevin Roose, "TikTok, a Chinese Video App, Brings Fun Back to Social Media," *New York Times*, December 3, 2018, https://www.nytimes.com/2018/12/03/technology/tiktok-a-chinese-video-app-brings-fun-back-to-social-media.html.

147 **President Trump's personal support for a proposed deal:** Bobby Allyn, "TikTok Ban Averted: Trump Gives Oracle-Walmart Deal His 'Blessing,'" *Weekend Edition Sunday*, September 20, 2020, https://www.npr.org/2020/09/20/914032065/tiktok-ban-averted-trump-gives-oracle-walmart-deal-his-blessing.

147 **control of the algorithm:** Ben Thompson, "The TikTok War," *Stratechery* (blog), July 14, 2020, https://stratechery.com/2020/the-tiktok-war/.

147 **algorithm plays a central role in shaping the content:** John Herrman, "How TikTok Is Rewriting the World," *New York Times*, March 10, 2019, https://www.nytimes.com/2019/03/10/style/what-is-tik-tok.html.

147 **algorithm's functionality is even more opaque than other platforms:** "How TikTok recommends videos #ForYou," TikTok, June 18, 2020, https://newsroom.tiktok.com/en-us/how-tiktok-recommends-videos-for-you.

147 **censor political content:** Fergus Ryan, Danielle Cave, and Vicky Xiuzhong Xu, *Mapping More of China's Technology Giants* (report no. 24/2019, Australian Strategic Policy Institute, 2019), https://www.aspi.org.au/report/mapping-more-chinas-tech-giants; Fergus Ryan, Audrey Fritz, and Daria Impiombato, *TikTok and WeChat* (report no. 37/2020, Australian Strategic Policy Institute, 2020), https://www.aspi.org.au/report/tiktok-wechat.

147 **"a technical glitch made it temporarily appear":** Vanessa Pappas and Kudzi Chikumbu, "A Message to Our Black Community," Tiktok news release, June 1, 2020, https://newsroom.tiktok.com/en-us/a-message-to-our-black-community.

148 **viral video criticizing the Chinese government's treatment of Muslims:** Brenda Goh, "TikTok Apologizes for Temporary Removal of Video on Muslims in China," Reuters, November 27, 2019, https://www.reuters.com/article/us-bytedance-tiktok-xinjiang/tiktok-apologizes-for-temporary-removal-of-video-on-muslims-in-china-idUSKBN1Y209E.

148 **"incorrectly partially restricted":** Yaqiu Wang, "Targeting TikTok's Privacy Alone Misses a Larger Issue: Chinese State Control," Human Rights Watch, January 24, 2020, https://www.hrw.org/news/2020/01/24/targeting-tiktoks-privacy-alone-misses-larger-issue-chinese-state-control.

148 **suspicious absence of videos of Hong Kong pro-democracy:** Drew Harwell and Tony Romm,

"TikTok's Beijing Roots Fuel Censorship Suspicion as It Builds a Huge U.S. Audience," *Washington Post*, September 15, 2019, https://www.washingtonpost.com/technology/2019/09/15/tiktoks-beijing-roots-fuel-censorship-suspicion-it-builds-huge-us-audience/.

148 **Houston Rockets basketball team:** Ben Thompson, "The China Cultural Clash," *Stratechery* (blog), October 8, 2019, https://stratechery.com/2019/the-china-cultural-clash/.

148 **propaganda videos about Xinjiang:** Ryan, Fritz, and Impiombato, *TikTok and WeChat*, 15–17.

148 **"highly controversial topics":** Alex Hern, "Revealed: How TikTok Censors Videos That Do Not Please Beijing," *The Guardian*, September 25, 2019, https://www.theguardian.com/technology/2019/sep/25/revealed-how-tiktok-censors-videos-that-do-not-please-beijing.

148 **"The old guidelines in question are outdated":** Hern, "Revealed: How TikTok Censors Videos That Do Not Please Beijing."

148 **ByteDance, like any other Chinese company, must comply:** Thompson, "The TikTok War"; Wang, "Targeting TikTok's Privacy Alone Misses a Larger Issue."

149 **"technology must be led by the socialist core value":** David Bandurski, "Tech Shame in the 'New Era,'" China Media Project, April 11, 2018, https://chinamediaproject.org/2018/04/11/tech-shame-in-the-new-era/.

149 **alternatives like Parler and Gab:** Mike Isaac and Kellen Browning, "Fact-Checked on Facebook and Twitter, Conservatives Switch Their Apps," *New York Times*, November 11, 2020, https://www.nytimes.com/2020/11/11/technology/parler-rumble-newsmax.html.

150 **"platforms are different from steel":** Eric Schmidt, interview by author, June 15, 2020.

150 **Conversative politicians have claimed for years—without evidence:** Elle Hunt, "Facebook to Change Trending Topics After Investigation into Bias Claims," *The Guardian*, May 23, 2016, https://www.theguardian.com/technology/2016/may/24/facebook-changes-trending-topics-anti-conservative-bias; John D. McKinnon and Alex Leary, "Trump Considers Forming Panel to Review Complaints of Online Bias," *Wall Street Journal*, May 23, 2020, https://www.wsj.com/articles/trump-considers-forming-panel-to-review-complaints-of-online-bias-11590238800.

150 **soft-pedal right-wing disinformation:** Jeff Horwitz and Deepa Seetharaman, "Facebook Executives Shut Down Efforts to Make the Site Less Divisive," *Wall Street Journal*, May 26, 2020, https://www.wsj.com/articles/facebook-knows-it-encourages-division-top-executives-nixed-solutions-11590507499.

150 **Facebook altered its algorithm to boost the rankings:** Kevin Roose, "Facebook Reverses Postelection Algorithm Changes That Boosted News from Authoritative Sources," *New York Times*, December 16, 2020, https://www.nytimes.com/2020/12/16/technology/facebook-reverses-postelection-algorithm-changes-that-boosted-news-from-authoritative-sources.html.

150 **incited a riot to storm the Capitol:** Twitter Inc., "Permanent Suspension of @realDonaldTrump," *Twitter Blog*, January 8, 2021, https://blog.twitter.com/en_us/topics/company/2020/suspension.html; Mark Zuckerberg, "The shocking events of the last 24 hours clearly demonstrate . . ." Facebook, January 7, 2021, https://www.facebook.com/zuck/posts/10112681480907401.

150 **account suspensions were clearly necessary:** Sheera Frenkel, "The Storming of Capitol Hill Was Organized on Social Media," *New York Times*, January 6, 2021, https://www.nytimes.com/2021/01/06/us/politics/protesters-storm-capitol-hill-building.html.

150 **Republican members of Congress objected to certifying:** Karen Yourish, Larry Buchanan, and Denise Lu, "The 147 Republicans Who Voted to Overturn Election Results," *New York Times*, January 7, 2021, https://www.nytimes.com/interactive/2021/01/07/us/elections/electoral-college-biden-objectors.html.

150 **debunked allegations of fraud:** Ann Gerhart, "Election Results Under Attack: Here Are the Facts," *Washington Post*, updated March 11, 2021, https://www.washingtonpost.com/elections/interactive/2020/election-integrity/.

19. FUSION

156 **Organizations on the Entity List:** "Addition of Certain Entities to the Entity List," 84 Fed. Reg. 54002 (October 9, 2019), https://www.federalregister.gov/documents/2019/10/09/2019-22210/addition-of-certain-entities-to-the-entity-list.

156 **seven more Chinese tech firms:** "Addition of Certain Entities to the Entity List; Revision of Existing Entries on the Entity List," 85 Fed. Reg. 34503, document no. 2020-10868 (June 5, 2020), https://www.federalregister.gov/documents/2020/06/05/2020-10868/addition-of-certain-entities-to-the-entity-list-revision-of-existing-entries-on-the-entity-list.

156 **objected to their inclusion on the Entity List:** In response to its 2019 Entity List designation, **Megvii** issued a statement saying "there are no grounds" for placing the company on the Entity List: "We are . . . in compliance with all laws and regulations in jurisdictions where we operate. We require our clients not to weaponize our technology or solutions or use them for illegal purposes." (Sherisse Pham, "The United States strikes a blow to China's AI ambitions," *CNN.com*, October 10, 2019, https://www.cnn.com/2019/10/09/tech/hikvision-sensetime-blacklist/index.html.)

After their 2019 Entity List designation, **SenseTime** released a statement on their website: "We are deeply disappointed with this decision by the US Department of Commerce. We will work closely with all relevant authorities to fully understand and resolve the situation. SenseTime is focused on computer vision and deep learning. We work with customers all over the world to leverage AI technology for a range of applications, including education, medical diagnosis, smart city, transportation, communications and entertainment, among many others. We abide by all relevant laws and regulations of the jurisdictions in which we operate. We have been actively developing our AI code of ethics to ensure our technologies are used in a responsible way. In the meantime, we remain focused on protecting the interests of our customers, partners, investors and employees." ("Statement on SenseTime Being Named on the US Entity List," SenseTime, October 8, 2019, https://www.sensetime.com/en/news-detail/54419?categoryId=1072.)

In response to its 2019 Entity List designation, **Dahua** released a statement: "With regard to U.S. Department of Commerce's decision on adding Dahua Technology to the Entity List, we express our strong protest to such decision, which is in lack of any factual basis, and call on the U.S. government to reconsider on it. As a global business entity, Dahua adheres to the business code of conduct, and follows market rules as well as international rules. Dahua is actively working to ensure our investment and business operations around the world to comply with all applicable laws and regulations. Regarding such decision of U.S. government, we have actively taken various measures, and we will continue providing outstanding products and services to our customers." ("Statement on 'adding Dahua Technology to the entity list,'" Dahua Technology, October 8, 2019, https://www.dahuasecurity.com/support/notice/647?us.) Additionally, Dahua's corporate statement, "Our Commitments," includes: "To be clear, Dahua Technology flatly denies the allegations implied by our inclusion on the Entity List or the NDAA 2019, and submitted two comment letters addressing these and other issues in response to the FCC proposal. Nevertheless, we respect the decision of the U.S. Government in this regard and are committed to complying with the limitations imposed on us. . . . And our hope is that, over time, the U.S.-China relationship will improve and some of the limitations currently imposed upon us may be lifted. Until then, we will do everything we can to earn the trust of our U.S. stakeholders. Dahua will always be open to a reasonable, fact-based dialogue on all issues of concern." ("Our Commitments," Dahua Technology, n.d., https:// us.dahuasecurity.com/?page_id=60083.)

Following its 2019 Entity List designation, **Hikvision Europe** released a statement: "We regret that Hikvision has been caught up in what is a broader political and trade dispute. Hikvision will request that the US Government remove the company from its list of Chinese entities facing trade restrictions. Any such decisions should reflect an international rules-based approach and be supported by evidence. Hikvision is a socially-responsible company. Our mission is to keep people, organizations, and property safe and secure. We are proud that our company is trusted in Europe and we will continue to invest in Europe's security. We are confident in our business continuity plan that ensures the sustainability of our global supply chain and we have the capability to continuously provide quality products to our valued partners and customers in Europe." ("Hikvision Europe's statement regarding the U.S. Commerce Department's decision," Hikvision, n.d., https:// www.hikvision.com/europe/newsroom/latest-news/2019/hikvision-europe-s-statement -regarding-the-u-s--commerce-departm/.) Additionally, in response to a press inquiry about the Entity List designation, a **Hikvision** representative stated: "Hikvision strongly opposes today's decision by the U.S. Government and it will hamper efforts by global companies to improve human rights around the world. Hikvision, as the security industry's global leader, respects human rights and takes our responsibility to protect people in the U.S. and the world seriously. Hikvision has been engaging with Administration officials over the past 12 months to clarify misunderstandings about the company and address their concerns." (Catherine Shu, "Eight Chinese Tech Firms Placed on US Entity List For Their Role in Human Rights Violations Against Muslim Minority Groups," *TechCrunch*, October 8, 2019, https://techcrunch.com/2019/10/07/eight-chinese-tech-firms-placed-on-u-s -entity-list-for-their-role-in-human rights-violations-against-muslim-minority-groups/.) A Hikvision spokesperson also said, "Punishing Hikvision, despite these engagements, will deter global companies from communicating with the U.S. government, hurt Hikvision's U.S. businesses partners and negatively impact the U.S. economy" (David Shepardson and Josh Horwitz, "U.S. Expands Blacklist to Include China's Top AI Startups Ahead of Trade Talks," Reuters, October 7, 2019, https://www.reuters.com/article/us-usa-trade -china-exclusive/u-s-expands-blacklist-to-include-chinas-top-ai-startups-ahead-of-trade -talks-idUSKBN1WM25M.)

In Chinese state-run media, **CloudWalk** representatives stated: "We formulate and implement strict ethical standards for the use of AI technologies and provide services to customers based on our self-developed technology and products with independent intellectual property rights to propel the healthy development of AI." (Fan Feifei, "US Blacklisting of Chinese High-Tech Firms Opposed," *China Daily*, May 25, 2020, https://global .chinadaily.com.cn/a/202005/25/WS5ecb023ba310a8b2411580a5.html.)

156 **"We will not be strangled":** Jane Zhang, "China's AI Champion iFlyTek Brushes Off US Entity List Inclusion with Bullish Profit Forecast," *South China Morning Post*, October 10, 2019, https://www.scmp.com/tech/big-tech/article/3032286/chinas-ai-champion-iflytek -says-it-wont-be-strangled-us-trade.

156 **MIT-SenseTime Alliance on Artificial Intelligence:** "MIT and SenseTime Announce Effort to Advance Artificial Intelligence Research," *MIT News*, February 28, 2018, https://

news.mit.edu/2018/mit-sensetime-announce-effort-advance-artificial-intelligence
-research-0228; Meg Murphy, "MIT-SenseTime Alliance Funds Projects from All Five
Schools," *MIT News*, August 24, 2018, https://news.mit.edu/2018/mit-sensetime-alliance
-funds-projects-human-machine-intelligence-0824.

156   **SenseTime's founder:** "The MIT-SenseTime Alliance on Artificial Intelligence," *Spectrum*, Spring 2018, https://spectrum.mit.edu/spring-2018/the-mit-sensetime-alliance-on
-artificial-intelligence/.

156   **five-year partnership with iFLYTEK:** Adam Conner-Simons, "CSAIL Launches New Five-
Year Collaboration with iFlyTek," *MIT News*, June 15, 2018, https://news.mit.edu/2018/
csail-launches-five-year-collaboration-with-iflytek-0615.

156   **million-dollar grant to Rutgers University:** Rutgers Business School, "China's iFlytek
partners with Rutgers on Big Data Lab," news release, April 4, 2017, updated April 25, 2019,
https://www.business.rutgers.edu/news/chinas-iflytek-partners-rutgers-big-data-lab.

156   **AI research at Princeton University:** Alexandra Harney, "Risky Partner: Top U.S. Universities Took Funds from Chinese Firm Tied to Xinjiang Security," Reuters, June 12, 2019,
https://www.reuters.com/article/us-china-xinjiang-mit-tech-insight/risky-partner-top-u
-s-universities-took-funds-from-chinese-firm-tied-to-xinjiang-security-idUSKCN1TE04
M?il=0; E. Weinan, Ma Chao, and Wu Lei, "A Comparative Analysis of Optimization and
Generalization Properties of Two-Layer Neural Network and Random Feature Models
Under Gradient Descent Dynamics," *SCIENCE CHINA Mathematics* 63, no. 7 (2020), 1235,
https://doi.org/10.1007/s11425-019-1628-5, also available at https://arxiv.org/pdf/1904
.04326.pdf.

156   **U.S. tech firms have come under fire:** "Congressional Letter Calls Out US Companies Supporting Dahua and Hikvision," IPVM.com, March 11, 2019, https://ipvm.com/
reports/letter-support. See also "Intel Movidius Helps Bring Artificial Intelligence to
Video Surveillance Cameras," Intel, April 5, 2017, https://newsroom.intel.com/news/intel
-movidius-helps-bring-artificial-intelligence-video-surveillance-cameras/#gs.76ouxy;
"Seagate Launches First Drive For AI-Enabled Surveillance," Seagate, October 28, 2017,
https://www.seagate.com/news/news-archive/seagate-launches-first-drive-for-ai-enabled
-surveillance-master-pr/; "Western Digital Enables Artificial-Intelligence-Powered Video
Surveillance With New High-Capacity Products," Western Digital, June 19, 2018, https://
www.westerndigital.com/company/newsroom/press-releases/2018/2018-06-19-western
-digital-enables-artificial-intelligence-powered-video-surveillance-with-new-high-capac-
ity-products. After public reports about their technology being used in Hikvision intelligent surveillance cameras, an NVIDIA spokesperson told the *Wall Street Journal* that the
company complied with all U.S. export control regulations. Seagate and Western Digital
also each told the *Wall Street Journal* that their companies comply with all U.S. laws and
are closely monitoring the situation in Xinjiang. Additionally, Western Digital stated "We
recognize the gravity of the allegations related to surveillance in the Xinjiang Province"
and that it does not sell products directly to the Chinese government. Hikvision told the
Wall Street Journal that it respects human rights and strongly opposed the U.S. government designating it on the Entity List. Additionally, Hikvision stated that it had hired a
former U.S. diplomat as an advisor on human rights compliance. Liza Lin and Josh Chin,
"U.S. Tech Companies Prop Up China's Vast Surveillance Network," *Wall Street Journal*,
November 26, 2019, https://www.wsj.com/articles/u-s-tech-companies-prop-up-chinas
-vast-surveillance-network-11574786846.

156   **Ürümqi Cloud Computing Center analyzes thousands of video surveillance feeds:** Intel
and NVIDIA chips were reportedly sold to Sugon, a Chinese supplier for the Ürümqi Cloud

Computing Center that was placed on the Entity List in 2019. Intel and NVIDIA both told the *New York Times* that they were unaware of what they described as a misuse of their technology. NVIDIA stated that at the time it had sold chips to support the Ürümqi Cloud Computing Center, it had no reason to believe they would be used "for any improper purpose." An NVIDIA spokesperson also said that Sugon had not been "a significant NVIDIA customer" since the Entity List designation and that NVIDIA had not provided technical assistance to Sugon after it was placed on the Entity List. Intel said that it would discontinue work with customers using its products to violate human rights. (Paul Mozur and Don Clark, "China's Surveillance State Sucks Up Data. U.S. Tech Is Key to Sorting It," *New York Times*, November 22, 2020, https://www.nytimes.com/2020/11/22/technology/china-intel-nvidia-xinjiang.html; 牟敏 [Mou Min], "乌鲁木齐市云计算中心正式运营 '最强大脑' [Urumqi cloud computing center officially operates 'strongest super brain']," news.sina.cn, August 30, 2017, https://news.sina.cn/gn/2017-08-30/detail-ifykiqfe2811033.d.html; "Addition of Certain Entities to the Entity List; Revision of Existing Entries on the Entity List" (document no. 2020-10868); "Addition of Entities to the Entity List and Revision of an Entry on the Entity List," 84 Fed. Reg. 29371 (June 24, 2019), https://www.federalregister.gov/documents/2019/06/24/2019-13245/addition-of-entities-to-the-entity-list-and-revision-of-an-entry-on-the-entity-list.)

156 **Uighur-detecting analytics:** Intel told IPVM that it was unaware its products were used to support Uighur-detecting analytics, it did not always have control over where its chips end up, and that it condemned human rights abuses using its products. Additionally, Intel said it would restrict or stop work with companies using its products to commit human rights abuses. ("China Uyghur Analytic Projects Require Intel And NVIDIA, Intel Condemns, NVIDIA Silent," IPVM.com, December 2, 2019, https://ipvm.com/reports/uyghur-intel-nvidia; "U.S. Lawmakers Ask Intel, Nvidia About Sale of Tech to China Used Against Uighurs," Reuters, December 8, 2020, https://www.reuters.com/article/us-usa-china-uighurs/u-s-lawmakers-ask-intel-nvidia-about-sale-of-tech-to-china-used-against-uighurs-idUSKBN28I2V8.)

156 **both companies that were later placed on the Entity List:** In response to reports that Intel sold chips to NetPosa, Intel told the *Wall Street Journal* that its products were used in a variety of applications around the world. At the time of the statement, NetPosa had not yet been placed on the Entity List. In response to news reports about its chips being used by Hikvision, Xilinx stated that the company takes human rights abuses seriously, complies with all U.S. laws, and doesn't always control how customers use its products. (Liza Lin and Josh Chin, "U.S. Tech Companies Prop Up China's Vast Surveillance Network," *Wall Street Journal*, November 26, 2019, https://www.wsj.com/articles/u-s-tech-companies-prop-up-chinas-vast-surveillance-network-11574786846.)

156 **U.S. investors have similarly backed a number of Chinese companies:** Paul Mozur, "One Month, 500,000 Face Scans: How China Is Using A.I. to Profile a Minority," *New York Times*, April 14, 2019, https://www.nytimes.com/2019/04/14/technology/china-surveillance-artificial-intelligence-racial-profiling.html.

157 **SenseTime:** CK Tan and James Hand-Cukierman, "Face Recognition Trailblazer SenseTime Rushes to Be Next Google," Nikkei Asia, August 9, 2019, https://asia.nikkei.com/Spotlight/Startups-in-Asia/Face-recognition-trailblazer-SenseTime-rushes-to-be-next-Google.

157 **Yitu:** "YITU Technology," Sequoia, n.d., https://www.sequoiacap.com/companies/yitu-technology; Mozur, "One Month, 500,000 Face Scans."

157 **Hikvision:** Fergus Ryan, Danielle Cave, and Vicky Xiuzhong Xu, *Mapping More of China's*

Technology Giants (report no. 24/2019, Australian Strategic Policy Institute, 2019), https://www.aspi.org.au/report/mapping-more-chinas-tech-giants.

157 **Hewlett Packard Enterprise had a 49 percent stake in New H3C Technologies:** Lin and Chin, "U.S. Tech Companies Prop Up China's Vast Surveillance Network." In response to press inquiries following New H3C Technologies' 2021 Entity List designation, Hewlett Packard Enterprise stated: "At this time, our due diligence suggests no indication that sales to the Chinese military have taken place . . . We're working to understand why the Commerce Department has taken this action. We remain engaged with all relevant stakeholders to research this matter." (Simon Sharwood, "HPE Sees 'No Indication' Its Tech Was Sold to Chinese Military, Seeks Answers From Uncle Sam on Sanctions," *The Register,* November 29, 2021, https://www.theregister.com/2021/11/29/hpe_china_sanctions/.)

157 **iFLYTEK's gift to Princeton and a grant from the U.S. Office of Naval Research:** Weinan, Ma, and Wu, "A Comparative Analysis of Optimization and Generalization Properties of Two-Layer Neural Network."

157 **MIT defended their partnership:** Madhumita Murgia and Christian Shepherd, "US Universities Reconsider Research Links with Chinese AI Company," *Financial Times*, June 13, 2019, https://www.ft.com/content/2f112da0-8e19-11e9-a1c1-51bf8f989972.

157 **AI research "is not expected to have immediate applications":** Alexandra Harney, "Risky Partner."

157 **"given that it had nothing to do with what the reported human rights issues were":** Maria Zuber, interview by author, August 26, 2021.

157 **MIT finally cancelled the iFLYTEK relationship:** Will Knight, "MIT Cuts Ties with a Chinese AI Firm Amid Human Rights Concerns," *Wired*, April 21, 2020, https://www.wired.com/story/mit-cuts-ties-chinese-ai-firm-human-rights/.

157 **"research that was already underway":** Zuber, interview.

157 **U.S. AI ecosystem also has links to the Chinese military:** Madhumita Murgia and Christian Shepherd, "Western AI Researchers Partnered with Chinese Surveillance Firms," *Financial Times*, April 19, 2019, https://www.ft.com/content/41be9878-61d9-11e9-b285-3acd5d43599e. **MIT** established a new review process for "elevated-risk" international proposals in April 2019. (Maria T. Zuber, "New Review Process for 'Elevated-Risk' International Proposals," *MIT*, April 3, 2019, https://orgchart.mit.edu/node/27/letters_to_community/new-review-process-elevated-risk-international-proposals.)

157 **National University of Defense Technology (NUDT):** "About," National University of Defense Technology, n.d., https://english.nudt.edu.cn/About/index.htm

157 **Commerce Department's Entity List:** "Addition of Certain Persons to the Entity List; and Removal of Person From the Entity List Based on a Removal Request," 80 Fed. Reg. 85224 (February 18, 2015), https://www.federalregister.gov/documents/2015/02/18/2015-03321/addition-of-certain-persons-to-the-entity-list-and-removal-of-person-from-the-entity-list-based-on-a.

157 **Google dismissed the papers:** In response to the *Financial Times* investigation, a Google spokesperson said: "These were academic papers written by researchers at universities—Google is not involved with these projects and has no partnerships with the Chinese universities in question." (Murgia and Shepherd, "Western AI Researchers Partnered with Chinese Surveillance Firms.")

157 **coauthored by researchers from Microsoft Research Asia:** Madhumita Murgia and Yuan Yang, "Microsoft Worked with Chinese Military University on Artificial Intelligence," *Financial Times*, April 10, 2019, https://www.ft.com/content/9378e7ee-5ae6-11e9-9dde-7aedca0a081a; Minghao Hu et al., *Read + Verify: Machine Reading Comprehension*

with *Unanswerable Questions* (arXiv.org, November 15, 2018), https://arxiv.org/pdf/1808
.05759.pdf; Renjiao Yi et al., *Faces as Lighting Probes via Unsupervised Deep Highlight
Extraction* (arXiv.org, July 21, 2018), https://arxiv.org/pdf/1803.06340.pdf; Minghao Hu et
al., *Attention-Guided Answer Distillation for Machine Reading Comprehension* (arXiv.org,
September 17, 2018), https://arxiv.org/pdf/1808.07644.pdf. In a statement to the *Financial
Times*, **Microsoft** said: "The research is guided by our principles, fully complies with US
and local laws, and . . . is published to ensure transparency so that everyone can benefit
from our work." (Murgia and Yang, "Microsoft Worked with Chinese Military University
on Artificial Intelligence.") In an interview with the author, Microsoft representatives disputed the accuracy of the *Financial Times* reporting. (Kevin Luo, interview by author, June
21, 2019.) Microsoft changed its policies for research in China in 2019, including no longer
working with organizations on the Entity List, no longer accepting visiting researchers
from any Chinese military institutions, and placing additional restrictions on research on
sensitive topics such as facial recognition. (Peter Lee, interview by author, July 26, 2021;
Brad Smith, remarks at the U.S.-China Series, Seattle, WA, January 15, 2020.)

158 **dual affiliation at Microsoft Research Asia and NUDT:** Wu et al., *ICTCP*; Huang et al.,
Link-Based Hidden Attribute Discovery. Microsoft representatives did not respond to a
request by the author for comment on the affiliation of these individuals.

158 **500 PLA scientists studied in the United States:** Alex Joske, *Picking Flowers, Making Honey:
The Chinese Military's Collaboration with Foreign Universities* (Australian Strategic Policy
Institute, October 2018), https://www.aspi.org.au/report/picking-flowers-making-honey.

158 **PLA scientists coauthored over 1,100 research papers:** Joske, *Picking Flowers, Making
Honey.*

158 **the PLA's other top targets for engagement abroad:** Joske, *Picking Flowers, Making
Honey.*

158 **study of DNA samples of Uighurs in the journal** *Human Genetics*: Sui-Lee Wee and Paul
Mozur, "China Uses DNA to Map Faces, With Help From the West," *New York Times*,
December 3, 2019, https://www.nytimes.com/2019/12/03/business/china-dna-uighurs
-xinjiang.html.

158 **denied being coauthor of a paper:** Dr. **Tang Kun** told the *New York Times* in 2019 that
"he did not know why he was named as an author of the April paper, though he said it
might have been because his graduate students worked on it," and that he had ended his
collaboration with Chinese police in 2017 "because he felt their biological samples and
research were subpar." A spokesperson for the **Max Planck Society** stated that its grant
funding Dr. Tang ended before his work with Chinese police began. Additionally, the Max
Planck Society stated that it "takes this issue very seriously" and that its ethics council
would review the issue. **Erasmus University Medical Center** stated that Dr. Liu Fan maintained a part-time position with the university but that Erasmus did not fund the research
papers in question, Erasmus was not responsible "for any research that has not taken place
under the auspices of Erasmus," and it had made inquiries and determined that no further
action was needed. (Wee and Mozur, "China Uses DNA to Map Faces, With Help From the
West.") The article in *Human Genetics* and another article published in the *International
Journal of Legal Medicine* were retracted in 2021 for ethical reasons. (Li, Y., Zhao, W.,
Li, D. et al., "Retraction Note: EDAR, LYPLAL1, PRDM16, PAX3, DKK1, TNFSF12, CAC-
NA2D3, and SUPT3H gene variants influence facial morphology in a Eurasian popula-
tion," *Human Genetics* 140, 1499 (2021), https://doi.org/10.1007/s00439-021-02352-6; Jing,
X., Sun, Y., Zhao, W. et al., "Retraction Note: Predicting adult height from DNA variants
in a European-Asian admixed population," *International Journal of Legal Medicine* 135,

2151 (2021), https://doi.org/10.1007/s00414-021-02692-y.) After the papers were retracted, **Erasmus University Medical Center** (Erasmus MC) issued a statement: "Dr. Liu is paid by the Erasmus MC for the work that he does in relation to his job at the Erasmus MC. His work regarding the retracted publications took place outside the Erasmus MC. Dr. Liu did not receive any funding for the research he conducted in China, which is described in these two articles. Dr. Xiong got a part time appointment at the Erasmus MC after publication of the article that he co-authored. The Erasmus MC has no cooperation agreement with the Bejing Institute of Genomics. . . . The Erasmus MC endorses the Dutch Code for Scientific Integrity. . . . In general, we consider ethical questions involving our employees to be very important, and the Board of Directors is attentive in this regard. Simultaneously, we have to be able to depend on other (international) research institutes complying with general rules of scientific integrity." (Annebelle de Bruijn and Siem Eikelenboom, "Controversial Studies of Erasmus MC Researcher into Uyghur DNA Retracted," *Follow the Money,* September 8, 2021, https://www.ftm.eu/articles/controversial-studies-erasmus-uyghur-dna-retracted.)

159 **Google later reconsidered:** Kaveh Waddell, "Why Google Quit China—and Why It's Heading Back," *The Atlantic,* January 19, 2016, https://www.theatlantic.com/technology/archive/2016/01/why-google-quit-china-and-why-its-heading-back/424482/.

159 **Microsoft Research Asia in Beijing:** "Microsoft Research Lab—Asia," Microsoft, 2021, https://www.microsoft.com/en-us/research/lab/microsoft-research-asia/.

159 **instrumental in the development of China's AI sector:** Matt Sheehan, "Who Benefits From American AI Research in China?" *Macro Polo,* October 21, 2019, https://macropolo.org/china-ai-research-resnet/?rp=m.

159 **U.S. government regulation of facial recognition:** Brad Smith, "Facial Recognition Technology: The Need for Public Regulation and Corporate Responsibility," *Microsoft on the Issues* (blog), July 13, 2018, https://blogs.microsoft.com/on-the-issues/2018/07/13/facial-recognition-technology-the-need-for-public-regulation-and-corporate-responsibility/.

159 **governance "to uphold Microsoft responsible AI principles":** "Our Approach to Responsible AI at Microsoft," Microsoft, 2021, https://www.microsoft.com/en-us/ai/our-approach.

159 **turned down offers for facial recognition contracts:** Brad Smith, remarks at the New Work Summit, Half Moon Bay, CA, February 26, 2019.

159 **"the single most important thing by far that Microsoft has done in China":** Brad Smith, remarks at the U.S.-China Series, Seattle, WA, January 15, 2020.

159 **"the world's hottest computer lab":** Gregory T. Huang, "The World's Hottest Computer Lab," *MIT Technology Review,* June 1, 2004, https://www.technologyreview.com/2004/06/01/232827/the-worlds-hottest-computer-lab/.

159 **"My Chinese Dream is to go to America!":** Xinmei Shen, "Microsoft's Xiaoice Chatbot to Become Its Own Company in China," *Abacus* (blog), *South China Morning Post,* July 13, 2020, https://www.scmp.com/abacus/tech/article/3092992/microsofts-xiaoice-chatbot-become-its-own-company-china; Yizhou (Joe) Xu, "Programmatic Dreams: Technographic Inquiry into Censorship of Chinese Chatbots," *Social Media + Society* 4, no. 4 (2018), https://doi.org/10.1177%2F2056305118808780.

159 **Xiaoice has since been programmed to sidestep questions:** Xu, "Programmatic Dreams."

160 **Bing search engine, which is permitted in China:** Tom Simonite, "US Companies Help Censor the Internet in China, Too," *Wired,* June 3, 2019, https://www.wired.com/story/us-companies-help-censor-internet-china/.

160 **"we're committed to providing our technology":** Colin Lecher, "Microsoft Workers' Letter Demands Company Drop Army HoloLens Contract," *The Verge,* February 22, 2019, https://www.theverge.com/2019/2/22/18236116/microsoft-hololens-army-contract-workers-letter.

160   **"Whampoa Academy of China's Internet":** Jeffrey Ding, translator, "The Whampoa Academy of China's Internet," Google Docs, n.d., https://docs.google.com/document/d/1ZG-SexF_PnnWMVOlJttQjr7slHdaQH6nJAGQ1vVDdAMY/edit.

160   **over 500 Microsoft Research Asia alums work in China's tech industry:** Ding, "The Whampoa Academy of China's Internet"; Will Knight, "Microsoft's Roots in China Have Positioned It to Buy TikTok," *Wired*, August 6, 2020, https://www.wired.com/story/micro-softs-roots-china-positioned-buy-tiktok/.

160   **surpass human-level performance in image classification:** Kaiming He et al., *Delving Deep into Rectifiers: Surpassing Human-Level Performance on ImageNet Classification* (Microsoft Research, February 6, 2015), https://arxiv.org/pdf/1502.01852.pdf; Richard Eckel, "Microsoft Researchers' Algorithm Sets ImageNet Challenge Milestone," Microsoft Research Blog, February 10, 2015, https://www.microsoft.com/en-us/research/blog/microsoft-researchers-algorithm-sets-imagenet-challenge-milestone/.

160   **team's 2015 paper on "deep residual learning":** Bec Crew, "Google Scholar Reveals Its Most Influential Papers for 2019," *nature index*, August 2, 2019, https://www.natureindex.com/news-blog/google-scholar-reveals-most-influential-papers-research-citations-twenty-nineteen; Kaiming He et al., *Deep Residual Learning for Image Recognition* (thecvf.com, n.d.), https://openaccess.thecvf.com/content_cvpr_2016/papers/He_Deep_Residual_Learning_CVPR_2016_paper.pdf.

160   **5,000 papers in top-tier journals:** Tim Pan, interview by author, June 21, 2019.

160   **"That's, on average, every working day":** Pan, interview.

161   **"very small number" of interns:** Kevin Luo, interview by author, June 21, 2019.

161   **approximately eleven such interns:** Information in this section comes from multiple interviews with Microsoft representatives during July and August 2021.

161   **also a PhD student in computer science at the PLA's NUDT:** 微软亚洲研究院 [Microsoft Research Asia] "实习派 | 胡明昊：在MSRA研究机器阅读理解是一种怎样的体验？ [Internship | Minghao Hu: What kind of experience is it to study machine reading comprehension at MSRA?]," Microsoft (China), January 22, 2019, https://www.msra.cn/zh-cn/news/outreach-articles/%E5%AE%9E%E4%B9%A0%E6%B4%BE-%E8%83%A1%E6%98%8E%E6%98%8A%EF%BC%9A%E5%9C%A8msra%E7%A0%94%E7%A9%B6%E6%9C%BA%E5%99%A8%E9%98%85%E8%AF%BB%E7%90%86%E8%A7%A3%E6%98%AF%E4%B8%80%E7%A7%8D%E6%80%8E%E6%A0%B7, (page discontinued), archived by the Internet Archive September 4, 2019, https://web.archive.org/web/20190904143341/https://www.msra.cn/zh-cn/news/outreach-articles/%E5%AE%9E%E4%B9%A0%E6%B4%BE-%E8%83%A1%E6%98%8E%E6%98%8A%EF%BC%9A%E5%9C%A8msra%E7%A0%94%E7%A9%B6%E6%9C%BA%E5%99%A8%E9%98%85%E8%AF%BB%E7%90%86%E8%A7%A3%E6%98%AF%E4%B8%80%E7%A7%8D%E6%80%8E%E6%A0%B7.

161   **interns "apply as individuals":** Luo, interview.

161   **"I am a professor myself":** Pan, interview.

161   **ties between U.S. AI researchers and the Chinese military:** John Eggerton, "Senate Bill Limits Visas for Chinese Engineers, Scientists," *Multichannel News*, May 14, 2019, https://www.multichannel.com/news/senate-bill-limits-visas-for-chinese-engineers-scientists; People's Liberation Army (PLA) Visa Security Act, H.R. 2713, 116th Congress (2019), https://www.congress.gov/bill/116th-congress/house-bill/2713.

161   **"Seven Sons of National Defense":** Glenn Tiffert, ed., *Global Engagement: Rethinking Risk in the Research Enterprise* (Hoover Institution, 2020), https://www.hoover.org/global-engagement-rethinking-risk-research-enterprise.

161 **"And those students, after they graduate, they tend to join us":** Pan, interview.

161 **seeking "to use U.S. technology for Chinese missile programs":** "Addition of Entities to the Entity List, Revision of Certain Entries on the Entity List," 85 Fed. Reg. 34495, document no. 10869, (June 5, 2020), https://www.federalregister.gov/documents/2020/06/05/2020 -10869/addition-of-entities-to-the-entity-list-revision-of-certain-entries-on-the-entity -list.

161 **Harbin Institute of Technology and the other Seven Sons of National Defense:** Alex Joske, *The China Defence Universities Tracker* (report no. 23/2019, Australian Strategic Policy Institute, November 2019), https://www.aspi.org.au/report/china-defence-universities -tracker.

162 **valuable feeder for talent into the Chinese defense industry:** Ryan Fedasiuk and Emily Weinstein, *Universities and the Chinese Defense Technology Workforce* (Center for Security and Emerging Technology, December 2020), https://cset.georgetown.edu/publication/ universities-and-the-chinese-defense-technology-workforce/.

162 **more than a quarter of Microsoft Research Asia's collaborative training projects with universities in China:** "2018年微软亚洲研究院-教育部产学合作协同育人项目（第一批）[2018 Microsoft Research Asia—Ministry of Education Industry—University Cooperation Collaborative Education Project (First Batch)]," Microsoft Research Asia, October 2018, captured by the Internet Archive October 15, 2020, https://web.archive.org/ web/20201015180833/https://www.msra.cn/zh-cn/connections/academic-programs/ academia-industry-cooperation-2018-1; Fedasiuk and Weinstein, *Universities and the Chinese Defense Technology Workforce*, 33–34. Microsoft changed its policies for research in China in 2019, including no longer working with organizations on the Entity List, no longer accepting visiting researchers from any Chinese military institutions, and placing additional restrictions on research on sensitive topics such as facial recognition. (Peter Lee, interview by author, July 26, 2021; Brad Smith, remarks at the U.S.-China Series, Seattle, WA, January 15, 2020.)

162 **U.S. companies as having training programs:** Fedasiuk and Weinstein, *Universities and the Chinese Defense Technology Workforce*, 15. In response to claims that Google's work in China indirectly aids the Chinese military, Google stated: "We are not working with the Chinese military. We are working with the U.S. government, including the Department of Defense, in many areas including cybersecurity, recruiting and healthcare." ("Trump Discusses China, 'Political Fairness' with Google CEO," Reuters, March 27, 2019, https://www .reuters.com/article/us-usa-trump-google/trump-discusses-china-political-fairness-with -google-ceo-idUSKCN1R82CB.)

162 **"it is likely that U.S. tech companies are inadvertently aiding in China's military modernization":** Fedasiuk and Weinstein, *Universities and the Chinese Defense Technology Workforce*, 13.

162 **eleven U.S. federal government research facilities:** Tiffert, ed., *Global Engagement*.

162 **concern over China's military-civil fusion:** Proclamation No. 10043, 85 Fed. Reg. 34353 (June 4, 2020), https://www.federalregister.gov/documents/2020/06/04/2020-12217/ suspension-of-entry-as-nonimmigrants-of-certain-students-and-researchers-from-the -peoples-republic.

162 **military-civil fusion is often mischaracterized:** Michael R. Pompeo, "Technology and the China Security Challenge" (remarks to the Silicon Valley Leadership Group, San Francisco, CA, January 14, 2020), https://id.usembassy.gov/remarks-by-secretary-pompeo-on -technology-and-the-china-security-challenge/.

162 **work in progress, and more of an aspiration:** Elsa B. Kania and Lorand Laskai, *Myths*

and Realities of China's Military-Civil Fusion Strategy (Center for a New American Security, January 28, 2021), https://www.cnas.org/publications/reports/myths-and-realities-of-chinas-military-civil-fusion-strategy.

162 **1994 paper by the now-defunct U.S. Office of Technology Assessments:** U.S. Congress, Office of Technology Assessment, *Assessing the Potential for Civil-Military Integration: Technologies, Processes, and Practices, OTA-ISS-611* (Washington, DC: U.S. Government Printing Office, September 1994), https://www.princeton.edu/~ota/disk1/1994/9402/9402.PDF.

163 **hampered by bureaucratic inefficiencies and ties to traditional defense contractors:** Kania and Laskai, *Myths and Realities of China's Military-Civil Fusion Strategy.*

163 **"a lot of basic research is not secret":** Smith, remarks at the U.S.-China Series.

163 **arXiv:** arXiv.org (homepage), n.d., https://arxiv.org/.

163 **"cultivate the talents that we want":** Pan, interview.

163 **NUDT graduate student who interned at Microsoft Research Asia:** 微软亚洲研究院 [Microsoft Research Asia] "实习派｜胡明昊：在MSRA研究机器阅读理解是一种怎样的体验？[Internship｜Minghao Hu: What kind of experience is it to study machine reading comprehension at MSRA?]."

163 **Chinese academic espionage, intellectual property (IP) theft, and tech transfer:** Michael Brown and Pavneet Singh, *China's Technology Transfer Strategy: How Chinese Investments in Emerging Technology Enable a Strategic Competitor to Access the Crown Jewels of U.S. Innovation* (Defense Innovation Unit Experimental, January 2018), https://admin.govexec.com/media/diux_chinatechnologytransferstudy_jan_2018_(1).pdf; U.S. Attorney's Office, Northern District of Illinois, "Suburban Chicago Woman Sentenced to Four Years in Prison for Stealing Motorola Trade Secrets Before Boarding Plane to China," news release, August 29, 2012, https://archives.fbi.gov/archives/chicago/press-releases/2012/suburban-chicago-woman-sentenced-to-four-years-in-prison-for-stealing-motorola-trade-secrets-before-boarding-plane-to-china; Rachel Lerman, "Jury Awards T-Mobile $4.8M in Trade-Secrets Case Against Huawei," *Seattle Times*, May 18, 2017, https://www.seattletimes.com/business/technology/july-awards-t-mobile-48m-in-trade-secrets-case-against-huawei/; Department of Justice, "U.S. Charges Five Chinese Military Hackers for Cyber Espionage Against U.S. Corporations and a Labor Organization for Commercial Advantage," news release May 19, 2014, https://www.justice.gov/opa/pr/us-charges-five-chinese-military-hackers-cyber-espionage-against-us-corporations-and-labor; "Preventing Loss of Academic Research," *Counterintelligence Strategic Partnership Intelligence Note (SPIN)* 15-006 (June 2015), https://info.publicintelligence.net/FBI-SPIN-ProtectingAcademicResearch.pdf; William C. Hannas, James Mulvenon, and Anna B. Puglisi, *Chinese Industrial Espionage: Technology Acquisition and Military Modernisation* (n.p., Routledge, 2013), https://www.routledge.com/Chinese-Industrial-Espionage-Technology-Acquisition-and-Military-Modernisation/Hannas-Mulvenon-Puglisi/p/book/9780415821421; William C. Hannas and Huey-meei Chang, *China's Access to Foreign AI Technology* (Center for Security and Emerging Technology, September 2019), https://cset.georgetown.edu/research/chinas-access-to-foreign-ai-technology/; Ryan Fedasiuk and Emily Weinstein, *Overseas Professionals and Technology Transfer to China* (Center for Security and Emerging Technology, July 21, 2020), https://cset.georgetown.edu/research/overseas-professionals-and-technology-transfer-to-china/; Tai Ming Cheung, William Lucyshyn, and John Rigilano, *The Role of Technology Transfers in China's Defense Technological and Industrial Development and the Implications for the United States* (Naval Postgraduate School, February 19, 2019), https://calhoun.nps.edu/bitstream/

handle/10945/61948/UCSD-AM-19-028.pdf?sequence=1&isAllowed=y; Office of the U.S. Trade Representative, *Findings of the Investigation into China's Acts, Policies, and Practices Related to Technology Transfer, Intellectual Property, and Innovation Under Section 301 of the Trade Act of 1974* (US Trade Representative, March 22, 2018), https://ustr.gov/sites/default/files/Section%20301%20FINAL.PDF; Commission on the Theft of American Intellectual Property, *The IP Commission Report: The Report of The Commission on the Theft of American Intellectual Property* (National Bureau of Asian Research, May 2013), https://www.nbr.org/wp-content/uploads/pdfs/publications/IP_Commission_Report.pdf.

164   **over 200 talent recruitment plans:** *Threats to the U.S. Research Enterprise: China's Talent Recruitment Plans* (staff report, Permanent Subcommittee on Investigations, Committee on Homeland Security and Governmental Affairs, U.S. Senate, n.d.), https://www.hsgac.senate.gov/imo/media/doc/2019-11-18%20PSI%20Staff%20Report%20-%20China's%20Talent%20Recruitment%20Plans.pdf.

164   **China's Thousand Talents Plan:** "The Recruitment Program for Innovative Talents (Long Term)," www.1000plan.org (site discontinued), https://web.archive.org/web/20190607222158/http://www.1000plan.org/en/.

164   **spent hundreds of millions:** Ryan Fedasluk, "If You Want to Keep Talent Out of China, Invest at Home," *Foreign Policy*, September 17, 2020, https://foreignpolicy.com/2020/09/17/china-thousand-talents-plan-invest-us-xenophobia/.

164   **7,600 scientists since 2008:** Hepeng Jia, "China's Science Ministry Gets Power to Attract More Foreign Scientists," *nature index*, March 23, 2018, https://www.natureindex.com/news-blog/chinas-science-ministry-gets-power-to-attract-more-foreign-scientists.

164   **"There is no country that poses a more severe counterintelligence threat":** Agence France-Presse, "FBI Has 1,000 Investigations into Chinese Intellectual Property Theft, Director Christopher Wray Says, Calling China the Most Severe Counter-Intelligence Threat to US," *South China Morning Post*, July 24, 2019, https://www.scmp.com/news/china/article/3019829/fbi-has-1000-probes-chinese-intellectual-property-theft-director.

164   **90 percent of Department of Justice espionage cases involving a state actor:** *China's Non-Traditional Espionage Against the United States: The Threat and Potential Policy Responses: Hearing Before the Senate Judiciary Committee*, 115th Cong. (2018) (statement of John C. Demers, Assistant Attorney General, National Security Division, US Department of Justice), https://www.justice.gov/sites/default/files/testimonies/witnesses/attachments/2018/12/18/12-05-2018_john_c._demers_testimony_re_china_non-traditional_espionage_against_the_united_states_the_threat_and_potential_policy_responses.pdf.

164   **IP theft by China:** Eric Rosenbaum, "1 in 5 Corporations Say China Has Stolen Their IP Within the Last Year: CNBC CFO survey," CNBC, March 1, 2019, https://www.cnbc.com/2019/02/28/1-in-5-companies-say-china-stole-their-ip-within-the-last-year-cnbc.html.

164   **Chinese IP theft results in an annual cost:** *Update to the IP Commission Report* (National Bureau of Asian Research, 2017), http://ipcommission.org/report/IP_Commission_Report_Update_2017.pdf.

164   **Department of Justice launched a new China Initiative:** Department of Justice, "Information About The Department Of Justice's China Initiative And A Compilation of China-Related Prosecutions Since 2018," news release, November 11, 2021, https://www.justice.gov/archives/nsd/information-about-department-justice-s-china-initiative-and-compilation-china-related.

164   **1,000 investigations under way:** Agence France-Presse, "FBI Has 1,000 Investigations into Chinese Intellectual Property Theft."

164 **investigations move slowly:** For examples of Justice Department criminal convictions, see: Department of Justice, "Harvard University Professor Convicted of Making False Statements and Tax Offenses," news release, December 21, 2021, https://www.justice.gov/usao-ma/pr/harvard-university-professor-convicted-making-false-statements-and-tax-offenses; Department of Justice, "Jury Convicts Chinese Intelligence Officer of Espionage Crimes, Attempting to Steal Trade Secrets," news release, November 5, 2021, https://www.justice.gov/opa/pr/jury-convicts-chinese-intelligence-officer-espionage-crimes-attempting-steal-trade-secrets; Department of Justice, "Ph.D. Chemist Convicted of Conspiracy to Steal Trade Secrets, Economic Espionage, Theft of Trade Secrets and Wire Fraud," news release, April 22, 2021, https://www.justice.gov/opa/pr/phd-chemist-convicted-conspiracy-steal-trade-secrets-economic-espionage-theft-trade-secrets; Department of Justice, "Hospital Researcher Sentenced to Prison for Conspiring to Steal Trade Secrets and Sell to China," news release, April 20, 2021, https://www.justice.gov/opa/pr/hospital-researcher-sentenced-prison-conspiring-steal-trade-secrets-and-sell-china; Department of Justice, "Information About The Department Of Justice's China Initiative And A Compilation of China-Related Prosecutions Since 2018."

164 **banning PLA-funded researchers:** Eggerton, "Senate Bill Limits Visas for Chinese Engineers, Scientists"; To Prohibit the Issuance of F or J Visas to Researchers Affiliated with the Chinese People's Liberation Army., S.—(draft), 116th Cong. (2020), https://www.cotton.senate.gov/files/documents/PLA%20Visa%20Security%20Act.pdf (page discontinued).

164 **"sensitive research projects":** The Protect Our Universities Act of 2019, S.—(draft), 116th Cong. (2019), https://www.hawley.senate.gov/sites/default/files/2019-06/Bill%20Text%20-%20The%20Protect%20Our%20Universities%20Act%20of%202019.pdf.

164 **revoked the visas of 1,000 Chinese "graduate students and research scholars":** Jennifer Hansler and James Griffiths, "US Reveals It Has Revoked More Than 1,000 Visas to Chinese Nationals Deemed Security Risks," CNN, September 10, 2020, https://edition.cnn.com/2020/09/09/politics/china-us-visas-intl-hnk/index.html; Proclamation No. 10043.

164 **prohibiting *any* Chinese national from undertaking graduate or post-graduate education:** Tom Cotton, Senator for Arkansas, "Cotton, Blackburn, Kustoff Unveil Bill to Restrict Chinese STEM Graduate Student Visas & Thousand Talents Participants," news release, May 27, 2020, https://www.cotton.senate.gov/?p=press_release&id=1371.

164 **"decouple" from China:** "Trump Again Raises Idea of Decoupling Economy from China," Reuters, September 15, 2020, https://www.reuters.com/article/us-usa-trump-china/trump-again-raises-idea-of-decoupling-economy-from-china-idUSKBN25Y1V9.

164 **"a pure decoupling of China would be very harmful":** Eric Schmidt, interview by author, June 15, 2020.

165 **over 90 percent—of Chinese AI PhD students:** Remco Zwetsloot, *Keeping Top AI Talent in the United States* (Center for Security and Emerging Technology, December 2019), 10, https://cset.georgetown.edu/wp-content/uploads/Keeping-Top-AI-Talent-in-the-United-States.pdf.

165 **over a quarter of AI researchers:** "The Global AI Talent Tracker," Macro Polo, n.d., https://macropolo.org/digital-projects/the-global-ai-talent-tracker/.

165 **"Clearly the Chinese have groups that are trying to infiltrate":** Schmidt interview.

165 **"We gain insight by being in that ecosystem":** Peter Lee, interview by author, July 26, 2021.

166 **"We do understand":** Zuber, interview.

166 **"protecting U.S. national and economic security while ensuring the open exchange**

of ideas": National Academies, "Co-Chairs Appointed to Lead New National Science, Technology, and Security Roundtable," news release, October 15, 2020, https://www.nationalacademies.org/news/2020/10/co-chairs-appointed-to-lead-new-national-science-technology-and-security-roundtable.

166 **"The Chinese market is not and has never been fully open":** Smith, remarks at the U.S.-China Series.

166 **"bifurcation" of the tech world:** Stu Woo and Asa Fitch, "The Great U.S.-China Tech Divide," *The Wall Street Journal*, January 20, 2020, https://www.wsj.com/articles/the-great-u-s-china-tech-divide-11579542441.

166 **"There is no longer a single internet":** Smith, remarks at the U.S.-China Series.

166 **public comment on possible export controls:** "Review of Controls for Certain Emerging Technologies" (proposed rule), 83 FR 58201 (November 19, 2018), https://www.federalregister.gov/documents/2018/11/19/2018-25221/review-of-controls-for-certain-emerging-technologies.

166 **businesses linked to the Chinese military:** Wilbur Ross, "Commerce Tightens Restrictions on Technology Exports to Combat Chinese, Russian and Venezuelan Military Circumvention Efforts," news release, April 27, 2020, https://www.commerce.gov/news/press-releases/2020/04/commerce-tightens-restrictions-technology-exports-combat-chinese-0 (page discontinued); Karen Freifeld, "U.S. Imposes New Rules on Exports to China to Keep Them from Its Military," Reuters, April 27, 2020, https://www.reuters.com/article/us-usa-china-exports/u-s-imposes-new-rules-on-exports-to-china-to-keep-them-from-its-military-idUSKCN2291SR.

166 **list of PLA-affiliated companies:** *Qualifying Entities Prepared in Response to Section 1237 of the National Defense Authorization Act for Fiscal Year 1999 (PUBLIC LAW 105-261)* (Department of Defense, June 12, 2020), https://media.defense.gov/2020/Aug/28/2002486659/-1/-1/1/LINK_2_1237_TRANCHE_1_QUALIFIYING_ENTITIES.PDF; (Correction to *Qualifying Entities* noting that the secretary of defense has removed the listed items from the CCMC list), Department of Defense, June 3, 2021, https://media.defense.gov/2020/Aug/28/2002486689/-1/-1/1/LINK_1_1237_TRANCHE-23_QUALIFYING_ENTITIES.PDF. In 2021, the Treasury Department established a new Non-SDN Chinese Military-Industrial Complex Companies List (NS-CMIC List) of companies engaged in the Chinese defense or surveillance sectors. The White House, "FACT SHEET: Executive Order Addressing the Threat from Securities Investments that Finance Certain Companies of the People's Republic of China," news release, June 3, 2021, https://www.whitehouse.gov/briefing-room/statements-releases/2021/06/03/fact-sheet-executive-order-addressing-the-threat-from-securities-investments-that-finance-certain-companies-of-the-peoples-republic-of-china/; "Non-SDN Chinese Military-Industrial Complex Companies List (NS-CMIC List)," U.S. Department of the Treasury, updated December 16, 2021, https://home.treasury.gov/policy-issues/financial-sanctions/consolidated-sanctions-list/ns-cmic-list.

166 **voluntary guidance on exports of surveillance technology:** *Guidance on Implementing the UN Guiding Principles for Transactions Linked to Foreign Government End-Users for Products or Services with Surveillance Capabilities* (US Department of State, n.d.), https://www.state.gov/wp-content/uploads/2020/09/DRL-Industry-Guidance-Project-FINAL-508.pdf.

166 **Entity List as a tool to blacklist various Chinese actors:** "Addition of Entities to the Entity List," 86 Fed. Reg 18437 (April 8, 2021), https://www.federalregister.gov/documents/2021/04/09/2021-07400/addition-of-entities-to-the-entity-list; "Addition of Certain Entities to the Entity List; Revision of Existing Entries on the Entity List" (document no. 2020-10868); "Addition of Entities to the Entity List and Revision of an Entry

on the Entity List," 84 Fed. Reg. 29371 (June 24, 2019), https://www.federalregister.gov/documents/2019/06/24/2019-13245/addition-of-entities-to-the-entity-list-and-revision-of-an-entry-on-the-entity-list; Jordan Brunner and Emily Weinstein, "The Strategic and Legal Implications of Biden's New China Sanctions," *Lawfare*, June 18, 2021, https://www.lawfareblog.com/strategic-and-legal-implications-bidens-new-china-sanctions.

167 **ended the Justice Department's China Initiative:** Matthew Olsen, remarks at George Mason University, Arlington, VA, February 23, 2022, https://www.justice.gov/opa/speech/assistant-attorney-general-matthew-olsen-delivers-remarks-countering-nation-state-threats; Josh Gerstein, "DOJ shuts down China-focused anti-espionage program," *Politico*, February 23, 2022, https://www.politico.com/news/2022/02/23/doj-shuts-down-china-focused-anti-espionage-program-00011065.

167 **"We have restrictions in place today in China":** Smith, remarks at the U.S.-China Series.

167 **"mass surveillance":** Smith, remarks at the U.S.-China Series.

167 **"We do not accept visiting researchers, for example":** Interview with Peter Lee, July 26, 2021.

167 **Microsoft also will not work with organizations on the U.S. Entity List:** Lee, interview. Brad Smith also stated this in remarks at the U.S.-China Series, Seattle, Washington, January 15, 2020.

167 **"sensitive topics like facial recognition":** Lee, interview.

20. HARMONY

169 **spread of China's model of techno-authoritarianism:** Nicholas Wright, "How Artificial Intelligence Will Reshape the Global Order," *Foreign Affairs*, July 10, 2018, https://www.foreignaffairs.com/articles/world/2018-07-10/how-artificial-intelligence-will-reshape-global-order.

169 **implement sometimes highly intrusive surveillance measures:** Nicholas Wright, "Coronavirus and the Future of Surveillance," *Foreign Affairs*, April 6, 2020, https://www.foreignaffairs.com/articles/2020-04-06/coronavirus-and-future-surveillance.

169 **Chinese government has been increasingly active in international standard-setting bodies:** Jeffrey Ding, Paul Triolo, and Samm Sacks, "Chinese Interests Take a Big Seat at the AI Governance Table," *DigiChina* (blog), NewAmerica.org, June 20, 2018, https://www.newamerica.org/cybersecurity-initiative/digichina/blog/chinese-interests-take-big-seat-ai-governance-table/; Anna Gross, Madhumita Murgia, and Yuan Yang, "Chinese Tech Groups Shaping UN Facial Recognition Standards," *Financial Times*, December 1, 2019, https://www.ft.com/content/c3555a3c-0d3e-11ea-b2d6-9bf4d1957a67; Justus Baron and Olia Kanevskaia Whitaker, "Global Competition for Leadership Positions in Standards Development Organizations," SSRN, March 31, 2021, https://ssrn.com/abstract=3818143; Marta Cantero Gamito, "From Private Regulation to Power Politics: The Rise of China in AI Private Governance Through Standardisation," SSRN, February 28, 2021, https://ssrn.com/abstract=3794761; U.S.-China Economic and Security Review Commission, *2021 Report to Congress*, November 2021, https://www.uscc.gov/sites/default/files/2021-11/2021_Annual_Report_to_Congress.pdf; U.S.-China Economic and Security Review Commission, Chapter 1, Section 2, "The China Model: Return of the Middle Kingdom," in 2020 Annual Report to Congress, December 2020, 80–135, https://www.uscc.gov/sites/default/files/2020-12/Chapter_1_Section_2--The_China_Model-Return_of_the_Middle_Kingdom.pdf; "Will China Set Global Tech Standards?," ChinaFile, March 22, 2022, https://www.chinafile.com/conversation/will-china-set-global-tech

-standards; "Chinese Involvement in International Technical Standards: A DigiChina Forum," DigiChina, December 6, 2021, https://digichina.stanford.edu/work/chinese -involvement-in-international-technical-standards-a-digichina-forum/; Daniel R. Russel and Blake H. Berger, *Stacking the Deck: China's Influence in International Technology Standards Setting* (Asia Society Policy Institute, November 2021), https://asiasociety.org/sites/ default/files/2021-11/ASPI_StacktheDeckreport_final.pdf; Bradley A. Thayer and Lianchao Han, "We Cannot Let China Set the Standards for 21st Century Technologies," *The Hill*, April 16, 2021, https://thehill.com/opinion/technology/548048-we-cannot-let-china -set-the-standards-for-21st-century-technologies/; Alexandra Bruer and Doug Brake, "Mapping the International 5G Standards Landscape and How It Impacts U.S. Strategy and Policy," Information Technology & Innovation Foundation, November 8, 2021, https://itif .org/publications/2021/11/08/mapping-international-5g-standards-landscape-and-how-it -impacts-us-strategy; Jacob Feldgoise and Matt Sheehan, "How U.S. Businesses View China's Growing Influence in Tech Standards," Carnegie Endowment for International Peace, December 23, 2021, https://carnegieendowment.org/2021/12/23/how-u.s.-businesses-view -china-s-growing-influence-in-tech-standards-pub-86084.

169 **"Encourage AI enterprises to participate in or lead the development"**: Graham Webster et al., "Full Translation: China's 'New Generation Artificial Intelligence Development Plan' (2017)," New America, August 1, 2017, https://www.newamerica.org/cybersecurity -initiative/digichina/blog/full-translation-chinas-new-generation-artificial-intelligence -development-plan-2017/.

169 **"White Paper on Artificial Intelligence Standardization"**: Ding, Triolo, and Sacks, "Chinese Interests Take a Big Seat at the AI Governance Table."

170 **national strategy for technical standards:** "中共中央国务院印发《国家标准化发展纲要》 [The Central Committee of the Communist Party of China and the State Council issued the "National Standardization Development Outline"], Central Committee of the Communist Party of China—State Council, October 10, 2021, http://www.gov.cn/zhengce/2021 -10/10/content_5641727.htm; English translation here: "Translation: The Chinese Communist Party Central Committee and the State Council Publish the 'National Standardization Development Outline'," Center for Strategic and Emerging Technology, November 19, 2021, https://cset.georgetown.edu/publication/the-chinese-communist-party-central -committee-and-the-state-council-publish-the-national-standardization-development -outline/; Matt Sheehan, Marjory Blumenthal, and Michael R. Nelson, *Three Takeaways From China's New Standards Strategy* (Carnegie Endowment for International Peace, October 28, 2021), https://carnegieendowment.org/2021/10/28/three-takeaways-from -china-s-new-standards-strategy-pub-85678.

170 **facilitate Chinese-style norms of surveillance:** Gross, Murgia, and Yang, "Chinese Tech Groups Shaping UN Facial Recognition Standards."

170 **tape recorders are regulated in eleven states:** "Recording Phone Calls and Conversations," Digital Media Law Project, 2021, https://www.dmlp.org/legal-guide/recording -phone-calls-and-conversations.

170 **"The world is essentially being put forward two fairly bad proposals" for tech governance**: Wang, interview.

171 **U.S. government needs to be more proactive in international standard-setting:** *U.S. Leadership in AI: A Plan for Federal Engagement in Developing Technical Standards and Related Tools* (National Institute of Standards and Technology, August 9, 2019), https:// www.nist.gov/system/files/documents/2019/08/10/ai_standards_fedengagement_ plan_9aug2019.pdf.

171 **briefly had to halt any academic interactions with Huawei:** "IEEE Lifts Restrictions on Editorial and Peer Review Activities," Institute of Electrical and Electronics Engineers, June 2, 2019, https://www.ieee.org/about/news/2019/statement-update-ieee-lifts-restrictions-on -editorial-and-peer-review-activities.html.

171 **permit U.S. companies to participate in international standard-setting bodies:** U.S. Department of Commerce, "Commerce Clears Way for U.S. Companies to More Fully Engage in Tech Standards-Development Bodies," news release, Monday, June 15, 2020, https://www.commerce.gov/news/press-releases/2020/06/commerce-clears-way-us-com panies-more-fully-engage-tech-standards (page discontinued); (Untitled document concerning BIS posting an advisory opinion and publishing a rule that rescinds the advisory opinion), doc.gov, n.d., https://www.bis.doc.gov/index.php/documents/advisory -opinions/2437-general-advisory-opinion-concerning-prohibited-activities-in-the-stan dards-setting-or-development-context-when-a-listed-entity-is-involved/file;   "Release of 'Technology' to Certain Entities on the Entity List in the Context of Standards Organizations," 85 Fed. Reg. 36719 (June 18, 2020), https://www.federalregister.gov/docu ments/2020/06/18/2020-13093/release-of-technology-to-certain-entities-on-the-entity-list -in-the-context-of-standards.

171 **AI ethics discussions in China:** Rebecca Arcesati, "Lofty Principles, Conflicting Incentives: AI Ethics and Governance in China," Mercator Institute for China Studies, June 24, 2021, https://merics.org/en/report/lofty-principles-conflicting-incentives-ai-ethics-and -governance-china; Matt Sheehan, "China's New AI Governance Initiatives Shouldn't Be Ignored," Carnegie Endowment for International Peace, January 4, 2022, https:// carnegieendowment.org/2022/01/04/china-s-new-ai-governance-initiatives-shouldn-t -be-ignored-pub-86127.

172 **company principles for ethical AI:** "司晓：打造伦理"方舟"，让人工智能可知、可控、可用、可靠 [Si Xiao: Create an ethical "Ark" to make artificial intelligence knowable, controllable, usable and reliable]," Tencent Research Institute, December 6, 2018, https://mp.weixin .qq.com/s/_CbBsrjrTbRkKjUNdmhuqQ; and "Li Yanhong unveiled after 'Baidu lost the land,'" *China IT News*, May 26, 2018, http://www.fonow.com/view/208592.html

172 **Beijing AI Principles:** Beijing AI Principles," Beijing Academy of Artificial Intelligence, May 25, 2019, https://www.baai.ac.cn/news/beijing-ai-principles-en.html.

172 **"Governance Principles for a New Generation of Artificial Intelligence":** Lorand Laskai and Graham Webster, "Translation: Chinese Expert Group Offers 'Governance Principles' for 'Responsible AI,'" *DigiChina* (blog), NewAmerica.org, June 17, 2019, https:// www.newamerica.org/cybersecurity-initiative/digichina/blog/translation-chinese-expert -group-offers-governance-principles-responsible-ai/.

172 **"Joint Pledge on Artificial Intelligence Industry Self-Discipline":** Graham Webster, "Translation: Chinese AI Alliance Drafts Self-Discipline 'Joint Pledge,'" *DigiChina* (blog), NewAmerica.org, June 17, 2019, https://www.newamerica.org/cybersecurity-initiative/ digichina/blog/translation-chinese-ai-alliance-drafts-self-discipline-joint-pledge/.

172 **"Ethical Norms for New Generation Artificial Intelligence":** The National New Generation Artificial Intelligence Governance Specialist Committee, "《新一代人工智能伦理规范》发布 [Ethical Norms for New Generation Artificial Intelligence Released]," Ministry of Science and Technology of the People's Republic of China, September 26, 2021, http://www .most.gov.cn/kjbgz/202109/t20210926_177063.html; English translation is available here: "Ethical Norms for New Generation Artificial Intelligence Released," Center for Security and Emerging Technology, October 21, 2021, https://cset.georgetown.edu/publication/ ethical-norms-for-new-generation-artificial-intelligence-released/.

172 **"community of common destiny"**: Liza Tobin, "Xi's Vision for Transforming Global Governance: A Strategic Challenge for Washington and Its Allies," *Texas National Security Review*, 2 no. 1 (November 2018), http://dx.doi.org/10.26153/tsw/863.

172 **"aim to incorporate ethics into the entire AI life cycle"**: "Ethical Norms for New Generation Artificial Intelligence Released."

172 **Yi Zeng:** Yi Zeng, "Research Interests," Yi Zeng (website), 2021, http://bii.ia.ac.cn/~yizeng/.

173 **Ministry of Science and Technology's expert committee:** Laskai and Webster, "Translation: Chinese Expert Group Offers 'Governance Principles' for 'Responsible AI.'"

173 **list of seventy-four different sets of AI principles released worldwide:** LAIP—Linking Artificial Intelligence Principles (website), 2021, http://www.linking-ai-principles.org/.

173 **"Harmonious AI Principles":** "Harmonious Artificial Intelligence Principles," harmonious-ai.org, 2018, http://harmonious-ai.org/?jdfwkey=wwyhh.

173 **AI governance website includes over thirty case studies:** English language version: http://www.ai-governance.online/; Chinese language version: http://www.ai-governance .online/cn

173 **his "life's work":** Ross Andersen, "The Panopticon Is Already Here," *The Atlantic*, September 2020, https://www.theatlantic.com/magazine/archive/2020/09/china-ai-surveillance/614197/.

173 **Beijing AI Principles had 5 million searches:** Yi Zeng, presentation at the World Peace Forum, Beijing, July 9, 2019.

173 **43 percent of Chinese youth cited AI privacy and ethics as a concern:** "Student Presentation: Risks and Governance of AI from the Perspective of Chinese Youth," World Peace Forum, Beijing, July 9, 2019.

173 **"We need to establish regulations, international laws, and principles":** Bo Zhang, remarks at the World Peace Forum, Beijing, July 9, 2019.

173 **World Peace Forum is a Chinese propaganda-fest:** *Chinese Influence & American Interests* (Hoover Institution, 2018), https://www.hoover.org/sites/default/files/research/docs/ chineseinfluence_americaninterests_fullreport_web.pdf.

173 **"ethics-washing":** James Vincent, "The Problem with AI Ethics," *The Verge*, April 3, 2019, https://www.theverge.com/2019/4/3/18293410/ai-artificial-intelligence-ethics-boards -charters-problem-big-tech.

174 **broader movement in China on data privacy:** "面对小区的人脸识别门禁，这位清华法学院教授决定说不 [Confronting facial recognition access control in the community, this professor of Tsinghua Law School decided to say no.]," oeeee.com, September 24, 2020, https://m.mp.oeeee.com/a/BAAFRD00002020923366254.html.

174 **series of data privacy scandals in China and globally:** Samm Sacks, Mingli Shi, and Graham Webster, "The Evolution of China's Data Governance Regime: A Timeline," *DigiChina* (blog), NewAmerica.org, February 8, 2019, https://www.newamerica.org/cybersecurity-initiative/ digichina/blog/china-data-governance-regime-timeline/; Karen Hao, "Inside China's Unexpected Quest to Protect Data Privacy," *MIT Technology Review*, August 19, 2020, https://www .technologyreview.com/2020/08/19/1006441/china-data-privacy-hong-yanqing-gdpr/.

174 **"very, very serious problems with data security":** Samantha Hoffman, interview by author, September 15, 2020.

174 **new consumer data privacy law:** Hao, "Inside China's Unexpected Quest"; Eva Xiao, "China Passes One of the World's Strictest Data-Privacy Laws," *Wall Street Journal*, August 20, 2021, https://www.wsj.com/articles/china-passes-one-of-the-worlds-strictest-data-pri vacy-laws-11629429138.

174 **"The [CCP] doesn't want anyone else to spy":** Maya Wang, interview by author, September 18, 2020.

174 **a number of sweeping laws:** William Evanina, remarks to International Legal Technology Association LegalSEC Summit 2019, June 4, 2019, https://www.dni.gov/files/NCSC/documents/news/20190606-NCSC-Remarks-ILTA-Summit_2019.pdf; Murray Scot Tanner, "Beijing's New National Intelligence Law: From Defense to Offense," *Lawfare,* July 20, 2017, https://www.lawfareblog.com/beijings-new-national-intelligence-law-defense-offense; "数据安全法：护航数据安全 助力数字经济发展 [Data Security Law: Escort data security, help the development of a digital economy]," The National People's Congress of the People's Republic of China, June 10, 2021, http://www.npc.gov.cn/npc/c30834/202106/b7b68bf8aca84f50a5bdef7f01acb6fe.shtml; Lester Ross, Kenneth Zhou, and Tingting Liu, "China Promulgates Data Security Law," WilmerHale, June 15, 2021, https://www.wilmerhale.com/en/insights/client-alerts/20210615-china-promulgates-data-security-law; Xiao, "China Passes One of the World's Strictest Data-Privacy Laws."

174 **"rule of law," where the law constrains even the government:** " 'Rule of Law' or 'Rule by Law'? In China, a Preposition Makes All the Difference," *Wall Street Journal,* October 20, 2014, https://www.wsj.com/articles/BL-CJB-24523.

175 **"The law is there to protect the Party's power":** Hoffman, interview.

175 **notably absent were any examples of Chinese government abuse of AI technology:** "Ai Governance Observatory," Artificial Intelligence Governance Online, updated 2021, http://www.ai-governance.online/cases-en.

175 **"Because of censorship, the government ensures that people know very, very little":** Wang, interview.

175 **Even Yi Zeng has dismissed the CCP's human rights abuses against Uighurs:** See remarks beginning at 29:00. Yi Zeng, remarks at Politico Live AI Summit 2021, virtual, May 31, 2021, https://www.youtube.com/watch?v=snIZRLDK0Rg.

176 **"tea" with the police, a polite euphemism:** "Drink Tea," China Digital Space, n.d, https://chinadigitaltimes.net/space/Drink_tea; Oiwan Lam, "China: Bloggers "Forced to Drink Tea" with Police," *Global Voices Advox,* February 19, 2013, https://advox.globalvoices.org/2013/02/19/china-bloggers-forced-to-drink-tea-with-police/.

176 **Personal Information Protection Law:** Xiao, "China Passes One of the World's Strictest Data-Privacy Laws."

177 **harassment of Westerners:** Paul Mozur, Alexandra Stevenson, and Edward Wong, "Koch Executive's Harassment in China Adds to Fears Among Visitors," *New York Times,* July 11, 2019, https://www.nytimes.com/2019/07/11/business/american-businesses-china.html.

177 **China arbitrarily detained Canadians:** "Michael Kovrig and Michael Spavor: Canada Renews Calls for China to Release Charged Pair," BBC News, June 19, 2020, https://www.bbc.com/news/world-asia-china-53113179.

177 **two and a half years in prison:** "Michael Kovrig and Michael Spavor"; Amanda Coletta, "Canada's 'two Michaels' back home after more than 1,000 days imprisoned in China as Huawei's Meng cuts deal with U.S.," *Washington Post,* September 25, 2021, https://www.washingtonpost.com/world/2021/09/24/canada-two-michaels-china-huawei/.

21. STRANGLEHOLD

178 **China's national efforts to boost its semiconductor industry:** VerWey, "Chinese Semiconductor Industrial Policy: Past and Present," 10.

178 **ten strategic plans and policy guidelines:** Duchâtel, *The Weak Links in China's Drive for Semiconductors,* 41.

178 **$150 billion to semiconductor investments:** Duchâtel, *The Weak Links in China's Drive for*

Semiconductors, 43; VerWey, "Chinese Semiconductor Industrial Policy: Past and Present," 13.

178 **massive capital needed to compete:** VerWey, "Chinese Semiconductor Industrial Policy: Past and Present," 15; Duchâtel, *The Weak Links in China's Drive for Semiconductors*, 43–46; Semiconductor Industry Association, "China's Share of Global Chip Sales Now Surpasses Taiwan's, Closing in on Europe's and Japan's," SIA blog, January 10, 2022, https://www.semiconductors.org/chinas-share-of-global-chip-sales-now-surpasses-taiwan-closing-in-on-europe-and-japan/.

178 **dearth of high-end talent:** Duchâtel, *The Weak Links in China's Drive for Semiconductors*, 47–51.

178 **3,000 semiconductor engineers from Taiwan:** 邱立玲 [Qiu Liling], "中國企業開出2至3倍薪資挖角 台灣已流失3000多名半導體業人才 [Chinese companies pay 2–3 times their salaries, Taiwan has lost more than 3,000 talents in the semiconductor industry]," cmmedia.com.tw, December 3, 2019, https://www.cmmedia.com.tw/home/articles/18815.

178 **massive raises:** Yimou Lee, "China Lures Chip Talent from Taiwan with Fat Salaries, Perks," Reuters, September 4, 2018, https://www.reuters.com/innovation/article/us-china-semiconductors-taiwan-insight/china-lures-chip-talent-from-taiwan-with-fat-salaries-perks-idUSKCN1LK0H1.

178 **partially government-owned:** "Topic: Semiconductor Manufacturing International Corporation (SMIC)," *South China Morning Post*, updated September 4, 2021, https://www.scmp.com/topics/semiconductor-manufacturing-international-corporation-smic; John VerWey, "Chinese Semiconductor Industrial Policy: Past and Present," *United States International Trade Commission Journal of International Commerce and Economics* (July 2019), 15, https://papers.ssrn.com/sol3/papers.cfm?abstract_id=3441951.

178 **hundreds of Taiwanese engineers along with top executives:** Duchâtel, *The Weak Links in China's Drive for Semiconductors*, 50–51.

178 **foreign acquisitions:** VerWey, "Chinese Semiconductor Industrial Policy: Past and Present," 15–16.

179 **over $5 billion in acquisitions of U.S. semiconductor firms:** VerWey, "Chinese Semiconductor Industrial Policy: Past and Present," 15, 29.

179 **$11 billion total in overseas acquisitions:** C. Patrick Yue and Tian Lu, "China's Latest Overseas M&A in the Semiconductor Industry," *IEEE Solid-State Circuits Magazine*, November 16, 2017, https://ieeexplore.ieee.org/stamp/stamp.jsp?arnumber=8110893.

179 **fab-building spree:** Dylan McGrath, "China to House Over 40% of Semi Fabs by 2020," *EE Times Asia*, December 19, 2016, https://www.eetasia.com/china-to-house-over-40-of-semi-fabs-by-2020/.

179 **largest and fastest-growing importer of semiconductor manufacturing equipment:** VerWey, *The Health and Competitiveness of the U.S. Semiconductor Manufacturing Equipment Industry*, 8.

179 **fastest growing share of global chip manufacturing:** Fitch and Santiago, "Why Fewer Chips Say 'Made in the U.S.A.'"

179 **at least two generations (roughly five to six years) behind:** VerWey, "Chinese Semiconductor Industrial Policy: Past and Present," 7, 20; Duchâtel, *The Weak Links in China's Drive for Semiconductors*, 22.

179 **spur domestic chip innovation:** Michaela D. Platzer, John F. Sargent Jr., and Karen M. Sutter, *Semiconductors: U.S. Industry, Global Competition, and Federal Policy* (Congressional Research Service, October 26, 2020), 47–49, https://fas.org/sgp/crs/misc/R46581.pdf.

179 **Hefty government subsidies by many countries:** Organisation for Economic Co-opera-

tion and Development, "Measuring Distortions in International Markets: The Semiconductor Value Chain," OECD iLibrary, November 21, 2019.

179 **U.S. chip manufacturing declined:** SIA Board of Directors, letter to President Joe Biden, February 11, 2021, https://www.semiconductors.org/wp-content/uploads/2021/02/SIA -Letter-to-Pres-Biden-re-CHIPS-Act-Funding.pdf.

179 **Committee on Foreign Investment in the United States (CFIUS):** "Summary of the Foreign Investment Risk Review Modernization Act of 2018," treasury.gov, n.d., https://home .treasury.gov/system/files/206/Summary-of-FIRRMA.pdf.

179 **TSMC began construction:** Stephen Nellis, "TSMC Says Has Begun Construction at Its Arizona Chip Factory Site," Reuters, June 1, 2021, https://www.reuters.com/technology/ tsmc-says-construction-has-started-arizona-chip-factory-2021-06-01/; Alan Patterson, "TSMC to Build 5nm Fab in Arizona," *EE Times*, May 15, 2020, https://www.eetimes.com/ tsmc-to-build-5nm-fab-in-arizona/.

179 **Samsung rolled out its plans:** Anton Shilov, "Samsung Foundry: New $17 Billion Fab in the USA by Late 2023," *AnandTech*, February 10, 2021, https://www.anandtech.com/ show/16483/samsung-in-the-usa-a-17-billion-usd-fab-by-late-2023.

179 **Intel broke ground:** Stephen Nellis, "Intel Breaks Ground on $20 bln Arizona Plants as U.S. Chip Factory Race Heats Up," Reuters, September 25, 2021, https://www.reuters.com/ technology/intel-breaks-ground-20-bln-arizona-plants-us-chip-factory-race-heats-up -2021-09-24/; Don Clark, "Intel to Invest at Least $20 Billion in New Chip Factories in Ohio," *New York Times,* January 21, 2022, https://www.nytimes.com/2022/01/21/technology/intel -chip-factories-ohio.html.

180 **U.S. government subsidies to help fund:** Clark, "Intel to Invest at Least $20 Billion in New Chip Factories in Ohio"; Stephen Nellis, "Phoenix Okays Development deal with TSMC for $12 Billion Chip Factory," Reuters, November 18, 2020, https://www.reuters .com/article/us-tsmc-arizona/phoenix-okays-development-deal-with-tsmc-for-12-bil- lion-chip-factory-idUSKBN27Y30E; "Samsung Considers Austin for $17 Billion Chip Plant, Seeks Tax Breaks of at Least $806 Million," Reuters, February 4, 2021, https://www .reuters.com/article/us-usa-semiconductors-samsung-elec/samsung-considers-austin -for-17-billion-chip-plant-eyes-tax-breaks-of-at-least-806-million-documents-idUSKB- N2A433B.

180 **CHIPS and Science Act:** *CHIPS and Science Act of 2022: Section-by-Section Summary* (Commerce.senate.gov, 2022), https://www.commerce.senate.gov/services/files/1201E1CA -73CB-44BB-ADEB-E69634DA9BB9. See also Sections 9902 and 9906: William M. (Mac) Thornberry National Defense Authorization Act for Fiscal Year 2021, H.R. 6395, 116th Cong. (2019), https://www.congress.gov/bill/116th-congress/house-bill/6395/text. Thanks to CNAS research assistant Katie Galgano for background research on U.S. innovation bills.

180 **rise of AI-specialized chips:** Gaurav Batra et al., "Artificial-Intelligence Hardware: New Opportunities for Semiconductor Companies," McKinsey & Company, January 2, 2019, Exhibit 6, https://www.mckinsey.com/industries/semiconductors/our-insights/artificial -intelligence-hardware-new-opportunities-for-semiconductor-companies.

180 **efficient hardware optimized for deep learning:** Saif M. Khan and Alexander Mann, *AI Chips: What They Are and Why They Matter* (Center for Security and Emerging Technology, April 2020), https://cset.georgetown.edu/research/ai-chips-what-they-are-and-why -they-matter/.

180 **opportunity for China:** Joy Dantong Ma, "Chip on the Shoulder: How China Aims to Compete in Semiconductors," Macro Polo, September 10, 2019, https://macropolo.org/ china-chips-semiconductors-artificial-intelligence/?rp=e.

180 **application-specific integrated circuits (ASICs):** Khan and Mann, *AI Chips*, 20; Batra et al., "Artificial-Intelligence Hardware," Exhibit 6; *Hitting the Accelerator: The Next Generation of Machine-Learning Chips* (Deloitte, 2017), https://www2.deloitte.com/content/dam/Deloitte/global/Images/infographics/technologymediatelecommunications/gx-deloitte-tmt-2018-nextgen-machine-learning-report.pdf.

180 **Google's Tensor Processing Unit (TPU):** *Hitting the Accelerator*; "Cloud TPU Beginner's Guide," Google Cloud, updated September 29, 2021, https://cloud.google.com/tpu/docs/beginners-guide.

180 **TPUs have been used to train:** Oriol Vinyals et al., "Grandmaster Level in StarCraft II Using Multi-Agent Reinforcement Learning," *Nature* 575 (2019), 350–354, https://doi.org/10.1038/s41586-019-1724-z.

180 **about 10 percent—of the global semiconductor market:** Batra et al., "Artificial-Intelligence Hardware," Exhibit 3.

180 **Google and Tesla:** Khan and Mann, *AI Chips*, 28-29.

181 **"Our dependence on core technology is the biggest hidden trouble":** "Core technology depends on one's own efforts: President Xi," *People's Daily Online*, April 19, 2018, http://en.people.cn/n3/2018/0419/c90000-9451186.html.

181 **manufacturing equipment used to make chips:** Saif M. Khan, *Securing Semiconductor Supply Chains* (Center for Security and Emerging Technology, January 2021), 12–15, https://cset.georgetown.edu/research/securing-semiconductor-supply-chains/; Saif M. Khan, Alexander Mann, and Dahlia Peterson, *The Semiconductor Supply Chain: Assessing National Competitiveness* (Center for Security and Emerging Technology, January 2021), https://cset.georgetown.edu/research/the-semiconductor-supply-chain/.

181 **90 percent of the global semiconductor manufacturing equipment market:** Khan, Mann, and Peterson, *The Semiconductor Supply Chain*, 26.

181 **a single company holds a monopoly:** John VerWey, *The Health and Competitiveness of the U.S. Semiconductor Manufacturing Equipment Industry* (SSRN, July 1, 2019), 17–18, https://papers.ssrn.com/sol3/papers.cfm?abstract_id=3413951; Bharath Ramsundar, "An Introduction to EUV Lithography," *Deep Into the Forest*, January 22, 2021, https://deepforest.substack.com/p/an-introduction-to-euv-lithography; Robert Castellano, "ASML's Dominance of the Semiconductor Lithography Sector Has Far-Reaching Implications," *Seeking Alpha*, January 23, 2018, https://seekingalpha.com/article/4139540-asmls-dominance-of-semiconductor-lithography-sector-far-reaching-implications.

181 **blocking Chinese foundries from adopting EUV technology:** Alexandra Alper, Toby Sterling, and Stephen Nellis, "Trump Administration Pressed Dutch Hard to Cancel China Chip-Equipment Sale: Sources," Reuters, January 6, 2020, https://www.reuters.com/article/us-asml-holding-usa-china-insight/trump-administration-pressed-dutch-hard-to-cancel-china-chip-equipment-sale-sources-idUSKBN1Z50HN.

181 **other tools that are only slightly less advanced:** Roberto Solé, "ASML Informs That It Will Continue to Send Its EUV Machines to China," HardwarEsfera, October 19, 2020, https://hardwaresfera.com/en/noticias/hardware/asml-china-estados-unidos/; Stephen Nellis, "ASML Extends Sales Deal with Chinese Chipmaker SMIC to End of 2021," *Yahoo! Finance*, March 3, 2021, https://finance.yahoo.com/amphtml/news/chinese-chipmaker-smic-buys-1-143115414.html.

181 **chip fabrication processes as advanced as the 7 nm node:** TSMC's original "N7" 7 nm process introduced in 2018 used deep ultraviolet lithography. TSMC's improved "N7+" 7 nm process, which entered full-scale production in 2019, uses EUV lithography. WikiChip,

s.v. "7 nm lithography process," n.d., https://en.wikichip.org/wiki/7_nm_lithography_ process; "7nm Technology," Taiwan Semiconductor Manufacturing Company, n.d., https://www.tsmc.com/english/dedicatedFoundry/technology/logic/l_7nm.

182 **supply of photoresist:** Samuel M. Goodman, Dan Kim, and John VerWey, "The South Korea-Japan Trade Dispute in Context: Semiconductor Manufacturing, Chemicals, and Concentrated Supply Chains" (working paper ID-062, Office of Industries, U.S. International Trade Commission, October 2019), 17–19, https://usitc.gov/publications/332/ working_papers/the_south_korea-japan_trade_dispute_in_context_semiconductor_ manufacturing_chemicals_and_concentrated_supply_chains.pdf.

182 **Japan controls roughly 90 percent of the global supply:** Goodman, Kim, and VerWey, "The South Korea-Japan Trade Dispute in Context," 18; Khan, Mann, and Peterson, *The Semiconductor Supply Chain*, 59.

182 **trade dispute with South Korea:** Goodman, Kim, and VerWey, "The South Korea-Japan Trade Dispute in Context," 4–5; "Japan Partially Reverses Curbs on Tech Materials Exports to South Korea," Reuters, December 20, 2019, https://www.reuters.com/article/us -southkorea-japan/japan-partially-reverses-curbs-on-tech-materials-exports-to-south -korea-idUSKBN1YO11L.

182 **South Korea depends on Japan:** Goodman, Kim, and VerWey, "The South Korea-Japan Trade Dispute in Context," 18–19.

182 **specialized software used to design chips:** Asa Fitch and Luis Santiago, "Why Fewer Chips Say 'Made in the U.S.A.,'" *Wall Street Journal*, November 3, 2020, https://www.wsj .com/articles/why-fewer-chips-say-made-in-the-u-s-a-11604411810?mod=article_inline; VerWey, *The Health and Competitiveness of the U.S. Semiconductor Manufacturing Equipment Industry*, 7; Mathieu Duchâtel, *The Weak Links in China's Drive for Semiconductors* (Institut Montaigne, January 2021), https://www.institutmontaigne.org/ressources/pdfs/ publications/weak-links-chinas-drive-semiconductors-note_0.pdf, 11; Khan, Mann, and Peterson, *The Semiconductor Supply Chain*, 8, 49–50.

182 **major international campaign against Huawei:** Robin Emmott, "U.S. Warns European Allies Not to Use Chinese Gear for 5G Networks," Reuters, February 5, 2019, https://www .reuters.com/article/us-usa-china-huawei-tech-eu/u-s-warns-european-allies-not-to-use -chinese-gear-for-5g-networks-idUSKCN1PU1TG.

182 **failed to persuade many European countries:** "Factbox: Huawei's Involvement in 5G Telecoms Networks Around the World," Reuters, October 20, 2020, https://www.reuters .com/article/us-sweden-huawei-global-factbox/factbox-huaweis-involvement-in-5g-tele- coms-networks-around-the-world-idUKKBN2751A1.

182 **Japan and Australia, by contrast, banned Huawei:** "Factbox: Huawei's Involvement in 5G Telecoms Networks Around the World"; Simon Denyer, "Japan Effectively Bans China's Huawei and ZTE from Government Contracts, Joining U.S.," *Washington Post*, December 10, 2018, https://www.washingtonpost.com/world/asia_pacific/japan-effectively-bans -chinas-huawei-zte-from-government-contracts-joining-us/2018/12/10/748fe98a-fc69 -11e8-ba87-8c7facdf6739_story.html. The Japanese government did not mention Huawei by name but effectively bans equipment from Huawei or Chinese telecom provider ZTE in Japanese networks.

182 **U.S. government added Huawei to the Commerce Department's Entity List:** U.S. Department of Commerce, "Department of Commerce Announces the Addition of Huawei Technologies Co. Ltd. to the Entity List," news release, May 15, 2019, https://www.commerce .gov/news/press-releases/2019/05/department-commerce-announces-addition-huawei

-technologies-co-ltd (page discontinued); "Addition of Entities to the Entity List," 84 Fed. Reg. 22961 (May 21, 2019), https://www.federalregister.gov/documents/2019/05/21/2019 -10616/addition-of-entities-to-the-entity-list.

182 **legal ways of sidestepping the Trump administration's ban:** Bloomberg, "US Companies Find Legal Ways Around Trump's Huawei Blacklist," *IndustryWeek*, June 26, 2019, https://www.industryweek.com/leadership/article/22027819/us-companies-find -legal-ways-around-trumps-huawei-blacklist; Paul Mozur and Cecilia Kang, "U.S. Tech Companies Sidestep a Trump Ban, to Keep Selling to Huawei," *New York Times*, June 25, 2019, https://www.nytimes.com/2019/06/25/technology/huawei-trump-ban -technology.html.

182 **25 percent or more U.S.-origin:** "*De minimis* Rules and Guidelines: § 734.4 and Supplement No. 2 to part 734 of the EAR," doc.gov, November 5, 2019, https://www.bis.doc.gov/ index.php/documents/pdfs/1382-de-minimis-guidance/file.

183 **officials criticized the companies' moves:** Mozur and Kang, "U.S. Tech Companies Sidestep a Trump Ban."

183 **$75 billion in state subsidies:** Chuin-Wei Yap, "State Support Helped Fuel Huawei's Global Rise," *Wall Street Journal*, December 25, 2019, https://www.wsj.com/articles/state-support -helped-fuel-huaweis-global-rise-11577280736.

183 **Made in China 2025:** Jason Fang and Michael Walsh, "Made in China 2025: Beijing's Manufacturing Blueprint and Why the World Is Concerned," abcnet.au, April 28, 2018, https://www.abc.net.au/news/2018-04-29/why-is-made-in-china-2025-making-people -angry/9702374; James McBride and Andrew Chatzky, "Is 'Made in China 2025' a Threat to Global Trade?" Council on Foreign Relations, updated May 13, 2019, https://www.cfr.org/ backgrounder/made-china-2025-threat-global-trade.

183 **intellectual property theft and technology transfer:** Michael Brown and Pavneet Singh, *China's Technology Transfer Strategy: How Chinese Investments in Emerging Technology Enable a Strategic Competitor to Access the Crown Jewels of U.S. Innovation* (Defense Innovation Unit Experimental, January 2018), https://admin.govexec.com/media/diux_ chinatechnologytransferstudy_jan_2018_(1).pdf.

183 **scale production to 1.5 million units:** Sijia Jiang, "Huawei Says It Has Begun Producing 5G Base Stations Without U.S. Parts," Reuters, September 26, 2019, https://www.reu-ters.com/article/uk-usa-china-huawei-tech/huawei-already-producing-5g-base-stations -without-u-s-parts-ceo-idUKKBN1WB0YH?edition-redirect=uk.

183 **Chinese appetite for imported chips:** "US Sanctions Help China Supercharge Its Chipmaking Industry," Bloomberg, June 20, 2022, https://www.bloomberg.com/news/articles/ 2022-06-20/us-sanctions-helped-china-supercharge-its-chipmaking-industry.

184 **whack-a-mole efforts against Huawei:** Sean Keane, "Huawei Ban Timeline: Detained CFO Makes Deal with US Justice Department," *CNET*, September 30, 2021, https://www.cnet .com/news/huawei-ban-full-timeline-us-sanctions-china-trump-biden-5g/.

184 **New Commerce Department rules expanded the ban:** U.S. Department of Commerce, "Commerce Addresses Huawei's Efforts to Undermine Entity List, Restricts Products Designed and Produced with U.S. Technologies," news release, May 15, 2020, https://2017 -2021.commerce.gov/news/press-releases/2020/05/commerce-addresses-huaweis-efforts -undermine-entity-list-restricts.html; Reuters, "U.S.-China tensions rise as Trump administration moves to cut Huawei off from global chip suppliers," CNBC, May 15, 2020, https:// www.cnbc.com/2020/05/15/us-china-tensions-rise-as-trump-administration-moves-to -cut-huawei-off-from-global-chip-suppliers.html.

184 **"The United States needs to strangle Huawei":** James Politi and Kiran Stacey, "US Esca-

lates China Tensions with Tighter Huawei Controls," *Financial Times*, May 15, 2020, https://www.ft.com/content/c284ee77-ddae-4133-b6a7-4b7443d94109.

184 **prohibiting U.S. equipment from being used to manufacture chips from *any* company:** "Addition of Huawei Non-U.S. Affiliates to the Entity List, the Removal of Temporary General License, and Amendments to General Prohibition Three (Foreign-Produced Direct Product Rule)," 85 Fed. Reg. 51596 (August 17, 2020), https://www.federalregister.gov/documents/2020/08/20/2020-18213/addition-of-huawei-non-us-affiliates-to-the-entity-list-the-removal-of-temporary-general-license-and; Jeanne Whalen and Ellen Nakashima, "U.S. Tightens Restrictions on Huawei Yet Again, Underscoring the Difficulty of Closing Trade Routes," *Washington Post*, August 17, 2020, https://www.washingtonpost.com/business/2020/08/17/us-cracks-down-huawei-again/.

184 **U.S. industry protested the expansive ban:** "SIA Statement on Export Control Rule Changes," Semiconductor Industry Association, August 17, 2020, https://www.semiconductors.org/sia-statement-on-export-control-rule-changes-2/.

184 **TSMC stated they would no longer ship chips to Huawei:** David Shepardson, "U.S. Tightening Restrictions on Huawei Access to Technology, Chips," Reuters, August 17, 2020, https://www.reuters.com/article/us-usa-huawei-tech-exclusive/exclusive-u-s-to-tighten-restrictions-on-huawei-access-to-technology-chips-sources-say-idUSKCN25D1CC.

184 **TSMC sales to China dropped:** Taiwan Semiconductor Manufacturing Company, *4Q20 Quarterly Management Report* (draft), January 14, 2021, https://investor.tsmc.com/english/encrypt/files/encrypt_file/reports/2021-01/4Q20ManagementReport.pdf; "The Struggle Over Chips Enters a New Phase," *The Economist*, January 21, 2021, https://www.economist.com/leaders/2021/01/23/the-struggle-over-chips-enters-a-new-phase.

184 **"This kills Huawei":** Whalen and Nakashima, "U.S. Tightens Restrictions on Huawei Yet Again."

184 **China's largest and most advanced chipmaker:** John VerWey, "Chinese Semiconductor Industrial Policy: Prospects for Future Success," *United States International Trade Commission Journal of International Commerce and Economics* (August 2019), 14, 20, https://papers.ssrn.com/sol3/papers.cfm?abstract_id=3441959.

184 **"entities of concern":** U.S. Department of Commerce, "Commerce Adds China's SMIC to the Entity List, Restricting Access to Key Enabling U.S. Technology," news release, December 18, 2020, https://2017-2021.commerce.gov/news/press-releases/2020/12/commerce-adds-chinas-smic-entity-list-restricting-access-key-enabling.html; "Addition of Entities to the Entity List, Revision of Entry on the Entity List, and Removal of Entities From the Entity List," 85 Fed. Reg. 83416 (December 18, 2020), http://www.federalregister.gov/d/2020-28031.

184 **technology "uniquely required" for 10 nm process nodes or below:** U.S. Department of Commerce, "Commerce Adds China's SMIC to the Entity List"; "Addition of Entities to the Entity List, Revision of Entry on the Entity List, and Removal of Entities From the Entity List."

184 **production capacity at the 14 nm node:** "About Us," Semiconductor Manufacturing International Corporation, 2022, captured by the Internet Archive February 1, 2022, https://web.archive.org/web/20220201031506/https://www.smics.com/en/site/about_summary; Khan, Mann, and Peterson, *The Semiconductor Supply Chain*, 21, 23; Anton Shilov, "China to Ramp Up High-Volume Production Using 14nm Node by End of 2022," Tom's Hardware, June 23, 2021, https://www.tomshardware.com/news/china-hopes-to-ramp-up-14nm-production-in-2022. In July 2022, SMIC was revealed to have developed a quasi-7 nm chip for bitcoin mining. Majeed Ahmad, "The truth about SMIC's 7nm chip fabrication ordeal," EDN Asia, August 26, 2022, https://www.ednasia.com/the-truth-about-smics-7nm-chip-fabrication-ordeal/; TechInsights, *7nm SMIC MinerVa Bitcoin Miner*, 2022.

184 **expansive new restrictions:** "Additional Export Controls: Certain Advanced Computing and Semiconductor Manufacturing Items; Supercomputer and Semiconductor End Use; Entity List Modification," document no. 2022-21658 (October 13, 2022), https://www.federalregister.gov/public-inspection/2022-21658/additional-export-controls-certain-advanced-computing-and-semiconductor-manufacturing-items.

184 **China announced a $1.4 trillion investment:** "China's Got a New Plan to Overtake the U.S. in Tech," Bloomberg, May 20, 2020, https://www.bloomberg.com/news/articles/2020-05-20/china-has-a-new-1-4-trillion-plan-to-overtake-the-u-s-in-tech.

185 **slow to develop a strategy for competing in AI hardware:** Christopher Darby and Sarah Sewall, "The Innovation Wars: America's Eroding Technological Advantage," *Foreign Affairs*, March/April 2021, https://www.foreignaffairs.com/articles/united-states/2021-02-10/technology-innovation-wars; Matt Pottinger, "Beijing's American Hustle," *Foreign Affairs*, September/October 2021, https://www.foreignaffairs.com/articles/asia/2021-08-23/beijings-american-hustle; Ben Buchanan, "The U.S. Has AI Competition All Wrong," *Foreign Affairs*, August 7, 2020, https://www.foreignaffairs.com/articles/united-states/2020-08-07/us-has-ai-competition-all-wrong; *A Strategy for the Chips for America Fund* (U.S. Department of Commerce, September 6, 2022), https://www.nist.gov/system/files/documents/2022/09/13/CHIPS-for-America-Strategy%20%28Sept%206%2C%202022%29.pdf.

185 **the ability to cut off China's access to chips:** Khan, *Securing Semiconductor Supply Chains*.

185 **a rare move:** Carrick Flynn, "The Chip-Making Machine at the Center of Chinese Dual-Use Concerns," Brookings Institution, June 30, 2020, https://www.brookings.edu/techstream/the-chip-making-machine-at-the-center-of-chinese-dual-use-concerns/; Ryan Fedasiuk, Karson Elmgren, and Ellen Lu, *Silicon Twist: Managing the Chinese Military's Access to AI Chips* (Center for Security and Emerging Technology, June 2022), https://cset.georgetown.edu/publication/silicon-twist/.

185 **fueling the growth of their domestic semiconductor industry:** Dan Wang, "China's Sputnik Moment? How Washington Boosted Beijing's Quest for Tech Dominance," *Foreign Affairs*, July 29, 2021, https://www.foreignaffairs.com/articles/united-states/2021-07-29/chinas-sputnik-moment; Jane Lanhee Lee and Stephen Nellis, "Analysis: U.S. ban on Nvidia, AMD chips seen boosting Chinese rivals," Reuters, September 8, 2022, https://www.reuters.com/technology/us-ban-nvidia-amd-chips-seen-boosting-chinese-rivals-2022-09-08/.

185 **China's ability to catch up in chip production:** Khan, *Securing Semiconductor Supply Chains*, 12–15; Saif M. Khan and Carrick Flynn, *Maintaining China's Dependence on Democracies for Advanced Computer Chips* (Brookings Institution, April 2020), https://www.brookings.edu/wp-content/uploads/2020/04/FP_20200427_computer_chips_khan_flynn.pdf.

185 **"control China's chip access":** Khan, *Securing Semiconductor Supply Chains*, 12.

185 **recommended the U.S. government control chip manufacturing technology:** National Security Commission on Artificial Intelligence, *Final Report* (n.d.), 231, https://www.nscai.gov/wp-content/uploads/2021/03/Full-Report-Digital-1.pdf.

185 **proposal endorsed by some:** Marco Rubio and Michael McCaul, letter to Gina Raimondo, March 17, 2022, https://www.rubio.senate.gov/public/_cache/files/3bb41687-81cf-4afd-a4a1-9710a23276e0/92A2622A0C8E981B853CE78C5E1720B5.03.17.22-rubio-mccaul-letter-to-commerce-re-smic.pdf.

185 **"sustainably effective":** Khan, *Securing Semiconductor Supply Chains*, 14.

186 **"as large of a lead as possible":** Jake Sullivan, remarks at the Special Competitive Studies Project Global Emerging Technologies Summit, September 16, 2022, https://www.white-

house.gov/briefing-room/speeches-remarks/2022/09/16/remarks-by-national-security
-advisor-jake-sullivan-at-the-special-competitive-studies-project-global-emerging
-technologies-summit/.

186 **diversify the geography of chip production:** Becca Wasser and Martijn Rasser, with Hannah Kelley, *When the Chips Are Down: Gaming the Global Semiconductor Competition* (Center for a New American Security, January 2022), https://www.cnas.org/publications/reports/when-the-chips-are-down; Julian E. Barnes, "How the Computer Chip Shortage Could Incite a U.S. Conflict With China," *New York Times*, January 26, 2022, https://www.nytimes.com/2022/01/26/us/politics/computer-chip-shortage-taiwan.html.

186 **100 miles off the coast of China:** John Lee and Jan-Peter Kleinhans, "Would China Invade Taiwan for TSMC?" *The Diplomat*, December 15, 2020, https://thediplomat.com/2020/12/would-china-invade-taiwan-for-tsmc/.

186 **the Chinese Communist Party has pledged to absorb:** Yew Lun Tian and Yimou Lee, "China Drops Word 'Peaceful' in Latest Push for Taiwan 'Reunification,'" Reuters, May 21, 2020, https://www.reuters.com/article/us-china-parliament-taiwan/china-drops-word-peaceful-in-latest-push-for-taiwan-reunification-idUSKBN22Y06S. A People's Republic of China white paper on Taiwan released in August 2022 stated, "We will work with the greatest sincerity and exert our utmost efforts to achieve peaceful reunification. But we will not renounce the use of force, and we reserve the option of taking all necessary measures." "Full Text: The Taiwan Question and China's Reunification in the New Era," Xinhua, August 10, 2022, https://english.news.cn/20220810/df9d3b8702154b34bbf1d451b99bf64a/c.html.

186 **moved Taiwan's semiconductor industry into the CCP's sphere of influence:** Wasser and Rasser, *When the Chips Are Down: Gaming the Global Semiconductor Competition.*

186 **expand multilateral export controls:** Saif M. Khan, *Maintaining the AI Chip Competitive Advantage of the United States and Its Allies* (Center for Security and Emerging Technology, December 2019), https://cset.georgetown.edu/wp-content/uploads/CSET-Maintaining-the-AI-Chip-Competitive-Advantage-of-the-United-States-and-its-Allies-20191206.pdf; Khan, *Securing Semiconductor Supply Chains.*

186 **China has 60 percent of the global demand:** Platzer, Sargent, and Sutter, *Semiconductors*, 26.

186 **buying power will tend to bend supply chains:** Antonio Varas and Raj Varadarajan, *How Restrictions to Trade with China Could End US Leadership in Semiconductors* (Boston Consulting Group, n.d.), https://media-publications.bcg.com/flash/2020-03-07-How-Restrictions-to-Trade-with-China-Could-End-US-Semiconductor-Leadership.pdf; Andre Barbe and Will Hunt, *Preserving the Choke Points* (Center for Security and Emerging Technology, May 2022), https://cset.georgetown.edu/publication/preserving-the-chokepoints/.

187 **technology-leading democracies to band together:** Anja Manuel, "How to Win the Technology Race with China," Freeman Spogli Institute for International Studies, June 18, 2019, https://fsi.stanford.edu/news/how-win-technology-race-china; Anja Manuel, Pavneet Singh, and Thompson Paine, "Compete, Contest and Collaborate: How to Win the Technology Race with China," Stanford Cyber Policy Center, October 17, 2019, https://fsi.stanford.edu/publication/compete-contest-and-collaborate-how-win-technology-race-china; Martijn Rasser et al., *Common Code: An Alliance Framework for Democratic Technology Policy* (Center for a New American Security, October 21, 2020), https://www.cnas.org/publications/reports/common-code; Jared Cohen and Richard Fontaine, "Uniting the Techno-Democracies: How to Build Digital Cooperation," *Foreign Affairs*, November/December 2020, https://www.foreignaffairs.com/articles/united-states/2020-10-13/uniting-techno-democracies; David Howell, "It's Time to Replace the Outmoded G7," *Japan Times*, February 15, 2021, https://

www.japantimes.co.jp/opinion/2021/02/15/commentary/world-commentary/g7-g20-d10
-uk-russia-us-boris-johnson/; Marietje Schaake, "How Democracies Can Claim Back Power
in the Digital World," *MIT Technology Review,* September 29, 2020, https://www.technolo-
gyreview.com/2020/09/29/1009088/democracies-power-digital-social-media-governance
-tech-companies-opinion/; Joe Biden, "My Trip to Europe Is About America Rallying
the World's Democracies," *Washington Post,* June 5, 2021, https://www.washingtonpost
.com/opinions/2021/06/05/joe-biden-europe-trip-agenda/.

187 **a new "D10" group of democratic, tech-leading countries:** Lucy Fisher, "Downing Street
Plans New 5G Club of Democracies," *Times* (London), May 29, 2020, https://www.thetimes
.co.uk/article/downing-street-plans-new-5g-club-of-democracies-bfnd5wj57.

187 **Potential areas of collaboration:** Rasser et al., *Common Code.*

187 **"critical- and emerging-technology working group":** The White House, "Quad Leaders'
Joint Statement: 'The Spirit of the Quad,'" March 12, 2021, https://www.whitehouse.gov/
briefing-room/statements-releases/2021/03/12/quad-leaders-joint-statement-the-spirit-of
-the-quad/.

187 **Trade and Technology Council (TTC):** The White House, "U.S.-EU Trade and Technology Council Inaugural Joint Statement," news release, September 29, 2021, https://
www.whitehouse.gov/briefing-room/statements-releases/2021/09/29/u-s-eu-trade
-and-technology-council-inaugural-joint-statement/.

22. ROBOTICS ROW

191 **periods of technological disruption:** Stephen Biddle, *Military Power: Explaining Victory
and Defeat in Modern Battle* (Princeton, NJ: Princeton University Press, 2004), https://
www.amazon.com/Military-Power-Explaining-Victory-Defeat/dp/0691128022; Max Boot,
War Made New: Weapons, Warriors, and the Making of the Modern World (New York:
Avery, August 16, 2007), https://www.amazon.com/War-Made-New-Weapons-Warriors/
dp/1592403158; Elting E. Morrison, "A Case Study of Innovation," *Engineering and Science
Monthly* XIII, no. 7 (April 1950): 5-11.

191 **Great Britain was the first nation to develop aircraft carriers:** Thomas C. Hone and Mark
D. Mandeles, "Interwar Innovation in Three Navies: U.S. Navy, Royal Navy, Imperial Japanese Navy," *Naval War College Review* 40, no. 2 (Spring 1987): 63-83, https://www.jstor
.org/stable/pdf/44636824.pdf.

191 **proper role of carriers:** Stephen Peter Rosen, *Winning the Next War: Innovation and the
Modern Military* (Ithaca, NY: Cornell University Press, May 3, 1994), 68-71, 76-88, https://
www.amazon.com/Winning-Next-War-Innovation-Military/dp/0801481961.

191 **Battle of Midway:** Sarah Pruitt, "5 Things You Might Not Know About the Battle of Midway," History.com, November 8, 2019, https://www.history.com/news/battle-midway
-facts.

192 **war games at the Naval War College:** Rosen, *Winning the Next War,* 68-71; Jan M. Van
Tol, "Military Innovation and Carrier Aviation—The Relevant History," *Joint Force Quar-
terly* (Summer 1997), 77-87, https://fas.org/man/dod-101/sys/ship/docs/1516pgs.pdf;
Jan M. Van Tol, "Military Innovation and Carrier Aviation—An Analysis," *Joint Force
Quarterly* (Autumn/Winter 1997-98), 97-109, https://fas.org/man/dod-101/sys/ship/
docs/2017pgs.pdf.

192 **bureaucratic missteps, rather than a lack of access to aircraft technology:** Hone and
Mandeles, "Interwar Innovation in Three Navies"; Van Tol, "Military Innovation and Car-

rier Aviation—The Relevant History"; Van Tol, "Military Innovation and Carrier Aviation—An Analysis."

192 **"by the time Germany invaded France in May 1940":** Kenneth A. Steadman, "The Evolution of the Tank in the U.S. Army," Combined Arms Research Library, April 21, 1982, National Archives and Records Administration, https://webharvest.gov/peth04/20041017175629/ http://www.cgsc.army.mil/carl/resources/csi/steadman2/steadman2.asp.

192 **New technologies are useless without the right organizations:** Michael C. Horowitz, *The Diffusion of Military Power: Causes and Consequences for International Politics* (Princeton, NJ: Princeton University Press, 2010).

193 **AI Task Force:** Matt Easley, interview by author, February 4, 2020.

194 **"a machine learning algorithm will be part of the fabric":** Isaac Faber, interview by author, February 4, 2020.

194 **use AI to accelerate targeting cycles:** Sydney J. Freedberg Jr., "Army AI Gets Live Fire Test Next Week," *Breaking Defense,* February 23, 2021, https://breakingdefense.com/2021/02/ army-ai-gets-live-fire-test-next-week/.

194 **fifteen different offices and departments across DoD:** Michael C. Horowitz and Lauren Kahn, "Why DoD's New Approach to Data and Artificial Intelligence Should Enhance National Defense," Council on Foreign Relations blog, March 11, 2022, https://www.cfr .org/blog/why-dods-new-approach-data-and-artificial-intelligence-should-enhance -national-defense.

23. PROJECT VOLTRON

195 **twenty-six business days:** Zach Walker, "VOLTRON: Disrupting DoD Cybersecurity with Artificial Intelligence," LinkedIn, August 2, 2018, https://www.linkedin.com/pulse/ voltron-disrupting-dod-cybersecurity-artificial-zach-walker/; Defense Innovation Unit, "Startups Highlight Ease and Benefits of Working with DoD," news release, March 13, 2019, https://www.diu.mil/latest/startups-highlight-ease-and-benefits-of-working-with-dod.

195 **"mission-critical cyber vulnerabilities":** *Weapon Systems Cybersecurity: DOD Just Beginning to Grapple with Scale of Vulnerabilities* (report no. GAO-19-128, US Government Accountability Office, October 2018), https://www.gao.gov/assets/700/694913.pdf, 21.

195 **vulnerabilities in fielded military aircraft:** *Artificial Intelligence Initiatives within the Defense Innovation Unit, Senate Armed Services Committee Subcommittee on Emerging Threats and Capabilities,* 116th Cong. (2019) (statement by Michael Brown, director of the Defense Innovation Unit), https://www.armed-services.senate.gov/imo/media/doc/ Brown_03-12-19.pdf.

195 **winner of the Cyber Grand Challenge:** "About Us," ForAllSecure, 2021, https://forallse-cure.com/about-us.

195 **Project Voltron:** Defense Innovation Unit, "Startups Highlight Ease and Benefits of Working with DoD"; Chris Bing, "The Tech Behind the DARPA Grand Challenge Winner Will Now Be Used by the Pentagon," *CyberScoop,* August 11, 2017, https://www.cyberscoop .com/mayhem-darpa-cyber-grand-challenge-dod-voltron/.

196 **"automating" cyber security functions:** Michael Brown, interview with author, February 25, 2020.

196 **deployment of small, autonomous drones:** "DIU Making Transformative Impact Five Years In," U.S. Department of Defense, August 27, 2020, https://www.defense.gov/Explore/ News/Article/Article/2327021/diu-making-transformative-impact-five-years-in/; Elliot

Ackerman, "A Navy SEAL, a Quadcopter, and a Quest to Save Lives in Combat," *Wired*, October 30, 2020, https://www.wired.com/story/shield-ai-quadcopter-military-drone/.

196 **poor state of Russian maintenance:** Trent Telenko (@TrentTelenko), "This is a thread that will explain the implied poor Russian Army truck maintenance practices . . . ," Twitter, March 2, 2022, https://twitter.com/trenttelenko/status/1499164245250002944.

196 **C3 AI:** "C3 AI Applications," C3.ai, 2021, https://c3.ai/products/c3-ai-applications/.

196 **C3 AI had an initial prototype:** "AI for Aircraft Readiness for the U.S. Department of Defense," C3.ai., 2021, https://c3.ai/customers/ai-for-aircraft-readiness/; *Artificial Intelligence Initiatives*.

196 **reduction in unscheduled maintenance:** *Artificial Intelligence Initiatives*, 6.

196 **"calculate the probability of failure on high-priority subsystems":** "AI for Aircraft Readiness for the U.S. Department of Defense."

196 **"actually, it was a small problem from their perspective":** Brown, interview.

196 **DIU expanded C3 AI's predictive maintenance work:** C3.ai, "US Defense Department Awards C3.ai $95M Contract Vehicle to Improve Aircraft Readiness Using AI," news release, January 15, 2020, https://c3.ai/us-defense-department-awards-c3-ai-95m-contract-vehicle-to-improve-aircraft-readiness-using-ai/; Philong Duong, "AI-Based Predictive Maintenance to Enhance Readiness, Reduce In-Flight Failures," C3.ai blog, July 21, 2020, https://c3.ai/blog/predictive-maintenance-to-enhance-readiness-reduce-in-flight-failures/.

196 **over $280 billion annually in operations and maintenance:** Office of the Under Secretary of Defense (Comptroller)/ Chief Financial Officer, *Operation and Maintenance Overview: Irreversible Implementation of the National Defense Strategy* (US Department of Defense, 2020), 2, https://comptroller.defense.gov/Portals/45/Documents/defbudget/fy2021/fy2021_OM_Overview.pdf.

196 **DIU has expanded their predictive maintenance work:** *Artificial Intelligence Initiatives*; "DIU Making Transformative Impact Five Years In."

197 **Navy ship maintenance:** Office of the Under Secretary of Defense (Comptroller), *National Defense Budget Estimates for FY 2021* (U.S. Department of Defense, April 2020), 55–56, https://comptroller.defense.gov/Portals/45/Documents/defbudget/fy2021/FY21_Green_Book.pdf.

197 **eight of every ten aircraft would be ready to fly:** Aaron Mehta, "Mattis Orders Fighter Jet Readiness to Jump to 80 Percent—in One Year," *DefenseNews*, October 9, 2018, https://www.defensenews.com/air/2018/10/09/mattis-orders-fighter-jet-readiness-to-jump-to-80-percent-in-one-year/.

197 **The Navy was in even worse shape:** David B. Larger, "The US Navy's Fight to Fix Its Worn-Out Super Hornet Fleet Is Making Way," *DefenseNews*, August 16, 2018, https://www.defensenews.com/naval/2018/08/16/the-us-navys-fight-to-fix-its-worn-out-super-hornet-fleet-is-making-way/.

197 **3 to 6 percent increase in mission capability:** "C3 AI Readiness: Maximize Mission Capability with AI-Driven Maintenance Operations," C3.ai., 2021, https://c3.ai/products/c3-ai-readiness/; "AI for Aircraft Readiness for the U.S. Department of Defense."

197 **"It was all about readiness":** Brown, interview.

197 **Air Force later abandoned Mattis's 80 percent readiness goal:** Senate Armed Service Committee, "Advance Policy Questions for General Charles Q. Brown, Jr., U.S. Air Force, Nominee for Appointment to be Chief of Staff of the Air Force," senate.gov, May 7, 2020, https://www.armed-services.senate.gov/imo/media/doc/Brown_APQs_05-07-20.pdf.

197 **"scaling machine learning solutions for predictive maintenance":** Mark Esper, "Con-

gratulations to the Defense Innovation Unit on Your Fifth Anniversary," memorandum to Defense Innovation Unit, August 25, 2020, https://media.defense.gov/2020/Aug/27/2002485583/-1/-1/1/DIU_BIRTHDAY_LETTER.PDF.

197 **Recent DoD Innovation Organizations:** Thanks to Xiaojing (JJ) Zeng, former CNAS Joseph S. Nye, Jr. Intern, for background research on DoD innovation organizations.

198 **DIU's founding in 2015:** Ash Carter, "Rewiring the Pentagon: Charting a New Path on Innovation and Cybersecurity," lecture to Stanford University, Palo Alto, CA, April 23, 2015, https://www.defense.gov/Newsroom/Speeches/Speech/Article/606666/drell-lecture-rewiring-the-pentagon-charting-a-new-path-on-innovation-and-cyber/; Billy Mitchell, " 'No Longer an Experiment'—DIUx Becomes DIU, Permanent Pentagon Unit," FedScoop, August 9, 2018, https://www.fedscoop.com/diu-permanent-no-longer-an-experiment/.

199 **120 "non-traditional" companies:** Esper, "Congratulations to the Defense Innovation Unit on Your Fifth Anniversary."

24. FOUNDATION

200 **"a protective response":** Brendan McCord, interview by author, February 5, 2020.

201 **"you have lots of data":** Jason Brown, interview by author, April 22, 2020.

201 **"the use case is: find the fire line":** Brown used the term "fire line" to refer to the perimeter of the fire. Firefighters use the term "fire line" differently, an example of some of the challenges in bringing together different communities.

202 **CrowdAI:** "We Are CrowdAI," CrowdAI, 2021, https://crowdai.com/about-us.

202 **Devaki Raj:** "Devaki Raj," *30 Under 30, Forbes*, 2019, https://www.forbes.com/profile/devaki-raj/?list=30under30-science&sh=4f95c961234a.

202 **build "best in class computer vision algorithms":** Devaki Raj, interview by author, July 29, 2021.

202 **"You need data to train":** Brown, interview.

202 **link the images to a real-world location:** Dominic Garcia, interview by author, May 19, 2020.

202 **1.5 terabytes of drone footage:** Brown, interview.

203 **"Once we had the labeled data set":** Garcia, interview.

203 **"The algorithm is always the easiest":** Jack Shanahan, interview by author, April 1, 2020.

203 **"just a few minutes" to develop a useful model:** Isaac Faber, interview by author, February 4, 2020.

203 **"A lot of folks are mesmerized":** Matt Cook, interview by author, April 28, 2020.

204 **JAIC's Fire Perimeter AI system began field testing:** "The JAIC Is Supporting National Guard Efforts to Combat Destructive Wildfires," Joint Artificial Intelligence Center, October 1, 2019, https://www.ai.mil/blog_09_16_19.html; The original name of "Fire Line" was changed to "Fire Perimeter" since "fire line" has a different meaning among firefighters. Erik Bates, interview, April 22, 2020.

204 **labeled dataset of over 850,000 buildings:** "xBD Dataset," xView2.org, n.d., https://xview2.org/dataset.

204 **AI model assessed building damage 300 times faster:** Erik Bates, interview by author, April 22, 2020.

205 **"I think we're probably two years away from having the data":** Shanahan, interview.

205 **nearly half the world's population had a smartphone:** Ash Turner, "How Many Smartphones Are in the World?" BankMyCell, 2021, https://www.bankmycell.com/blog/how-many-phones-are-in-the-world.

205 **AI was his "number one" technology priority:** Mark T. Esper, remarks at National Security Commission on Artificial Intelligence public conference, November 5, 2019, https://www.defense.gov/Newsroom/Transcripts/Transcript/Article/2011960/remarks-by-secretary-esper-at-national-security-commission-on-artificial-intell/.

205 **DoD spends approximately 1 percent:** Figure 5.2.2 in Daniel Zhang et al., *The AI Index 2022 Annual Report* (Stanford, CA: AI Index Steering Committee, March 2022), 189, https://aiindex.stanford.edu/wp-content/uploads/2022/03/2022-AI-Index-Report_Master.pdf.

206 **AI's hype:** Julia Ciocca, Michael C. Horowitz, and Lauren Kahn, "The Perils of Overhyping Artificial Intelligence: For AI to Succeed, It First Must Be Able to Fail," *Foreign Affairs*, April 6, 2021, https://www.foreignaffairs.com/articles/united-states/2021-04-06/perils-overhyping-artificial-intelligence; Marc Losito and John Anderson, "The Department of Defense's Looming AI Winter," *War on the Rocks*, May 10, 2021, https://warontherocks.com/2021/05/the-department-of-defenses-looming-ai-winter/; Esper, remarks at National Security Commission on Artificial Intelligence public conference; Jackson Barnett, "Esper Announces New Initiatives to Boost U.S. Position in AI Race," *FedScoop*, September 9, 2020, https://www.fedscoop.com/esper-ai-announcements-ai-race/.

206 **"either introduce efficiencies, or find cost savings":** Rachael Martin, interview by author, April 29, 2020.

206 **"Game Changer":** "The JAIC's Business Process Transformation Mission Initiative Delivers," Joint Artificial Intelligence Center, May 14, 2020, https://www.ai.mil/blog_05_14_20-mi_business_process_transformation_mission.html.

206 **"amateurs talk tactics":** "Where does the quote of 'Amateurs talk strategy; professionals talk logistics' come from? Is it true or not?" Quora, June 20, 2019, https://www.quora.com/Where-does-the-quote-of-Amateurs-talk-strategy-professionals-talk-logistics-come-from-Is-it-true-or-not.

207 **precision-guided weapons:** Barry D. Watts, *Six Decades of Guided Munitions and Battle Networks: Progress and Prospects* (Center for Strategic and Budgetary Assessments, March 2007), https://csbaonline.org/research/publications/six-decades-of-guided-munitions-and-battle-networks-progress-and-prospects; Lauren Kahn and Michael C. Horowitz, *Who Gets Smart: Explaining How Precision Bombs Proliferate* (SSRN.com, 2021), https://papers.ssrn.com/sol3/papers.cfm?abstract_id=3792071.

207 **predictive maintenance tool for helicopters:** The Robotics Institute, Carnegie Mellon University, "Carnegie Mellon AI Collaborates with Pentagon to Improve Reliability of Army's Black Hawk Helicopters," news release, February 3, 2021, https://www.ri.cmu.edu/carnegie-mellon-ai-collaborates-with-pentagon-to-improve-reliability-of-armys-black-hawk-helicopters/; "JAIC Partners with USSOCOM to Deliver AI-Enabled Predictive Maintenance Capabilities," Joint Artificial Intelligence Center, December 17, 2020, https://www.ai.mil/news_12_17_20-jaic_partners_with_ussocom_to_deliver_ai-enabled_predictive_maintenance_capabilities.html; Sydney J. Freedberg Jr, "Fix It Before It Breaks: SOCOM, JAIC Pioneer Predictive Maintenance AI," *Breaking Defense*, February 19, 2019, https://breakingdefense.com/2019/02/fix-it-before-it-breaks-socom-jaic-pioneer-predictive-maintenance-ai/; Shanahan, interview.

207 **"That's fantastic that we did that for one engine":** Nand Mulchandani, interview by author, May 12, 2020.

207 **"We empower your workforce":** Raj, interview.

207 **cloud-based AI platform called the Joint Common Foundation:** Joint Artificial Intelligence Center (website), 2019, https://www.ai.mil/.

208 **the JAIC worked to accelerate the process:** "A Roadmap to Getting 'AI-Ready,'" Joint Artificial intelligence Center, June 18, 2020, https://www.ai.mil/blog_06_18_20-a_roadmap_to_getting_ai_ready.html.

25. THE WRONG KIND OF LETHALITY

209 **Deep Learning Analytics:** "Deep Learning Analytics Center of Excellence," General Dynamics Mission Systems, 2021, https://gdmissionsystems.com/about-us/engineering/deep-learning.

209 **top American performer in several AI competitions:** John Kaufhold, interview by author, February 7, 2020; "Private Leaderboard" in "iNaturalist Challenge at FGVC5," Kaggle, June 4, 2018, https://www.kaggle.com/c/inaturalist-2018/leaderboard; "Private Leaderboard" in "iNaturalist 2019 at FGVC6," Kaggle, June 10, 2019, https://www.kaggle.com/c/inaturalist-2019-fgvc6/leaderboard; "Deep Learning Analytics Places 2nd in International Machine Learning Challenge," General Dynamics Mission Systems, August 19, 2018, https://gdmissionsystems.com/articles/2018/08/19/deep-learning-analytics-places-2nd-in-international-machine-learning-challenge.

209 **Eastern Foundry:** Eastern Foundry (website), 2019, https://www.eastern-foundry.com/.

210 **paper showing groundbreaking performance on ImageNet:** Alex Krizhevsky, Ilya Sutskever, and Geoffrey E. Hinton, *ImageNet Classification with Deep Convolutional Neural Networks* (nips.cc, 2012), https://papers.nips.cc/paper/2012/file/c399862d3b9d6b76c8436e924a68c45b-Paper.pdf.

210 **Deep Learning Analytics won a $6 million contract:** Kaufhold, interview; John Keller, "DARPA TRACE program using advanced algorithms, embedded computing for radar target recognition," *Military & Aerospace Electronics*, July 24, 2015, https://www.militaryaerospace.com/computers/article/16714226/darpa-trace-program-using-advanced-algorithms-embedded-computing-for-radar-target-recognition.

211 **government contracting requirements:** Kaufhold, interview; "Business Rx: The Story of How One Tiny Start-Up Bested the World's Biggest Federal Contractors," On Small Business, *Washington Post*, August 24, 2016, https://www.washingtonpost.com/news/on-small-business/wp/2016/08/24/business-rx-the-story-of-how-one-tiny-start-up-bested-the-worlds-biggest-federal-contractors/.

211 **iNaturalist challenge:** Yang Song and Serge Belongie, "Introducing the iNaturalist 2018 Challenge," Google AI Blog, March 9, 2018, https://ai.googleblog.com/2018/03/introducing-inaturalist-2018-challenge.html.

211 **average of 1,000 images per category:** "About ImageNet," ImageNet, updated March 11, 2021, http://www.image-net.org/about.

212 **Deep Learning Analytics came in second place:** "Private Leaderboard" in "iNaturalist Challenge at FGVC5."

212 **officer responsible for meeting security requirements for handling classified data:** "Facility Security Officers," Defense Counterintelligence and Security Agency, n.d., https://www.dcsa.mil/mc/ctp/fso/

213 **"It takes a very long time":** Devaki Raj, interview by author, July 29, 2021.

213 **Federal Risk and Authorization Management Program:** FedRAMP (website), n.d., https://www.fedramp.gov/.

214 **DIU transitioned thirty-five commercial projects:** Defense Innovation Unit, "Annual Report: FY 2021," 8, https://assets.ctfassets.net/3nanhbfkr0pc/5JPfbtxBv4HLjn8eQKiUW9/cab09a726c2ad2ed197bdd2df343f385/Digital_Version_-_Final_-_DIU_-_2021_Annual_Report.pdf.

214 **the bespoke nature of much of DoD's current innovation:** Jackson Barnett, "The Pentagon Is Failing to Scale Emerging Technology, Senior Leaders Say," *FedScoop*, August 7, 2020, https://www.fedscoop.com/dod-innovation-emerging-technology-acquisition-aspen-security-summit/.

214 **"the classic hack-the-bureaucracy organizations":** Jack Shanahan, interview by author, April 1, 2020.

214 **two million full-time military and civilian employees:** "About the Department of Defense (DOD)," U.S. Department of Defense website, n.d., https://www.defense.gov/about/.

214 **leveraged business model:** Brett Bivens, "Business Model Leverage: Spotify, the Audio Market, and the Negative Churn Consumer SaaS Company," *Venture Desktop* (blog), December 10, 2019, https://venturedesktop.substack.com/p/business-model-leverage.

214 **"Well, it needs lots of data":** Nand Mulchandani, interview by author, May 12, 2020.

214 **"hitting the infrastructure wall":** Will Roper, interview by author, August 6, 2021.

215 **Jim Mattis flew out to the West Coast:** Alan Boyle, "Pentagon Chief James Mattis Meets With Amazon Chief Jeff Bezos During Tech Tour," *GeekWire*, August 10, 2017, https://www.geekwire.com/2017/pentagon-chief-james-mattis-meets-amazons-jeff-bezos-west-coast-tech-sub-tour/; Jeff Bezos (@JeffBezos), "A pleasure to host #SecDef James Mattis at Amazon HQ in Seattle today," Twitter, August 10, 2017, https://twitter.com/JeffBezos/status/895714205822730241.

215 **Joint Enterprise Defense Infrastructure:** "About JEDI Cloud," Enterprise Cloud, U.S. Department of Defense, n.d,. https://www.cloud.mil/JEDI-Cloud/ (page discontinued), https://web.archive.org/web/20210608000716/https://www.cloud.mil/JEDI-Cloud/; Heidi M. Peters, *The Department of Defense's JEDI Cloud Program* (Congressional Research Service, updated August 2, 2019), https://fas.org/sgp/crs/natsec/R45847.pdf; Monica Nickelsburg, "What Is JEDI? Explaining the $10B Military Cloud Contract That Microsoft Just Won over Amazon," *GeekWire*, October 28, 2019, https://www.geekwire.com/2019/jedi-explaining-10b-military-cloud-contract-microsoft-just-won-amazon/.

215 **challenging the terms of the RFP:** Inspector General, U.S. Department of Defense, *Report on the Joint Enterprise Defense Infrastructure (JEDI) Cloud Procurement* (report no. DODIG-2020-079, US Department of Defense, April 13, 2020), https://media.defense.gov/2020/Apr/21/2002285087/-1/-1/1/REPORT%20ON%20THE%20JOINT%20ENTERPRISE%20DEFENSE%20INFRASTRUCTURE%20(JEDI)%20CLOUD%20PRO-CUREMENT%20DODIG-2020-079.PDF;

215 **contract provisions "seem to be tailored to one specific contractor":** Steve Womack and Tom Cole, letter to Glenn A. Fine, October 22, 2018, https://www.nextgov.com/media/gbc/docs/pdfs_edit/102318fk1ng.pdf.

215 **letter didn't mention which contractor:** May Jeong, "'Everybody Immediately Knew That It Was for Amazon': Has Bezos Become More Powerful in D.C. Than Trump?" *Vanity Fair*, August 13, 2018, https://www.vanityfair.com/news/2018/08/has-bezos-become-more-powerful-in-dc-than-trump.

215 **GAO denied Oracle's protest:** Government Accountability Office, "GAO Statement on Oracle Bid Protest," news release, November 14, 2018, https://www.gao.gov/press-release/gao-statement-oracle-bid-protest.

215 **dismissed IBM's:** "International Business Machines Corporation" (information on 2018 protest), Government Accountability Office, December 11, 2018, https://www.gao.gov/products/b-416657.5%2Cb-416657.6#mt=e-report.

215 **protest in the U.S. Court of Federal Claims:** Inspector General, U.S. Department of Defense, *Report on the Joint Enterprise Defense Infrastructure (JEDI) Cloud Procurement.*

215 **"swampy dealings":** Ronn Blitzer, "Amazon, Pentagon Accused of Swampy Dealings over $10B Contract," Fox News, June 19, 2019, https://www.foxnews.com/politics/amazon-pentagon-accused-of-swampy-dealings-over-10b-contract.

215 **review complaints of favoritism:** Alina Selyukh, "Pentagon Pauses $10 Billion Contract That Embroiled Amazon in Controversy," *Morning Edition*, August 1, 2019, https://www.npr.org/2019/08/01/747374991/pentagon-pauses-10-billion-cloud-contract-after-months-of-controversy; "Key Dates Leading Up to the U.S. Pentagon's Cloud-Computing Award to Microsoft," Reuters, October 27, 2019, https://www.reuters.com/article/us-pentagon-jedi-timeline/key-dates-leading-up-to-the-u-s-pentagons-cloud-computing-award-to-microsoft-idUSKBN1X60KZ.

215 **Microsoft was the winner:** "Contracts for Oct. 25, 2019," U.S. Department of Defense, 2019, https://www.defense.gov/Newsroom/Contracts/Contract/Article/1999639/.

215 **"unmistakable bias":** Jay Green and Aaron Gregg, "Amazon Will Challenge Pentagon's Award of $10 Billion JEDI Contract to Microsoft," *Washington Post*, November 14, 2019, https://www.washingtonpost.com/business/2019/11/14/amazon-will-challenge-pentagons-award-billion-jedi-contract-microsoft/.

215 **claimed the process was biased in *favor* of Amazon:** Inspector General, U.S. Department of Defense, *Report on the Joint Enterprise Defense Infrastructure (JEDI) Cloud Procurement*, 1–2.

215 **Amazon's protest was considered:** Jared Serbu, "Court Temporarily Blocks Work on DoD's JEDI Cloud Contract," Federal News Network, February 13, 2020, https://federalnewsnetwork.com/defense-main/2020/02/court-temporarily-blocks-work-on-dods-jedi-cloud-contract/.

215 **sweeping investigation:** Inspector General, U.S. Department of Defense, *Report on the Joint Enterprise Defense Infrastructure (JEDI) Cloud Procurement*, 5–6.

216 **Trump's antipathy toward Amazon:** Chris Cillizza, "Donald Trump's Long and Dramatic History with Jeff Bezos," *The Point with Chris Cillizza*, February 8, 2019, https://www.cnn.com/2019/02/08/politics/donald-trump-jeff-bezos-amazon-affair-national-enquirer.

216 **"DoD personnel who evaluated the contract proposals":** Inspector General, U.S. Department of Defense, *Report on the Joint Enterprise Defense Infrastructure (JEDI) Cloud Procurement*, 8.

216 **no "swampy dealings":** Blitzer, "Amazon, Pentagon Accused of Swampy Dealings."

216 **a "comprehensive re-evaluation":** U.S. Department of Defense, "DOD Reaffirms Original JEDI Cloud Award to Microsoft," news release, September 4, 2020, https://www.defense.gov/Newsroom/Releases/Release/Article/2337557/dod-reaffirms-original-jedi-cloud-award-to-microsoft/.

216 **"continue to protest":** "JEDI: Why We Will Continue to Protest This Politically Corrupted Contract Award," *AWS Public Sector Blog*, September 4, 2020, https://aws.amazon.com/blogs/publicsector/jedi-why-we-will-continue-protest-politically-corrupted-contract-award/.

216 **seemingly endless legal battles:** Aaron Gregg, "With a $10 Billion Cloud-Computing Deal Snarled in Court, the Pentagon May Move Forward Without It," *Washington Post*, February 10, 2021, https://www.washingtonpost.com/business/2021/02/10/jedi-contract

-pentagon-biden/; Naomi Nix, "Microsoft's US$10B Pentagon Deal at Risk Amid Amazon Fight," BNN Bloomberg, March 5, 2021, https://www.bnnbloomberg.ca/microsoft-s-us-10b-pentagon-deal-at-risk-amid-amazon-fight-1.1572730.

216 **Pentagon cancelled the JEDI contract:** U.S. Department of Defense, "Future of the Joint Enterprise Defense Infrastructure Cloud Contract," news release, July 6, 2021, https://www.defense.gov/Newsroom/Releases/Release/Article/2682992/future-of-the-joint-enterprise-defense-infrastructure-cloud-contract/; Toni Townes-Whitley, "Microsoft's Commitment to the DoD Remains Steadfast," Official Microsoft Blog, July 6, 2021, https://blogs.microsoft.com/blog/2021/07/06/microsofts-commitment-to-the-dod-remains-steadfast/; Robert Burns, "Pentagon Cancels Disputed JEDI Cloud Contract with Microsoft," Associated Press, July 6, 2021, https://apnews.com/article/amazoncom-inc-technology-business-government-and-politics-83dae68a0ed4e24246900a1d1d1d00be

216 **a new "multi-cloud/multi-vendor" contract:** Jared Serbu, "DoD Picks Amazon, Microsoft, Google and Oracle for Multibillion Dollar Project to Replace JEDI Cloud," Federal News Network, November 19, 2021, https://federalnewsnetwork.com/defense-main/2021/11/dod-picks-amazon-microsoft-google-and-oracle-for-multibillion-dollar-project-to-replace-jedi-cloud/.

216 **Protesting DoD contracts:** "DoD Ready for Tanker Protest," *Military.com*, February 18, 2011, https://www.military.com/dodbuzz/2011/02/18/dod-ready-for-tanker-protest.

216 **contract for a new stealth bomber:** "The Boeing Company" (information on 2016 protest), Government Accountability Office, February 16, 2016, https://www.gao.gov/products/b-412441.

216 **overturning a contract decision:** Jared Serbu, "Pentagon Loses Two Bid Protests That Challenged $7 Billion Moving Contract," Federal News Network, October 21, 2020, https://federalnewsnetwork.com/defense-main/2020/10/pentagon-loses-two-bid-protests-that-challenged-7-billion-moving-contract/.

216 **Boeing protested a 2008 decision:** *Air Force KC-46A Pegasus Tanker Aircraft Program* (Congressional Research Service, updated April 21, 2020), 11, https://fas.org/sgp/crs/weapons/RL34398.pdf.

216 **Microsoft filed a protest:** Aaron Gregg, "NSA Quietly Awards $10 Billion Cloud Contract to Amazon, Drawing Protest from Microsoft," *Washington Post*, August 11, 2021, https://www.washingtonpost.com/business/2021/08/11/amazon-nsa-contract/; "Microsoft Corporation (H98230-20-R-0225)" (information about 2021 protest), Government Accountability Office, July 21, 2021, https://www.gao.gov/docket/b-420004.1.

216 **Protesting is endemic:** Thomas H. Armstrong, "Re: GAO Bid Protest Annual Report to Congress for Fiscal Year 2020," letter to congressional committees, December 23, 2020, https://www.gao.gov/assets/gao-21-281sp.pdf.

217 **"No question":** Mulchandani, interview.

217 **"total rewrite" of defense acquisition policy:** Genevieve Hatfield, "A Hard Talk About Software with USD(A&S) Ellen Lord," Defense Acquisition University, November 12, 2020, https://www.dau.edu/News/A-Hard-Talk-about-Software.

217 **DoD has also expanded its use of "other transaction":** *Defense Acquisitions: DOD's Use of Other Transactions for Prototype Projects Has Increased* (report no. GAO-20-84, Government Accountability Office, November 2019), https://www.gao.gov/assets/gao-20-84.pdf.

217 **Other transaction authority:** "Other Transaction Authority (OTA)," AcqNotes, updated August 9, 2021, https://acqnotes.com/acqnote/careerfields/other-transaction-authority-ota; "What Is an 'Other Transaction,'" AiDA—MITRE Corporation, 2021, https://aida.mitre.org/ota/; Office of the Under Secretary of Defense for Acquisition and Sustainment,

Other Transactions Guide (U.S. Department of Defense, November 2018), https://www.dau
.edu/guidebooks/Shared%20Documents/Other%20Transactions%20(OT)%20Guide.pdf

217 **OTAs may still be protested:** "What Is an 'Other Transaction' "; Office of the Under Secretary of Defense for Acquisition and Sustainment, *Other Transactions Guide*, 26.

217 **companies that did not traditionally work with DoD:** *Defense Acquisitions.*

217 **scaling up to large contracts:** Husch Blackwell LLP and George Steward III, "The Army's Newest $21 Billion Contract Is Not Your Typical Government Contract," JD Supra, April 14, 2021, https://www.jdsupra.com/legalnews/the-army-s-newest-21-billion-contract -3958057/.

217 **augmented reality headsets:** Program Executive Office Soldier, "IVAS Production Contract Award," news release, March 31, 2021, https://www.peosoldier.army.mil/News/ Article-Display/Article/2556870/ivas-production-contract-award/; Alex Kipman, "Army Moves Microsoft HoloLens-Based Headset from Prototyping to Production Phase," *Official Microsoft Blog*, March 31, 2021, https://blogs.microsoft.com/blog/2021/03/31/army-moves -microsoft-hololens-based-headset-from-prototyping-to-production-phase/; Sydney J. Freedberg Jr., "IVAS: Microsoft Award by Army Worth up to $21.9B," *Breaking Defense*, March 31, 2021, https://breakingdefense.com/2021/03/ivas-microsoft-award-worth-up-to -21-9b/.

218 **DIU helped AI start-up Anduril:** Defense Innovation Unit, "Generating Meaningful Revenue Opportunities for Commercial Vendors," February 2022.

27. DISRUPTION

219 **superior technology over its adversaries:** Rebecca Grant, "The Second Offset," *Air Force Magazine*, June 24, 2016, https://www.airforcemag.com/article/the-second-offset/

219 **median technology difference:** Stephen Biddle, *Military Power: Explaining Victory and Defeat in Modern Battle* (Princeton, NJ: Princeton University Press, 2004), 66–67, https:// www.amazon.com/Military-Power-Explaining-Victory-Defeat/dp/0691128022.

219 **1991 Gulf War:** Biddle, *Military Power*, 25, 66.

219 **how militaries use their forces:** Biddle, *Military Power*, 66–69.

219 **much larger and more modern Russian military:** European Parliament, "Russia's War on Ukraine: Military Balance of Power," March 2022, https://www.europarl.europa.eu/ RegData/etudes/ATAG/2022/729292/EPRS_ATA(2022)729292_EN.pdf.

219 **fund more of the same kinds of weapons:** Paul Scharre, "Esper's Convenient Lie," *Defense One*, September 18, 2020, https://www.defenseone.com/ideas/2020/09/espers-convenient -lie/168596/.

220 **Pentagon is starting to undertake much-needed reforms:** For an independent analysis of DoD efforts at AI adoption, see *Artificial Intelligence: Status of Developing and Acquiring Capabilities for Weapon Systems* (report no. GAO-22-104765, Government Accountability Office, February 2022), https://www.gao.gov/assets/gao-22-104765.pdf.

220 **"I made the fateful decision":** Brett Darcey, interview by author, October 6, 2021.

222 **"traditionalist," "hidebound" culture:** Elsa Kania, interview by author, June 4, 2021.

223 **promotion opportunities:** *Unmanned Aerial Systems: Air Force Pilot Promotion Rates Have Increased but Oversight Process of Some Positions Could Be Enhanced* (report no. GAO-19-155, Government Accountability Office, February 2019), https://www.gao.gov/ assets/gao-19-155.pdf.

223 **combat medals:** US Air Force, "Air Force Releases Criteria for New Remote Combat Effects Campaign Medal," news release, October 28, 2019, https://www.af.mil/News/

Article-Display/Article/2000789/air-force-releases-criteria-for-new-remote-combat-effects
-campaign-medal/; Kyle Rempfer, "Air Force Awards First-Ever 'R' Devices for Remote
Combat Ops," *Air Force Times*, July 12, 2018, https://www.airforcetimes.com/news/your-air
-force/2018/07/12/air-force-awards-first-ever-r-devices-for-remote-combat-ops/; Charlsy
Panzino, "Air Force Releases Awards Criteria for New 'C' and 'R' Devices," *Air Force Times*,
June 25, 2017, https://www.airforcetimes.com/news/your-air-force/2017/06/25/air-force
-releases-awards-criteria-for-new-c-and-r-devices/.

223 **"The PLA is the Party's army. The Party controls the gun":** Kania, interview.
223 **"When it comes to innovation":** Hal Brands, "China's Creative Challenge—and the Threat
to America," *Commentary*, May 2021, https://www.commentarymagazine.com/articles/
hal-brands/chinas-geopolitical-challenge-threat-to-america/.
223 **"You can have innovation occur without people being happy":** Kania, interview.
224 **Maven controversy:** Ryan Browne, "Top US General Says Google 'Is Indirectly Benefiting
the Chinese Military,'" CNN, March 14, 2019, https://www.cnn.com/2019/03/14/politics/
dunford-china-google/index.html.
224 **"We have ethics discussions":** Devaki Raj, interview, July 29, 2021.
224 **"it's a huge uphill battle":** Will Roper, interview by author, August 6, 2021.
225 **fleet of 355 ships:** *Navy Force Structure and Shipbuilding Plans: Background and Issues
for Congress* (Congressional Research Service, September 30, 2021), https://fas.org/sgp/crs/
weapons/RL32665.pdf.
225 **386 operational squadrons:** U.S. Air Force, "The Air Force We Need: 386 Operational
Squadrons," news release, September 17, 2018, https://www.af.mil/News/Article-Display/
Article/1635070/the-air-force-we-need-386-operational-squadrons/.
225 **500,000 troops:** Meghann Myers, "Esper: The Ultimate Size of the Army Is a Moving Target," *Army Times*, April 17, 2019, https://www.armytimes.com/news/your
-army/2019/04/17/esper-the-ultimate-size-of-the-army-is-a-moving-target/.

28. CONTROL

230 **"really impressed":** Gabriel Kocher, interview, November 15, 2019.
230 **drone racing:** Autonomous AI-piloted drone racing has continued to improve, including beating human pilots in head-to-head competitions. Evan Ackerman, "Autonomous
Drones Challenge Human Champions in First 'Fair' Race," *IEEE Spectrum*, July 6, 2022,
https://spectrum.ieee.org/amp/zurich-autonomous-drone-race-2657587538.
230 **"Managing this transition to the real world":** "Collaborative Air Combat Autonomy
Program Makes Strides," Defense Advanced Research Projects Agency, March 18, 2021,
https://www.darpa.mil/news-events/2021-03-18a.
230 **Machine learning systems:** Pedro A. Ortega, Vishal Maini, and the DeepMind safety
team, "Building Safe Artificial Intelligence: Specification, Robustness, and Assurance,"
Medium, September 27, 2018, https://medium.com/@deepmindsafetyresearch/building
-safe-artificial-intelligence-52f5f75058f1; Ram Shankar Siva Kumar et al., "Failure Modes
in Machine Learning," Microsoft Docs, November 11, 2019, https://docs.microsoft.com/
en-us/security/engineering/failure-modes-in-machine-learning#unintended-failures
-summary; Dario Amodei et al., *Concrete Problems in AI Safety* (arXiv.org, July 25, 2016),
https://arxiv.org/pdf/1606.06565.pdf.
230 **AlphaGo reportedly could not play well:** James Hendler and Alice M. Mulvehill, *Social
Machines: The Coming Collision of Artificial Intelligence, Social Networking, and Humanity*
(New York: Apress, 2016), 57.

230 **Failures in real-world applications:** Sean Mcgregor, "When AI Systems Fail: Introducing the AI Incident Database," *Partnership on AI Blog*, November 18, 2020, https://www.partnershiponai.org/aiincidentdatabase/.

230 **multiple fatalities:** Jim Puzzanghera, "Driver in Tesla Crash Relied Excessively on Autopilot, but Tesla Shares Some Blame, Federal Panel Finds," *Los Angeles Times*, September 12, 2017, http://www.latimes.com/business/la-fi-hy-tesla-autopilot-20170912-story.html; "Driver Errors, Overreliance on Automation, Lack of Safeguards, Led to Fatal Tesla Crash," National Transportation Safety Board Office of Public Affairs, press release, September 12, 2017, https://www.ntsb.gov/news/press-releases/Pages/PR20170912.aspx; "Collision Between a Car Operating with Automated Vehicle Control Systems and a Tractor-Semitrailer Truck Near Williston, Florida" NTSB/HAR-17/02/ PB2017-102600 (National Transportation Safety Board, May 7, 2016), https://www.ntsb.gov/news/events/Documents/2017-HWY16FH018-BMG-abstract.pdf; James Gilboy, "Officials Find Cause of Tesla Autopilot Crash Into Fire Truck: Report," *The Drive*, May 17, 2018, http://www.thedrive.com/news/20912/cause-of-tesla-autopilot-crash-into-fire-truck-cause-determined-report; "Tesla Hit Parked Police Car 'While Using Autopilot,'" BBC, May 30, 2018, https://www.bbc.com/news/technology-44300952; and Raphael Orlove, "This Test Shows Why Tesla Autopilot Crashes Keep Happening," Jalopnik, June 13, 2018, https://jalopnik.com/this-test-shows-why-tesla-autopilot-crashes-keep-happen-1826810902.

231 **"dominate their local battle spaces":** Phil Root, interview, February 6, 2020.

232 **machine learning was "alchemy":** Ali Rahimi and Ben Recht, "Reflections on Random Kitchen Sinks," *arg minblog*, December 5, 2017, http://www.argmin.net/2017/12/05/kitchen-sinks/.

232 **fatal crashes of two 737 MAX airliners:** Jon Ostrower, "What Is the Boeing 737 Max Maneuvering Characteristics Augmentation System?" *Air Current*, November 13, 2018, https://theaircurrent.com/aviation-safety/what-is-the-boeing-737-max-maneuvering-characteristics-augmentation-system-mcas-jt610/.

232 **failures can arise at multiple stages:** Ram Shankar Siva Kumar et al., "Failure Modes in Machine Learning," Microsoft Docs, November 11, 2019, https://docs.microsoft.com/en-us/security/engineering/failure-modes-in-machine-learning#details-on-unintended failures; Ortega, Maini, and the DeepMind safety team, "Building Safe Artificial Intelligence"; Amodei et al., *Concrete Problems in AI Safety*.

232 **three main types:** Ben Buchanan and Taylor Miller, *Machine Learning for Policymakers: What It Is and Why It Matters* (Belfer Center for Science and International Affairs, Harvard University, June 2017), https://www.belfercenter.org/sites/default/files/files/publication/MachineLearningforPolicymakers.pdf; Greg Allen, *Understanding AI Technology* (Joint Artificial Intelligence Center, U.S. Department of Defense, April 2020), https://www.ai.mil/docs/Understanding%20AI%20Technology.pdf.

232 **Large language models:** "Better Language Models and Their Implications," openai.com, n.d., https://openai.com/blog/better-language-models/; Alec Radford et al., *Language Models Are Unsupervised Multitask Learners* (openai.com, n.d.), https://cdn.openai.com/better-language-models/language_models_are_unsupervised_multitask_learners.pdf; Tom B. Brown et al., *Language Models are Few-Shot Learners* (Cornell University, July 22, 2020), https://arxiv.org/pdf/2005.14165.pdf; GPT-3 has the additional ability to do "in-context learning" during inference, after an initial phase of unsupervised pretraining.

233 **"distributional shift":** Sunil Thulasidasan et al., *An Effective Baseline for Robustness to Distributional Shift* (arXiv.org, May 15, 2021), https://arxiv.org/pdf/2105.07107.pdf; Jessica Dai and Sarah M. Brown, "Label Bias, Label Shift: Fair Machine Learning with Unreliable

Labels" (paper presented at 34th Conference on Neural Information Processing Systems, Vancouver, Canada, December 2020), https://dynamicdecisions.github.io/assets/pdfs/29 .pdf.

233 **trained on one set of data:** Lack of robustness to distributional shift is a consistent problem with facial recognition systems across gender and racial groups. Joy Adowaa Buolamwini, "Gender Shades: Intersectional Phenotypic and Demographic Evaluation of Face Datasets and Gender Classifiers" (master's thesis, MIT, September 2017), https://dam -prod.media.mit.edu/x/2018/02/05/buolamwini-ms-17_WtMjoGY.pdf; Joy Buolamwini and Timnit Gebru, "Gender Shades: Intersectional Accuracy Disparities in Commercial Gender Classification," *Proceedings of Machine Learning Research* 81 (2018), 1–15, https:// dam-prod.media.mit.edu/x/2018/02/06/Gender%20Shades%20Intersectional%20Accuracy%20Disparities.pdf.

233 **Neural networks don't know:** Thulasidasan et al., *An Effective Baseline for Robustness to Distributional Shift.*

233 **deep learning systems in the real world:** Chuan Guo et al., "On Calibration of Modern Neural Networks," *Proceedings of the 34th International Conference on Machine Learning* 70 (August 2017), 1321–1330, https://arxiv.org/pdf/1706.04599.pdf; Dan Hendrycks et al., *Scaling Out-of-Distribution Detection for Real-World Settings* (arXiv.org, December 7, 2020), https://arxiv.org/pdf/1911.11132.pdf; "Overview," ICML 2021 Workshop on Uncertainty & Robustness in Deep Learning, July 23, 2021, https://sites.google.com/view/ udlworkshop2021/home.

233 **shallow "world model":** David Ha and Jürgen Schmidhuber, World Models (arXiv.org, May 9, 2018), https://arxiv.org/pdf/1803.10122.pdf.

233 **"mistaking performance for competence":** Rodney A. Brooks, "Mistaking Performance for Competence Misleads Estimates Of AI's 21st Century Promise And Danger," in *What to Think About Machines That Think: Today's Leading Thinkers on the Age of Machine Intelligence (Edge Question Series)* (New York: Harper Perennial, October 6, 2015), https://www .edge.org/response-detail/26057.

234 **gender, racial, and religious biases:** Brown et al., *Language Models are Few-Shot Learners*; Emily M. Bender et al., "On the Dangers of Stochastic Parrots: Can Language Models Be Too Big?" *FAccT '21: Proceedings of the 2021 ACM Conference on Fairness, Accountability, and Transparency* (March 2021), 610–623, https://dl.acm.org/doi/pdf/10.1145/3442188.3445922.

234 **Google Translate:** James Kuczmarski, "Reducing Gender Bias in Google Translate," *The Keyword* (blog), Google, December 6, 2018, https://blog.google/products/translate/ reducing-gender-bias-google-translate/.

234 **gender distribution of nurses and doctors:** "Professionally Active Physicians by Gender," Kaiser Family Foundation, updated September 2021, https://www.kff.org/other/state -indicator/physicians-by-gender/; "Labor Force Statistics from the Current Population Survey: Household Data Annual Averages," U.S. Bureau of Labor Statistics, updated January 22, 2021, https://www.bls.gov/cps/cpsaat11.htm.

234 **existing social biases:** Bender et al., "On the Dangers of Stochastic Parrots."

234 **option to choose the gender:** Kuczmarski, "Reducing Gender Bias in Google Translate."

234 **résumé-sorting model:** Jeffrey Dastin, "Amazon Scraps Secret AI Recruiting Tool That Showed Bias Against Women," Reuters, October 10, 2018, https://www.reuters.com/ article/us-amazon-com-jobs-automation-insight/amazon-scraps-secret-ai-recruiting -tool-that-showed-bias-against-women-idUSKCN1MK08G.

234 **Learning systems will sometimes find shortcuts:** Ortega, Maini, and the DeepMind safety team, "Building Safe Artificial Intelligence."

234 **learned to alternate from the previous input:** Joel Lehman et al., "The Surprising Creativity of Digital Evolution: A Collection of Anecdotes from the Evolutionary Computation and Artificial Life Research Communities," *Artificial Life* 26, no. 2 (2020), 281–282, https://doi.org/10.1162/artl_a_00319.

234 **Simulated digital creatures:** Lehman et al., "The Surprising Creativity of Digital Evolution," 279–281.

235 **deception and concealment tactics:** Lehman et al., "The Surprising Creativity of Digital Evolution," 288–289.

235 **optimal scoring strategy was not to race at all:** Jack Clark and Dario Amodei, "Faulty Reward Functions in the Wild," *OpenAI Blog*, December 21, 2016, https://openai.com/blog/faulty-reward-functions/.

235 **Q*bert:** Lehman et al., "The Surprising Creativity of Digital Evolution," 285.

235 **win by crashing opposing algorithms:** Lehman et al., "The Surprising Creativity of Digital Evolution," 284.

235 **exploiting bugs in the simulation:** Lehman et al., "The Surprising Creativity of Digital Evolution," 283–285.

235 **evolved circuit on an FPGA chip:** Adrian Thompson, "An Evolved Circuit, Intrinsic in Silicon, Entwined with Physics," in: Tetsuya Higuchi, Masaya Iwata, and Liu Weixin, eds., *Evolvable Systems: From Biology to Hardware* (Berlin: Springer, 1996), https://doi.org/10.1007/3-540-63173-9_61.

235 **"game" or "hack" their reward functions:** Victoria Krakovna et al., "Specification Gaming: the Flip Side of AI Ingenuity," *Deepmind Blog*, April 21, 2020, https://deepmind.com/blog/article/Specification-gaming-the-flip-side-of-AI-ingenuity; Clark and Amodei, "Faulty Reward Functions in the Wild"; Amodei et al., *Concrete Problems in AI Safety*.

235 **deleted the files containing the "correct" answers:** Lehman et al., "The Surprising Creativity of Digital Evolution," 281.

235 **take credit for other rules:** Douglas B. Lenat, "EURISKO: A Program That Learns New Heuristics and Domain Concepts," *Artificial Intelligence* 21 (1983), 90, http://www.cs.northwestern.edu/~mek802/papers/not-mine/Lenat_EURISKO.pdf.

235 **Tetris-playing bot learned to pause the game:** Tom Murphy VII, *The First Level of Super Mario Bros. Is Easy with Lexicographic Orderings and Time Travel . . . After That It Gets a Little Tricky* (cmu.edu, April 1, 2013), https://www.cs.cmu.edu/~tom7/mario/mario.pdf.

235 **clever hacks:** "Specification Gaming Examples in AI—Master List : Sheet 1," Google Sheets, n.d., https://docs.google.com/spreadsheets/d/e/2PACX-1vRPiprOaC3HsCf5Tuum8bRfzYUiKLRqJmbOoC-32JorNdfyTiRRsR7Ea5eWtvsWzuxo8bjOxCG84dAg/pubhtml.

235 **"It is often functionally simpler":** Lehman et al., "The Surprising Creativity of Digital Evolution," 6.

236 **bias and fairness:** James Manyika, Jake Silberg, and Brittany Presten, "What Do We Do About the Biases in AI?" *Harvard Business Review*, October 25, 2019, https://hbr.org/2019/10/what-do-we-do-about-the-biases-in-ai.

236 **"train as you fight":** Melody Everly, " 'Train as You Fight, Fight as You Train,' " U.S. Army, June 8, 2017, https://www.army.mil/article/189059/train_as_you_fight_fight_as_you_train.

236 **"no plan survives contact with the enemy":** "No Plan Survives Contact with the Enemy," Boot Camp & Military Fitness Institute, February 28, 2016, https://bootcampmilitaryfitnessinstitute.com/military-and-outdoor-fitness-articles/no-plan-survives-contact-with-the-enemy/.

237 **Google:** "Explainable AI," Google Cloud, n.d., https://cloud.google.com/explainable-ai.

237 **DARPA:** Matt Turek, "Explainable Artificial Intelligence (XAI)," Defense Advanced

Research Projects Agency, n.d., https://www.darpa.mil/program/explainable-artificial
-intelligence.

237 **"explainable AI":** Giulia Vilone and Luca Longo, *Explainable Artificial Intelligence: a Systematic Review* (arXiv.org, October 12, 2020), https://arxiv.org/pdf/2006.00093.pdf

237 **black box of neural networks:** Nicolas Papernot and Nicholas Frosst, "How to Know When Machine Learning Does Not Know," *cleverhans-blog*, May 20, 2019, http://www.cleverhans
.io/security/2019/05/20/dknn.html.

237 **making them more transparent:** Ribana Roscher et al., "Explainable Machine Learning for Scientific Insights and Discoveries," *IEEE Access* 8 (February 24, 2020), https://ieeexplore.ieee.org/document/9007737.

29. POISON

239 **"machine learning works":** Nicolas Papernot and Ian Goodfellow, "Breaking Things Is Easy," *cleverhans-blog*, December 16, 2016, http://www.cleverhans.io/security/privacy/
ml/2016/12/16/breaking-things-is-easy.html.

239 **target machine learning systems at multiple stages:** Ram Shankar Siva Kumar et al., "Failure Modes in Machine Learning," Microsoft Docs, November 11, 2019, https://
docs.microsoft.com/en-us/security/engineering/failure-modes-in-machine-learning;
Papernot and Goodfellow, "Breaking Things Is Easy"; Andrew J. Lohn, *Poison in the Well:
Securing the Shared Resources of Machine Learning* (Center for Security and Emerging
Technology, June 2021), https://cset.georgetown.edu/publication/poison-in-the-well/;
Nicolas Papernot et al., *SoK: Towards the Science of Security and Privacy in Machine
Learning* (arXiv.org, November 11, 2016), https://arxiv.org/pdf/1611.03814.pdf; Battista
Biggio and Fabio Roly, *Wild Patterns: Ten Years After the Rise of Adversarial Machine
Learning* (arXiv.org, July 19, 2018), https://arxiv.org/pdf/1712.03141.pdf.

239 **"adversarial example":** Ian Goodfellow et al., "Attacking Machine Learning with
Adversarial Examples," *OpenAI Blog*, February 24, 2017, https://openai.com/blog/
adversarial-example-research/; Papernot and Goodfellow, "Breaking Things Is Easy";
Ian Goodfellow and Nicolas Papernot, "Is Attacking Machine Learning Easier Than
Defending It?" *cleverhans-blog*, February 15, 2017, http://www.cleverhans.io/security/
privacy/ml/2017/02/15/why-attacking-machine-learning-is-easier-than-defending-it
.html; Christian Szegedy et al., *Intriguing Properties of Neural Networks* (arXiv.org, February 19, 2014), https://arxiv.org/pdf/1312.6199.pdf; Ian J. Goodfellow, Jonathon Shlens,
and Christian Szegedy, "Explaining and Harnessing Adversarial Examples" (paper presented at ICLR 2015, San Diego, CA, May 7–9, 2015), https://arxiv.org/pdf/1412.6572.pdf.

239 **Some look, to a human, like abstract patterns:** Anh Nguyen, Jason Yosinski, and Jeff
Clune, "Deep Neural Networks are Easily Fooled: High Confidence Predictions for
Unrecognizable Images" (presented at Conference on Computer Vision and Pattern Recognition, Boston, MA, 2015), https://arxiv.org/pdf/1412.1897.pdf.

239 **Adversarial Examples:** Nguyen, Yosinski, and Clune, "Deep Neural Networks are Easily
Fooled."

239 **subtle ways that a human can't see:** Szegedy et al., *Intriguing Properties of Neural Networks*;
Goodfellow, Shlens, and Szegedy, "Explaining and Harnessing Adversarial Examples."

240 **"black box" attacks:** Papernot et al., *SoK*; Nicolas Papernot, Patrick McDaniel, and Ian
Goodfellow, *Transferability in Machine Learning: From Phenomena to Black-Box Attacks
Using Adversarial Samples* (arXiv.org, May 24, 2016), https://arxiv.org/pdf/1605.07277.pdf.

241 **Adversarial examples are transferable:** Goodfellow, Shlens, and Szegedy, "Explaining and

Harnessing Adversarial Examples"; Papernot et al., *SoK*; Papernot, McDaniel, and Goodfellow, *Transferability in Machine Learning*; Vahid Behzadan and Arslan Munir, *Vulnerability of Deep Reinforcement Learning to Policy Induction Attacks* (arXiv.org, January 16, 2017), https://arxiv.org/pdf/1701.04143.pdf; Sandy Huang et al., *Adversarial Attacks on Neural Network Policies* (arXiv.org, February 8, 2017), https://arxiv.org/pdf/1702.02284 .pdf.

241 **attacks against image classifiers using printed pictures:** Alexey Kurakin, Ian J. Goodfellow, and Samy Bengio, *Adversarial Examples in the Physical World* (arXiv.org, February 11, 2017), https://arxiv.org/pdf/1607.02533.pdf.

241 **fool facial recognition systems using manipulated glasses:** Mahmood Sharif et al., "Accessorize to a Crime: Real and Stealthy Attacks on State-of-the-Art Face Recognition," in *CCS '16: Proceedings of the 2016 SIGSAC Conference on Computer and Communications Security* (New York: Association for Computing Machinery, 2016), https://doi.org/10 .1145/2976749.2978392. In this project, researchers demonstrated an effective black box attack against the Face++ facial recognition algorithm and a physical white box attack against a customized algorithm. They did not attempt a physical black box attack.

241 **misidentifying a stop sign:** Kevin Eykholt et al., "Robust Physical-World Attacks on Deep Learning Visual Classification" (paper presented at CVPR 2018, Salt Lake City, UT, June 18–22, 2018), https://arxiv.org/pdf/1707.08945.pdf.

241 **stickers to fool image classifiers:** Kevin Eykholt et al., "Physical Adversarial Examples for Object Detectors" (paper presented at WOOT '18, 12th USENIX Workshop on Offensive Technologies, Baltimore, MD, August 13–14, 2018), https://www.usenix.org/system/files/ conference/woot18/woot18-paper-eykholt.pdf.

241 **3D-printed turtle:** Anish Athalye et al., "Synthesizing Robust Adversarial Examples," *Proceedings of the 35th International Conference on Machine Learning* 80 (2018), https://arxiv .org/pdf/1707.07397.pdf.

241 **evade detection by the laser-based detection systems:** Yulong Cao et al., *Adversarial Objects Against LiDAR-Based Autonomous Driving Systems* (arXiv.org, July 11, 2019), https://arxiv.org/pdf/1907.05418 .pdf.

241 **manipulated clothing:** Researchers have shown proof-of-concept demonstrations of physical adversarial attacks using manipulated hats, clothing, and eyewear, but the generalizability and robustness of these attacks under a variety of settings, conditions, AI systems, and human subjects has not been demonstrated. Kendra Albert et al., *Ethical Testing in the Real World: Evaluating Physical Testing of Adversarial Machine Learning* (arXiv.org, December 3, 2020,) https://arxiv.org/pdf/2012.02048.pdf.

241 **cognitive land mines:** Kurakin, Goodfellow, and Bengio, *Adversarial Examples in the Physical World*; Mahmood Sharif, "A General Framework for Adversarial Examples with Objectives," *ACM Transactions on Privacy and Security* 1, no. 1 (January 2019), https:// doi.org/10.1145/3317611; Eykholt et al., "Robust Physical-World Attacks on Deep Learning Visual Classification"; Anish Athalye et al., "Fooling Neural Networks in the Physical World with 3D Adversarial Objects," LabSix, October 31, 2017, https://www.labsix.org/ physical-objects-that-fool-neural-nets/; Athalye et al., "Synthesizing Robust Adversarial Examples."

242 **Adversarial Patch:** Norman Mu, "Adversarial Patches for Deep Neural Networks," normanmu.com, January 17, 2019, https://www.normanmu.com/2019/01/17/adversarial -patches.html.

242 **hide objects from detectors:** Eykholt et al., "Physical Adversarial Examples for Object Detectors." Adversarial patches themselves can be detected by AI patch detectors, however.

Adam Ven Etten, *The Weaknesses of Adversarial Camouflage in Overhead Imagery* (arXiv. org, July 6, 2022), https://arxiv.org/pdf/2207.02963.pdf.

242 **they may be mistaken at a glance for graffiti:** For examples, see Tom B. Brown et al., "Adversarial Patch" (paper presented at the 31st Conference on Neural Information Processing Systems [NIPS 2017], Long Beach, CA, December 4–9, 2017), https://arxiv.org/ pdf/1712.09665.pdf; Eykholt et al., "Physical Adversarial Examples for Object Detectors"; Eykholt et al., "Robust Physical-World Attacks on Deep Learning Visual Classification."

242 **problems of a lack of robustness:** Eykholt et al., "Physical Adversarial Examples for Object Detectors."

242 **white box methods:** Eykholt et al., "Robust Physical-World Attacks on Deep Learning Visual Classification."

242 **black box attacks:** Eykholt et al., "Physical Adversarial Examples for Object Detectors"; Nicolas Papernot et al., "Practical Black-Box Attacks Against Machine Learning," in *ASIA CCS '17: Proceedings of the 2017 ACM on Asia Conference on Computer Security* (New York: Association for Computing Machinery, April 2017), http://dx.doi.org/10.1145/3052973 .3053009; Sharif et al., "Accessorize to a Crime."

243 **Adversarial Attack in the Physical World:** Kevin Eykholt et al., "Robust Physical-World Attacks on Deep Learning Visual Classification."

243 **Vulnerability to adversarial attacks:** Papernot et al., "Practical Black-Box Attacks Against Machine Learning"; Papernot, McDaniel, and Goodfellow, *Transferability in Machine Learning*; Xiaoyong Yuan et al., *Adversarial Examples: Attacks and Defenses for Deep Learning* (arXiv.org, July 7, 2018), https://arxiv.org/pdf/1712.07107.pdf.

243 **evade malware detectors:** Battista Biggio et al., *Evasion Attacks Against Machine Learning at Test Time* (arXiv.org, August 21, 2017), https://arxiv.org/pdf/1708.06131.pdf; Nedim Šrndić and Pavel Laskov, *Practical Evasion of a Learning-Based Classifier: A Case Study* (utdallas.edu, n.d.), https://personal.utdallas.edu/~muratk/courses/dmsec_files/srndic -laskov-sp2014.pdf; Ambra Demontis et al., *On Security and Sparsity of Linear Classifiers for Adversarial Settings* (arXiv.org, August 31, 2017), https://arxiv.org/pdf/1709.00045 .pdf; Yuan et al., *Adversarial Examples*; "CVE-2019-20634 Detail," National Institute of Standards and Technology, April 27, 2022, https://nvd.nist.gov/vuln/detail/CVE-2019 -20634; "Security Notice: Response to CVE-2019-20634," Proofpoint, n.d., https://www .proofpoint.com/us/security/security-advisories/pfpt-sn-2020-0001.

243 **perturbing pixels on the video game screen:** Behzadan and Munir, *Vulnerability of Deep Reinforcement Learning*.

243 **imperceptible to human observers:** Huang et al., *Adversarial Attacks on Neural Network Policies*.

243 **defending against adversarial attacks:** Yuan et al., *Adversarial Examples*; Nicolas Papernot and Nicholas Frosst, "How to Know When Machine Learning Does Not Know," *cleverhans-blog*, May 20, 2019, http://www.cleverhans.io/security/2019/05/20/dknn.html; Austin Short, Trevor La Pay, and Apurva Gandhi, Defending Against Adversarial Examples (Sandia National Laboratories, September 2019), https://doi.org/10.2172/1569514; Kui Ren et al., "Adversarial Attacks and Defenses in Deep Learning," *Engineering* 6, no. 3 (March 2020), https://doi.org/10.1016/j.eng.2019.12.012; Naveed Akhtar et al., "Attack to Fool and Explain Deep Networks," *Journal of LaTeX Class Files* (August 2020), https://arxiv.org/ pdf/2106.10606.pdf; Aditi Raghunathan, Jacob Steinhardt, and Percy Liang, "Certified Defenses Against Adversarial Examples" (paper presented at International Conference on Learning Representations 2018 (ICLR 2018), Vancouver, Canada, April 30–May 3, 2018), https://arxiv.org/pdf/1801.09344.pdf.

243 **models can usually be defeated:** Ren et al., "Adversarial Attacks and Defenses in Deep Learning."

244 **Camouflaged Adversarial Attack:** Kevin Eykholt et al., "Robust Physical-World Attacks on Deep Learning Visual Classification."

244 **no known method of fully inoculating algorithms:** Yuan et al., *Adversarial Examples.*

244 **Data poisoning:** Battista Biggio, Blaine Nelson, and Pavel Laskov, "Poisoning Attacks against Support Vector Machines," in *Proceedings of the 29th International Conference on Machine Learning* (Madison, WI: Omnipress, 2012), https://arxiv.org/pdf/1206.6389.pdf.

244 **without knowledge of the model's architecture:** Mengchen Zhao et al., "Efficient Label Contamination Attacks Against Black-Box Learning Models," in *Proceedings of the 26th International Joint Conference on Artificial Intelligence* (IJCAI-17) (AAAI Press, 2012), https://www.ijcai.org/proceedings/2017/0551.pdf.

244 **image classifiers:** Loc Truong et al., *Systematic Evaluation of Backdoor Data Poisoning Attacks on Image Classifiers* (arXiv.org, April 24, 2020), https://arxiv.org/pdf/2004.11514 .pdf.

244 **facial recognition:** Xinyun Chen et al., *Targeted Backdoor Attacks on Deep Learning Systems Using Data Poisoning* (arXiv.org, December 15, 2017), https://arxiv.org/pdf/1712 .05526.pdf.

244 **malware detectors:** Huang Xiao et al., "Is Feature Selection Secure Against Training Data Poisoning?" in *Proceedings of the 32nd International Conference on Machine Learning* (Lille, France, 2015), https://arxiv.org/pdf/1804.07933.pdf; ilmoi, "Poisoning Attacks on Machine Learning," *towards data science*, July 14, 2019, https://towardsdatascience.com/ poisoning-attacks-on-machine-learning-1ff247c254db.

245 **recommendation algorithms:** Hai Huang, "Data Poisoning Attacks to Deep Learning Based Recommender Systems," (paper, Network and Distributed Systems Security (NDSS) Symposium 2021, February 21–25, 2021), https://arxiv.org/pdf/2101.02644.pdf.

245 **poison a medical AI model:** Matthew Jagielski et al., *Manipulating Machine Learning: Poisoning Attacks and Countermeasures for Regression Learning* (arXiv.org, September 28, 2021), https://arxiv.org/pdf/1804.00308.pdf.

245 **manipulate real-world data:** Ricky Laishram and Vir Virander Phoha, *Curie: A method for protecting SVM Classifier from Poisoning Attack* (arXiv.org, June 7, 2016), https://arxiv .org/pdf/1606.01584.pdf; Zhao et al., "Efficient Label Contamination Attacks."

245 **data from external sources:** Zhao et al., "Efficient Label Contamination Attacks."

245 **alter the data or even just the label:** Zhao et al., "Efficient Label Contamination Attacks."

245 **insert adversarial noise into the training data:** Adrien Chan-Hon-Tong, "An Algorithm for Generating Invisible Data Poisoning Using Adversarial Noise That Breaks Image Classification Deep Learning," *Machine Learning & Knowledge Extraction* 1, no. 1 (November 9, 2018), https://doi.org/10.3390/make1010011; Ali Shafahi et al., "Poison Frogs! Targeted Clean-Label Poisoning Attacks on Neural Networks," (paper, 32nd Conference on Neural Information Processing Systems [NIPS 2018], Montreal, Canada, December 3–8, 2018), https://arxiv.org/pdf/1804.00792.pdf.

245 **"strong poisons":** Liam Fowl et al., *Adversarial Examples Make Strong Poisons* (arXiv.org, June 21, 2021), https://arxiv.org/pdf/2106.10807.pdf.

245 **backdoor key:** Chen et al., *Targeted Backdoor Attacks on Deep Learning Systems.*

245 **limited number of poisoned samples:** Chen et al., *Targeted Backdoor Attacks on Deep Learning Systems.*

245 **does not degrade model performance:** Truong et al., *Systematic Evaluation of Backdoor Data Poisoning Attacks on Image Classifiers.*

246 **Defending against data poisoning attacks:** Jacob Steinhardt, Pang Wei Koh, and Percy Liang, *Certified Defenses for Data Poisoning Attacks* (arXiv, November 24, 2017), https://arxiv.org/pdf/1706.03691.pdf; Laishram and Phoha, *Curie*; Truong et al., *Systematic Evaluation of Backdoor Data Poisoning Attacks on Image Classifiers*; ilmoi, "Poisoning Attacks on Machine Learning."

246 **supply chain attacks:** Lohn, *Poison in the Well.*

246 **publicly available pretrained model:** Tianyu Gu, Brendan Dolan-Gavitt, and Siddharth Garg, *BadNets: Identifying Vulnerabilities in the Machine Learning Model Supply Chain* (arXiv.org, March 11, 2019), https://arxiv.org/pdf/1708.06733.pdf; Tianyu Gu et al., "Bad-Nets: Evaluating Backdooring Attacks on Deep Neural Networks," *IEEE Access* 7 (2019), http://dx.doi.org/10.1109/ACCESS.2019.2909068.

246 **"The security of the AI [model] is thus dependent":** "TrojAI: Trojans in Artificial Intelligence," Intelligence Advanced Research Projects Activity, n.d., https://www.iarpa.gov/index.php/research-programs/trojai.

246 **SolarWinds:** Dina Temple-Raston, "A 'Worst Nightmare' Cyberattack: The Untold Story Of The SolarWinds Hack," *All Things Considered*, April 16, 2021, https://www.npr.org/2021/04/16/985439655/a-worst-nightmare-cyberattack-the-untold-story-of-the-solarwinds-hack; Kevin Poulsen, Robert McMillan, and Dustin Volz, "SolarWinds Hack Victims: From Tech Companies to a Hospital and University," *Wall Street Journal*, December 21, 2020, https://www.wsj.com/articles/solarwinds-hack-victims-from-tech-companies-to-a-hospital-and-university-11608548402.

246 **model stealing attacks:** Kumar et al., "Failure Modes in Machine Learning"; Florian Tramèr et al., "Stealing Machine Learning Models via Prediction APIs," in *Proceedings of the 25th USENIX Security Symposium* (Berkeley, CA: USENIX Association, 2016), https://www.usenix.org/system/files/conference/usenixsecurity16/sec16_paper_tramer.pdf.

247 **Model inversion attacks:** Matt Fredrikson, Somash Jha, and Thomas Ristenpart, "Model Inversion Attacks that Exploit Confidence Information and Basic Countermeasures," in *CCS '15: Proceedings of the 22nd ACM SIGSAC Conference on Computer and Communications Security* (New York: Association for Computing Machinery, 2015), http://dx.doi.org/10.1145/2810103.2813677.

247 **Tay may have learned from others':** Peter Lee, "Learning from Tay's Introduction," Official Microsoft Blog, March 25, 2016, https://blogs.microsoft.com/blog/2016/03/25/learning-tays-introduction/; Oscar Schwartz, "In 2016, Microsoft's Racist Chatbot Revealed the Dangers of Online Conversation," IEEE Spectrum, November 25, 2019, https://spectrum.ieee.org/tech-talk/artificial-intelligence/machine-learning/in-2016-microsofts-racist-chatbot-revealed-the-dangers-of-online-conversation; James Vincent, "Twitter Taught Microsoft's AI Chatbot to Be a Racist Asshole in Less Than a Day," *The Verge*, March 24, 2016, https://www.theverge.com/2016/3/24/11297050/tay-microsoft-chatbot-racist.

247 **system was trained on past conversations:** L. Kumar et al., "Failure Modes in Machine Learning."

247 **TrojAI:** "Introduction," TrojAI (documentation website), 2020, https://trojai.readthedocs.io/en/latest/intro.html.

247 **Trojan attack:** "TrojAI: Trojans in Artificial Intelligence."

247 **"the brittleness of the attack":** Nathan Drenkow, interview by author, March 11, 2020.

248 **"the real world will continue to be the biggest adversary":** Ashley Llorens, interview by author, March 11, 2020.

248 **Cyberattacks cost:** Zhanna Malekos Smith and Eugenia Lostri, *The Hidden Costs of*

Cybercrime (McAfee, 2020), https://www.mcafee.com/enterprise/en-us/assets/reports/rp-hidden-costs-of-cybercrime.pdf.

248 **"relatively simple tools":** *Weapon Systems Cybersecurity: DOD Just Beginning to Grapple with Scale of Vulnerabilities* (report no. GAO-19-128, US Government Accountability Office, October 2018), https://www.gao.gov/assets/700/694913.pdf.

30. TRUST

249 **"resilient, robust, reliable, and secure":** *Summary of the 2018 Department of Defense Artificial Intelligence Strategy* (U.S. Department of Defense, 2018), 8, 15, https://media.defense.gov/2019/Feb/12/2002088963/-1/-1/1/SUMMARY-OF-DOD-AI-STRATEGY.PDF.

249 **"I don't think the answer is that we don't":** Ashley Llorens, interview by author, March 11, 2020.

249 **"How do you create a safe agent?":** Brett Darcey, interview by author, October 6, 2021.

250 **Training safe and robust AI agents:** Jack Clark and Dario Amodei, "Faulty Reward Functions in the Wild," *OpenAI Blog*, December 21, 2016, https://openai.com/blog/faulty-reward-functions/; Victoria Krakovna et al., "Specification Gaming: the Flip Side of AI Ingenuity," *Deepmind Blog*, April 21, 2020, https://deepmind.com/blog/article/Specification-gaming-the-flip-side-of-AI-ingenuity.

250 **Micro Air Vehicle Lab (MAVLab):** Micro Air Vehicle Lab—TUDelft (website), 2021, https://mavlab.tudelft.nl/.

250 **"mix of neural networks and control theory":** Federico Paredes, interview by author, January 15, 2019.

250 **"for a lot of what we want to do":** Chuck Howell, interview by author, May 25, 2021.

251 **"model distillation":** Geoffrey Hinton, Oriol Vinyals, and Jeff Dean, *Distilling the Knowledge in a Neural Network* (arXiv.org, March 9, 2015), https://arxiv.org/pdf/1503.02531.pdf

251 **some pharmaceuticals that are approved:** Paul Gerrard and Robert Malcolm, "Mechanisms of Modafinil: A Review of Current Research," *Neuropsychiatric Disease and Treatment* 3, no. 3 (June 2007): 349–64, https://www.ncbi.nlm.nih.gov/pmc/articles/PMC2654794/; PROVIGIL(R) (Modafinil) Tablets [C-IV], package insert, October 2010, https://www.accessdata.fda.gov/drugsatfda_docs/label/2010/020717s030s034s036lbl.pdf; Jonathan Zittrain, "Intellectual Debt: With Great Power Comes Great Ignorance," Berkman Klein Center, July 24, 2019, https://medium.com/berkman-klein-center/from-technical-debt-to-intellectual-debt-in-ai-e05ac56a502c; Jonathan Zittrain, "The Hidden Costs of Automated Thinking," *New Yorker*, July 23, 2019, https://www.newyorker.com/tech/annals-of-technology/the-hidden-costs-of-automated-thinking.

251 **"We rely on a complex socio-technical system":** Howell, interview.

251 **necessary processes for AI assurance to establish justified confidence:** Pedro A. Ortega, Vishal Maini, and the DeepMind safety team, "Building Safe Artificial Intelligence: Specification, Robustness, and Assurance," *Medium*, September 27, 2018, https://medium.com/@deepmindsafetyresearch/building-safe-artificial-intelligence-52f5f75058f1.

251 **"test and evaluation":** Jim Alley et al., *Autonomy Community of Interest (COI) Test and Evaluation, Verification and Validation (TEVV) Working Group Technology Investment Strategy 2015-2018* (Office of the Assistant Secretary of Defense for Research & Engineering, May 2015), https://defenseinnovationmarketplace.dtic.mil/wp-content/uploads/2018/02/OSD_ATEVV_STRAT_DIST_A_SIGNED.pdf

251 **adequate TEVV for autonomous systems:** United States Air Force Office of the Chief Scientist, "Autonomous Horizons: System Autonomy in the Air Force—A Path to the Future,"

AF/ST TR 15-01, (2015); Alley et al., *Autonomy Community of Interest (COI) Test and Evaluation, Verification and Validation (TEVV) Working Group Technology Investment Strategy.*

251 **"immature as regards the 'illities'":** The MITRE Corporation, "Perspectives on Research in Artificial Intelligence and Artificial General Intelligence Relevant to DoD," JSR-16-Task-003 (The MITRE Corporation, January 2017), 27, 55.

251 **"We know the fundamentals":** Howell, interview.

252 **DoD needs improve its processes for AI:** Flournoy, Haines, and Chefitz, "Building Trust through Testing."

252 **"nowhere close to ensuring the performance":** Tarraf et al., "The Department of Defense Posture for Artificial Intelligence: Assessment and Recommendations," xiii, xv.

252 **"TEVV of traditional legacy systems is not sufficient":** National Security Commission on Artificial Intelligence, *Final Report* (n.d.), 137, https://www.nscai.gov/wp-content/uploads/2021/03/Full-Report-Digital-1.pdf.

252 **raft of recommendations:** National Security Commission on Artificial Intelligence, *Final Report*, 131–140.

252 **DoD bureaucratic structures to ensure "responsible AI":** Kathleen Hicks, "Implementing Responsible Artificial Intelligence in the Department of Defense," memorandum for senior Pentagon leadership et al., May 26, 2021, https://media.defense.gov/2021/May/27/2002730593/-1/-1/0/IMPLEMENTING-RESPONSIBLE-ARTIFICIAL-INTELLIGENCE-IN-THE-DEPARTMENT-OF-DEFENSE.PDF.

252 **AI "safety":** Patrick Tucker, "US Needs to Defend Its Artificial Intelligence Better, Says Pentagon No. 2," *Defense One*, June 22, 2021, https://www.defenseone.com/technology/2021/06/us-needs-defend-its-artificial-intelligence-better-says-pentagon-no-2/174876/.

252 **"responsible AI guidelines":** Jared Dunnmon, Bryce Goodman, Peter Kirechu, Carol Smith, and Alexandrea Van Deusen, "Responsible AI Guidelines in Practice," Defense Innovation Unit, November 15, 2021, https://assets.ctfassets.net/3nanhbfkr0pc/acoo1Fj5u-ungnGNPJ3QWy/6ec382b3b5a20ec7de6defdb33b04dcd/2021_RAI_Report.pdf.

252 *Responsible Artificial Intelligence Strategy:* *U.S. Department of Defense Responsible Artificial Intelligence Strategy and Implementation Pathway* (U.S. Department of Defense, June 2022), https://media.defense.gov/2022/Jun/22/2003022604/-1/-1/0/Department-of-Defense-Responsible-Artificial-Intelligence-Strategy-and-Implementation-Pathway.PDF.

252 **consolidating AI and data-related functions:** Kathleen Hicks, "Establishment of the Chief Digital and Artificial Intelligence Officer," memorandum for senior Pentagon leadership et al., December 8, 2021, https://media.defense.gov/2021/Dec/08/2002906075/-1/-1/1/MEMORANDUM-ON-ESTABLISHMENT-OF-THE-CHIEF-DIGITAL-AND-ARTIFICIAL-INTELLIGENCE-OFFICER.PDF; Kathleen Hicks, "Initial Operating Capability of the Chief Digital and Artificial Intelligence Officer," memorandum for senior Pentagon leadership et al., February 1, 2022, https://media.defense.gov/2022/Feb/02/2002931807/-1/-1/1/MEMORANDUM-ON-THE-INITIAL-OPERATING-CAPABILITY-OF-THE-CHIEF-DIGITAL-AND-ARTIFICIAL-INTELLIGENCE-OFFICER.PDF; Kathleen Hicks, "Role Clarity for the Chief Digital and Artificial Intelligence Officer," memorandum for senior Pentagon leadership et al., February 1, 2022, https://media.defense.gov/2022/Feb/02/2002931802/-1/-1/1/MEMORANDUM-ON-ROLE-CLARITY-FOR-THE-CHIEF-DIGITAL-AND-ARTIFICIAL-INTELLIGENCE-OFFICER.PDF; Mark Pomerleau, "David Spirk, DOD Chief Data Officer, to Depart," FedScoop, March 10, 2022, https://www.fedscoop.com/david-spirk-cdo-departing-dod/;

Michael C. Horowitz and Lauren Kahn, "Why DoD's New Approach to Data and Artificial Intelligence Should Enhance National Defense," Council on Foreign Relations blog, March 11, 2022, https://www.cfr.org/blog/why-dods-new-approach-data-and-artificial-intelligence-should-enhance-national-defense; Jaspreet Gill, "Say Goodbye to JAIC and DDS, As Offices Cease to Exist As Independent Bodies June 1," *Breaking Defense*, May 24, 2022, https://breakingdefense.com/2022/05/say-goodbye-to-jaic-and-dds-as-offices-cease-to-exist-as-independent-bodies-june-1/.

252 **technical innovation:** Ian Goodfellow and Nicolas Papernot, "The Challenge of Verification and Testing of Machine Learning," *cleverhans-blog*, June 14, 2017, http://www.cleverhans.io/security/privacy/ml/2017/06/14/verification.html.

253 **Patriot air and missile defense system:** For more on the Patriot fratricides, see Paul Scharre, *Army of None: Autonomous Weapons and the Future of War* (New York: W. W. Norton, April 24, 2018), 137–145.

31. RACE TO THE BOTTOM

254 **"race to the bottom":** Portions of this chapter are adapted, with permission, from Paul Scharre, "Debunking the AI Arms Race Theory," *Texas National Security Review* 4, no. 3 (Summer 2021): 121–132, http://dx.doi.org/10.26153/tsw/13985.

254 **"move fast and break things":** Steven Levy, "Mark Zuckerberg on Facebook's Future, from Virtual Reality to Anonymity," *Wired*, April 30, 2014, https://www.wired.com/2014/04/zuckerberg-f8-interview/.

254 **"We are under so much pressure":** Jack Shanahan, interview by author, April 1, 2020.

254 **twenty-five years from initial concept:** *F-35 Joint Strike Fighter (JSF) Program* (Congressional Research Service, updated May 27, 2020) https://fas.org/sgp/crs/weapons/RL30563.pdf; The Joint Advanced Strike Technology (JAST) program, which later became the Joint Strike Fighter program, was created in 1993. "JAST: History," JSF.mil, http://www.jsf.mil/history/his_jast.htm (page discontinued), https://web.archive.org/web/20190715052740/http://www.jsf.mil/history/his_jast.htm; and "Lockheed F-35 Jet Used by U.S. in Combat for First Time: Official," Reuters, September 27, 2018, https://www.reuters.com/article/us-usa-pentagon-f35/lockheed-f-35-jet-used-by-u-s-in-combat-for-first-time-official-idUSKCN1M72BT.

254 **still not in full-rate production:** Valerie Insinna, "Full Rate Production for F-35 Is At Least Another Year Away," *Breaking Defense*, March 8, 2022, https://breakingdefense.com/2022/03/full-rate-production-for-f-35-is-at-least-another-year-away/.

254 **"acquisition malpractice":** Colin Clark, "F-35 Production Move Was 'Acquisition Malpractice': Top DoD Buyer," *Breaking Defense*, February 6, 2012, https://breakingdefense.com/2012/02/f-35-production-was-acquisition-malpractice-top-dod-weapons-b/.

254 **testing the jet concurrently:** Robert N. Charette, "F-35 Joint Strike Fighter Program Management Was 'Acquisition Malpractice' DoD Says," IEEE Spectrum, February 13, 2012, https://spectrum.ieee.org/riskfactor/aerospace/military/f35-joint-strike-fighter-program-management-was-acquisition-malpractice-dod-says; *F-35 Joint Strike Fighter (JSF) Program*.

255 **four crashes during development:** Jeremiah Gertler, *V-22 Osprey Tilt-Rotor Aircraft: Background and Issues for Congress* (Congressional Research Service, March 10, 2011), https://fas.org/sgp/crs/weapons/RL31384.pdf.

255 **"Meeting a funding deadline was more important":** Ron Berler, "Saving the Pentagon's Killer Chopper-Plane," *Wired*, July 1, 2005, https://www.wired.com/2005/07/osprey/.

255 **"schedule pressures":** Berler, "Saving the Pentagon's Killer Chopper-Plane"; Mary Pat Flaherty and Thomas E. Ricks, "Key Tests Omitted on the Osprey," *Washington Post,* February 19, 2001, https://www.washingtonpost.com/archive/politics/2001/02/19/key-tests-omitted-on-the-osprey/a657accd-d14c-4235-a781-6e05e12b25fd/.

255 **Accidents:** *Trends in Active-Duty Military Deaths Since 2006* (Congressional Research Service, updated May 17, 2021), https://fas.org/sgp/crs/natsec/IF10899.pdf.

255 **"peacetime naval accidents":** William M. Arkin and Joshua Handler, *Naval Accidents 1945–1988* (Neptune Paper No. 3, Greenpeace Institute for Policy Studies, June 1989), https://fas.org/wp-content/uploads/2014/05/NavalAccidents1945-1988.pdf.

255 **Air and ground operations:** *Aviation Class A Mishap Summary* (U.S. Air Force, August 30, 2021), https://www.safety.af.mil/Portals/71/documents/Aviation/Mishap%20Summaries/USAF_Aviation_Class_A_Summary.pdf.

255 **much higher accident rate:** "Major Russian Submarine Accidents Since 2000," *Radio Free Europe/Radio Liberty,* July 2, 2019, https://www.rferl.org/a/major-russian-submarine-accidents-since-2000/30033592.html; Peter Suciu, "Steel Tomb: The Worst Russian Submarine Disasters of All Time," *National Interest,* May 12, 2020, https://nationalinterest.org/blog/buzz/steel-tomb-worst-russian-submarine-disasters-all-time-153216.

256 *Challenger* **explosion:** Diane Vaughan, *The Challenger Launch Decision: Risky Technology, Culture, and Deviance at NASA* (Chicago: University of Chicago Press, 1996, 2016).

256 **desire to beat others to market:** Charles Duhigg, "Did Uber Steal Google's Intellectual Property?" *The New Yorker,* October 15, 2018, https://www.newyorker.com/magazine/2018/10/22/did-uber-steal-googles-intellectual-property; David Gelles, et al., "Boeing Was 'Go, Go, Go' to Beat Airbus with the 737 Max," *New York Times,* March 23, 2019, https://www.nytimes.com/2019/03/23/business/boeing-737-max-crash.html.

256 **"I'm less worried right now about autonomous weapons":** Shanahan, interview.

257 **United States demonstrated a swarm:** Aaron Mehta, "Pentagon Launches 103 Unit Drone Swarm," *Defense News,* January 10, 2017, https://www.defensenews.com/air/2017/01/10/pentagon-launches-103-unit-drone-swarm/.

257 **China followed with its own swarm:** Xinhua, "China Launches Record-Breaking Drone Swarm," *China Daily,* June 11, 2017, https://www.chinadaily.com.cn/china/2017-06/11/content_29702465.htm.

257 **superhuman AI dogfighting system:** Liu Xuanzun, "PLA Deploys AI in Mock Warplane Battles, 'Trains Both Pilots and AIs,'" *Global Times,* June 14, 2021, https://www.globaltimes.cn/page/202106/1226131.shtml.

257 **"There might be an artificial intelligence arms race":** Brandon Knapp, "DoD Official: US Not Part of AI Arms Race," c4isrnet.com, April 10, 2018, https://www.c4isrnet.com/it-networks/2018/04/10/dod-official-us-not-part-of-ai-arms-race/.

257 **"digital arms race with China":** Will Roper, "There's No Turning Back on AI in the Military," *Wired,* October 24, 2020, https://www.wired.com/story/opinion-theres-no-turning-back-on-ai-in-the-military/.

257 **Security scholars define an arms race:** Michael D. Wallace, "Arms Races and Escalation," *Journal of Conflict Resolution* 23 no. 1 (March 1979), 5–6, https://www.jstor.org/stable/173649; Colin Gray, "The Arms Race Phenomenon," *World Politics* 24 no. 1 (October 1971), 41, https://www.cambridge.org/core/journals/world-politics/article/abs/arms-race-phenomenon/B780FDD0C24BCD543FC27129DB6ACC93; Theresa Claire Smith, "Arms Race Instability and War," *Journal of Conflict Resolution* 24 no. 2 (June 1980), 255–56, https://doi.org/10.1177%2F002200278002400204; Michael F. Altfeld, "Arms Races?—

And Escalation? A Comment on Wallace," *International Studies Quarterly* 27 no. 2 (1983), 225–26, https://doi.org/10.2307/2600547; Paul F. Diehl, "Arms Races and Escalation: A Closer Look," *Journal of Peace Research* 20 no. 3 (1983), 206–8, https://www.jstor.org/stable/423792; Toby J. Rider, Michael G. Findley, and Paul F. Diehl, "Just Part of the Game? Arms Races, Rivalry, and War," *Journal of Peace Research* 48 no. 1 (January 2011), 90, https://www.jstor.org/stable/29777471.

257 **$9.3 billion in DoD AI-related research and development:** Figure 5.2.2 in Daniel Zhang et al., *The AI Index 2022 Annual Report* (Stanford, CA: AI Index Steering Committee, March 2022), 189, https://aiindex.stanford.edu/wp-content/uploads/2022/03/2022-AI-Index -Report_Master.pdf.

257 **Chinese official military spending:** *Military and Security Developments Involving the People's Republic of China, 2020*, annual report to Congress, Office of the Secretary of Defense, 2020,   https://media.defense.gov/2020/Sep/01/2002488689/-1/-1/1/2020-DOD-CHINA -MILITARY-POWER-REPORT-FINAL.PDF.

258 **"Russia and China are likely to field AI-enabled systems":** National Security Commission on Artificial Intelligence, *Final Report* (n.d.), 99, https://www.nscai.gov/wp-content/ uploads/2021/03/Full-Report-Digital-1.pdf.

258 **"How do you know when you're fielding":** Shanahan, interview.

32. ALIEN INTELLIGENCE

263 **On the battlefield:** Christian Brose, *The Kill Chain: Defending America in the Future of High-Tech Warfare* (New York: Hachette Books, April 21, 2020), https://www.amazon .com/Kill-Chain-Defending-America-High-Tech/dp/031653353X; Kenneth Payne, *I, Warbot: The Dawn of Artificially Intelligent Conflict* (London: Hurst Publishers, June 2021), https://www.amazon.com/Warbot-Dawn-Artificially-Intelligent-Conflict/dp/0197611699.

263 **automation could accelerate the "kill chain":** "Here's How the US Air Force Is Automating the Future Kill Chain," *Defense News*, November 16, 2019, https://www.defensenews .com/video/2019/11/16/heres-how-the-us-air-force-is-automating-the-future-kill-chain -dubai-airshow-2019/.

263 **reducing flexibility in a crisis:** Paul Scharre, "Autonomous Weapons and Stability" (master's thesis, King's College London, March 2020), https://kclpure.kcl.ac.uk/portal/ files/129451536/2020_Scharre_Paul_1575997_ethesis.pdf.

263 **Cognitive tasks that are best done by machines:** Payne, *I, Warbot*, 186.

265 **unprecedented increases in standards of living:** Clark Nardinelli, "Industrial Revolution and the Standard of Living," Econlib Collection: Economic History, n.d., https:// www.econlib.org/library/Enc/IndustrialRevolutionandtheStandardofLiving.html; Luke Muehlhauser, "How Big a Deal Was the Industrial Revolution?" Luke Muehlhauser (personal website), n.d., http://lukemuehlhauser.com/industrial-revolution/.

265 **tens of thousands of tanks and airplanes:** Paul Kennedy, *The Rise and Fall of the Great Powers* (New York, Random House, 1987), 353–354.

265 **Clinical methods of mathematical optimization:** *The Fog of War* (film), directed by Errol Morris, 2003.

265 **untethered by the limits of the human body:** Paul Scharre, *Robotics on the Battlefield - Part I: Range, Persistence and Daring* (Center for a New American Security, May 21, 2014), https://www.cnas.org/publications/reports/robotics-on-the-battlefield-part-i-range -persistence-and-daring.

266 **robotic systems can be made cheaper:** Paul Scharre, *Robotics on the Battlefield Part II: The Coming Swarm* (Center for a New American Security, October 15, 2014), https://www.cnas.org/publications/reports/robotics-on-the-battlefield-part-ii-the-coming-swarm.

266 **a "superhuman capability":** Joseph Trevithick, "AI Claims 'Flawless Victory' Going Undefeated In Digital Dogfight With Human Fighter Pilot," *The Drive*, August 20, 2020, https://www.thedrive.com/the-war-zone/35888/ai-claims-flawless-victory-going-undefeated-in-digital-dogfight-with-human-fighter-pilot.

266 **AlphaGo calculated the odds:** Cade Metz, "In Two Moves, AlphaGo and Lee Sedol Redefined the Future," *Wired*, March 16, 2016, https://www.wired.com/2016/03/two-moves-alphago-lee-sedol-redefined-future/.

266 **plays differently than humans:** Dawn Chan, "The AI That Has Nothing to Learn from Humans," *The Atlantic*, October 20, 2017, https://www.theatlantic.com/technology/archive/2017/10/alphago-zero-the-ai-that-taught-itself-go/543450/.

266 **"It splits its bets":** Cade Metz, "A Mystery AI Just Crushed the Best Human Players at Poker," *Wired*, January 31, 2017, https://www.wired.com/2017/01/mystery-ai-just-crushed-best-human-players-poker/.

267 **"ferocious, unexpected attacks":** Matthew Sadler and Natasha Regan, *Game Changer: AlphaZero's Groundbreaking Chess Strategies and the Promise of AI* (Amsterdam: New in Chess, February 15, 2019), 135, https://www.amazon.com/Game-Changer-AlphaZeros-Groundbreaking-Strategies/dp/9056918184.

267 **play deviates in important ways:** Sadler and Regan, *Game Changer*, 135–136.

267 **sacrifice chess pieces early:** Natasha Regan and Matthew Sadler, "Game Changer: AlphaZero revitalizing the attack," interview by Aditya Pai, Chess News, January 31, 2019, https://en.chessbase.com/post/interview-with-natasha-regan-and-matthew-sadler; Sadler and Regan, *Game Changer*, 102, 136.

267 **combining attacks and maximizing its use of mobility:** Sadler and Regan, *Game Changer*, 136.

267 **ignores some conventional wisdom that humans have developed:** Sadler and Regan, *Game Changer*, 122–123.

267 **ability to search 60,000 moves per second:** David Silver et al., "AlphaZero: Shedding New Light on Chess, Shogi, and Go," *DeepMind Blog*, December 6, 2018, https://deepmind.com/blog/article/alphazero-shedding-new-light-grand-games-chess-shogi-and-go.

267 **valuable test beds for AI agents:** Michael Buro, "Real-Time Strategy Games: A New AI Research Challenge," in *Proceedings of the 18th International Joint Conference on Artificial Intelligence* (International Joint Conferences on Artificial Intelligence, 2003), http://citeseerx.ist.psu.edu/viewdoc/summary?doi=10.1.1.96.6742.

267 **StarCraft II:** Oriol Vinyals et al., "Grandmaster Level in StarCraft II Using Multi-Agent Reinforcement Learning," *Nature* 575 (2019), 350, https://doi.org/10.1038/s41586-019-1724-z.

268 **approximately 20,000 time steps:** Open AI et al., *Dota 2 with Large Scale Deep Reinforcement Learning* (arXiv.org, December 13, 2019), 2, https://arxiv.org/pdf/1912.06680.pdf.

268 **command and control:** Congressional Research Service, "Defense Primer: What Is Command and Control?," November 29, 2021, https://sgp.fas.org/crs/natsec/IF11805.pdf.

268 **micro play:** An example of AI micro on display in *StarCraft II*: Automaton2000Micro, "Automaton 2000 Micro—Dodging Siege Tanks," April 4, 2011, https://www.youtube.com/watch?v=IKVFZ28ybQs.

268 **much faster than even the top professional human gamers:** Aleksi Pietkäinen, "An Analysis on How Deepmind's Starcraft 2 AI's Superhuman Speed Is Probably a Band-Aid Fix for the Limitations of Imitation Learning," *Medium*, January 26, 2019, https://blog.usejournal

.com/an-analysis-on-how-deepminds-starcraft-2-ai-s-superhuman-speed-could-be-a
-band-aid-fix-for-the-1702fb8344d6.

268 **dodge enemy fire:** Automaton2000Micro, "Automaton 2000 Micro—Dodging Siege
Tanks"; Micro A.I., "Micro AI in Real Game Scenarios," YouTube, November 3, 2015,
https://www.youtube.com/watch?v=3PLplRDSgpo; Automaton2000Micro, "Automaton 2000 Micro - Drops Part I," YouTube, April 10, 2011, https://www.youtube.com/
watch?v=0EYH-csTttw.

268 **greater coordination among multiple disparate units:** DeepMind, "DeepMind StarCraft
II Demonstration," streamed on YouTube January 24, 2019, https://www.youtube.com/
watch?v=cUTMhmVh1qs&t=6122s; "Takeaways from OpenAI Five (2019) [AI/ML, Dota
Summary," senrigan.io, April 22, 2019, updated June 25, 2020, https://senrigan.io/blog/
takeaways-from-openai-5/.

268 **OpenAI's *Dota 2* agents:** Mike, "OpenAI & DOTA 2: Game Is Hard," *Games by Angelina*,
updated August 10, 2018, http://www.gamesbyangelina.org/2018/08/openai-dota-2-game
-is-hard/; "Open AI Five Benchmark," streamed on Twitch, 2018, https://www.twitch
.tv/videos/293517383?t=2h11m08s; (deleted user), "OpenAI Hex was Within the 200ms
Response Time," r/DotA2, Reddit, 2018, https://www.reddit.com/r/DotA2/comments/
94vdpm/openai_hex_was_within_the_200ms_response_time/e3ofipk/; OpenAI et al.,
Dota 2, 52.

269 **precisely coordinate their attacks:** Mike, "OpenAI & DOTA 2: Game Is Hard."

269 **excel in team fights:** ProGuides Dota 2 Tips Tricks and Guides, "Dota2: What Can We
Learn from OpenAI Five? | Pro Dota 2 Guides," YouTube, August 7, 2018, https://www
.youtube.com/watch?v=rTtg_DdOqPQ.

269 **"It felt like I was pressured":** Mike, "OpenAI & DOTA 2: Game Is Hard."

269 **human grandmasters can look only fifteen to twenty moves ahead:** Magnus Carlsen,
"Magnus Carlsen: The 19-Year-Old King of Chess," interview by Eben Harrell, *Time*,
December 25, 2009, http://content.time.com/time/world/article/0,8599,1948809,00.html

269 **AlphaZero's 60,000 positions per second:** David Silver, et al., *A General Reinforcement Learning Algorithm That Masters Chess, Shogi and Go Through Self-Play* (googleusercontent.com,
n.d.,) https://kstatic.googleusercontent.com/files/2f51b2a749a284c2e2dfa13911da965f4855
092a179469aedd15fbe4efe8f8cbf9c515ef83ac03a6515fa990e6f85fd827dcd477845e
806f23a17845072dc7bd.

269 **capture-the-flag computer games:** Max Jaderberg et al., "Human-Level Performance in
3D Multiplayer Games with Population-Based Reinforcement Learning," *Science* 364, no.
6443 (May 31, 2019), 3, https://doi.org/10.1126/science.aau6249.

269 **take in information about the whole map:** OpenAI et al., *Dota 2*, 4, 39.

269 **redeploying pieces that are no longer needed:** Regan and Sadler, "Game Changer:
AlphaZero revitalizing the attack."

270 **superhuman attentiveness of AI agents:** AlphaZero has committed blunders in chess but
they are rare. Sadler and Regan, *Game Changer*, 130.

270 **"I've realized how much my gameplay relies on forcing mistakes":** "AlphaStar: Mastering the Real-Time Strategy Game StarCraft II," *DeepMind Blog*, January 24, 2019, https://
deepmind.com/blog/article/alphastar-mastering-real-time-strategy-game-starcraft-ii.

270 **AI agents' superhuman precision:** OpenAI et al., *Dota 2*, 10.

270 **AlphaZero excels at combining multiple attacks:** Sadler and Regan, *Game Changer*, 136.

270 **In *Dota 2*, AI agents demonstrate superhuman coordination:** ProGuides Dota 2 Tips
Tricks and Guides, "Dota2: What Can We Learn from OpenAI Five?"; Mike, "OpenAI &
DOTA 2: Game Is Hard."

270 **OpenAI Five's five AI agents switched their characters' locations:** OpenAI et al., *Dota 2,* 10; ProGuides Dota 2 Tips Tricks and Guides, "Dota2: What Can We Learn from OpenAI Five?"

270 **long-term positional advantage:** Chan, "The AI That Has Nothing to Learn from Humans."

270 **apparent lack of long-term planning:** Kyle Wiggers, "OpenAI's Dota 2 Bot Defeated 99.4% of Players in Public Matches," *GamesBeat,* April 22, 2019, https://venturebeat .com/2019/04/22/openais-dota-2-bot-defeated-99-4-of-players-in-public-matches/; Mike, "OpenAI & DOTA 2: Game Is Hard"; Nick Statt, "OpenAI's Dota 2 AI Steamrolls World Champion e-Sports Team with Back-to-Back Victories," *The Verge,* April 13, 2019, https:// www.theverge.com/2019/4/13/18309459/openai-five-dota-2-finals-ai-bot-competition-og -e-sports-the-international-champion.

270 **greater range in behaviors than human players:** Andrew Lohn, "What Chess Can Teach Us About the Future of AI and War," War on the Rocks, January 3, 2020, https:// warontherocks.com/2020/01/what-chess-can-teach-us-about-the-future-of-ai-and-war/; Payne, *I, Warbot,* 170–173.

270 **"The agent demonstrated strategies I hadn't thought of before":** "AlphaStar: Mastering the Real-Time Strategy Game StarCraft II."

270 **expanded how humans think about the game:** Regan and Sadler, "Game Changer: AlphaZero revitalizing the attack."

271 **If AlphaGo is ahead, it will play conservatively:** Elizabeth Gibney, "Google AI Algorithm Masters Ancient Game of Go," *Nature* 529 (2016): 445–446, https://www.nature.com/ articles/529445a; John Ribeiro, "AlphaGo's Unusual Moves Prove Its AI Prowess, Experts Say," *PCWorld,* March 14, 2016, https://www.pcworld.com/article/3043668/alphagos-unusual -moves-prove-its-ai-prowess-experts-say.html; Tanguy Chouard, "The Go Files: AI Computer Clinches Victory Against Go Champion," *Nature* (2016), https://doi.org/10.1038/nature.2016 .19553; David Ormerod, "AlphaGo Shows Its True Strength in 3rd Victory Against Lee Sedol," *Go Game Guru,* March 12, 2016, https://gogameguru.com/alphago-shows-true-strength-3rd -victory-lee-sedol/ (site discontinued), https://web.archive.org/web/20160312154540/https:// gogameguru.com/alphago-shows-true-strength-3rd-victory-lee-sedol/.

271 **constant pressure on human players:** Mike, "OpenAI & DOTA 2: Game Is Hard."; "Takeaways from OpenAI Five"; Statt, "OpenAI's Dota 2 AI Steamrolls World Champion e-Sports Team."

271 **"Human players are often cautious":** OpenAI et al., *Dota 2,* 10.

271 **"Unexpectedly, increasing [actions per minute]":** Vinyals et al., "Grandmaster Level in StarCraft II Using Multi-Agent Reinforcement Learning," 353.

271 **settling for suboptimal strategies:** OpenAI et al., *Dota 2,* 62.

272 **overly reliant on their team-fighting skills**: Wiggers, "OpenAI's Dota 2 Bot Defeated 99.4% of Players in Public Matches"; Mike, "OpenAI & DOTA 2: Game Is Hard"; Statt, "OpenAI's Dota 2 AI Steamrolls World Champion e-Sports Team."

272 **poor lineup of characters:** "OpenAI Five Benchmark: Results," *OpenAI Blog,* August 6, 2018, https://openai.com/blog/openai-five-benchmark-results/.

272 **AI agents performed poorly and inflexibly:** Mike, "OpenAI & DOTA 2: Game Is Hard."

272 **certain characters and types of actions off-limits:** "OpenAI Five Benchmark," *OpenAI Blog,* July 18, 2018, https://openai.com/blog/openai-five-benchmark/; OpenAI et al., *Dota 2.*

272 **99.4 percent win average:** OpenAI et al., *Dota 2.*

272 **perform surgery:** OpenAI et al., *Dota 2,* 7–8, 10–13, 25–29.

272 **Superhuman precision and speed:** Vinyals et al., "Grandmaster Level in StarCraft II";

Pietkäinen, "An Analysis on How Deepmind's Starcraft 2 AI's Superhuman Speed Is Probably a Band-Aid."

272 **forward-quarter gunshots:** Colin "Farva" Price, "Navy F/A-18 Squadron Commander's Take on AI Repeatedly Beating Real Pilot In Dogfight," *The Drive*, August 24, 2020, https://www.thedrive.com/the-war-zone/35947/navy-f-a-18-squadron-commanders-take-on-ai-repeatedly-beating-real-pilot-in-dogfight.

272 **capture-the-flag computer game:** Jaderberg et al., "Human-Level Performance in 3D Multiplayer Games," 3.

272 **AlphaStar's superhuman click rate:** In refining their *StarCraft II* agent, AlphaStar, Deep-Mind went to great lengths to handicap the AI agent so that it was limited to playing at the rough equivalent to a human level. This includes slowing down its rate of actions, introducing delays, and limiting its field of observation to be equivalent to human players. Pietkäinen, "An Analysis on How Deepmind's Starcraft 2 AI's Superhuman Speed Is Probably a Band-Aid"; "AlphaStar: Mastering the Real-Time Strategy Game StarCraft II"; Vinyals et al., "Grandmaster Level in StarCraft II."

273 **better combat performance:** Kenneth Payne, *Strategy, Evolution, and War: From Apes to Artificial Intelligence* (Washington, DC: Georgetown University Press, April 18, 2018), 181.

273 **Human soldiers suffer fear:** U.S. Marine Corps, *MCDP 1: Warfighting* (U.S. Marine Corps, 1997), 15–16, https://www.marines.mil/Portals/1/Publications/MCDP%201%20Warfighting.pdf

274 **"The relative psychological advantages of defense":** Payne, *Strategy, Evolution, and War*, 178–179.

274 **"the mental strain of operating far from home":** Payne, *Strategy, Evolution, and War*, 179.

274 **"attackers enjoy the initiative":** Payne, *Strategy, Evolution, and War*, 179.

274 **Combat action among humans ebbs and flows:** U.S. Marine Corps, *MCDP 1: Warfighting*, 10.

274 **"I kind of felt powerless":** Christopher Moyer, "How Google's AlphaGo Beat a Go World Champion," *The Atlantic*, March 28, 2016, https://www.theatlantic.com/technology/archive/2016/03/the-invisible-opponent/475611/.

275 **AI "cannot be defeated":** "(Yonhap Interview) Go Master Lee Says He Quits Unable to Win over AI Go Players," Yonhap News Agency, November 27, 2019, https://en.yna.co.kr/view/AEN20191127004800315.

275 **overestimation of Deep Blue's abilities:** Nate Silver, *The Signal and the Noise: Why So Many Predictions Fail—but Some Don't* (New York: Penguin Books, February 3, 2015), 277–289.

33. BATTLEFIELD SINGULARITY

276 **Battlefield Singularity:** The chapter title comes from the title of Elsa Kania's report, *Battlefield Singularity*. Elsa B. Kania, *Battlefield Singularity: Artificial Intelligence, Military Revolution, and China's Future Military Power* (Center for a New American Security, November 28, 2017), https://www.cnas.org/publications/reports/battlefield-singularity-artificial-intelligence-military-revolution-and-chinas-future-military-power.

276 **higher rate of fire:** Stephen Biddle, *Military Power: Explaining Victory and Defeat in Modern Battle* (Princeton, NJ: Princeton University Press, 2004), 29, https://www.amazon.com/Military-Power-Explaining-Victory-Defeat/dp/0691128022.

277 **Battle of the Somme:** Wikipedia, s.v. "First Day on the Somme," updated September 12, 2021, https://en.wikipedia.org/wiki/First_day_on_the_Somme.

277 **military tactics had finally adapted:** Biddle, *Military Power*, 33–35.
277 **swarming:** John Arquilla and David Ronfeldt, *Swarming and the Future of Conflict* (RAND Corporation, 2000), https://www.rand.org/pubs/documented_briefings/DB311.html; Sean J. A. Edwards, *Swarming on the Battlefield: Past, Present, and Future* (RAND Corporation, 2000), https://www.rand.org/pubs/monograph_reports/MR1100.html; Sean J. A. Edwards, *Swarming and the Future of Warfare* (RAND Corporation, 2005), https://www.rand.org/pubs/rgs_dissertations/RGSD189.html; Paul Scharre, *Robotics on the Battlefield Part II: The Coming Swarm* (Center for a New American Security, October 15, 2014), https://www.cnas.org/publications/reports/robotics-on-the-battlefield-part-ii-the-coming-swarm.
277 **maneuver warfare:** The term "maneuver warfare" sometimes is used differently to describe a philosophy of combat, rather than the more narrow meaning in which it is used here pertaining to the physical movements of units in spatial relation to each other. For more on this more narrow meaning of maneuver, see *Doctrine for the Armed Forces of the United States*, Joint Publication 1 (U.S. Army, U.S. Navy, U.S. Air Force, U.S. Coast Guard, U.S. Marine Corps, March 25, 2013, updated July 12, 2017), https://www.jcs.mil/Portals/36/Documents/Doctrine/pubs/jp1_ch1.pdf?ver=2019-02-11-174350-967. For more on the philosophy of maneuver warfare, see U.S. Marine Corps, *MCDP 1: Warfighting* (U.S. Marine Corps, 1997), https://www.marines.mil/Portals/1/Publications/MCDP%201%20Warfighting.pdf.
277 **sports team:** "Official Numbers of Players on a Team," Factmonster.com, updated February 21, 2017, https://www.factmonster.com/sports/sports-section/official-numbers-players-team.
278 **Swarming tactics:** Arquilla and Ronfeldt, *Swarming and the Future of Conflict*; Edwards, *Swarming on the Battlefield*; Edwards, *Swarming and the Future of Warfare*; Scharre, *Robotics on the Battlefield Part II*.
278 **mass drone attacks:** David Reid, "A Swarm of Armed Drones Attacked a Russian Military Base in Syria," CNBC, January 11, 2018, https://www.cnbc.com/2018/01/11/swarm-of-armed-diy-drones-attacks-russian-military-base-in-syria.html.
278 **first true drone swarm:** David Hambling, "Israel Used World's First AI-Guided Combat Drone Swarm in Gaza Attacks," *NewScientist*, June 30, 2021, https://www.newscientist.com/article/2282656-israel-used-worlds-first-ai-guided-combat-drone-swarm-in-gaza-attacks/; Zak Kallenborn, "Israel's Drone Swarm Over Gaza Should Worry Everyone," *Defense One*, July 7, 2021, https://www.defenseone.com/ideas/2021/07/israels-drone-swarm-over-gaza-should-worry-everyone/183156/.
278 **Nonmilitary robot swarms:** Self-Organizing Systems Research Group (website), Harvard University, 2021, https://ssr.seas.harvard.edu/.
279 **"span of control":** *Doctrine for the Armed Forces of the United States*.
279 **AI command and control:** See also Kenneth Payne, *I, Warbot: The Dawn of Artificially Intelligent Conflict* (London: Hurst Publishers, June 2021), 127, https://www.amazon.com/Warbot-Dawn-Artificially-Intelligent-Conflict/dp/0197611699.
279 **hand over execution of swarm behavior:** Payne, *I, Warbot*, 110.
279 **"'shepherd' model":** Garry Kasparov, "AlphaZero and the Knowledge Revolution," foreword to Matthew Sadler and Natasha Regan, *Game Changer: AlphaZero's Groundbreaking Chess Strategies and the Promise of AI* (Amsterdam: New in Chess, February 15, 2019), 10, https://www.amazon.com/Game-Changer-AlphaZeros-Groundbreaking-Strategies/dp/9056918184.
279 **Chen Hanghui of the PLA's Army Command College:** *US-China Economic and Security Review Commission Hearing on Trade, Technology, and Military-Civil Fusion*, June 7, 2019 (testimony of Elsa B. Kania, Adjunct Senior Fellow, Technology and National Security

Program, Center for a New American Security), https://www.uscc.gov/sites/default/files/June%207%20Hearing_Panel%201_Elsa%20Kania_Chinese%20Military%20Innovation%20in%20Artificial%20Intelligence.pdf.

279 **"In the future battlefield":** Chen, Hanghui 陈航辉. "Rengong Zhineng: Dianfu Xing Gaibian "Youxi Guize" 人工智能 :颠覆性改变 "游戏规则"" [Artificial intelligence: disruptively changing the "rules of the game"]. Zhongguo Junwang 中国军网, March 18, 2016. http://www.81.cn/jskj/2016-03/18/content_6966873_2.htm. [Translation by Peter Hansen.]

280 **"hyperwar":** John R. Allen and Amir Husain, "On Hyperwar," *Proceedings*, July 2017, https://www.usni.org/magazines/proceedings/2017/july/hyperwar.

280 **lose the ability to control escalation or terminate a war:** Paul Scharre, "Autonomous Weapons and Stability" (master's thesis, King's College London, March 2020), https://kcl-pure.kcl.ac.uk/portal/files/129451536/2020_Scharre_Paul_1575997_ethesis.pdf.

280 **battlefield singularity:** Kania, *Battlefield Singularity*.

280 **ever-changing character of warfare:** For example, see: Colin S. Gray, "War—Continuity in Change, and Change in Continuity," *Parameters* 40, no. 2 (Summer 2010): 5–13, https://press.armywarcollege.edu/parameters/vol40/iss2/5/; U.S. Marine Corps, *MCDP 1: Warfighting* (U.S. Marine Corps, 1997), https://www.marines.mil/Portals/1/Publications/MCDP%201%20Warfighting.pdf; and Christopher Mewitt, "Understanding War's Enduring Nature Alongside Its Changing Character," *War on the Rocks*, January 21, 2014, https://warontherocks.com/2014/01/understanding-wars-enduring-nature-alongside-its-changing-character/.

280 **War is a violent struggle among competing groups:** The political nature of war is taken as an unquestioned assumption in contemporary Western defense circles, but there are dissenting points of view. John Keegan states in *A History of Warfare*, "War is not the continuation of policy by other means. The world would be a simpler place to understand if this dictum of Clausewitz's were true.... [W]ar embraces much more than politics: ... it is always an expression of culture, often a determinant of cultural forms, in some societies the culture itself." John Keegan, *A History of Warfare* (New York: Alfred A. Knopf, 1993), 3, 12.

280 **"I'm certainly questioning my original premise":** Aaron Mehta, "AI Makes Mattis Question 'Fundamental' Beliefs About War," C4ISRNET, February 17, 2018, https://www.c4isrnet.com/intel-geoint/2018/02/17/ai-makes-mattis-question-fundamental-beliefs-about-war/.

281 **AI could, in theory, change the nature of war:** Frank Hoffman, "Squaring Clausewitz's Trinity in the Age of Autonomous Weapons," *Orbis* 63, no. 1 (Winter 2019): 44–63, https://doi.org/10.1016/j.orbis.2018.12.011; and Paul Scharre, "White Walkers and the Nature of War" in *Winning Westeros: How Game of Thrones Explains Modern Military Conflict* (Sterling, VA: Potomac Books, 2019), 253–264.

282 **a war without political purpose:** It is possible to imagine extreme political purposes for which human extinction would, in fact, be the goal, such as a madman's act of revenge on humanity or an extreme act of ecoterrorism to wipe humanity from the face of the earth.

283 **The very first internet worm:** Ted Eisenberg et al., "The Cornell Commission: On Morris and the Worm," *Communications of the ACM* 32, no. 6 (June 1989): 706–709, http://dx.doi.org/10.1145/63526.63530.

282 **spread far beyond its intended target:** Nicolas Falliere, Liam O. Murchu, and Eric Chien, *W32.Stuxnet Dossier* (Symantec Security Response, February 2011), https://www.symantec.com/content/en/us/enterprise/media/security_response/whitepapers/w32_stuxnet_dossier.pdf (page discontinued).

282 **an instrumental goal that intelligent systems adopt:** Stephen M. Omohundro, *The Basic*

AI Drives (wordpress.com, n.d.), httpsaselfawaresystems.files.wordpress.com/2008/01/ai_
drives_final.pdf; Nick Bostrom, *Superintelligence* (Oxford, UK: Oxford University Press,
May 5, 2015), 131–139, https://www.amazon.com/Superintelligence-Dangers-Strategies
-Nick-Bostrom/dp/0199678111/.

284 **variation, selection, and replication:** Joel Lehman et al., "The Surprising Creativity of
Digital Evolution: A Collection of Anecdotes from the Evolutionary Computation and
Artificial Life Research Communities," *Artificial Life* 26, no. 2 (2020).

284 **artificial general intelligence (AGI):** Vincent C. Müller and Nick Bostrom, "Future Progress in Artificial Intelligence: A Survey of Expert Opinion," in Vincent C. Müller, ed.,
Fundamentals of Artificial Intelligence (Berlin: Springer, 2014), https://nickbostrom.com/
papers/survey.pdf; and Katja Grace et al., *When Will AI Exceed Human Performance? Evidence From AI Experts* (arXiv.org, May 3, 2018), https://arxiv.org/pdf/1705.08807.pdf.

284 **superintelligence:** Nick Bostrom, "How Long Before Superintelligence?" *International
Journal of Future Studies* 2 (1998), https://www.nickbostrom.com/superintelligence.html;
Bostrom, *Superintelligence.*

284 **pinnacle of intelligence:** For definitions of intelligence, see Shane Legg and Marcus Hut-
ter, *A Collection of Definitions of Intelligence* (Technical Report IDSIA-07-07, arXiv.org,
June 15, 2007), 9.

284 **"There seem to be almost as many definitions of intelligence":** R. J. Sternberg, "Quantitative Integration: Definitions of Intelligence: A Comparison of the 1921 and 1986 Sympo-
sia," in *What Is Intelligence? Contemporary Viewpoints on its Nature and Definition*, ed. R.
J. Sternberg and C. A. Berg (Norwood, NJ: Ablex Publishing Corporation, 1986), quoted in
R. L. Gregory, The Oxford Companion to the Mind (Oxford, UK: Oxford University Press,
1998), quoted in Shane Legg, "Machine Super Intelligence" (doctoral diss., University of
Lugano, June 2008), 3–4.

284 **Copernican revolution:** Kevin Kelly, "The Next 30 Digital Years," YouTube, April 13, 2020,
https://www.youtube.com/watch?v=XhduPAy2bxo.

284 **Cambrian explosion:** Gill Pratt has made this analogy with respect to robotics. Gill A.
Pratt, "Is a Cambrian Explosion Coming for Robotics?" *Journal of Economic Perspectives,*
29, no. 3 (Summer 2015): 51–60, http://dx.doi.org/10.1257/jep.29.3.51.

285 **AI researchers vary widely in their predictions:** Seth D. Baum, Ben Goertzel, and Ted G.
Goertzel, "How Long Until Human-Level AI? Results from an Expert Assessment," *Techno-
logical Forecasting and Social Change* 78, no. 1 (January 2011): 185–195, https://doi.org/10
.1016/j.techfore.2010.09.006; Grace et al., *When Will AI Exceed Human Performance?*; Katja
Grace, "Update on All the AI Predictions," AI Impacts, June 5, 2015, https://aiimpacts.org/
update-on-all-the-ai-predictions; Katja Grace, "Predictions of Human-Level AI Timelines,"
AI Impacts, June 5, 2015, https://aiimpacts.org/predictions-of-human-level-ai-timelines/;
Müller and Bostrom, "Future Progress in Artificial Intelligence"; Ross Gruetzemacher,
David Paradice, and Kang Bok Lee, *Forecasting Transformative AI: An Expert Survey* (arXiv.
org, n.d.), https://arxiv.org/pdf/1901.08579.pdf; Luke Muehlhauser, "What Should We Learn
from Past AI Forecasts?," Open Philanthropy Project, September 2016, https://www.open-
philanthropy.org/focus/global-catastrophic-risks/potential-risks-advanced-artificial-intel-
ligence/what-should-we-learn-past-ai-forecasts; "List of Analyses of Time to Human-Level
AI," AI Impacts, n.d., https://aiimpacts.org/list-of-analyses-of-time-to-human-level-ai/.

285 **Surveys of several hundred AI researchers:** Grace et al., *When Will AI Exceed Human Performance?*; Baobao Zhang et al., *Forecasting AI Progress: Evidence From a Survey of Machine
Learning Researchers* (arXiv.org, June 10, 2022), https://arxiv.org/pdf/2206.04132.pdf.

285 **predictions should be taken with a grain of salt:** Grace, "Update on All the AI Predic-

tions"; "Accuracy of AI Predictions," AI Impacts, updated June 4, 2015, https://aiimpacts
.org/accuracy-of-ai-predictions/.

285 **reliable predictions about a major, disruptive shift in** *any* **technology:** Luke Meuhl-
hauser, "When Will AI Be Created?" Machine Intelligence Research Institute, May 15,
2013, https://intelligence.org/2013/05/15/when-will-ai-be-created/.

34. RESTRAINT

286 **AI applications that could be dangerous to international stability:** Vincent Boulanin
et al., *Artificial Intelligence, Strategic Stability and Nuclear Risk* (Stockholm International
Peace Research Institute, June 2020), https://www.sipri.org/publications/2020/other-pub-
lications/artificial-intelligence-strategic-stability-and-nuclear-risk; T4GS, *AI and the
Military: Forever Altering Strategic Stability* (T4GS Reports, February 13, 2019), https://
securityandtechnology.org/wp-content/uploads/2020/07/ai_and_the_military_forever_
altering_strategic_stability__IST_research_paper.pdf; Forrest E. Morgan et al., *Military
Applications of Artificial Intelligence: Ethical Concerns in an Uncertain World* (RAND Corporation, 2020), https://www.rand.org/pubs/research_reports/RR3139-1.html; Michael
C. Horowitz, Paul Scharre, and Alexander Velez-Green, *A Stable Nuclear Future? The
Impact of Autonomous Systems and Artificial Intelligence* (arXiv.org, 2019), https://arxiv
.org/abs/1912.05291; Edward Geist and Andrew J. Lohn, *How Might Artificial Intelligence
Affect the Risk of Nuclear War?* (RAND Corporation, 2018), https://www.rand.org/pubs/
perspectives/PE296.html.

286 **Lethal autonomous weapons:** Paul Scharre, *Army of None: Autonomous Weapons and the
Future of War* (New York: W.W. Norton, April 24, 2018).

286 **intersection of AI and cyber systems:** Micah Musser and Ashton Garriott, *Machine Learning and Cybersecurity: Hype and Reality* (Center for Security and Emerging Technology,
June 2021), https://cset.georgetown.edu/publication/machine-learning-and-cybersecurity/

286 **computer program called RYaN:** RYaN is an acronym for Raketno Yadernoye Napadenie
(Ракетно ядерное нападение), which translates to "nuclear missile attack." The program
is sometimes referred to as Operation RYaN or VRYAN. President's Foreign Intelligence
Advisory Board, *The Soviet "War Scare,"* National Security Archive, George Washington
University, February 15, 1990, https://nsarchive2.gwu.edu/nukevault/ebb533-The-Able
-Archer-War-Scare-Declassified-PFIAB Report-Released/2012-0238-MR.pdf.

287 **indicators of a surprise attack:** Bernd Schaefer, Nate Jones, and Benjamin B. Fischer,
"Forecasting Nuclear War," Wilson Center, n.d., https://www.wilsoncenter.org/publica-
tion/forecasting-nuclear-war; *Ministry of State Security (Stasi), Report on Development
and Achieved State of Work Regarding Early Recognition of Adversarial Attack and Surprise
Intentions (Complex RYAN)*, Wilson Center Digital Archive, May 6, 1986, translated by
Bernd Schaefer, https://digitalarchive.wilsoncenter.org/document/119334.

287 **"self-reinforcing cycle":** President's Foreign Intelligence Advisory Board, *The Soviet "War
Scare,"* 81–82.

287 **NATO's Able Archer military exercise:** The scariness of the 1983 war scare is highly
debated and remains contested. President's Foreign Intelligence Advisory Board, *The
Soviet "War Scare,"* vi; Schaefer, Jones, and Fischer, "Forecasting Nuclear War."

287 **"Although it may seem absurd to some":** President's Foreign Intelligence Advisory Board,
The Soviet "War Scare," 46.

288 **intelligence agencies are likely to use AI:** Anthony Vinci, "The Coming Revolution in
Intelligence Affairs: How Artificial Intelligence and Autonomous Systems Will Transform

Espionage," *Foreign Affairs*, August 31, 2020, https://www.foreignaffairs.com/articles/north-america/2020-08-31/coming-revolution-intelligence-affairs.

288 **United States publicly shared intelligence:** Katie Bo Lillis, Natasha Bertrand, and Kylie Atwood, "How the Biden Administration Is Aggressively Releasing Intelligence in an Attempt to Deter Russia," CNN.com, February 11, 2022, https://www.cnn.com/2022/02/11/politics/biden-administration-russia-intelligence/index.html.

288 **opaque nature of complex AI systems:** Michael Horowitz and Paul Scharre, *AI and International Stability: Risks and Confidence-Building Measures* (Center for a New American Security, January 12, 2021), https://www.cnas.org/publications/reports/ai-and-international-stability-risks-and-confidence-building-measures.

288 **nuclear stability:** Keir A. Lieber and Daryl G Press, "The New Era of Counterforce: Technological Change and the Future of Nuclear Deterrence," *International Security* 41, no. 4 (Spring 2017): 9–49, https://doi.org/10.1162/ISEC_a_00273; Charles L. Glaser and Steve Fetter, "Should the United States Reject MAD? Damage Limitation and US Nuclear Strategy toward China," *International Security* 41, no. 1 (Summer 2016): 49–98, https://doi.org/10.1162/ISEC_a_00248; Austin Long and Brendan Rittenhouse Green, "Stalking the Secure Second Strike: Intelligence, Counterforce, and Nuclear Strategy," *Journal of Strategic Studies* 38, no. 1-2 (2015): 38–73, http://dx.doi.org/10.1080/01402390.2014.958150. Also see Brendan Rittenhouse Green et al., "The Limits of Damage Limitation," *International Security* 42, no. 1 (2017): 193–207, https://doi.org/10.1162/ISEC_c_00279.

288 **AI could affect the risk of nuclear war:** Geist and Andrew J. Lohn, *How Might Artificial Intelligence Affect the Risk of Nuclear War?*; Vincent Boulanin and Maaike Verbruggen, *Mapping the Development of Autonomy in Weapon Systems* (Stockholm International Peace Research Institute, November 2017), https://www.sipri.org/publications/2017/other-publications/mapping-development-autonomy-weapon-systems; T4GS, *AI and the Military*; Horowitz, Scharre, and Velez-Green, *A Stable Nuclear Future?*; Boulanin et al., *Artificial Intelligence, Strategic Stability and Nuclear Risk*; T4GS, *AI and the Military*; Morgan et al., *Military Applications of Artificial Intelligence*; Michael C. Horowitz et al., "Policy Roundtable: Artificial Intelligence and International Security," *Texas National Security Review*, June 2, 2020, https://tnsr.org/roundtable/policy-roundtable-artificial-intelligence-and-international-security/; Melanie Sisson et al., *The Militarization of Artificial Intelligence* (Stanley Center for Peace and Security, June 2020), https://stanleycenter.org/publications/militarization-of-artificial-intelligence/; Andrew Imbrie and Elsa B. Kania, AI *Safety, Security, and Stability Among Great Powers: Options, Challenges, and Lessons Learned for Pragmatic Engagement* (Center for Security and Emerging Technology, December 2019), https://cset.georgetown.edu/publication/ai-safety-security-and-stability-among-great-powers-options-challenges-and-lessons-learned-for-pragmatic-engagement/.

289 **Status-6, or Poseidon:** U.S. Department of Defense, *Nuclear Posture Review 2018*, 8–9, https://media.defense.gov/2018/Feb/02/2001872886/-1/-1/1/2018-NUCLEAR-POSTURE-REVIEW-FINAL-REPORT.PDF; and Vladimir Putin, presidential address to the Federal Assembly, March 1, 2018, http://en.kremlin.ru/events/president/news/56957.

289 **intended use of the Status-6:** H. I. Sutton, "Countering Russian Poseidon Torpedo," *Covert Shores*, August 15, 2018, http://www.hisutton.com/Countering_Russian_Poseidon_Torpedo.html; U.S. Department of Defense, *Nuclear Posture Review 2018*, 8–9; Michael Kofman, "Emerging Russian Weapons: Welcome to the 2020s (Part 2—9M730?, Status-6, Klavesin-2R)," *Russia Military Analysis* (blog), March 6, 2018, https://russianmilitaryanalysis.wordpress.com/2018/03/06/emerging-russian-weapons-welcome-to-the-2020s-part-2-9m730-status-6-klavesin-2r/.

289   **loss of human control over nuclear weapons:** Horowitz, Scharre, and Velez-Green, *A Stable Nuclear Future?*

289   **The U.S. Air Force has repeatedly expressed unease:** *RPA Vector: Vision and Enabling Concepts, 2013–2038* (U.S. Air Force, February 17, 2014), 54, http://www.globalsecurity .org/military/library/policy/usaf/usaf-rpa-vector_vision-enabling-concepts_2013-2038 .pdf; and Hope Hodge Seck, "Air Force Wants to Keep 'Man in the Loop' with B-21 Raider," *Defencetech.org*, September 19, 2016, https://www.military.com/defensetech/2016/09/19/ air-force-wants-to-keep-man-in-the-loop-with-b-21-raider.

289   **different risk calculus:** "Russia Could Deploy Unmanned Bomber After 2040—Air Force," RIA Novosti, *GlobalSecurity.org*, February 8, 2012, http://www.globalsecurity.org/wmd/ library/news/russia/2012/russia-120802-rianovosti01.htm; Kyle Mizokami, "Experts: North Korea May Be Developing a Dirty Bomb Drone," *Popular Mechanics*, December 28, 2016, http://www.popularmechanics.com/military/weapons/a24525/north-korea-dirty -bomb-drone/; H.I. Sutton, "Poseidon Torpedo," *Covert Shores*, February 22, 2019, http:// www.hisutton.com/Poseidon_Torpedo.html; Horowitz, Scharre, and Velez-Green, *A Stable Nuclear Future?*

289   **semiautomated "dead hand" device called "Perimeter":** Nicholas Thompson, "Inside the Apocalyptic Soviet Doomsday Machine," *Wired*, September 21, 2009, https://www.wired .com/2009/09/mf-deadhand/; Vitalii Leonidovich Kataev, interview by Ellis Mishulovich, May 1993, http://nsarchive.gwu.edu/nukevault/ebb285/vol%20II%20Kataev.PDF; Varfolo- mei Vladimirovich Korobushin, interviewed by John G. Hines, December 10, 1992, http:// nsarchive.gwu.edu/nukevault/ebb285/vol%20II%20Korobushin.PDF; Andrian A. Dani- levich, interview by John G. Hines, March 5, 1990, http://nsarchive.gwu.edu/nukevault/ ebb285/vol%20iI%20Danilevich.pdf, 62–63; and Viktor M. Surikov, interview by John G. Hines, September 11, 1993, http://nsarchive.gwu.edu/nukevault/ebb285/vol%20II%20 Surikov.PDF, 134–135.

289   **operational in Russia today:** Some accounts by former Soviet officials state that the Dead Hand was investigated and possibly even developed, but never deployed oper- ationally (Danilevich, interview, 62–63; Surikov, interview, 134–135). It is unclear, though, whether this refers or not to a fully automatic system. Multiple sources con- firm the system was active, although the degree of automation is ambiguous in their accounts (Kataev, interview, 100–101; Korobushin, interview, 107). Other sources claim the system remains active today. Thompson, "Inside the Apocalyptic Soviet Doomsday Machine."

289   **"This is the ultimate human decision":** Sydney Freedberg Jr., "No AI for Nuclear Com- mand & Control: JAIC's Shanahan," *Breaking Defense*, September 25, 2019, https:// breakingdefense.com/2019/09/no-ai-for-nuclear-command-control-jaics-shanahan/.

289   **consequences of AI for international stability:** Paul Scharre, "Autonomous Weapons and Stability" (master's thesis, King's College London, March 2020), https://kclpure.kcl.ac.uk/ portal/files/129451536/2020_Scharre_Paul_1575997_ethesis.pdf; Horowitz, Scharre, and Velez-Green, *A Stable Nuclear Future?*; Horowitz and Scharre, *AI and International Stabil- ity*; Kenneth Payne, *I, Warbot: The Dawn of Artificially Intelligent Conflict* (London: Hurst Publishers, June 2021), 186–192, https://www.amazon.com/Warbot-Dawn-Artificially -Intelligent-Conflict/dp/0197611699; and Yuna Huh Wong et al., *Deterrence in the Age of Thinking Machines* (RAND Corporation, 2020), https://www.rand.org/pubs/research_ reports/RR2797.html.

289   **security dilemma:** John H. Herz, "Idealist Internationalism and the Security Dilemma," *World Politics* 2, no. 2 (January 1950): 157–180, https://doi.org/10.2307/2009187; John H.

Herz, *Political Realism and Political Idealism* (Chicago: University of Chicago Press, 1951); Robert Jervis, "Cooperation Under the Security Dilemma," *World Politics* 30, no. 2 (January 1978): 169, https://doi.org/10.2307/2009958; and Charles L. Glaser, "The Security Dilemma Revisited," *World Politics* 50, no. 1 (October 1997): 174, https://www.jstor.org/stable/25054031.

289 **race to the bottom on safety:** Paul Scharre, "Debunking the AI Arms Race Theory," *Texas National Security Review* 4, no. 3 (Summer 2021): 121–132, http://dx.doi.org/10.26153/tsw/13985.

290 **reduce the risks of military competition:** Michael C. Horowitz, Lauren Kahn, and Casey Mahoney, "The Future of Military Applications of Artificial Intelligence: A Role for Confidence-Building Measures?" *Orbis* 64, no. 4 (2020): 528–543, https://doi.org/10.1016/j.orbis.2020.08.003; Imbrie and Kania, *AI Safety, Security, and Stability Among Great Powers*; Giacomo Persi Paoli et al., *Modernizing Arms Control: Exploring Responses to the Use of AI in Military Decision-Making* (UNIDIR, 2020).

290 **Confidence-building measures:** Marie-France Desjardins, *Rethinking Confidence-Building Measures* (New York: Routledge, February 28, 1997), 5; Horowitz and Scharre, *AI and International Stability.*

290 **variety of measures that countries could adopt:** Horowitz and Scharre, *AI and International Stability.*

290 **"severe challenges that artificial intelligence military applications pose":** Li, Chijiang 李驰江. "[Shijie Zhishi] Rengong Zhineng Junshi Yingyong De Guoji Jun Kong Changyi He Jinzhan 【世界知识】人工智能军事应用的国际军控倡议和进展" [[World Affairs] International Arms Control Initiatives and Progress of Military Applications of Artificial Intelligence]. *Weixin* 微信. *Shijie Zhishi* 世界知识, Last modified May 13, 2021. https://mp.weixin.qq.com/s/46vaQlyUD0DQHHycYHy5zw. [Translation by Peter Hansen.]

290 **adopt confidence-building measures, including in AI:** Zhou Bo, "China and America Can Compete and Coexist," *New York Times,* February 3, 2020, https://www.nytimes.com/2020/02/03/opinion/pla-us-china-cold-war-military-sea.html.

290 **1972 U.S.-Soviet Incidents at Sea Agreement:** Agreement on the Prevention of Incidents On and Over the High Seas, U.S.–U.S.S.R., May 25, 1972, 23 U.S.T. 1168; 852 U.N.T.S. 151, https://2009-2017.state.gov/t/isn/4791.htm.

291 **confidence-building measure that was highly successful:** Eric A. McVadon, "The Reckless and the Resolute: Confrontation in the South China Sea," *China Security* 5, no. 2 (Spring 2009), 10, https://www.files.ethz.ch/isn/117001/Issue14full.pdf; Pete Pedrozo, "The U.S.-China Incidents at Sea Agreement: A Recipe for Disaster," *Journal of National Security Law & Policy* 6, no. 207 (2012), https://jnslp.com/wp-content/uploads/2012/08/07_Pedrozo-Master.pdf.

291 **"In the Cold War, the United States and the Soviet Union developed a lot of cooperation":** Li Bin, remarks at the World Peace Forum, Beijing, China, 2019.

291 **"some limits, some guidelines":** Jack Shanahan, interview by author, April 1, 2020.

291 **"Both sides should clarify the strategic boundaries":** Zhu Qichao and Long Kun, "How Will Artificial Intelligence Impact Sino–US Relations?" *China International Strategy Review* 1 (2019): 139–151, https://doi.org/10.1007/s42533-019-00008-9.

291 **"We need to enhance the efforts to regulate military applications":** "Position Paper of the People's Republic of China on Regulating Military Applications of Artificial Intelligence (AI)," Permanent Mission of the People's Republic of China to the United Nations Office at Geneva and other International Organizations in Switzerland, December 13, 2021, http://www.china-un.ch/eng/dbdt/202112/t20211213_10467517.htm.

292 **"China has taken the lead in demonstrating a clear attitude":** Zhu and Long, "How Will Artificial Intelligence Impact Sino–US relations?"

292 **"The ones most ardent about arms control statements":** Shanahan, interview.

292 **U.S.-China air and naval incidents have continued:** Maritime Matters: Military Safety, U.S.-China, January 19, 1998, T.I.A.S. 12924, https://www.state.gov/wp-content/uploads/2019/02/12924-China-Maritime-Matters-Misc-Agreement-1.19.1998.pdf; David Griffiths, *U.S.-China Maritime Confidence Building: Paradigms, Precedents, and Prospects* (study no. 6, U.S. Naval War College's China Maritime Studies Institute, July 2010), https://digital-commons.usnwc.edu/cmsi-red-books/4/; *Memorandum of Understanding Between the Department of Defense of the United States of America and the Ministry of National Defense of the People's Republic of China Regarding the Rules of Behavior for Safety of Air and Maritime Encounters* (November 2014), https://archive.defense.gov/pubs/141112_MemorandumOfUnderstandingRegardingRules.pdf (site discontinued); Yeganeh Torbati, "Despite Agreements, Risks Linger of U.S.-China Naval Mishaps," Reuters, October 30, 2015, https://www.reuters.com/article/us-southchinasea-usa-communications/despite-agreements-risks-linger-of-u-s-china-naval-mishaps-idUSKCN-0SO0E220151030. Both nations are also signatories to the 2014 multinational Code for Unplanned Encounters at Sea. "Document: Code for Unplanned Encounters at Sea," USNI News, August 22, 2016, https://news.usni.org/2014/06/17/document-conduct-unplanned-encounters-sea.

292 **"China has generally resisted any effective efforts":** Julian Borger, "Hotlines 'Ring Out': China's Military Crisis Strategy Needs Rethink, Says Biden Asia Chief," *The Guardian*, May 6, 2021, https://www.theguardian.com/world/2021/may/06/hotlines-ring-out-chinas-military-crisis-strategy-needs-rethink-says-biden-asia-chief-kurt-campbell.

292 **refused a request by U.S. Defense Secretary Lloyd Austin:** "Pentagon Chief Unable to Talk to Chinese Military Leaders Despite Repeated Attempts," Reuters, May 21, 2021, https://www.reuters.com/world/china/pentagon-chief-unable-talk-chinese-military-leaders-despite-repeated-attempts-2021-05-21/; Tom Fox, "When Defense Secretary Austin Tried to Call His Chinese Counterpart, Here's What Really Got in the Way," *Washington Post*, June 24, 2021, https://www.washingtonpost.com/politics/2021/06/24/when-defense-secretary-austin-tried-call-his-chinese-counterpart-heres-what-really-got-way/.

292 **China and India have a number of agreements:** United Nations, *Agreement on the Maintenance of Peace and Tranquility Along the Line of Actual Control in the India-China Border Areas* (September 7, 1993), https://peacemaker.un.org/sites/peacemaker.un.org/files/CN%20IN_930907_Agreement%20on%20India-China%20Border%20Areas.pdf; United Nations, *Agreement Between the Government of the Republic of India and the Government of the People's Republic of China on Confidence-Building Measures in the Military Field Along the Line of Actual Control in the India-China Border Areas* (November 29, 1996), https://peacemaker.un.org/sites/peacemaker.un.org/files/CN%20IN_961129_Agreement%20between%20China%20and%20India.pdf; United Nations, *Protocol Between the Government of the Republic of India and the Government of the People's Republic of China on Modalities for the Implementation of Confidence Building Measures in the Military Field Along the Line of Actual Control in the India-China Border Areas* (April 11, 2005), https://peacemaker.un.org/sites/peacemaker.un.org/files/CN%20IN_050411_Protocol%20between%20India%20and%20China.pdf.

35. THE FUTURE OF AI

294 **rapid growth in size for large language models:** Deep Ganguli et al., *Predictability and Surprise in Large Generative Models* (arXiv.org, February 15, 2022), https://arxiv.org/pdf/2202.07785.pdf.

294 **BERT$_{LARGE}$:** Jacob Devlin et al., *BERT: Pre-training of Deep Bidirectional Transformers for Language Understanding* (Google AI Language, October 11, 2018), https://arxiv.org/pdf/1810.04805v2.pdf.

294 **GPT-2:** "Better Language Models and Their Implications," openai.com, n.d., https://openai.com/blog/better-language-models/.

294 **GPT-3:** Tom B. Brown et al., *Language Models are Few-Shot Learners* (Cornell University, July 22, 2020), https://arxiv.org/pdf/2005.14165.pdf.

294 **Switch-C:** William Fedus, Barret Zoph, and Noam Shazeer. *Switch Transformers: Scaling to Trillion Parameter Models with Simple and Efficient Sparsity* (arXiv.org, January 11, 2021), https://arxiv.org/pdf/2101.03961.pdf.

294 **745 GB of text:** Emily M. Bender et al., "On the Dangers of Stochastic Parrots: Can Language Models Be Too Big?" *FAccT '21: Proceedings of the 2021 ACM Conference on Fairness, Accountability, and Transparency* (March 2021), 610–623, https://dl.acm.org/doi/pdf/10.1145/3442188.3445922.

294 **Megatron-Turing NLG:** Ali Alvi and Paresh Kharya, "Using DeepSpeed and Megatron to Train Megatron-Turing NLG 530B, the World's Largest and Most Powerful Generative Language Model," Microsoft Research Blog, October 11, 2021, https://www.microsoft.com/en-us/research/blog/using-deepspeed-and-megatron-to-train-megatron-turing-nlg-530b-the-worlds-largest-and-most-powerful-generative-language-model/.

294 **825 GB of text:** Leo Gao et al., *The Pile: An 800GB Dataset of Diverse Text for Language Modeling* (arXiv, December 31, 2020), https://arxiv.org/pdf/2101.00027.pdf.

294 **270 billion "tokens":** Alvi and Kharya, "Using DeepSpeed and Megatron to Train Megatron-Turing NLG 530B."

294 **sixth-largest supercomputer:** "SELENE," Top500, https://www.top500.org/system/179842/.

294 **over 4,000 GPUs:** Alvi and Kharya, "Using DeepSpeed and Megatron to Train Megatron-Turing NLG 530B."

294 **PaLM:** The 540 billion parameter version of PaLM was trained using "6144 TPU v4 chips running for 1,200 hours and 3072 TPU v4 chips running for 336 hours including some downtime and repeated steps." The training dataset for PaLM contains 200 billion words. Aakanksha Chowdhery et al., *PaLM: Scaling Language Modeling with Pathways* (arXiv.org, April 19, 2022), https://arxiv.org/pdf/2204.02311.pdf, 3, 36, 65.

295 **compute and model size more than thousandfold:** PaLM used 350,000 TPU-days for training compared to 256 TPU-days for training BERT$_{LARGE}$. However, this does not account for improvements in compute power with more advanced TPU chips. Sevilla et al. estimated 2.9×10^{20} FLOPs (floating-point operations per second) to train BERT$_{LARGE}$. (Jaime Sevilla et al., "Parameter, Compute and Data Trends in Machine Learning," 2021, https://docs.google.com/spreadsheets/d/1AAIebjNsnJj_uKALHbXNfn3_YsT6sHXtCU0q7OI-Puc4/). PaLM employed 2.5×10^{24} FLOPs for training. (Chowdhery et al., *PaLM: Scaling Language Modeling with Pathways*, 48). Using estimated FLOPs arrives at an 8,000X compute increase from BERT$_{LARGE}$ to PaLM. See also Or Sharir et al., *The Cost of Training NLP Models: A Concise Overview* (AI21 Labs, April 19, 2020), https://arxiv.org/pdf/2004.08900.pdf, 2. Some research suggests that the optimal balance with a fixed amount of compute would be to scale training data size and model size equally and that many recent large

language models would perform better if a smaller model were trained on a larger dataset. Jordan Hoffman et al., *Training Compute-Optimal Large Language Models* (arXiv.org, March 29, 2022), https://arxiv.org/pdf/2203.15556.pdf. For an analysis of overall trends in dataset size in machine learning research, see Pablo Villalobos, "Trends in Training Dataset Sizes," Epoch, September 20, 2022, https://epochai.org/blog/trends-in-training-dataset-sizes. For an analysis of overall trends in model size, see Pablo Villalobos et al., *Machine Learning Model Sizes and the Parameter Gap* (arXiv.org, July 5, 2022), https://arxiv.org/pdf/2207.02852.pdf.

295 **multimodal models:** Ilya Sutskever, "Multimodal," *OpenAI Blog*, January 2021, https://openai.com/blog/tags/multimodal/; Aditya Ramesh et al., "DALL·E: Creating Images from Text," OpenAI Blog, January 5, 2021, https://openai.com/blog/dall-e/; Aditya Ramesh et al., *Zero-Shot Text-to-Image Generation* (arXiv.org, February 26, 2021), https://arxiv.org/pdf/2102.12092.pdf; Alec Radford et al., "CLIP: Connecting Text and Images," OpenAI Blog, January 5, 2021, https://openai.com/blog/clip/; Alec Radford et al., *Learning Transferable Visual Models From Natural Language Supervision* (arXiv.org, February 26, 2021), https://arxiv.org/pdf/2103.00020.pdf; Gabriel Goh et al., "Multimodal Neurons in Artificial Neural Networks," OpenAI Blog, March 4, 2021, https://openai.com/blog/multimodal-neurons/; Romero, "GPT-3 Scared You?"

295 **Text-to-image models:** Ramesh et al., "DALL·E"; Ramesh et al., *Zero-Shot Text-to-Image Generation*; Aditya Ramesh et al., "DALL·E 2," OpenAI Blog, n.d., https://openai.com/dall-e-2/; Aditya Ramesh et al., *Hierarchical Text-Conditional Image Generation with CLIP Latents* (arXiv.org, April 13, 2022), https://arxiv.org/pdf/2204.06125.pdf; Chitwan Saharia et al., "Imagen," Google Research, n.d., https://imagen.research.google/; Chitwan Saharia et al., *Photorealistic Text-to-Image Diffusion Models with Deep Language Understanding* (arXiv.org, May 23, 2022), https://arxiv.org/pdf/2205.11487.pdf; Emad Mostaque, "Stable Diffusion Public Release," *Stability AI* blog, August 22, 2022, https://stability.ai/blog/stable-diffusion-public-release; Emad Mostaque, "Stable Diffusion Launch Announcement," *Stability AI* blog, August 10, 2022, https://stability.ai/blog/stable-diffusion-announcement.

295 **artificial neurons tied to underlying concepts:** Goh et al., "Multimodal Neurons in Artificial Neural Networks" (OpenAI Blog); Gabriel Goh et al., "Multimodal Neurons in Artificial Neural Networks" (full paper), distill.pub, March 4, 2021, https://distill.pub/2021/multimodal-neurons/; "Unit 550," OpenAI Microscope, n.d., https://microscope.openai.com/models/contrastive_4x/image_block_4_5_Add_6_0/550

295 **larger, more diverse datasets:** Radford et al., *Learning Transferable Visual Models From Natural Language Supervision*.

295 **Gato:** Scott Reed et al., "A Generalist Agent," *DeepMind blog*, May 12, 2022, https://www.deepmind.com/publications/a-generalist-agent; Scott Reed et al., *A Generalist Agent* (arXiv.org, May 19, 2022), https://arxiv.org/pdf/2205.06175.pdf.

295 **interrogate the inner workings of multimodal models:** Goh et al., "Multimodal Neurons in Artificial Neural Networks" (full paper).

295 **new ways of attacking models:** Goh et al., "Multimodal Neurons in Artificial Neural Networks" (full paper).

296 **trend toward ever-larger AI models:** Jared Kaplan et al., *Scaling Laws for Neural Language Models* (arXiv.org, January 23, 2020), https://arxiv.org/pdf/2001.08361.pdf. See also Jonathan S. Rosenfeld et al., *A Constructive Prediction of the Generalization Error Across Scales* (arXiv.org, December 20, 2019), https://arxiv.org/pdf/1909.12673.pdf; Tom Henighan et al., *Scaling Laws for Autoregressive Generative Modeling* (arXiv.org, November 6, 2020),

https://arxiv.org/pdf/2010.14701.pdf; Rishi Bommasani et al., *On the Opportunities and Risks of Foundation Models* (Center for Research on Foundation Models, Stanford Institute for Human-Centered Artificial Intelligence, August 18, 2021), https://arxiv.org/pdf/2108 .07258.pdf; Neil C. Thompson et al., *The Computational Limits of Deep Learning* (arXiv.org, July 10, 2020), https://arxiv.org/pdf/2007.05558.pdf.

296 **compute appears likely to be the biggest limiting factor:** Thompson et al., *The Computational Limits of Deep Learning.*

296 **amount of compute used for training cutting-edge machine learning research:** Jaime Sevilla et al., *Compute Trends Across Three Eras of Machine Learning* (arXiv.org, March 9, 2022), https://arxiv.org/pdf/2202.05924.pdf. Other researchers have come up with somewhat different rates of progress in the deep learning era, see Dario Amodei and Danny Hernandez, "AI and Compute," openai.com, May 16, 2018, https://openai.com/blog/ai-and -compute/; Thompson et al., *The Computational Limits of Deep Learning.*

296 **Compute for training the largest models:** Sevilla et al., *Compute Trends Across Three Eras of Machine Learning*, 5–6.

296 **millions of dollars per research project:** Andrew J. Lohn and Micah Musser, "AI and Compute: How Much Longer Can Computing Power Drive Artificial Intelligence Progress?," (Center for Security and Emerging Technology, January 2022), 9, https://cset .georgetown.edu/publication/ai-and-compute/; Sharir et al., *The Cost of Training NLP Models*; Saif M. Khan and Alexander Mann, *AI Chips: What They Are and Why They Matter* (Center for Security and Emerging Technology, April 2020), 26, https://cset.george- town.edu/publication/ai-chips-what-they-are-and-why-they-matter/. Other experts have estimated higher costs, up to tens of millions of dollars, for training some AI models: Sevilla et al., *Compute Trends Across Three Eras of Machine Learning*, 22; Lennart Heim, "Estimating PaLM's training cost," blog.heim.xyz, April 5, 2022, https://blog.heim.xyz/ palm-training-cost/; Dan H, "How much did AlphaGo Zero cost?" Dansplaining, updated June 2020, https://www.yuzeh.com/data/agz-cost.html; and Ryan Carey, "Interpreting AI Compute Trends," AI Impacts, n.d., https://aiimpacts.org/interpreting-ai-compute -trends/.

296 **compute-intensive research out of reach for some:** Bommasani et al., *On the Opportunities and Risks of Foundation Models*; Ganguli et al., *Predictability and Surprise in Large Generative Models*, 11.

296 **increased federal resources for cloud computing:** Gil Alterovitz et al., *Recommendations for Leveraging Cloud Computing Resources for Federally Funded Artificial Intelligence Research and Development* (Select Committee on Artificial Intelligence, National Science & Technology Council, November 17, 2020), https://www.nitrd.gov/pubs/Recommendations-Cloud -AI-RD-Nov2020.pdf; "About the Task Force," National Artificial Intelligence Research Resource Task Force, 2021, https://www.ai.gov/nairrtf/; Interim NAIRR Task Force, *Envisioning a National Artificial Intelligence Research Resource (NAIRR): Preliminary Findings and Recommendations*, May 2022, https://www.ai.gov/wp-content/uploads/2022/05/NAIRR -TF-Interim-Report-2022.pdf; Lynne Parker, "Bridging the Resource Divide for Artificial Intelligence Research," OSTP blog, May 22, 2022, https://www.whitehouse.gov/ostp/news -updates/2022/05/25/bridging-the-resource-divide-for-artificial-intelligence-research/.

296 **$1 billion investment from Microsoft:** "OpenAI Forms Exclusive Computing Partnership with Microsoft to Build New Azure AI Supercomputing Technologies," Microsoft, July 22, 2019, https://news.microsoft.com/2019/07/22/openai-forms-exclusive-computing -partnership-with-microsoft-to-build-new-azure-ai-supercomputing-technologies/.

296 **AI Research SuperCluster:** "Introducing the AI Research SuperCluster—Meta's Cut-

ting-Edge AI Supercomputer for AI Research," Meta AI Blog, January 24, 2022, https://ai
.facebook.com/blog/ai-rsc.

297 **outstrip the spending capacity of large corporations:** Lohn and Musser, "AI and Compute: How Much Longer Can Computing Power Drive Artificial Intelligence Progress?";
Carey, "Interpreting AI Compute Trends"; Thompson et al., *The Computational Limits of
Deep Learning*; Ross Gruetzemacher, "2018 Trends in DeepMind Operating Costs," Ross
Gruetzemacher (personal website), August 8, 2019, http://www.rossgritz.com/uncate-
gorized/updated-deepmind-operating-costs/. Other estimates suggest that compute for
training large scale "flagship" AI models (e.g., AlphaGo, GPT-3) is doubling roughly every
10 months, a slightly slower pace than other deep learning models, perhaps due to the
higher cost or greater engineering challenges associated these larger models. Sevilla et al.,
Compute Trends Across Three Eras of Machine Learning, 5–6, 22–24.

297 **highest revenue of any tech company in the world:** "Fortune 500: Amazon," *Fortune*,
updated August 2, 2021, https://fortune.com/company/amazon-com/fortune500/.

297 **Alphabet and Microsoft:** "Fortune 500: Alphabet," *Fortune*, updated August 2, 2021,
https://fortune.com/company/alphabet/fortune500/; "Fortune 500: Microsoft," *Fortune*,
updated August 2, 2021, https://fortune.com/company/microsoft/fortune500/.

297 **Manhattan project:** "Manhattan Project," Comprehensive Nuclear-Test-Ban Treaty
Organization, n.d., https://www.ctbto.org/nuclear-testing/history-of-nuclear-testing/
manhattan-project/

297 **Apollo Program:** "Apollo Program Budget Appropriations ($000)," NASA, n.d., https://
history.nasa.gov/SP-4029/Apollo_18-16_Apollo_Program_Budget_Appropriations.htm.

297 **U.S. Defense Department's budget:** *Defense Budget Overview, United States Department of Defense Fiscal Year 2022 Budget Request* (Office of the Under Secretary of Defense
[Comptroller]/Chief Financial Officer, May 2021), https://comptroller.defense.gov/Por-
tals/45/Documents/defbudget/FY2022/FY2022_Budget_Request_Overview_Book.pdf.

297 **over 12 percent of its gross domestic product (GDP) annually:** Office of the Under Sec-
retary of Defense (Comptroller), *National Defense Budget Estimates for FY 2021* (U.S.
Department of Defense, April 2020), Table 7-7, https://comptroller.defense.gov/Portals/45/
Documents/defbudget/fy2021/FY21_Green_Book.pdf.

297 **significant technical hurdles:** Alvi and Kharya, "Using DeepSpeed and Megatron to Train
Megatron-Turing NLG 530B;" Amir Gholami, "AI and Memory Wall," *Medium*, March 29,
2021, https://medium.com/riselab/ai-and-memory-wall-2cb4265cb0b8.

297 **increases in compute efficiency:** Thompson et al., *The Computational Limits of Deep
Learning*; Sharir et al., *The Cost of Training NLP Models*, 3. For example, GPU price-performance (FLOPs per dollar) is doubling approximately every 2.5 years. Marius Hobbhahn
and Tamay Besiroglu, "Trends in GPU Price-Performance," Epoch, June 27, 2022, https://
epochai.org/blog/trends-in-gpu-price-performance.

297 **forty-four-fold improvement in compute efficiency:** Danny Hernandez and Tom B.
Brown, *Measuring the Algorithmic Efficiency of Neural Networks* (arXiv.org, n.d.), https://
arxiv.org/pdf/2005.04305.pdf.

298 **compute efficiency for both training and inference:** Hernandez and Brown, *Measuring
the Algorithmic Efficiency of Neural Networks*, 9–10; Radosvet Desislavov et al., *Compute
and Energy Consumption Trends in Deep Learning Inference* (arXiv.org, September 12,
2021), https://arxiv.org/pdf/2109.05472.pdf.

298 **progress in algorithmic efficiency:** Katja Grace, *Algorithmic Progress in Six Domains*
(technical report no. 2013-3, Machine Intelligence Research Institute, 2013), https://intelli-
gence.org/files/AlgorithmicProgress.pdf.

298 **compute-heavy models much more accessible:** Desislavov et al., *Compute and Energy Consumption Trends in Deep Learning Inference.*

298 **ASIC optimized for deep learning:** "Cloud TPU," Google Cloud, n.d., https://cloud .google.com/tpu; "Cloud Tensor Processing Units (TPUs)," Google Cloud, n.d., https:// cloud.google.com/tpu/docs/tpus.

298 **reduced energy consumption:** The metric DeepMind used to compare AlphaGo versions, thermal design power (TDP), is not a direct measure of energy consumption. It is a rough first-order proxy, however, for power consumption. David Silver and Demis Hassabis, "AlphaGo Zero: Starting From Scratch," *DeepMind Blog*, October 18, 2017, https:// deepmind.com/blog/article/alphago-zero-starting-scratch.

298 **reduced compute usage to only 4 TPUs:** Silver and Hassabis, "AlphaGo Zero: Starting From Scratch"; "AlphaGo," DeepMind, n.d., https://deepmind.com/research/case-studies/ alphago-the-story-so-far; David Silver et al., "Mastering the Game of Go without Human Knowledge," *Nature* 550 (October 19 2017), 354–355, https://www.nature.com/articles/ nature24270.epdf.

298 **reduced the compute needed for training by a factor of eight:** Hernandez and Brown, *Measuring the Algorithmic Efficiency of Neural Networks*, 18.

298 **may make AI models available:** Desislavov et al., *Compute and Energy Consumption Trends in Deep Learning Inference*; Sharir et al., *The Cost of Training NLP Models*, 3.

298 **AI training costs could be as much as thirty times higher:** Khan and Mann, *AI Chips*, 26.

299 **costly and locks out university researchers:** Rodney Brooks, "A Better Lesson," Rodney Brooks (personal website), March 19, 2019, https://rodneybrooks.com/a-better-lesson/; Kevin Vu, "Compute Goes Brrr: Revisiting Sutton's Bitter Lesson for Artificial Intelligence," DZone.com, March 11, 2021, https://dzone.com/articles/compute-goes-brrr -revisiting-suttons-bitter-lesson; Bommasani et al., *On the Opportunities and Risks of Foundation Models.*

299 **contributes to carbon emissions:** "On the Dangers of Stochastic Parrots"; Brooks, "A Better Lesson"; Vu, "Compute Goes Brrr"; Lasse F. Wolff Anthony, Benjamin Kanding, and Raghavendra Selvan, "Carbontracker: Tracking and Predicting the Carbon Footprint of Training Deep Learning Models" (paper presented at International Conference on Machine Learning 2020, virtual, July 12–18, 2020), https://arxiv.org/pdf/2007.03051.pdf; Emma Strubell, Ananya Ganesh, and Andrew McCallum, *Energy and Policy Considerations for Deep Learning in NLP* (arXiv.org, June 5, 2019), https://arxiv.org/pdf/1906.02243 .pdf; Peter Henderson et al., "Towards the Systematic Reporting of the Energy and Carbon Footprints of Machine Learning," *Journal of Machine Learning Research* 21 (November 2020): 1–43, https://jmlr.org/papers/volume21/20-312/20-312.pdf; Bommasani et al., *On the Opportunities and Risks of Foundation Models*, 139–144. For an example of estimates of energy consumption and environmental impact for training large language models, see Emma Strubell et al., *Energy and Policy Considerations for Deep Learning in NLP* (arXiv. org, June 5, 2019), https://arxiv.org/pdf/1906.02243.pdf; Chowdhery et al., *PaLM: Scaling Language Modeling with Pathways*, 65. Even though training is more compute-intensive, the total energy consumption and carbon footprint is likely to be much higher for inference than training because of the multiplicative effect of inference being done many times. Desislavov et al., *Compute and Energy Consumption Trends in Deep Learning Inference.*

299 **"real intelligence":** Gary Marcus and Ernest Davis, *Rebooting AI: Building Artificial Intelligence We Can Trust* (New York: Pantheon Books, 2019), 64.

299 **value of compute-heavy methods:** Sharir et al., *The Cost of Training NLP Models*, 3.

299 **The biggest lesson that can be read from seventy years of AI research:** Rich Sutton, "The

Bitter Lesson," incompleteideas.net, March 13, 2019, http://incompleteideas.net/IncIdeas/ BitterLesson.html.

299 **Simpler methods that apply vast amounts of data:** Sutton's argument is backed by empirical findings by multiple research teams across multiple types of neural network models, both for language models and image classification. Researchers concluded in one paper that for neural language models, "Performance depends strongly on scale, weakly on model shape." Jared Kaplan et al., *Scaling Laws for Neural Language Models* (arXiv.org, January 23, 2020), https://arxiv.org/pdf/2001.08361.pdf. See also Rosenfeld et al., *A Constructive Prediction of the Generalization Error Across Scales*.

299 **backlash to Sutton's article:** Brooks, "A Better Lesson"; Shimon Whiteson (@shimon8282), "Rich Sutton has a new blog post entitled 'The Bitter Lesson' (http://incompleteideas.net/ IncIdeas/BitterLesson.html) that I strongly disagree with. In it, he argues that the history of AI teaches us that leveraging computation always eventually wins out over leveraging human knowledge," Twitter, March 15, 2019, https://twitter.com/shimon8282/ status/1106534178676506624; Andy Kitchen, "A Meta Lesson," Andy Kitchen (personal website), March 21, 2019, http://andy.kitchen/a-meta-lesson.html; Katherine Bailey, "The Wrong Classroom," katbailey.github.io, March 23, 2019, https://katbailey.github.io/post/ the-wrong-classroom/; Vu, "Compute Goes Brrr."

299 **level of expenditures only possible by major governments:** Carey, "Interpreting AI Compute Trends."

299 **Chinese researchers have already signaled:** In June 2021, the Beijing Academy of Artificial Intelligence reported a 1.75 trillion parameter model, WuDao 2.0, trained on 4.9 terabytes (4,900 GB) of text and images, although little information is publicly available about the model. (Coco Feng, "US-China tech war: Beijing-Funded AI Researchers Surpass Google and OpenAI with New Language Processing model," *South China Morning Post*, June 2, 2021, https://www.scmp.com/tech/tech-war/article/3135764/us-china-tech-war -beijing-funded-ai-researchers-surpass-google-and; Alberto Romero, "GPT-3 Scared You? Meet Wu Dao 2.0: A Monster of 1.75 Trillion Parameters," *Towards Data Science*, June 5, 2021, https://towardsdatascience.com/gpt-3-scared-you meet-wu-dao-2-0-a-monster -of-1-75-trillion-parameters-832cd83db484.) In April 2022, researchers from several labs, including Tsinghua University, Alibaba, and the Beijing Academy of Artificial Intelligence, announced a framework for scaling up training to 14.5 trillion parameter models, with the long-term intent of training "brain scale" models of over 100 trillion parameters. Zixuan Ma et al., "BaGuaLu: Targeting Brain Scale Pretrained Models with over 37 Million Cores," *PPoPP '22: Proceedings of the 27th ACM SIGPLAN Symposium on Principles and Practice of Parallel Programming* (April 2022), 192–204, https://doi.org/10.1145/3503221.3508417.

300 **Denying Chinese companies access to chips aids the Chinese:** James Andrew Lewis, *China's Pursuit of Semiconductor Independence* (Center for Strategic & International Studies, February 27, 2019), https://www.csis.org/analysis/chinas-pursuit-semiconductor-independence; Christopher A. Thomas, "Lagging but Motivated: The State of China's Semiconductor Industry," TechStream (blog), Brookings Institution, January 7, 2021, https://www.brookings.edu/techstream/lagging-but-motivated-the-state-of-chinas -semiconductor-industry/; Raymond Zhong and Cao Li, "With Money, and Waste, China Fights for Chip Independence," *New York Times*, December 24, 2020, https://www .nytimes.com/2020/12/24/technology/china-semiconductors.html; Asa Fitch, "China's Chip-Independence Goals Helped by U.S.-Developed Tech," *Wall Street Journal*, January 11, 2021, https://www.wsj.com/articles/chinas-chip-independence-goals-helped-by-u-s -developed-tech-11610375472.

300 **research breakthroughs quickly proliferate:** For example, within eighteen months of OpenAI's announcement of GPT-3, similar scale language models had been announced by research teams in China, South Korea, and Israel. Ganguli et al., *Predictability and Surprise in Large Generative Models*, 10.

300 **improved computational efficiency:** Desislavov et al., *Compute and Energy Consumption Trends in Deep Learning Inference*.

CONCLUSION

302 **inherently political act:** Rishi Bommasani et al., *On the Opportunities and Risks of Foundation Models* (Center for Research on Foundation Models, Stanford Institute for Human-Centered Artificial Intelligence, August 18, 2021), 148–149, 157, https://arxiv.org/pdf/2108.07258.pdf.

304 **genocide against Uighurs:** "China Cuts Uighur Births with IUDs, Abortion, Sterilization," Associated Press, June 29, 2020, https://apnews.com/269b3de1af34e17c1941a514f78d764c; "Opinion: What's Happening in Xinjiang Is Genocide," editorial, *Washington Post*, July 6, 2020, https://www.washingtonpost.com/opinions/global-opinions/whats-happening-in-xinjiang-is-genocide/2020/07/06/cde3f9da-bfaa-11ea-9fdd-b7ac6b051dc8_story.html; Adrian Zenz, interview by Scott Simon, NPR, July 4, 2020, https://www.npr.org/2020/07/04/887239225/china-suppression-of-uighur-minorities-meets-u-n-definition-of-genocide-report-s; Humeyra Pamuk and David Brunnstrom, "New U.S. Secretary of State Favors Cooperation with China Despite Genocide of Uighurs," Reuters, January 27, 2021, https://www.reuters.com/article/us-usa-china-blinken/new-u-s-secretary-of-state-favors-cooperation-with-china-despite-genocide-of-uighurs-idUSKBN29W2RC; "Canada's Parliament Declares China's Treatment of Uighurs 'Genocide,'" BBC News, February 23, 2021, https://www.bbc.com/news/world-us-canada-56163220; "Dutch Parliament: China's Treatment of Uighurs Is Genocide," Reuters, February 25, 2021, https://www.reuters.com/article/us-netherlands-china-uighurs/dutch-parliament-chinas-treatment-of-uighurs-is-genocide-idUSKBN2AP2CI; Donald Clarke, "The Economist on Xinjiang: Don't Call It Genocide," China Collection, February 13, 2021, https://thechinacollection.org/economist-xinjiang-dont-call-genocide/; Elizabeth M. Lynch, "The Economist's Recent Piece about Genocide in Xinjiang Is Wrong," *China Law & Policy*, February 15, 2021, https://chinalawandpolicy.com/2021/02/15/the-economists-recent-piece-about-genocide-in-xinjiang-is-wrong/.

304 **China produces more top AI researchers:** "The Global AI Talent Tracker," Macro Polo, n.d., https://macropolo.org/digital-projects/the-global-ai-talent-tracker/.

304 **brain gain for the United States:** "The Global AI Talent Tracker"; Remco Zwetsloot, *Keeping Top AI Talent in the United States* (Center for Security and Emerging Technology, December 2019), https://cset.georgetown.edu/wp-content/uploads/Keeping-Top-AI-Talent-in-the-United-States.pdf.

304 **"will become the ruler of the world":** "'Whoever Leads in AI Will Rule the World': Putin to Russian Children on Knowledge Day," RT News, September 1, 2017, https://www.rt.com/news/401731-ai-rule-world-putin/

INDEX

Page numbers after 313 refer to notes.